Lazy Day
Cookin'

More than 900 Fix-It and Forget-It™ Recipes

Lazy Day
Cookin'
Slow-cooker meals
that simmer to delicious
perfection while you
work, play, or sleep!

Reader's Digest

The Reader's Digest Association, Inc.
Pleasantville, New York / Montreal

LAZY DAY COOKIN'

The recipes in this book originally appeared in *Fix-It and Forget-It™ Cookbook* and *Fix-It and Forget-It™ Recipes for Entertaining* and are published in this special edition, arranged by Reader's Digest, by permission of Good Books, Intercourse, PA 17534.

Cover and spot illustrations by Bill Reynolds.

Address any comments about *Lazy Day Cookin'* to:
Editor in Chief
Reader's Digest Home and Health Books
Reader's Digest Road
Pleasantville, NY 10570-7000

To order additional copies of *LazyDay Cookin'*, call 1-800-846-2100.

For more Reader's Digest products and information, visit our website: **rd.com**

Library of Congress Cataloging in Publication Data

Good, Phyllis Pellman, 1948-
  Lazy day cookin' : slow-cooker meals that simmer to delicious
perfection while you work, play or sleep! / Phyllis Pellman Good, Dawn J. Ranck.-- 1st ed.
    p. cm.
Includes index.
  ISBN 0-7621-0519-4 (Hardcover)
  1. Electric cookery, Slow. I. Ranck, Dawn J. II. Title.
  TX827.G6623 2003
  641.5'884--dc22
                        2003021042

Printed in the United States of America.
  3 5 7 9 10 8 6 4 2

US 4592/G

Cookin' the Lazy Way

You know what's the best thing about cooking dinner? It's having the time to read a good book. Or, perhaps, the leisure to putter in the garden, spiff up your button collection, go for a walk—or maybe, even do a little shopping or take in a movie. If this is your idea of how to spend your time cooking—and still put a piping hot, soul satisfying meal on the table—then welcome to *Lazy Day Cookin'.*

To get started, you have to find your slow cooker. If, like most, it's buried in the back of the pantry, it's time to dig it out, dust it off, and restore it to its rightful place among your most frequently used cooking gear. When it comes to freeing you from the bonds that bind you to the kitchen, fancy gourmet ranges, sealed cooktops, and convection ovens can't compete with an old workhouse like the slow cooker. With this tried-and-true time-saver, all you need to do is spend a few minutes in the morning—or the night before—getting the ingredients ready. Then you can be gone all day while your cooker quietly and safely simmers your dinner to its flavor peak, having it perfectly ready to serve when you get home. Just ask a gourmet range to do that!

After you've found your slow cooker, give this book a test drive by trying one of the super easy recipes that you'll find at the beginning of every chapter. Try the Rich and Tasty Beef Roast on p. 88, for example—it has only three ingredients. Or try the Barbecue Pork Chops on page 153—it has only two. You'll be out of the kitchen in no time. And very soon, as you try more and more dishes, you'll be like the die-hard slow-cooker users who provided the 954 family-tested favorites in this collection: you won't know what do with all the extra time you got on your hands. Maybe, take a nap . . .

Contents

Breakfast

Creamy Old-Fashioned Oatmeal

Mary Wheatley/Mashpee, MA

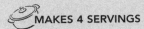 **MAKES 4 SERVINGS**

1 1/3 cups dry old-fashioned rolled oats
2 1/2 cups, plus 1 Tbsp., water
dash of salt

1. Mix together cereal, water, and salt in slow cooker.

2. Cook on Low 6 hours.

note
● The formula is this: for one serving, use 1/3 cup dry oats and 2/3 cup water, plus a few grains salt. Multiply by the number of servings you need.

variation
● Before cooking, stir in a few chopped dates or raisins for each serving, if you wish.
Cathy Boshart/Lebanon, PA

Hot Wheatberry Cereal

Rosemarie Fitzgerald
Gibsonia, PA

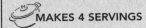 **MAKES 4 SERVINGS**

1 cup wheatberries
5 cups water
butter
milk
honey

1. Rinse and sort berries. Cover with water and soak all day (or 8 hours) in slow cooker.

2. Cover. Cook on Low overnight (or 10 hours).

3. Drain, if needed. Serve hot with honey, milk, and butter.

variations and notes
● Eat your hot wheatberries with raisins and maple syrup as a variation.
● Wheatberries can also be used in pilafs or grain salads. Cook as indicated, drain and cool.

Dulce Leche (Sweet Milk)

Dorothy Horst/Tiskilwa, IL

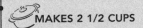 **MAKES 2 1/2 CUPS**

2 14-oz. cans sweetened condensed milk

1. Place unopened cans of milk in slow cooker. Fill cooker with warm water so that it comes above the cans by 1 1/2–2 inches.

2. Cover cooker. Cook on High 2 hours.

3. Cool unopened cans.

4. When opened, the contents should be thick and spreadable. Use as a filling between 2 cookies or crackers.

When on a tour in Argentina, we were served this at breakfast time as a spread on toast or thick slices of bread. We were also presented with a container of prepared Dulce Leche as a parting gift to take home. This dish also sometimes appears on Mexican menus.
— • —

Cheese Souffle Casserole

Iva Schmidt/Fergus Falls, MN

 **MAKES 6 SERVINGS**

8 slices bread (crusts removed), cubed or torn into squares
2 cups (8 oz.) grated cheddar, Swiss, or American, cheese
1 cup cooked, chopped ham
4 eggs
1 cup light cream, or milk
1 cup evaporated milk
1/4 tsp. salt
1 Tbsp. parsley
paprika

1. Lightly grease slow cooker. Alternate layers of bread and cheese and ham.

2. Beat together eggs, milk, salt, and parsley. Pour over bread in slow cooker.

3. Sprinkle with paprika.

4. Cover and cook on Low 3–4 hours. (The longer cooking time yields a firmer, dryer dish.)

Breakfast Casserole

Shirley Hinh/Wayland, IA

 **MAKES 8–10 SERVINGS**

6 eggs, beaten
1 lb. little smokies (cocktail wieners), or 1 1/2 lbs. bulk sausage, browned and drained
1 1/2 cups milk
1 cup shredded cheddar cheese
8 slices bread, torn into pieces
1 tsp. salt
1/2 tsp. dry mustard
1 cup shredded mozzarella cheese

1. Mix together all ingredients except cheese. Pour into greased slow cooker.

2. Sprinkle mozzarella cheese over top.

3. Cover and cook 2 hours on High, and then 1 hour on Low.

Egg and Cheese Bake

Evie Hershey/Atglen, PA

 **MAKES 6 SERVINGS**

3 cups toasted bread cubes
1 1/2 cups shredded cheese
fried, crumbled bacon, or ham chunks, optional
6 eggs, beaten
3 cups milk
3/4 tsp. salt
1/4 tsp. pepper

1. Combine bread cubes, cheese, and meat in greased slow cooker.

2. Mix together eggs, milk, salt, and pepper. Pour over bread.

3. Cook on Low 4–6 hours.

Egg and Broccoli Casserole

Joette Droz/Kalona, IA

MAKES 6 SERVINGS

24-oz. carton small-curd cottage cheese
10-oz. pkg. frozen chopped broccoli, thawed and drained
2 cups (8 oz.) shredded cheddar cheese
6 eggs, beaten
1/3 cup flour
1/4 cup melted butter, or margarine
3 Tbsp. finely chopped onion
1/2 tsp. salt
shredded cheese, optional

1. Combine first 8 ingredients. Pour into greased slow cooker.

2. Cover and cook on High 1 hour. Stir. Reduce heat to Low. Cover and cook 2 1/2–3 hours, or until temperature reaches 160°F and eggs are set.

3. Sprinkle with cheese and serve.

Breakfast Skillet

Sue Hamilton/Minooka, IL

MAKES 4–5 SERVINGS

3 cups milk
5.5 oz. box au gratin potatoes
1 tsp. hot sauce
5 eggs, lightly beaten
1 Tbsp. prepared mustard
4-oz. can sliced mushrooms
8 slices bacon, fried and crumbled
1 cup cheddar cheese, shredded

1. Combine milk, au gratin-sauce packet, hot sauce, eggs, and mustard.

2. Stir in dried potatoes, mushrooms, and bacon.

3. Cover. Cook on High 2 1/2–3 hours or on Low 5–6 hours.

4. Sprinkle cheese over top. Cover until melted.

Western Omelet Casserole

Mary Louise Martin/Boyd, WI

MAKES 10 SERVINGS

32-oz. bag frozen hash brown potatoes
1 lb. cooked ham, cubed
1 medium onion, diced
1 1/2 cups shredded cheddar cheese
12 eggs
1 cup milk
1 tsp. salt
1 tsp. pepper

1. Layer one-third each of frozen potatoes, ham, onions, and cheese in bottom of slow cooker. Repeat 2 times.

2. Beat together eggs, milk, salt, and pepper. Pour over mixture in slow cooker.

3. Cover. Cook on Low 8–9 hours.

4. Serve with orange juice and fresh fruit.

Baked Oatmeal

Ellen Ranck/Gap, PA

MAKES 4–6 SERVINGS

1/3 cup oil
1/2 cup sugar
1 large egg, beaten
2 cups dry quick oats
1 1/2 tsp. baking powder
1/2 tsp. salt
3/4 cup milk

1. Pour the oil into the slow cooker to grease bottom and sides.

2. Add remaining ingredients. Mix well.

3. Bake on Low 2 1/2–3 hours.

Mexican-Style Grits

Mary Sommerfeld
Lancaster, PA

MAKES 10–12 SERVINGS

1 1/2 cups instant grits
1 lb. Velveeta cheese, cubed
1/2 tsp. garlic powder
2 4-oz. cans diced chilies
1/2 cup (1 stick) butter, or margarine

1. Prepare grits according to package directions.

2. Stir in cheese, garlic powder, and chilies, until cheese is melted.

3. Stir in butter. Pour into greased slow cooker.

4. Cover. Cook on High 2–3 hours or on Low 4–6 hours.

Apple Oatmeal

Frances B. Musser
Newmanstown, PA

MAKES 4–5 SERVINGS

2 cups milk
2 Tbsp. honey
1 Tbsp. butter (no substitute!)
1/4 tsp. salt
1/2 tsp. cinnamon
1 cup dry old-fashioned oats
1 cup chopped apples
1/2 cup chopped walnuts
2 Tbsp. brown sugar

1. Mix together all ingredients in greased slow cooker.

2. Cover. Cook on Low 5–6 hours.

3. Serve with milk or ice cream.

variation
● Add 1/2 cup light or dark raisins to mixture.

Jeanette Oberholtzer
Manheim, PA

Slow Cooker Oatmeal

Betty B. Dennison
Grove City, PA

 MAKES 2 SERVINGS

1 cup uncooked rolled oats
2 cups water
salt
1/3–1/2 cup raisins
1/4 tsp. ground nutmeg
1/4 tsp. ground cinnamon

1. Combine ingredients in slow cooker.

2. Cover. Cook on Low 6–8 hours.

3. Eat with milk and brown sugar.

Peanut Butter Granola

Dawn Ranck/Harrisonburg, VA

MAKES 16–20 SERVINGS

6 cups dry oatmeal
1/2 cup wheat germ
1/2 cup toasted coconut
1/2 cup sunflower seeds
1/2 cup raisins
1 cup butter
1 cup peanut butter
1 cup brown sugar

1. Combine oatmeal, wheat germ, coconut, sunflower seeds, and raisins in large slow cooker.

2. Melt together butter, peanut butter, and brown sugar. Pour over oatmeal in cooker. Mix well.

3. Cover. Cook on Low 1 1/2 hours, stirring every 15 minutes.

4. Allow to cool in cooker, stirring every 30 minutes or so, or spread onto cookie sheet. When thoroughly cooled, break into chunks and store in airtight container.

Breakfast Apple Cobbler

Anona M. Teel/Banga, PA

MAKES 6–8 SERVINGS

8 medium apples, cored, peeled, sliced
1/4 cup sugar
dash of cinnamon
juice of 1 lemon
1/4 cup (1/2 stick) butter, melted
2 cups granola

1. Combine ingredients in slow cooker.

2. Cover. Cook on Low 7–9 hours (while you sleep!), or on High 2–3 hours (after you're up in the morning).

Breakfast Prunes

Jo Haberkamp/Fairbank, IA

MAKES 6 SERVINGS

2 cups orange juice
1/4 cup orange marmalade
1 tsp. ground cinnamon
1/4 tsp. ground cloves
1/4 tsp. ground nutmeg
1 cup water
12-oz. pkg. pitted dried
 prunes (1 3/4 cups)
2 thin lemon slices

1. Combine orange juice, marmalade, cinnamon, cloves, nutmeg, and water in slow cooker.

2. Stir in prunes and lemon slices.

3. Cover. Cook on Low 8–10 hours, or overnight.

4. Serve warm as a breakfast food, or warm or chilled as a side dish with a meal later in the day.

variation

● If you prefer more citrus flavor, eliminate the ground cloves and reduce the cinnamon to 1/2 tsp. and the nutmeg to 1/8 tsp.

Hot Applesauce Breakfast

Colleen Konetzni
Rio Rancho, NM

MAKES 8 SERVINGS

10 apples, peeled and sliced
1/2–1 cup sugar
1 Tbsp. ground cinnamon
1/4 tsp. ground nutmeg

1. Combine ingredients in slow cooker.

2. Cover. Cook on Low 8–10 hours.

variations and notes

● Yummy over oatmeal or with vanilla yogurt. Or serve it over pancakes or waffles.
● Add chopped nuts for an extra treat.

Breakfast Wassail

Lori Berezovsky/Salina, KS

MAKES 4 QUARTS

64-oz. bottle cranberry juice
32-oz. bottle apple juice
12-oz. can frozen pineapple
 juice concentrate
12-oz. can frozen lemonade
 concentrate
3–4 cinnamon sticks
1 qt. water, optional

1. Combine all ingredients except water in slow cooker. Add water if mixture is too sweet.

2. Cover. Cook on Low 3 hours.

Even though the name of this recipe conjures up thoughts of Christmas, it is the perfect breakfast substitute for juice, especially when entertaining a houseful of overnight guests.

— • —

Appetizers
and Snacks

...supereasy

Chili Nuts

Barbara Aston/Ashdown, AR

 **MAKES 5 CUPS NUTS**

1/4 cup melted butter
2 12-oz. cans cocktail
  peanuts
1 5/8-oz. pkg. chili
  seasoning mix

1. Pour butter over nuts in slow cooker. Sprinkle in dry chili mix. Toss together.

2. Cover. Heat on Low 2–2 1/2 hours. Turn to High. Remove lid and cook 10–15 minutes.

3. Serve warm or cool.

Cheese Spread

Barbara Kuhns
Millersburg, OH

 **MAKES APPROXIMATELY 12–15 SERVINGS**

1 lb. white American
  cheese, cubed
1 1/2 cups milk
crackers

1. Combine cheese and milk in slow cooker.

2. Cover. Cook on Low about 2 hours, or until cheese is melted, stirring occasionally.

3. Serve on crackers.

Mexicana Dip

Julia B. Boyd/Memphis, TN
Sue Williams/Gulfport, MS

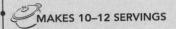 **MAKES 10–12 SERVINGS**

2 lbs. American, or
  Velveeta, cheese, cubed
10-oz. can tomatoes with
  green chilies
tortilla chips, corn chips,
  or potato chips

1. Combine cheese and tomatoes in slow cooker.

2. Cover. Cook on Low 2–3 hours, stirring until cheese is melted. If mixture is too thick, add a little milk.

3. Serve as a dip, or pour over platter of favorite chips.

variation
● Stir in 1/2 lb. browned bulk sausage, crumbled into small pieces.
Jane Steele/Moore, OK

...supereasy

Chili Bean Dip

Glenna Fay Bergey
Lebanon, OR

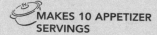

MAKES 10 APPETIZER SERVINGS

15-oz. can chili
1 small green or red sweet pepper, diced
8-oz. jar Cheese Whiz
1 lb. cheddar cheese, cubed

1. Combine all ingredients in slow cooker.

2. Cover. Cook on High 45–60 minutes, or until cheese is melted. Turn cooker to Low for up to 6 hours.

3. Serve dip warm from the cooker with nacho chips.

Red Pepper-Cheese Dip

Ann Bender/Ft. Defiance, VA

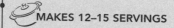

MAKES 12–15 SERVINGS

2 Tbsp. olive oil
4–6 large red peppers, cut into 1-inch squares
1/2 lb. feta-cheese
crackers or pita bread

1. Pour oil into slow cooker. Stir in peppers.

2. Cover. Cook on Low 2 hours.

3. Serve with feta cheese on crackers.

Lilli's Nacho Dip

Lilli Peters/Dodge City, KS

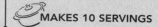

MAKES 10 SERVINGS

3-lbs. Velveeta cheese, cubed
10 3/4-oz. can cream of chicken soup
2 4-oz. cans chopped green chilies and juice
tortilla chips

1. Place cheese in slow cooker. Cook on Low until cheese melts, stirring occasionally.

2. Add soup and chilies. Stir. Heat on Low 1 hour.

3. Pour over tortilla chips just before serving.

note
● If you want to speed up the process, melt the cheese in the microwave. Heat on High for 1 1/2 minutes, stir, and continue heating at 1 1/2-minute intervals as long as needed.

variations
● Instead of using 2 4-oz. cans chilies, use 10-oz. can tomatoes and chilies.
● For a heartier dip, add 1/2–1 lb. bulk sausage, browned, crumbled into small pieces, and drained.

Jeanne's Chile Con Queso

Jeanne Allen/Rye, CO

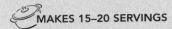 MAKES 15–20 SERVINGS

40-oz. can chili without beans
2-lbs. Velveeta cheese, cubed
16-oz. jar picante sauce (mild, medium, or hot, whichever you prefer)
tortilla chips

1. Combine all ingredients except chips in slow cooker.

2. Cover. Cook on Low 1–2 hours, until cheese is melted. Stir.

3. Serve with tortilla chips.

Tina's Cheese Dip

Tina Houk/Clinton, MO

MAKES 12 SERVINGS

2 8-oz. pkgs. cream cheese, softened
3 15 1/2-oz. cans chili
2 cups shredded cheddar or mozzarella cheese
tortilla chips

1. Spread cream cheese in bottom of slow cooker.

2. Spread chili on top of cream cheese.

3. Top with shredded cheese.

4. Cover. Cook on Low 1–1 1/2 hours, until shredded cheese is melted. Stir.

5. Serve with tortilla chips.

Chili Con Queso Dip

Jenny R. Unternahrer
Wayland, IA

MAKES APPROXIMATELY 12 SERVINGS

1 lb. Velveeta cheese, cubed
1 cup salsa (mild, medium, or hot, whichever you prefer)
1 cup sour cream
tortilla chips

1. Combine cheese, salsa, and sour cream in slow cooker.

2. Cover. Heat on Low, stirring occasionally until cheese melts and dip is well blended, about 1–1 1/2 hours.

3. Serve with tortilla chips.

...supereasy

Hot Chili Dip

Lavina Hochstedler
Grand Blanc, MI

Anna Stoltzfus
Honey Brook, PA

Kathi Rogge/Alexandria, IN

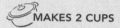 MAKES 2 CUPS

24-oz. jar hot salsa
15-oz. can chili with beans
2 2 1/4-oz. cans sliced ripe
olives, drained
12 ozs. mild cheese, cubed

1. Combine all ingredients in slow cooker.

2. Cover. Cook on Low 1–2 hours, or until cheese is melted, stirring halfway through.

3. Serve with tortilla chips.

Chili Dip

Sue Tjon/Austin, TX

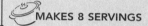 MAKES 8 SERVINGS

1 large can chili without
beans
8-oz. pkg. cream cheese
10-oz. pkg. jalapeño Jack
cheese, shredded
tortilla chips

1. Pour chili into slow cooker.

2. Cut cream cheese into chunks and add to chili.

3. Add shredded cheese. Stir well.

4. Cover. Cook on Low 4 hours.

5. Serve with tortilla chips.

This is best served warm, so I keep it in the slow cooker to serve. You can refrigerate leftovers and reheat them.

— • —

Mexican Bean and Cheese Dip

Mary Sommerfeld
Lancaster, PA

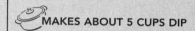 MAKES ABOUT 5 CUPS DIP

15-oz. can refried beans
8-oz. jar taco sauce
1 lb. Velveeta cheese,
cubed
1 pkg. dry taco seasoning

1. Combine ingredients in slow cooker.

2. Cover. Cook on Low 2–3 hours, or until cheese is melted.

3. Serve warm from the cooker with tortilla chips.

note
● If you're cautious about salt, choose minimally salted chips.

Sweet and Sour Vienna Sausages

Judy Denney
Lawrenceville, GA

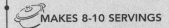 MAKES 10 FULL-SIZED SERVINGS, OR 20 APPETIZER-SIZED SERVINGS

8 cans Vienna sausages, drained
2 cups grape jelly
2 cups ketchup

1. Put sausages in slow cooker.

2. Combine jelly and ketchup. Pour over sausages. Stir lightly. (Add more jelly and ketchup if sausages are not covered.)

3. Cover. Cook on High 1 hour, then turn to Low for 5 hours.

variations
● Instead of Vienna sausages, use smoky links. Add 1 can pineapple chunks and juice to jelly and ketchup.

Spicy Franks

Char Hagner/Montague, MI

MAKES 4–6 FULL-SIZED SERVINGS, OR 32 APPETIZER-SIZED SERVINGS

2 1-lb. pkgs. cocktail wieners
1 cup chili sauce
1 cup bottled barbecue sauce
8-oz. can jellied cranberry sauce

1. Place wieners in slow cooker.

2. In separate bowl, combine chili sauce, barbecue sauce, and cranberry sauce. Pour over wieners.

3. Cover. Cook on Low 3–4 hours, or High 1 1/2–2 hours.

Crockpot Smokies

Dede Peterson/Rapid City, SD

MAKES 8-10 SERVINGS

2 lbs. Little Smokies
18-oz. bottle barbecue sauce (your choice of flavors)

1. Put Little Smokies in slow cooker.

2. Cover with barbecue sauce.

3. Cover. Cook on Low 3–4 hours.

...supereasy

Super-Bowl Little Smokies

Mary Sommerfeld
Lancaster, PA

Alicia Denlinger
Lancaster, PA

MAKES 9–10 MAIN-DISH SERVINGS, OR 15–20 APPETIZER SERVINGS

3 1-lb. pkgs. Little Smokies
8-oz. bottle Catalina dressing
splash of liquid smoke

1. Combine all ingredients in slow cooker.

2. Cover. Cook on Low 2 hours.

3. Use toothpicks to serve.

These are always a hit at parties, whether it's Christmas, New Year's, or the Super Bowl. They are good any time that you'd like to serve food beyond dessert, but you don't want to have a sitdown meal.

— • —

Little Smokies

Sharon Kauffman
Harrisonburg, VA

MAKES 6–8 FULL-SIZED SERVINGS, OR 12–15 APPETIZER-SIZED SERVINGS

2 pkgs. Li'l Smokies
1 bottle chili sauce
1 small jar grape jelly

1. Combine all ingredients in slow cooker.

2. Cover. Cook on Low 1–2 hours, or until heated through.

Party Meatballs

Marie Miller/Scotia, NY

MAKES 8–10 MAIN-DISH SERVINGS

16-oz. jar salsa
16-oz. can jellied cranberry sauce
2 lbs. frozen meatballs

1. Melt cranberry sauce in saucepan. Stir in salsa and meatballs. Bring to boil. Stir. Pour into slow cooker.

2. Cover. Cook on Low 2–4 hours.

Artichokes

Susan Yoder Graber/Eureka, IL

MAKES 4 SERVINGS

4 artichokes
1 tsp. salt
2 Tbsp. lemon juice
melted butter

1. Wash and trim artichokes by cutting off the stems flush with the bottoms of the artichokes and by cutting 3/4–1 inch off the tops. Stand upright in slow cooker.

2. Mix together salt and lemon juice and pour over artichokes. Pour in water to cover 3/4 of artichokes.

3. Cover. Cook on Low 8–10 hours, or High 2–4 hours.

4. Serve with melted butter. Pull off individual leaves and dip bottom of each into butter. Using your teeth, strip the individual leaf of the meaty portion at the bottom of each leaf.

Easy Meatballs

Carlene Horne/Bedford, NH

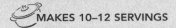 **MAKES 10–12 SERVINGS**

2 10 3/4-oz. cans cream of
mushroom soup
2 8-oz. pkgs. cream cheese,
softened
4-oz. can sliced mushrooms,
undrained
1 cup milk
2–3 lbs. frozen meatballs

1. Combine soup, cream
cheese, mushrooms, and
milk in slow cooker.

2. Add meatballs. Stir.

3. Cover. Cook on Low
4–5 hours.

4. Serve over noodles.

Easy Meatballs
for a Group

Penny Blosser
Beavercreek, OH

 **MAKES 10–12 MAIN-DISH
SERVINGS**

80–100 frozen small
meatballs
16-oz. jar barbecue sauce
16-oz. jar apricot jam

1. Fill slow cooker with
meatballs.

2. Combine sauce and jam.
Pour over meatballs.

3. Cover. Cook on Low
4 hours, stirring occasionally.

4. This works well as an
appetizer, or as a main dish
over rice.

Holiday
Meat Balls

Jean Robinson
Cinnaminson, NJ

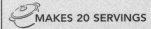 **MAKES 20 SERVINGS**

2 15-oz. bottles hot ketchup
2 cups blackberry wine
2 12-oz. jars apple jelly
2 lbs. frozen, precooked
meatballs, or your own
favorite meatballs, cooked

1. Heat ketchup, wine, and
jelly in slow cooker on High.

2. Add frozen meatballs.

3. Cover. Cook on High
4–6 hours. (If the meatballs
are not frozen, cook on
High 3–4 hours.)

variations

● For those who like it hotter
and spicier, put a bottle of
XXXtra hot sauce on the table
for them to add to their
individual servings.
● If you prefer a less wine-y
flavor, use 1 cup water and
only 1 cup wine.

Super Bowl Super Dip

Colleen Heatwole/Burton, MI

MAKES 4–5 CUPS, OR
APPROXIMATELY
12 SERVINGS

1 lb. ground beef
1 lb. Mexican Velveeta
   cheese spread
8-oz. salsa (mild, medium,
   or hot)
tortilla chips

1. Brown ground beef,
crumble into fine pieces, and
drain. Place in slow cooker.
Add cheese.

2. Cover. Cook on High
for 45 minutes, stirring
occasionally until cheese
melts.

3. Add salsa. Reduce heat
to Low and cook until
heated through.

4. Serve warm with tortilla
chips.

Hamburger Cheese Dip

Carol Eberly/Harrisonburg, VA

MAKES ABOUT 6 CUPS DIP

1 2-lb. box Velveeta cheese,
   cubed
1 lb. ground beef
1 onion, chopped
10 3/4-oz. can cream of
   mushroom soup
14.5-oz. can diced tomatoes
   with green chilies

1. While cutting up cheese,
brown beef and onions in
skillet. Drain meat mixture
and place in slow cooker.

2. Place all remaining
ingredients in slow cooker
and combine.

3. Cover. Cook on Low
2 hours, or until cheese is
melted, stirring occasionally.

4. Serve over baked
potatoes or with tortilla
chips.

variation
● For more snap, add 4.5-oz.
can green chilies in Step 2.

Hot Beef Dip

Paula Showalter
Weyers Cave, VA

MAKES ABOUT 3 CUPS DIP

2 8-oz. pkgs. cream cheese,
   softened
8 ozs. mild cheddar cheese,
   grated
1 green pepper, chopped
   fine
1 small onion, chopped fine
1/4 lb. chipped dried beef,
   shredded

1. Combine cheeses.

2. Fold in onions, peppers,
and beef.

3. Place in slow cooker.

4. Cover. Cook on Low
2–3 hours.

5. Serve hot with crackers.

variation
● For more kick, add a few
finely diced chili peppers to
Step 2.

Hearty Beef Dip Fondue

Ann Bender/Ft. Defiance, VA
Charlotte Shaffer/East Earl, PA

 MAKES 2 1/2 CUPS DIP

1 3/4 cups milk
2 8-oz. pkgs. cream cheese, cubed
2 tsp. dry mustard
1/4 cup chopped green onions
2 1/2 ozs. sliced dried beef, shredded or torn into small pieces
French bread, cut into bite-size pieces, each having a side of crust

1. Heat milk on High.

2. Add cheese. Stir until melted.

3. Add mustard, onions, and dried beef. Stir well.

4. Cover. Cook on Low for up to 6 hours.

5. Serve by dipping bread on long forks into mixture.

variations
● Add 1/2 cup chopped pecans, 2 Tbsp. chopped olives, or 1 tsp. minced onion in Step 3. I make this on cold winter evenings, and we sit around the table playing games.

Short-Cut Fondue Dip

Jean Butzer/Batavia, NY

 MAKES 8–10 SERVINGS

2 10 3/4-oz. cans condensed cheese soup
2 cups grated sharp cheddar cheese
1 Tbsp. Worcestershire sauce
1 tsp. lemon juice
2 Tbsp. dried chopped chives
celery sticks
cauliflower florets
corn chips

1. Combine soup, cheese, Worcestershire sauce, lemon juice, and chives in slow cooker.

2. Cover. Heat on Low 2–2 1/2 hours. Stir until smooth and well blended.

3. Serve warm dip with celery sticks, cauliflower, and corn chips.

Cheese Queso Dip

Janie Steele/Moore, OK

 MAKES ABOUT 2 QUARTS DIP

2-lbs. Velveeta cheese, cubed
10-oz. can diced tomatoes and chilies
1 lb. bulk sausage, browned, crumbled fine, and drained
tortilla chips

1. Combine cheese, tomatoes, and sausage in slow cooker.

2. Cover. Heat on Low 1–2 hours.

3. Serve with tortilla chips.

Broccoli Cheese Dip

Carla Koslowsky/Hillsboro, KS

MAKES 6 CUPS DIP

1 cup chopped celery
1/2 cup chopped onion
10-oz. pkg. frozen chopped
   broccoli, cooked
1 cup cooked rice
10 3/4-oz. can cream of
   mushroom soup
16-oz. jar cheese spread,
   or 15 slices American
   cheese, melted and mixed
   with 2/3 cup milk
snack breads or crackers

1. Combine all ingredients
in slow cooker.

2. Cover. Heat on Low
2 hours.

3. Serve with snack breads
or crackers.

Cheesy Sausage Dip

Reba Rhodes/Bridgewater, VA

MAKES 12–14 SERVINGS

1 lb. smoked sausage,
   chopped
1 lb. Velveeta cheese,
   cubed
1 1/4 cups salsa

1. Brown sausage in skillet.
Drain and place in slow
cooker.

2. Add cheese. Pour salsa
over top.

3. Cover. Cook on Low
1 1/2–2 hours.

4. Serve with tortilla chips
or party rye bread.

Sausage Cheese Dip

Fannie Miller/Hutchinson, KS

MAKES 20 SERVINGS

1 lb. sausage, either sliced
   thin, or with casings
   removed and crumbled
1 medium onion, chopped
1 green pepper, chopped
2 lbs. Velveeta cheese, or
   American cheese, cubed
16-oz. jar medium salsa

1. Brown sausage and
onions in skillet. Drain off
drippings and transfer meat
and onions to slow cooker.

2. Add remaining
ingredients to slow cooker
and stir well.

3. Cover. Cook on Low 4–5
hours.

4. Serve warm from cooker
with tortilla chips.

Refried Bean Dip

Maryann Markano
Wilmington, DE

 **MAKES 6 SERVINGS**

20-oz. can refried beans
1 cup shredded cheddar
  cheese
1/2 cup chopped green
  onions
1/4 tsp. salt
2–4 Tbsp. bottled taco
  sauce (depending upon
  how spicy a dip you like)
tortilla chips

1. Combine beans, cheese, onions, salt, and taco sauce in slow cooker.

2. Cover. Cook on Low 2–2 1/2 hours, or cook on High 30 minutes and then on Low 30 minutes.

3. Serve with tortilla chips.

Black-Eyed Pea Dip

Audrey Romonosky/Austin, TX

 **MAKES 12 SNACK-SIZED SERVINGS**

8 ozs. Velveeta cheese,
  cubed
15.5-oz. can black-eyed
  peas, drained
4.5-oz. can chopped green
  chilies
1/2 cup (1 stick) butter,
  melted
4 chopped green onions
tortilla chips

1. Combine cheese, peas, chilies, butter, and onions in slow cooker.

2. Cover. Cook on Low, stirring occasionally, until cheese melts. Cook an additional 1 1/2 hours on Low.

3. Serve warm from cooker with tortilla chips.

Southwest Hot Chip Dip

Annabelle Unternahrer
Shipshewana, IN

 **MAKES 15–20 SERVINGS**

1 lb. ground beef, browned,
  crumbled fine, and drained
2 15-oz. cans refried beans
2 10-oz. cans diced
  tomatoes and chilies
1 pkg. taco seasoning
1 lb. Velveeta cheese, cubed
tortilla chips

1. Combine ground beef, beans, tomatoes, and taco seasoning in slow cooker.

2. Cover. Cook on Low 3–4 hours, or on High 1 1/2 hours.

3. Add cheese. Stir occasionally. Heat until cheese is melted.

4. Serve with tortilla chips.

note
● Serve as a main dish alongside a soup.

Chili-Cheese Dip

Ruth Hofstetter
Versailles, Missouri
Paula King/Harrisonburg, VA

 **MAKES 10 SERVINGS**

1 lb. ground beef, browned, crumbled fine, and drained
2 lbs. Velveeta cheese, cubed
10-oz. can tomatoes with chilies
1 tsp. Worcestershire sauce
1/2 tsp. chili powder
tortilla or corn chips

1. Combine all ingredients except chips in slow cooker. Mix well.

2. Cover. Cook on High 1 hour, stirring occasionally until cheese is fully melted.

3. Serve immediately or turn to Low for serving up to 6 hours later.

4. Serve with tortilla or corn chips.

variation
● For a thicker dip, make a smooth paste of 2 Tbsp. flour mixed with 3 Tbsp. cold water. Stir into hot dip.

Chili-Cheese Taco Dip

Kim Stoltzfus
New Holland, PA

 **MAKES 10–12 SERVINGS**

1 lb. ground beef
1 can chili, without beans
1 lb. mild Mexican Velveeta cheese, cubed
taco or tortilla chips

1. Brown beef, crumble into small pieces, and drain.

2. Combine beef, chili, and cheese in slow cooker.

3. Cover. Cook on Low 1–1 1/2 hours, or until cheese is melted, stirring occasionally to blend ingredients.

4. Serve warm with taco or tortilla chips.

Michelle's Taco Dip

Michelle Strite
Harrisonburg, VA

 **MAKES 6–8 SERVINGS**

1 1/2 lbs. ground beef, browned, crumbled fine, and drained
1 pkg. taco seasoning mix
10-oz. jar salsa
1 lb. Velveeta cheese, cubed
1/4 cup chopped onion
tortilla chips

1. Combine all ingredients except chips in slow cooker.

2. Cover. Heat on Low for 2–3 hours.

3. Serve with tortilla chips.

variation
● The recipe can be made with half the amount of meat called for, if you prefer.

Karen's Nacho Dip

Karen Stoltzfus/Alto, MI

MAKES 10–12 SERVINGS

1 lb. ground beef
2 lbs. American cheese, cubed
16-oz. jar salsa (mild, medium, or hot, whichever you prefer)
1 Tbsp. Worcestershire sauce
tortilla or corn chips

1. Brown beef, crumble into small pieces, and drain.

2. Combine beef, cheese, salsa, and Worcestershire sauce in slow cooker.

3. Cover. Cook on High 1 hour, stirring occasionally until cheese is fully melted.

4. Serve immediately, or turn to Low for serving up to 6 hours later.

Mexican Chip Dip Ole'

Joy Sutter/Iowa City, IA

MAKES 10–12 SERVINGS

2 lbs. ground turkey
1 large onion, chopped
15-oz. can tomato sauce
4-oz. can green chilies, chopped
3-oz. can jalapeño peppers, chopped
2 lbs. Velveeta cheese, cubed
tortilla chips

1. Brown turkey and onion. Drain.

2. Add tomato sauce, chilies, jalapeño peppers, and cheese. Pour into slow cooker.

3. Cover. Cook on Low 4 hours, or High 2 hours.

4. Serve warm with tortilla chips.

Barbara's Chili Cheese Dip

Barbara Shie
Colorado Springs, CO

MAKES 8–10 SERVINGS

1 lb. ground beef
1 lb. Velveeta cheese, cubed
8-oz. can green chilies and tomato sauce
2 tsp. Worcestershire sauce
1/2 tsp., or more, chili powder
1/4 cup salsa with jalapeño peppers
tortilla or corn chips

1. Brown ground beef, crumble fine, and drain.

2. Combine all ingredients except chips in slow cooker. Stir well.

3. Cover. Cook on High 1 hour, stirring until cheese is melted. Serve immediately, or turn on Low for serving up to 6 hours later.

4. Serve with tortilla or corn chips.

note
● Serve over rice, noodles, or baked potatoes as a main dish, making 4–5 servings.

Chili Con Queso Cheese Dip

Melanie Thrower
McPherson, KS

 **MAKES 8 SERVINGS**

1 lb. ground beef
1/2 cup chopped onion
1 cup Velveeta cheese, cubed
10-oz. can diced tomatoes and green chilies
1 can evaporated milk
2 Tbsp. chili powder
tortilla chips

1. Brown ground beef and onion. Crumble beef into fine pieces. Drain.

2. Combine all ingredients except tortilla chips in slow cookers.

3. Cover. Heat on Low 1–2 hours, until cheese is melted.

4. Serve with tortilla chips.

Good 'n' Hot Dip

Joyce B. Suiter/Garysburg, NC

 **MAKES 30–50 SERVINGS**

1 lb. ground beef
1 lb. bulk sausage
10 3/4-oz. can cream of chicken soup
10 3/4-oz. can cream of celery soup
24-oz. jar salsa (use hot for some zing)
1 lb. Velveeta cheese, cubed
chips

1. Brown beef and sausage, crumbling into small pieces. Drain.

2. Combine meat, soups, salsa, and cheese in slow cooker.

3. Cover. Cook on High 1 hour. Stir. Cook on Low until ready to serve.

4. Serve with chips.

Maryann's Chili Cheese Dip

Maryann Westerberg
Rosamond, CA

 **MAKES ABOUT 10 SERVINGS**

2 lbs. Velveeta cheese, cubed
16-oz. can chili without beans
10-oz. can diced tomatoes with chilies, drained
10 3/4-oz. can cream of mushroom soup
tortilla chips

1. Combine cheese and chili in slow cooker. Heat on Low until cheese melts, stirring occasionally.

2. Add tomatoes and soup.

3. Cover. Cook on Low 2 hours. Stir before serving.

4. Serve with tortilla chips.

Chili Verde con Queso Dip

Bonita Ensenberger
Albuquerque, NM

**MAKES 1 QUART
(8–10 SERVINGS)**

2 10 3/4-oz. cans cheddar cheese soup
7-oz. can chopped green chilies
1 garlic clove, minced
1/2 tsp. dried cilantro leaves
1/2 tsp. ground cumin
corn chips

1. Mix together all ingredients except corn chips in slow cooker.

2. Cover. Cook on Low 1–1 1/2 hours. Stir well. Cook an additional 1 1/2 hours.

3. Serve with corn chips.

variation
● Make this a main dish by serving over baked potatoes.

Chili Con Queso

Arlene Leaman Kliewer
Lakewood, CO

MAKES 12–16 SERVINGS

2 Tbsp. oil
1 medium onion, chopped
2 4-oz. cans chopped green chilies
14 1/2-oz. can Mexican-style stewed tomatoes, drained
1 lb. Velveeta cheese, cubed

1. In skillet, sauté onion in oil until transparent. Add chilies and tomatoes. Bring to boil.

2. Add cheese. Pour into slow cooker on Low. Cook for 2 hours.

3. Keep warm in slow cooker, stirring occasionally.

4. Serve with tortilla chips.

Cheesy Hot Bean Dip

John D. Allen/Rye, CO

MAKES 4–5 CUPS DIP

16-oz. can refried beans
1 cup salsa
2 cups (8 ozs.) shredded Jack and cheddar cheeses, mixed
1 cup sour cream
3-oz. pkg. cream cheese, cubed
1 Tbsp. chili powder
1/4 tsp. ground cumin
tortilla chips

1. Combine all ingredients except chips in slow cooker.

2. Cover. Cook on High 2 hours. Stir 2–3 times during cooking.

3. Serve warm from the cooker with chips.

This bean dip is a favorite. Once you start on it, it's hard to leave it alone. We have been known to dip into it even when it's cold.

— ● —

Mexican Meat Dip

Deborah Swartz/Grottoes, VA

 MAKES 20 SERVINGS

1 lb. ground beef
3/4–1 cup chopped onions
15-oz. can refried beans
1 pkg. dry taco seasoning mix
1 cup sour cream
1 1/2 cups grated mozzarella cheese

1. Brown ground beef and onions in skillet. Drain. Place meat and onions in slow cooker.

2. Add beans and taco seasoning mix. Mix together well.

3. Spread sour cream over mixture. Sprinkle cheese over top.

4. Cover. Cook on Low 1 1/2 hours or on High 3/4 hour.

5. Serve warm from the cooker with tortilla chips.

TNT Dip

Sheila Plock/Boalsburg, PA

 MAKES 8 CUPS

1 1/2 lbs. ground beef, browned
10 3/4-oz. can cream of mushroom soup
1/4 cup butter, melted
1 lb. Velveeta cheese, cubed
1 cup salsa
2 Tbsp. chili powder

1. Combine all ingredients in slow cooker.

2. Cover. Cook on High 1–1 1/4 hours, or until cheese is melted, stirring occasionally.

3. Serve with tortilla chips, corn chips, or party rye bread.

variation
● To change the balance of flavors, use 1 lb. browned ground beef and 1 1/2 cups salsa. My son has hosted a Super Bowl party for his college friends at our house the past two years. He served this dip the first year, and the second year it was requested. His friends claim it's the best dip they've ever eaten. With a bunch of college kids it disappears quickly.

Nacho Dip

Beth Maurer/Harrisonburg, VA

 MAKES 10–12 SERVINGS

2 lbs. ground beef, browned
1 lb. sausage, browned
16-oz. jar medium-hot salsa
1 pkg. dry taco seasoning mix
2-lb. box Velveeta cheese, cubed
10 3/4-oz. can cream of mushroom soup

1. Stir salsa and seasoning mix into meat. Then spread in bottom of slow cooker.

2. Cover and cook on High one hour.

3. Stir in cheese and soup.

4. Cover. Cook on Low 3–4 hours, until ingredients are hot and cheese and soup are melted.

5. Serve with unsalted chips, tortilla or nacho chips, pita wedges, chopped tomatoes, refried beans, onions, and sour cream.

This is a delight at any party or get-together. We serve it at every Christmas party.

— ● —

Cheese and Crab Dip

Donna Lantgen/Rapid City, SD

MAKES 10–12 SERVINGS

3 8-oz. pkgs. cream cheese, at room temperature
2 6-oz. cans crabmeat, drained
1 can broken shrimp, drained
6 Tbsp. finely chopped onions
1 tsp. horseradish
1/2 cup toasted almonds, broken

1. Combine all ingredients in slow cooker.

2. Cover. Cook on Low 2 hours.

3. Serve with crackers or bread cubes.

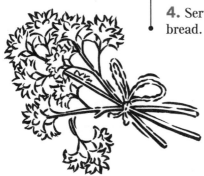

Hot Crab Dip

Cassandra Ly/Carlisle, PA
Miriam Nolt/New Holland, PA

MAKES 15–20 SERVINGS

1/2 cup milk
1/3 cup salsa
3 8-oz. pkgs. cream cheese, cubed
2 8-oz. pkgs. imitation crabmeat, flaked
1 cup thinly sliced green onions
4-oz. can chopped green chilies
assorted crackers or bread cubes

1. Combine milk and salsa. Transfer to greased slow cooker.

2. Stir in cream cheese, crabmeat, onions, and chilies.

3. Cover. Cook on Low 3–4 hours, stirring every 30 minutes.

4. Serve with crackers or bread.

Reuben Spread

Clarice Williams/Fairbank, IA
Julie McKenzie
Punxsutawney, PA

MAKES 5 CUPS SPREAD

1/2 lb. corned beef, shredded or chopped
16-oz. can sauerkraut, well drained
1–2 cups shredded Swiss cheese
1–2 cups shredded cheddar cheese
1 cup mayonnaise
snack rye bread
Thousand Island dressing, optional

1. Combine all ingredients except bread and Thousand Island dressing in slow cooker. Mix well.

2. Cover. Cook on High 1–2 hours until heated through, stirring occasionally.

3. Turn to Low to keep warm while serving. Put spread on bread slices. Top with Thousand Island dressing, if desired.

note
● Low-fat cheese and mayonnaise are not recommended.

variation
● Use dried beef instead of corned beef.

Slow Cooker Reuben Dip

Allison Ingels/Maynard, IA

MAKES 8–12 SERVINGS

8-oz. carton sour cream
2 8-oz. pkgs. cream cheese, softened
8-oz. can sauerkraut, drained
3 2 1/2-oz. pkgs. dried corned beef, finely chopped
6-oz. pkg. shredded Swiss cheese

1. Combine ingredients in slow cooker.

2. Cover. Heat on Low 3–4 hours, or until cheeses are melted.

3. Serve from cooker with rye crackers or rye party bread.

Reuben Appetizer

Joleen Albrecht/Gladstone, MI

MAKES 12 SERVINGS

1/2 cup mayonnaise
10 ozs. Swiss cheese, shredded
1/2 lb. chipped, or thinly sliced, corned beef
16-oz. can sauerkraut, drained and cut up
sliced party rye bread

1. Combine all ingredients except bread in slow cooker.

2. Heat until cheese is melted.

3. Serve hot on rye bread.

Roasted Pepper and Artichoke Spread

Sherril Bieberly/Salina, KS

MAKES 3 CUPS, OR ABOUT 12 SERVINGS

1 cup grated Parmesan cheese
1/2 cup mayonnaise
8-oz. pkg. cream cheese, softened
1 garlic clove, minced
14-oz. can artichoke hearts, drained and chopped finely
1/3 cup finely chopped roasted red bell peppers (from 7 1/4-oz. jar)
crackers, cut-up fresh vegetables, or snack-bread slices

1. Combine Parmesan cheese, mayonnaise, cream cheese, and garlic in food processor. Process until smooth. Place mixture in slow cooker.

2. Add artichoke hearts and red bell pepper. Stir well.

3. Cover. Cook on Low 1 hour. Stir again.

4. Use as spread for crackers, cut-up fresh vegetables, or snack-bread slices.

Hot Artichoke Dip

Mary E. Wheatley
Mashpee, MA

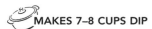

MAKES 7–8 CUPS DIP

2 14 3/4 oz. jars marinated artichoke hearts, drained
1 cup mayonnaise
1 cup sour cream
1 cup water chestnuts, chopped
2 cups grated Parmesan cheese
1/4 cup finely chopped scallions

1. Cut artichoke hearts into small pieces. Add mayonnaise, sour cream, water chestnuts, cheese, and scallions. Pour into slow cooker.

2. Cover. Cook on High 1–2 hours or on Low 3–4 hours.

3. Serve with crackers or crusty French bread.

Festive Cocktail Meatballs

Sharon Timpe/Mequon, WI

MAKES ABOUT 4 DOZEN MEATBALLS

Sauce:
2 cups ketchup
1 cup brown sugar
2 Tbsp. Worcestershire sauce

Meatballs:
2 lbs. ground beef
1 envelope dry onion soup mix
1/2 cup milk

1. Mix together ketchup, brown sugar, and Worcestershire sauce in slow cooker. Turn on High while mixing up meatballs.

2. Combine ground beef, soup mix, and milk. Mix well. Shape into 1" balls. Bake at 325°F for 20 minutes. Drain. Add to slow cooker.

3. Cover. Cook on Low 2–2 1/2 hours, stirring gently, twice throughout the cooking time.

Barbecued Mini-Franks

Zona Mae Bontrager
Kokomo, IN

MAKES 8–10 FUN-SIZED SERVINGS, OR 16–20 APPETIZER-SIZED SERVINGS

1 cup finely chopped onions
1 cup ketchup
1/3 cup Worcestershire sauce
1/4 cup sugar
1/4 cup vinegar
4 tsp. prepared mustard
1 tsp. pepper
4-lbs. miniature hot dogs

1. Combine all ingredients except hot dogs in slow cooker.

2. Cover. Heat on High 1 1/2 hours, or until hot. Add hot dogs.

3. Reduce heat to Low and simmer 4 hours.

variations
● Add 1 Tbsp. finely chopped green pepper and 2 garlic cloves, pressed.
● Use miniature smoked sausages instead of mini-hot dogs.

Frankwiches

Esther Mast
East Petersburg, PA

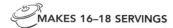

MAKES 16–18 SERVINGS

2 10 3/4-oz. cans cheddar
cheese soup
1/2 cup finely chopped
onions
1/2 cup sweet pickle relish
4 tsp. prepared mustard
2 lbs. hot dogs, thinly sliced
8-oz. container sour cream

1. Combine soup, onions,
relish, and mustard. Stir in
sliced hot dogs.

2. Cover. Cook on Low
4 hours.

3. Stir in sour cream.

4. Cover. Cook on High
10–15 minutes, stirring
occasionally.

5. Serve over toasted
English muffin halves or
squares of hot cornbread.

notes
● You can also serve this over
rice as a main dish. Add a
green vegetable and a Jell-O
salad and you have an easy,
refreshing, quick meal!
This will also bring smiles to
the faces of your grandchildren!
Add a relish tray and some
chips, and you have a quick
summer meal on the patio.
Top it off with frozen Popsicles.

Cranberry Franks

Loretta Krahn
Mountain Lake, MN

MAKES 15–20 SERVINGS

2 pkgs. cocktail wieners or
little smoked sausages
16-oz. can jellied cranberry
sauce
1 cup ketchup
3 Tbsp. brown sugar
1 Tbsp. lemon juice

1. Combine all ingredients
in slow cooker.

2. Cover. Cook on High
1–2 hours.

> Great picnic, potluck,
> or buffet food.

— • —

Curried Almonds

Barbara Aston/Ashdown, AR

MAKES 4 CUPS NUTS

2 Tbsp. melted butter
1 Tbsp. curry powder
1/2 tsp. seasoned salt
1 lb. blanched almonds

1. Combine butter with
curry powder and seasoned
salt.

2. Pour over almonds in
slow cooker. Mix to coat
well.

3. Cover. Cook on Low
2–3 hours. Turn to High.
Uncover cooker and cook
1–1 1/2 hours.

4. Serve hot or cold.

Soups
and Stews

Salsa Soup

Sue Hamilton/Minooka, IL

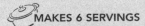 **MAKES 6 SERVINGS**

3 cups (26 oz.) corn-black bean mild salsa

6 cups beef broth

1/4 cup white long grain rice, uncooked

1. Combine all ingredients in slow cooker.

2. Cover. Cook on Low 4–6 hours, or until rice is tender.

Buffalo Chicken Wing Soup

Anna Stoltzfus
Honey Brook, PA

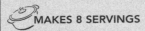 **MAKES 8 SERVINGS**

6 cups milk

3 10 3/4-oz. cans cream of chicken soup

3 cups shredded cooked chicken

1 cup sour cream

1/4–1/2 cup hot pepper sauce (or if you're timid, use 2 Tbsp.)

1. Combine ingredients in slow cooker.

2. Cover. Cook on Low 4–5 hours.

Sauerkraut-Sausage Bean Soup

Bonnie Goering
Bridgewater, VA

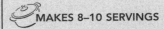 **MAKES 8–10 SERVINGS**

3 15-oz. cans white beans, undrained

16-oz. can sauerkraut, drained and rinsed

1 lb. link sausage, sliced

1/4 brown sugar

1/2 cup ketchup

1. Combine all ingredients in slow cooker.

2. Cover. Cook on High 2–3 hours.

3. Serve with cornbread, applesauce, or coleslaw.

note
● You may add tomato juice or water if you prefer a thinner soup.

...super**easy**

Rich and Easy Clam Chowder

Rhonda Burgoon
Collingswood, NJ

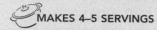 MAKES 4–5 SERVINGS

3 10 3/4-oz. cans cream of potato soup
2 10 3/4-oz. cans New England clam chowder
1/2 cup butter
1 small onion, diced
1 pint half-and-half
2 6 1/2-oz. cans clams, chopped

1. Combine all ingredients in slow cooker.

2. Cover. Cook on Low 2–4 hours.

Easy Cheese Soup

Nancy Wagner Graves
Manhattan, KS

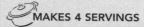 MAKES 4 SERVINGS

2 10 3/4-oz. cans cream of mushroom, or cream of chicken, soup
1 cup beer or milk
1 lb. cheddar cheese, grated
1 tsp. Worcestershire sauce
1/4 tsp. paprika
croutons

1. Combine all ingredients except croutons in slow cooker.

2. Cover. Cook on Low 4–6 hours.

3. Stir thoroughly 1 hour before serving, to make sure cheese is well distributed and melted.

4. Serve topped with croutons or in bread bowls.

Hearty Alphabet Soup

Maryann Markano
Wilmington, DE

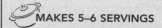 MAKES 5–6 SERVINGS

1/2 lb. beef stewing meat, or round steak, cubed
14 1/2-oz. can stewed tomatoes
8-oz. can tomato sauce
1 cup water
1 envelope dry onion soup mix
10-oz. pkg. frozen vegetables, partially thawed
1/2 cup uncooked alphabet noodles

1. Combine meat, tomatoes, tomato sauce, water, and soup mix in slow cooker.

2. Cover. Cook on Low 6–8 hours. Turn to High.

3. Stir in vegetables and noodles. Add more water if mixture is too dry and thick.

4. Cover. Cook on High 30 minutes, or until vegetables are tender.

Nancy's Vegetable Beef Soup

Nancy Graves/Manhattan, KS

MAKES 6–8 SERVINGS

2-lb. roast cut into bite-size
  pieces, or 2 lbs. stewing
  meat
15-oz. can corn
15-oz. can green beans
1-lb. bag frozen peas
40-oz. can stewed tomatoes
5 beef bouillon cubes
Tabasco to taste
2 tsp. salt

1. Combine all ingredients
in slow cooker. Do not drain
vegetables.

2. Add water to fill slow
cooker to within 3 inches
of top.

3. Cover. Cook on Low
8 hours, or until meat
is tender and vegetables
are soft.

variation
● Add 1 large onion, sliced,
2 cups sliced carrots, and
3/4 cup pearl barley to mixture
before cooking.

"Absent Cook" Stew

Kathy Hertzler/Lancaster, PA

MAKES 5–6 SERVINGS

2 lbs. stewing beef, cubed
2–3 carrots, sliced
1 onion, chopped
3 large potatoes, cubed
3 ribs celery, sliced
10 3/4-oz. can tomato soup
1 soup can water
1 tsp. salt
dash of pepper
2 Tbsp. vinegar

1. Combine all ingredients
in slow cooker.

2. Cover. Cook on Low
10–12 hours.

Ruby's Vegetable Beef Soup

Ruby Stoltzfus/Mount Joy, PA

MAKES 8–10 SERVINGS

1 lb. beef cubes
1 cup beef broth
1 1/2 cups chopped
  cabbage
1 1/2 cups stewed
  tomatoes, undrained
1 1/2 cups frozen, or
  canned, corn
1 1/2 cups frozen peas
1 1/2 cups frozen green
  beans
1 1/2 cups sliced carrots
3/4 tsp. salt
1/4–1/2 tsp. pepper

1. Combine all ingredients
in slow cooker.

2. Cover. Cook on Low 6–8
hours, or High 3–4 hours.

Sharon's Vegetable Soup

Sharon Wantland
Menomonee Falls, WI

MAKES 6–8 SERVINGS

46-oz. can tomato juice
5 beef bouillon cubes
4 celery ribs, sliced
4 large carrots, sliced
1 onion, chopped
one-quarter head of
  cabbage, chopped
1-lb. can green beans
2 cups water
1 lb. beef stewing meat,
  browned
4-oz. can sliced mushrooms

1. Combine all ingredients
in slow cooker.

2. Cover. Cook on Low
8 hours, or until meat and
vegetables are tender.

Old-Fashioned Vegetable Beef Soup

Pam Hochstedler/Kalona, IA

MAKES 8–10 SERVINGS

1–2 lbs. beef short ribs
2 qts. water
1 tsp. salt
1 tsp. celery salt
1 small onion, chopped
1 cup diced carrots
1/2 cup diced celery
2 cups diced potatoes
1-lb. can whole kernel corn,
  undrained
1-lb. can diced tomatoes
  and juice

1. Combine meat, water,
salt, celery salt, onion,
carrots, and celery in slow
cooker.

2. Cover. Cook on Low
4–6 hours.

3. Debone meat, cut into
bite-size pieces, and return
to pot.

4. Add potatoes, corn, and
tomatoes.

5. Cover and cook on High
2–3 hours.

Slow-Cooker Minestrone

Dorothy Shank/Sterling, IL

MAKES 8 SERVINGS

3 cups water
1 1/2 lbs. stewing meat,
  cut into bite-size pieces
1 medium onion, diced
4 carrots, diced
14 1/2-oz. can tomatoes
2 tsp. salt
10-oz. pkg. frozen mixed
  vegetables, or your choice
  of frozen vegetables
1 Tbsp. dried basil
1/2 cup dry vermicelli
1 tsp. dried oregano
grated Parmesan cheese

1. Combine all ingredients
except cheese in slow
cooker. Stir well.

2. Cover. Cook on Low
10–12 hours, or on High
4–5 hours.

3. Top individual servings
with Parmesan cheese.

Vegetable Beef Soup

Ruth Ann Swartzendruber
Hydro, OK

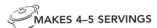 MAKES 4–5 SERVINGS

1 lb. ground beef, browned and drained
2 cups tomato juice
2 cups beef broth
1 lb. frozen mixed vegetables, or your choice of vegetables

1. Combine all ingredients in slow cooker.

2. Cover. Cook on High 3 hours, and then on Low 3–4 hours.

Hearty Beef and Cabbage Soup

Carolyn Mathias
Williamsville, NY

 MAKES 8 SERVINGS

1 lb. ground beef
1 medium onion, chopped
40-oz. can tomatoes
2 cups water
15-oz. can kidney beans
1 tsp. salt
1/2 tsp. pepper
1 Tbsp. chili powder
1/2 cup chopped celery
2 cups thinly sliced cabbage

1. Sauté beef in skillet. Drain.

2. Combine all ingredients except cabbage in slow cooker.

3. Cover. Cook on Low 3 hours. Add cabbage. Cook on High 30–60 minutes longer.

Spicy Beef Vegetable Stew

Melissa Raber/Millersburg, OH

 MAKES 12 SERVINGS

1 lb. ground beef
1 cup chopped onions
30-oz. jar meatless spaghetti sauce
3 1/2 cups water
1 lb. frozen mixed vegetables
10-oz. can diced tomatoes with green chilies
1 cup sliced celery
1 tsp. beef bouillon granules
1 tsp. pepper

1. Cook beef and onion in skillet until meat is no longer pink. Drain. Transfer to slow cooker.

2. Stir in remaining ingredients.

3. Cover. Cook on Low 8 hours.

Vegetable Soup with Potatoes

Annabelle Unternahrer
Shipshewana, IN

 MAKES 6–8 SERVINGS

1 lb. hamburger, browned and drained
2 15-oz. cans diced tomatoes
2 carrots, sliced or cubed
2 onions, sliced or cubed
2 potatoes, diced
1–2 garlic cloves, minced
12-oz. can V-8 vegetable juice
1 1/2–2 cups sliced celery
2 tsp. beef stock concentrate, or 2 beef bouillon cubes
2–3 cups vegetables (cauliflower, peas, corn, limas, or your choice of leftovers from your freezer)

1. Combine all ingredients in slow cooker.

2. Cover. Cook on Low 12 hours, or High 4–6 hours.

note
● If using leftover vegetables that are precooked, add during last hour if cooking on Low, or during last half hour if cooking on High.

variation
● Use 3 cups pre-cooked dried beans or lentils instead of hamburger.

Vegetable Soup with Noodles

Glenda S. Weaver
New Holland, PA

 MAKES 6 SERVINGS

1 pint water
2 beef bouillon cubes
1 onion, chopped
1 lb. ground beef
1/4 cup ketchup
1 tsp. salt
1/8 tsp. celery salt
1/2 cup uncooked noodles
12–16 oz. pkg. frozen mixed vegetables, or vegetables of your choice
1 pint tomato juice

1. Dissolve bouillon cubes in water.

2. Brown onion and beef in skillet. Drain.

3. Combine all ingredients in slow cooker.

4. Cover. Cook on Low 6 hours, or on High 2–3 hours, until vegetables are tender.

Dottie's Creamy Steak Soup

Debbie Zeida/Mashpee, MA

 MAKES 4–6 SERVINGS

1 lb. ground beef
half a large onion, chopped
12-oz. can V-8 vegetable juice
2–3 medium potatoes, diced
10 3/4-oz. can cream of mushroom soup
10 3/4-oz. can cream of celery soup
16-oz. pkg. frozen mixed vegetables, or your choice of frozen vegetables
2 tsp. salt
1/2–3/4 tsp. pepper

1. Sauté beef and onions in skillet. Drain.

2. Combine all ingredients in slow cooker.

3. Cover. Cook on Low 8–10 hours.

Hamburger Soup

Naomi Ressler
Harrisonburg, VA

Kay Magruder/Seminole, OK

MAKES 8 SERVINGS

1 1/2 lbs. ground beef, browned
1 medium onion, chopped
1 cup sliced carrots
1 cup sliced celery
1 cup sliced cabbage
6-oz. can tomato paste
2 tsp. Worcestershire sauce
2–3 cups beef broth, depending upon how thick or thin you like your soup

1. Combine beef, onions, carrots, celery, and cabbage in slow cooker.

2. Combine tomato paste, Worcestershire sauce, and broth. Pour into slow cooker. Mix to blend.

3. Cover. Cook on Low 8–10 hours or on High 3–4 hours.

variation
● Stir in 1/4 tsp. black or cayenne pepper and 2 bay leaves in Step 2 for added flavor.

Ground Beef Soup

Nadine L. Martinitz/Salina, KS

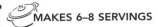MAKES 6–8 SERVINGS

1 lb. ground beef
1 medium onion, chopped
1 Tbsp. oil
15.8-oz. can Great Northern Beans, undrained
15-oz. can tomato sauce
1 1/2–2 tomato-sauce cans water
2 large potatoes, cubed
14.5-oz. can tomatoes
1 tsp. salt

1. Brown ground beef and onions in oil in skillet. Drain. Place in slow cooker.

2. Add remaining ingredients.

3. Cook on High 1 hour, then Low 6–8 hours.

4. Serve with grilled cheese sandwiches.

Ruth's Ground Beef Vegetable Soup

Ruth Ann Penner
Hillsboro, KS

MAKES 6 SERVINGS

1 lb. ground beef
1 1/2 qts. water
3/4 cup chopped celery
1 cup chopped carrots
1 large onion, chopped
2 cups cubed potatoes
1 1/2 tsp. salt
1/2 cup uncooked rice
1/4 tsp. pepper
10 3/4-oz. can tomato soup

1. Crumble ground beef in slow cooker. Add water.

2. Add remaining ingredients except soup. Mix together well.

3. Cover. Cook on Low 8–10 hours.

4. Add soup 30 minutes before serving and stir through.

Beef Barley Soup

Michelle Showalter
Bridgewater, VA

MAKES 10–12 SERVINGS

1 lb. ground beef, browned
1 1/2 qts. water
1 qt. canned tomatoes, stewed, crushed, or whole
3 cups sliced carrots
1 cup diced celery
1 cup diced potatoes
1 cup diced onions
3/4 cup quick-cooking barley
3 tsp. beef bouillon granules, or 3 beef bouillon cubes
2–3 tsp. salt
1/4 tsp. pepper

1. Combine ingredients in slow cooker.

2. Cover. Cook on Low 8–10 hours or High 4–5 hours.

3. Serve with fresh bread and cheese cubes.

variation
● You may use pearl barley instead of quick-cooking barley. Cook it according to package directions and add halfway through cooking time of soup.

Easy Vegetable Soup

Dawn Day/Westminster, CA

MAKES 6–8 SERVINGS

4 cups vegetable, beef, or chicken stock
4 cups vegetables (use any or all of corn, peas, carrots, broccoli, green beans, cauliflower, mushrooms), either fresh or frozen
leftover meat, cut in small pieces, or 1 lb. cubed beef, browned in oil in skillet
15-oz. can chopped tomatoes
1 bay leaf
1/4 cup uncooked rice or barley, or 1/2 cup cooked orzo or small shells

1. Combine all ingredients in slow cooker except pasta.

2. Cover. Cook on Low 6 hours, adding pasta 1/2 hour before serving.

3. Serve with rolls and a salad for a great comfort meal.

Taco Soup with Black Beans

Alexa Slonin/Harrisonburg, VA

MAKES 6–8 SERVINGS

1 lb. ground beef, browned and drained
28-oz. can crushed tomatoes
15 1/4-oz. can corn, undrained
15-oz. can black beans, undrained
15 1/2-oz. can red kidney beans, undrained
1 envelope dry Hidden Valley Ranch Dressing mix
1 envelope dry taco seasoning
1 small onion, chopped
tortilla, or corn, chips
shredded cheese
sour cream

1. Combine all ingredients except chips, shredded cheese, and sour cream in slow cooker.

2. Cover. Cook on Low 4–6 hours.

3. Garnish individual servings with chips, cheese, and sour cream.

Taco Soup with Pinto Beans

Janie Steele/Moore, OK

MAKES 10–12 SERVINGS

1 lb. ground beef
1 large onion, chopped
3 14-oz. cans pinto beans
14-oz. can tomatoes with chilies
14 1/2-oz. can chopped tomatoes
15-oz. can tomato sauce
1 pkg. dry Hidden Valley Ranch Dressing mix
1 pkg. dry taco seasoning
15 1/4-oz. can corn, drained

1. Brown beef and onions in skillet. Drain.

2. Combine all ingredients in slow cooker.

3. Cover. Cook on Low 4 hours, or until ingredients are heated through.

Sante Fe Soup with Melted Cheese

Carla Koslowsky/Hillsboro, KS

MAKES 8 SERVINGS

1 lb. Velveeta cheese, cubed
1 lb. ground beef, browned and drained
15 1/4-oz. can corn, undrained
15-oz. can kidney beans, undrained
14 1/2-oz. can diced tomatoes with green chilies
14 1/2-oz. can stewed tomatoes
2 Tbsp. dry taco seasoning
corn chips, or soft tortillas

1. Combine all ingredients except chips or tortillas in slow cooker.

2. Cover. Cook on High 3 hours.

3. Serve with corn chips as a side, or dip soft tortillas in individual servings in soup bowls.

Taco Soup with Pizza Sauce

Barbara Kuhns
Millersburg, OH

MAKES 8–10 SERVINGS

2 lbs. ground beef, browned
1 small onion, chopped and sautéed in ground beef drippings
3/4 tsp. salt
1/2 tsp. pepper
1 1/2 pkgs. dry taco seasoning
1 qt. pizza sauce
1 qt. water
tortilla chips
shredded mozzarella cheese
sour cream

1. Combine ground beef, onion, salt, pepper, taco seasoning, pizza sauce, and water in 5-quart, or larger, slow cooker.

2. Cover. Cook on Low 3–4 hours.

3. Top individual servings with tortilla chips, cheese, and sour cream.

variation
● Add 15-oz. can black beans and 4-oz. can chilies to mixture before cooking. (Be sure to use one very large cooker, or two medium-sized cookers.)

Chicken Tortilla Soup

Becky Harder/Monument, CO

MAKES 6–8 SERVINGS

- 4 chicken breast halves
- 2 15-oz. cans black beans, undrained
- 2 15-oz. cans Mexican stewed tomatoes, or Rotel tomatoes
- 1 cup salsa (mild, medium, or hot, whichever you prefer)
- 4-oz. can chopped green chilies
- 14 1/2-oz. can tomato sauce
- tortilla chips
- 2 cups grated cheese

1. Combine all ingredients except chips and cheese in large slow cooker.

2. Cover. Cook on Low 8 hours.

3. Just before serving, remove chicken breasts and slice into bite-size pieces. Stir into soup.

4. To serve, put a handful of chips in each individual soup bowl. Ladle soup over chips. Top with cheese.

Tex-Mex Chicken Chowder

Janie Steele/Moore, OK

MAKES 8–10 SERVINGS

- 1 cup chopped onions
- 1 cup thinly sliced celery
- 2 garlic cloves, minced
- 1 Tbsp. oil
- 1 1/2 lbs. boneless, skinless chicken breasts, cubed
- 32-oz. can chicken broth
- 1 pkg. country gravy mix
- 2 cups milk
- 16-oz. jar chunky salsa
- 32-oz. bag frozen hash brown potatoes
- 4 1/2-oz. can chopped green chilies
- 8 oz. Velveeta cheese, cubed

1. Combine onions, celery, garlic, oil, chicken, and broth in 5-quart or larger slow cooker.

2. Cover. Cook on Low 2 1/2 hours, until chicken is no longer pink.

3. In separate bowl, dissolve gravy mix in milk. Stir into chicken mixture. Add salsa, potatoes, chilies, and cheese and combine well. Cook on Low 2–4 hours, or until potatoes are fully cooked.

Taco Soup

Suzanne Slagel/Midway, OH

MAKES 6–8 SERVINGS

- 1 lb. ground beef
- 1 large onion, chopped
- 16-oz. can Mexican-style tomatoes
- 16-oz. can ranch-style beans
- 16-oz. can whole-kernel corn, undrained
- 16-oz. can kidney beans, undrained
- 16-oz. can black beans, undrained
- 16-oz. jar picante sauce
- corn or tortilla chips
- sour cream
- shredded cheddar cheese

1. Brown meat and onions in skillet. Drain.

2. Combine with all other vegetables and picante sauce in slow cooker.

3. Cover. Cook on Low 4–6 hours.

4. Serve with corn or tortilla chips, sour cream, and shredded cheese as toppings.

Taco Soup

Sue Tjon/Austin, TX

MAKES 8 SERVINGS

1 lb. ground beef
1 envelope dry ranch dressing mix
1 envelope dry taco seasoning mix
3 12-oz. cans Rotel tomatoes, undrained
2 24-oz. cans pinto beans, undrained
24-oz. can hominy, undrained
14.5-oz. can stewed tomatoes, undrained
1 onion, chopped
2 cups water

1. Brown meat in skillet. Pour into slow cooker.

2. Add remaining ingredients. Mix well.

3. Cover. Cook on Low 4 hours.

notes
● Increase or decrease the amount of water you add to make the dish either stew-like or soup-like.
● A serving suggestion is to line each individual soup bowl with tortilla chips, ladle taco soup on top, and sprinkle with grated cheese.

Sauerkraut Soup

Barbara Tenny/Delta, PA

MAKES 8 SERVINGS

1 lb. smoked Polish sausage, cut into 1/2-inch pieces
5 medium potatoes, cubed
2 large onions, chopped
2 large carrots, cut into 1/4-inch slices
42–45-oz. can chicken broth
32-oz. can or bag sauerkraut, rinsed and drained
6-oz. can tomato paste

1. Combine all ingredients in large slow cooker. Stir to combine.

2. Cover. Cook on High 2 hours, and then on Low 6–8 hours.

3. Serve with rye bread.

Kielbasa Soup

Bernice M. Gnidovec
Streator, IL

MAKES 8 SERVINGS

16-oz. pkg. frozen mixed vegetables, or your choice of vegetables
6-oz. can tomato paste
1 medium onion, chopped
3 medium potatoes, diced
1 1/2 lbs. kielbasa, cut into 1/4-inch pieces
4 qts. water
fresh parsley

1. Combine all ingredients except parsley in large slow cooker.

2. Cover. Cook on Low 12 hours.

3. Garnish individual servings with fresh parsley.

Delicious Sausage Soup

Karen Waggoner/Joplin, MO

MAKES 4 SERVINGS

5 1/2 cups chicken broth
1/2 cup heavy cream
3 carrots, grated
4 potatoes, sliced or cubed
4 cups kale, chopped
1 lb. spicy Italian sausage, browned
1/2 tsp. salt
1/2 tsp. crushed red pepper flakes

1. Combine broth and cream in slow cooker. Turn on High.

2. Add carrots, potatoes, kale, and sausage.

3. Sprinkle spices over top.

4. Cover. Cook on High 4–5 hours, stirring occasionally.

Curried Pork and Pea Soup

Kathy Hertzler/Lancaster, PA

MAKES 6–8 SERVINGS

1 1/2-lb. boneless pork shoulder roast
1 cup yellow, or green, split peas, rinsed and drained
1/2 cup finely chopped carrots
1/2 cup finely chopped celery
1/2 cup finely chopped onions
49 1/2-oz. can (approximately 6 cups) chicken broth
2 tsp. curry powder
1/2 tsp. Paprika
1/4 tsp. ground cumin
1/4 tsp. pepper
2 cups torn fresh spinach

1. Trim fat from pork and cut pork into 1/2-inch pieces.

2. Combine split peas, carrots, celery, and onions in slow cooker.

3. Stir in broth, curry powder, paprika, cumin, and pepper. Stir in pork.

4. Cover. Cook on Low 10–12 hours, or on High 4 hours.

5. Stir in spinach. Serve immediately.

Ruth's Split Pea Soup

Ruth Conrad Liechty
Goshen, IN

MAKES 6–8 SERVINGS

1 lb. bulk sausage, browned and drained
6 cups water
1 bag (2 1/4 cups) dry split peas
2 medium potatoes, diced
1 onion, chopped
1/2 tsp. dried marjoram, or thyme
1/2 tsp. pepper

1. Wash and sort dried peas, removing any stones. Then combine all ingredients in slow cooker.

2. Cover. Cook on Low 12 hours.

Kelly's Split Pea Soup

Kelly Evenson/Pittsboro, NC

MAKES 8 SERVINGS

2 cups dry split peas
2 quarts water
2 onions, chopped
2 carrots, peeled and sliced
4 slices Canadian bacon, chopped
2 Tbsp. chicken bouillon granules, or 2 chicken bouillon cubes
1 tsp. salt
1/4–1/2 tsp. pepper

1. Combine all ingredients in slow cooker.

2. Cover. Cook on Low 8–9 hours.

variation
● For a creamier soup, remove half of soup when done and puree. Stir back into rest of soup.

Sally's Split Pea Soup

Sally Holzem/Schofield, WI

MAKES 8 SERVINGS

1-lb. pkg. split peas
1 ham hock
1 carrot, diced
1 onion, diced
1 rib celery, diced
2 qts. water
1/4 tsp. pepper
1 bay leaf
2 whole allspice
3 potatoes, diced
1 tsp. sugar

1. Wash and sort split peas, removing any stones. Then combine ingredients in slow cooker.

2. Cover. Cook on Low 8–10 hours.

3. Remove ham bone. Cut meat off and dice. Return meat to soup. Stir through.

4. Remove bay leaf before serving.

Rosemarie's Pea Soup

Rosemarie Fitzgerald
Gibsonia, PA

Shirley Sears/Tiskilwa, IL

MAKES 4–6 SERVINGS

2 cups dried split peas
4 cups water
1 rib celery, chopped
1 cup chopped potatoes
1 large carrot, chopped
1 medium onion, chopped
1/4 tsp. dried thyme, or marjoram
1 bay leaf
1/2 tsp. salt
1 garlic clove
1/2 tsp. dried basil

1. Combine all ingredients in slow cooker.

2. Cover. Cook on Low 8–12 hours, or on High 6 hours, until peas are tender.

variations
● For increased flavor, use chicken broth instead of water. Stir in curry powder, coriander, or red pepper flakes to taste.

Chet's Trucker Stew

Janice Muller/Derwood, MD

 MAKES 8 SERVINGS

1 lb. bulk pork sausage, cooked and drained

1 lb. ground beef, cooked and drained

31-oz. can pork and beans

16-oz. can light kidney beans

16-oz. can dark kidney beans

14 1/2-oz. can waxed beans, drained

14 1/2-oz. can lima beans, drained

1 cup ketchup

1 cup brown sugar

1 Tbsp. spicy prepared mustard

1. Combine all ingredients in slow cooker.

2. Cover. Simmer on High 2–3 hours.

French Market Soup

Ethel Mumaw/Berlin, OH

 MAKES 2 1/2 QUARTS SOUP

2 cups dry bean mix, washed, with stones removed

2 quarts water

1 ham hock

1 tsp. salt

1/4 tsp. pepper

16-oz. can tomatoes

1 large onion, chopped

1 garlic clove, minced

1 chili pepper, chopped, or 1 tsp. chili powder

1/4 cup lemon juice

1. Combine all ingredients in slow cooker.

2. Cover. Cook on Low 8 hours. Turn to High and cook an additional 2 hours, or until beans are tender.

3. Debone ham, cut meat into bite-size pieces, and stir back into soup.

Easy Lima Bean Soup

Barbara Tenney/Delta, PA

 MAKES 8–10 SERVINGS

1 lb. bag large dry lima beans

1 large onion, chopped

6 ribs celery, chopped

3 large potatoes, cut in 1/2-inch cubes

2 large carrots, cut in 1/4-inch rounds

2 cups ham, sausage, or kielbasa

1 Tbsp. salt

1 tsp. pepper

2 bay leaves

3 quarts water, or combination water and beef broth

1. Sort beans. Soak overnight. Drain.

2. Combine all ingredients in slow cooker.

3. Cover. Cook on Low 8–10 hours.

variation

● For extra flavor, add 1 tsp. dried oregano before cooking.

Slow Cooked Navy Beans with Ham

Julia Lapp/New Holland, PA

 **MAKES 8–10 SERVINGS**

1 lb. dry navy beans
   (2 1/2 cups)
5 cups water
1 garlic clove, minced
1 ham hock
1 tsp. salt

1. Soak beans in water at least 4 hours in slow cooker.

2. Add garlic and ham hock.

3. Cover. Cook on Low 7–8 hours, or High 4 hours. Add salt during last hour of cooking time.

4. Remove ham hock from cooker. Allow to cool. Cut ham from hock and stir back into bean mixture. Correct seasonings and serve in soup bowls with hot corn bread.

variation
● For added flavor, stir 1 chopped onion, 2–3 chopped celery stalks, 2–3 sliced carrots, and 3–4 cups canned tomatoes into cooker with garlic and ham hock.

Navy Bean Soup

Joyce Bowman/Lady Lake, FL

MAKES 8 SERVINGS

1 lb. dry navy beans
8 cups water
1 onion, finely chopped
2 bay leaves
1/2 tsp. ground thyme
1/2 tsp. nutmeg
2 tsp. salt
1/2 tsp. lemon pepper
3 garlic cloves, minced
one ham hock, or 1-lb.
   ham pieces

1. Soak beans in water overnight. Strain out stones but reserve liquid.

2. Combine all ingredients in slow cooker.

3. Cover. Cook on Low 8–10 hours. Debone meat and cut into bite-size pieces. Set ham aside.

4. Puree three-fourths of soup in blender in small batches. When finished blending, stir in meat.

variation
● Add small chunks of cooked potatoes when stirring in ham pieces after blending.

Old-Fashioned Bean Soup

Gladys M. High/Ephrata, PA

MAKES 6 SERVINGS

1 lb. dry navy beans, or
   dry green split peas
1-lb. meaty ham bone,
   or 1 lb. ham pieces
1–2 tsp. salt
1/4 tsp. ground pepper
1/2 cup chopped celery
   leaves
2 qts. water
1 medium onion, chopped
1 bay leaf, optional

1. Soak beans or peas overnight. Drain, discarding soaking water.

2. Combine all ingredients in slow cooker.

3. Cover. Cook on High 8–9 hours.

4. Debone ham bone, cut meat into bite-size pieces, and stir back into soup.

Vegetable Bean Soup

Kathi Rogge/Alexandria, IN

MAKES 6–8 SERVINGS

6 cups cooked beans: navy, pinto, Great Northern, etc.
1 meaty ham bone
1 cup cooked ham, diced
1/4 tsp. garlic powder
1 small bay leaf
1 cup cubed potatoes
1 cup chopped onions
1 cup chopped celery
1 cup chopped carrots
water

1. Combine all ingredients except water in 3 1/2-quart slow cooker. Add water to about 1 inch from top.

2. Cover. Cook on Low 5–8 hours.

3. Remove bay leaf before serving.

Baked Bean Soup

Maryann Markano
Wilmington, DE

MAKES 5–6 SERVINGS

1-lb. 12-oz. can baked beans
6 slices browned bacon, chopped
2 Tbsp. bacon drippings
2 Tbsp. finely chopped onions
14 1/2-oz. can stewed tomatoes
1 Tbsp. brown sugar
1 Tbsp. vinegar
1 tsp. seasoning salt

1. Combine all ingredients in slow cooker.

2. Cover. Cook on Low 4–6 hours.

Katelyn's Black Bean Soup

Katelyn Bailey
Mechanicsburg, PA

MAKES 4–6 SERVINGS

1/3 cup chopped onions
1 garlic clove, minced
1–2 Tbsp. oil
2 15 1/2-oz. cans black beans, undrained
1 cup water
1 chicken bouillon cube
1/2 cup diced, cooked, smoked ham
1/2 cup diced carrots
1 dash, or more, cayenne pepper
1–2 drops, or more, Tabasco sauce
sour cream

1. Sauté onion and garlic in oil in saucepan.

2. Puree or mash contents of one can of black beans. Add to sautéed ingredients.

3. Combine all ingredients except sour cream in slow cooker.

4. Cover. Cook on Low 6–8 hours.

5. Add dollop of sour cream to each individual bowl before serving.

Black Bean and Corn Soup

Joy Sutter/Iowa City, IA

MAKES 6–8 SERVINGS

2 15-oz. cans black beans, drained and rinsed

14 1/2-oz. can Mexican stewed tomatoes, undrained

14 1/2-oz. can diced tomatoes, undrained

11-oz. can whole kernel corn, drained

4 green onions, sliced

2–3 Tbsp. chili powder

1 tsp. ground cumin

1/2 tsp. dried minced garlic

1. Combine all ingredients in slow cooker.

2. Cover. Cook on High 5–6 hours.

variations
● Use 2 cloves fresh garlic, minced, instead of dried garlic.
● Add 1 large rib celery, sliced thinly, and 1 small green pepper, chopped.

Tuscan Garlicky Bean Soup

Sara Harter Fredette
Williamsburg, MA

MAKES 8–10 SERVINGS

1 lb. dry Great Northern, or other dry white, beans

1 qt. water

1 qt. beef broth

3 Tbsp. olive oil

2 garlic cloves, minced

4 Tbsp. chopped parsley

olive oil

2 tsp. salt

1/2 tsp. pepper

1. Place beans in large soup pot. Cover with water and bring to boil. Cook 2 minutes. Remove from heat. Cover pot and allow to stand for 1 hour. Drain, discarding water.

2. Combine beans, 1 quart fresh water, and beef broth in slow cooker.

3. Sauté garlic and parsley in olive oil in skillet. Stir into slow cooker. Add salt and pepper.

4. Cover. Cook on Low 8–10 hours, or until beans are tender.

Bean Soup

Joyce Cox/Port Angeles, WA

MAKES 10–12 SERVINGS

1 cup dry Great Northern beans

1 cup dry red beans, or pinto beans

4 cups water

28-oz. can diced tomatoes

1 medium onion, chopped

2 Tbsp. vegetable bouillon granules, or 4 bouillon cubes

2 garlic cloves, minced

2 tsp. Italian seasoning, crushed

9-oz. pkg. frozen green beans, thawed

1. Soak and rinse dried beans.

2. Combine all ingredients except green beans in slow cooker.

3. Cover. Cook on High 5 1/2–6 1/2 hours, or on Low 11–13 hours.

4. Stir green beans into soup during last 2 hours.

Winter Squash and White Bean Stew

Mary E. Herr/Three Rivers, MI

MAKES 6 SERVINGS

1 cup chopped onions
1 Tbsp. olive oil
1/2 tsp. ground cumin
1/4 tsp. salt
1/4 tsp. cinnamon
1 garlic clove, minced
3 cups peeled, butternut squash, cut into 3/4-inch cubes
1 1/2 cups chicken broth
19-oz. can cannellini beans, drained
14 1/2-oz. can diced tomatoes, undrained
1 Tbsp. chopped fresh cilantro

1. Combine all ingredients in slow cooker.

2. Cover. Cook on High 1 hour. Reduce heat to Low and heat 2–3 hours.

variations
● Beans can be pureed in blender and added during the last hour.
● Eight ounces dried beans can be soaked overnight, cooked until soft, and used in place of canned beans.

Black Bean Soup

Sue Tjon/Austin, TX

MAKES 6 SERVINGS

1-lb. bag black beans
2 10-oz. cans Rotel tomatoes
1 medium onion, chopped
1 medium green bell pepper, chopped
1 Tbsp. minced garlic
14 1/2-oz. can chicken or vegetable broth
water
Cajun seasoning to taste

1. Cover beans with water and soak for 8 hours or overnight. Drain well. Place beans in slow cooker.

2. Add tomatoes, onions, pepper, garlic, and chicken or vegetable broth. Add water just to cover beans. Add Cajun seasoning.

3. Cover. Cook on High 8 hours. Mash some of the beans before serving for a thicker consistency.

4. Serve over rice or in black bean tacos.

note
● Leftovers freeze well.

Many-Bean Soup

Trudy Kutter/Corfu, NY

MAKES 12 SERVINGS

20-oz. pkg. dried 15-bean soup mix, or 2 1/4 cups dried beans
5 14 1/2-oz. cans chicken, or vegetable, broth
2 cups chopped carrots
1 1/2 cups chopped celery
1 cup chopped onions
2 Tbsp. tomato paste
1 tsp. Italian seasoning
1/2 tsp. pepper
14 1/2-oz. can diced tomatoes

1. Combine all ingredients except tomatoes in slow cooker.

2. Cover. Cook on Low 8–10 hours, or until beans are tender.

3. Stir in tomatoes.

4. Cover. Cook on High 10–20 minutes, or until soup is heated through.

5. Serve with bread and salad.

Navy Bean Soup

Lucille Amos/Greensboro, NC

MAKES 8 SERVINGS

2 cups navy beans
1 cup chopped onions
1 bay leaf
1 tsp. salt
1 tsp. pepper
1/2 lb. ham, chopped

1. Soak beans in water overnight. Drain.

2. Combine ingredients in slow cooker. Add water to cover.

3. Cover. Cook on Low 10–12 hours or on High 5–6 hours.

4. Remove bay leaf and serve.

Lentil Soup with Ham Bone

Rhoda Atzeff/Harrisburg, PA

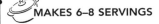

MAKES 6–8 SERVINGS

1 lb. lentils, washed and drained
1 celery rib, chopped
1 large carrot, grated
1/2 cup chopped onions
1 bay leaf
1/4 tsp. dried thyme
7–8 cups water
1 ham bone, thinly sliced kielbasa, or hot smoked sausage
1/4–1/2 tsp. crushed red hot pepper flakes
pepper to taste
salt to taste

1. Combine all ingredients except pepper and salt in slow cooker.

2. Cover. Cook on Low 8–9 hours. Remove bay leaf and ham bone. Dice meat from bone and return to cooker.

3. Season to taste with pepper and salt.

4. Serve alone, or over rice with grated cheese on top.

Cassoulet Chowder

Miriam Friesen/Staunton, VA

MAKES 8–10 SERVINGS

1 1/4 cups dry pinto beans
4 cups water
12-oz. pkg. brown-and-serve sausage links, cooked and drained
2 cups cubed cooked chicken
2 cups cubed cooked ham
1 1/2 cups sliced carrots
8-oz. can tomato sauce
3/4 cup dry red wine
1/2 cup chopped onions
1/2 tsp. garlic powder
1 bay leaf

1. Combine beans and water in large saucepan. Bring to boil. Reduce heat and simmer 1 1/2 hours. Refrigerate beans and liquid 4–8 hours.

2. Combine all ingredients in slow cooker.

3. Cover. Cook on Low 8–10 hours or on High 4 hours. If the chowder seems too thin, remove lid during last 30 minutes of cooking time to allow it to thicken.

4. Remove bay leaf before serving.

Chicken Broth

Ruth Conrad Liechty
Goshen, IN

MAKES ABOUT 6 CUPS BROTH

bony chicken pieces from 2 chickens
1 onion, quartered
3 whole cloves, optional
3 ribs celery, cut up
1 carrot, quartered
1 1/2 tsp. salt
1/4 tsp. pepper
4 cups water

1. Place chicken in slow cooker.

2. Stud onion with cloves. Add to slow cooker with other ingredients.

3. Cover. Cook on High 4–5 hours.

4. Remove chicken and vegetables. Discard vegetables. Debone chicken. Cut up meat and add to broth. Use as stock for soups.

Chicken Noodle Soup

Beth Shank/Wellman, IA

MAKES 6–8 SERVINGS

5 cups hot water
2 Tbsp. chicken bouillon granules, or 2 chicken bouillon cubes
46-oz. can chicken broth
2 cups cooked chicken
1 tsp. salt
4 cups "homestyle" noodles, uncooked
1/3 cup thinly sliced celery, lightly pre-cooked in microwave
1/3 cup shredded, or chopped, carrots

1. Dissolve bouillon in water. Pour into slow cooker.

2. Add remaining ingredients. Mix well.

3. Cover. Cook on Low 4–6 hours.

Brown Jug Soup

Dorothy Shank/Sterling, IL

MAKES 10–12 SERVINGS

10 1/2-oz. can chicken broth
4 chicken bouillon cubes
1 qt. water
2 cups (3–4 ribs) diced celery
2 cups (2 medium-sized) diced onions
4 cups (4 large) diced potatoes
3 cups (8 medium-sized) diced carrots
10-oz. pkg. frozen whole kernel corn
2 10 3/4-oz. cans cream of chicken soup
1/2 lb. Velveeta cheese, cubed

1. Combine all ingredients except cheese in slow cooker.

2. Cover. Cook on Low 10–12 hours, or until vegetables are tender.

3. Just before serving, add cheese. Stir until cheese is melted. Serve.

Chili, Chicken, Corn Chowder

Jeanne Allen/Rye, CO

MAKES 6–8 SERVINGS

1/4 cup oil
1 large onion, diced
1 garlic clove, minced
1 celery stalk, finely chopped
2 cups frozen, or canned, corn
2 cups cooked, deboned, diced chicken
4-oz. can diced green chilies
1/2 tsp. black pepper
2 cups chicken broth
salt to taste
1 cup half-and-half

1. In saucepan, sauté onion, garlic, and celery in oil until limp.

2. Stir in corn, chicken, and chilies. Sauté for 2–3 minutes.

3. Combine all ingredients except half-and-half in slow cooker.

4. Cover. Heat on Low 4 hours.

5. Stir in half-and-half before serving. Do not boil, but be sure cream is heated through.

Chicken and Ham Gumbo

Barbara Tenney/Delta, PA

MAKES 4 SERVINGS

1 1/2 lbs. boneless, skinless chicken thighs
1 Tbsp. oil
10-oz. pkg. frozen okra
1/2 lb. smoked ham, cut into small chunks
1 1/2 cups coarsely chopped onions
1 1/2 cups coarsely chopped green peppers
2 or 3 10-oz. cans cannellini beans, drained
6 cups chicken broth
2 10-oz. cans diced tomatoes with green chilies
2 Tbsp. chopped fresh cilantro

1. Cut chicken into bite-size pieces. Cook in oil in skillet until no longer pink.

2. Run hot water over okra until pieces separate easily.

3. Combine all ingredients except cilantro in slow cooker.

4. Cover. Cook on Low 6–8 hours. Stir in cilantro before serving.

variation
● Stir in 1/2 cup long grain, dry rice with rest of ingredients.

Joy's Brunswick Stew

Joy Sutter/Iowa City, IA

MAKES 8 SERVINGS

1 lb. skinless, boneless chicken breasts, cut into bite-size pieces
2 potatoes, thinly sliced
10 3/4-oz. can tomato soup
16-oz. can stewed tomatoes
10-oz. pkg. frozen corn
10-oz. pkg. frozen lima beans
3 Tbsp. onion flakes
1/4 tsp. salt
1/8 tsp. pepper

1. Combine all ingredients in slow cooker.

2. Cover. Cook on High 2 hours. Reduce to Low and cook 2 hours.

variation
● For more flavor, add 1, or 2, bay leaves during cooking.

Leftover Turkey Soup

Janie Steele/Moore, OK

MAKES 8–10 SERVINGS

1 small onion, chopped
1 cup chopped celery
1 Tbsp. oil
2–3 cups diced turkey
1 cup cooked rice
leftover gravy, or
    combination of leftover
    gravy and chicken broth

1. Sauté onion and celery in oil in saucepan until translucent.

2. Combine all ingredients in slow cooker, adding gravy and/or broth until you have the consistency you want.

3. Cover. Cook on Low for at least 2–3 hours, or until heated through.

Pixie's Chicken Stew

Janice Muller/Derwood, MD

MAKES 8–10 SERVINGS

2–3-lb. chicken
2 qts. water
1 pkg. dry chicken noodle
    soup
2 chicken bouillon cubes
15-oz. can whole-kernel
    corn, undrained
1 Tbsp. onion flakes
1/2 tsp. dried thyme, or
    to taste

1. Place chicken in slow cooker. Add water.

2. Cover. Cook on High 3–4 hours. Cool.

3. Strain liquid into container. Debone chicken. Return cut-up meat and strained broth to slow cooker.

4. Stir in other ingredients.

5. Cover. Cook on High 2 hours.

note
● Make this a day ahead and refrigerate overnight to make it easier to skim fat off the top. Pixie would invite friends in for soup after long walks in the snow. She always served this with fresh bread in front of a roaring fire.

Chicken Noodle Soup

Jennifer J. Gehman
Harrisburg, PA

MAKES 6–8 SERVINGS

2 cups cubed chicken
15 1/4-oz. can corn, or
    2 cups frozen corn
1 cup frozen peas, or green
    beans
10 cups water
10–12 chicken bouillon
    cubes
3 Tbsp. bacon drippings
1/2 pkg. dry Kluski (or other
    very sturdy) noodles

1. Combine all ingredients except noodles in slow cooker.

2. Cover. Cook on High 4–6 hours or Low 6–8 hours. Add noodles during last 2 hours.

3. Serve with potato rolls and butter or grilled cheese sandwiches.

Santa Fe Chicken Soup

Sherry Conyers
McPherson, KS

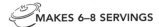MAKES 6–8 SERVINGS

4 whole chicken breasts, cooked and shredded
1 small onion, diced
15 1/4-oz. can whole-kernel corn, undrained
24-oz. can pinto beans, undrained
14 1/2-oz. can diced tomatoes, undrained
10-oz. can Rotel tomatoes, undrained
1/2 lb. mild Velveeta cheese, cubed
1/2 lb. regular Velveeta cheese, cubed
1/4 cup milk

1. Place chicken and onions in slow cooker.

2. Add corn, beans, tomatoes, cubed cheese, and milk.

3. Cover. Cook on Low 3–4 hours, or until cheese is melted. Try not to let soup boil.

Cabbage Soup

Margaret Jarrett/Anderson, IN

MAKES 8 SERVINGS

half a head of cabbage, sliced thin
2 ribs celery, sliced thin
2–3 carrots, sliced thin
1 onion, chopped
2 chicken bouillon cubes
2 garlic cloves, minced
1 qt. tomato juice
1 tsp. salt
1/4 tsp. pepper
water

1. Combine all ingredients except water in slow cooker. Add water to within 3 inches of top of slow cooker.

2. Cover. Cook on High 3 1/2–4 hours, or until vegetables are tender.

Cream of Broccoli Soup

Barb Yoder/Angola, IN

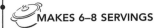MAKES 6–8 SERVINGS

1 small onion, chopped
oil
20-oz. pkg. frozen broccoli
2 10 3/4-oz. cans cream of celery soup
10 3/4-oz. can cream of mushroom soup
1 cup grated American cheese
2 soup cans milk

1. Sauté onion in oil in skillet until soft.

2. Combine all ingredients in slow cooker.

3. Cover. Cook on Low 3–4 hours.

Broccoli-Cheese Soup

Darla Sathre/Baxter, MN

**MAKES 8 SERVINGS**

2 16-oz. pkgs. frozen chopped broccoli
2 10 3/4-oz. cans cheddar cheese soup
2 12-oz. cans evaporated milk
1/4 cup finely chopped onions
1/2 tsp. seasoned salt
1/4 tsp. pepper
sunflower seeds, optional
crumbled bacon, optional

1. Combine all ingredients except sunflower seeds and bacon in slow cooker.

2. Cover. Cook on Low 8–10 hours.

3. Garnish with sunflower seeds and bacon.

Broccoli-Cheese with Noodles Soup

Carol Sherwood/Batavia, NY

**MAKES 8 SERVINGS**

2 cups cooked noodles
10-oz. pkg. frozen chopped broccoli, thawed
3 Tbsp. chopped onions
2 Tbsp. butter
1 Tbsp. flour
2 cups cubed processed cheese
1/2 tsp. salt
5 1/2 cups milk

1. Cook noodles just until soft in saucepan while combining rest of ingredients in slow cooker. Mix well.

2. Drain cooked noodles and stir into slow cooker.

3. Cover. Cook on Low 4 hours.

Double Cheese Cauliflower Soup

Zona Mae Bontrager
Kokomo, IN

**MAKES 6 SERVINGS**

4 cups (1 small head) cauliflower pieces
2 cups water
8-oz. pkg. cream cheese, cubed
5 oz. American cheese spread
1/4 lb. dried beef, torn into strips or shredded
1/2 cup potato flakes, or potato buds

1. Combine cauliflower and water in saucepan. Bring to boil. Set aside.

2. Heat slow cooker on Low. Add cream cheese and cheese spread. Pour in cauliflower and water. Stir to be sure the cheese is dissolved and mixed through the cauliflower.

3. Add dried beef and potato flakes. Mix well.

4. Cover. Cook on Low 2–3 hours.

Broccoli, Potato, and Cheese Soup

Ruth Shank/Gridley, IL

 MAKES 6 SERVINGS

2 cups cubed or diced potatoes

3 Tbsp. chopped onion

10-oz. pkg. frozen broccoli cuts, thawed

2 Tbsp. butter, or margarine, melted

1 Tbsp. flour

2 cups cubed Velveeta cheese

1/2 tsp. salt

5 1/2 cups milk

1. Cook potatoes and onion in boiling water in saucepan until potatoes are crisp-tender. Drain. Place in slow cooker.

2. Add remaining ingredients. Stir together.

3. Cover. Cook on Low 4 hours.

Cheesy Broccoli Soup

Dede Peterson/Rapid City, SD

 MAKES 4 SERVINGS

1 lb. frozen chopped broccoli, thawed

1 lb. Velveeta cheese, cubed

10 3/4-oz. can cream of celery soup

14 1/2-oz. can chicken, or vegetable, broth

dash of pepper

dash of salt

1. Combine ingredients in slow cooker.

2. Cover. Cook on Low 5–6 hours.

Spicy Potato Soup

Sharon Kauffman
Harrisonburg, VA

 MAKES 6–8 SERVINGS

1 lb. ground beef, or bulk sausage, browned

4 cups cubed peeled potatoes

1 small onion, chopped

3 8-oz. cans tomato sauce

2 tsp. salt

1 1/2 tsp. pepper

1/2–1 tsp. hot pepper sauce

water

1. Combine all ingredients except water in slow cooker. Add enough water to cover ingredients.

2. Cover. Cook on Low 8–10 hours, or High 5 hours, until potatoes are tender.

Potato Soup

Deborah Santiago
Lancaster, PA

 MAKES 6 SERVINGS

6 potatoes, peeled and cubed
2 onions, chopped
1 carrot, sliced
1 rib celery, sliced
4 chicken, or vegetable, bouillon cubes
1 Tbsp. parsley flakes
5 cups water
1/4 tsp. pepper
1 Tbsp. salt
1/3 cup butter, melted
13-oz. can evaporated milk

1. Combine all ingredients except evaporated milk in slow cooker.

2. Cover. Cook on High 3–4 hours or Low 10–12 hours.

3. Stir in evaporated milk during last hour of cooking time.

4. Serve with sandwiches, crackers, and beverage.

Potato Soup

Zona Mae Bontrager
Kokomo, IN

 MAKES 4 SERVINGS

1/2 cup chopped onions
1 tsp. butter
14 1/2-oz. can beef, chicken, or vegetable, broth
1 potato, chopped
1 carrot, shredded
1 rib celery, chopped
1/2–3/4 tsp. salt
1/8–1/4 tsp. pepper
2 cups mashed potatoes
1/2 cup shredded mild cheese, optional

1. Sauté onions in butter in skillet.

2. Stir in broth, 1 potato, carrot, celery, and seasonings. Cook until vegetables are tender. Pour into hot slow cooker.

3. Add mashed potatoes and cheese. Stir well.

4. Cover. Heat on Low until ready to serve.

Potato Cheddar-Cheese Soup

Marla Folkerts/Holland, OH

 MAKES 4 SERVINGS

6–10 potatoes, peeled and cubed
1/2 cup vegetable broth
1 cup water
1 large onion, finely chopped
1/2 tsp. garlic powder
1/8 tsp. white pepper
2 cups milk, heated
1 cup shredded sharp, or extra sharp, cheddar cheese
paprika

1. Place potatoes, broth, water, onions, and garlic powder in slow cooker.

2. Cover. Cook on Low 7–9 hours, or on High 4–6 hours.

3. Mash potatoes, leaving them a bit lumpy. Stir in pepper and milk a little at a time. Add cheese. Cook until cheese has melted, about 5 minutes. Add more milk if you'd like a thinner or creamier soup.

4. Garnish each serving with paprika.

5. Serve with homemade bread, salad, and fruit.

Ham and Potato Chowder

Penny Blosser
Beavercreek, OH

MAKES 5 SERVINGS

5-oz. pkg. scalloped
potatoes
sauce mix from potato pkg.
1 cup cooked ham, cut into
narrow strips
4 cups chicken broth
1 cup chopped celery
1/3 cup chopped onions
salt to taste
pepper to taste
2 cups half-and-half
1/3 cup flour

1. Combine potatoes, sauce mix, ham, broth, celery, onions, salt, and pepper in slow cooker.

2. Cover. Cook on Low 7 hours.

3. Combine half-and-half and flour. Gradually add to slow cooker, blending well.

4. Cover. Cook on Low up to 1 hour, stirring occasionally until thickened.

Corn Chowder

Charlotte Fry/St. Charles, MO
Jeanette Oberholtzer
Manheim, PA

MAKES 4 SERVINGS

6 slices bacon, diced
1/2 cup chopped onions
2 cups diced peeled
potatoes
2 10-oz. pkgs. frozen corn
16-oz. can cream-style corn
1 Tbsp. sugar
1 tsp. Worcestershire sauce
1 tsp. seasoned salt
1/4 tsp. pepper
1 cup water

1. In skillet, brown bacon until crisp. Remove bacon, reserving drippings.

2. Add onions and potatoes to skillet and sauté for 5 minutes. Drain.

3. Combine all ingredients in slow cooker. Mix well.

4. Cover. Cook on Low 6–7 hours.

variations
● To make Clam Corn Chowder, drain and add 2 cans minced clams during last hour of cooking.
● Substitute 1 quart home-frozen corn for the store-bought frozen and canned corn.

Cheese and Corn Chowder

Loretta Krahn/Mt. Lake, MN

MAKES 8 SERVINGS

3/4 cup water
1/2 cup chopped onions
1 1/2 cups sliced carrots
1 1/2 cups chopped celery
1 tsp. salt
1/2 tsp. pepper
15 1/4-oz. can whole kernel
corn, drained
15-oz. can cream-style corn
3 cups milk
1 1/2 cup grated cheddar
cheese

1. Combine water, onions, carrots, celery, salt, and pepper in slow cooker.

2. Cover. Cook on High 4–6 hours.

3. Add corn, milk, and cheese. Heat on High 1 hour, and then turn to Low until you are ready to eat.

French Onion Soup

Jenny R. Unternahrer
Wayland, IA

Janice Yoskovich
Carmichaels, PA

MAKES 10 SERVINGS

8–10 large onions, sliced
1/2 cup butter or margarine
6 10 1/2-oz. cans condensed beef broth
1 1/2 tsp. Worcestershire sauce
3 bay leaves
10 slices French bread, toasted
grated Parmesan and/or shredded mozzarella cheese

1. Sauté onions in butter until crisp-tender. Transfer to slow cooker.

2. Add broth, Worcestershire sauce, and bay leaves.

3. Cover. Cook on Low 5–7 hours, or until onions are tender. Discard bay leaves.

4. Ladle into bowls. Top each with a slice of bread and some cheese.

note
● For a more intense beef flavor, add one beef bouillon cube, or use home-cooked beef broth instead of canned broth.

Onion Soup

Rosemarie Fitzgerald
Gibsonia, PA

MAKES 6–8 SERVINGS

3 medium onions, thinly sliced
1/4 cup butter
1 tsp. salt
1 Tbsp. sugar
2 Tbsp. flour
1 qt. beef, or vegetable, broth
1/2 cup dry white wine
slices of French bread
Swiss or Parmesan cheese, grated

1. Sauté onions in butter in covered skillet until soft. Uncover. Add salt and sugar. Cook 15 minutes. Stir in flour. Cook 3 more minutes.

2. Combine onions, broth, and wine in slow cooker.

3. Cover. Cook on Low 6–8 hours.

4. Toast bread. Sprinkle with grated cheese and then broil.

5. Dish soup into individual bowls; then float a slice of broiled bread on top of each serving of soup.

Heart Happy Tomato Soup

Anne Townsend
Albuquerque, NM

MAKES 6 SERVINGS

46-oz. can tomato juice
8-oz. can tomato sauce
1/2 cup water
1 Tbsp. bouillon granules
1 sprig celery leaves, chopped
half an onion, thinly sliced
1/2 tsp. dried basil
2 Tbsp. sugar
1 bay leaf
1/2 tsp. whole cloves

1. Combine all ingredients in greased slow cooker. Stir well.

2. Cover. Cook on Low 5–8 hours. Remove bay leaf and cloves before serving.

note
● If you prefer a thicker soup, add 1/4 cup instant potato flakes. Stir well and cook 5 minutes longer.

Grandma's Barley Soup

Andrea O'Neil/Fairfield, CT

MAKES 10–12 SERVINGS

2 smoked ham hocks
4 carrots, sliced
4 potatoes, cubed
1 cup dried lima beans
1 cup tomato paste
1 1/2–2 cups cooked barley
salt, if needed

1. Combine all ingredients in slow cooker, except salt.

2. Cover with water.

3. Cover. Simmer on Low 6–8 hours.

4. Debone ham hocks and return cut-up meat to soup.

5. Taste before serving. Add salt if needed.

note
● If you want to reduce the amount of meat you eat, this dish is flavorful using only 1 ham hock.

Green Bean Soup

Loretta Krahn
Mountain Lake, MN

MAKES 6 SERVINGS

1 meaty ham bone, or 2 cups cubed ham
1 1/2 qts. water
1 large onion, chopped
2–3 cups cut-up green beans
3 large carrots, sliced
2 large potatoes, peeled and cubed
1 Tbsp. parsley
1 Tbsp. summer savory
1/2 tsp. salt
1/4 tsp. pepper
1 cup cream or milk

1. Combine all ingredients except cream in slow cooker.

2. Cover. Cook on High 4–6 hours.

3. Remove ham bone. Cut off meat and return to slow cooker.

4. Turn to Low. Stir in cream or milk. Heat through and serve.

Lidia's Egg Drop Soup

Shirley Unternahrer Hinh
Wayland, IA

MAKES 8 SERVINGS

2 14 1/2-oz. cans chicken broth
1 qt. water
2 Tbsp. fish sauce
1/4 tsp. salt
4 Tbsp. cornstarch
1 cup cold water
2 eggs, beaten
1 chopped green onion
pepper to taste

1. Combine broth and water in large saucepan.

2. Add fish sauce and salt. Bring to boil.

3. Mix cornstarch into cold water until smooth. Add to soup. Bring to boil while stirring. Remove from heat.

4. Pour beaten eggs into thickened broth, but do not stir. Instead, pull fork through soup with 2 strokes.

5. Transfer to slow cooker. Add green onions and pepper.

6. Cover. Cook on Low 1 hour. Keep warm in cooker.

7. Eat plain or with rice.

Special Seafood Chowder

Dorothea K. Ladd
Ballston Lake, NY

MAKES 8–10 SERVINGS

1/2 cup chopped onions
2 Tbsp. butter
1 lb. fresh or frozen cod,
  or haddock
4 cups diced potatoes
15-oz. can creamed corn
1/2 tsp. salt
dash pepper
2 cups water
1 pint half-and-half

1. Sauté onions in butter in skillet until transparent but not brown.

2. Cut fish into 3/4-inch cubes. Combine fish, onions, potatoes, corn, seasonings, and water in slow cooker.

3. Cover. Cook on Low 6 hours, until potatoes are tender.

4. Add half-and-half during last hour.

variation
● To cut milk fat, use 1 cup half-and-half and 1 cup skim milk, instead of 1 pint half-and-half.

Wonderful Clam Chowder

Carlene Horne/Bedford, NH

MAKES 4–6 SERVINGS

2 12-oz. cans evaporated milk
1 evaporated milk can of water
2 6-oz. cans whole clams, undrained
6-oz. can minced clams, undrained
1 small onion, chopped
2 small potatoes, diced
2 Tbsp. cornstarch
1/4 cup water

1. Combine all ingredients except cornstarch and 1/4 cup water in slow cooker.

2. Cover. Cook on Low 6–7 hours.

3. One hour before end of cooking time, mix cornstarch and 1/4 cup water together. When smooth, stir into soup. Stir until soup thickens.

Clam Chowder

Ruth Shank/Gridley, IL

MAKES 8-12 SERVINGS

2 10 3/4-oz. cans cream of potato soup
10 3/4-oz. can cream of celery soup
2 6 1/2-oz. cans minced clams, drained
3 slices bacon, diced and fried
1 soup can of water
1 small onion, minced
1 Tbsp. fresh parsley
dash of dried marjoram
1 Tbsp. Worcestershire sauce
pepper to taste
2 soup cans of milk

1. Combine all ingredients, except 2 soup cans of milk, in slow cooker.

2. Cover. Cook on Low 6-8 hours.

3. Twenty minutes before end of cooking time, stir in milk. Continue cooking until heated through.

Chili

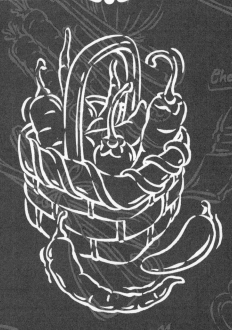

Extra Easy Chili

Jennifer Gehman
Harrisburg, PA

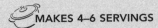
MAKES 4–6 SERVINGS

1 lb. ground beef, or turkey, uncooked
1 pkg. dry chili seasoning mix
16-oz. can chili beans in sauce
2 28-oz. cans crushed, or diced, tomatoes seasoned with garlic and onion

1. Crumble meat in bottom of slow cooker.

2. Add remaining ingredients. Stir.

3. Cover. Cook on High 4–6 hours or Low 6–8 hours. Stir halfway through cooking time.

4. Serve over white rice, topped with shredded cheddar cheese and chopped raw onions.

I decided to make this chili one year for Christmas. We had had guests for about a week prior to Christmas. Needless to say, I was tired of cooking so this seemed easy enough. Put the ingredients in the slow cooker and let it cook all day. It was a welcomed change from the traditional Christmas meal. It has been my tradition ever since!

— • —

Beans and Tomato Chili

Becky Harder/Monument, CO

MAKES 6–8 SERVINGS

15-oz. can black beans, undrained
15-oz. can pinto beans, undrained
16-oz. can kidney beans, undrained
15-oz. can garbanzo beans, undrained
2 14 1/2-oz. cans stewed tomatoes and juice
1 pkg. prepared chili seasoning

1. Pour beans, including their liquid, into slow cooker.

2. Stir in tomatoes and chili seasoning.

3. Cover. Cook on Low 4–8 hours.

4. Serve with crackers, and topped with grated cheddar cheese, sliced green onions, and sour cream, if desired.

variation
● Add additional cans of white beans or 1 tsp. dried onion.

Turkey Chili

Reita F. Yoder/Carlsbad, NM

MAKES 6–8 SERVINGS

2 lbs. ground turkey
16-oz. can pinto, or kidney, beans
2 cups fresh, or canned, tomatoes, chopped
2 cups tomato sauce
1 garlic clove, minced
1 small onion, chopped
16-oz. can Rotel tomatoes
1-oz. pkg. Williams chili seasoning

1. Crumble ground turkey in bottom of slow cooker.

2. Add remaining ingredients. Mix well.

3. Cover. Cook on Low 6–8 hours.

Easy Chili

Sheryl Shenk
Harrisonburg, VA

 MAKES 10–12 SERVINGS

1 lb. ground beef
1 onion, chopped
1 green pepper, chopped
1 1/2 tsp. salt
1 Tbsp. chili powder
2 tsp. Worcestershire sauce
29-oz. can tomato sauce
3 16-oz. cans kidney beans, drained
14 1/2-oz. can crushed, or stewed, tomatoes
6-oz. can tomato paste
2 cups grated cheddar cheese

1. Brown meat in skillet. Add onion and green pepper halfway through browning process. Drain. Pour into slow cooker.

2. Stir in remaining ingredients except cheese.

3. Cover. Cook on High 3 hours, or Low 7–8 hours.

4. Serve in bowls topped with cheddar cheese.

note
● This chili can be served over cooked rice.

Berenice's Favorite Chili

Berenice M. Wagner
Dodge City, KS

 MAKES 6 SERVINGS

2 16-oz. cans red kidney beans, drained
2 14 1/2-oz. cans diced tomatoes
2 lbs. coarsely ground beef, browned and drained
2 medium onions, coarsely chopped
1 green pepper, coarsely chopped
2 garlic cloves, minced
2–3 Tbsp. chili powder
1 tsp. pepper
2 1/2 tsp. salt

1. Combine all ingredients in slow cooker in order listed. Stir once.

2. Cover. Cook on Low 10–12 hours, or High 5–6 hours.

variations
● Top individual servings with green onion, sour cream, and cheese.
Judy Govotsus/Monrovia, MD

● Increase proportion of tomatoes in chili by adding 8-oz. can tomato sauce before cooking.
Bernice A. Esau
North Newton, KS

Slow-Cooker Chili

Wanda S. Curtin
Bradenton, FL

Ann Sunday McDowell
Newtown, PA

 MAKES 10 SERVINGS

2 lbs. ground beef, browned and drained
2 16-oz. cans red kidney beans, drained
2 14 1/2-oz. cans diced tomatoes, drained
2 medium onions, chopped
2 garlic cloves, crushed
2–3 Tbsp. chili powder
1 tsp. ground cumin
1 tsp. black pepper
1 tsp. salt

1. Combine all ingredients in slow cooker.

2. Cover. Cook on Low 8–10 hours.

note
● Use leftovers over lettuce and other fresh vegetables to make a taco salad.

variations
● For more flavor, add cayenne pepper or a jalapeño pepper before cooking.
Dorothy Shank/Sterling, IL

● Add 1 cup chopped green peppers before cooking.
Mary V. Warye
West Liberty, OH

Chili Con Carne

Donna Conto/Saylorsburg, PA

MAKES 8 SERVINGS

1 lb. ground beef
1 cup chopped onions
3/4 cup chopped green peppers
1 garlic clove, minced
14 1/2-oz. can tomatoes, cut up
16-oz. can kidney beans, drained
8-oz. can tomato sauce
2 tsp. chili powder
1/2 tsp. dried basil

1. Brown beef, onion, green pepper, and garlic in saucepan. Drain.

2. Combine all ingredients in slow cooker.

3. Cover. Cook on Low 5–6 hours.

4. Serve in bread bowl.

variation
● Add 16-oz. can pinto beans, 1/4 tsp. salt, and 1/4 tsp. pepper in Step 2.
Alexa Slonin
Harrisonburg, VA

Judy's Chili Soup

Judy Buller/Bluffton, OH

MAKES 6 SERVINGS

1 lb. ground beef
1 onion, chopped
10 3/4-oz. can condensed tomato soup
16-oz. can kidney beans, drained
1 qt. tomato juice
1/8 tsp. garlic powder
1 Tbsp. chili powder
1/2 tsp. pepper
1/2 tsp. ground cumin
1/2 tsp. salt

1. Brown hamburger and onion in skillet. Drain.

2. Combine all ingredients in slow cooker. Mix well.

3. Cover. Cook on Low 7–8 hours.

variation
● Use ground venison instead of ground beef.

Cindy's Chili

Cindy Krestynick
Glen Lyon, PA

MAKES 4–6 SERVINGS

1 lb. ground beef, browned and drained
3 15 1/2-oz. cans chili beans (hot or mild)
28-oz. can stewed tomatoes, chopped
1 celery stalk, chopped
4 cups tomato juice
1/2 tsp. garlic salt
1/2 tsp. chili powder
1/4 tsp. pepper
1/4 tsp. Tabasco sauce

1. Combine all ingredients in large slow cooker.

2. Cover. Cook on Low 4–6 hours.

Chili and Cheese on Rice

Dale and Shari Mast
Harrisonburg, VA

 **MAKES 6 SERVINGS**

1 lb. ground beef
1 onion, diced
1 tsp. dried basil
1 tsp. dried oregano
16-oz. can light red kidney beans
15 1/2-oz. can chili beans
1 pint stewed tomatoes, drained
cooked rice
grated cheddar cheese

1. Brown ground beef and onion in skillet. Season with basil and oregano.

2. Combine all ingredients except rice and cheese in slow cooker.

3. Cover. Cook on Low 4 hours.

4. Serve over cooked rice. Top with cheese.

So-Easy Chili

Sue Graber/Eureka, IL

MAKES 4 SERVINGS

1 lb. ground beef
1 onion, chopped
15-oz. can chili, with or without beans
14.5-oz. can diced tomatoes with green chilies, or with basil, garlic, and oregano
1 cup tomato juice
chopped onion
grated cheddar cheese

1. Brown ground beef and onion in skillet. Drain and put in slow cooker.

2. Add chili, diced tomatoes, and tomato juice.

3. Cover. Cook on Low 4–6 hours.

4. Serve with onion and cheese on top of each individual serving.

note
● This chili is of a good consistency for serving over rice. For a thicker chili, add 4–6 ozs. tomato paste 20 minutes before end of cooking time.

Slow-Cooked Chili

Jean A. Shaner/York, PA

 **MAKES 10 SERVINGS**

2 lbs. ground beef, browned
2 16-oz. cans kidney beans, rinsed and drained
2 14 1/2-oz. cans diced tomatoes
8-oz. can tomato sauce
2 onions, chopped
1 green pepper, chopped
2 garlic cloves, minced
2 Tbsp. chili powder
2 tsp. salt
1 tsp. pepper
shredded cheddar cheese

1. Combine all ingredients except cheese in slow cooker.

2. Cover. Cook on Low 8–10 hours.

3. Ladle chili into individual bowls and top with cheese just before serving.

The Chili Connection

Anne Townsend
Albuquerque, NM

MAKES 6 SERVINGS

1 1/2 lbs. ground beef
1 cup chopped onions
28-oz. can tomatoes, chopped
15-oz. can kidney beans, undrained
1 Tbsp. brown, or granulated, sugar
2–4 tsp. chili powder, to taste
1 tsp. salt

1. Brown ground beef and onions in skillet.

2. Combine all ingredients in slow cooker.

3. Cover. Cook on Low 3–5 hours.

variation

● For thicker chili, stir in a 6-oz. can of tomato paste in Step 2.

notes

● An assortment of toppings can take the place of a salad with this chili. I usually offer chopped onions, tomatoes, grated cheddar cheese, picante sauce, and, when avocados are in season, guacamole. Cornbread or refrigerated twist rolls sprinkled with garlic salt are delicious.

Chili Soup

Glenna Fay Bergey
Lebanon, OR

MAKES 5 QUARTS

3 lbs. ground beef
3/4 cup chopped onions
2 Tbsp. celery flakes
2 tsp. salt
1 Tbsp. chili powder, or more, according to taste
3 15-oz. cans kidney beans
1 qt. tomato juice
2 10 3/4-oz. cans tomato soup
1 cup ketchup
1/4 cup brown sugar

1. Brown meat, onions, and seasonings in large skillet. Transfer to large bowl and stir in remaining ingredients.

2. Divide between 2 4- or 5-qt. slow cookers (this is a large recipe!).

3. Cover. Cook on High 2 hours or Low 4–6 hours.

4. Serve with cornbread.

Country Auction Chili Soup

Clara Newswanger
Gordonville, PA

MAKES 20 SERVINGS

1 1/2 lbs. ground beef
1/4 cup chopped onions
1/2 cup flour
1 Tbsp. chili powder
1 tsp. salt
6 cups water
2 cups ketchup
1/3 cup brown sugar
3 15.5-oz. cans kidney beans, undrained

1. Brown ground beef and onions in skillet. Drain. Spoon meat mixture into slow cooker.

2. Stir flour into meat and onions. Add seasonings.

3. Slowly stir in water. Add ketchup, brown sugar, and beans.

4. Cover. Cook on High 4 hours or Low 8 hours.

Hot and Good Chili

Rose Hankins/Stevensville, MD

MAKES 12 SERVINGS

1 lb. ground beef
1 cup chopped onions
1 cup chopped celery
1 cup chopped green
   peppers
28-oz. can tomatoes
14-oz. can tomato sauce
2 14-oz. cans kidney beans,
   undrained
2 Tbsp. chili powder
1 Tbsp. garlic powder
1 Tbsp. hot sauce

1. Brown beef in skillet. Reserve drippings and transfer drained beef to slow cooker.

2. Sauté onions, celery, and green peppers in drippings. Drain and transfer to slow cooker.

3. Stir in remaining ingredients.

4. Cover. Cook on High 4–5 hours or on Low 8–10 hours.

Slowly Cooked Chili

Beatrice Martin/Goshen, IN

MAKES 6–8 SERVINGS

2 lbs. ground beef, or
   turkey, browned in skillet
15 1/2-oz. can kidney
   beans, undrained
3 cups tomato juice
3 Tbsp. chili powder
1 tsp. minced garlic
1 pkg. dry onion soup mix
1/2–1 tsp. salt, according
   to taste
1/4 tsp. pepper

1. Combine all ingredients in slow cooker.

2. Cover. Cook on Low 10–12 hours or on High 5–6 hours.

3. Serve in soup bowls with crackers, or over rice.

note
● This chili freezes well.

Dorothea's Slow-Cooker Chili

Dorothea K. Ladd
Ballston Lake, NY

MAKES 6–8 SERVINGS

1 lb. ground beef
1 lb. bulk pork sausage
1 large onion, chopped
1 large green pepper,
   chopped
2–3 celery stalks, chopped
2 15 1/2-oz. cans kidney
   beans
29-oz. can tomato puree
6-oz. can tomato paste
2 cloves garlic, minced
2 Tbsp. chili powder
2 tsp. salt

1. Brown ground beef and sausage in skillet. Drain.

2. Combine all ingredients in slow cooker.

3. Cover. Cook on Low 8–10 hours.

variations
● For extra flavor, add 1 tsp. cayenne pepper.
● For more zest, use mild or hot Italian sausage instead of regular pork sausage.
● Top individual servings with shredded sharp cheddar cheese.

Three-Bean Chili

Chris Kaczynski
Schenectady, NY

 MAKES 8–10 SERVINGS

2 lbs. ground beef
2 medium onions, diced
16-oz. jar medium salsa
2 pkgs. dry chili seasoning
2 16-oz. cans red kidney beans, drained
2 16-oz. cans black beans, drained
2 16-oz. cans white kidney, or garbanzo, beans drained
28-oz. can crushed tomatoes
16-oz. can diced tomatoes
2 tsp. sugar

1. Brown beef and onions in skillet.

2. Combine all ingredients in 6-qt. Slow cooker, or in 2 4- or 5-qt. cookers.

3. Cover. Cook on Low 8–10 hours.

4. Serve with chopped raw onion and/or shredded cheddar cheese.

note
This recipe can be cut in half without injuring the flavor, if you don't have a cooker large enough to handle the full amount.

Hearty Potato Chili

Janice Muller/Derwood, MD

 MAKES 8 SERVINGS

1 lb. ground beef
1/2 cup chopped onions, or 2 Tbsp. Dried minced onions
1/2 cup chopped green peppers
1 Tbsp. poppy seeds (optional)
1 tsp. salt
1/2 tsp. chili powder
1 pkg. au gratin, or scalloped, potato mix
1 cup hot water
15-oz. can kidney beans, undrained
16-oz. can stewed tomatoes
4-oz. can mushroom pieces, undrained

1. Brown ground beef in skillet. Remove meat and place in slow cooker. Sauté onions and green peppers in drippings until softened.

2. Combine all ingredients in slow cooker.

3. Cover. Cook on High 4 hours, or until liquid is absorbed and potatoes are tender.

Chili Soup

Fannie Miller/Hutchinson, KS

MAKES 12–15 SERVINGS

4 lbs. ground beef
1 large onion, diced
2 cups cold water
2 Tbsp. brown sugar
2 Tbsp. chili powder
2 tsp. salt
2 tsp. dried oregano
1/2 tsp. garlic salt
1/4 tsp. ground coriander

1. Brown hamburger and onion in skillet. Drain and transfer to slow cooker.

2. Add remaining ingredients. Mix well.

3. Cover. Cook on Low 4–6 hours.

M&T's Chili

Sherry Conyers
McPherson, KS

MAKES 4 SERVINGS

1 lb. ground beef, browned
1/2 lb. sausage links, sliced
  and browned
1 pkg. Williams chili
  seasoning
2 10-oz. cans Mexican
  tomatoes
15-oz. can chili with no beans
2 10-oz. cans Rotel
  tomatoes
1-lb. can refried beans
1/4 cup diced onions

1. Combine ingredients in
slow cooker.

2. Cover. Cook on Low 5–6
hours.

variations

● If you want a soupier, and
less spicy, chili, add a 1-lb. can
of stewed tomatoes or 2 cups
tomato juice.

Slow-Cooker Black Bean Chili

Mary Seielstad/Sparks, NV

MAKES 8 SERVINGS

1 lb. pork tenderloin, cut
  into 1-inch chunks
16-oz. jar thick chunky salsa
3 15-oz. cans black beans,
  rinsed and drained
1/2 cup chicken broth
1 medium red bell pepper,
  chopped
1 medium onion, chopped
1 tsp. ground cumin
2–3 tsp. chili powder
1–1 1/2 tsp. dried oregano
1/4 cup sour cream

1. Combine all ingredients
except sour cream in slow
cooker.

2. Cover. Cook on Low 6–8
hours, or until pork is tender.

3. Garnish individual
servings with sour cream.

note

● This is good served over
brown rice.

White Chili Speciality

Barbara McGinnis/Jupiter, FL

MAKES 8–10 SERVINGS

1 lb. large Great Northern
  beans, soaked overnight
2 lbs. boneless, skinless
  chicken breasts, cut up
1 medium onion, chopped
2 4 1/2-oz. cans chopped
  green chilies
2 tsp. cumin
1/2 tsp. salt
14 1/2-oz. can chicken broth
1 cup water

1. Put soaked beans in
medium-size saucepan and
cover with water. Bring to
boil and simmer 20 minutes.
Discard water.

2. Brown chicken, if desired,
in 1–2 Tbsp. oil in skillet.

3. Combine pre-cooked and
drained beans, chicken, and
all remaining ingredients in
slow cooker.

4. Cover. Cook on Low
10–12 hours, or High 5–6
hours.

Joyce's Slow-Cooked Chili

Joyce Slaymaker/Strasburg, PA

MAKES 10 SERVINGS

2 lbs. ground turkey
2 16-oz. cans kidney beans, rinsed and drained
2 14 1/2-oz. cans diced tomatoes, undrained
8-oz. can tomato sauce
2 medium onions, chopped
1 green pepper, chopped
2 cloves garlic, minced
2 Tbsp. chili powder
2 tsp. salt, optional
1 tsp. pepper
shredded cheddar cheese, optional

1. Brown ground turkey in skillet. Drain. Transfer to slow cooker.

2. Stir in remaining ingredients except cheese.

3. Cover. Cook on Low 8–10 hours, or on High 4 hours.

4. Garnish individual servings with cheese.

Turkey Chili

Dawn Day/Westminster, CA

MAKES 6–8 SERVINGS

1 large chopped onion
2–3 Tbsp. oil
1 lb. ground turkey
1/2 tsp. salt
3 Tbsp. chili powder
6-oz. can tomato paste
3 1-lb. cans small red beans with liquid
1 cup frozen corn

1. Sauté onion in oil in skillet until transparent. Add turkey and salt and brown lightly in skillet.

2. Combine all ingredients in slow cooker. Mix well.

3. Cover. Cook on Low 8–9 hours.

note
● Ground beef can be used in place of turkey.

variation
● Serve over rice, topped with shredded cheddar cheese and sour cream.

Chili Sans Cholesterol

Dolores S. Kratz
Souderton, PA

MAKES 4 SERVINGS

1 lb. ground turkey
1/2 cup chopped celery
1/2 cup chopped onions
8-oz. can tomatoes
14-oz. can pinto beans
14 1/2-oz. can diced tomatoes
1/2 tsp., or more, chili powder
1/2 tsp. salt
dash pepper

1. Sauté turkey in skillet until browned. Drain.

2. Combine all ingredients in slow cooker.

3. Cover. Cook on Low 6 hours.

Chilly-Chili

Alix Nancy Botsford
Seminole, OK

MAKES 6–8 SERVINGS

2 cups dried beans
1 tsp. salt
2 Tbsp. olive oil
1 large onion, chopped
1 lb. ground turkey
2 tsp. minced garlic oil
1 tsp. salt
2 celery stalks, chopped
1 green pepper, diced
10-oz. can tomatoes and
  green chilies

1. Sort, wash, and cover beans with water. Soak 6–8 hours. Drain.

2. Place beans in slow cooker. Cover with fresh water. Add 1 tsp. salt.

3. Cover. Cook on High 2–3 hours, or until you can crush a bean with a fork. Drain all but 1–2 cups liquid.

4. Brown onion, turkey, and garlic in oil in skillet. Add 1 tsp. salt, celery, and green pepper. Cook until vegetables start to soften. Add tomatoes. Place in slow cooker.

5. Cover. Cook on Low 1–8 hours.

6. Serve with slices of cheese and crackers.

Wintertime Vegetable Chili

Maricarol Magill/Freehold, NJ

MAKES 6 SERVINGS

1 medium butternut squash, peeled and cubed
2 medium carrots, peeled and diced
1 medium onion, diced
3 tsp.—3 Tbsp. chili powder, depending upon how hot you like your chili
2 14-oz. cans diced tomatoes
4-oz. can chopped mild green chilies
1 tsp. salt, optional
1 cup vegetable broth
2 16-oz. cans black beans, drained and rinsed
sour cream, optional

1. In slow cooker, layer ingredients in order given— except sour cream.

2. Cover. Cook on Low 6–8 hours, or until vegetables are tender.

3. Stir before serving.

4. Top individual servings with dollops of sour cream.

5. Serve with crusty French bread.

Vegetarian Chili

Connie Johnson/Loudon, NH

MAKES 6 SERVINGS

3 garlic cloves, minced
2 onions, chopped
1 cup textured vegetable protein (T.V.P.)
1-lb. can beans of your choice, drained
1 green bell pepper, chopped
1 jalapeño pepper, seeds removed, chopped
28-oz. can diced Italian tomatoes
1 bay leaf
1 Tbsp. dried oregano
1/2-1 tsp. salt
1/4 tsp. pepper

1. Combine all ingredients in slow cooker.

2. Cover. Cook on Low 6–8 hours.

Beef

There's-No-Easier Roast Beef

Sue Pennington
Bridgewater, VA

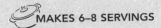 **MAKES 6–8 SERVINGS**

12-oz. bottle barbecue
  sauce
3–4-lb. beef roast

1. Pour half of barbecue
sauce into bottom of slow
cooker.

2. Add roast. Top with
remaining barbecue sauce.

3. Cover. Cook on Low 6–8
hours.

4. Slice roast and serve with
sauce.

variation
● Use an 18-oz. bottle of
barbecue sauce if you prefer
a juicier outcome.

Easy Roast

Lisa Warren / Parkesburg, PA

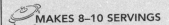 **MAKES 6–8 SERVINGS**

3–4-lb. beef roast
1 envelope dry onion soup
  mix
14 1/2-oz. can stewed
  tomatoes, or seasoned
  tomatoes

1. Place roast in slow
cooker. Cover with onion
soup and tomatoes.

2. Cover. Cook on Low
8 hours.

Cola Roast

Janice Yoskovich
Carmichaels, PA

MAKES 8–10 SERVINGS

3-lb. beef roast
1 envelope dry onion soup
  mix
2 cans cola

1. Place roast in slow
cooker. Sprinkle with soup
mix. Pour soda over all.

2. Cover. Cook on Low
7–8 hours.

note
● Diet cola does not work with
this recipe.

Italian Beef

Joyce Bowman / Lady Lake, FL

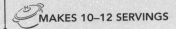 **MAKES 10–12 SERVINGS**

3–4-lb. beef roast
1 pkg. dry Italian dressing
  mix
12-oz. can beer

1. Place roast in slow
cooker. Sprinkle with dry
Italian dressing mix. Pour
beer over roast.

2. Cover. Cook on Low 8–10
hours, or High 3–4 hours.

3. When beef is done, shred
and serve with juice on
crusty rolls.

variation
● In place of beef, use pork
chops or chicken legs and
thighs (skin removed).

...super**easy**

Dale & Shari's Beef Stroganoff

Dale and Shari Mast
Harrisonburg, VA

 MAKES 4 SERVINGS

4 cups beef cubes
10 3/4-oz. can cream of
   mushroom soup
1 cup sour cream

1. Place beef in slow cooker. Cover with mushroom soup.

2. Cover. Cook on Low 8 hours, or High 4–5 hours.

3. Before serving stir in sour cream.

4. Serve over cooked rice, pasta, or baked potatoes.

8-Hour Tangy Beef

Mary Martins/Fairbank, IA

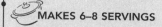 **MAKES 6–8 SERVINGS**

3 1/2–4-lb. beef roast
12-oz. can ginger ale
1 1/2 cups ketchup

1. Put beef in slow cooker.

2. Pour ginger ale and ketchup over roast.

3. Cover. Cook on Low 8–9 hours.

4. Shred with 2 forks and serve on buns. Or break up into chunks and serve over rice, potatoes, or pasta.

variations

● This recipe produces a lot of juice. You can add chopped onions, potatoes, and green beans in Step 2, if you want. Or stir in sliced mushrooms and/or peas 30 minutes before the end of the cooking time.
● For a tangier finished dish, add chili powder or cumin, along with black pepper, in Step 2.

Beef Roast in Beer

Evelyn Page/Riverton, WY

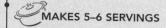 **MAKES 5–6 SERVINGS**

2–3-lb. beef roast
1 can beer
1 onion, sliced

1. Place roast in slow cooker. Poke all over surface with fork.

2. Pour beer over roast. Cover. Refrigerate for 8 hours.

3. Add sliced onion to slow cooker.

4. Cover. Cook on Low 6–8 hours.

variations

● Brown roast in oil in skillet on top and bottom before placing in cooker.
● Mix together 1 cup cider vinegar and 2 Tbsp. Worcestershire sauce. Marinate roast in mixture in refrigerator for 2–4 hours. Either discard marinade when placing roast in cooker, or add it to the cooker. To thicken broth, mix together 1/4 cup flour and 1 cup water until smooth. Twenty minutes before end of cooking time, remove roast from cooker. Stir flour paste into beef broth until smooth. Return roast to cooker and continue cooking. When finished, cut roast into chunks and serve with gravy.

Pot Roast with Creamy Mushroom Sauce

Colleen Konetzni
Rio Rancho, NM

Janet V. Yocum
Elizabethtown, PA

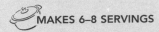

MAKES 6–8 SERVINGS

2–2 1/2-lb. boneless beef chuck roast
1 envelope dry onion soup mix
10 3/4-oz. can condensed cream of mushroom soup

1. Place roast in slow cooker. Sprinkle with dry soup mix. Top with mushroom soup.

2. Cover. Cook on High 1 hour, and then on Low 8 hours, or until meat is tender.

3. Slice. Serve with mashed potatoes or cooked noodles.

variation

● Add cubed potatoes and sliced carrots to beef. Proceed with directions above.
Marla Folkert/Holland, OH

Slow-Cooker Beef Sandwiches

Elaine Unruh
Minneapolis, MN

Winifred Ewy/Newton, KS

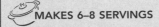

MAKES 6–8 SERVINGS

2–3-lb. chuck roast, cubed
1 pkg. dry onion soup mix
12-oz. can cola

1. Place meat in slow cooker.

2. Sprinkle soup mix over meat. Pour cola over all.

3. Cover. Cook on Low 8–10 hours.

4. Serve as roast or shred the beef, mix with sauce, and serve on buns.

variation

● Layer 4 medium potatoes, sliced, and 4 carrots, sliced, in bottom of pot. Place meat and rest of ingredients on top, and follow recipe for cooking.

Corned Beef

Margaret Jarrett/Anderson, IN

MAKES 6–7 SERVINGS

2–3-lb. cut of marinated corned beef
2–3 garlic cloves, minced
10–12 peppercorns

1. Place meat in bottom of cooker. Top with garlic and peppercorns. Cover with water.

2. Cover. Cook on High 4–5 hours, or until tender.

3. Cool meat, slice thin, and use to make Reuben sandwiches along with sliced Swiss cheese, sauerkraut, and Thousand Island dressing on toasted pumpernickel bread.

...**supereasy**

Rich and Tasty Beef Roast

Reita F. Yoder/Carlsbad, NM

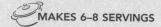MAKES 6–8 SERVINGS

10 3/4-oz. can cream of
  mushroom soup
3–5-lb. beef roast
oil
1 pkg. dry onion soup mix

1. Spread mushroom soup
in bottom of slow cooker.

2. Sear roast on all sides
in oil in hot skillet. Add to
slow cooker.

3. Sprinkle meat with dry
onion soup mix.

4. Cook on High 5–6 hours.

Beef Ribs with Sauerkraut

Rosaria Strachan/Fairfield, CT

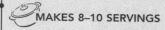MAKES 8–10 SERVINGS

3–4 lbs. beef short ribs
32-oz. bag, or 27-oz. can,
  sauerkraut, drained
2 Tbsp. caraway seeds
1/4 cup water

1. Put ribs in 6-qt. slow
cooker.

2. Place sauerkraut and
caraway seeds on top of ribs.

3. Pour in water.

4. Cover. Cook on High 3–4
hours or on Low 7–8 hours.

5. Serve with mashed
potatoes.

variation
● If you really enjoy
sauerkraut, double the amount
of sauerkraut, and divide the
recipe between two 4- or 5-qt.
cookers.

Pepsi Pot Roast

Mrs. Don Martins/Fairbank, IA

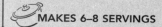MAKES 6–8 SERVINGS

3–4-lb. pot roast
10 3/4-oz. can cream of
  mushroom soup
1 envelope dry onion
  soup mix
16-oz. bottle Pepsi, or
  other cola

1. Place meat in slow
cooker.

2. Top with mushroom soup
and onion soup mix. Pour in
Pepsi.

3. Cover. Cook on High
6 hours.

Can-It-Really-Be-So-Easy? Roast Beef

Laverne Stoner/Scottdale, PA

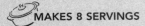MAKES 8 SERVINGS

4-lb. beef roast
10 3/4-oz. can cream of
   mushroom soup
1 pkg. dry onion soup mix
1 cup water

1. Place beef roast on double layer of aluminum foil.

2. Combine soup and dry soup mix. Spread on all sides of roast. Wrap foil around roast. Place in slow cooker. Pour water around roast.

3. Cover. Cook on Low 6–8 hours.

Easy Company Beef

Joyce B. Suiter/Garysburg, NC

MAKES 8 SERVINGS

3 lbs. stewing beef, cubed
10 3/4-oz. can cream of
   mushroom soup
7-oz. jar mushrooms,
   undrained
1/2 cup red wine
1 envelope dry onion
   soup mix

1. Combine all ingredients in slow cooker.

2. Cover. Cook on Low 10 hours.

3. Serve over noodles, rice, or pasta.

Good 'n Easy Beef 'n Gravy

Janice Crist/Quinter, KS

MAKES 8 SERVINGS

3-lb. beef roast, cubed
1 envelope dry onion soup
   mix
1/2 cup beef broth
10 3/4-oz. can cream of
   mushroom, or cream of
   celery, soup
4-oz. can sliced mushrooms,
   drained

1. Combine all ingredients in slow cooker.

2. Cover. Cook on Low 10–12 hours.

variation

● Use 1/2 cup sauterne instead of beef broth.

Joyce Shackelford
Green Bay, WI

...super**easy**

Easy Dinner Surprise

Nancy Graves/Manhattan, KS

 MAKES 4–5 SERVINGS

1–1 1/2 lbs. stewing meat, cubed
10 3/4-oz. can cream of mushroom soup
10 3/4-oz. can cream of celery soup
1 pkg. dry onion soup mix
4-oz. can mushroom pieces

1. Combine all ingredients in slow cooker.

2. Cover. Cook on Low 8–10 hours.

3. Serve over rice or baked potatoes.

variation
● Add 1/4 cup finely chopped celery for color and texture.

Slow-Cooker Roast Beef

Ernestine Schrepfer
Trenton, MO

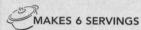 MAKES 6 SERVINGS

3-lb. sirloin tip roast
1/2 cup flour
1 envelope dry onion soup mix
1 envelope brown gravy mix
2 cups ginger ale

1. Coat roast with flour (reserve remaining flour). Place in slow cooker.

2. Combine soup mix, gravy mix, remaining flour, and ginger ale in bowl. Mix well. Pour over roast.

3. Cover. Cook on Low 8–10 hours.

Zippy Beef Tips

Maryann Westerberg
Rosamond, CA

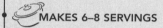 MAKES 6–8 SERVINGS

2 lbs. stewing meat, cubed
2 cups sliced fresh mushrooms
10 3/4-oz. can cream of mushroom soup
1 envelope dry onion soup mix
1 cup 7-Up, or other lemon-lime carbonated drink

1. Place meat and mushrooms in slow cooker.

2. Combine mushroom soup, soup mix, and soda. Pour over meat.

3. Cover. Cook on Low 8 hours.

4. Serve over rice.

French Dip Roast

Patti Boston/Newark, OH

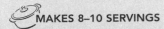 **MAKES 8–10 SERVINGS**

1 large onion, sliced
3-lb. beef bottom roast
1/2 cup dry white wine, or water
1 pkg. dry au jus gravy mix
2 cups beef broth

1. Place onion in slow cooker. Add roast.

2. Combine wine and gravy mix. Pour over roast.

3. Add enough broth to cover roast.

4. Cover. Cook on High 5–6 hours, or Low 10–12 hours.

5. Remove meat from liquid. Let stand 5 minutes before slicing thinly across grain.

Hickory Smoked Brisket

Janet Roggie/Lowville, NY

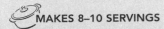 **MAKES 12–14 SERVINGS**

3–4-lb. beef brisket
1/4 cup liquid smoke
1/2 tsp. celery salt
1/2 tsp. garlic salt
1/2 tsp. onion powder

1. Place beef on piece of foil.

2. Sprinkle with remaining ingredients. Wrap foil securely around beef. Place in slow cooker.

3. Cover. Cook on Low 8–12 hours.

4. Serve warm with juice ladled over each slice.

Delicious, Easy Chuck Roast

Mary Jane Musser
Manheim, PA

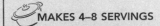 **MAKES 4–8 SERVINGS**

2–4-lb. chuck roast
salt to taste
pepper to taste
1 onion, sliced
10 3/4-oz. can cream of mushroom soup

1. Season roast with salt and pepper and place in slow cooker.

2. Add onion. Pour soup over all.

3. Cover. Cook on Low 8–10 hours, or on High 6 hours.

Pot Roast

Carole Whaling
New Tripoli, PA

MAKES 8 SERVINGS

4 medium potatoes, cubed

4 carrots, sliced

1 onion, sliced

3–4-lb. rump roast, or pot roast, cut into serving-size pieces

1 tsp. salt

1/2 tsp. pepper

1 bouillon cube

1/2 cup boiling water

1. Put vegetables and meat in slow cooker. Stir in salt and pepper.

2. Dissolve bouillon cube in water, then pour over other ingredients.

3. Cover. Cook on Low 10–12 hours.

Powerhouse Beef Roast with Tomatoes, Onions, and Peppers

Donna Treloar/Gaston, IN

MAKES 5–6 SERVINGS

3-lb. boneless chuck roast

1 garlic clove, minced

1 Tbsp. oil

2–3 onions, sliced

2–3 sweet green and red peppers, sliced

16-oz. jar salsa

2 14 1/2-oz. cans Mexican-style stewed tomatoes

1. Brown roast and garlic in oil in skillet. Place in slow cooker.

2. Add onions and peppers.

3. Combine salsa and tomatoes and pour over ingredients in slow cooker.

4. Cover. Cook on Low 8–10 hours.

5. Slice meat to serve.

Easy Pot Roast and Veggies

Tina Houk/Clinton, MO

Arlene Wiens/Newton, KS

MAKES 6 SERVINGS

3–4-lb. chuck roast

4 medium-sized potatoes, cubed

4 medium-sized carrots, sliced, or 1 lb. baby carrots

2 celery stalks, sliced thin, optional

1 envelope dry onion soup mix

3 cups water

1. Put roast, potatoes, carrots, and celery in slow cooker.

2. Add onion soup mix and water.

3. Cover. Cook on Low 6–8 hours.

variations

● To add flavor to the broth, stir 1 tsp. kitchen bouquet, 1/2 tsp. salt, 1/2 tsp. black pepper, and 1/2 tsp. garlic powder into water before pouring over meat and vegetables.

Bonita Ensenberger
Albuquerque, NM

● Before putting roast in, sprinkle it with the dry soup mix, patting it on so it adheres.

Betty Lahman/Elkton, VA

Pot Roast

Janet L. Roggie/Linville, NY

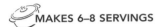MAKES 6–8 SERVINGS

3 potatoes, thinly sliced
2 large carrots, thinly sliced
1 onion, thinly sliced
1 tsp. salt
1/2 tsp. pepper
3–4-lb. pot roast
1/2 cup water

1. Put vegetables in bottom of slow cooker. Stir in salt and pepper. Add roast. Pour in water.

2. Cover. Cook on Low 10–12 hours.

variations
● Add 1/2 tsp. dried dill, a bay leaf, and 1/2 tsp. dried rosemary for more flavor.
● Brown roast on all sides in saucepan in 2 Tbsp. oil before placing in cooker.
Debbie Zeida/Mashpee, MA

Pot Roast

Julie McKenzie
Punxsutawney, PA

MAKES 8 SERVINGS

3-lb. rump roast
1/2 envelope dry onion soup mix
1 small onion, sliced
4-oz. can mushrooms with liquid
1/3 cup dry red wine
1/3 cup water
1 garlic clove, minced
1 bay leaf
1/2 tsp. dried thyme
2 Tbsp. chopped fresh basil, or 1 tsp. dried basil

1. Combine all ingredients in slow cooker.

2. Cover. Cook on Low 10–12 hours.

variations
● Add 1/2 tsp. salt, if desired.
● Mix 3 Tbsp. cornstarch into 1/2 cup cold water. At the end of the cooking time remove bay leaf and discard. Remove meat to serving platter and keep warm. Stir dissolved cornstarch into hot liquid in slow cooker. Stir until absorbed. Cover and cook on High 10 minutes, until sauce thickens. Serve over top or alongside sliced meat.

Forget It Pot Roast

Mary Mitchell
Battle Creek, MI

MAKES 6 SERVINGS

6 potatoes, quartered
6 carrots, sliced
3–3 1/2-lb. chuck roast
1 envelope dry onion soup mix
10 3/4-oz. can cream of mushroom soup
2–3 Tbsp. flour
1/4 cup cold water

1. Place potatoes and carrots in slow cooker. Add meat. Top with soups.

2. Cover. Cook on Low 8–9 hours.

3. To make gravy, remove meat and vegetables to serving platter and keep warm. Pour juices into saucepan and bring to boil. Mix 2–3 Tbsp. flour with 1/4 cup cold water until smooth. Stir into juices in pan until thickened. Serve over meat and vegetables, or alongside as a gravy.

Beef Pot Roast

Julia B. Boyd/Memphis, TN

MAKES 6–8 SERVINGS

3–4-lb. chuck, or English-cut, beef roast
1 envelope dry onion-mushroom soup mix
10 3/4-oz. can cream of celery soup
1 soup can water
2–3 Tbsp. flour
2–3 beef bouillon cubes
1 medium onion, chopped

1. Combine all ingredients in slow cooker.

2. Cover. Cook on Low 10–12 hours.

variations
● Use leftover meat to make soup. Add one large can tomatoes and any leftover vegetables you have on hand. Add spices such as minced onion, garlic powder, basil, bay leaf, celery seed. To increase the liquid, use V-8 juice and season with 1–2 tablespoons butter for a richer soup base. Cook on Low 6–12 hours. If you wish, stir in cooked macaroni or rice just before serving.

Chuck Roast

· Hazel L. Propst/Oxford, PA

MAKES 6–8 SERVINGS

4–5-lb. boneless chuck roast
1/3 cup flour
3 Tbsp. oil
1 envelope dry onion soup mix
water
1/4 cup flour
1/3 cup cold water

1. Rub roast with flour on both sides. Brown in oil in saucepan. Place in slow cooker (cutting to fit if necessary).

2. Sprinkle dry soup mix over roast. Add water to cover roast.

3. Cover. Cook on Low 8 hours.

4. Stir flour into 1/3 cup cold water until smooth. Remove roast to serving platter and keep warm. Stir paste into hot sauce and stir until dissolved. Cover and cook on High until sauce is thickened.

Roast Beef

Judy Buller/Bluffton, OH

MAKES 6 SERVINGS

2 1/2–3-lb. bottom round roast
2 cups water
2 beef bouillon cubes
1/2 tsp. cracked pepper
1/4 cup flour
1/2 tsp. salt
3/4 cup cold water

1. Cut roast into 6–8 pieces and place in slow cooker. Add water and bouillon cubes. Sprinkle with pepper.

2. Cover. Cook on High 2 hours. Reduce heat to Low and cook 4–5 hours, or until meat is tender.

3. Dissolve flour and salt in cold water. Remove roast from cooker and keep warm. Stir flour paste into hot broth in cooker until smooth. Cover and cook on High for 5 minutes. Serve gravy with sliced roast beef.

Roast

Tracey Yohn/Harrisburg, PA

MAKES 6 SERVINGS

2–3-lb. shoulder roast
1 tsp. salt
1 tsp. pepper
1 tsp. garlic salt
1 small onion, sliced in rings
1 cup boiling water
1 beef bouillon cube

1. Place roast in slow cooker. Sprinkle with salt, pepper, and garlic salt. Place onion rings on top.

2. Dissolve bouillon cube in water. Pour over roast.

3. Cover. Cook on Low 10–12 hours, or on High 5–6 hours.

Savory Sweet Roast

Martha Ann Auker
Landisburg, PA

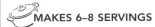

MAKES 6–8 SERVINGS

3–4-lb. blade, or chuck, roast
oil
1 onion, chopped
10 3/4-oz. can cream of mushroom soup
1/2 cup water
1/4 cup sugar
1/4 cup vinegar
2 tsp. salt
1 tsp. prepared mustard
1 tsp. Worcestershire sauce

1. Brown meat in oil on both sides in saucepan. Put in slow cooker.

2. Blend together remaining ingredients. Pour over meat.

3. Cover. Cook on Low 12–16 hours.

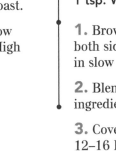

Dilled Pot Roast

C. J. Slagle/Roann, IN

MAKES 6 SERVINGS

3–3 1/2-lb. beef pot roast
1 tsp. salt
1/4 tsp. pepper
2 tsp. dried dillweed, divided
1/4 cup water
1 Tbsp. vinegar
3 Tbsp. flour
1/2 cup water
1 cup sour cream

1. Sprinkle both sides of meat with salt, pepper, and 1 tsp. dill. Place in slow cooker. Add water and vinegar.

2. Cover. Cook on Low 7–9 hours, or until tender. Remove meat from pot. Turn to High.

3. Dissolve flour in water. Stir into meat drippings. Stir in additional 1 tsp. dill. Cook on High 5 minutes. Stir in sour cream. Cook on High another 5 minutes.

4. Slice meat and serve with sour cream sauce over top.

Herbed Roast with Gravy

Sue Williams/Gulfport, MS

 MAKES 8–10 SERVINGS

4-lb. roast
2 tsp. salt
1/2 tsp. pepper
2 medium onions, sliced
half a can (10 3/4-oz.)
    condensed cheddar
    cheese soup
8-oz. can tomato sauce
4-oz. can mushroom pieces
    and stems, drained
1/4 tsp. dried basil
1/4 tsp. dried oregano

1. Season roast with salt and pepper. Place in slow cooker.

2. Combine remaining ingredients and pour over meat.

3. Cover. Cook on Low 8–10 hours, or on High 4–5 hours.

4. Serve with gravy.

Pot Roast

Judi Manos/West Islip, NY

 MAKES 8 SERVINGS

4-lb. chuck roast or stewing
    meat, cubed
1 Tbsp. oil
3/4 can beer
1/2 cup, plus 1 Tbsp.,
    ketchup
1 onion, sliced
1/2 cup cold water
1 1/2 Tbsp. flour

1. Brown meat in oil in saucepan.

2. Combine beer and ketchup in slow cooker. Stir in onion and browned meat.

3. Cover. Cook on Low 8 hours.

4. Remove meat and keep warm. Blend flour into cold water until dissolved. Stir into hot gravy until smooth.

5. Serve gravy and meat together.

Horseradish Beef

Barbara Nolan
Pleasant Valley, NY

MAKES 6–8 SERVINGS

3–4-lb. pot roast
2 Tbsp. oil
1/2 tsp. salt
1/2 tsp. pepper
1 onion, chopped
6-oz. can tomato paste
1/3 cup horseradish sauce

1. Brown roast on all sides in oil in skillet. Place in slow cooker. Add remaining ingredients.

2. Cover. Cook on Low 8–10 hours.

French Dip

Barbara Walker/Sturgis, SD

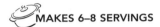MAKES 6–8 SERVINGS

3-lb. rump roast
1/2 cup soy sauce
1 beef bouillon cube
1 bay leaf
1 tsp. dried thyme
3–4 peppercorns
1 tsp. garlic powder

1. Combine all ingredients in slow cooker. Add water to almost cover meat.

2. Cover. Cook on Low 10–12 hours.

Spicy Pot Roast

Jane Talso/Albuquerque, NM

MAKES 6–8 SERVINGS

3–4-lb. beef pot roast
salt to taste
pepper to taste
3/4-oz. pkg. brown gravy mix
1/4 cup ketchup
2 tsp. Dijon mustard
1 tsp. Worcestershire sauce
1/8 tsp. garlic powder
1 cup water

1. Sprinkle meat with salt and pepper. Place in slow cooker.

2. Combine remaining ingredients. Pour over meat.

3. Cover. Cook on Low 8–10 hours, or High 4–5 hours.

Chinese Pot Roast

Marsha Sabus/Fallbrook, CA

MAKES 6 SERVINGS

3-lb. boneless beef pot roast
2 Tbsp. flour
1 Tbsp. oil
2 large onions, chopped
salt to taste
pepper to taste
1/2 cup soy sauce
1 cup water
1/2 tsp. ground ginger

1. Dip roast in flour and brown on both sides in oil in saucepan. Place in slow cooker.

2. Top with onions, salt and pepper.

3. Combine soy sauce, water, and ginger. Pour over meat.

4. Cover. Cook on High 10 minutes. Reduce heat to Low and cook 8–10 hours.

5. Slice and serve with rice.

Beef Au Jus

Jean Weller/State College, PA

MAKES 6–8 SERVINGS

3-lb. eye, or rump, roast
1 pkg. dry au jus gravy mix
1 tsp. garlic powder
1 tsp. onion powder
1/2 tsp. salt
1/4–1/2 tsp. pepper

1. Place roast in slow cooker.

2. Prepare gravy according to package directions. Pour over roast.

3. Sprinkle with garlic powder, onion powder, salt, and pepper.

4. Cover. Cook on Low 6 hours. After 6 hours, remove meat and trim fat. Shred meat and return to slow cooker, cooking until desired tenderness. Add more water if roast isn't covered with liquid when returning it to cooker.

Dripped Beef

Mitzi McGlynchey
Downingtown, PA

MAKES 8 SERVINGS

3–4-lb. chuck roast
1 tsp. salt
1 tsp. seasoned salt
1 tsp. white pepper
1 Tbsp. rosemary
1 Tbsp. dried oregano
1 Tbsp. garlic powder
1 cup water

1. Combine all ingredients in slow cooker.

2. Cover. Cook on Low 6–7 hours.

3. Shred meat using two forks. Strain liquid and return liquid and meat to slow cooker. Serve meat and au jus over mashed potatoes, noodles, or rice.

Deep Pit Beef

Kristina Shull/Timberville, VA

MAKES 6–8 SERVINGS

1 tsp. garlic salt, or powder
1 tsp. celery salt
1 tsp. lemon pepper
1 1/2 Tbsp. liquid smoke
2 Tbsp. Worcestershire sauce
3–4-lb. beef roast

1. Combine seasonings in small bowl. Spread over roast as a marinade. Cover tightly with foil. Refrigerate for at least 8 hours.

2. Place roast in slow cooker. Cover with marinade sauce.

3. Cover. Cook on Low 6–7 hours. Save juice for gravy and serve with roast.

note
● This is also good served cold, along with picnic foods.

Italian Roast Beef

Elsie Russett/Fairbank, IA

MAKES 6–8 SERVINGS

4-lb. beef rump roast
flour
1 onion
2 garlic cloves
1 large celery stalk
2-oz. salt pork, or bacon
1 onion, sliced

1. Lightly flour roast.

2. In blender, grind onion, garlic, celery, and salt pork together. Rub ground mixture into roast.

3. Place sliced onion in slow cooker. Place roast on top of onion.

4. Cover. Cook on Low 8–10 hours.

Diane's Gutbuster

Joyce Cox/Port Angeles, WA

MAKES 10–15 SERVINGS

5-lb. chuck roast
1 large onion, sliced
2 tsp. salt
3/4 tsp. pepper
28-oz. can stewed tomatoes
1 Tbsp. brown sugar
1 cup water
half a bottle barbecue sauce
1 Tbsp. Worcestershire sauce

1. Combine all ingredients except barbecue sauce and Worcestershire sauce in slow cooker.

2. Cover. Cook on Low 6–7 hours. Refrigerate for at least 8 hours.

3. Shred meat and place in slow cooker. Add barbecue sauce and Worcestershire sauce.

4. Cover. Cook on Low 4–5 hours.

5. Serve as main dish or in hamburger buns.

Easy Barbecued Venison

Tracey B. Stenger/Gretna, LA

MAKES 6 SERVINGS

2–3-lb. venison, or beef, roast, cubed
2 large onions, sliced in rings
1–2 18-oz. bottles barbecue sauce

1. Put layer of meat and layer of onion rings in slow cooker. Drizzle generously with barbecue sauce. Repeat layers until meat and onion rings are all in place.

2. Cover. Cook on Low 8–10 hours.

3. Eat with au gratin potatoes and a vegetable, or slice thin and pile into steak rolls, drizzled with juice.

note
● To be sure venison cooks tender, marinate overnight in 1 cup vinegar and 2 Tbsp. dried rosemary. In the morning, discard marinade, cut venison into cubes, and proceed with recipe.

Sour Beef

Rosanne Hankins
Stevensville, MD

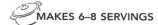 MAKES 6–8 SERVINGS

3–4-lb. pot roast
1/3 cup cider vinegar
1 large onion, sliced
3 bay leaves
1/2 tsp. salt
1/4 tsp. ground cloves
1/4 tsp. garlic powder

1. Place roast in slow cooker. Add remaining ingredients.

2. Cover. Cook on Low 8–10 hours.

Saucy Italian Roast

Sharon Miller/Holmesville, OH

 MAKES 8–10 SERVINGS

3–3 1/2-lb. boneless rump
 roast
1/2 tsp. salt
1/2 tsp. garlic powder
1/4 tsp. pepper
4 1/2-oz. jar mushroom
 pieces, drained
1 medium onion, diced
14-oz. jar spaghetti sauce
1/4–1/2 cup beef broth
hot cooked pasta

1. Cut roast in half.

2. Combine salt, garlic powder, and pepper. Rub over both halves of the roast. Place in slow cooker.

3. Top with mushrooms and onions.

4. Combine spaghetti sauce and broth. Pour over roast.

5. Cover. Cook on Low 8–9 hours.

6. Slice roast. Serve in sauce over pasta.

Italian Beef Au Jus

Carol Sherwood/Batavia, NY

 MAKES 8 SERVINGS

3–5-lb. boneless beef roast
10-oz. pkg. au jus mix
1 pkg. Italian salad dressing
 mix
14 1/2-oz. can beef both
half a soup can water

1. Place beef in slow cooker.

2. Combine remaining ingredients. Pour over roast.

3. Cover. Cook on Low 8 hours.

4. Slice meat and spoon onto hard rolls with straining spoon to make sandwiches. Or shred with 2 forks and serve over noodles or rice in broth thickened with flour.

note
● To thicken broth, mix 3 Tbsp. cornstarch into 1/4 cup cold water. Stir until smooth. Remove 1/2 cup beef broth from cooker and blend into cornstarch-water. Stir back into broth in cooker, stirring until smooth. Cook 10–15 minutes on High until broth becomes of gravy consistency.

Simply Super Supper

Anne Townsend
Albuquerque, NM

MAKES 4 SERVINGS

2 celery stalks, sliced
3 carrots, cut in strips
2 potatoes, cubed
2 onions, coarsely chopped
2-lb. beef roast
1 pkg. dry onion soup mix
1 Tbsp. liquid smoke
1 1/2 cups water

1. Place vegetables in slow cooker.

2. Place roast on top of vegetables.

3. Sprinkle with dry soup mix.

4. Combine liquid smoke and water. Pour over roast.

5. Cover. Cook on Low 7–8 hours, or until vegetables are tender.

6. Slice meat and serve with cole slaw and French bread. Lemon pie makes a nice finish.

This is a welcoming dinner to come home to because the house smells so yummy as you walk in. And the wonderful aroma lingers.

— • —

Favorite Sunday Pot Roast

Amber Swarey/Donalds, SC

MAKES 6 SERVINGS

4-lb. chuck roast
meat tenderizer
1 pkg. dry onion soup mix
fresh mushrooms, sliced
carrots, sliced
potatoes, chunked
1 cup boiling water

1. Place roast in slow cooker. Sprinkle with meat tenderizer and onion soup mix.

2. Layer mushrooms over roast.

3. Add carrots and potatoes around roast.

4. Pour water over vegetables.

5. Cover. Cook on High 4–5 hours.

6. Add a fresh salad and your meal is ready.

This is a recipe I grew up with at home. When Sunday came around, we looked forward to roast, potatoes, and carrots.

— • —

Beef Pot Roast

Nancy Wagner Graves
Manhattan, KS

MAKES 6–8 SERVINGS

4–5-lb. beef chuck roast
1 garlic clove, cut in half
salt to taste
pepper to taste
1 carrot, chopped
1 celery stalk, chopped
1 small onion, sliced
3/4 cup sour cream
3 Tbsp. flour
1/2 cup dry white wine

1. Rub roast with garlic. Season with salt and pepper. Place in slow cooker.

2. Add carrots, celery, and onion.

3. Combine sour cream, flour, and wine. Pour into slow cooker.

4. Cover. Cook on Low 6–7 hours.

Easy Roast Beef Barbecue

Rose Hankins
Stevensville, MD

 MAKES 12–16 SERVINGS

3–4-lb. beef roast
12-oz. bottle barbecue
  sauce
1/2 cup water
1/2 cup ketchup
1/2 cup chopped onions
1/2 cup chopped green
  pepper
12–16 sandwich rolls

1. Combine ingredients in slow cooker.

2. Cover. Cook on Low 12 hours.

3. Shred meat using 2 forks. Mix thoroughly through sauce.

4. Serve on rolls with cole slaw.

Salsa Chuck Roast

Hazel L. Propst/Oxford, PA

MAKES 6 SERVINGS

3–4-lb. chuck or round roast
1 Tbsp. oil
1 pkg. dry onion soup mix
2 cups water
1 cup salsa

1. Brown meat in skillet in oil on both sides. Place in slow cooker.

2. Add remaining ingredients to drippings in pan. Simmer 2–3 minutes. Add to slow cooker.

3. Cover. Cook on Low 7–8 hours.

4. Serve with broth over noodles or rice.

Salsa Beef

Sarah Niessen/Akron, PA

MAKES 5–6 SERVINGS

2–2 1/2 lbs. beef, cut up
  in bite-size cubes
1 Tbsp. oil
16-oz. jar salsa
8-oz. can tomato sauce
2 garlic cloves, minced
2 Tbsp. brown sugar
1 Tbsp. soy sauce
1 cup canned tomatoes

1. Brown beef in skillet in oil. Place in slow cooker.

2. Add remaining ingredients.

3. Cover. Cook on Low 6–8 hours.

4. Serve over rice.

variation
● For added flavor, use Italian tomato sauce.

Green Chili Roast

Anna Kenagy/Carlsbad, NM

 MAKES 8–10 SERVINGS

3–4-lb. beef roast
1 tsp. seasoned meat tenderizer
oil, optional
1 tsp. salt
3–4 green chili peppers, or 4-oz. can green chilies, undrained
1 Tbsp. Worchestershire sauce
1/2 tsp. black pepper

1. Sprinkle roast with meat tenderizer. Brown under broiler or in skillet in oil. Place in slow cooker.

2. Pour in water until roast is half covered.

3. Add remaining ingredients over top.

4. Cover. Cook on Low 8 hours.

5. Serve with mashed potatoes and green beans.

Barbecue Brisket

Patricia Howard
Albuquerque, NM

 MAKES 8–10 SERVINGS

4–5-lb. beef brisket
1/8 tsp. celery salt
1/4 tsp. garlic salt
1/4 tsp. onion salt
1/4 tsp. salt
1.5-oz. bottle liquid smoke
1 1/2 cups barbecue sauce

1. Place brisket in slow cooker.

2. Sprinkle with celery salt, garlic salt, onion salt, and salt.

3. Pour liquid smoke over brisket. Cover. Refrigerate for 8 hours.

4. Cook on Low 8–10 hours, or until tender. During last hour pour barbecue sauce over brisket.

Smoky Brisket

Angeline Lang/Greeley, CO

MAKES 8–10 SERVINGS

2 medium onions, sliced
3–4-lb. beef brisket
1 Tbsp. smoke-flavored salt
1 tsp. celery seed
1 Tbsp. mustard seed
1/2 tsp. pepper
12-oz. bottle chili sauce

1. Arrange onions in bottom of slow cooker.

2. Sprinkle both sides of meat with smoke-flavored salt.

3. Combine celery seed, mustard seed, pepper, and chili sauce. Pour over meat.

4. Cover. Cook on Low 10–12 hours.

Corned Beef and Cabbage

Rhoda Burgoon
Collingswood, NJ

Jo Ellen Moore/Pendleton, IN

 MAKES 6–8 SERVINGS

3 carrots, cut in 3-inch pieces

3–4-lb. corned beef brisket

2–3 medium onions, quartered

3/4–1 1/4 cups water

half a small head of cabbage, cut in wedges

1. Layer all ingredients except cabbage in cooker.

2. Cover. Cook on Low 8–10 hours, or High 5–6 hours.

3. Add cabbage wedges to liquid, pushing down to moisten. Turn to High and cook an additional 2–3 hours.

note

● To cook more cabbage separately in a skillet, remove 1 cup broth from slow cooker during last hour of cooking. Pour over cabbage wedges in skillet. Cover and cook slowly for 20–30 minutes.

variations

● Add 4 medium potatoes, halved, with the onions.

● Top individual servings with sour cream-horseradish mixture.

Kathi Rogge/Alexandria, IN

Eleanor's Corned Beef and Cabbage

Eleanor J. Ferreira
N. Chelmsford, MA

 MAKES 6 SERVINGS

2 medium onions, sliced

2 1/2–3-lb. corned beef brisket

1 cup apple juice

1/4 cup brown sugar, packed

2 tsp. finely shredded orange peel

6 whole cloves

2 tsp. prepared mustard

6 cabbage wedges

1. Place onions in slow cooker. Place beef on top of onions.

2. Combine apple juice, brown sugar, orange peel, cloves, and mustard. Pour over meat.

3. Place cabbage on top.

4. Cover. Cook on Low 10–12 hours, or High 5–6 hours.

Corned Beef

Elaine Vigoda/Rochester, NY

 MAKES 8 SERVINGS

3 large carrots, cut into chunks

1 cup chopped celery

1 tsp. salt

1/2 tsp. pepper

1 cup water

3–4-lb. corned beef

1 large onion, cut into pieces

half a small head of cabbage, cut in wedges

4 potatoes, peeled and chunked

1. Place carrots, celery, seasonings, and water in slow cooker.

2. Add beef. Cover with onions.

3. Cover. Cook on Low 8–10 hours, or on High 5–6 hours.

4. Lift corned beef out of cooker and add cabbage and potatoes, pushing them to bottom of slow cooker. Return beef to cooker.

5. Cover. Cook on High 2 hours.

6. Remove corned beef. Cool and slice on the diagonal. Serve surrounded by vegetables.

Corned Beef and Cabbage with Potatoes and Carrots

Rosaria Strachan/Fairfield, CT

 MAKES 6–7 SERVINGS

3–4 carrots, sliced
3–4 potatoes, cubed
1 onion, sliced
2 1/2–3 1/2-lb. corned beef brisket
10–12 peppercorns
4–6 cabbage wedges

1. Place carrots, potatoes, and onions in bottom of slow cooker.

2. Place beef over vegetables.

3. Cover with water.

4. Add peppercorns.

5. Cover. Cook on Low 8–10 hours or on High 5–6 hours.

6. Add cabbage. Cook on High 2–3 hours more.

7. Cut up meat and serve on large platter with mustard or horseradish as condiments. Pass vegetables with meat or in their own serving dish.

Corned Beef Dinner

Shirley Sears/Tiskilwa, IL

 MAKES 6 SERVINGS

2 onions, sliced
2 garlic cloves, minced
3 potatoes, pared and quartered
3 carrots, sliced
2 bay leaves
1 small head cabbage, cut into 4 wedges
3–4-lb. corned beef brisket
1 cup water
1/2 cup brown sugar
1 Tbsp. prepared mustard
dash of ground cloves

1. Layer onions, garlic, potatoes, carrots, bay leaves, and cabbage in slow cooker.

2. Place brisket on top.

3. Add water.

4. Cover. Cook on Low 10–11 hours.

5. During last hour of cooking, combine brown sugar, mustard, and cloves. Spread over beef.

6. Discard bay leaves. Slice meat and arrange on platter of vegetables.

Baked Steak

Shirley Thieszen/Lakin, KS

MAKES 6 SERVINGS

2 1/2 lbs. round steak, cut into 10 pieces
1 Tbsp. salt
1/2 tsp. pepper
oil
1/2 cup chopped onions
1/2 cup chopped green peppers
1 cup cream of mushroom soup
1/2 cup water

1. Season the steak with salt and pepper. Brown on both sides in oil in saucepan. Place in slow cooker.

2. Stir in onions, green peppers, mushroom soup, and water.

3. Cover. Cook on High 1 hour, and then on Low 3–4 hours.

Scrumptious Beef

Julia Lapp/New Holland, PA

MAKES 4–8 SERVINGS
(DEPENDING UPON
AMOUNT OF BEEF USED)

1–2 lbs. beef, cubed
1/2 lb. mushrooms, sliced
10 1/2-oz. can beef broth,
  or 1 cup water and
  1 cube beef bouillon
1 onion, chopped
10 3/4-oz. can cream of
  mushroom soup
3 Tbsp. dry onion soup mix

1. Combine all ingredients in slow cooker.

2. Cover. Cook on High 3–4 hours, or on Low 7–8 hours.

3. Serve over hot cooked rice.

Elaine's Beef Stroganoff

Elaine Unruh
Minneapolis, MN

MAKES 4 SERVINGS

1-lb. round steak, cubed
1 Tbsp. shortening
1/2 cup chopped onions
1/2 cup chopped celery
10 3/4-oz. can cream of
  celery soup
4-oz. can mushroom pieces,
  drained
1 cup sour cream
1/4 tsp. garlic salt

1. Brown meat in shortening in saucepan. Add onions and celery and sauté until just tender.

2. Combine all ingredients in slow cooker.

3. Cover. Cook on Low 6–8 hours.

4. Serve over hot cooked noodles.

Slow Cooker Beef

Sara Harter Fredette
Williamsburg, MA

MAKES 4–6 SERVINGS

1/2 cup flour
2 tsp. salt
1/4 tsp. pepper
2–3 lbs. stewing beef,
  cubed
2 Tbsp. oil
10 3/4-oz. can cream of
  mushroom soup
1 envelope dry onion soup
  mix
1/2 cup sour cream

1. Combine flour, salt, and pepper in plastic bag. Add beef in small batches. Shake to coat beef. Sauté beef in oil in saucepan. Place browned beef in slow cooker.

2. Stir in mushroom soup and onion soup mix.

3. Cover. Cook on Low 6–8 hours.

4. Stir in sour cream before serving. Heat for a few minutes.

5. Serve with noodles or mashed potatoes.

Beef and Gravy

Arlene Groff/Lewistown, PA

 MAKES 8 SERVINGS

1 onion, chopped
1 Tbsp. butter
3–4-lb. beef roast, cubed
1 tsp. salt
1/4 tsp. pepper
2 cups water
3 beef bouillon cubes
1/2 cup flour

1. Saute onion in skillet in butter until brown. Place onion in slow cooker, but reserve drippings.

2. Brown roast in skillet in drippings. Add meat to slow cooker, again reserving drippings.

3. Combine salt, pepper, water, bouillon, and flour. Add to meat drippings. Cook until thickened. Pour over meat.

4. Cover. Cook on Low 6–8 hours.

5. Serve over noodles.

Easy Stroganoff

Vicki Dinkel
Sharon Springs, KS

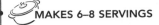 MAKES 6–8 SERVINGS

10 3/4-oz. can cream of mushroom soup
14 1/2-oz. can beef broth
1 lb. beef stewing meat or round steak, cut in 1-inch pieces
1 cup sour cream
2 cups cooked noodles

1. Combine soup and broth in slow cooker. Add meat.

2. Cover. Cook on High 3–4 hours. Reduce heat to Low and cook 3–4 hours.

3. Stir in sour cream.

4. Stir in noodles.

5. Cook on High 20 minutes.

Since I'm in school part-time and work two part-time jobs, this nearly complete meal is great to come home to. It smells wonderful when you open the door. A vegetable or salad and some crispy French bread are good additions.

— • —

Barbecue Roast Beef

Vicki Dinkel
Sharon Springs, KS

 MAKES 6–8 SERVINGS

1 1/2–2-lb. beef roast, cooked

Sauce:
1 cup ketchup
1/2 cup minced onions
2 tsp. Worcestershire sauce
1 cup water
1 Tbsp. brown sugar

1. Cut roast into cubes and place in slow cooker.

2. Combine sauce ingredients and pour over meat.

3. Cover. Cook on High 2 hours, then on Low for 4. Return to High 30 minutes before serving.

Tender Texas-Style Steaks

Janice Muller/Derwood, MD

MAKES 4–6 SERVINGS

steaks or chops
1 cup brown sugar
1 cup ketchup
salt to taste
pepper to taste
few dashes of
Worcestershire sauce

1. Lay steaks in bottom of slow cooker.

2. Combine sugar and ketchup. Pour over steaks.

3. Sprinkle with salt and pepper and a few dashes of Worcestershire sauce.

4. Cover. Cook on High 3 hours and Low 3 hours.

5. Serve with wide egg noodles, green beans, and applesauce. Use some of the juice from the cooker over the noodles. Thicken the juice if you like with a little flour.

Slow Cooker Beef with Mushrooms

Grace W. Yoder
Harrisonburg, VA

MAKES 6 SERVINGS

2 medium onions, thinly sliced
1/2 lb. mushrooms, sliced, or 2 4-oz. cans sliced mushrooms, drained
2 1/2-lb. beef flank, or round steak
salt to taste
pepper to taste
1 Tbsp. Worcestershire sauce
1 Tbsp. oil
paprika to taste

1. Place sliced onions and mushrooms in slow cooker.

2. Score top of meat about 1/2" deep in diamond pattern.

3. Season with salt and pepper. Rub in Worcestershire sauce and oil. Sprinkle top with paprika.

4. Place meat on top of onions.

5. Cover. Cook on Low 7–8 hours.

6. To serve, cut beef across grain in thin slices. Top with mushrooms and onions.

Barbecued Chuck Steak

Rhonda Burgoon
Collingswood, NJ

MAKES 4 SERVINGS

1 1/2-lb. boneless chuck steak, 1 1/2" thick
1 clove garlic, minced
1/4 cup wine vinegar
1 Tbsp. brown sugar
1 tsp. paprika
2 Tbsp. Worcestershire sauce
1/2 cup ketchup
1 tsp. salt
1 tsp. prepared mustard
1/4 tsp. black pepper

1. Cut beef on diagonal across the grain into 1"-thick slices. Place in slow cooker.

2. Combine remaining ingredients. Pour over meat. Stir to mix.

3. Cover. Cook on Low 3–5 hours.

Fruited Flank Steak

Ruth A. Feister/Narvon, PA

MAKES 6 SERVINGS

1 flank steak
salt to taste
pepper to taste
14 1/2-oz. can mixed fruit, or your choice of canned fruit
1 Tbsp. salad oil
1 Tbsp. lemon juice
1/4 cup teriyaki sauce
1 tsp. vinegar
1 garlic clove, minced

1. Sprinkle steak with salt and pepper. Place in slow cooker.

2. Drain fruit, saving 1/4 cup syrup. Combine 1/4 cup syrup with remaining ingredients. Pour over steak.

3. Cover. Cook on Low 6–8 hours. Add drained fruit during the last 15 minutes of cooking.

4. Lift from cooker onto platter. Using sharp knife slice across the grain making thin slices. Spoon fruit over meat.

5. Serve with baked rice.

Swiss Steak

Marilyn Mowry/Irving, TX

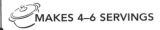

MAKES 4–6 SERVINGS

3–4 Tbsp. flour
1/2 tsp. salt
1/4 tsp. pepper
1 1/2 tsp. dry mustard
1 1/2–2 lbs. round steak
oil
1 cup sliced onions
1 lb. carrots
14 1/2-oz. can whole tomatoes
1 Tbsp. brown sugar
1 1/2 Tbsp. Worcestershire sauce

1. Combine flour, salt, pepper, and dry mustard.

2. Cut steak into serving pieces. Dredge in flour mixture. Brown on both sides in oil in saucepan. Place in slow cooker.

3. Add onions and carrots.

4. Combine tomatoes, brown sugar, and Worcestershire sauce. Pour into slow cooker.

5. Cover. Cook on Low 8–10 hours, or High 3–5 hours.

Pigs in Blankets

Linda Sluiter/Schererville, IN

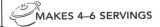

MAKES 4–6 SERVINGS

2–3-lb. round steak, cut about 1 inch thick
1 lb. bacon
1 cup ketchup
3/4 cup brown sugar
1 cup water
half a yellow onion, chopped

1. Cut steak into strips 1" thick x 3" long.

2. Lay a bacon strip down, then a strip of beef on top of the bacon slice. Roll up and secure with toothpick. Place in slow cooker.

3. Combine remaining ingredients. Pour over meat roll-ups.

4. Cover. Cook on High 8 hours.

Jacqueline's Swiss Steak

Jacqueline Stafl
East Bethany, NY

 **MAKES 4 SERVINGS**

1 1/2 lbs. round steak
2–4 Tbsp. flour
1/2 lb. sliced carrots, or
  1 lb. baby carrots
1 pkg. dry onion soup mix
8-oz. can tomato sauce
1/2 cup water

1. Cut steak into serving-size pieces. Dredge in flour.

2. Place carrots in bottom of slow cooker. Top with steak.

3. Combine soup mix, tomato sauce, and water. Pour over all.

4. Cover. Cook on Low 8–10 hours.

5. Serve over mashed potatoes.

Margaret's Swiss Steak

Margaret Rich
North Newton, KS

 **MAKES 6 SERVINGS**

1 cup chopped onions
1/2 cup chopped celery
2-lb. 1/2-inch-thick round
  steak
1/4 cup flour
3 Tbsp. oil
1 tsp. salt
1/4 tsp. pepper
16-oz. can diced tomatoes
1/4 cup flour
1/2 cup water

1. Place onions and celery in bottom of slow cooker.

2. Cut steak in serving-size pieces. Dredge in 1/4 cup flour. Brown on both sides in oil in saucepan. Place in slow cooker.

3. Sprinkle with salt and pepper. Pour on tomatoes.

4. Cover. Cook on Low 9 hours. Remove meat from cooker and keep warm.

5. Turn heat to High. Blend together 1/4 cup flour and water. Stir into sauce in slow cooker. Cover and cook 15 minutes. Serve with steak.

Creamy Swiss Steak

Jo Ellen Moore/Pendleton, IN

 **MAKES 6 SERVINGS**

1 1/2-lb. 3/4-inch-thick
  round steak
2 Tbsp. flour
1 tsp. salt
1/4 tsp. pepper
1 medium onion, sliced
10 3/4-oz. can cream of
  mushroom soup
1 carrot, chopped
1 small celery rib, chopped

1. Cut steak into serving-size pieces.

2. Combine flour, salt, and pepper. Dredge meat in flour.

3. Place onions in bottom of slow cooker. Add meat.

4. Spread cream of mushroom soup over meat. Top with carrots and celery.

5. Cover. Cook on Low 8–10 hours, or High 3–5 hours.

Creamy Swiss Steak

Connie B. Weaver
Bethlehem, PA

 **MAKES 4–6 SERVINGS**

2 lbs. round, or Swiss steak, cut 3/4 inch thick
salt to taste
pepper to taste
1 large onion, thinly sliced
10 3/4 oz. can cream of mushroom soup
1/2 cup water

1. Cut steak into serving-size pieces. Season with salt and pepper. Place in slow cooker. Layer onion over steak.

2. Combine soup and water. Pour into slow cooker.

3. Cover. Cook on Low 8–10 hours.

4. Serve over noodles or rice.

Swiss Steak

Marie Shank/Harrisonburg, VA

MAKES 6–8 SERVINGS

2-lb. round steak, cut into serving pieces
1 tsp. salt
1/2 tsp. pepper
1 large onion, sliced, or 1 pkg. dry onion soup mix
16-oz. can tomatoes

1. Combine ingredients in slow cooker.

2. Cover. Cook on Low 6–10 hours or High 3–4 hours.

note
● You may want to omit the salt if you use the onion soup mix.

Hearty Beef Stew

Charlotte Shaffer/East Earl, PA

MAKES 4–5 SERVINGS

2 lbs. stewing beef, cubed
5 carrots, sliced
1 large onion, cut in chunks
3 ribs celery, sliced
22-oz. can stewed tomatoes
1/2 tsp. ground cloves
2 bay leaves
1 1/2 tsp. salt
1/4–1/2 tsp. pepper

1. Combine all ingredients in slow cooker.

2. Cover. Cook on High 5–6 hours.

variations
● Substitute 1 whole clove for the 1/2 tsp. ground cloves. Remove before serving.
● Use venison instead of beef.
● Cut back the salt to 1 tsp. and use 1 tsp. soy sauce.

Betty B. Dennison
Grove City, PA

Italian Stew

Ann Gouinlock/Alexander, NY

MAKES 6 SERVINGS

1 1/2 lbs. beef cubes

2–3 carrots, cut in 1-inch chunks

3–4 ribs celery, cut in 3/4–1-inch pieces

1–1 1/2 cups coarsely chopped onions

14 1/2-oz. can stewed, or diced, tomatoes

1/3 cup minute tapioca

1 1/2 tsp. salt

1/4 tsp. pepper

1/4 tsp. Worcestershire sauce

1/2 tsp. Italian seasoning

1. Combine all ingredients in slow cooker.

2. Cover. Cook on Low 8–10 hours.

Judy's Beef Stew

Judy Koczo/Plano, IL

MAKES 4–6 SERVINGS

2 lbs. stewing meat, cubed

5 carrots, sliced

1 onion, diced

3 ribs celery, diced

5 potatoes, cubed

28-oz. can tomatoes

1/3–1/2 cup quick-cooking tapioca

2 tsp. salt

1/2 tsp. pepper

1. Combine all ingredients in slow cooker.

2. Cover. Cook on Low 10–12 hours, or High 5–6 hours.

variation
● Add 1 whole clove and 2 bay leaves to stew before cooking.
L. Jean Moore/Pendleton, IN

Slow-Cooker Stew

Trudy Kutter/Corfu, NY

MAKES 6–8 SERVINGS

2 lbs. boneless beef, cubed

4–6 celery ribs, sliced

6–8 carrots, sliced

6 potatoes, cubed

2 onions, sliced

28-oz. can tomatoes

1/4 cup minute tapioca

1 tsp. salt

1/4 tsp. pepper

1/2 tsp. dried basil, or oregano

1 garlic clove, pressed or minced

1. Combine all ingredients in slow cooker.

2. Cover. Cook on Low 8–10 hours.

variation
● Add 2 10 1/2-oz. cans beef gravy and 1/2 cup water in place of the tomatoes. Reduce tapioca to 2 Tbsp.

Waldorf Astoria Stew

Mary V. Warye
West Liberty, OH

 MAKES 6–8 SERVINGS

3 lbs. beef stewing meat,
cubed
1 medium onion, chopped
1 cup celery, sliced
2 cups carrots, sliced
4 medium potatoes, cubed
3 Tbsp. minute tapioca
1 Tbsp. sugar
1 Tbsp. salt
1/2 tsp. pepper
10 3/4-oz. can tomato soup
1/3 cup water

1. Layer meat, onion,
celery, carrots, and potatoes
in slow cooker. Sprinkle
with seasonings and tapioca.
Add soup and water.

2. Cover. Cook on Low 7–9
hours.

Busy Day Beef Stew

Dale Peterson/Rapid City, SC

MAKES 6–8 SERVINGS

2 lbs. stewing meat, cubed
2 medium onions, diced
1 cup chopped celery
2 cups sliced carrots
4 medium potatoes, diced
2 1/2 Tbsp. quick-cooking
tapioca
1 Tbsp. sugar
1 tsp. salt
1/2 tsp. pepper
10 3/4-oz. can tomato soup
1 1/2 soup cans water

1. Layer meat and vegetables
in slow cooker. Sprinkle with
tapioca, sugar, salt, and
pepper. Combine soup and
water and pour into slow
cooker. Do not stir.

2. Cover. Cook on Low 6–8
hours.

Donna's Beef Stew

Donna Treloar/Gaston, IN

MAKES 6 SERVINGS

2 lbs. beef, cubed
4–5 potatoes, cubed
4–5 carrots, sliced
3 ribs celery, sliced
2 onions, chopped
1 Tbsp. sugar
2 tsp. salt
1/4–1/2 tsp. pepper
2 Tbsp. instant tapioca
3 cups V-8, or tomato, juice

1. Place meat and vegetables
in slow cooker. Sprinkle
with sugar, salt, pepper, and
tapioca. Toss lightly. Pour
juice over the top.

2. Cover. Cook on Low
8–10 hours.

variation
● Add 10-oz. pkg. frozen
succotash or green beans.

Beef, Tomatoes, & Noodles

Janice Martins/Fairbank, IA

MAKES 8 SERVINGS

1 1/2 lbs. stewing beef, cubed
1/4 cup flour
2 cups stewed tomatoes (if you like tomato chunks), or 2 cups crushed tomatoes (if you prefer a smoother gravy)
1 tsp. salt
1/4–1/2 tsp. pepper
1 medium onion, chopped
water
12-oz. bag noodles

1. Combine meat and flour until cubes are coated. Place in slow cooker.

2. Add tomatoes, salt, pepper, and onion. Add water to cover.

3. Cover. Simmer on Low 6–8 hours.

4. Serve over cooked noodles.

Big Beef Stew

Margaret H. Moffitt
Bartlett, TN

MAKES 6–8 SERVINGS

3-lb. beef roast, cubed
1 large onion, sliced
1 tsp. dried parsley flakes
1 green pepper, sliced
3 ribs celery, sliced
4 carrots, sliced
28-oz. can tomatoes with juice, undrained
1 garlic clove, minced
2 cups water

1. Combine all ingredients.

2. Cover. Cook on High 1 hour. Reduce heat to Low and cook 8 hours.

3. Serve on rice or noodles.

note
● This is a low-salt recipe. For more zest, add 2 tsp. salt and 3/4 tsp. black pepper.

Steak San Morco

Susan Tjon/Austin, TX

MAKES 4–6 SERVINGS

2 lbs. stewing meat, cubed
1 envelope dry onion soup mix
29-oz. can peeled, or crushed, tomatoes
1 tsp. dried oregano
garlic powder to taste
2 Tbsp. oil
2 Tbsp. wine vinegar

1. Layer meat evenly in bottom of slow cooker.

2. Combine soup mix, tomatoes, spices, oil, and vinegar in bowl. Blend with spoon. Pour over meat.

3. Cover. Cook on High 6 hours, or Low 8–10 hours.

Pat's Meat Stew

Pat Bishop/Bedminster, PA

MAKES 4–5 SERVINGS

1–2 lbs. beef roast, cubed
2 tsp. salt
1/4 tsp. pepper
2 cups water
2 carrots, sliced
2 small onions, sliced
4–6 small potatoes, cut up in chunks, if desired
1/4 cup quick-cooking tapioca
1 bay leaf
10-oz. pkg. frozen peas, or mixed vegetables

1. Brown beef in saucepan. Place in slow cooker.

2. Sprinkle with salt and pepper. Add remaining ingredients except frozen vegetables. Mix well.

3. Cover. Cook on Low 8–10 hours, or on High 4–5 hours. Add vegetables during last 1–2 hours of cooking.

Ernestine's Beef Stew

Ernestine Schrepfer
Trenton, MO

MAKES 5–6 SERVINGS

1 1/2 lbs. stewing meat, cubed
2 1/4 cups tomato juice
10 1/2-oz. can consommé
1 cup chopped celery
2 cups sliced carrots
4 Tbsp. quick-cooking tapioca
1 medium onion, chopped
3/4 tsp. salt
1/4 tsp. pepper

1. Combine all ingredients in slow cooker.

2. Cover. Cook on Low 7–8 hours. (Do not peek.)

Beef Stew with Vegetables

Joyce B. Suiter/Garysburg, NC

MAKES 8 SERVINGS

3 lbs. stewing beef, cubed
1 cup water
1 cup red wine
1.2-oz. envelope beef-mushroom soup mix
2 cups diced potatoes
1 cup thinly sliced carrots
10-oz. pkg. frozen peas and onions

1. Layer all ingredients in order in slow cooker.

2. Cover. Cook on Low 8–10 hours.

note
● You may increase all vegetable quantities with good results!

Becky's Beef Stew

Becky Harder/Monument, CO

MAKES 6–8 SERVINGS

1 1/2 lbs. beef stewing meat, cubed
2 10-oz. pkgs. frozen vegetables—carrots, corn, peas
4 large potatoes, cubed
1 bay leaf
1 onion, chopped
15-oz. can stewing tomatoes of your choice—Italian, Mexican, or regular
8-oz. can tomato sauce
2 Tbsp. Worcestershire sauce
1 tsp. salt
1/4 tsp. pepper

1. Put meat on bottom of slow cooker. Layer frozen vegetables and potatoes over meat.

2. Mix remaining ingredients together in large bowl and pour over other ingredients.

3. Cover. Cook on Low 6–8 hours.

Irish Beef Stew

Teena Wagner/Waterloo, ON

MAKES 4–6 SERVINGS

2 lbs. stewing beef, cubed
1 envelope dry onion soup mix
2 10 3/4-oz. cans tomato soup
1 soup can water
1 tsp. salt
1/2 tsp. pepper
2 cups diced carrots
2 cups diced potatoes
1-lb. package frozen peas
1/4 cup water

1. Place beef, onion soup, tomato soup, soup can of water, salt, pepper, carrots, and potatoes in slow cooker.

2. Cover. Cook on Low 8 hours.

3. Add peas and 1/4 cup water. Cover. Cook on Low 1 more hour.

Full-Flavored Beef Stew

Stacy Petersheim
Mechanicsburg, PA

MAKES 6 SERVINGS

2-lb. beef roast, cubed
2 cups sliced carrots
2 cups diced potatoes
1 medium onion, sliced
1 1/2 cups peas
2 tsp. quick-cooking tapioca
1 Tbsp. salt
1/2 tsp. pepper
8-oz. can tomato sauce
1 cup water
1 Tbsp. brown sugar

1. Combine beef and vegetables in slow cooker. Sprinkle with tapioca, salt, and pepper.

2. Combine tomato sauce and water. Pour over ingredients in slow cooker. Sprinkle with brown sugar.

3. Cover. Cook on Low 8 hours.

variation
● Add peas one hour before cooking time ends to keep their color and flavor.

Hearty Beef Stew

Lovina Baer/Conrath, WI

MAKES 4–6 SERVINGS

2-lb. round steak
4 large potatoes, cubed
2 large carrots, sliced
2 ribs celery, sliced
1 medium onion, chopped
1 qt. tomato juice
1 Tbsp. Worcestershire sauce
2 tsp. salt
1/2 tsp. pepper
1/4 cup sugar
1 Tbsp. Clear Jel

1. Combine meat, potatoes, carrots, celery, and onion in slow cooker.

2. Combine tomato juice, Worcestershire sauce, salt, and pepper. Pour into slow cooker.

3. Mix together sugar and clear jel. Add to remaining ingredients, stirring well.

4. Cover. Cook on High 6–7 hours.

variation
● Instead of Clear Jel, use 1/4 cup instant tapioca.

Virginia's Beef Stew

Virginia Bender/Dover, DE

MAKES 6 SERVINGS

3 lbs. boneless beef
1 envelope dry onion soup
28-oz. can diced tomatoes, undrained
1 Tbsp. minute tapioca
4–5 potatoes, cubed
1 onion, chopped
6 carrots, sliced
1 tsp. sugar
1 Tbsp. salt
1/2 tsp. pepper

1. Combine all ingredients in slow cooker.

2. Cover. Bake on High 5 hours.

variation
● Add 2 cups frozen peas during last 10 minutes of cooking.

Beef Stew with Mushrooms

Dorothy M. Pittman
Pickens, SC

MAKES 6 SERVINGS

2 lbs. stewing beef, cubed
10 3/4-oz. can cream of mushroom soup
4-oz. can mushrooms
1 envelope dry onion soup mix
1/2 tsp. salt
1/4 tsp. pepper
half a soup can of water

1. Sprinkle bottom of greased slow cooker with one-fourth of dry soup mix. Layer in meat, mushroom soup, canned mushrooms, and remaining dry onion soup mix. Pour water over.

2. Cover. Cook on Low 8 hours, or High 4 hours.

3. Serve over potatoes, rice, or noodles.

Paul's Beef Bourguignon

Janice Muller/Derwood, MD

 **MAKES 4 SERVINGS**

3-lb. chuck roast, cubed
2 Tbsp. oil
2 10 3/4-oz. cans golden cream of mushroom soup
1 envelope dry onion soup mix
1 cup cooking sherry

1. Brown meat in oil in skillet. Drain. Place in slow cooker. Add remaining ingredients and cover.

2. Refrigerate 6–8 hours, or up to 14 hours, to marinate.

3. Remove from refrigerator, cover, and cook on Low 8–10 hours.

4. Serve over cooked egg noodles or rice.

Beef Burgundy

Jacqueline Stefl
East Bethany, NY

 **MAKES 6 SERVINGS**

5 medium onions, thinly sliced
2 lbs. stewing meat, cubed
1 1/2 Tbsp. flour
1/2 lb. fresh mushrooms, sliced
1 tsp. salt
1/4 tsp. dried marjoram
1/4 tsp. dried thyme
1/8 tsp. pepper
3/4 cup beef broth
1 1/2 cups burgundy wine

1. Place onions in slow cooker.

2. Dredge meat in flour. Put in slow cooker.

3. Add mushrooms, salt, marjoram, thyme, and pepper.

4. Pour in broth and wine.

5. Cover. Cook 8–10 hours on Low.

6. Serve over cooked noodles.

Tomato-y Beef Stew

Janie Steele/Moore, OK

 **MAKES 6–8 SERVINGS**

5 lbs. stewing meat, cubed
2 onions, chopped
14 1/2-oz. can chopped tomatoes
10 3/4-oz. can tomato soup
5–6 carrots, sliced
5–6 potatoes, peeled and cubed
1 cup sliced celery
1 bell pepper, sliced
2 tsp. salt
1/2 tsp. pepper
2 cloves minced garlic

1. Combine all ingredients in slow cooker.

2. Cover. Cook on Low 8 hours.

3. Serve with warm bread or cornbread.

note
● This recipe is very adaptable. You can reduce the amount of meat and increase the vegetables as you wish.

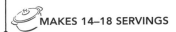

After-Work Stew

Vera M. Kuhns
Harrisonburg, VA

**MAKES 5 SERVINGS**

3 medium-sized potatoes, pared and cubed
4 medium-sized carrots, quartered
2 celery ribs, sliced
2 medium-sized onions, sliced
1 1/2 lbs. beef, cut into 1 1/2-inch cubes, browned
2 tsp. salt
1/2 tsp. dried basil
1/2 tsp. pepper
10 3/4-oz. can tomato soup
half a soup can water

1. Layer potatoes, carrots, celery, and onions in slow cooker.

2. Mix beef with salt, basil, and pepper in bowl and place on top of vegetables.

3. Combine soup and water. Pour into slow cooker.

4. Cover. Bake on Low 8–9 hours, or until vegetables and meat are tender.

Best Ever Beef Stew

Barbara Walker/Sturgis, SD

MAKES 6 SERVINGS

2 cups water
1 pkg. beef stew mix
2 lbs. stewing meat, cubed
3 15-oz. cans whole new potatoes, or 3 lbs. fresh new potatoes
1 cup sliced celery
10–12 small white onions, peeled
1–1 1/2 cups sliced carrots
8 ozs. fresh mushrooms

1. Combine water and beef stew mix in slow cooker.

2. Layer meat in slow cooker.

3. Add remaining ingredients.

4. Cover. Cook on High 6–7 hours.

Easy Beef Stew

Janie Steele/Moore, OK

MAKES 14–18 SERVINGS

2–3 lbs. beef, cubed
16-oz. pkg. frozen green beans or mixed vegetables
16-oz. pkg. frozen corn
16-oz. pkg. frozen peas
2 lbs. carrots, chopped
1 large onion, chopped
4 medium potatoes, peeled and chopped
10 3/4-oz. can tomato soup
10 3/4-oz. can celery soup
10 3/4-oz. can mushroom soup
bell pepper chopped, optional

1. Combine all ingredients in 2 4-qt. slow cookers (this is a very large recipe).

2. Cover. Cook on Low 10–11 hours.

Hungarian Goulash

Kim Stoltzfus
New Holland, PA

MAKES 8 SERVINGS

2-lb. round steak, cubed
1/2 tsp. onion powder
1/2 tsp. garlic powder
2 Tbsp. flour
1/2 tsp. salt
1/2 tsp. pepper
1 1/2 tsp. paprika
10 3/4-oz. can tomato soup
1/2 soup can water
1 cup sour cream

1. Mix meat, onion powder, garlic powder, and flour together in slow cooker until meat is well coated.

2. Add remaining ingredients, except sour cream. Stir well.

3. Cover. Cook on Low 8–10 hours, or High 4–5 hours.

4. Add sour cream 30 minutes before serving.

5. Serve over hot noodles.

Hungarian Beef Stew

Esther Becker/Gordonville, PA

MAKES 6 SERVINGS

2 lbs. beef cubes
1 onion, chopped
2 medium potatoes, peeled and cubed
2 carrots, sliced
10-oz. pkg. frozen lima beans
2 tsp. parsley
1/2 cup beef broth
2 tsp. paprika
1 tsp. salt
16-oz. can diced tomatoes

1. Combine beef, onion, potatoes, carrots, lima beans, and parsley in slow cooker.

2. Combine remaining ingredients and pour into slow cooker.

3. Cover. Cook on Low 10–12 hours.

4. Serve with seven layer salad and homemade rolls.

Pepper Beef Goulash

Anna Stoltzfus
Honey Brook, PA

MAKES 4–6 SERVINGS

1/2 cup water
6-oz. can tomato paste
2 Tbsp. vinegar
1 pkg. dry sloppy Joe seasoning
2–2 1/4 lbs. beef stewing meat, cubed
1 rib celery, sliced
1 medium green pepper, cut into 1/2-inch pieces

1. Combine water, tomato paste, vinegar, and seasoning mix in slow cooker.

2. Stir in beef, celery, and green peppers.

3. Cover. Cook on High 4–5 hours.

4. Serve over noodles.

Round Steak Casserole

Gladys High/Ephrata, PA

 **MAKES 6 SERVINGS**

2 lbs. round steak, cut 1/2 inch thick

1 tsp. salt

1/4 tsp. pepper

1 onion, thinly sliced

3–4 potatoes, pared and quartered

16-oz. can French-style green beans, drained

1 clove garlic, minced

10 3/4-oz. can tomato soup

14 1/2-oz. can tomatoes

1. Season roast with salt and pepper. Cut into serving pieces and place in slow cooker.

2. Add onion, potatoes, green beans, and garlic. Top with soup and tomatoes.

3. Cover and cook on Low 8–10 hours, or High 4–5 hours. Remove cover during last half hour if too much liquid has collected.

Pepper Steak Oriental

Donna Lantgen/Rapid City, SD

MAKES 6 SERVINGS

1 lb. round steak, sliced thin

3 Tbsp. soy sauce

1/2 tsp. ground ginger

1 garlic clove, minced

1 green pepper, thinly sliced

4-oz. can mushrooms, drained, or 1 cup fresh mushrooms

1 onion, thinly sliced

1/2 tsp. crushed red pepper

1. Combine all ingredients in slow cooker.

2. Cover. Cook on Low 6–8 hours.

3. Serve as steak sandwiches topped with provolone cheese, or over rice.

note

● Round steak is easier to slice into thin strips if it is partially frozen when cut.

Gone All-Day Casserole

Beatrice Orgish
Richardson, TX

MAKES 12 SERVINGS

1 cup uncooked wild rice, rinsed and drained

1 cup chopped celery

1 cup chopped carrots

2 4-oz. cans mushrooms, stems and pieces, drained

1 large onion, chopped

1 clove garlic, minced

1/2 cup slivered almonds

3 beef bouillon cubes

2 1/2 tsp. seasoned salt

2-lb. boneless round steak, cut into 1-inch cubes

3 cups water

1. Please ingredients in order listed in slow cooker.

2. Cover. Cook on Low 6–8 hours or until rice is tender. Stir before serving.

variations

● Brown beef in saucepan in 2 Tbsp. oil before putting in slow cooker for deeper flavor.

● Add a bay leaf and 4–6 whole peppercorns to mixture before cooking. Remove before serving.

● Substitute chicken legs and thighs (skin removed) for beef.

"Smothered" Steak

Susan Yoder Graber/Eureka, IL

 **MAKES 6 SERVINGS**

1 1/2-lb. chuck, or round, steak, cut into strips
1/3 cup flour
1/2 tsp. salt
1/4 tsp. pepper
1 large onion, sliced
1–2 green peppers, sliced
14 1/2-oz. can stewed tomatoes
4-oz. can mushrooms, drained
2 Tbsp. soy sauce
10-oz. pkg. frozen French-style green beans

1. Layer steak in bottom of slow cooker. Sprinkle with flour, salt, and pepper. Stir well to coat steak.

2. Add remaining ingredients. Mix together gently.

3. Cover. Cook on Low 8 hours.

4. Serve over rice.

Variations:
● Use 8-oz. can tomato sauce instead of stewed tomatoes.
● Substitute 1 Tbsp. Worcestershire sauce in place of soy sauce.

Mary E. Martin/Goshen, IN

Round Steak Casserole

Cheryl Bartel/Hillsboro, KS
Barbara Walker/Sturgis, SD

 MAKES 4–6 SERVINGS

2-lb. 1/2-inch-thick round steak
1/2 tsp. garlic salt
1 tsp. salt
1/4–1/2 tsp. pepper
1 onion, thinly sliced
3–4 potatoes, quartered
3–4 carrots, sliced
14 1/2-oz. can French-style green beans, drained, or 1 lb. frozen green beans
10 3/4-oz. can tomato soup
14 1/2-oz. can stewed tomatoes

1. Cut meat into serving-size pieces, place in slow cooker, stir in seasonings, and mix well.

2. Add potatoes, carrots, and green beans. Top with soup and tomatoes.

3. Cover. Cook on High 1 hour. Reduce heat to Low and cook 8 hours, or until done. Remove cover during last half hour if there is too much liquid.

Veal and Peppers

Irma H. Schoen/Windsor, CT

 **MAKES 4 SERVINGS**

1 1/2 lbs. boneless veal, cubed
3 green peppers, quartered
2 onions, thinly sliced
1/2 lb. fresh mushrooms, sliced
1 tsp. salt
1/2 tsp. dried basil
2 cloves garlic, minced
28-oz. can tomatoes

1. Combine all ingredients in slow cooker.

2. Cover. Cook on Low 7 hours, or on High 4 hours.

3. Serve over rice or noodles.

variation
● Use boneless, skinless chicken breast, cut into chunks, instead of veal.

Beef and Beans

Robin Schrock
Millersburg, OH

MAKES 8 SERVINGS

1 Tbsp. prepared mustard
1 Tbsp. chili powder
1/2 tsp. salt
1/4 tsp. pepper
1 1/2-lb. boneless round
   steak, cut into thin slices
2 14 1/2-oz. cans diced
   tomatoes, undrained
1 medium onion, chopped
1 beef bouillon cube,
   crushed
16-oz. can kidney beans,
   rinsed and drained

1. Combine mustard, chili powder, salt, and pepper. Add beef slices and toss to coat. Place meat in slow cooker.

2. Add tomatoes, onion, and bouillon.

3. Cover. Cook on Low 6–8 hours.

4. Stir in beans. Cook 30 minutes longer.

5. Serve over rice.

Round Steak

Janet V. Yocum
Elizabethtown, PA

MAKES 4 SERVINGS

2-lb. round steak, cut into
   serving-size chunks
1 onion, chopped
4 ribs celery, chopped
4 carrots, chopped
4 potatoes, cut into bite-
   size pieces
2 tsp. salt
1 tsp. seasoning salt
1/2 tsp. pepper
10 3/4-oz. can cream of
   celery, or cream of
   mushroom, soup
water

1. Put steak in bottom of slow cooker.

2. Stir vegetables, seasonings, and soup together in large bowl. Pour over meat.

3. Add water if needed to cover meat and vegetables.

4. Cover. Cook on Low 8 hours.

Saucy Round Steak Supper

Shirley Sears/Tiskilwa, IL

MAKES 6–8 SERVINGS

2 lbs. round steak, sliced
   diagonally into 1/8-inch
   strips (reserve meat bone)
1/2 cup chopped onions
1/2 cup chopped celery
8-oz. can mushrooms, stems
   and pieces, drained
   (reserve liquid)
1/3 cup French dressing
2 1/2-oz. pkg. sour cream
   sauce mix
1/3 cup water
1 tsp. Worcestershire sauce

1. Place steak and bone in slow cooker. Add onions, celery, and mushrooms.

2. Combine dressing, sour cream sauce mix, water, Worcestershire sauce, and mushroom liquid. Pour over mixture in slow cooker.

3. Cover. Cook on Low 8–9 hours.

4. Serve over noodles.

variation
● Instead of using the sour cream sauce mix, remove meat from cooker at end of cooking time and keep warm. Stir 1 cup sour cream into gravy, cover, and cook on High 10 minutes. Serve over steak.

Round Steak

Dorothy Hess
Willow Street, PA

Betty A. Holt/St. Charles, MO

Betty Moore/Plano, IL

Michelle Strite
Harrisonburg, VA

Barbara Tenney/Delta, PA

Sharon Timpe/Mequon, WI

 **MAKES 4–5 SERVINGS**

2-lb. boneless round steak
oil
1 envelope dry onion soup
    mix
10 3/4-oz. can cream of
    mushroom soup
1/2 cup water

1. Cut steak into serving-size pieces. Brown in oil in saucepan. Place in slow cooker. Sprinkle with soup mix.

2. Combine soup and water. Pour over meat.

3. Cover. Cook on Low 7–8 hours.

Beef Mushroom Casserole

Susan Stephani Smith
Monument, CO

 **MAKES 12 SERVINGS**

4 lbs. lean beef sirloin, cut
    into 1-inch cubes
2 10 3/4-oz. cans cream of
    mushroom soup
2 pkgs. dry onion soup mix
1/4–1 tsp. pepper,
    according to your taste
    preference
1/2 tsp. salt
1–2 cups red Burgundy
    wine, optional
1 1/2 lbs. fresh mushrooms,
    quartered
1/4 cup sour cream,
    optional

1. Combine all ingredients except wine, mushrooms, and sour cream in slow cooker.

2. Cover. Cook on Low 4–5 hours, stirring occasionally.

3. Add mushrooms and wine. Cook 30 minutes longer.

4. Ten minutes before end of cooking time, stir in sour cream, if you wish.

5. Serve over egg noodles.

Crockery Cooking

Betty Sue Good/Broadway, VA

 **MAKES 8 SERVINGS**

2 lbs. beef cubes
oil
1 large onion, chopped
2 potatoes, cubed
2 carrots, sliced
1 pt. frozen lima beans,
    thawed
1 qt. stewed tomatoes
1–1 1/2 tsp. salt, according
    to your taste preference
1/4–1/2 tsp. pepper,
    according to your taste
    preference

1. Brown beef on all sides in oil in skillet. Place in slow cooker.

2. Layer onions, potatoes, carrots, and lima beans over beef.

3. Mix tomatoes and seasonings together in bowl. Pour over meat and vegetables.

4. Cover. Cook on Low 8–10 hours.

5. Serve over rice with warm rolls, pickles, pecan pie, and vanilla ice cream.

Yum-Yums

Evelyn L. Ward/Greeley, CO

MAKES 12 SERVINGS

3 lbs. ground beef
2 onions, chopped
10 3/4-oz. can cream of
   chicken soup
1 1/2 cups tomato juice
1 tsp. prepared mustard
1 tsp. Worcestershire sauce
1 tsp. salt
1/4 tsp. pepper

1. Brown beef and onions in skillet. Drain.

2. Add remaining ingredients. Pour into slow cooker.

3. Cover. Cook on Low 4–6 hours.

4. Serve on hamburger buns.

This is a great recipe for serving a crowd. A club I am a part of serves it when we do fund raisers. Our menu is Yum-Yums, marinated bean salad, and strawberry short cake. We make the food in our homes and carry it to the meeting site.

— • —

Reuben Sandwiches

Maryann Markano
Wilmington, DE

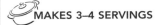

MAKES 3–4 SERVINGS

1-lb. can sauerkraut
1 lb. sliced corned beef
   brisket
1/4-lb. Swiss cheese, sliced
sliced rye bread
sandwich spread, or
   Thousand Island Dressing

1. Drain sauerkraut in sieve, then on paper towels until very day. Place in bottom of slow cooker.

2. Arrange layer of corned beef slices over sauerkraut. Top with cheese slices.

3. Cover. Cook on Low 3–4 hours.

4. Toast bread. Spread generously with sandwich spread or dressing. Spoon ingredients from slow cooker onto toasted bread, maintaining layers of sauerkraut, meat, and cheese.

New Mexico Cheeseburgers

Colleen Konetzni
Rio Rancho, NM

MAKES 8 SERVINGS

1 lb. ground beef, browned
6 potatoes, peeled and
   sliced
1/2 cup chopped green
   chilies
1 onion, chopped
10 3/4-oz. can cream of
   mushroom soup
2 cups cubed Velveeta
   cheese

1. Layer beef, potatoes, green chilies, and onions in slow cooker.

2. Spread soup over top.

3. Top with cheese.

4. Cover. Cook on High 1 hour. Reduce heat to Low and cook 6–8 hours.

Piquant French Dip

Marcella Stalter
Flanagan, IL

 **MAKES 8 SERVINGS**

3-lb. chuck roast
2 cups water
1/2 cup soy sauce
1 tsp. dried rosemary
1 tsp. dried thyme
1 tsp. garlic powder
1 bay leaf
3–4 whole peppercorns
8 French rolls

1. Place roast in slow cooker. Add water, soy sauce, and seasonings.

2. Cover. Cook on High 5–6 hours, or until beef is tender.

3. Remove beef from broth. Shred with fork. Keep warm.

4. Strain broth. Skim fat. Pour broth into small cups for dipping. Serve beef on rolls.

note
● If you have leftover broth, freeze it to use later for gravy or as a soup base.

Carol's Italian Beef

Carol Findling/Princeton, IL

 **MAKES 6–8 SERVINGS**

3–4-lb. lean rump roast
2 tsp. salt, divided
4 garlic cloves
2 tsp. Romano, or Parmesan, cheese, divided
12-oz. can beef broth
1 tsp. dried oregano

1. Place roast in slow cooker. Cut 4 slits in top of roast. Fill each slit with 1/2 tsp. salt, 1 garlic clove, and 1/2 tsp. cheese.

2. Pour broth over meat. Sprinkle with oregano.

3. Cover. Cook on Low 10–12 hours, or High 4–6 hours.

4. Remove meat and slice or shred. Serve on buns with meat juices on the side.

Lauren's Italian Beef

Lauren Eberhard/Seneca, IL

 **MAKES 16 SERVINGS**

4–5-lb. boneless roast, cubed
1 medium onion, chopped
1–2 garlic cloves, minced
2–3 pkgs. dry Good Seasons Italian dressing mix
1/2 cup water
16 steak rolls
mozzarella cheese, shredded

1. Combine first five ingredients in slow cooker.

2. Cover. Cook on Low 10 hours. Stir occasionally.

3. Slice meat into thin slices. Pile on rolls, top with cheese, and serve immediately.

Barbecue Beef

Elizabeth Yoder
Millersburg, OH

**MAKES 12 SERVINGS**

3-lb. boneless chuck roast
1 cup barbecue sauce
1/2 cup apricot preserves
1/3 cup chopped green
  peppers
1 small onion, chopped
1 Tbsp. Dijon mustard
2 tsp. brown sugar
12 sandwich rolls

1. Cut roast into quarters.
Place in greased slow cooker.

2. Combine barbecue sauce,
preserves, green peppers,
onion, mustard, and brown
sugar. Pour over roast.

3. Cover. Cook on Low 6–8
hours. Remove roast and
slice thinly. Return to slow
cooker. Stir gently.

4. Cover. Cook 20–30
minutes.

5. Serve beef and sauce
on rolls.

Barbecue Beef Sandwiches

Eleanor Larson/Glen Lyon, PA

**MAKES 18–20
SANDWICHES**

3 1/2–4-lb. beef round
  steak, cubed
1 cup finely chopped onions
1/2 cup firmly packed
  brown sugar
1 Tbsp. chili powder
1/2 cup ketchup
1/3 cup cider vinegar
12-oz. can beer
6-oz. can tomato paste
buns

1. Combine all ingredients
except buns in slow cooker.

2. Cover. Cook on Low
10–12 hours.

3. Remove beef from sauce
with slotted spoon. Place
in large bowl. Shred with
2 forks.

4. Add 2 cups sauce from
slow cooker to shredded
beef. Mix well.

5. Pile into buns and serve
immediately.

6. Reserve any remaining
sauce for serving over pasta,
rice, or potatoes.

Potluck Beef Barbecue Sandwiches

Carol Sommers
Millersburg, OH

MAKES 16 SERVINGS

4-lb. beef chuck roast
1 cup brewed coffee or
  water
1 Tbsp. cider or red-wine
  vinegar
1 tsp. salt
1/2 tsp. pepper
14-oz. bottle ketchup
15-oz. can tomato sauce
1 cup sweet pickle relish
2 Tbsp. Worcestershire
  sauce
1/4 cup brown sugar

1. Place roast, coffee,
vinegar, salt, and pepper in
slow cooker.

2. Cover. Cook on High 6–8
hours, or until meat is very
tender.

3. Pour off cooking liquid.
Shred meat with two forks.

4. Add remaining
ingredients. Stir well.

5. Cover. Cook on High
30–45 minutes. Reduce heat
to Low for serving.

Hot Beef Sandwiches

Evelyn L. Ward/Greeley, CO

 MAKES 10 SERVINGS

3 lbs. beef chuck roast
1 large onion, chopped
1/4 cup vinegar
1 clove garlic, minced
1–1 1/2 tsp. salt
1/4–1/2 tsp. pepper

1. Place meat in slow cooker. Top with onions.

2. Combine vinegar, garlic, salt, and pepper. Pour over meat.

3. Cover. Cook on Low 8–10 hours.

4. Drain broth but save for dipping.

5. Shred meat.

6. Serve on hamburger buns with broth on side.

> I volunteer with Habitat for Humanity. I don't do construction, but I provide lunch sometimes for work crews. This sandwich is a favorite. I make the most colorful tossed salad that I can and serve fresh fruit that is in season and pie.

— • —

Herby Beef Sandwiches

Jean A. Shaner/York, PA

 MAKES 10–12 SERVINGS

3–4-lb. boneless beef chuck roast
3 Tbsp. fresh basil, or 1 Tbsp. dried basil
3 Tbsp. fresh oregano, or 1 Tbsp. dried oregano
1 1/2 cups water
1 pkg. dry onion soup mix
10–12 Italian rolls

1. Place roast in slow cooker.

2. Combine basil, oregano, and water. Pour over roast.

3. Sprinkle with onion soup mix.

4. Cover. Cook on Low 7–8 hours. Shred meat with fork.

5. Serve on Italian rolls.

Shredded Beef for Tacos

Dawn Day/Westminster, CA

 MAKES 6–8 SERVINGS

2–3-lb. round roast, cut into large chunks
1 large onion, chopped
3 Tbsp. oil
2 serrano chilies, chopped
3 garlic cloves, minced
1 tsp. salt
1 cup water

1. Brown meat and onion in oil. Transfer to slow cooker.

2. Add chilies, garlic, salt, and water.

3. Cover. Cook on High 6–8 hours.

4. Pull meat apart with two forks until shredded.

5. Serve with fresh tortillas, lettuce, tomatoes, cheese, and guacamole.

Ground Meat

Bean Tator Tot Casserole

Marjora Miller/Archbold, OH

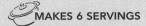 **MAKES 6 SERVINGS**

1 lb. ground beef
1/2 tsp. salt
1/4 tsp. pepper
1 onion, chopped
1-lb. bag frozen string beans
10 3/4-oz. can cream of mushroom soup
1 cup shredded cheese
21-oz. bag. frozen tator tots

1. Crumble raw ground beef in bottom of slow cooker. Sprinkle with salt and pepper.

2. Layer remaining ingredients on beef in order listed.

3. Cover. Cook on High 1 hour. Reduce heat to Low and cook 3 hours.

variation

● In order to reduce the calorie content of this dish, use raw shredded potatoes instead of tater tots.

Nancy's Meatballs

Betty Richards/Rapid City, SD

MAKES 8 MAIN-DISH SERVINGS

3–4-lb. bag prepared meatballs
3 10 3/4-oz. cans cream of mushroom, or cream of celery, soup
4-oz. can button mushrooms
16-oz. jar Cheese Whiz
1 medium onion, diced

1. Combine all ingredients in slow cooker.

2. Cover. Cook on Low 6–8 hours.

3. Use as an appetizer, or as a main dish served over noodles or rice.

Meatloaf Sensation

Andrea O'Neil/Fairfield, CT

MAKES 8 SERVINGS

2 1/2 lbs. ground beef
half of an 8-oz. jar salsa
1 pkg. dry taco seasoning, divided
1 egg, slightly beaten
1 cup bread crumbs
12-oz. pkg. shredded Mexican-mix cheese
2 tsp. salt
1/2 tsp. pepper

1. Combine all ingredients, except half of taco seasoning. Mix well. Shape into loaf and place in slow cooker. Sprinkle with remaining taco seasoning.

2. Cover. Cook on Low 8–10 hours.

Beef Stroganoff

Julette Leaman
Harrisonburg, VA

 MAKES 6 SERVINGS

2 lbs. ground beef
2 medium onions, chopped
2 garlic cloves, minced
6 1/2-oz. can mushrooms
1 1/2 cups sour cream
4 Tbsp. flour
2 1/2 tsp. salt
1/4 tsp. pepper
1 cup bouillon
3 Tbsp. tomato paste

1. In skillet, brown beef, onions, garlic, and mushrooms until meat and onions are brown. Drain. Pour into slow cooker.

2. Combine sour cream and flour. Add to mixture in. slow cooker. Stir in remaining ingredients.

3. Cover. Cook on Low 6–8 hours.

4. Serve over hot buttered noodles.

A Hearty Western Casserole

Karen Ashworth
Duenweg, MO

 MAKES 5 SERVINGS

1 lb. ground beef, browned
16-oz. can whole corn, drained
16-oz. can red kidney beans, drained
10 3/4-oz. can condensed tomato soup
1 cup (4 oz.) Colby cheese
1/4 cup milk
1 tsp. minced dry onion flakes
1/2 tsp. chili powder

1. Combine beef, corn, beans, soup, cheese, milk, onion, and chili powder in slow cooker.

2. Cover. Cook on Low 1 hour.

variation

1 pkg. (of 10) refrigerator biscuits
2 Tbsp. margarine
1/4 cup yellow cornmeal

● Dip biscuits in margarine and then in cornmeal. Bake 20 minutes or until brown. Top beef mixture with biscuits before serving.

Cowboy Casserole

Lori Berezovsky/Salina, KS

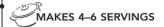 MAKES 4–6 SERVINGS

1 onion, chopped
1 1/2 lbs. ground beef, browned and drained
6 medium potatoes, sliced
1 clove garlic, minced
16-oz. can kidney beans
15-oz, can diced tomatoes mixed with 2 Tbsp. flour, or 10 3/4-oz. can tomato soup
1 tsp. salt
1/4 tsp. pepper

1. Layer onions, ground beef, potatoes, garlic, and beans in slow cooker.

2. Spread tomatoes or soup over all. Sprinkle with salt and pepper.

3. Cover. Cook on Low 5–6 hours, or until potatoes are tender.

Hamburger Potatoes

Juanita Marner
Shipshewana, IN

MAKES 3–4 SERVINGS

3 medium potatoes, sliced
3 carrots, sliced
1 small onion, sliced
2 Tbsp. dry rice
1 tsp. salt
1/2 tsp. pepper
1 lb. ground beef, browned
    and drained
1 1/2–2 cups tomato juice,
    as needed to keep dish
    from getting too dry

1. Combine all ingredients in slow cooker.

2. Cover. Cook on Low 6–8 hours.

Shipwreck

Betty Lahman/Elkton, VA

MAKES 8 SERVINGS

1 lb. ground beef, browned
4–5 potatoes, cut in
    French-fry-like strips
1–2 onions, chopped
16-oz. can light red kidney
    beans, drained
1/4-lb. Velveeta cheese,
    cubed
10 3/4-oz. can tomato soup
1 1/2 tsp. salt
1/4 tsp. pepper
butter

1. Layer in slow cooker in this order: ground beef, potatoes, onions, kidney beans, and cheese. Pour soup over top. Season with salt and pepper. Dot with butter.

2. Cover. Cook on Low 6–8 hours.

note
● This is particularly good served with Parmesan cheese sprinkled on top at the table.

Judy's Hamburger Stew

Judy Koczo/Plano, IL

MAKES 6–8 SERVINGS

3 large potatoes, sliced
3 carrots, sliced
1 lb. frozen peas
1 onion, diced
2 ribs celery, sliced thin
salt to taste
pepper to taste
1 1/2 lbs. ground beef,
    browned and drained
10 3/4-oz. can tomato soup
1 soup can water

1. Put vegetables in slow cooker in layers as listed. Season each layer with salt and pepper.

2. Layer beef on top of celery. Mix together soup and water. Pour over ground beef.

3. Cover. Cook on Low 6–8 hours, or High 2–4 hours, stirring occasionally.

variation
● Substitute 28-oz. can whole or diced tomatoes in place of tomato soup and water.

Ann Bender/Fort Defiance, VA

Taters n' Beef

Maryland Massey
Millington, MD

MAKES 6–8 SERVINGS

2 lbs. ground beef,
    browned
1 tsp. salt
1/2 tsp. pepper
1/4 cup chopped onions
1 cup canned tomato soup
6 potatoes, sliced
1 cup milk

1. Combined beef, salt,
pepper, onions, and soup.

2. Place a layer of potatoes
in bottom of slow cooker.
Cover with a portion of the
meat mixture. Repeat layers
until ingredients are used.

3. Cover. Cook on Low 4–6
hours. Add milk and cook
on High 15–20 minutes.

variations
● Use home-canned spaghetti
sauce instead of tomato soup.
● Add a layer of chopped raw
cabbage after each layer of
sliced potatoes to add to the
flavor, texture, and nutritional
value of the meal.

Working-Woman Favorite

Martha Ann Auker
Landisburg, PA

MAKES 6–8 SERVINGS

2 lbs. ground beef,
    browned and drained
4 ribs celery, chopped
1 small green pepper,
    chopped
1 onion, chopped
2 tsp. sugar
1/2 tsp. salt
dash of pepper
10 3/4-oz. can cream of
    mushroom soup

1. Combine all ingredients
in slow cooker.

2. Cover. Cook on Low
8–10 hours.

3. Serve over warm biscuits.

note
● Sprinkle individual servings
with shredded cheddar cheese.

Ground Beef Casserole

Lois J. Cassidy
Willow Street, PA

MAKES 6–8 SERVINGS

1 1/2 lbs. ground beef
6–8 potatoes, sliced
1 medium onion, sliced
14 1/2-oz. can cut green
    beans with juice
1/2 tsp. salt
dash of pepper
10 3/4-oz. can cream of
    mushroom soup

1. Crumble uncooked
ground beef in bottom of
slow cooker. Add potatoes,
onion, salt, and pepper. Pour
beans over all. Spread can of
mushroom soup over beans.

2. Cover. Cook on Low 6–8
hours.

variation
● Brown the beef before
putting in the slow cooker.
Mix half a soup can of water
with the mushroom soup
before placing over beans.

Chinese Hamburger

Esther J. Yoder/Hartville, OH

MAKES 8 SERVINGS

1 lb. ground beef, browned and drained
1 onion, diced
2 ribs celery, diced
10 3/4-oz. can chicken noodle soup
10 3/4-oz. can cream of mushroom soup
12-oz. can Chinese vegetables
salt to taste, about 1/4–1/2 tsp.
pepper to taste, about 1/4 tsp.
1 green pepper, diced
1 tsp. soy sauce

1. Combine all ingredients in slow cooker.

2. Cover. Cook on High 3–4 hours.

3. Serve over rice.

Tater Tot Casserole

Shirley Hinh/Wayland, IA

MAKES 6–8 SERVINGS

32-oz. bag frozen tater tots
1 lb. ground beef, browned
1/2 tsp. salt
1/4 tsp. pepper
2 14 1/2-oz. cans green beans, drained
10 3/4-oz. can cream of mushroom soup
1 Tbsp. dried onions
1/4 cup milk

1. Line slow cooker with frozen tater tots.

2. Combine remaining ingredients. Pour over potatoes.

3. Cover. Cook on High 3 hours.

note
● Sprinkle individual servings with your choice of grated cheese.

Family Favorite Casserole

Lizzie Weaver/Ephrata, PA

MAKES 6–8 SERVINGS

1 1/2 lbs. ground beef
1 onion, chopped
1 1/2 cups diced potatoes
1 1/2 cups sliced carrots
1 1/2 cups peas
1 1/2 cups macaroni, cooked
10 3/4-oz. can cream of celery soup
1/2 lb. cheddar cheese, grated
2 cups milk
1 1/2 tsp. salt

1. Fry beef and onion in saucepan until brown. Drain.

2. Cook vegetables just until soft.

3. Combine all ingredients in slow cooker.

4. Cover. Cook on High 2 hours, or Low 4–5 hours.

variation
● Skip pre-cooking the vegetables; add them raw to the slow cooker. Increase cooking time to 4 hours on High, or 8–10 hours on Low. Add the cooked macaroni and the milk during the last 15 minutes if cooking on High, or during the last 30 minutes if cooking on Low.

Tastes-Like-Turkey

Lizzie Weaver/Ephrata, PA

MAKES 6 SERVINGS

2 lbs. hamburger, browned
1 tsp. salt
1/2 tsp. pepper
2 10 3/4-oz. cans cream of chicken soup
10 3/4-oz. can cream of celery soup
4 scant cups milk
1 large pkg. bread stuffing, or large loaf of bread, torn in pieces

1. Combine all ingredients in large buttered slow cooker.

2. Cover. Cook on High 3 hours, or Low 6–8 hours.

Cooker Casserole

Carol Eberly
Harrisonburg, VA

MAKES 6–8 SERVINGS

2 cups grated carrots
1 medium-sized onion, sliced
4 cups grated raw potatoes
1 lb. ground beef, browned
1 tsp. salt
1/4 tsp. pepper
1 Tbsp. Worcestershire sauce
10 3/4-oz. can cream of mushroom soup

1. Layer carrots, onions, potatoes, and ground beef in slow cooker.

2. Combine salt, pepper, Worcestershire sauce, and soup in bowl. Pour over ground beef.

3. Cover. Cook on Low 8–10 hours.

Hamburger Potato Casserole

Sue Pennington
Bridgewater, VA

MAKES 6–10 SERVINGS

1 lb. ground beef
1 Tbsp. oil
6–8 potatoes, peeled and sliced
4–6 carrots, sliced
2 medium onions, sliced
1 cup peas
1 cup grated cheddar cheese
1 tsp. salt
1/4 tsp. pepper
10-oz. can cream of chicken soup

1. Brown ground beef in oil in skillet.

2. Layer half of beef, potatoes, carrots, onions, peas and cheese in cooker. Sprinkle with salt and pepper. Repeat layers.

3. Pour cream of chicken soup over top.

4. Cover. Cook on Low 8–10 hours.

My husband came up with this recipe. Our family loves it and often requests it when I ask them what they want to eat.

— • —

Hamburger Casserole

Kelly Evenson/Pittsboro, NC

MAKES 6–8 SERVINGS

2 large potatoes, sliced

2–3 medium carrots, sliced

1 cup frozen peas, thawed and drained

3 medium onions, sliced

2 celery ribs, sliced

garlic salt to taste

pepper to taste

salt to taste

1 lb. ground beef, browned and drained

10 3/4-oz. can tomato soup

1 soup can of water

1. Layer vegetables in order given into slow cooker.

2. Sprinkle each layer with garlic salt, pepper, and salt.

3. Place meat on top of celery.

4. Combine soup and water. Pour over all.

5. Cover. Cook on Low 8 hours.

6. Serve with applesauce.

Wholesome Hamburger Dinner

Reba Rhodes/Bridgewater, VA

MAKES 6–8 SERVINGS

1 lb. ground beef

1 tsp. salt

1/4 tsp. pepper

1 cup sliced carrots

1 cup coarsely chopped celery

1 medium onion, sliced

1 cup green beans

2 tsp. sugar

2–3 cups tomato juice

1/2 lb. grated cheese

1. Brown ground beef in skillet. Place in bottom of slow cooker.

2. Layer remaining ingredients, except cheese, over ground beef in order given.

3. Cover. Cook on High 3–4 hours or Low 5–6 hours.

4. Thirty minutes before the end of the cooking time, layer cheese on top. Cover and resume cooking.

5. Serve with cornbread.

Prompt

Mary Martins/Fairbank, IA

MAKES 6–8 SERVINGS

4–6 medium-sized potatoes, sliced

1/2–3/4 cup minute rice

1 onion, sliced

1 1/2 lbs. ground beef

1 diced green pepper, optional

1 qt. tomatoes with juice

salt to taste

pepper to taste

1. Layer ingredients in order given in greased slow cooker. Salt and pepper each layer to taste.

2. Cover. Cook on High for 1 1/2–2 hours.

variation
● You may substitute 1 qt. V-8 juice for the quart of tomatoes with juice.

Hamburger/ Green Bean Dish

Hazel L. Propst/Oxford, PA

MAKES 4–5 SERVINGS

1 lb. ground beef
1 onion, chopped
1 qt. string beans
10 3/4-oz. can tomato soup
3/4 tsp. salt
1/4 tsp. pepper
6–7 cups mashed potatoes
1 egg, beaten

1. Brown meat and onion in skillet. Stir in beans, soup, and seasonings. Pour into slow cooker.

2. Combine mashed potatoes with egg. Spread over meat mixture in slow cooker.

3. Cover. Cook on Low 5–6 hours, or until beans are tender.

Cheeseburger Casserole

Erma Kauffman
Cochranville, PA

MAKES 6 SERVINGS

1 lb. ground beef
1 small onion, chopped
1 tsp. salt
dash of pepper
1/2 cup bread crumbs
1 egg
tomato juice to moisten
4 1/2 cups mashed potatoes (leftover mashed potatoes work well)
9 slices American cheese

1. Combine beef, onions, salt, pepper, bread crumbs, egg, and tomato juice. Place one-third of mixture in slow cooker.

2. Spread with one-third of mashed potatoes and 3 slices cheese. Repeat 2 times.

3. Cover. Cook on Low 3 hours.

Meal-in-One

Melanie L. Thrower
McPherson, KS

MAKES 6–8 SERVINGS

2 lbs. ground beef
1 onion, diced
1 green bell pepper, diced
1 tsp. salt
1/4 tsp. pepper
1 large bag frozen hash brown potatoes
16-oz. container sour cream
24-oz. container cottage cheese
1 cup Monterey Jack cheese, shredded

1. Brown ground beef, onion, and green pepper in skillet. Drain. Season with salt and pepper.

2. In slow cooker, layer one-third of the potatoes, meat, sour cream, and cottage cheese. Repeat twice.

3. Cover. Cook on Low 4 hours, sprinkling Monterey Jack cheese over top during last hour.

4. Serve with red or green salsa.

Cedric's Casserole

Kathy Purcell/Dublin, OH

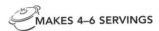

MAKES 4–6 SERVINGS

1 medium onion, chopped
3 Tbsp. butter, or margarine
1 lb. ground beef
1/2–3/4 tsp. salt
1/4 tsp. pepper
3 cups shredded cabbage
10 3/4-oz. can tomato soup

1. Saute onion in skillet in butter.

2. Add ground beef and brown. Season with salt and pepper.

3. Layer half of cabbage in slow cooker, followed by half of meat mixture. Repeat layers.

4. Pour soup over top.

5. Cover. Cook on Low 3–4 hours.

6. Serve with garlic bread and canned fruit.

I grew up with this recipe and remember my mother serving it often. It makes a wonderful potluck take-a-long.

— • —

Stuffed Cabbage

Barbara Nolan
Pleasant Valley, NY

MAKES 6 SERVINGS

4 cups water
12 large cabbage leaves
1 lb. ground beef, lamb, or turkey
1/2 cup cooked rice
1/2 tsp. salt
1/8 tsp. pepper
1/4 tsp. dried thyme
1/4 tsp. nutmeg
1/4 tsp. cinnamon
6-oz. can tomato paste
3/4 cup water

1. Boil 4 cups water in deep kettle. Remove kettle from heat. Soak cabbage leaves in hot water 5 minutes, or just until softened. Remove. Drain. Cool.

2. Combine ground beef, rice, salt, pepper, thyme, nutmeg, and cinnamon. Place 2 Tbsp. of mixture on each leaf. Roll up firmly. Stack stuffed leaves in slow cooker.

3. Combine tomato paste and 3/4 cup water until smooth. Pour over cabbage rolls.

4. Cover. Cook on Low 6–8 hours.

Stuffed Green Peppers

Lois Stoltzfus
Honey Brook, PA

MAKES 6 SERVINGS

6 large green peppers
1 lb. ground beef, browned
2 Tbsp. minced onion
1 tsp. salt
1/8 tsp. garlic powder
2 cups cooked rice
15-oz. can tomato sauce
3/4 cup shredded mozzarella cheese

1. Cut peppers in half and remove seeds.

2. Combine all ingredients except peppers and cheese.

3. Stuff peppers with ground beef mixture. Place in slow cooker.

4. Cover. Cook on Low 6–8 hours, or High 3–4 hours. Sprinkle with cheese during last 30 minutes.

Stuffed Bell Peppers

Mary Puterbaugh/Elwood, IN

MAKES 8 SERVINGS

8 large bell peppers
2 lbs. ground beef, lightly browned
1 large onion, chopped
1 cup cooked rice
2 eggs, beaten
1/2 cup milk
1/2 cup ketchup
dash hot pepper sauce
2 tsp. salt
1/2 tsp. pepper

1. Combine all ingredients except peppers. Gently pack mixture into peppers which have been capped and seeded. Place in greased slow cooker.

2. Cover. Cook on Low 9–11 hours, or High 5–6 hours.

Stuffed Peppers

Eleanor J. Ferreira
N. Chelmsford, MA

MAKES 6-8 SERVINGS

6–8 green peppers
1–2 lbs. ground beef
1 onion, chopped
1/4 tsp. salt
1/4 tsp. pepper
1 egg
1 slice white bread
28-oz. can whole, or stewed, tomatoes

1. Cut peppers in half and remove seeds.

2. Combine ground beef, onion, salt, pepper, and egg. Tear bread into small pieces. Add to ground beef mixture. Stuff into peppers.

3. Form remaining meat into oblong shape. Place meatloaf and peppers into slow cooker. Pour in tomatoes.

4. Cover. Cook on Low 6–12 hours, or High 4–5 hours.

Stuffed Green Peppers

Patricia Howard
Albuquerque, NM

MAKES 6 SERVINGS

6 green peppers
1 lb. ground beef
1/4 cup chopped onions
1 tsp. salt
1/4 tsp. pepper
1 1/4 cups cooked rice
1 Tbsp. Worcestershire sauce
8-oz. can tomato sauce
1/4 cup beef broth

1. Cut stem ends from peppers. Carefully remove seeds and membrane. Parboil in water for 5 minutes. Drain. Set aside.

2. Brown ground beef and onions in skillet. Drain off drippings. Place meat and onions in mixing bowl.

3. Add seasonings, rice, and Worcestershire sauce to meat and combine well. Stuff green peppers with mixture. Stand stuffed peppers upright in large slow cooker.

4. Mix tomato sauce and broth. Pour over peppers.

5. Cover. Cook on Low 5–7 hours.

Stuffed Peppers with Cheese

Rosaria Strachan/Fairfield, CT

 MAKES 6–8 SERVINGS

6–8 medium-sized green peppers
1–2 lbs. ground beef
1 onion, chopped and sauteed
salt to taste
pepper to taste
1 egg
1 1/2 cups cooked rice
15-oz. can tomato sauce, divided
1/2–3/4 cup shredded cheddar cheese

1. Remove caps and seeds from peppers, but keep them whole.

2. Combine ground beef, onion, salt, pepper, egg, rice, 1/3 can tomato sauce, and cheddar cheese. Stuff into peppers. Stand in large slow cooker, or two smaller cookers.

3. Cover with remaining tomato sauce.

4. Cover. Cook on Low 8–10 hours.

Spanish Stuffed Peppers

Katrine Rose/Woodbridge, VA

 MAKES 4 SERVINGS

1 lb. ground beef
7-oz. pkg. Spanish rice mix
1 egg
1/4 cup chopped onions
4 medium-sized green bell peppers, halved lengthwise, cored, and seeded
28-oz. can tomatoes
10 3/4-oz. can tomato soup
1 cup water
shredded cheese, optional

1. Combine beef, rice mix (reserving seasoning packet), egg, and onions. Divide meat mixture among pepper halves.

2. Pour tomatoes into slow cooker. Arrange pepper halves over tomatoes.

3. Combine tomato soup, rice-mix seasoning packet, and water. Pour over peppers.

4. Cover. Cook on Low 8–10 hours.

5. Twenty minutes before the end of the cooking time, top stuffed peppers with cheese.

Poor Man's Steak

Elsie Schlabach
Millersburg, OH

 MAKES 8–10 SERVINGS

1 1/2 lbs. ground beef
1 cup milk
1/4 tsp. pepper
1 tsp. salt
1 small onion, finely chopped
1 cup cracker crumbs
1 tsp. brown sugar
10 3/4-oz. can cream of mushroom soup
1 soup can water

1. Mix together all ingredients except soup and water. Shape into narrow loaf. Refrigerate for at least 8 hours.

2. Slice and fry until brown in skillet.

3. Mix soup and water together until smooth. Spread diluted soup on each piece. Place slices into cooker. Pour any remaining soup over slices in cooker.

4. Cover. Cook on Low 2–3 hours.

Pizzaburgers

Deborah Swartz/Grottoes, VA

MAKES 4–6 SERVINGS

1 lb. ground beef
1/2 cup chopped onions
1/4 tsp. salt
1/8 tsp. pepper
8 ozs. pizza sauce
10 3/4-oz. can cream of
   mushroom soup
2 cups shredded cheddar
   cheese

1. Brown ground beef and
onion in skillet. Drain.

2. Add remaining
ingredients. Mix well. Pour
into slow cooker.

3. Cover. Cook on Low
1–2 hours.

4. Serve on hamburger
buns.

Meat Loaf Burgers

Lafaye M. Musser/Denver, PA

MAKES 6 SERVINGS

1 large onion, sliced
1 rib celery, chopped
2 lbs. ground beef
1 tsp. salt
1 1/4 tsp. pepper
2 cups tomato juice
4 garlic cloves, minced
1 Tbsp. ketchup
1 tsp. Italian seasoning
1/2 tsp. salt
6 hamburger buns

1. Place onion and celery in
slow cooker.

2. Combine beef, salt, and
pepper. Shape into 6 patties.
Place in slow cooker.

3. Combine tomato juice,
garlic, ketchup, Italian
seasoning, and salt. Pour
over patties.

4. Cover. Cook on Low
7–9 hours.

5. Serve on hamburger
buns.

Barbecue Sauce and Hamburgers

Dolores Kratz/Souderton, PA

MAKES 6 SERVINGS

14 3/4-oz. can beef gravy
1/2 cup ketchup
1/2 cup chili sauce
1 Tbsp. Worcestershire
   sauce
1 Tbsp. prepared mustard
6 grilled hamburger patties
6 slices cheese, optional

1. Combine all ingredients
except hamburger patties and
cheese slices in slow cooker.

2. Add hamburger patties.

3. Cover. Cook on Low 5–6
hours.

4. Serve in buns, each
topped with a slice of cheese
if you like.

notes
● Freeze leftover sauce for
future use.
● This is both a practical and a
tasty recipe for serving a crowd
(picnics, potlucks, etc). You can
grill the patties early in the day,
rather than at the last minute
when your guests are arriving.

Barbecued Hamburgers

Martha Hershey/Ronks, PA

 MAKES 4 SERVING

1 lb. ground beef
1/4 cup chopped onions
3 Tbsp. ketchup
1 tsp. salt
1 egg, beaten
1/4 cup seasoned bread crumbs
18-oz. bottle of your favorite barbecue sauce

1. Combine beef, onions, ketchup, salt, egg, and bread crumbs. Form into 4 patties. Brown both sides lightly in skillet. Place in slow cooker.

2. Cover with barbecue sauce.

3. Cover. Bake on High 3 hours or Low 6 hours.

note
● Mix the hamburger patties, brown them, and freeze them in advance, and you'll have little to do at the last minute.

We first had Barbecued Hamburgers at a 4-H picnic, and they have been a family favorite ever since.

— ● —

Meatloaf Dinner

Esther Lehman/Croghan, NY

 MAKES 4 SERVINGS

6 potatoes, cubed
4 carrots, thinly sliced
1/4 tsp. salt
1 egg, slightly beaten
1 large shredded wheat biscuit, crushed
1/4 cup chili sauce
1/4 cup finely chopped onion
1/2 tsp. salt
1/4 tsp. dried marjoram
1/8 tsp. pepper
1 lb. ground beef

1. Place potatoes and carrots in slow cooker. Season with salt.

2. Combine egg, shredded wheat, chili sauce, onion, salt, marjoram, and pepper. Add ground beef. Mix well. Shape into loaf, slightly smaller in diameter than the cooker. Place on top of vegetables, not touching sides of cooker.

3. Cover. Cook on Low 9–10 hours.

variation
● Substitute 1/2 cup bread crumbs or dry oatmeal for crushed shredded wheat biscuit.

— ● —

Easy, All-Day Meatloaf and Vegetables

Ann Sunday McDowell Newtown, PA

 MAKES 6 SERVINGS

4 large, or 6 medium, potatoes, sliced
6 carrots, sliced
1/4 tsp. salt
1 1/2 lbs. ground beef
2 eggs, beaten
3/4 cup cracker crumbs
1/3 cup ketchup
1/3 cup finely chopped onions
3/4 tsp. salt
1/4 tsp. dried marjoram
1/4 tsp. black pepper

1. Place potatoes and carrots in slow cooker. Sprinkle with 1/4 tsp. salt.

2. Combine remaining ingredients. Mix well and shape into loaf. Place loaf on top of vegetables, making sure that it doesn't touch sides of slow cooker.

3. Cover. Cook on Low 8–10 hours.

Betty's Meatloaf

Betty B. Dennison
Grove City, PA

MAKES 4–6 SERVINGS

2 lbs. ground beef
1/2 cup chopped green
  peppers
1/2 cup chopped onions
1/2 tsp. salt
1 cup cracker crumbs
1 egg
7/8-oz. envelope brown
  gravy mix
1 cup milk
4–6 small potatoes, cut up,
  optional

1. Combine all ingredients
except potatoes in large
bowl. Shape into loaf. Place
in slow cooker.

2. Place potatoes alongside
meatloaf.

3. Cover. Cook on Low
8–10 hours, or High 4–5
hours.

Tracey's Italian Meatloaf

Tracey Yohn / Harrisburg, PA

MAKES 8 SERVINGS

2 lbs. ground beef
2 cups soft bread crumbs
1/2 cup spaghetti sauce
1 large egg
2 Tbsp. dried onion
1/4 tsp. pepper
1 1/4 tsp. salt
1 tsp. garlic salt
1/2 tsp. dried Italian herbs
1/4 tsp. garlic powder
2 Tbsp. spaghetti sauce

1. Fold a 30"-long piece of
foil in half lengthwise. Place
in bottom of slow cooker with
both ends hanging over the
edge of cooker. Grease foil.

2. Combine beef, bread
crumbs, 1/2 cup spaghetti
sauce, egg, onion, and
seasonings. Shape into loaf.
Place on top of foil in slow
cooker. Spread 2 Tbsp.
spaghetti sauce over top.

3. Cover. Cook on High
2 1/2–3 hours, or Low 5–6
hours.

Mary Ann's Italian Meatloaf

Mary Ann Wasick
West Allis, WI

MAKES 8–10 SERVINGS

2 lbs. ground beef
2 eggs, beaten
2/3 cup quick-cooking oats
1 envelope dry onion soup
  mix
1/2 cup pasta sauce
  (your favorite)
1 tsp. garlic powder
onion slices

1. Combine ground beef,
eggs, oats, soup mix, pasta
sauce, and garlic powder.
Shape into a loaf. Place in
slow cooker. Garnish top
of loaf with onion slices.

2. Cover. Cook on Low
8 hours.

3. Serve with pasta and
more of the sauce that you
mixed into the meatloaf.

Barbecue Hamburger Steaks

Jeanette Oberholtzer
Manheim, PA

MAKES 4 SERVINGS

1 lb. ground beef
1 tsp. salt
1 tsp. pepper
1/2 cup milk
1 cup soft bread crumbs
2 Tbsp. brown sugar
2 Tbsp. vinegar
3 Tbsp. Worcestershire sauce
1 cup ketchup

1. Combine beef, salt, pepper, milk, and bread crumbs. Mix well. Form into patties. Brown in saucepan and drain.

2. Combine brown sugar, vinegar, Worcestershire sauce, and ketchup in slow cooker. Add ground beef patties, pushing them down into the sauce, so that each one is well covered.

3. Cover. Cook on Low 4–6 hours.

Meat Loaf

Colleen Heatwole/Burton, MI

MAKES 8 SERVINGS

2 lbs. ground beef
2 eggs
2/3 cup quick oats
1 pkg. dry onion soup mix
1/2–1 tsp. liquid smoke
1 tsp. ground mustard
1/2 cup ketchup, divided

1. Combine ground beef, eggs, dry oats, dry soup mix, liquid smoke, ground mustard, and all but 2 Tbsp. ketchup. Shape into loaf and place in slow cooker.

2. Top with remaining ketchup.

3. Cover. Cook on Low 8–10 hours or on High 4–6 hours.

Nutritious Meatloaf

Elsie Russett/Fairbank, IA

MAKES 6 SERVINGS

1 lb. ground beef
2 cups finely shredded cabbage
1 medium green pepper, diced
1 Tbsp. dried onion flakes
1/2 tsp. caraway seeds
1 tsp. salt

1. Combine all ingredients. Shape into loaf and place on rack in slow cooker.

2. Cover. Cook on High 3–4 hours.

Comfort Meat Loaf

Trudy Kutter/Corfu, NY

 **MAKES 6 SERVINGS**

2 eggs, beaten
1/2 cup milk
2/3 cup bread crumbs
2 Tbsp. grated or finely chopped onion
1 tsp. salt
1/2 tsp. sage
1 1/2 lbs. ground beef
2–3 Tbsp. tomato sauce or ketchup

1. Combine everything but tomato sauce. Shape into 6" round loaf and place in cooker.

2. Cover. Cook on Low 6 hours.

3. Spoon tomato sauce over meat loaf.

4. Cover. Cook on High 30 minutes.

Cheese Meat Loaf

Mary Sommerfeld
Lancaster, PA

 **MAKES 8 SERVINGS**

2 lbs. ground chuck or ground beef
2 cups shredded sharp cheddar or American cheese
1 tsp. salt
1 tsp. dry mustard
1/4 tsp. pepper
1/2 cup chili sauce
2 cups crushed cornflakes
2 eggs
1/2 cup milk

1. Combine all ingredients. Shape into loaf. Place in greased slow cooker.

2. Cover. Cook on Low 6–8 hours.

3. Slice and serve with your favorite tomato sauce or ketchup.

variation

● Before baking, surround meat loaf with quartered potatoes, tossed lightly in oil.

Barbecued Meatballs

Esther Becker/Gordonville, Pa
Ruth Shank/Gridley, IL

 **MAKES 30 SMALL MEATBALLS**

1 1/2 cups chili sauce
1 cup grape, or apple, jelly
3 tsp. brown spicy mustard
1 lb. ground beef
1 egg
3 Tbsp. dry bread crumbs
1/2 tsp. salt

1. Combine chili sauce, jelly, and mustard in slow cooker. Mix well.

2. Cover. Cook on High while preparing meatballs.

3. Mix together remaining ingredients. Shape into 30 balls. Place in baking pan and bake at 400°F for 15–20 minutes. Drain well. Spoon into slow cooker. Stir gently to coat well.

4. Cover. Cook on Low 6–10 hours.

variations

● To increase flavor, add 1/4 tsp. pepper, 1/4 tsp. Italian spice, and a dash of garlic powder to the meatball mixture. Sandra Thom/Jenks, OK

● Make meatballs larger and serve with rice or noodles.

Great Meatballs

Judy Denney
Lawrenceville, GA

MAKES 12–16 MAIN DISH-SIZE SERVINGS, OR 24 APPETIZER-SIZE SERVINGS

4 lbs. ground beef
2 eggs
4 slices fresh bread, torn into bread crumbs
1 1/2 tsp. salt
1/2 tsp. pepper
1 cup tomato juice
2 10-oz. jars chili sauce
2 cans whole cranberry sauce

1. Mix together beef, eggs, bread crumbs, seasonings, and tomato juice. Form into small meatballs. Place in slow cooker.

2. Pour chili sauce and cranberry sauce on top of meatballs. Stir lightly.

3. Cover. Cook on High 2 hours. Reduce heat to Low and cook 3 more hours.

Sweet 'n Tangy Meatballs

Donna Lantgen/Rapid City, SD

MAKES 8 SERVINGS

1 1/2 lbs. ground beef
1/4 cup plain dry bread crumbs
3 Tbsp. prepared mustard
1 tsp. Italian seasoning
3/4 cup water
1/4 cup ketchup
2 Tbsp. honey
1 Tbsp. red-hot cayenne pepper sauce
3/4-oz. pkg. brown gravy mix

1. Combine ground beef, bread crumbs, mustard, and Italian seasoning. Shape into 1" balls. Bake or microwave until cooked. Drain. Place meatballs in slow cooker.

2. Cover. Cook on Low 3 hours.

3. Combine remaining ingredients in saucepan. Cook for 5 minutes. Pour over meatballs.

4. Cover. Cook on Low 2 hours.

variation
● For a fuller flavor, use orange juice instead of water in sauce.

Applesauce Meatballs

Mary E. Wheatley
Mashpee, MA

MAKES 6 SERVINGS

3/4 lb. ground beef
1/4 lb. ground pork
1 egg
3/4 cup soft bread crumbs
1/2 cup unsweetened applesauce
3/4 tsp. salt
1/4 tsp. pepper
oil
1/4 cup ketchup
1/4 cup water

1. Combine beef, pork, egg, bread crumbs, applesauce, salt, and pepper. Form into 1 1/2" balls.

2. Brown in oil in batches in skillet. Transfer meat to slow cooker, reserving drippings.

3. Combine ketchup and water and pour into skillet. Stir up browned drippings and mix well. Spoon over meatballs.

4. Cover. Cook on Low 4–6 hours.

5. Serve with steamed rice and green salad.

Tamale Pie

Jeannine Janzen/Elbing, KS

MAKES 8 SERVINGS

3/4 cup cornmeal
1 1/2 cups milk
1 egg, beaten
1 lb. ground beef, browned and drained
1 envelope dry chili seasoning mix
16-oz. can diced tomatoes
16-oz. can corn, drained
1 cup grated cheddar cheese

1. Combine cornmeal, milk, and egg.

2. Stir in meat, chili seasoning mix, tomatoes, and corn until well blended. Pour into slow cooker.

3. Cover. Cook on High 1 hour, then on Low 3 hours.

4. Sprinkle with cheese. Cook another 5 minutes until cheese is melted.

Pecos River Red Frito Pie

Donna Barnitz/Jerks, OK

MAKES 6 SERVINGS

1 large onion, chopped coarsely
3 lbs. coarsely ground hamburger
2 garlic cloves, minced
3 Tbsp. ground hot red chili peppers
2 Tbsp. ground mild red chili peppers
1 1/2 cups water
corn chips
shredded Monterey Jack cheese
shredded cheddar cheese

1. Combine onion, hamburger, garlic, chilies, and water in slow cooker.

2. Cover. Cook on Low 8–10 hours. Drain.

3. Serve over corn chips. Top with mixture of Monterey Jack and cheddar cheeses.

Tortilla Bake

Kelly Evenson/Pittsboro, NC

MAKES 6–8 SERVINGS

10 3/4-oz. can cheddar cheese soup
1 1/2-oz. pkg. dry taco seasoning mix
8 corn tortillas
1 1/2 lbs. ground beef, browned and drained
3 medium tomatoes, coarsely chopped
toppings: sour cream, grated cheese, thinly sliced green onions, cut-up bell peppers, diced avocado, shredded lettuce

1. Combine soup and taco seasoning.

2. Cut each tortilla into 6 wedges. Spoon one-quarter of ground beef into slow cooker. Top with one-quarter of all tortilla wedges. Spoon one-quarter of soup mixture on tortillas. Top with one-quarter of tomatoes. Repeat layers 3 times.

3. Cover. Cook on Low 6–8 hours.

4. To serve, spoon onto plates and offer toppings as condiments.

Cheddar Parmesan Swiss

Taco Casserole

Marcia S. Myer/Manheim, PA

MAKES 6 SERVINGS

1 1/2 lbs. ground beef, browned
14 1/2-oz. can diced tomatoes with chilies
10 3/4-oz. can cream of onion soup
1 pkg. dry taco seasoning mix
1/4 cup water
6 corn tortillas cut in 1/2-inch strips
1/2 cup sour cream
1 cup shredded cheddar cheese
2 green onions, sliced, optional

1. Combine beef, tomatoes, soup, seasoning mix, and water in slow cooker.

2. Stir in tortilla strips.

3. Cover. Cook on Low 7–8 hours.

4. Spread sour cream over casserole. Sprinkle with cheese.

5. Cover. Let stand 5 minutes until cheese melts.

6. Remove cover. Garnish with green onions. Allow to stand for 15 more minutes before serving.

Hearty Italian Sandwiches

Rhonda Lee Schmidt
Scranton, PA

Robin Schrock
Millersburg, OH

MAKES 8 SERVINGS

1 1/2 lbs. ground beef
1 1/2 lbs. bulk Italian sausage
2 large onions, chopped
2 large green peppers, chopped
2 large sweet red peppers, chopped
1 tsp. salt
1 tsp. pepper
shredded Monterey Jack cheese
8 sandwich rolls

1. In skillet brown beef and sausage. Drain.

2. Place one-third onions and peppers in slow cooker. Top with half of meat mixture. Repeat layers. Sprinkle with salt and pepper.

3. Cover. Cook on Low 6 hours, or until vegetables are tender.

4. With a slotted spoon, serve about 1 cup mixture on each roll. Top with cheese.

Jean & Tammy's Sloppy Joes

Jean Shaner/York, PA

Tammy Smoker
Cochranville, PA

MAKES 12 SERVINGS

3 lbs. ground beef, browned and drained
1 onion, finely chopped
1 green pepper, chopped
2 8-oz. cans tomato sauce
3/4 cup ketchup
1 Tbsp. Worcestershire sauce
1 tsp. chili powder
1/4 tsp. pepper
1/4 tsp. garlic powder
sandwich rolls

1. Combine all ingredients except rolls in slow cooker.

2. Cover. Cook on Low 8–10 hours, or High 3–4 hours.

3. Serve in sandwich rolls.

Penny's Sloppy Joes

Penny Blosser
Beavercreek, OH

MAKES 6 SERVINGS

1 lb. ground beef, browned
  and drained
10 3/4-oz. can cream of
  mushroom soup
1/4 cup ketchup
1 small onion, diced

1. Combine all ingredients
in slow cooker.

2. Cover. Cook on Low
1–2 hours.

3. Serve on rolls or over
baked potatoes.

Nan's Sloppy Joes

Nan Decker/Albuquerque, NM

MAKES 4–6 SERVINGS

1 lb. ground beef
1 onion, chopped
3/4 cup ketchup
2 Tbsp. chili sauce
1 Tbsp. Worcestershire
  sauce
1 Tbsp. prepared mustard
1 Tbsp. vinegar
1 Tbsp. sugar
whole wheat buns

1. Brown beef and onion in
saucepan. Drain.

2. Combine all ingredients
in slow cooker.

3. Cover. Cook on Low 4–5
hours.

4. Serve on buns.

Dianna's Barbecue

Lauren Eberhard/Seneca, IL

MAKES 12 SERVINGS

4 lbs. ground beef,
  browned
24-oz. bottle ketchup
4 Tbsp. prepared mustard
2 Tbsp. vinegar
4 Tbsp. sugar
3/4 cup water
1 tsp. pepper
1 Tbsp. paprika
1 cup chopped celery
1 cup chopped onion
sandwich rolls

1. Combine all ingredients
except rolls in slow cooker.

2. Cover. Cook on High 1–2
hours or on Low 4 hours.

3. Serve in sandwich rolls.

Pork

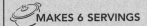

Barbecue Pork Chops

Annabelle Unternahrer
Shipshewana, IN

Evelyn L. Ward/Greeley, CO

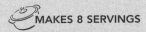
MAKES 8 SERVINGS

8 pork chops
1 cup (or more) barbecue, or sweet-sour, sauce

1. Brush each pork chop generously with sauce, then place in slow cooker.

2. Cover. Cook on Low 7–8 hours.

Italian Chops

Jan Moore/Wellsville, KS

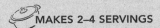
MAKES 2–4 SERVINGS

16-oz. bottle Italian salad dressing (use less if cooking only 2 chops)
2–4 pork chops

1. Place pork chops in slow cooker. Pour salad dressing over chops.

2. Cover. Cook on High 6–8 hours.

Autumn Pork Chops

Leesa Lesenski/Whately, MA

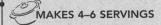
MAKES 4–6 SERVINGS

4–6 boneless pork chops
2 cups apple juice
1/2 tsp. ground cinnamon

1. Place pork chops in slow cooker.

2. Cover with apple juice.

3. Sprinkle with cinnamon.

4. Cover. Cook on Low 10 hours.

Simply Pork and Sauerkraut

Gladys Longacre
Susquehanna, PA

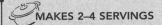
MAKES 2–4 SERVINGS

2–4 pork chops
14-oz. can sauerkraut, or more if you like sauerkraut

1. Place pork chops in slow cooker. Cover with sauerkraut.

2. Cover. Cook on Low 7–8

Chops and Kraut

Willard E. Roth/Elkhart, IN

MAKES 6 SERVINGS

1-lb. bag fresh sauerkraut
2 large Vidalia onions, sliced
6 pork chops

1. Make 3 layers in well-greased cooker: kraut, onions, and chops.

2. Cover. Cook on Low 6 hours.

3. Serve with mashed potatoes and applesauce or cranberry sauce.

...super**easy**

Cooker Chops

Lucille Metzler/Wellsboro, PA

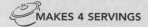 **MAKES 4 SERVINGS**

4 pork chops
10 3/4-oz. can cream of
    mushroom soup
1/4 cup ketchup
2 tsp. Worcestershire sauce

1. Put chops in slow cooker.

2. Combine remaining
ingredients. Pour over chops.

3. Cover. Cook on High 3–4
hours, or Low 8–10 hours.

variation
• Add one sliced onion to
mixture.
Maryland Massey
Mellington, MD

Easy Sweet and Sour Pork Chops

Jeanne Hertzog/Bethlehem, PA

 **MAKES 6 SERVINGS**

16-oz. bag frozen Oriental
    vegetables
6 pork chops
12-oz. bottle sweet and
    sour sauce
1/2 cup water
1 cup frozen pea pods

1. Place partially thawed
Oriental vegetables in slow
cooker. Arrange chops on
top.

2. Combine sauce and
water. Pour over chops

3. Cover. Cook on Low
7–8 hours.

4. Turn to High and add
pea pods.

5. Cover. Cook on High
5 minutes.

Baked Beans and Chops

John D. Allen/Rye, CO

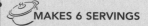 **MAKES 6 SERVINGS**

2 16 1/2-oz. cans baked
    beans
6 rib pork chops, 1/2 inch
    thick
1 1/2 tsp. prepared mustard
1 1/2 Tbsp. brown sugar
1 1/2 Tbsp. ketchup
6 onion slices, 1/4 inch thick

1. Pour baked beans into
bottom of greased slow
cooker.

2. Layer pork chops over
beans.

3. Spread mustard over
pork chops. Sprinkle with
brown sugar and drizzle
with ketchup.

4. Top with onion slices.

5. Cover. Cook on High
4–6 hours.

1-2-3 Barbecued Country Ribs

Barbara Walker/Sturgis, SD

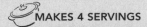 **MAKES 4 SERVINGS**

4 lbs. spareribs, or 3 lbs. country-style ribs, cut in serving-size pieces
18-oz. bottle prepared barbecue sauce

1. Pour a little sauce into bottom of slow cooker. Put in a layer of ribs, meaty side up. Cover with barbecue sauce.

2. Continue layering until all ribs are in the pot. Submerge them as much as possible in the sauce.

3. Cover. Cook on Low 8–10 hours.

note
● No need to precook the ribs if they're lean. If they're fattier than you like, parboil in water in stockpot before placing in cooker, to cook off some of the grease.

Pork Roast

Lucille Amos/Greensboro, NC

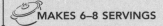 **MAKES 6–8 SERVINGS**

1 Boston butt roast
1 cup Worcestershire sauce
1 cup brown sugar

1. Place roast in greased slow cooker.

2. Pour Worcestershire sauce over roast.

3. Pat brown sugar on roast.

4. Cover. Cook on High 1 hour. Reduce heat to Low for 8–10 hours.

5. Slice and serve topped with broth and drippings from cooker.

Ham in Foil

Jeanette Oberholtzer
Manheim, PA

Vicki Dinkel
Sharon Springs, KS

Janet Roggie/Lowville, NY

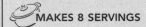 **MAKES 8 SERVINGS**

1/2 cup water
3–4-lb. precooked ham
liquid smoke

1. Pour water into slow cooker.

2. Sprinkle ham with liquid smoke. Wrap in foil. Place in slow cooker.

3. Cover. Cook on High 1 hour, then on Low 6 hours.

4. Cut into thick chunks or 1/2" slices and serve.

...super**easy**

Ham and Cabbage Supper

Louise Stackhouse/Benten, PA

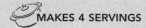**MAKES 4 SERVINGS**

1 medium-size cabbage
 head, cut into quarters
4-lb. smoked picnic ham
1/4 cup water

1. Place cabbage quarters in bottom of slow cooker. Place ham on top. Pour in water.

2. Cover. Cook on Low 8–10 hours.

variation

● To cabbage quarters, add
2 sliced carrots, 1 sliced onion,
2 potatoes cut into cubes, and
2 bay leaves for additional
flavor and nutrition.

Ham Barbecue

Janet V. Yocum
Elizabethtown, PA

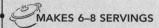**MAKES 6–8 SERVINGS**

1 lb. boiled ham, cut into
 cubes
1 cup cola-flavored soda
1 cup ketchup

1. Place ham in slow cooker. Pour cola and ketchup over ham.

2. Cover. Cook on Low 8 hours.

3. Serve in hamburger rolls.

Glazed Ham in a Bag

Eleanor J. Ferreira
North Chelmsford, MA

**MAKES 12 SERVINGS**

5-lb. cooked ham
3 Tbsp. orange juice
1 Tbsp. Dijon mustard

1. Rinse meat. Place in cooking bag.

2. Combine orange juice and mustard. Spread over ham.

3. Seal bag with twist tie. Poke 4 holes in top of bag. Place in slow cooker.

4. Cover. Cook on Low 6–8 hours.

5. To serve, remove ham from bag, reserving juices. Slice ham and spoon juices over. Serve additional juice alongside in small bowl.

Savory Pork Roast

Betty A. Holt/St. Charles, MO

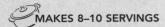 MAKES 8–10 SERVINGS

4–5-lb. pork loin roast
large onion, sliced
1 bay leaf
2 Tbsp. soy sauce
1 Tbsp. garlic powder

1. Place roast and onion in slow cooker. Add bay leaf, soy sauce, and garlic powder.

2. Cover. Cook on High 1 hour and then on Low 6 hours.

3. Slice and serve.

Country-Style Ribs and Sauerkraut

Rhonda Burgoon
Collingswood, NJ

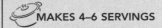 MAKES 4–6 SERVINGS

16-oz. bag sauerkraut, rinsed and drained
1 onion, diced
1 red-skinned apple, chopped
2–3 lbs. country-style pork ribs
1 cup beer

1. Combine sauerkraut, onion, and apple in bottom of slow cooker.

2. Layer ribs over sauerkraut.

3. Pour beer over ribs just before turning on cooker.

4. Cover. Cook on Low 8–10 hours.

5. Serve with homemade cornbread and mashed potatoes, or serve deboned on a kaiser roll as a sandwich.

Barbecued Ribs

Virginia Bender/Dover, DE

MAKES 6 SERVINGS

4 lbs. pork ribs
1/2 cup brown sugar
12-oz. jar chili sauce
1/4 cup balsamic vinegar
2 Tbsp. Worcestershire sauce
2 Tbsp. Dijon mustard
1 tsp. hot sauce

1. Place ribs in slow cooker.

2. Combine remaining ingredients. Pour half of sauce over ribs.

3. Cover. Cook on Low 8–10 hours.

4. Serve with remaining sauce.

Spicy Pork Chops

Mary Puskar/Forest Hill, MD

 **MAKES 5 SERVINGS**

5–6 center-cut loin pork chops
3 Tbsp. oil
1 onion, sliced
1 green pepper, cut in strips
8-oz. can tomato sauce
3–4 Tbsp. brown sugar
1 Tbsp. vinegar
1 1/2 tsp. salt
1–2 tsp. Worcestershire sauce

1. Brown chops in oil in skillet. Transfer to slow cooker.

2. Add remaining ingredients to cooker.

3. Cover. Cook on Low 6–8 hours.

4. Serve over rice.

Pork Chops in Bean Sauce

Shirley Sears/Tiskilwa, IL

 **MAKES 6 SERVINGS**

6 pork chops
1/3 cup chopped onions
1/2 tsp. salt
1/3 tsp. garlic salt
1/8 tsp. pepper
28-oz. can vegetarian, or baked, beans
1/4 tsp. hot pepper sauce
13 1/2-oz. can crushed pineapple, undrained
1/3 cup chili sauce

1. Brown pork chops in skillet five minutes per side. Place in slow cooker.

2. Sauté onion in skillet in meat juices. Spread over pork chops.

3. Sprinkle with salt, garlic salt, and pepper.

4. Combine beans and hot sauce. Pour over chops.

5. Combine pineapple and chili sauce. Spread evenly over beans.

6. Cover. Cook on Low 7–8 hours.

Saucy Pork Chops

Bonita Ensenberger
Albuquerque, NM

 **MAKES 4 SERVINGS**

4 pork chops
salt to taste
pepper to taste
1 tsp. garlic powder
1 Tbsp. oil
2–2 1/2 cups ketchup
1/2 cup brown sugar
1 Tbsp. hickory-flavored liquid smoke
1 cup onions, chopped

1. Season chops with salt, pepper, and garlic powder. Brown on both sides in oil in skillet. Drain.

2. Combine ketchup, brown sugar, and liquid smoke in bowl.

3. Place onions in slow cooker. Dip browned pork chops in sauce mixture and place on onions. Pour remaining sauce over chops.

4. Cover. Cook on Low 7–9 hours, or High 4–5 hours.

5. Makes a great meal served with cole slaw and oven-roasted, cut-up root vegetables.

Chicken-Fried Pork Chops

Martha Ann Auker
Landisburg, PA

MAKES 6 SERVINGS

1/2 cup flour
3/4 tsp. salt
1 1/2 tsp. dry mustard
3/4 tsp. garlic powder
6 pork chops
2 Tbsp. oil
10 3/4-oz. can cream of chicken soup
1 soup can water

1. Combine flour, salt, dry mustard, and garlic powder. Dredge pork chops in flour mixture. Brown in oil in skillet. Place in slow cooker.

2. Combine soup and water. Pour over meat.

3. Cover. Cook on High 6–8 hours.

Golden Glow Pork Chops

Pam Hochstedler/Kalona, IA

MAKES 5–6 SERVINGS

5–6 pork chops
salt to taste
pepper to taste
29-oz. can cling peach halves, drained (reserve juice)
1/4 cup brown sugar
1/2 tsp. ground cinnamon
1/4 tsp. ground cloves
8-oz. can tomato sauce
1/4 cup vinegar

1. Lightly brown pork chops on both sides in saucepan. Drain. Arrange in slow cooker. Sprinkle with salt and pepper.

2. Place drained peach halves on top of pork chops.

3. Combine brown sugar, cinnamon, cloves, tomato sauce, 1/4 cup peach syrup, and vinegar. Pour over peaches and pork chops.

4. Cover. Cook on Low 3–4 hours.

Perfect Pork Chops

Brenda Pope/Dundee, OH

MAKES 2 SERVINGS

2 small onions
2 3/4-inch thick, boneless, center loin pork chops, frozen
fresh ground pepper to taste
1 chicken bouillon cube
1/4 cup hot water
2 Tbsp. prepared mustard with white wine
fresh parsley sprigs, or lemon slices, optional

1. Cut off ends of onions and peel. Cut onions in half crosswise to make 4 thick "wheels." Place in bottom of slow cooker.

2. Sear both sides of frozen chops in heavy skillet. Place in cooker on top of onions. Sprinkle with pepper.

3. Dissolve bouillon cube in hot water. Stir in mustard. Pour into slow cooker.

4. Cover. Cook on High 3–4 hours.

5. Serve topped with fresh parsley sprigs or lemon slices, if desired.

Pork Chops and Gravy

Sharon Wantland
Menomonee Falls, WI

MAKES 8 SERVINGS

8 pork chops
salt to taste
pepper to taste
2 Tbsp. oil
2 10 3/4-oz. cans cream
   of mushroom soup
1 large onion, sliced
12-oz. can evaporated milk

1. Season pork chops with salt and pepper. Brown in oil. Drain. Transfer to slow cooker.

2. In separate bowl, whisk together mushroom soup, onion, and evaporated milk until smooth. Pour over chops.

3. Cook on High 3–4 hours, or Low 6–8 hours.

variations
● To increase flavor, stir 1/2–1 cup sour cream, or 1/4 cup sherry, into mixture during last 30 minutes of cooking time.

Pork Chops and Mushrooms

Michele Ruvola/Selden, NY

MAKES 4 SERVINGS

4 boneless pork chops,
   1/2 inch thick
2 medium onions, sliced
4-oz. can sliced mushrooms,
   drained
1 envelope dry onion soup
   mix
1/4 cup water
10 3/4-oz. can golden cream
   of mushroom soup

1. Place pork chops in greased slow cooker. Top with onions and mushrooms.

2. Combine soup mix, water, and mushroom soup. Pour over mushrooms.

3. Cover. Cook on Low 6–8 hours.

Pork Chops with Mushroom Sauce

Jennifer J. Gehman
Harrisburg, PA

MAKES 4–6 SERVINGS

4–6 boneless thin or thick
   pork chops
10 3/4-oz. can cream of
   mushroom soup
3/4 cup white wine
4-oz. can sliced mushrooms
2 Tbsp. quick cooking
   tapioca
2 tsp. Worcestershire sauce
1 tsp. beef bouillon
   granules, or 1 beef
   bouillon cube
1/4 tsp. minced garlic
3/4 tsp. dried thyme,
   optional

1. Place pork chops in slow cooker.

2. Combine remaining ingredients and pour over pork chops.

3. Cook on Low 8–10 hours, or on High 4 1/2–5 hours.

4. Serve over rice.

Pork Chops and Gravy

Barbara J. Fabel/Wausau, WI

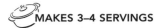 MAKES 3–4 SERVINGS

3 large onions, quartered or sliced
3 ribs of celery, chunked or sliced
3–4 pork chops
10 3/4-oz. can cream of mushroom, or cream of celery, soup

1. Place onions and celery in slow cooker. Wash pork chops and place on top of onions and celery. Pour soup over all.

2. Cover. Cook on High 1 hour. Reduce heat to Low and cook 3–4 hours, or until chops are tender.

Pork Chop Surprise

Jan Moore/Wellsville, KS

 MAKES 4 SERVINGS

4 pork chops
6 potatoes, sliced
10 3/4-oz. can cream of mushroom soup
water

1. Brown pork chops on both sides in skillet. Transfer to slow cooker.

2. Add potatoes. Pour soup over top. Add enough water to cover all ingredients.

3. Cover. Cook on High 6–8 hours.

variation
● Combine 1 envelope dry onion soup mix with mushroom soup before pouring over chops and potatoes.
Trudy Kutter/Corfu, NY

Pork Chop Casserole

Doris Bachman/Putnam, IL

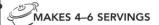 MAKES 4–6 SERVINGS

4–6 pork chops
3 cups water
1 cup rice, uncooked
10 3/4-oz. can cream of mushroom soup
1 tsp. salt
1 tsp. dried parsley
1/4 tsp. pepper

1. Sauté pork chops in skillet until brown. Transfer to slow cooker.

2. Mix remaining ingredients and pour over chops in cooker.

3. Cover. Cook on Low 6–8 hours, or High 3–4 hours.

Jean's Pork Chops

Jean Weller/State College, PA

 **MAKES 6 SERVINGS**

1/2 cup flour
1 Tbsp. salt
1 1/2 tsp. dry mustard
1/2 tsp. garlic powder
6–8 1-inch-thick pork chops
2 Tbsp. oil
15 1/2-oz. can chicken and rice soup

1. Combine flour, salt, dry mustard, and garlic powder. Dredge pork chops in flour mixture. Brown in oil in skillet. Transfer to slow cooker. Add soup.

2. Cover. Cook on Low 6–8 hours, or on High 3 1/2 hours.

variation

● For increased flavor, step up the dry mustard to 1 Tbsp. and add 1 tsp. pepper.
Mary Puskar/Forest Hill, MD

Tender Pork Chops

Dawn M. Propst
Levittown, PA
Kim McEuen
Lincoln University, PA

 **MAKES 6 SERVINGS**

6 pork chops
1/2 cup flour
1 tsp. salt
1/2 tsp. garlic powder
1 1/2 tsp dry mustard
2 Tbsp. oil
15-oz. can chicken gumbo soup

1. Coat chops with a combination of flour, salt, garlic powder, and mustard. Brown chops in skillet. Place in slow cooker. Drain drippings from skillet.

2. Add soup to skillet. Stir to loosen brown bits from pan. Pour over pork chops.

3. Cover. Cook on Low 6–8 hours.

Pork and Cabbage Dinner

Mrs. Paul Gray/Beatrice, NE

 **MAKES 8 SERVINGS**

2 lbs. pork steaks, or chops, or shoulder
3/4 cup chopped onions
1/4 cup chopped fresh parsley, or 2 Tbsp. dried parsley
4 cups shredded cabbage
1 tsp. salt
1/8 tsp. pepper
1/2 tsp. caraway seeds
1/8 tsp. allspice
1/2 cup beef broth
2 cooking apples, cored and sliced 1/4 inch thick

1. Place pork in slow cooker. Layer onions, parsley, and cabbage over pork.

2. Combine salt, pepper, caraway seeds, and allspice. Sprinkle over cabbage. Pour broth over cabbage.

3. Cover. Cook on Low 5–6 hours.

4. Add apple slices 30 minutes before serving.

Pork Chops

Linda Sluiter/Schererville, IN

 MAKES 4 SERVINGS

4 boneless pork chops,
  1 inch thick
1/2 tsp. dry mustard
1/4 cup flour
1/2 tsp. sugar
1 tsp. vinegar
1/2 cup water
1/2 cup ketchup
1/2 tsp. salt

1. Place pork chops in slow cooker.

2. Combine remaining ingredients and pour over pork chops.

3. Cover. Cook on High 2–3 hours, and then Low 3–4 hours, or cook on Low 8 hours.

Pork Chops Hong Kong

Marjorie Y. Guengerich
Harrisonburg, VA

 MAKES 6–8 SERVINGS

10-oz. bottle soy sauce
6–8 Tbsp. sugar
6–8 pork chops
10 3/4-oz. can cream of
  mushroom soup

1. Combine soy sauce and sugar. Pour over pork chops. Marinate for 60 minutes.

2. Transfer pork chops to slow cooker.

3. Add soup.

4. Cover. Cook on Low 6 hours or High 3 hours.

Sauerkraut and Pork

Ethel Mumaw/Berlin, OH

MAKES 6–8 SERVINGS

2 lbs. pork cutlets
2 14-oz. cans sauerkraut
2 apples, chopped
2 Tbsp. brown sugar

1. Cut pork into serving-size pieces. Brown under broiler or in 2 Tbsp. oil in skillet. Place in slow cooker.

2. Add remaining ingredients.

3. Cover. Cook on Low 7–8 hours.

Barbecued Pork Chops

LaVerne A. Olson/Lititz, PA

 **MAKES 6–8 SERVINGS**

6–8 pork chops, lightly browned in skillet
1/2 cup ketchup
1 tsp. salt
1 tsp. celery seed
1/2 tsp. ground nutmeg
1/3 cup vinegar
1/2 cup water
1 bay leaf

1. Place pork chops in slow cooker.

2. Combine remaining ingredients. Pour over chops.

3. Cover. Cook on Low 2–3 hours, or until chops are tender.

4. Remove bay leaf before serving.

Pork Chop Casserole

Nancy Wagner Graves
Manhattan, KS

 **MAKES 4–6 SERVINGS**

6–8 pork chops
salt to taste
pepper to taste
oil
2 medium potatoes, peeled and sliced
1 large onion, sliced
1 large green pepper, sliced
1/2 tsp. dried oregano
16-oz. can tomatoes

1. Season pork chops with salt and pepper. Brown in oil in skillet. Transfer to slow cooker.

2. Add remaining ingredients in order listed.

3. Cover. Cook on Low 8–10 hours or on High 3–4 hours.

Pork Chop Slow Cooker Casserole

Janice Crist/Quinter, KS

 **MAKES 5 SERVINGS**

5 pork chops
4–5 medium potatoes, quartered or sliced
10 3/4-oz. can cream of chicken soup
10 3/4-oz. can cream of celery soup
15-oz. can green beans, drained

1. Layer ingredients in slow cooker in order listed.

2. Cover. Cook on Low 5–6 hours or on High 4 hours.

Pork Chops with Vegetables

LaVerne A. Olson/Lititz, PA

 MAKES 6 SERVINGS

6 boneless pork chops
2 Tbsp. butter or margarine
1 1/2 cups sliced
   mushrooms
1 tsp. crushed rosemary
10 3/4-oz. can cream of
   mushroom soup
2 Tbsp. water
1/2–1 lb. green beans, cut
   in 2-inch pieces

1. Brown pork chops in skillet in 1 Tbsp. butter. Transfer to slow cooker.

2. Cook mushrooms and rosemary in 1 Tbsp. butter until just wilted. Add to chops.

3. Combine soup, rosemary, mushrooms, water, and beans. Pour over chops.

4. Cover. Cook on Low 6–8 hours or on High 4 hours.

5. Serve over hot noodles.

Cherry Pork Chops

Jo Haberkamp/Fairbank, IA

 MAKES 6 SERVINGS

6 pork chops, each cut
   3/4 inch thick
1 Tbsp. oil
salt
pepper
1 cup cherry pie filling
2 tsp. lemon juice
1/2 tsp. instant chicken
   bouillon granules
1/8 tsp. ground mace

1. Brown pork chops in oil in skillet. Sprinkle each chop with salt and pepper.

2. Combine remaining ingredients in slow cooker. Mix well.

3. Place browned pork chops on top of cherry mixture.

4. Cover. Cook on Low 4–5 hours.

5. Place chops on platter. Spoon some of the cherry sauce on top. Pass remaining sauce and serve with rice or baked potatoes.

Pork Chops with Stuffing

Erma Kauffman
Cochranville, PA

 MAKES 2 SERVINGS

4 slices bread, cubed
1 egg
1/4 cup grated, or finely
   chopped, celery
1/4–1/2 tsp. salt
1/8 tsp. pepper
2 thickly cut pork chops
1 cup water

1. Combine bread cubes, eggs, celery, salt, and pepper.

2. Cut pork chops part way through, creating a pocket. Fill with stuffing.

3. Pour water into slow cooker. Add chops.

4. Cover. Cook on Low 4–5 hours.

Pork Chops and Stuffing with Curry

Mary Martins/Fairbank, IA

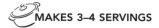 **MAKES 3–4 SERVINGS**

1 box stuffing mix
1 cup water
10 3/4-oz. can cream of mushroom soup
1 tsp., or more, curry powder, according to your taste preference
3–4 pork chops

1. Combine stuffing mix and water. Place half in bottom of slow cooker.

2. Combine soup and curry powder. Pour half over stuffing. Place pork chops on top.

3. Spread remaining stuffing over pork chops. Pour rest of soup on top.

4. Cover. Cook on Low 6–7 hours.

5. Serve with a tossed salad and a cooked vegetable.

Cranberry Pork Roast

Barbara Aston/Ashdown, AR

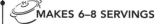 **MAKES 6–8 SERVINGS**

3–4-lb. pork roast
salt to taste
pepper to taste
1 cup ground, or finely chopped, cranberries
1/4 cup honey
1 tsp. grated orange peel
1/8 tsp. ground cloves
1/8 tsp. ground nutmeg

1. Sprinkle roast with salt and pepper. Place in slow cooker.

2. Combine remaining ingredients. Pour over roast.

3. Cover. Cook on Low 8–10 hours.

Teriyaki Pork Roast

Janice Yoskovich
Carmichaels, PA

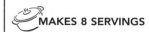 **MAKES 8 SERVINGS**

3/4 cup unsweetened apple juice
2 Tbsp. sugar
2 Tbsp. soy sauce
1 Tbsp. vinegar
1 tsp. ground ginger
1/4 tsp. garlic powder
1/8 tsp. pepper
3-lb. boneless pork loin roast, halved
2 1/2 Tbsp. cornstarch
3 Tbsp. cold water

1. Combine apple juice, sugar, soy sauce, vinegar, ginger, garlic powder, and pepper in greased slow cooker.

2. Add roast. Turn to coat.

3. Cover. Cook on Low 7–8 hours. Remove roast and keep warm.

4. In saucepan, combine cornstarch and cold water until smooth. Stir in juices from roast. Bring to boil. Cook and stir for 2 minutes, or until thickened. Serve with roast.

Pork Roast with Potatoes and Onions

Trudy Kutter/Corfu, NY

MAKES 6–8 SERVINGS

2 1/2–3-lb. boneless pork loin roast
1 large garlic clove, slivered
5–6 potatoes, cubed
1 large onion, sliced
3/4 cup broth, tomato juice, or water
1 1/2 Tbsp. soy sauce
1 Tbsp. cornstarch
1 Tbsp. cold water

1. Make slits in roast and insert slivers of garlic. Put under broiler to brown.

2. Put potatoes in slow cooker. Add half of onions. Place roast on onions and potatoes. Cover with remaining onions.

3. Combine broth and soy sauce. Pour over roast.

4. Cover. Cook on Low 8 hours. Remove roast and vegetables from liquid.

5. Combine cornstarch and water. Add to liquid in slow cooker. Turn to High until thickened. Serve over sliced meat and vegetables.

Chalupa

Jeannine Janzen/Elbing, KS

MAKES 12–16 SERVINGS

3-lb. pork roast
1 lb. dry pinto beans
2 garlic cloves, minced
1 Tbsp. ground cumin
1 Tbsp. dried oregano
2 Tbsp. chili powder
1 Tbsp. salt
4-oz. can chopped green chilies
water

1. Cover beans with water in cooker. Soak overnight.

2. In the morning, remove beans (reserve soaking water), and put roast in bottom of cooker. Add remaining ingredients (including the beans and their soaking water) and more water if needed to cover all the ingredients.

3. Cook on High 1 hour, and then on Low 6 hours. Remove meat and shred with two forks. Return meat to slow cooker.

4. Cook on High 1 more hour.

5. Serve over a bed of lettuce. Top with grated cheese and chopped onions and tomatoes.

Shredded Pork

Sharon Easter/Yuba City, CA

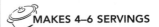MAKES 4–6 SERVINGS

2–3-lb. pork butt roast, or boneless country-style spareribs
1/2–1 cup water
1 pkg. dry taco seasoning mix

1. Place meat in slow cooker. Add water and seasoning mix.

2. Cover. Cook on Low 24 hours. Shred meat with two forks.

3. Use in tacos or in rolls, or use the sauce as gravy and serve over rice.

Autumn Harvest Pork Loin

Stacy Schmucker Stoltzfus
Enola, PA

MAKES 4–6 SERVINGS

1 cup cider or apple juice
1 1/2–2-lb. pork loin
salt
pepper
2 large Granny Smith apples, peeled and sliced
1 1/2 whole butternut squashes, peeled and cubed
1/2 cup brown sugar
1/4 tsp. cinnamon
1/4 tsp. dried thyme
1/4 tsp. dried sage

1. Heat cider in hot skillet. Sear pork loin on all sides in cider.

2. Sprinkle meat with salt and pepper on all sides. Place in cooker, with juices.

3. Combine apples and squash. Sprinkle with sugar and herbs. Stir. Place around pork loin.

4. Cover. Cook on Low 5–6 hours.

5. Remove pork from cooker. Let stand 10–15 minutes. Slice into 1/2"-thick slices.

6. Serve topped with apples and squash.

Pork Roast with Sauerkraut

Betty K. Drescher
Quakertown, PA

MAKES 8–10 SERVINGS

3–4-lb. pork roast
32-oz. bag sauerkraut
2 apples, peeled and sliced
1 medium onion, sliced thin
14 1/2-oz. can Italian tomatoes, drained and smashed

1. Place roast in slow cooker.

2. Add sauerkraut.

3. Layer apples and onion over roast.

4. Top with tomatoes.

5. Cover. Cook on Low 7–9 hours, or until meat is tender.

variation
● If you like a brothy dish, add 1 cup water along with sauerkraut in Step 2.

Flautas with Pork Filling

Donna Lantgen/Rapid City, SD

MAKES 6–8 SERVINGS

1 lb. pork roast or chops, cubed
1/4 cup chopped onions
4-oz. can diced green chilies
7-oz. can green chile salsa or chile salsa
1 tsp. cocoa powder
16-oz. can chili

1. Brown cubed pork in skillet. Drain. Place in slow cooker.

2. Add remaining ingredients except chili.

3. Cover. Cook on Low 2–3 hours.

4. Add chili. Cook 2–3 hours longer.

5. Serve on flour tortillas with guacamole dip.

note
● This is especially good on spinach-herb tortillas.

Barbecued Spareribs

Mrs. Paul Gray/Beatrice, NE

MAKES 4 SERVINGS

4-lb. country-style spareribs, cut into serving-size pieces
10 3/4-oz. can tomato soup
1/2 cup cider vinegar
1/2 cup brown sugar
1 Tbsp. soy sauce
1 tsp. celery seed
1 tsp. salt
1 tsp. chili powder
dash cayenne pepper

1. Place ribs in slow cooker.

2. Combine remaining ingredients and pour over ribs.

3. Cover. Cook on Low 6–8 hours.

4. Skim fat from juices before serving.

Tender and Tangy Ribs

Betty Moore/Plano, IL
Renee Shirk/Mount Joy, PA

MAKES 2–3 SERVINGS

3/4–1 cup vinegar
1/2 cup ketchup
2 Tbsp. sugar
2 Tbsp. Worcestershire sauce
1 garlic clove, minced
1 tsp. dry mustard
1 tsp. paprika
1/2 tsp. salt
1/8 tsp. pepper
2 lbs. pork spareribs
1 Tbsp. oil

1. Combine all ingredients except spareribs and oil in slow cooker.

2. Brown ribs in oil in skillet. Transfer to slow cooker.

3. Cover. Cook on Low 4–6 hours.

Michele's Barbecued Ribs

Michele Ruvola/Selden, NY

MAKES 8 SERVINGS

3 lbs. pork loin back ribs, cut into serving-size pieces
2 Tbsp. instant minced onion
1 tsp. crushed red pepper
1/2 tsp. ground cinnamon
1/2 tsp. garlic powder
1 medium onion, sliced
1/2 cup water
1 1/2 cups barbecue sauce

1. Combine onion, red pepper, cinnamon, and garlic powder. Rub mixture into ribs. Layer ribs and onion in slow cooker. Pour water around ribs.

2. Cover. Cook on Low 8–9 hours.

3. Remove ribs from slow cooker. Drain and discard liquid. Pour barbecue sauce in bowl and dip ribs in sauce. Return ribs to slow cooker. Pour remaining sauce over ribs.

4. Cover. Cook on Low 1 hour.

Sharon's Barbecued Ribs

Sharon Easter/Yuba City, CA

MAKES 4–6 SERVINGS

3–4-lb. boneless pork ribs, cut into serving-size pieces
1 cup barbecue sauce
1 cup Catalina salad dressing

1. Place ribs in slow cooker.

2. Combine barbecue sauce and salad dressing. Pour over ribs.

3. Cover. Cook on Low 8 hours.

variation
● Add 1 garlic clove sliced thin to top of sauce before cooking.

Just Peachy Ribs

Amymarlene Jensen
Fountain, CO

MAKES 4–6 SERVINGS

4-lb. boneless pork spareribs
1/2 cup brown sugar
1/4 cup ketchup
1/4 cup white vinegar
1 garlic clove, minced
1 tsp. salt
1 tsp. pepper
2 Tbsp. soy sauce
15-oz. can spiced cling peaches, cubed, with juice

1. Cut ribs in serving-size pieces and brown in broiler or in saucepan in oil. Drain. Place in slow cooker.

2. Combine remaining ingredients. Pour over ribs.

3. Cover. Cook on Low 8–10 hours.

Awfully Easy Barbecued Ribs

Sara Harter Fredette, Williamsburg, MA
Colleen Konetzni
Rio Rancho, NM
Mary Mitchell/Battle Creek, MI
Audrey Romonosky/Austin, TX
Iva Schmidt/Fergus Falls, MN
Susan Tjon/Austin, TX

MAKES 4–6 SERVINGS

3–4-lb. baby back, or country-style, spareribs
1/2 tsp. salt, optional
1/2 tsp. pepper, optional
2 onions, sliced
16–24-oz. bottle barbecue sauce (depending upon how saucy you like your chops)

1. Brown ribs under broiler. Slice into serving-size pieces, season, and place in slow cooker.

2. Add onions and barbecue sauce.

3. Cover. Cook on Low 6 hours. These are good served with baked beans and corn on the cob.

variation
● Instead of broiling the ribs, place them in slow cooker with other ingredients and cook on High 1 hour. Turn to Low and cook 8 more hours.

Tender 'N Tangy Ribs

Sherri Grindle/Goshen, IN

MAKES 2–3 SERVINGS

3/4–1 cup vinegar
1/2 cup ketchup
2 Tbsp. sugar
2 Tbsp. Worcestershire sauce
1 clove garlic, minced
1 tsp. ground mustard
1 tsp. paprika
1/2–1 tsp. salt
1/8 tsp. pepper
2 lbs. pork spareribs, or country-style ribs
1 Tbsp. oil

1. Combine first nine ingredients in slow cooker.

2. Cut ribs into serving-size pieces. Brown in oil in skillet. Transfer to slow cooker.

3. Cover. Cook on Low 4–6 hours.

4. Serve with baked potatoes and rice.

> I often use this recipe if I am having company for Sunday lunch.

— • —

Barbecued Pork

Grace Ketcham/Marietta, GA

Mary Seielstad/Sparks, NV

MAKES 6 SERVINGS

3 lbs. pork, cubed
2 cups chopped onions
3 green peppers, chopped
1/2 cup brown sugar
1/4 cup vinegar
6-oz. can tomato paste
1 1/2 Tbsp. chili powder
1 tsp. dry mustard
2 tsp. Worcestershire sauce
2 tsp. salt

1. Combine all ingredients in slow cooker.

2. Cover. Cook on High 8 hours.

3. Shred meat with fork. Mix into sauce and heat through.

4. Serve on hamburger buns with grated cheese and cole slaw on top.

variation
● Substitute cubed chuck roast or stewing beef for the pork, or use half beef, half pork.

Barbecued Pork in the Slow Cooker

Dawn Day/Westminster, CA

MAKES 6–8 SERVINGS

2–3-lb. boneless pork roast, cubed
2 onions, chopped
12-oz. bottle barbecue sauce
1/4 cup honey
sandwich rolls

1. Place meat in slow cooker. Add onions, barbecue sauce, and honey.

2. Cover. Cook on Low 6–8 hours.

3. Use 2 forks to shred meat.

4. Serve on rolls with sauce.

Pork Barbecue

Mary Sommerfeld
Lancaster, PA

MAKES 8–12 SANDWICHES

2 onions, sliced
4–5-lb. pork roast, or fresh
  picnic ham
5–6 whole cloves
2 cups water

Sauce:
1 large onion, chopped
16-oz. bottle barbecue
  sauce

1. Put half of sliced onions in bottom of slow cooker. Add meat, cloves, and water. Cover with remaining sliced onions.

2. Cover. Cook on Low 8–12 hours.

3. Remove bone from meat. Cut up meat. Drain liquid.

4. Return meat to slow cooker. Add chopped onion and barbecue sauce.

5. Cover. Cook on High 1–3 hours, or Low 4–8 hours, stirring two or three times.

6. Serve on buns.

note
● This freezes well.

Barbecue Sandwiches

Sherry L. Lapp/Lancaster, PA

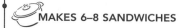

MAKES 6–8 SANDWICHES

1 1/2 lbs. cubed pork
1 lb. stewing beef, cubed
6-oz. can tomato paste
1/4 cup vinegar
1/2 cup brown sugar
1 tsp. salt
1 Tbsp. chili powder
1 large onion, chopped
1 green pepper, chopped

1. Combine ingredients in slow cooker.

2. Cover. Cook on Low 8 hours.

3. Shred meat with fork before serving on rolls.

4. Bring to the table with creamy cole slaw.

Pork Barbecue

Barbara L. McGinnis
Jupiter, FL

MAKES 6 SERVINGS

3–4-lb. pork loin
salt to taste
pepper to taste
2 cups cider vinegar
2 tsp. sugar
1/2 cup ketchup
crushed red pepper to taste
Tabasco sauce to taste
sandwich rolls

1. Sprinkle pork with salt and pepper. Place in cooker.

2. Pour vinegar over meat. Sprinkle sugar on top.

3. Cover. Cook on Low 8 hours.

4. Remove pork from cooker and shred meat.

5. In bowl mix together ketchup, red pepper, Tabasco sauce, and 1/2 cup vinegar-sugar drippings. Stir in shredded meat.

6. Serve on sandwich rolls with cole slaw.

variation
● To increase the tang, add 1 tsp. dry mustard in Step 5. Use 1/4 cup ketchup and 1/4 cup orange juice, instead of 1/2 cup ketchup.

Ham 'n Cola

Carol Peachey/Lancaster, PA

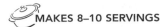MAKES 8–10 SERVINGS

1/2 cup brown sugar
1 tsp. dry mustard
1 tsp. prepared horseradish
1/4 cup cola-flavored soda
3–4-lb. precooked ham

1. Combine brown sugar, mustard, and horseradish. Moisten with just enough cola to make a smooth paste. Reserve remaining cola.

2. Rub entire ham with mixture. Place ham in slow cooker and add remaining cola.

3. Cover. Cook on Low 6–10 hours, or High 2–3 hours.

Ham and Scalloped Potatoes

Penny Blosser
Beavercreek, OH
Jo Haberkamp/Fairbank, IA
Ruth Hofstetter/Versailles, MO
Rachel Kauffman/Alto, MI
Mary E. Martin/Goshen, IN
Brenda Pope/Dundee, OH
Joyce Slaymaker/Strasburg, PA

MAKES 6–8 SERVINGS

6–8 slices ham
8–10 medium potatoes, thinly sliced
2 onions, thinly sliced
salt to taste
pepper to taste
1 cup grated cheddar, or American, cheese
10 3/4-oz. can cream of celery, or mushroom, soup
paprika

1. Put half of ham, potatoes, and onions in slow cooker. Sprinkle with salt, pepper, and cheese. Repeat layers.

2. Spoon soup over top. Sprinkle with paprika.

3. Cover. Cook on Low 8–10 hours, or High 4 hours.

Miriam's Scalloped Potatoes with Ham

Miriam Christophel
Battle Creek, MI

MAKES 6 SERVINGS

6 cups raw potatoes, cut into small cubes
1 medium onion, minced
1 tsp. salt
1/2 lb. cooked ham, cubed
4 Tbsp. butter
4 Tbsp. flour
1 tsp. salt
2 cups milk
1 1/2 cups shredded cheddar cheese

1. Layer potatoes, onion, 1 tsp. salt, and ham into slow cooker.

2. Melt butter in saucepan. Stir in flour and 1 tsp. salt. Cook until bubbly. Gradually add milk. Cook until smooth and thickened. Add cheese and stir until melted. Pour over potato-ham mixture, stirring lightly.

3. Cover. Cook on Low 6–7 hours, or High 3–4 hours.

Michelle's Scalloped Potatoes and Ham

Michelle Strite
Harrisonburg, VA

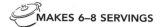

MAKES 6–8 SERVINGS

6 cups cooked, shredded potatoes
4 cups diced ham
dash pepper, if desired
10 3/4-oz. can cream of mushroom soup
10 3/4-oz. can cream of celery soup
1 cup milk

1. Combine all ingredients in slow cooker.

2. Cover. Cook on Low 3–4 hours.

Potatoes and Ham

Janice Martins/Fairbank, IA

MAKES 8 SERVING

5 potatoes, sliced
1/2 lb. ham, diced
1/4-lb. Velveeta cheese, cubed
half a small onion, diced
10 3/4-oz. can cream of chicken soup

1. Layer potatoes, ham, cheese, and onion in slow cooker. Top with soup.

2. Cover. Cook on Low 6 hours.

Barbara's Scalloped Potatoes with Ham

Barbara Katrine Rose
Woodbridge, VA

MAKES 10–12 SERVINGS

4-lb. potatoes, sliced
1 1/2 lbs. cooked ham, cut into 1/4-inch strips
3 Tbsp. minced dried onions
1 cup water
2 11-oz. cans condensed cheddar cheese soup

1. Layer potatoes, ham, and onions in very large slow cooker.

2. Combine soup and water. Pour over layers in pot.

3. Cover. Cook on Low 6–8 hours.

Country Scalloped Potatoes and Ham

Deb Unternahrer/Wayland, IA

MAKES 10 SERVINGS

8 potatoes, thinly sliced
1 onion, chopped
1 lb. fully-cooked ham, cubed
1-oz. pkg. dry country-style gravy mix
10 3/4-oz. can cream of mushroom soup
2 cups water
2 cups shredded cheddar cheese

1. Combine potatoes, onion, and ham in lightly greased slow cooker.

2. Combine gravy mix, mushroom soup, and water. Whisk until combined. Pour over potatoes.

3. Cover. Cook on Low 7–9 hours, or High 3–4 hours.

4. Top with cheese during last 30 minutes of cooking.

Au Gratin Potatoes and Ham

Donna Lantgen/Rapid City, SD

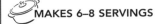MAKES 6–8 SERVINGS

10 potatoes, thinly sliced
1 onion, chopped
2 Tbsp. flour
1/4 tsp. pepper, optional
1/2 lb. Velveeta cheese, cubed
1/2 cup milk
1/2–1 cup fully cooked ham, or sliced hot dogs

1. Combine all ingredients in slow cooker.

2. Cover. Cook on Low 7–8 hours.

Ham and Potatoes

Ruth Shank/Gridley, IL

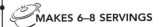MAKES 6–8 SERVINGS

6–8 medium red, or russet, potatoes, cut into chunks
2–3-lb. boneless ham
1/2 cup brown sugar
1 tsp. dry mustard

1. Prick potato pieces with fork. Place in slow cooker.

2. Place ham on top of potatoes. Crumble brown sugar over ham. Sprinkle with dry mustard.

3. Cover. Cook on Low 10 or more hours, until potatoes are tender.

4. Pour juices over ham and potatoes to serve.

Ham, Bean, and Potato Dish

Hazel L. Propst/Oxford, PA

MAKES 6–8 SERVINGS

8–10 small potatoes
3–4 cans string beans, undrained
ham hock, or leftover ham
salt to taste
pepper to taste

1. Place potatoes in bottom of slow cooker.

2. Alternate layers of beans and ham over potatoes. Sprinkle with salt and pepper.

3. Cover. Cook on Low 8 hours if using ham hock; 6 hours if using leftover ham.

Cheesy Potatoes and Ham

Beth Maurer/Harrisonburg, VA

MAKES 4–6 SERVINGS

6 cups sliced, peeled potatoes
2 1/2 cups cooked ham, cubed
1 1/2 cups shredded cheddar cheese
10 3/4-oz. can cream of mushroom soup
1/2 cup milk

1. In slow cooker, layer one-third of potatoes, of ham, and of cheese. Repeat two more times.

2. Combine soup and milk. Pour over ingredients in slow cooker.

3. Cover. Cook on High 1 hour. Reduce to Low for 6–8 hours, or just until potatoes are soft.

Ham and Lima Beans

Charlotte Shaffer
East Earl, PA

MAKES 6 SERVINGS

1 lb. dry lima beans
1 onion, chopped
1 bell pepper, chopped
1 tsp. dry mustard
1 tsp. salt
1 tsp. pepper
1/2 lb. ham, finely cubed
1 cup water
10 3/4-oz. can tomato soup

1. Cover beans with water. Soak 8 hours. Drain.

2. Combine ingredients in slow cooker.

3. Cover. Cook on Low 7 hours or High 4 hours.

4. If mixture begins to dry out, add 1/2 cup water or more and stir well.

5. This is delicious served with hot cornbread.

Ham and Hash Browns

Evelyn Page/Riverton, WY
Anna Stoltzfus
Honey Brook, PA

MAKES 6–8 SERVINGS

28-oz. pkg. frozen hash
  brown potatoes
2 1/2 cups cubed cooked
  ham
2-oz. jar pimentos, drained
  and chopped
10 3/4-oz. can cheddar
  cheese soup
3/4 cup half-and-half, or
  milk
dash of pepper
salt to taste

1. Combine potatoes, ham,
and pimentos in slow cooker.

2. Combine soup, half-and-
half, and seasonings. Pour
over potatoes.

3. Cover. Cook on Low
6–8 hours. (If you turn
the cooker on when you
go to bed, you'll have a
wonderfully tasty breakfast
in the morning.)

variation
●Add a 4-oz. can of
mushrooms, drained,
or 1/4 lb. sliced fresh
mushrooms, to Step 1.

Ham 'n Cabbage Stew

Dede Peterson/Rapid City, SD

MAKES 4–5 SERVINGS

1/2 lb. cooked ham, cubed
1/2 cup diced onions
1 garlic clove, minced
4-oz. can sliced mushrooms
4 cups shredded cabbage
2 cups sliced carrots
1/4 tsp. pepper
1/4 tsp. caraway seeds
2/3 cup beef broth
1 Tbsp. cornstarch
2 Tbsp. water

1. Combine all ingredients
except cornstarch and water
in slow cooker.

2. Cover. Cook on Low 4–6
hours.

3. Mix cornstarch into
water until smooth. Stir into
slow cooker during last hour
to thicken slightly.

Cheesy Ham and Broccoli

Dolores Kratz/Souderton, PA

MAKES 6 SERVINGS

1 bunch fresh broccoli
1 1/2 cups chopped ham
3/4 cup uncooked rice
4-oz. can mushrooms,
  drained
1 small onion, chopped
10 3/4-oz. can cheddar
  cheese soup
3/4 cup water
1/4 cup half-and-half, or
  milk
dash of pepper
1/2–1 can chow mein
  noodles

1. Cut broccoli into pieces
and steam for 4 minutes in
microwave. Place in slow
cooker.

2. Add remaining ingredients
except noodles. Mix well.

3. Sprinkle with noodles.

4. Cover. Cook on Low
6–7 hours.

5. Serve with tossed salad
or applesauce.

Broccoli Casserole

Rebecca Meyerkorth
Wamego, KS

**MAKES 4 SERVINGS**

16-oz. pkg. frozen broccoli cuts, thawed and drained
2–3 cups cubed, cooked ham
10 3/4-oz. can cream of mushroom soup
4 ozs. of your favorite mild cheese, cubed
1 cup milk
1 cup instant rice, uncooked
1 rib celery, chopped
1 small onion, chopped

1. Combine broccoli and ham in slow cooker.

2. Combine soup, cheese, milk, rice, celery, and onion. Stir into broccoli.

3. Cover. Cook on Low 4–5 hours.

Casserole in the Cooker

Ruth Ann Hoover
New Holland, PA

**MAKES 4 SERVINGS**

16-oz. pkg. frozen broccoli, thawed and drained
3 cups cubed fully cooked ham
10 3/4-oz. can cream of mushroom soup
8-oz. jar processed cheese sauce
1 cup milk
1 cup instant rice
1 celery rib, chopped
1 small onion, chopped

1. Combine broccoli and ham in slow cooker.

2. Combine remaining ingredients. Stir into broccoli/ham mixture.

3. Cover. Cook on Low 4–5 hours.

Ham and Broccoli

Dede Peterson/Rapid City, SD

**MAKES 6–8 SERVINGS**

3/4 lb. fresh broccoli, chopped, or 10-oz. pkg. frozen chopped broccoli
10 3/4-oz. can cream of mushroom soup
8-oz. jar processed cheese sauce
2 1/2 cups milk
1 1/4 cups long-grain rice, uncooked
1 rib celery, sliced
1/8 tsp. pepper
3 cups cooked and cubed ham
8-oz. can water chestnuts, drained and sliced
1/2 tsp. paprika

1. Combine all ingredients except ham, water chestnuts, and paprika in slow cooker.

2. Cover. Cook on High 3–4 hours.

3. Stir in ham and water chestnuts. Cook 15–20 minutes, until heated through. Let stand 10 minutes before serving.

4. Sprinkle with paprika before serving.

Ham with Sweet Potatoes and Oranges

Esther Becker/Gordonville, PA

MAKES 4 SERVINGS

2–3 sweet potatoes, peeled and sliced 1/4 inch thick
1 large ham slice
3 seedless oranges, peeled and sliced
3 Tbsp. orange juice concentrate
3 Tbsp. honey
1/2 cup brown sugar
2 Tbsp. cornstarch

1. Place sweet potatoes in slow cooker.

2. Arrange ham and orange slices on top.

3. Combine remaining ingredients. Drizzle over ham and oranges.

4. Cover. Cook on Low 7–8 hours.

5. Delicious served with lime jello salad.

Southwest Hominy

Reita F. Yoder/Carlsbad, NM

MAKES 12–14 SERVINGS

4 20-oz. cans hominy, drained
10 3/4-oz. can cream of mushroom soup
10 3/4-oz. can cream of chicken soup
1 cup diced green chilies
1/2 lb. Velveeta cheese, cubed
1 lb. hot dogs or ham, diced

1. Combine all ingredients in slow cooker.

2. Cover. Cook on Low 2–4 hours. Stir before serving.

Verenike Casserole

Jennifer Yoder Sommers
Harrisonburg, VA

MAKES 8–10 SERVINGS

24 ozs. cottage cheese
3 eggs
1 tsp. salt
1/2 tsp. pepper
1 cup sour cream
2 cups evaporated milk
2 cups cubed cooked ham
7–9 dry lasagna noodles

1. Combine all ingredients except noodles.

2. Place half of creamy ham mixture in bottom of cooker. Add uncooked noodles.

Cover with remaining half of creamy ham sauce. Be sure noodles are fully submerged in sauce.

3. Cover. Cook on Low 5–6 hours.

4. Serve with green salad, peas, and zwiebach or bread.

This is an easy way to make the traditional Russian Mennonite dish— verenike, or cheese pockets. Its great taste makes up for its appearance!

— • —

Pork and Kraut

Joyce B. Suiter/Garysburg, NC

MAKES 6 SERVINGS

4-lb. pork loin
29-oz. can sauerkraut
1/4 cup water
1 onion, sliced
1 large white potato, sliced
10 3/4-oz. can cheddar
   cheese soup
1 Tbsp. caraway seeds
1 large Granny Smith apple,
   peeled and sliced
salt to taste
pepper to taste

1. Brown roast on all sides in skillet. Place in slow cooker.

2. Rinse sauerkraut and drain well. Combine sauerkraut, water, onion, potato, soup, caraway seeds, and apple. Pour over roast.

3. Cover. Cook on Low 10 hours.

4. Season with salt and pepper before serving.

note
● Apple and potato disappear into the cheese soup as they cook, making a good sauce.

Pork Roast with Sauerkraut

Gail Bush/Landenberg, PA

MAKES 8 SERVINGS

2 3-lb. pork shoulder roasts
1 large can sweet Bavarian
   sauerkraut with caraway
   seeds
1/4 cup brown sugar
1 envelope dry onion soup
   mix
1/2 cup water

1. Place roasts in slow cooker.

2. Rinse and drain sauerkraut. Combine sauerkraut, brown sugar, and onion soup mix. Layer over roasts. Pour water over all.

3. Cover. Cook on Low 7 hours.

note
● If you can't find Bavarian sauerkraut with caraway seeds, substitute with a 27-oz. can regular sauerkraut and 1/2 tsp. caraway seeds.

Pork and Sauerkraut

Carole Whaling
New Tripoli, PA

MAKES 6 SERVINGS

4 large potatoes, cubed
32-oz. bag sauerkraut,
   drained
1 large onion, chopped
1 large tart apple, chopped
2 Tbsp. packed brown sugar
1 tsp. caraway seeds
1 tsp. minced garlic
1/2 tsp. pepper
2 1/2-lb. boneless pork
   loin roast

1. Put potatoes in slow cooker.

2. Combine remaining ingredients, except pork, in slow cooker. Place half of the sauerkraut mixture on top of the potatoes. Add roast. Top with remaining sauerkraut mixture.

3. Cover. Cook on High 3–4 hours.

Sauerkraut and Ribs

Margaret H. Moffitt
Bartlett, TN

 MAKES 6 SERVINGS

27–oz. can sauerkraut with juice
1 small onion, chopped
2 lbs. pork, or beef, ribs, cut into serving-size pieces
1 tsp. salt
1/4 tsp. pepper
half a sauerkraut can of water

1. Pour sauerkraut and juice into slow cooker. Add onion.

2. Season ribs with salt and pepper. Place on top of sauerkraut. Add water.

3. Cover. Cook on High until mixture boils. Reduce heat to Low and cook 4 hours.

4. Serve with mashed potatoes.

Country Ribs and Sauerkraut

Andrea O'Neil/Fairfield, CT

 MAKES 4–6 SERVINGS

2 27-oz. cans sauerkraut, drained and rinsed
2–3 lbs. country-style pork ribs, cut into serving-size pieces
6 slices bacon, browned
3–4 Tbsp. caraway seeds
2 cups water

1. Place alternating layers of sauerkraut and ribs in slow cooker, starting and ending with sauerkraut.

2. Crumble bacon and mix gently into top layer of sauerkraut. Sprinkle with caraway seeds. Pour water over all.

3. Cover. Cook on Low 7–8 hours.

Pork Spareribs with Sauerkraut

Char Hagner/Montague, MI

MAKES 4–6 SERVINGS

2 small cooking apples, sliced in rings
1 1/2–2 lbs. spareribs, cut into serving-size pieces and browned
1 qt. sauerkraut
1/2 cup apple cider, or juice
1/2 tsp. caraway seeds, optional

1. Layer apples, ribs, and sauerkraut into slow cooker. Pour on juice. Sprinkle with caraway seeds.

2. Cover. Cook on Low 8 hours, or High 4 hours.

Pork Rib and Kraut Dinner

Betty A. Holt/St. Charles, MO

MAKES 6–8 SERVINGS

3–4 lbs. country-style ribs
4 Tbsp. brown rice
1 Tbsp. caraway seeds
28-oz. can sauerkraut, rinsed
12-oz. can V-8 juice

1. Place ingredients in slow cooker in order listed.

2. Cover. Cook on Low 6–8 hours, or High 3–4 hours.

variation

● To take the edge off the sour flavor of sauerkraut, stir in 3 Tbsp. mild molasses or honey before cooking.

Ham Hock and Sauerkraut

Bernice M. Gnidovec
Streator, IL

MAKES 2 SERVINGS

2 small ham hocks, or pork chops
14-oz. can sauerkraut, rinsed
1 large potato, cubed
1 Tbsp. butter
half a small onion, diced
1 Tbsp. flour
2 Tbsp. cold water

1. Place ham hocks or chops in slow cooker. Top with sauerkraut. Add enough water to cover meat and sauerkraut.

2. Cover. Cook on High 4 hours, or Low 6–8 hours.

3. Sauté onions in butter in saucepan until transparent. Stir in flour and brown. Add 2 Tbsp. cold water, stirring until thickened. Pour over ingredients in slow cooker. Cover and cook on High 5–10 minutes.

No Fuss Sauerkraut

Vera M. Kuhns
Harrisonburg, VA

MAKES 12 SERVINGS

3-lb. pork roast
3 2-lb. pkgs. sauerkraut (drain off juice from 1 pkg.)
2 apples, peeled and sliced
1/2 cup brown sugar
1 cup apple juice

1. Place meat in large slow cooker.

2. Place sauerkraut on top of meat.

3. Add apples and brown sugar. Add juice.

4. Cover. Cook on High 4–5 hours.

5. Serve with mashed potatoes.

note

● If your slow cooker isn't large enough to hold all the ingredients, cook one package of sauerkraut and half the apples, brown sugar, and apple juice in another cooker. Mix the ingredients of both cookers together before serving.

Sausage

Perfection Hot Dogs

Audrey L. Kneer
Williamsfield, IL

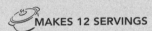MAKES 12 SERVINGS

12 hot dogs, bratwurst,
or Polish sausage links

1. Place hot dogs or
sausages in slow cooker.

2. Cover. Cook on High
1–2 hours.

Sauerkraut and Kielbasa

Mary Ellen Wilcox/Scotia, NY

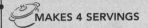MAKES 4–6 SERVINGS

64-oz. can sauerkraut
1 medium onion, chopped
1 large bay leaf
1 lb. kielbasa, cut into
serving-sized pieces

1. Combine all ingredients
in slow cooker. Add enough
water to cover all ingredients.

2. Cover. Cook on High
30 minutes, and then on
Low 6 hours. Remove bay
leaf before serving.

Kraut and Sausage

Kathi Rogge/Alexandria, IN

MAKES 4 SERVINGS

2 16-oz. cans sauerkraut,
drained and rinsed
2 Tbsp. dark brown sugar
1 large onion, chopped
2 strips bacon, diced
1 lb. fully-cooked sausage,
sliced

1. Combine sauerkraut and
brown sugar. Place in slow
cooker. Add layers of onion,
bacon, and sausage. Add
enough water to cover half
of sausage.

2. Cover. Cook on Low 5–6
hours, or on High 3 hours.

Cabbage Dinner

Kathi Rogge/Alexandria, IN

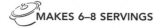MAKES 6–8 SERVINGS

medium head of cabbage
6–8 medium-sized potatoes
2 lbs. smoked sausage, or
    turkey sausage
salt to taste
1 qt. water

1. Cut cabbage into 1–2
inch-wide wedges. Place in
slow cooker.

2. Wash and quarter
potatoes. Do not peel. Add
to cabbage in slow cooker.

3. Cut sausage into bite-size
pieces. Add to slow cooker.
Add salt and mix well.

4. Pour water into slow
cooker.

5. Cover. Cook on High
2 hours, and then on Low
6–8 hours, or until vegetables
are tender.

Green Beans and Sausage

Alma Weaver/Ephrata, PA

MAKES 4–6 SERVINGS

1 qt. green beans, cut into
    2-inch pieces
1 carrot, chopped
1 small green pepper,
    chopped
8-oz. can tomato sauce
1/4 tsp. dried thyme
1/2 tsp. salt
1 lb. bulk pork sausage,
    or link sausage cut into
    1-inch pieces

1. Combine all ingredients
except sausage in slow
cooker.

2. Cover. Cook on High 3–4
hours. Add sausage and cook
another 2 hours on Low.

Sausage Supreme

Jan Moore/Wellsville, KS

MAKES 4 SERVINGS

1 lb. fresh sausage, cut into
    1-inch pieces and browned
2 10 3/4-oz. cans cream of
    mushroom soup
1 onion, chopped
4 potatoes, cubed

1. Combine all ingredients
in slow cooker.

2. Cover. Cook on Low
8 hours. If mixture becomes
too dry, stir in half a soup
can or more of water.

variation
● Substitute 1 can cheese
soup for 1 can cream of
mushroom soup.

Sausage and Apples

Evelyn L. Ward / Greeley, CO

MAKES 4 SERVINGS

20-oz. can apple pie filling
1/4 cup water
ground nutmeg
10-oz. pkg. fully cooked and
  browned sausage patties

1. Spoon pie filling into slow cooker. Stir in water. Sprinkle with nutmeg. Top with sausage.

2. Cover. Cook on Low 4–6 hours.

Barbecued Sausage Pieces

Elizabeth Yutzy / Wauseon, OH

MAKES 4–5 MAIN-DISH SERVINGS, OR 8–10 SNACK-SIZED SERVINGS

1 lb. smoked sausage
1 cup hickory-flavored
  barbecue sauce
1/4 cup honey
2 Tbsp. brown sugar

1. Cut sausage in 1/2-inch pieces. Brown in skillet. Place in slow cooker.

2. Combine remaining ingredients. Pour over sausage.

3. Cover. Cook on Low 2 hours.

4. Serve over rice or noodles as a main dish or with toothpicks as a party snack.

Beer Brats

Mary Ann Wasick
West Allis, WI

MAKES 6 SERVINGS

6 fresh bratwurst
2 garlic cloves, minced
2 Tbsp. olive oil
12-oz. can beer

1. Brown sausages and garlic in olive oil in skillet. Pierce sausage casings and cook 5 more minutes. Transfer to slow cooker.

2. Pour beer into cooker to cover sausages.

3. Cover. Cook on Low 6–7 hours.

Italian Sausage

Lauren Eberhard Seneca, IL

**MAKES 15 SERVINGS**

5 lbs. Italian sausage
  in casing
4 large green peppers sliced
3 large onions, sliced
1 or 2 garlic cloves, minced
28-oz. can tomato puree
14-oz. can tomato sauce
12-oz. can tomato paste
1 Tbsp. dried oregano
1 Tbsp. dried basil
1/2 tsp. garlic powder
1 1/2 tsp. salt
2 tsp. sugar

1. Cut sausage into 4" or 5" pieces and brown on all sides in batches in skillet.

2. Saute peppers, onions, and garlic in drippings.

3. Combine tomato puree, sauce, and paste in bowl. Add seasonings and sugar.

4. Layer half of sausage, onions, and peppers in 6-qt cooker or in 2 4-qt. cookers. Cover with half the tomato mixture. Repeat layers.

5. Cover. Cook on high 1 hour and low 5–6 hours.

6. Serve over pasta, or dip mixture with a straining spoon onto Italian rolls.

Dawn's Sausage and Peppers

Dawn Day/Westminster, CA

**MAKES 8–10 SERVINGS**

3 medium onions, sliced
1 sweet red pepper, sliced
1 sweet green pepper,
  sliced
1 sweet yellow pepper,
  sliced
4 garlic cloves, minced
1 Tbsp. oil
28 oz.-can chopped
  tomatoes
1 tsp. salt
1/2 tsp. red crushed pepper
2–3 lbs. sweet Italian
  sausage, cut into 3-inch
  pieces

1. Sauté onions, peppers, and garlic in oil in skillet. When just softened, place in slow cooker.

2. Add tomatoes, salt, and crushed red pepper. Mix well.

3. Add sausage links.

4. Cover. Cook on Low 6 hours.

5. Serve on rolls, or over pasta or baked potatoes.

variation

● For a thicker sauce, stir in 3 Tbsp. ClearJell during the last 15 minutes of the cooking time.

Savory Sausage Sandwiches

Mary Jane Musser
Manheim, PA

**MAKES 8 SERVINGS**

2 lbs. fresh sausage, cut
  into bun-length pieces
2 pkgs. dry spaghetti sauce
  mix
12-oz. can tomato paste
3 cups water
1/2 cup brown sugar
1/4 cup vinegar
8 Italian, or hot dog, rolls
grated cheese

1. Cook sausage in skillet in water for 10 minutes. Drain. Place in slow cooker.

2. Combine remaining ingredients. Simmer 5 minutes in saucepan. Pour over sausage.

3. Cover. Cook on High 3 hours or Low 6 hours.

4. Serve in rolls topped with grated cheese.

variation

● Use 1 qt. spaghetti sauce, either homemade or bought, instead of sauce mix, tomato paste, and water.

Sausage-Potato Slow Cooker Dinner

Deborah Swartz/Grottoes, VA

MAKES 6–8 SERVINGS

1 cup water
1/2 tsp. cream of tartar
6 medium potatoes, thinly sliced
3/4 lb. sausage, casings removed and browned
1 onion, chopped
1/4 cup flour
salt to taste
pepper to taste
1 1/2 cups grated cheddar cheese, divided
2 Tbsp. butter or margarine
10 3/4-oz. can cream of mushroom soup

1. Combine water and cream of tartar. Toss sliced potatoes in water. Drain.

2. Layer potatoes, sausage, onion, flour, a sprinkling of salt and pepper, and half of cheddar cheese in slow cooker. Repeat layers until ingredients are used.

3. Dot butter over top. Pour soup over all.

4. Cover. Cook on Low 7–9 hours or on High 3–4 hours.

5. Sprinkle reserved cheese over top just before serving.

Sausage and Scalloped Potatoes

Carolyn Baer/Conrath, WI

MAKES 5 SERVINGS

2 1/2 lbs. potatoes, sliced 1/4 inch thick
1 lb. fully cooked smoked sausage links, sliced 1/2 inch thick
2 medium onions, chopped
10 3/4-oz. can cheddar cheese soup
10 3/4-oz. can cream of celery soup

1. Layer one-third of potatoes, one-third of sausage, one-third of onions, one-third of cheddar cheese soup, and one-third of celery soup into slow cooker. Repeat 2 times.

2. Cover. Cook on Low 10 hours or High 5 hours.

I like to prepare this delicious dish when I will be gone for the day, but know I will have guests for the evening meal. When I get home, the meat and potatoes are already cooked. I simply have to heat the peas, fix a salad, and slice the dessert.

— • —

Sausage and Sweet Potatoes

Ruth Hershey/Paradise, PA

MAKES 4–6 SERVINGS

1 lb. bulk sausage, browned in skillet
2 sweet potatoes, peeled and sliced
3 apples, peeled and sliced
2 Tbsp. brown sugar
1 Tbsp. flour
1/4 tsp. ground cinnamon
1/4 tsp. salt
1/4 cup water

1. Layer sausage, sweet potatoes, and apples in slow cooker.

2. Combine remaining ingredients and pour over ingredients in slow cooker.

3. Cover. Cook on Low 8–10 hours or High 4 hours.

Spiced Hot Dogs

Tracey Yohn/Harrisburg, PA

 **MAKES 3–4 SERVINGS**

1 lb. hot dogs, cut in pieces
2 Tbsp. brown sugar
3 Tbsp. vinegar
1/2 cup ketchup
2 tsp. prepared mustard
1/2 cup water
1/2 cup chopped onions

1. Place hot dogs in slow cooker.

2. Combine all ingredients except hot dogs in saucepan. Simmer. Pour over hot dogs.

3. Cover. Cook on Low 2 hours.

Barbecued Hot Dogs

Jeanette Oberholtzer
Manheim, PA

 **MAKES 8 SERVINGS**

1 cup apricot preserves
4 oz. tomato sauce
1/3 cup vinegar
2 Tbsp. soy sauce
2 Tbsp. honey
1 Tbsp. oil
1 tsp. salt
1/4 tsp. ground ginger
2 lbs. hot dogs, cut into
    1-inch pieces

1. Combine all ingredients except hot dogs in slow cooker.

2. Cover. Cook on High 30 minutes. Add hot dog pieces. Cook on Low 4 hours.

3. Serve over rice as a main dish, or as an appetizer.

Bits and Bites

Betty Richards/Rapid City, SD

 **MAKES 12 SERVINGS**

12-oz. can beer
1 cup ketchup
1 cup light brown sugar
1/2–1 cup barbecue sauce
1 lb. all-beef hot dogs,
    sliced 1 1/2 inches thick
2 lbs. cocktail sausages

1. Combine beer, ketchup, brown sugar, and barbecue sauce. Pour into slow cooker.

2. Add hot dogs and sausages. Mix well.

3. Cover. Cook on Low 3–4 hours.

Bandito Chili Dogs

Sue Graber/Eureka, IL

MAKES 10 SERVINGS

1 lb. hot dogs
2 15-oz. cans chili, with or without beans
10 3/4-oz. can condensed cheddar cheese soup
4-oz. can chopped green chilies
10 hot dog buns
1 medium onion, chopped
1-2 cups corn chips, coarsely crushed
1 cup shredded cheddar cheese

1. Place hot dogs in slow cooker.

2. Combine chili, soup, and green chilies. Pour over hot dogs.

3. Cover. Cook on Low 3–3 1/2 hours.

4. Serve hot dogs in buns. Top with chili mixture, onion, corn chips, and cheese.

This is a fun recipe for after a football game or outside activity. The main part of your meal is ready when you get home.

— • —

Zesty Wieners

Lisa F. Good
Harrisonburg, VA

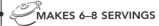MAKES 6–8 SERVINGS

1 dozen hot dogs
1/2 cup chopped onions
1 tsp. butter
1 tsp. pepper
2 Tbsp. sugar
2 tsp. prepared mustard
1 cup ketchup
3 Tbsp. Worcestershire sauce

1. Place hot dogs in slow cooker.

2. Sauté onions in butter in skillet until almost tender.

3. Add remaining ingredients. Pour over hot dogs in slow cooker.

4. Cover. Cook on Low 4 hours.

Harvest Kielbasa

Christ Kaczynski
Schenectady, NY

MAKES 6 SERVINGS

2 lbs. smoked kielbasa
3 cups unsweetened applesauce
1/2 cup brown sugar
3 medium onions, sliced

1. Slice kielbasa into 1/4" slices. Brown in skillet. Drain.

2. Combine applesauce and brown sugar.

3. Layer kielbasa, onions, and applesauce mixture in slow cooker.

4. Cover. Cook on Low 4–8 hours.

The longer it cooks, the better the flavor.

— • —

Sauerkraut & Trail Bologna

Carol Sommers
Millersburg, OH

MAKES 10 SERVINGS

32-oz. bag sauerkraut, rinsed
1/4–1/2 cup brown sugar
1 ring Trail Bologna

1. Combine sauerkraut and brown sugar in slow cooker.

2. Remove casing from bologna and cut into 1/4-inch slices. Add to sauerkraut. Stir.

3. Cover. Cook on Low 6–8 hours.

note
● If you don't have access to Holmes County, Ohio's specialty Trail Bologna, use 1 large ring bologna.

Polish Kraut 'n Apples

Lori Berezovsky/Salina, KS
Marie Morucci/Glen Lyon, PA

MAKES 4 SERVINGS

1 lb. fresh, or canned, sauerkraut
1 lb. lean smoked Polish sausage
3 tart cooking apples, thinly sliced
1/2 cup packed brown sugar
3/4 tsp. salt
1/8 tsp. pepper
1/2 tsp. caraway seeds, optional
3/4 cup apple juice, or cider

1. Rinse sauerkraut and squeeze dry. Place half in slow cooker.

2. Cut sausage into 2-inch lengths and add to cooker.

3. Continue to layer remaining ingredients in slow cooker in order given. Top with remaining sauerkraut. Do not stir.

4. Cover. Cook on High 3–3 1/2 hours, or Low 6–7 hours. Stir before serving.

Keilbasa Stew

Fannie Miller/Hutchinson, KS

MAKES 6–8 SERVINGS

6 strips of bacon
1 onion, chopped
1–1 1/2 lbs. smoked, fully cooked kielbasa, thinly sliced
2 15 1/2-oz. cans Great Northern beans
2 8-oz. cans tomato sauce
4-oz. can chopped green chilies
2 medium carrots, thinly sliced
1 medium green pepper, chopped
1/2 tsp. Italian seasoning
1/2 tsp. dried thyme
1/2 tsp. black pepper

1. Fry bacon in skillet until crisp. Crumble bacon and place in large slow cooker. Add onions and sausage to drippings in skillet. Cook until onions are soft.

2. Transfer onions and sausage to slow cooker.

3. Add all remaining ingredients to cooker and stir together well.

4. Cover. Cook on Low 8–10 hours, or until vegetables are tender.

Old World Sauerkraut Supper

Josie Bollman/Maumee, OH
Joyce Bowman/Lady Lake, FL
Vera Schmucker/Goshen, IN

 **MAKES 8 SERVINGS**

3 strips bacon, cut into
   small pieces
2 Tbsp. flour
2 15-oz. cans sauerkraut
2 small potatoes, cubed
2 small apples, cubed
3 Tbsp. brown sugar
1 1/2 tsp. caraway seeds
3 lbs. Polish sausage, cut
   into 3-inch pieces
1/2 cup water

1. Fry bacon until crisp.
Drain, reserving drippings.

2. Add flour to bacon
drippings. Blend well. Stir
in sauerkraut and bacon.
Transfer to slow cooker.

3. Add remaining
ingredients.

4. Cover. Cook on Low 6–8
hours, or High 3–4 hours.

Polish Sausage Stew

Jeanne Heyerly/Chenoa, IL
Joyce Kaut/Rochester, NY
Joyce B. Suiter/Garysburg, NC

 **MAKES 6–8 SERVINGS**

10 3/4-oz. can cream of
   celery soup
1/3 cup packed brown
   sugar
27-oz. can sauerkraut,
   drained
1 1/2 lbs. Polish sausage,
   cut into 2-inch pieces
   and browned
4 medium potatoes, cubed
1 cup chopped onions
1 cup (4 oz.) shredded
   Monterey Jack cheese

1. Combine soup, sugar, and
sauerkraut. Stir in sausage,
potatoes, and onions.

2. Cover. Cook on Low
8 hours, or on High 4 hours.

3. Stir in cheese and serve.

Sausage Sauerkraut Supper

Ruth Ann Hoover,
New Holland, PA

Robin Schrock,
Millersburg, OH

 **MAKES 10–12 SERVINGS**

4 cups cubed carrots
4 cups cubed red potatoes
2 14-oz. cans sauerkraut,
   rinsed and drained
2 1/2 lbs. fresh Polish
   sausage, cut into 3-inch
   pieces
1 medium onion, thinly
   sliced
3 garlic cloves, minced
1 1/2 cups dry white wine,
   or chicken broth
1/2 tsp. pepper
1 tsp. caraway seeds

1. Layer carrots, potatoes,
and sauerkraut in cooker.

2. Brown sausage in skillet.
Transfer to slow cooker.
Reserve 1 Tbsp. drippings
in skillet.

3. Sauté onion and garlic
in drippings until tender.
Stir in wine. Bring to boil.
Stir to loosen brown bits.
Stir in pepper and caraway
seeds. Pour over sausage.

4. Cover. Cook on Low
8–9 hours.

Aunt Lavina's Sauerkraut

Pat Unternahrer/Wayland, IA

 **MAKES 8–12 SERVINGS**

2–3 lbs. smoked sausage, cut into 1-inch pieces
2 Tbsp. water, or oil
2 bell peppers, chopped
2 onions, sliced
1/2 lb. fresh mushrooms, sliced
1 qt. sauerkraut, drained
2 14 1/2-oz. cans diced tomatoes with green peppers
1 tsp. salt
1/2 tsp. pepper
2 Tbsp. brown sugar

1. Place sausage in slow cooker. Heat on Low while you prepare other ingredients.

2. Sauté peppers, onions, and mushrooms in small amount of water or oil in saucepan.

3. Combine all ingredients in slow cooker.

4. Cover. Cook on Low 5–6 hours, or High 3–4 hours.

5. Serve with mashed potatoes.

Brats and Spuds

Kathi Rogge/Alexandria, IN

 **MAKES 6 SERVINGS**

5–6 bratwurst links, cut into 1-inch pieces
5 medium-sized potatoes, peeled and cubed
27-oz. can sauerkraut, rinsed and drained
1 medium tart apple, chopped
1 small onion, chopped
1/4 cup packed brown sugar
1/2 tsp. salt

1. Brown bratwurst on all sides in skillet.

2. Combine remaining ingredients in slow cooker. Stir in bratwurst and pan drippings.

3. Cover. Cook on High 4–6 hours, or until potatoes and apples are tender.

variation
● Add a small amount of caraway seeds or crisp bacon pieces, just before serving.

Sausage and Sauerkraut

Eileen Lehman/Kidron, OH

 MAKES 12 SERVINGS

2–3 lbs. fresh sausage, cut in 3-inch lengths, or removed from casings
3 32-oz. cans sauerkraut

1. Brown sausage in skillet.

2. Combine sausage and sauerkraut in slow cooker.

3. Cover. Cook on Low 4–8 hours.

4. Serve with mashed potatoes, a jello salad, and pumpkin pie.

It is traditional to serve sauerkraut on New Year's Day in Kidron.

— • —

Chicken

Chicken-at-the-Ready

Mary Mitchell/Battle Creek, MI

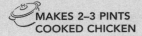 **MAKES 2–3 PINTS COOKED CHICKEN**

1 large whole chicken, skinned
1 cup water

1. Place chicken in greased slow cooker. Add water.

2. Cover. Cook on Low 6–8 hours.

3. Remove meat from bones, pack cooked meat into plastic boxes, and store in freezer to use in recipes that call for cooked chicken.

note
● I frequently put this on late at night so that it is done when I wake up in the morning.

Lemon Honey Chicken

Carolyn W. Carmichael
Berkeley Heights, NJ

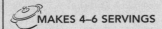 **MAKES 4–6 SERVINGS**

1 lemon
1 whole roasting chicken, rinsed
1/2 cup orange juice
1/2 cup honey

1. Pierce lemon with fork. Place in chicken cavity. Place chicken in slow cooker.

2. Combine orange juice and honey. Pour over chicken.

3. Cover. Cook on Low 8 hours. Remove lemon and squeeze over chicken.

4. Carve chicken and serve.

Valerie's & Stacy's Roast Chicken

Valerie Hertzler
Weyers Cave, VA

Stacy Petersheim
Mechanicsburg, PA

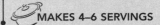 **MAKES 4–6 SERVINGS**

3–4-lb. chicken
salt to taste
pepper to taste
butter
basil to taste

1. Wash chicken thoroughly. Pat dry. Sprinkle cavity with salt and pepper. Place in slow cooker. Dot with butter. Sprinkle with basil.

2. Cover. Cook on High 1 hour, and then on Low 8–10 hours.

...**supereasy**

Hot Chicken Sandwiches

Glenna Fay Bergey
Lebanon, OR

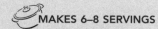 MAKES 6–8 SERVINGS

1 large chicken
1 cup water

1. Place chicken in slow cooker. Add water.

2. Cover. Cook on Low 6–7 hours.

3. Debone chicken. Mix cut-up chicken with broth.

4. Spoon into dinner rolls with straining spoon to make small hot sandwiches. Top with your favorite condiments.

note

● This is also a great way to prepare a chicken for soups or casseroles. Save the broth if you're making soup.

Super Easy Chicken

Mary Seielstad/Sparks, NV

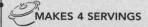 MAKES 4 SERVINGS

4 frozen chicken-breast halves
1 pkg. dry Italian dressing mix
1 cup warm water, or chicken stock

1. Place chicken in slow cooker. Sprinkle with dressing mix. Pour water over chicken.

2. Cover. Cook on Low 8–10 hours.

Sloppy Chicken

Marjora Miller/Archbold, OH

MAKES 4–6 SERVINGS

28-oz. can boneless chicken
10 3/4-oz. can cream of chicken soup
1 stack butter crackers, crushed
15-oz. can chicken broth
10 3/4-oz. can cream of mushroom soup

1. Combine all ingredients in slow cooker.

2. Cover. Cook on Low 5–6 hours, stirring occasionally.

Awfully Easy Chicken

Martha Hershey/Ronks, PA

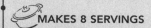 MAKES 8 SERVINGS

1/2 cup water
4 lbs. chicken legs and thighs
14-oz. bottle barbecue sauce

1. Place water in bottom of slow cooker. Add chicken. Pour barbecue sauce over top.

2. Cover. Cook on Low 8 hours.

note

● Serve any additional sauce over mashed potatoes.

Judy Denney
Lawrenceville, GA

variation

● Place 3 large onions, quartered or sliced, in bottom of slow cooker. Then add chicken and sauce.

Barbara J. Fabel/Wausau, WI

Saucy Apricot Chicken

Anna Stoltzfus
Honey Brook, PA

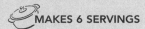MAKES 6 SERVINGS

6 boneless, skinless chicken breast halves
2 12-oz. jars apricot preserves
1 pkg. dry onion soup mix

1. Place chicken in slow cooker.

2. Combine preserves and onion soup mix in separate bowl. Spoon over chicken.

3. Cover. Cook on Low 4–5 hours.

4. Serve over rice.

Chicken in Wine

Mary Seielstad/Sparks, NV

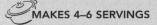MAKES 4–6 SERVINGS

2–3 lbs. chicken breasts, or pieces
10 3/4-oz. can cream of mushroom soup
10 3/4-oz. can French onion soup
1 cup dry white wine, or chicken broth

1. Put chicken in slow cooker.

2. Combine soups and wine. Pour over chicken.

3. Cover. Cook on Low 6–8 hours.

4. Serve over rice, pasta, or potatoes.

Easy Teriyaki Chicken

Barbara Shie
Colorado Springs, CO

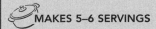MAKES 5–6 SERVINGS

2–3 lbs. skinless chicken pieces
20-oz. can pineapple chunks
dash of ground ginger
1 cup teriyaki sauce

1. Place chicken in slow cooker. Pour remaining ingredients over chicken.

2. Cover. Cook on Low 6–8 hours, or High 4–6 hours.

...supereasy

Blue Ribbon Cranberry Chicken

Marjorie Y. Guengerich
Harrisonburg, VA

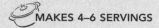 MAKES 4–6 SERVINGS

2 1/2–3-lb. chicken, cut up
16-oz. can whole cranberry
  sauce
8-oz. bottle Russian salad
  dressing
1 pkg. dry onion soup mix

1. Rinse chicken. Pat dry with paper towel. Place in slow cooker.

2. Combine cranberry sauce, salad dressing, and soup mix. Pour over chicken.

3. Cover and chill 1–8 hours, or overnight.

4. Cover. Cook on High 4 hours or on Low 6–8 hours.

5. Serve over rice or noodles.

Donna's Cooked Chicken

Donna Treloar/Gaston, IN

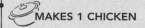 MAKES 1 CHICKEN

chicken (boneless, skinless
  breasts are the easiest,
  but any chicken pieces
  will do)
1 onion, sliced
seasoned salt
pepper
minced garlic, or garlic
  powder

1. Layer onion in bottom of slow cooker. Add chicken and with seasoned salt, pepper, minced garlic, or garlic powder.

2. Cook on Low 4 hours or until done but not dry. (Time will vary according to amount of chicken and size of pieces.)

3. Use in stir-frys, chicken salads, or casseroles, slice for sandwiches, shred for enchiladas, or cut up and freeze for later use.

variation
● Splash chicken with 2 Tbsp. soy sauce before cooking.

Scalloped Chicken

Carolyn W. Carmichael
Berkeley Heights, NJ

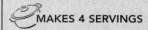 MAKES 4 SERVINGS

5-oz. pkg. scalloped
  potatoes
scalloped potatoes dry
  seasoning pack
4 chicken-breast halves,
  or 8 legs
10-oz. pkg. frozen peas
2 cups water

1. Put potatoes, seasoning pack, chicken, and peas in slow cooker. Pour water over all.

2. Cover. Cook on Low 8–10 hours, or High 4 hours.

Easy Chicken

Ruth Liebelt/Rapid City, SD

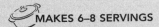 **MAKES 6–8 SERVINGS**

8–10 chicken wings or legs
    and thighs
1/2 cup soy sauce
1/2 cup sugar
1/2 tsp. Tabasco sauce
pinch of ground ginger

1. Place chicken in greased slow cooker.

2. Combine remaining ingredients and pour over chicken.

3. Cover. Cook on Low 8 hours.

4. Serve with cooked rice, rolls, and salad.

Chicken in a Hurry

Yvonne Boettger
Harrisonburg, VA

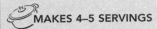 **MAKES 4–5 SERVINGS**

2 1/2–3 lbs. skinless chicken
    drumsticks
1/2 cup ketchup
1/4 cup water
1/4 cup brown sugar
1 pkg. dry onion soup mix

1. Arrange chicken in slow cooker.

2. Combine remaining ingredients. Pour over chicken.

3. Cover. Cook on High 4–5 hours or Low 7–8 hours.

Creamy Chicken Breasts

Judy Buller/Bluffton, OH

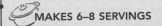 **MAKES 6–8 SERVINGS**

6–8 chicken breast halves
salt to taste
pepper to taste
paprika to taste
10 3/4-oz. can cream of
    mushroom soup
1/2 cup sour cream

1. Season chicken breasts with salt, pepper, and paprika. Place in slow cooker.

2. Combine mushroom soup and sour cream. Pour over chicken.

3. Cover. Cook on Low 6 hours.

4. Serve with rice, noodles, or mashed potatoes.

Baked Chicken Breasts

Janice Crist/Quinter, KS
Tracy Supcoe/Barclay, MD

 MAKES 4–6 SERVINGS

2–3 whole chicken breasts, halved
2 Tbsp. butter, or margarine
10 3/4-oz. can cream of chicken soup
1/2 cup dry sherry
1 tsp. dried tarragon, or rosemary, or both
1 tsp. Worcestershire sauce
1/4 tsp. garlic powder
4-oz. can sliced mushrooms, drained

1. Place chicken breasts in slow cooker.

2. In saucepan, combine remaining ingredients. Heat until smooth and hot. Pour over chicken.

3. Cover. Cook on Low 8–10 hours.

Chicken Delicious

Janice Crist/Quinter, KS

 MAKES 8–12 SERVINGS

4–6 whole skinless chicken breasts, boned and halved
lemon juice
salt to taste
pepper to taste
celery salt to taste
paprika to taste
10 3/4-oz. can cream of mushroom soup
10 3/4-oz. can cream of celery soup
1/3 cup dry sherry, or white wine
grated Parmesan cheese

1. Season chicken with lemon juice, salt, pepper, celery salt, and paprika. Place in slow cooker.

2. Combine soups with sherry. Pour over chicken. Sprinkle with cheese.

3. Cover. Cook on Low 8–10 hours.

4. Serve with rice.

Chicken in Mushroom Gravy

Rosemarie Fitzgerald
Gibsonia, PA

Audrey L. Kneer
Williamsfield, IL

MAKES 6 SERVINGS

6 boneless, skinless chicken-breast halves
salt to taste
pepper to taste
1/4 cup dry white wine, or chicken broth
10 3/4-oz. can cream of mushroom soup
4-oz. can sliced mushrooms, drained

1. Place chicken in slow cooker. Season with salt and pepper.

2. Combine wine and soup. Pour over chicken. Top with mushrooms.

3. Cover. Cook on Low 7–9 hours.

Creamy Cooker Chicken

Violette Harris Denney
Carrollton, GA

MAKES 6 SERVINGS

1 envelope dry onion soup mix
2 cups sour cream
10 3/4-oz. can cream of mushroom soup
6 boneless, skinless chicken-breast halves

1. Combine soup mix, sour cream, and cream of mushroom soup in slow cooker. Add chicken, pushing it down so it is submerged in the sauce.

2. Cover. Cook on Low 8 hours.

3. Serve over rice or noodles.

Ruth's Slow-Cooker Chicken

Sara Harter Fredette
Williamsburg, MA

MAKES 6 SERVINGS

6 boneless chicken-breast halves
10 3/4-oz. can cream of mushroom soup
1 pkg. dry mushroom soup mix
1/4–1/2 cup sour cream
4-oz. can mushrooms, drained

1. Combine chicken and soups in slow cooker.

2. Cover. Cook on Low 6–8 hours.

3. Just before serving, stir in sour cream and mushrooms. Reheat briefly.

4. Serve on noodles.

note
● Leftover sauce makes a flavorful topping for grilled hamburgers.

Mushroom Chicken

Brenda Pope/Dundee, OH

MAKES 4 SERVINGS

1 lb. boneless, skinless chicken breast
1 pkg. dry chicken gravy mix
10 3/4-oz. can cream of mushroom, or chicken, soup
1 cup white wine
8-oz. pkg. cream cheese, softened

1. Put chicken in slow cooker. Sprinkle gravy mix on top. In separate bowl, combine soup and wine and pour over gravy mix.

2. Cover. Cook on Low 8 hours.

3. During last 30 minutes of cooking time, stir in cream cheese. Before serving, remove chicken (keeping it warm) and whisk the sauce until smooth.

4. Serve chicken and sauce over noodles or rice.

Creamy Mushroom Chicken

Patricia Howard
Albuquerque, NM

 MAKES 4–5 SERVINGS

2–3 lbs. chicken parts, skinned
4-oz. can mushrooms
2 10 3/4-oz. cans cream of chicken soup
1 envelope dry onion soup mix
1/2–1 cup chicken broth

1. Place chicken in slow cooker.

2. Combine remaining ingredients and pour over chicken.

3. Cover. Cook on Low 5–6 hours.

So You Forgot to Defrost!

Mary Seielstad/Sparks, NV

 MAKES 6 SERVINGS

6 boneless, skinless frozen chicken-breast halves
2 10 3/4-oz. cans cream of chicken soup
4-oz. can sliced mushrooms, or 1/2 cup sliced fresh mushrooms
3/4 tsp. salt
1/4 tsp. pepper

1. Place frozen chicken in slow cooker.

2. Mix together soup, mushrooms, salt, and pepper and pour over chicken.

3. Cover. Cook on Low 10–12 hours.

4. Serve over rice.

Continental Chicken

Jennifer J. Gehman
Harrisburg, PA

Gladys M. High
Ephrata, PA

L. Jean Moore/Pendleton, IN

 MAKES 4–6 SERVINGS

2 1/4-oz. pkg. dried beef
3–4 whole chicken breasts, halved, skinned, and boned
6–8 slices bacon
10 3/4-oz. can cream of mushroom soup, undiluted
1/4 cup sour cream
1/4 cup flour

1. Arrange dried beef in bottom of slow cooker.

2. Wrap each piece of chicken with a strip of bacon. Place on top of dried beef.

3. Combine soup, sour cream, and flour. Pour over chicken.

4. Cover. Cook on Low 7–9 hours, or High 3–4 hours.

5. Serve over hot buttered noodles.

Creamy Chicken Italiano

Sharon Easter/Yuba City, CA
Rebecca Meyerkorth
Wamego, KS
Bonnie Miller/Cochranville, PA

MAKES 4 SERVINGS

4 boneless, skinless chicken-breast halves
1 envelope dry Italian salad dressing mix
1/4 cup water
8-oz. pkg. cream cheese, softened
10 3/4-oz. can cream of chicken soup
4-oz. can mushroom stems and pieces, drained

1. Place chicken in slow cooker.

2. Combine salad dressing mix and water. Pour over chicken.

3. Cover. Cook on Low 3 hours.

4. Combine cheese and soup until blended. Stir in mushrooms. Pour over chicken.

5. Cover. Cook on Low 1 hour, or until chicken juices run clear.

6. Serve over noodles or rice.

Creamy Mushroom Chicken

Barbara Shie
Colorado Springs, CO

MAKES 4–6 SERVINGS

4–6 boneless, skinless chicken-breast halves
12-oz. jar mushroom gravy
1 cup milk
8-oz. pkg. cream cheese, cubed
4 1/2-oz. can chopped green chilies
1 pkg. dry Italian salad dressing

1. Combine all ingredients in slow cooker.

2. Cover. Cook on Low 6 hours.

3. Serve over noodles or rice.

Darla's Chicken Cacciatore

Darla Sathre/Baxter, MN

MAKES 6 SERVINGS

2 onions, thinly sliced
4 boneless chicken breasts, cubed
3 garlic cloves, minced
1/4 tsp. pepper
2 tsp. dried oregano
1 tsp. dried basil
1 bay leaf
2 15-oz. cans diced tomatoes
8-oz. can tomato sauce
4-oz. can sliced mushrooms

1. Place onions in bottom of slow cooker. Add remaining ingredients.

2. Cover. Cook on Low 8 hours.

3. Serve over hot spaghetti.

Dale & Shari's Chicken Cacciatore

Dale and Shari Mast
Harrisonburg, VA

 MAKES 4 SERVINGS

4 chicken quarters, or
  4 boneless, skinless
  chicken-breast halves
15-oz. can tomato, or
  spaghetti, sauce
4-oz. can sliced mushrooms,
  drained
1/2 cup water
1 tsp. dry chicken broth
  granules
1/2 tsp. Italian seasoning

1. Place chicken in slow cooker. Pour on sauce, mushrooms, and water. Sprinkle with granules and seasoning.

2. Cover. Cook on High 3–4 hours, or Low 6–8 hours.

3. Serve over rice.

Easy Chicken A la King

Jenny R. Unternahrer
Wayland, IA

 MAKES 4 SERVINGS

1 1/2 lbs. boneless, skinless
  chicken breasts
10 3/4-oz. can cream of
  chicken soup
3 Tbsp. flour
1/4 tsp. pepper
9-oz. pkg. frozen peas and
  onions, thawed and
  drained
2 Tbsp. chopped pimentos
1/2 tsp. paprika

1. Cut chicken into bite-size pieces and place in slow cooker.

2. Combine soup, flour, and pepper. Pour over chicken. Do not stir.

3. Cover. Cook on High 2 1/2 hours, or Low 5–5 1/2 hours.

4. Stir in peas and onions, pimentos, and paprika.

5. Cover. Cook on High 20–30 minutes.

variation
● Add 1/4–1/2 cup chopped green peppers to Step 2.
Sharon Brubaker
Myerstown, PA

Lemon Garlic Chicken

Cindy Krestynick
Glen Lyon, PA

 MAKES 4 SERVINGS

1 tsp. dried oregano
1/2 tsp. seasoned salt
1/4 tsp. pepper
2 lbs. chicken-breast halves,
  skinned and rinsed
2 Tbsp. butter, or margarine
1/4 cup water
3 Tbsp. lemon juice
2 garlic cloves, minced
1 tsp. chicken bouillon
  granules
1 tsp. minced fresh parsley

1. Combine oregano, salt, and pepper. Rub all of mixture into chicken. Brown chicken in butter or margarine in skillet. Transfer to slow cooker.

2. Place water, lemon juice, garlic, and bouillon cubes in skillet. Bring to boil, loosening browned bits from skillet. Pour over chicken.

3. Cover. Cook on High 2–2 1/2 hours, or Low 4–5 hours.

4. Add parsley and baste chicken. Cover. Cook on High 15–30 minutes, until chicken is tender.

Chicken Reuben Bake

Gail Bush/Landenberg, PA

MAKES 4 SERVINGS

4 boneless, skinless chicken-breast halves

2-lb. bag sauerkraut, drained and rinsed

4–5 slices Swiss cheese

1 1/4 cups Thousand Island salad dressing

2 Tbsp. chopped fresh parsley

1. Place chicken in slow cooker. Layer sauerkraut over chicken. Add cheese. Top with salad dressing. Sprinkle with parsley.

2. Cover. Cook on Low 6–8 hours.

Garlic Lime Chicken

Loretta Krahn
Mountain Lake, MN

MAKES 5 SERVINGS

5 chicken breast halves

1/2 cup soy sauce

1/4–1/3 cup lime juice, according to your taste preference

1 Tbsp. Worcestershire sauce

2 garlic cloves, minced, or 1 tsp. garlic powder

1/2 tsp. dry mustard

1/2 tsp. ground pepper

1. Place chicken in slow cooker.

2. Combine remaining ingredients and pour over chicken.

3. Cover. Cook on High 4–6 hours or on Low 6–8 hours.

Herbed Chicken

LaVerne A. Olson/Lititz, PA

MAKES 8 SERVING

4 whole chicken breasts, halved

10 3/4-oz. can cream of mushroom or chicken soup

1/4 cup soy sauce

1/4 cup oil

1/4 cup wine vinegar

3/4 cup water

1/2 tsp. minced garlic

1 tsp. ground ginger

1/2 tsp. dried oregano

1 Tbsp. brown sugar

1. Place chicken in slow cooker.

2. Combine remaining ingredients. Pour over chicken.

3. Cover. Cook on Low 2–2 1/2 hours. Uncover and cook 15 minutes more. Serve with rice.

A favorite with the whole family, even grandchildren. The gravy is delicious.

— • —

Teriyaki Chicken

Colleen Konetzni
Rio Rancho, NM

MAKES 6 SERVINGS

6–8 skinless chicken thighs
1/2 cup soy sauce
2 Tbsp. brown sugar
2 Tbsp. grated fresh ginger
2 garlic cloves, minced

1. Wash and dry chicken. Place in slow cooker.

2. Combine remaining ingredients. Pour over chicken.

3. Cover. Cook on High 1 hour. Reduce heat to Low and cook 6–7 hours.

4. Serve over rice with a fresh salad.

Scrumptious Chicken

Kathi Rogge/Alexandria, IN

MAKES 8 SERVINGS

8 skinned chicken breast halves
10 3/4-oz. can cream of mushroom, or cream of chicken, soup
16 ozs. sour cream
1 pkg. dry onion soup mix
fresh basil or oregano, chopped

1. Place chicken in slow cooker.

2. Combine all remaining ingredients except fresh herbs. Pour over chicken.

3. Cover. Cook on Low 6 hours. (If convenient for you, stir after 3 hours of cooking.)

4. Sprinkle with fresh herbs just before serving.

5. Serve with brown and wild rice, mixed, or couscous.

Miriam's Chicken

Arlene Leaman Kliewer
Lakewood, CO

MAKES 6 SERVINGS

4 chicken breast halves, cut up into 1-inch chunks
8-oz. pkg. cream cheese, cubed
2 10 3/4-oz. cans cream soup (your favorite—or a combination of your favorites)
6 croissants
paprika
fresh parsley, minced

1. Place chicken in slow cooker.

2. Combine cream cheese and soups. Pour over chicken. Stir.

3. Cover. Cook on Low 8 hours.

4. Serve over croissants split in half. Sprinkle with paprika and parsley.

Elegant Chicken with Gravy

Leesa Lesenski
South Deerfield, MA

 MAKES 6 SERVING

6 boneless chicken breast halves
10 3/4-oz. can cream of broccoli, or broccoli cheese, soup
10 3/4-oz. can cream of chicken soup
1/2 cup white wine
4-oz. can sliced mushrooms, undrained, optional

1. Place chicken breasts in slow cooker.

2. In bowl mix together soups, wine, and mushroom slices. Pour over chicken.

3. Cover. Cook on High 3 hours or on Low 6 hours, or until chicken is tender but not dry.

4. Serve over rice or noodles.

Savory Chicken

Shari Mast/Harrisonburg, VA

 MAKES 8–10 SERVINGS

4 boneless, skinless chicken breast halves
4 skinless chicken quarters
10 3/4-oz. can cream of chicken soup
1 Tbsp. water
1/4 cup chopped sweet red peppers
1 Tbsp. chopped fresh parsley, or 1 tsp. dried parsley
1 Tbsp. lemon juice
1/2 tsp. paprika

1. Layer chicken in slow cooker.

2. Combine remaining ingredients and pour over chicken.

3. Cover. Cook on High 4–5 hours.

Savory Chicken, Meal #2

Shari Mast/Harrisonburg, VA

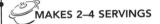 MAKES 2–4 SERVINGS

leftover chicken and broth from first Savory Chicken Meal
2 carrots
1 rib celery
2 medium-sized onions
2 Tbsp. flour or cornstarch
1/4 cup cold water

1. For a second Savory Chicken Meal, pick leftover chicken off bone. Set aside.

2. Return remaining broth to slow cooker and stir in thinly sliced carrots and celery and onions cut up in chunks. Cook 3–4 hours on High.

3. In separate bowl, mix flour or cornstarch with cold water. When smooth, stir into hot broth.

4. Stir in cut-up chicken. Heat 15–20 minutes, or until broth thickens and chicken is hot.

5. Serve over rice or pasta.

Gourmet Chicken Breasts

Sharon Swartz Lambert
Dayton, VA

Deborah Santiago
Lancaster, PA

MAKES 4–6 SERVINGS

6–8 slices dried beef

4–6 boneless, skinless chicken breast halves

2–3 slices bacon, cut in half lengthwise

10 3/4-oz. cream of mushroom soup

8-oz. carton sour cream

1/2 cup flour

1. Line bottom of slow cooker with dried beef.

2. Roll up each chicken breast half and wrap with a half-slice of bacon. Place in slow cooker.

3. Combine remaining ingredients in bowl. Pour over breasts.

4. Cover. Cook on Low 6–8 hours.

5. Serve with cooked noodles, rice, or mashed potatoes.

Creamy Nutmeg Chicken

Amber Swarey/Donalds, SC

MAKES 6 SERVINGS

6 boneless chicken breast halves

oil

1/4 cup chopped onions

1/4 cup minced parsley

2 10 3/4-oz. cans cream of mushroom soup

1/2 cup sour cream

1/2 cup milk

1 Tbsp. ground nutmeg

1/4 tsp. sage

1/4 tsp. dried thyme

1/4 tsp. crushed rosemary

1. Brown chicken in skillet in oil. Reserve drippings and place chicken in slow cooker.

2. Saute onions and parsley in drippings until onions are tender.

3. Stir in remaining ingredients. Mix well. Pour over chicken.

4. Cover. Cook on Low 3 hours, or until juices run clear.

5. Serve over mashed or fried potatoes, or rice.

Slow Cooker Creamy Chicken Italian

Sherri Grindle/Goshen, IN

MAKES 6 SERVINGS

8 boneless, skinless chicken breast halves

1 pkg. dry Italian salad dressing mix

1/4 cup water

8-oz. pkg. cream cheese, softened

10 3/4-oz. can cream of chicken soup

4-oz. can mushrooms, drained

1. Place chicken in greased slow cooker.

2. Combine salad dressing and water. Pour over chicken.

3. Cover. Cook on Low 4–5 hours.

4. In saucepan, combine cream cheese and soup. Heat slightly to melt cream cheese. Stir in mushrooms. Pour over chicken.

5. Cover. Cook 1 additional hour on Low.

6. Serve over noodles or rice.

variation
● Add frozen vegetables along with the mushrooms.

Chicken in a Pot

Carolyn Baer/Conrath, WI
Evie Hershey/Atglen, PA
Judy Koczo/Plano, IL
Mary Puskar/Forest Hill, MD
Mary Wheatley/Mashpee, MA

MAKES 6 SERVINGS

2 carrots, sliced
2 onions, sliced
2 celery ribs, cut in 1-inch
   pieces
3 lb. chicken, whole or
   cut up
2 tsp. salt
1/2 tsp. dried coarse black
   pepper
1 tsp. dried basil
1/2 cup water, chicken
   broth, or white cooking
   wine

1. Place vegetables in bottom of slow cooker. Place chicken on top. Add seasonings and water.

2. Cover. Cook on Low 8–10 hours, or High 3 1/2–5 hours (use 1 cup liquid if cooking on High).

3. This is a great foundation for soups—chicken vegetable, chicken noodle…

note
● To make this a full meal, add 2 medium-sized potatoes, quartered, to vegetables before cooking.

Savory Slow-Cooker Chicken

Sara Harter Fredette
Williamsburg, MA

MAKES 4 SERVINGS

2 1/2 lbs. chicken pieces,
   skinned
1 lb. fresh tomatoes,
   chopped, or 15-oz. can
   stewed tomatoes
2 Tbsp. white wine
1 bay leaf
1/4 tsp. pepper
2 garlic cloves, minced
1 onion, chopped
1/2 cup chicken broth
1 tsp. dried thyme
1 1/2 tsp. salt
2 cups broccoli, cut into
   bite-size pieces

1. Combine all ingredients except broccoli in slow cooker.

2. Cover. Cook on Low 8–10 hours.

3. Add broccoli 30 minutes before serving.

Another Chicken in a Pot

Jennifer J. Gehman
Harrisburg, PA

MAKES 4–6 SERVINGS

1-lb. bag baby carrots
1 small onion, diced
14 1/2-oz. can green beans
3-lb. whole chicken, cut into
   serving-size pieces
2 tsp. salt
1/2 tsp. black pepper
1/2 cup chicken broth
1/4 cup white wine
1/2–1 tsp. dried basil

1. Put carrots, onion, and beans on bottom of slow cooker. Add chicken. Top with salt, pepper, broth, and wine. Sprinkle with basil.

2. Cover. Cook on Low 8–10 hours, or High 3 1/2–5 hours.

Chicken and Vegetables

Rosanne Hankins
Stevensville, MD

MAKES 6 SERVINGS

1 chicken, cut up
salt to taste
pepper to taste
1 bay leaf
2 tsp. lemon juice
1/4 cup diced onions
1/4 cup diced celery
1 lb. frozen mixed
vegetables

1. Sprinkle salt and pepper over chicken and place chicken in slow cooker. Add bay leaf and lemon juice.

2. Cover. Cook on Low 6–8 hours, or High 3–5 hours. Remove chicken from bones. Reserve liquid, skimming fat if desired.

3. Cook 1/2 cup liquid, celery and onions in microwave on High for 2 minutes. Add frozen vegetables and microwave until cooked through.

4. Return all ingredients to slow cooker and cook on High 30 minutes.

5. Serve over cooked rice.

Chicken-Vegetable Dish

Cheri Jantzen/Houston, TX

MAKES 4 SERVINGS

4 skinless chicken-breast
halves, with bone in
15-oz. can crushed
tomatoes
10-oz. pkg. frozen green
beans
2 cups water, or chicken
broth
1 cup brown rice, uncooked
1 cup sliced mushrooms
2 carrots, chopped
1 onion, chopped
1/2 tsp. minced garlic
1/2 tsp. herb-blend
seasoning
1/4 tsp. dried tarragon

1. Combine all ingredients in slow cooker.

2. Cover. Cook on High 2 hours, and then on Low 3–5 hours.

Chicken and Vegetables

Jeanne Heyerly/Chenoa, IL

MAKES 2 SERVINGS

2 medium potatoes,
quartered
2–3 carrots, sliced
2 frozen chicken breasts, or
2 frozen drumstick/thigh
pieces
salt to taste
pepper to taste
1 medium onion, chopped
2 garlic cloves, minced
1–2 cups shredded cabbage
16-oz. can chicken broth

1. Place potatoes and carrots in slow cooker. Layer chicken on top. Sprinkle with salt, pepper, onion, and garlic. Top with cabbage. Carefully pour chicken broth around edges.

2. Cover. Cook on Low 8–9 hours.

African Chicken Treat

Anne Townsend
Albuquerque, NM

MAKES 4 SERVINGS

1 1/2 cups water
2 tsp. chicken bouillon granules
2 ribs celery, thinly sliced
2 onions, thinly sliced
1 red bell pepper, sliced
1 green bell pepper, sliced
8 chicken thighs, skinned
1/2 cup extra crunchy peanut butter
crushed chili pepper of your choice

1. Combine water, chicken bouillon granules, celery, onions, and peppers in slow cooker.

2. Spread peanut butter over both sides of chicken pieces. Sprinkle with chili pepper. Place on top of ingredients in slow cooker.

3. Cover. Cook on Low 5–6 hours.

Chicken Kapaman

Judy Govotsus/Monrovia, MD

MAKES 4–6 SERVINGS

4–6 potatoes, quartered
4–6 carrots, sliced
2–3-lbs. chicken pieces
2 onions, chopped
1 whole garlic bulb, minced
2 Tbsp. tomato paste
1 1/2 cups water
1 cinnamon stick
1/2 tsp. salt
1/4 tsp. pepper

1. Layer potatoes and carrots in slow cooker. Add chicken.

2. In separate bowl, mix remaining ingredients together and pour over vegetables and chicken in cooker.

3. Cover. Cook on High 4 hours. Remove lid and cook on Low an additional 1–1 1/2 hours.

Greek Chicken

Judy Govotsus/Monrovia, MD

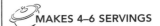MAKES 4–6 SERVINGS

4–6 potatoes, quartered
2–3 lbs. chicken pieces
2 large onions, quartered
1 whole bulb garlic, minced
3 tsp. dried oregano
1 tsp. salt
1/2 tsp. pepper
1 Tbsp. olive oil

1. Place potatoes in bottom of slow cooker. Add chicken, onions, and garlic. Sprinkle with seasonings. Top with oil.

2. Cover. Cook on High 5–6 hours, or on Low 9–10 hours.

Old-Fashioned Stewed Chicken

Bonnie Goering
Bridgewater, VA

MAKES 6–8 SERVINGS

3–4-lb. chicken, cut up
1 small onion, cut into wedges
1 rib celery, sliced
1 carrot, sliced
1 Tbsp. chopped fresh parsley (1 tsp. dried)
1 Tbsp. chopped fresh thyme (1 tsp. dried)
1 Tbsp. chopped fresh rosemary (1 tsp. dried)
3 tsp. salt
1/4 tsp. pepper
3–4 cups hot water

1. Place chicken in slow cooker. Add remaining ingredients.

2. Cover. Cook on Low 8 hours.

3. Use broth as a base to make gravy. Debone chicken and set aside. Thicken broth with flour-water paste. When bubbly and thickened, stir chicken pieces into gravy.

4. Serve with mashed potatoes or noodles and creamed peas.

Janie's Chicken a La King

Lafaye M. Musser/Denver, PA

MAKES 4 SERVINGS

10 3/4-oz. can cream of chicken soup
3 Tbsp. flour
1/2 tsp. salt
1/4 tsp. pepper
dash cayenne pepper
1 lb. boneless chicken, uncooked and cut in pieces
1 rib celery, chopped
1/2 cup chopped green pepper
1/4 cup chopped onions
9-oz. bag frozen peas, thawed

1. Combine soup, flour, salt, pepper, and cayenne pepper in slow cooker.

2. Stir in chicken, celery, green pepper, and onion.

3. Cover. Cook on Low 7–8 hours.

4. Stir in peas.

5. Cover. Cook 30 minutes longer.

6. Serve in pastry cups or over rice, waffles, or toast.

Creamy Chicken and Vegetables

Dawn M. Propst
Levittown, PA

MAKES 4 SERVINGS

10 3/4-oz. can cream of mushroom soup, divided
4 boneless, skinless chicken breast halves
16-oz. pkg. frozen vegetable medley (broccoli, cauliflower, and carrots), thawed and drained
1/2 tsp. salt
1/8–1/4 tsp. pepper
1 cup shredded cheddar cheese, divided

1. Pour small amount of soup in bottom of slow cooker.

2. Add chicken breasts, vegetables, and seasonings.

3. Mix in 1/2 cup cheddar cheese. Cover with remaining soup.

4. Cover. Cook on Low 5–6 hours, or until vegetables are cooked and chicken is no longer pink.

5. Sprinkle with remaining cheese 10–15 minutes before serving.

Szechwan-Style Chicken and Broccoli

Jane Meiser/Harrisonburg, VA

MAKES 4 SERVINGS

2 whole boneless, skinless
  chicken or turkey breasts
oil
1/2 cup picante sauce
2 Tbsp. soy sauce
1/2 tsp. sugar
1/2 Tbsp. quick-cooking
  tapioca
1 medium onion, chopped
2 garlic cloves, minced
1/2 tsp. ground ginger
2 cups broccoli florets
1 medium red pepper, cut
  into pieces

1. Cut chicken into 1"
cubes and brown lightly in
oil in skillet. Place in slow
cooker.

2. Stir in remaining
ingredients.

3. Cover. Cook on High
1–1 1/2 hours or on Low
2–3 hours.

Chicken Gumbo

Virginia Bender/Dover, DE

MAKES 6–8 SERVINGS

1 large onion, chopped
3–4 garlic cloves, minced
1 green pepper, diced
2 cups okra, sliced
2 cups tomatoes, chopped
4 cups chicken broth
1 lb. chicken breast, cut into
  1-inch pieces
2 tsp. Old Bay Seasoning

1. Combine all ingredients
in slow cooker.

2. Cover. Cook on Low 8–10
hours or High 3–4 hours.

3. Serve over rice.

California Chicken

Shirley Sears/Tiskilwa, IL

MAKES 4–6 SERVINGS

3-lb. chicken, quartered
1 cup orange juice
1/3 cup chili sauce
2 Tbsp. soy sauce
1 Tbsp. molasses
1 tsp. dry mustard
1 tsp. garlic salt
2 Tbsp. chopped green
  peppers
3 medium oranges, peeled
  and separated into slices,
  or 13 1/2-oz. can
  mandarin oranges

1. Arrange chicken in slow
cooker.

2. In separate bowl,
combine juice, chili sauce,
soy sauce, molasses, dry
mustard, and garlic salt.
Pour over chicken.

3. Cover. Cook on Low 8–9
hours.

4. Stir in green peppers and
oranges. Heat 30 minutes
longer.

variation
● Stir 1 tsp. curry powder in
with sauces and seasonings.
Stir 1 small can pineapple
chunks and juice in with green
peppers and oranges.

Cranberry Chicken

Teena Wagner / Waterloo, ON

MAKES 6–8 SERVINGS

3–4-lb. chicken pieces
1/2 tsp. salt
1/4 tsp. pepper
1/2 cup diced celery
1/2 cup diced onions
16-oz. can whole berry cranberry sauce
1 cup barbecue sauce

1. Combine all ingredients in slow cooker.

2. Cover. Bake on High for 4 hours, or on Low 6–8 hours.

Chicken with Tropical Barbecue Sauce

Lois Stoltzfus
Honey Brook, PA

MAKES 6 SERVINGS

1/4 cup molasses
2 Tbsp. cider vinegar
2 Tbsp. Worcestershire sauce
2 tsp. prepared mustard
1/8–1/4 tsp. hot pepper sauce
2 Tbsp. orange juice
3 whole chicken breasts, halved

1. Combine molasses, vinegar, Worcestershire sauce, mustard, hot pepper sauce, and orange juice. Brush over chicken.

2. Place chicken in slow cooker.

3. Cover. Cook on Low 7–9 hours, or High 3–4 hours.

Fruited Barbecue Chicken

Barbara Katrine Rose
Woodbridge, VA

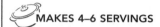
MAKES 4–6 SERVINGS

29-oz. can tomato sauce
20-oz. can unsweetened crushed pineapple, undrained
2 Tbsp. brown sugar
3 Tbsp. vinegar
1 Tbsp. instant minced onion
1 tsp. paprika
2 tsp. Worcestershire sauce
1/4 tsp. garlic powder
1/8 tsp. pepper
3 lbs. chicken, skinned and cubed
11-oz. can mandarin oranges, drained

1. Combine all ingredients except chicken and oranges. Add chicken pieces.

2. Cover. Cook on High 4 hours.

3. Just before serving, stir in oranges. Serve over hot rice.

Orange-Glazed Chicken Breasts

Leona Miller/Millersburg, OH

MAKES 6 SERVINGS

6-oz. can frozen orange
 juice concentrate, thawed
1/2 tsp. dried marjoram
6 boneless, skinless chicken-
 breast halves
1/4 cup cold water
2 Tbsp. cornstarch

1. Combine orange juice
and marjoram in shallow
dish. Dip each breast in
orange-juice mixture and
place in slow cooker. Pour
remaining sauce over breasts.

2. Cover. Cook on Low, 7–9
hours, or High 3 1/2–4 hours.

3. Remove chicken from
slow cooker. Turn cooker to
High and cover.

4. Combine water and
cornstarch. Stir into liquid
in slow cooker. Place cover
slightly ajar on slow cooker.
Cook until sauce is thick and
bubbly, about 15–20
minutes. Serve over chicken.

variation
● To increase "spice" in dish,
add 1/2–1 tsp. Worcestershire
sauce to orange juice-
marjoram glaze.

Oriental Chicken

Marcia S. Myer/Manheim, PA

MAKES 6 SERVINGS

2 2 1/2–3 lb. broiler/fryer
 chickens, cut up
1/4 cup flour
1 1/2 tsp. salt
2 Tbsp. oil
6-oz. can lemonade
 concentrate, thawed
2 Tbsp. brown sugar
3 Tbsp. ketchup
1 Tbsp. vinegar
2 Tbsp. cold water
2 Tbsp. cornstarch

1. Combine flour with salt.
Coat chicken. Brown
chicken in oil in skillet.
Transfer to slow cooker.

2. Combine lemonade
concentrate, brown sugar,
ketchup, and vinegar. Pour
over chicken.

3. Cover. Cook on High 3–4
hours.

4. Remove chicken. Pour
liquid into saucepan. Return
chicken to cooker and cover
to keep warm. Skim fat from
liquid.

5. Combine water and
cornstarch. Stir into hot
liquid. Cook and stir until
thick and bubbly.

6. Serve over rice.

Sweet Aromatic Chicken

Anne Townsend
Albuquerque, NM

MAKES 4 SERVINGS

1/2 cup coconut milk
1/2 cup water
8 chicken thighs, skinned
1/2 cup brown sugar
2 Tbsp. soy sauce
1/8 tsp. ground cloves
2 garlic cloves, minced

1. Combine coconut milk
and water. Pour into greased
slow cooker.

2. Add remaining ingredients
in order listed.

3. Cover. Cook on Low
5–6 hours.

note
What to do with leftover
coconut milk?
● Two or three spoonfuls over
vanilla ice cream, topped with
a cherry, makes a flavorful,
quick dessert.
● Family Pina Coladas are
good. Pour the coconut milk
into a pitcher and add one
large can pineapple juice,
along with some ice cubes.
Decorate with pineapple
chunks and cherries.

Maui Chicken

John D. Allen/Rye, CO

MAKES 6 SERVINGS

6 boneless chicken breast halves
2 Tbsp. oil
14 1/2-oz. can chicken broth
20-oz. can pineapple chunks
1/4 cup vinegar
2 Tbsp. brown sugar
2 tsp. soy sauce
1 garlic clove, minced
1 medium green bell pepper, chopped
3 Tbsp. cornstarch
1/4 cup water

1. Brown chicken in oil. Transfer chicken to slow cooker.

2. Combine remaining ingredients. Pour over chicken.

3. Cover. Cook on High 4–6 hours.

4. Serve over rice.

Spicy Sweet Chicken

Carolyn Baer/Conrath, WI

MAKES 4 SERVINGS

2 1/2–3 lbs. chicken breasts, thighs, and/or legs, skinned
1 Tbsp. oil
16-oz. can whole cranberry sauce
1/4 cup spicy-sweet Catalina salad dressing
2 Tbsp. dry onion soup mix
1 Tbsp. cornstarch

1. Rinse chicken. Pat dry. Brown in hot oil in skillet. Place in slow cooker.

2. Combine half of cranberry sauce, and all of salad dressing and soup mix. Pour over chicken.

3. Cover. Cook on Low 6 hours or High 3 hours.

4. Stir cornstarch into remaining cranberry sauce. Stir into chicken mixture.

5. Turn slow cooker to High. Cover and cook 30–45 minutes more, or until thickened and bubbly.

6. Serve over cooked noodles or rice.

Chicken with Applesauce

Kelly Evenson/Pittsboro, NC

MAKES 4 SERVINGS

4 boneless, skinless chicken breast halves
salt to taste
pepper to taste
4–5 Tbsp. oil
2 cups applesauce
1/4 cup barbecue sauce
1/2 tsp. poultry seasoning
2 tsp. honey
1/2 tsp. lemon juice

1. Season chicken with salt and pepper. Brown in oil for 5 minutes per side.

2. Cut up chicken into 1" chunks and transfer to slow cooker.

3. Combine remaining ingredients. Pour over chicken and mix together well.

4. Cover. Cook on High 2–3 hours, or until chicken is tender.

5. Serve over rice or noodles.

Chicken ala Orange

Carlene Horne/Bedford, NH

 **MAKES 8 SERVINGS**

8 boneless, skinless chicken
   breast halves
1/2 cup chopped onion
12-oz. jar orange
   marmalade
1/2 cup Russian dressing
1 Tbsp. dried parsley, or
   to taste

1. Place chicken and onion
in slow cooker.

2. Combine marmalade and
dressing. Pour over chicken.

3. Sprinkle with parsley.

4. Cover. Cook on Low 4–6
hours.

5. Serve with rice.

Marcy's Barbecued Chicken

Marcy Engle/Harrisonburg, VA

 **MAKES 6 SERVINGS**

2 lbs. chicken pieces
1/4 cup flour
1 cup ketchup
2 cups water
1/3 cup Worcestershire
   sauce
1 tsp. chili powder
1/2 tsp. salt
1/2 tsp. pepper
2 drops Tabasco sauce
1/4 tsp. garlic salt
1/4 tsp. onion salt

1. Dust chicken with flour.
Transfer to slow cooker.

2. Combine remaining
ingredients. Pour over
chicken.

3. Cover. Cook on Low
5 hours.

Barbecued Chicken

Joanne Kennedy
Plattsburgh, NY

 **MAKES 4 SERVINGS**

2 whole boneless, skinless
   chicken breasts, cubed
1 medium onion, sliced
1 green pepper, sliced
1 cup chopped celery
2 Tbsp. Worcestershire
   sauce
2 Tbsp. brown sugar
1 1/2 cups ketchup
1 1/2 cups water
1/2 tsp. pepper

1. Combine all ingredients
in slow cooker.

2. Cover. Cook on Low
8 hours or High 4 hours.

3. Serve over rice with a
tossed salad.

Tender Barbecued Chicken

Betty Stoltzfus
Honeybrook, PA

MAKES 4–6 SERVINGS

3–4 lb. broiler chicken
1 medium onion, thinly sliced
1 medium lemon, thinly sliced
18-oz. bottle barbecue sauce
3/4 cup cola-flavored soda

1. Place chicken in slow cooker.

2. Top with onion and lemon.

3. Combine barbecue sauce and cola. Pour into slow cooker.

4. Cover. Cook on Low 8–10 hours, or until chicken juices run clear.

5. Cut into serving-sized pieces and serve with barbecue sauce. Slice any leftovers and use in sandwiches.

Tracy's Barbecued Chicken Wings

Tracy Supcoe/Barclay, MD

MAKES 8 FULL-SIZED SERVINGS

4 lbs. chicken wings
2 large onions, chopped
2 6-oz. cans tomato paste
2 large garlic cloves, minced
1/4 cup Worcestershire sauce
1/4 cup cider vinegar
1/2 cup brown sugar
1/2 cup sweet pickle relish
1/2 cup red, or white, wine
2 tsp. salt
2 tsp. dry mustard

1. Cut off wing tips. Cut wings at joint. Place in slow cooker.

2. Combine remaining ingredients. Add to slow cooker. Stir.

3. Cover. Cook on Low 5–6 hours.

Mary's Chicken Wings

Mary Casey/Scranton, PA

MAKES 8–12 FULL-SIZED SERVINGS

3–6 lbs. chicken wings
1–3 Tbsp. oil
3/4–1 cup vinegar
1/2 cup ketchup
2 Tbsp. sugar
2 Tbsp. Worcestershire sauce
3 garlic cloves, minced
1 Tbsp. dry mustard
1 tsp. paprika
1/2–1 tsp. salt
1/8 tsp. pepper

1. Brown wings in oil in skillet, or brush wings with oil and broil, watching carefully so they do not burn.

2. Combine remaining ingredients in 5–6 1/2-quart slow cooker. Add wings. Stir gently so that they are all well covered with sauce.

3. Cover. Cook on Low 4–6 hours, or until tender.

Chicken Wings Colorado

Nancy Rexrode Clark
Woodstock, MD

MAKES 6–8 SERVINGS

1 1/2 cups sugar
1/4 tsp. salt
1 chicken bouillon cube
1 cup cider vinegar
1/2 cup ketchup
2 Tbsp. soy sauce
12–16 chicken wings
1/4 cup cornstarch
1/2 cup cold water
red hot sauce to taste,
    optional

1. Combine sugar, salt, bouillon cube, vinegar, ketchup, and soy sauce and bring to boil in slow cooker.

2. Add chicken wings, pushing them down into the sauce.

3. Cover. Cook on Low 6–7 hours.

4. Combine cornstarch and cold water. Add to slow cooker.

5. Cover. Cook on High until liquid thickens, about 30 minutes.

6. Season with red hot sauce, or let each diner add to his or her own serving.

Rosemarie's Barbecued Chicken Wings

Rosemarie Fitzgerald
Gibsonia, PA

MAKES 10 FULL-SIZED SERVINGS

5 lbs. chicken wings, tips cut off
12-oz. bottle chili sauce
1/3 cup lemon juice
1 Tbsp. Worcestershire sauce
2 Tbsp. molasses
1 tsp. salt
2 tsp. chili powder
1/4 tsp. hot pepper sauce
dash garlic powder

1. Place wings in cooker.

2. Combine remaining ingredients and pour over chicken.

3. Cover. Cook on Low 6–8 hours, or High 2–3 hours.

note
● These wings are also a great appetizer, yielding about 15 appetizer-size servings. Take any leftover chicken off the bone and combine with leftover sauce. Serve over cooked pasta for a second meal.

Donna's Chicken Wings

Donna Conto/Saylorsburg, PA

MAKES 10 FULL-SIZED SERVINGS

5 lbs. chicken wings
28-oz. jar spaghetti sauce
1 Tbsp. Worcestershire sauce
1 Tbsp. molasses
1 Tbsp. prepared mustard
1 tsp. salt
1/2 tsp. pepper

1. Place wings in slow cooker.

2. Combine remaining ingredients. Pour over wings and stir them gently, making sure all are covered with sauce.

3. Cover. Cook on High 3–4 hours.

Chicken Olé

Barb Yoder/Angola, IN

 MAKES 8 SERVINGS

10 3/4-oz. can cream of mushroom soup
10 3/4-oz. can cream of chicken soup
1 cup sour cream
2 Tbsp. grated onion
1 1/2 cups grated cheddar cheese
12 flour tortillas, each torn into 6–8 pieces
3–4 cups cubed, cooked chicken
7-oz. jar salsa
1/2 cup grated cheddar cheese

1. In separate bowl, combine soups, sour cream, onion, and 1 1/2 cups cheese.

2. Place one-third of each of the following in layers in slow cooker: torn tortillas, soup mixture, chicken, and salsa. Repeat layers 2 more times.

3. Cover. Cook on Low 4–5 hours. (This recipe does not respond well to cooking on High.)

4. Gently stir. Sprinkle with remaining 1/2 cup cheese. Cover. Cook on Low another 15–30 minutes.

5. Serve with tortilla chips and lettuce.

Chicken Tortillas

Julette Leaman
Harrisonburg, VA

 MAKES 4 SERVINGS

1 fryer chicken, cooked and cubed
10 3/4-oz. can cream of chicken soup
1/2 cup (can) tomatoes with chilies
2 Tbsp. quick-cooking tapioca
6–8 tortillas, torn into pieces
1 medium onion, chopped
2 cups grated cheddar cheese

1. Combine chicken, soup, tomatoes with chilies, and tapioca.

2. Line bottom of slow cooker with one-third tortilla pieces. Add one-third chicken mixture. Sprinkle with one-third onion and cheese. Repeat layers.

3. Cover. Cook on Low 6–8 hours. (This recipe does not respond well to being cooked on High.)

4. Serve with shredded lettuce, chopped fresh tomatoes, diced raw onions, sour cream, and salsa.

Chicken Azteca

Katrine Rose/Woodbridge, VA

 MAKES 10–12 SERVINGS

2 15-oz. cans black beans, drained
4 cups frozen corn kernels
2 garlic cloves, minced
3/4 tsp. ground cumin
2 cups chunky salsa, divided
10 skinless, boneless chicken breast halves
2 8-oz. pkgs. cream cheese, cubed
cooked rice
shredded cheddar cheese

1. Combine beans, corn, garlic, cumin, and half of salsa in slow cooker.

2. Arrange chicken breasts over top. Pour remaining salsa over top.

3. Cover. Cook on High 2–3 hours or on Low 4–6 hours.

4. Remove chicken and cut into bite-size pieces. Return to cooker.

5. Stir in cream cheese. Cook on High until cream cheese melts.

6. Spoon chicken and sauce over cooked rice. Top with shredded cheese.

Red Pepper Chicken

Sue Graber/Eureka, IL

 **MAKES 4 SERVINGS**

4 boneless, skinless chicken breast halves
15-oz. can black beans, drained
12-oz. jar roasted red peppers, undrained
14 1/2-oz. can Mexican stewed tomatoes, undrained
1 large onion, chopped
1/2 tsp. salt
pepper to taste
hot cooked rice

1. Place chicken in slow cooker.

2. Combine beans, red peppers, stewed tomatoes, onion, salt, and pepper. Pour over chicken.

3. Cover. Cook on Low 4–6 hours, or until chicken is no longer pink.

4. Serve over rice.

Frances' Roast Chicken

Frances Schrag/Newton, KS

 **MAKES 6 SERVINGS**

3–4-lb. whole frying chicken
half an onion, chopped
1 rib celery, chopped
salt to taste
pepper to taste
1/2 tsp. poultry seasoning
1/4 tsp. dried basil

1. Sprinkle chicken cavity with salt, pepper, and poultry seasoning. Put onion and celery inside cavity. Put chicken in slow cooker. Sprinkle with basil.

2. Cover. Cook on Low 8–10 hours, or High 4–6 hours.

Con Pollo

Dorothy Van Deest
Memphis, TN

 **MAKES 4–6 SERVINGS**

3–4-lb. whole chicken
salt to taste
pepper to taste
paprika to taste
garlic salt to taste
6-oz. can tomato paste
1/2 cup beer
3-oz. jar stuffed olives with liquid

1. Wash chicken. Sprinkle all over with salt, pepper, paprika, and garlic salt. Place in slow cooker.

2. Combine tomato paste and beer. Pour over chicken. Add olives.

3. Cover. Cook on Low 8–10 hours or High 3–4 hours.

4. Serve over rice or noodles, along with salad and cornbread, and sherbet for dessert.

This is chicken with a Spanish flair. This easy supper is quick, too, by slow-cooker standards, if you use the High temperature. Let your slow cooker be the chef.

— • —

Basil Chicken

Sarah Niessen/Akron, PA

 **MAKES 4–6 SERVINGS**

1 lb. baby carrots
2 medium onions, sliced
1–2 cups celery slices and
  leaves
3-lb. chicken
1/2 cup chicken broth, or
  white cooking wine
2 tsp. salt
1/2 tsp. black pepper
1 tsp. dried basil

1. Place carrots, onions, and celery in bottom of slow cooker.

2. Add chicken.

3. Pour broth over chicken.

4. Sprinkle with salt, pepper, and basil.

5. Cover. Cook on Low 7–10 hours, or until chicken and vegetables are tender.

One-Dish Chicken Supper

Louise Stackhouse/Benton, PA

 **MAKES 4 SERVINGS**

4 boneless, skinless chicken-
  breast halves
10 3/4-oz. can cream of
  chicken, or celery, or
  mushroom, soup
1/3 cup milk
1 pkg. Stove Top stuffing
  mix and seasoning packet
1 2/3 cups water

1. Place chicken in slow cooker.

2. Combine soup and milk. Pour over chicken.

3. Combine stuffing mix, seasoning packet, and water. Spoon over chicken.

4. Cover. Cook on Low 6–8 hours.

Chicken and Stuffing Dinner

Trudy Kutter/Corfu, NY

 **MAKES 4–6 SERVINGS**

4–6 skinless chicken breast
  halves
10 3/4-oz. can cream of
  chicken, or celery soup
4–6 potatoes, peeled and
  sliced
6-oz. pkg. stuffing mix
1 1/4 cups water
2 Tbsp. melted butter
1–1 1/2 cups frozen green
  beans, thawed

1. Place chicken in slow cooker.

2. Spoon soup over chicken.

3. Top with potatoes.

4. Combine stuffing mix, water, and butter. Spoon over potatoes.

5. Cover. Cook on Low 6 hours.

6. Sprinkle green beans over stuffing.

7. Cover. Cook on Low 45–60 minutes, or until beans are just tender.

8. Serve with a salad.

Ham and Swiss Chicken

Nanci Keatley/Salem, OR

Janice Yoskovich
Carmichaels, PA

 MAKES 6 SERVINGS

2 eggs, beaten
1 1/2 cups milk
2 Tbsp. butter, melted
1/2 cup chopped celery
1/4 cup diced onion
10 slices bread, cubed
12 thin slices deli ham, rolled up
2 cups grated Swiss cheese
2 1/2 cups cubed cooked chicken
10 3/4-oz. can cream of chicken soup
1/2 cup milk

1. Combine eggs and milk. Add butter, celery, and onion. Stir in bread cubes. Place half of mixture in greased slow cooker. Top with half the ham, cheese, and chicken.

2. Combine soup and milk. Pour half over chicken. Repeat layers.

3. Cover. Cook on Low 4–5 hours.

Easy Casserole

Ruth Conrad Liechty
Goshen, IN

 MAKES 6–8 SERVINGS

2 10 3/4-oz. cans chicken gumbo soup
2 10 3/4-oz. cans cream of mushroom soup
1–2 cups cut up chicken, or turkey
1 cup milk
6-oz. can chow mein noodles
1 pint frozen green beans, or corn, cooked

1. Combine all ingredients in slow cooker.

2. Cover. Cook on Low 7–8 hours, or High 3–4 hours.

Elizabeth's Hot Chicken Sandwiches

Elizabeth Yutzy/Wauseon, OH

 MAKES 8 SERVINGS

3 cups cubed cooked chicken
2 cups chicken broth
1 cup crushed soda crackers
1/4–1/2 tsp. salt
dash pepper
8 sandwich buns

1. Combine chicken, broth, crackers, and seasoning in slow cooker.

2. Cover. Cook on Low 2–3 hours, until mixture thickens and can be spread.

3. Fill sandwich buns and serve while warm.

Oriental Chicken Cashew Dish

Dorothy Horst/Tiskilwa, IL

 **MAKES 6 SERVINGS**

14-oz. can bean sprouts, drained
3 Tbsp. butter, or margarine, melted
4 green onions, chopped
4-oz. can mushroom pieces
10 3/4-oz. can cream of mushroom soup
1 cup sliced celery
12 1/2-oz. can chunk chicken breast, or 1 cup cooked chicken cubed
1 Tbsp. soy sauce
1 cup cashew nuts

1. Combine all ingredients except nuts in slow cooker.

2. Cover. Cook on Low 4–9 hours or on High 2–3 hours.

3. Stir in cashew nuts before serving.

4. Serve over rice.

Scalloped Chicken

Brenda Joy Sonnie/Newton, PA

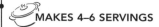 **MAKES 4–6 SERVINGS**

4 cups cooked chicken
1 box stuffing mix for chicken
2 eggs
1 cup water
1 1/2 cups milk
1 cup frozen peas

1. Combine chicken and dry stuffing mix. Place in slow cooker.

2. Beat together eggs, water, and milk. Pour over chicken and stuffing.

3. Cover. Cook on High 2–3 hours. Add frozen peas during last hour of cooking.

variation

● For more flavor use chicken broth instead of water.

Loretta's Hot Chicken Sandwiches

Loretta Krahn/Mt. Lake, MN

 **MAKES 12 SERVINGS**

8 cups cubed cooked chicken, or turkey
1 medium onion, chopped
1 cup chopped celery
2 cups mayonnaise
1 cup cubed American cheese
buns

1. Combine all ingredients except buns in slow cooker.

2. Cover. Cook on High 2 hours.

3. Serve on buns.

Turkey

Easy Turkey Breast

Susan Stephani Smith
Monument, CO

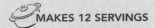

MAKES 12 SERVINGS

1 Jenny O'Turkey Breast—
   with bone in and with
   gravy packet
salt

1. Wash frozen breast and
sprinkle with salt.

2. Place turkey, gravy
packet up, in slow cooker
that's large enough to be
covered when the turkey
breast is in it.

3. Cover. Cook turkey on
Low 6–7 hours, or until
tender, removing gravy
packet when the turkey
is partially thawed.(Keep
packet in refrigerator.)

4. Make gravy according to
directions on packet. Warm
before serving.

No-Fuss Turkey Breast

Dorothy Miller/Gulfport, MI

**MAKES 3–4 PINTS
COOKED MEAT**

1 turkey breast
olive oil
1–2 Tbsp. water

1. Rub turkey breast with
oil. Place in slow cooker.
Add water.

2. Cover. Cook on High
1 hour, or Low 4–5 hours.

3. Cool. Debone and cut
into bite-size pieces and
store in pint-size plastic
boxes in freezer. Use when
cooked turkey or chicken is
called for.

Onion Turkey Breast

Mary Ann Wasick
West Allis, WI

MAKES 6–8 SERVINGS

4–6-lb. boneless, skinless
   turkey breast
1 tsp. garlic powder
1 envelope dry onion soup
   mix

1. Place turkey in slow
cooker. Sprinkle garlic
powder and onion soup
mix over breast.

2. Cover. Cook on Low
8–10 hours.

note
● Use au jus over rice or pasta.

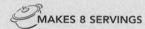

...supereasy

Turkey Crockpot

Arlene Leaman Kliewer
Lakewood, CO

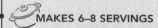 MAKES 8 SERVINGS

5-lb. turkey breast
1 pkg. dry onion soup mix
16-oz. can whole cranberry
sauce

1. Place turkey in slow cooker.

2. Combine soup mix and cranberry sauce. Spread over turkey.

3. Cover. Cook on Low 8 hours.

Turkey Breast

Barbara Katrine Rose
Woodbridge, VA

MAKES 6–8 SERVINGS

1 large boneless turkey
breast
1/4 cup apple cider, or juice
1 tsp. salt
1/4 tsp. pepper

1. Put turkey breast in slow cooker. Drizzle apple cider over turkey. Sprinkle on both sides with salt and pepper.

2. Cover. Cook on High 3–4 hours.

3. Remove turkey breast. Let stand for 15 minutes before slicing.

Easy and Delicious Turkey Breast

Gail Bush/Landenberg, PA

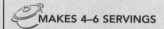 MAKES 4–6 SERVINGS

1 turkey breast
15-oz. can whole berry
cranberry sauce
1 envelope dry onion
soup mix
1/2 cup orange juice
1/2 tsp. salt
1/4 tsp. pepper

1. Place turkey in slow cooker.

2. Combine remaining ingredients. Pour over turkey.

3. Cover. Cook on Low 6–8 hours.

Turkey in a Pot

Dorothy M. Pittman
Pickens, SC

MAKES 10–12 SERVINGS

4–5 lb. turkey breast (if
   frozen, it doesn't have
   to be thawed)
1 medium onion, chopped
1 rib celery, chopped
1/4 cup melted margarine
salt to taste
lemon-pepper seasoning
   to taste
1 1/2 cups chicken broth

1. Wash turkey breast. Pat
dry. Place in greased slow
cooker. Put onion and celery
in cavity.

2. Pour margarine over
turkey. Sprinkle with
seasonings. Pour broth
around turkey.

3. Cover. Cook on
High 6 hours. Let stand
10 minutes before carving.

Slow Cooker Turkey Breast

Liz Ann Yoder/Hartville, OH

MAKES 8–10 SERVINGS

6-lb. turkey breast
2 tsp. oil
salt to taste
pepper to taste
1 medium onion, quartered
4 garlic cloves, peeled
1/2 cup water

1. Rinse turkey and pat dry
with paper towels.

2. Rub oil over turkey.
Sprinkle with salt and
pepper. Place, meaty side
up, in large slow cooker.

3. Place onion and garlic
around sides of cooker.

4. Cover. Cook on Low
9–10 hours, or until meat
thermometer stuck in meaty
part of breast registers 170°.

5. Remove from slow cooker
and let stand 10 minutes
before slicing.

6. Serve with mashed
potatoes, cranberry salad,
and corn or green beans.

variation
● Add carrot chunks and
chopped celery to Step 3
to add more flavor to the
turkey broth.

Turkey Breast with Orange Sauce

Jean Butzer/Batavia, NY

MAKES 4–6 SERVINGS

1 large onion, chopped
3 garlic cloves, minced
1 tsp. dried rosemary
1/2 tsp. pepper
2–3-lb. boneless, skinless
   turkey breast
1 1/2 cups orange juice

1. Place onions in slow
cooker.

2. Combine garlic,
rosemary, and pepper.

3. Make gashes in turkey,
about 3/4 of the way
through at 2" intervals.
Stuff with herb mixture.
Place turkey in slow cooker.

4. Pour juice over turkey.

5. Cover. Cook on Low 7–8
hours, or until turkey is no
longer pink in center.

This very easy, impressive-
looking and -tasting recipe
is perfect for company.

— ● —

Slow Cooker Turkey and Dressing

Carol Sherwood/Batavia, NY

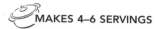 **MAKES 4–6 SERVINGS**

8-oz. pkg., or 2 6-oz. pkgs., stuffing mix
1/2 cup hot water
2 Tbsp. butter, softened
1 onion, chopped
1/2 cup chopped celery
1/4 cup sweetened, dried cranberries
3-lb. boneless turkey breast
1/4 tsp. dried basil
1/2 tsp. salt
1/2 tsp. pepper

1. Spread dry stuffing mix in greased slow cooker.

2. Add water, butter, onion, celery, and cranberries. Mix well.

3. Sprinkle turkey breast with basil, salt, and pepper. Place over stuffing mixture.

4. Cover. Cook on Low 5–6 hours, or until turkey is done but not dry.

5. Remove turkey. Slice and set aside.

6. Gently stir stuffing and allow to sit for 5 minutes before serving.

Turkey Stew

Ruth S. Weaver/Reinholds, PA

 **MAKES 8 SERVINGS**

2 lbs. skinless turkey thighs
1 lb., or 5 large, carrots, sliced
2 medium onions, chopped
8 medium potatoes, cubed
4 ribs celery, chopped
3 garlic cloves, minced
1 tsp. salt
1/4 tsp. pepper
2 Tbsp. Worcestershire sauce
15-oz. can tomato sauce
2 bay leaves

1. Place turkey in large slow cooker.

2. In separate bowl, mix together carrots, onions, potatoes, celery, garlic, salt, pepper, Worcestershire sauce, tomato sauce, and bay leaves.

3. Pour over turkey. Cover. Cook on Low 8–12 hours, or High 6–8 hours. Remove bay leaves before serving.

Slow-Cooked Turkey Dinner

Miriam Nolt/New Holland, PA

 **MAKES 4–6 SERVINGS**

1 onion, diced
6 small red potatoes, quartered
2 cups sliced carrots
1 1/2-2 lbs. boneless, skinless turkey thighs
1/4 cup flour
2 Tbsp. dry onion soup mix
10 3/4-oz. can cream of mushroom soup
2/3 cup chicken broth or water

1. Place vegetables in bottom of slow cooker.

2. Place turkey thighs over vegetables.

3. Combine remaining ingredients. Pour over turkey.

4. Cover. Cook on High 30 minutes. Reduce heat to Low and cook 7 hours.

Turkey and Sweet Potato Casserole

Michele Ruvola/Selden, NY

 MAKES 4 SERVINGS

3 medium sweet potatoes, peeled and cut into 2-inch pieces
10-oz. pkg. frozen cut green beans
2 lbs. turkey cutlets
12-oz. jar home-style turkey gravy
2 Tbsp. flour
1 tsp. parsley flakes
1/4–1/2 tsp. dried rosemary leaves, crumbled
1/8 tsp. pepper

1. Layer sweet potatoes, green beans, and turkey in slow cooker.

2. Combine remaining ingredients until smooth. Pour over mixture in slow cooker.

3. Cover. Cook on Low 8–10 hours.

4. Remove turkey and vegetables and keep warm. Stir sauce. Serve with sauce over meat and vegetables, or with sauce in a gravy boat.

5. Serve with biscuits and cranberry sauce.

Barbecued Turkey Cutlets

Maricarol Magill/Freehold, NJ

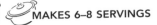 MAKES 6–8 SERVINGS

6–8 (1 1/2–2 lbs. each) turkey cutlets
1/4 cup molasses
1/4 cider vinegar
1/4 cup ketchup
3 Tbsp. Worcestershire sauce
1 tsp. garlic salt
3 Tbsp. chopped onion
2 Tbsp. brown sugar
1/4 tsp. pepper

1. Place turkey cutlets in slow cooker.

2. Combine remaining ingredients. Pour over turkey.

3. Cover. Cook on Low 4 hours.

4. Serve over white or brown rice.

Barbecued Turkey Legs

Barbara Walker/Sturgis, SC

MAKES 4–6 SERVINGS

4 turkey drumsticks
1-2 tsp. salt
1/4–1/2 tsp. pepper
1/3 cup molasses
1/4 cup vinegar
1/2 cup ketchup
3 Tbsp. Worcestershire sauce
3/4 tsp. hickory smoke
2 Tbsp. instant minced onion

1. Sprinkle turkey with salt and pepper. Place in slow cooker.

2. Combine remaining ingredients. Pour over turkey.

3. Cover. Cook on Low 5–7 hours.

Turkey Barbecue

Marcia S. Myer/Manheim, PA

MAKES 8 SERVINGS

2 lbs. chopped cooked
  turkey
1 1/4 cups ketchup
1 tsp. dry mustard
4 tsp. vinegar
4 tsp. Worcestershire sauce
2 Tbsp. sugar
1 tsp. onion salt
8 hamburger buns

1. Combine all ingredients
in slow cooker.

2. Cover. Cook on Low 3–4
hours.

3. Serve on hamburger buns.

note
● You can make the turkey
by putting 2 lbs. uncooked
turkey tenderloins in slow
cooker, adding 1/2 cup
water, and cooking the meat
on Low for 6 hours, or until
juices run clear.

Turkey Sloppy Joes

Marla Folkerts/Holland, OH

MAKES 6 SERVINGS

1 red onion, chopped
1 sweet pepper, chopped
1 1/2 lbs. boneless turkey,
  finely chopped
1 cup chili sauce, or ketchup
1/4 tsp. salt
1 garlic clove, minced
1 tsp. Dijon-style mustard
1/8 tsp. pepper
thickly sliced homemade
  bread, or 6 sandwich rolls

1. Place onion, sweet pepper,
and turkey in slow cooker.

2. Combine chili sauce, salt,
garlic, mustard, and pepper.
Pour over turkey mixture.
Mix well.

3. Cover. Cook on Low
4 1/2–6 hours.

4. Serve on homemade
bread or sandwich rolls.

Turkey Loaf and Potatoes

Lizzie Weaver/Ephrata, PA

MAKES 6–7 SERVINGS

2 lbs. ground turkey
1 1/2 cups soft bread
  crumbs, or oatmeal
2 eggs, slightly beaten
1 small onion, chopped
1 tsp. salt
1 tsp. dry mustard
1/4 cup ketchup
1/4 cup evaporated milk
6 medium-sized potatoes,
  quartered

1. Combine all ingredients
except potatoes. Form into
loaf to fit in slow cooker.

2. Tear 4 strips of aluminum
foil, each 18" x 2". Position
them in the slow cooker,
spokefashion, with the ends
sticking out over the edges
of the cooker to act as
handles. Place loaf down
in the cooker, centered over
the foil strips.

3. Place potatoes around
meat.

4. Cover. Cook on High
4–5 hours, or until potatoes
are soft.

5. Serve with gravy, green
vegetable, and cole slaw.

Pasta
and Rice

Easy Stuffed Shells

Rebecca Plank Leichty
Harrisonburg, VA

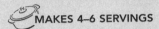 MAKES 4–6 SERVINGS

20-oz. bag frozen stuffed
  shells
15-oz. can marinara, or
  spaghetti, sauce
15-oz. can green beans,
  drained

1. Place shells around edge
of greased slow cooker.

2. Cover with marinara
sauce.

3. Pour green beans in
center.

4. Cover. Cook on Low
8 hours or on High 3 hours.

5. Serve with garlic toast
and salad.

variation
● Reverse Steps 2 and 3.
Double the amount of
marinara sauce and pour over
both the shells and the beans.

Crockpot Macaroni

Lisa F. Good/Harrisonburg, VA

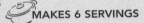 MAKES 6 SERVINGS

1 1/2 cups dry macaroni
3 Tbsp. butter
1 tsp. salt
1/2 lb. Velveeta cheese,
  sliced
1 qt. milk

1. Combine macaroni,
butter, and salt.

2. Layer cheese over top.

3. Pour in milk.

4. Cover. Cook on High
3–4 hours, or until macaroni
are soft.

Mjeddrah

Dianna Milhizer/Brighton, MI

MAKES 20–24 SERVINGS

10 cups water
4 cups dried lentils, rinsed
2 cups uncooked brown rice
1/4 cup olive oil
2 tsp. salt

1. Combine ingredients in
large slow cooker.

2. Cover. Cook on High
8 hours, then on Low
2 hours. Add 2 more cups
water, if needed, to allow
rice to cook and to prevent
dish from drying out.

3. This is traditionally
eaten with a salad with an
oil-and-vinegar dressing over
the lentil-rice mixture,
similar to a tostada without
the tortilla.

Melt-in-Your-Mouth Sausages

Ruth Ann Gingrich,
New Holland, PA

Ruth Hershey/Paradise, PA

Carol Sherwood/Batavia, NY

Nancy Zimmerman
Loysville, PA

 MAKES 6–8 SERVINGS

2 lbs. sweet Italian sausage,
cut into 5-inch lengths

48-oz. jar spaghetti sauce

6-oz. can tomato paste

1 large green pepper, thinly
sliced

1 large onion, thinly sliced

1 Tbsp. grated Parmesan
cheese

1 tsp. dried parsley, or
1 Tbsp. chopped fresh
parsley

1 cup water

1. Place sausage in skillet.
Cover with water. Simmer
10 minutes. Drain.

2. Combine remaining
ingredients in slow cooker.
Add sausage.

3. Cover. Cook on Low
6 hours.

4. Serve in buns, or cut
sausage into bite-size pieces
and serve over cooked
spaghetti. Sprinkle with
more Parmesan cheese.

Chunky Spaghetti Sauce

Patti Boston/Newark, OH

 MAKES 6 CUPS

1 lb. ground beef, browned
and drained

1/2 lb. bulk sausage,
browned and drained

14 1/2-oz. can Italian
tomatoes with basil

15-oz. can Italian tomato
sauce

1 medium onion, chopped

1 green pepper, chopped

8-oz. can sliced mushrooms

1/2 cup dry red wine

2 tsp. sugar

1 tsp. minced garlic

1. Combine all ingredients
in slow cooker.

2. Cover. Cook on High
3 1/2–4 hours, or Low 7–8
hours.

variations
● For added texture and zest,
add 3 fresh, medium-sized
tomatoes, chopped, and 4 large
fresh basil leaves, torn. Stir in
1 tsp. salt and 1/2 tsp. pepper.
● To any leftover sauce, add
chickpeas or kidney beans and
serve chili!

Sausage-Beef Spaghetti Sauce

Jeannine Janzen/Elbing, KS

 MAKES 16–20 SERVINGS

1 lb. ground beef

1 lb. Italian sausage, sliced

2 28-oz. cans crushed
tomatoes

3/4 can (28-oz. tomato can)
water

2 tsp. garlic powder

1 tsp. pepper

2 Tbsp. or more parsley

2 Tbsp. dried oregano

2 12-oz. cans tomato paste

2 12-oz. cans tomato puree

1. Brown ground beef and
sausage in skillet. Drain.
Transfer to large slow cooker.

2. Add crushed tomatoes,
water, garlic powder, pepper,
parsley, and oregano.

3. Cover. Cook on High
30 minutes. Add tomato
paste and tomato puree.
Cook on Low 6 hours.

note
● Leftovers freeze well.

Easy-Does-It Spaghetti

Rachel Kauffman/Alto, MI

Lois Stoltzfus
Honey Brook, PA

Deb Unternahrer/Wayland, IA

MAKES 8 SERVINGS

2 lbs. ground chuck, browned and drained
1 cup chopped onions
2 cloves garlic, minced
2 15-oz. cans tomato sauce
2–3 tsp. Italian seasoning
1 1/2 tsp. salt
1/4 tsp. pepper
2 4-oz. cans sliced mushrooms, drained
6 cups tomato juice
16-oz. dry spaghetti, broken into 4–5-inch pieces
grated Parmesan cheese

1. Combine all ingredients except spaghetti and cheese in 4-quart (or larger) slow cooker.

2. Cover. Cook on Low 6–8 hours, or High 3–5 hours. Turn to High during last 30 minutes and stir in dry spaghetti. (If spaghetti is not fully cooked, continue cooking another 10 minutes, checking to make sure it is not becoming over-cooked.)

3. Sprinkle each serving with Parmesan cheese.

Italian Sausage Spaghetti

Eleanor Larson/Glen Lyon, PA

MAKES 12 SERVINGS

6 Italian turkey sausage links (1 1/2 lbs.), cut into 1 1/2-inch pieces
1 cup diced onions
3 Tbsp. sugar
1 tsp. dried oregano
1/2 tsp. salt
2 garlic cloves, minced
28-oz. can crushed tomatoes, undrained
15-oz. can tomato sauce
12-oz. can tomato paste
1 1/2 lbs. dry spaghetti

1. Combine all ingredients except spaghetti in slow cooker.

2. Cover. Cook on Low 8–10 hours.

3. Cook spaghetti in large soup pot. Drain and top with sauce.

Nancy's Spaghetti Sauce

Nancy Graves/Manhattan, KS

MAKES 4–6 SERVINGS

1/4 cup minced onion
garlic powder to taste
3 cups chopped fresh tomatoes, or 1-lb., 12-oz. can diced tomatoes with juice
6-oz. can tomato paste
3 1/2 tsp. salt
dash of pepper
1 basil leaf
1 chopped green pepper
1 lb. ground beef, browned and drained
4-oz. can sliced mushrooms

1. Combine all ingredients in slow cooker.

2. Cover. Cook on Low 3 hours.

Pasta Sauce with Meat and Veggies

Marla Folkerts/Holland, OH

MAKES 6 SERVINGS

1/2 lb. ground turkey
1/2 lb. ground beef
1 rib celery, chopped
2 medium carrots, chopped
1 garlic clove, minced
1 medium onion, chopped
28-oz. can diced tomatoes
  with juice
1/2 tsp. salt
1/4 tsp. dried thyme
6-oz. can tomato paste
1/8 tsp. pepper

1. Combine turkey, beef, celery, carrots, garlic, and onion in slow cooker.

2. Add remaining ingredients. Mix well.

3. Cover. Cook on Low 7–8 hours.

4. Serve over pasta or rice.

Katelyn's Spaghetti Sauce

Katelyn Bailey
Mechanicsburg, PA

MAKES 10–12 SERVINGS

1 lb. ground beef, browned
  and drained
3/4 cup chopped onions
1 garlic clove, minced
3 Tbsp. oil
2 6-oz. cans tomato paste
1 Tbsp. sugar
1 1/2 tsp. salt
1–1 1/2 tsp. dried oregano
1/2 tsp. pepper
1 bay leaf
2 qts. tomatoes, or tomato
  sauce

1. Combine all ingredients in slow cooker.

2. Cover. Cook on Low 8–10 hours. Remove bay leaf before serving.

note
● This sauce freezes well.

Char's Spaghetti Sauce

Char Hagner/Montague, MI

MAKES 16–20 SERVINGS

4 lbs. ground beef
2 large onions, chopped
1/4 lb. bacon, cut into small
  squares
5 garlic cloves, minced
1 Tbsp. salt
1/4 tsp. celery salt
4 10 3/4-oz. cans tomato
  soup
2 6-oz. cans tomato paste
8-oz. can mushrooms
3 green peppers, chopped

1. Brown ground beef, onions, bacon, and garlic in saucepan. Drain.

2. Combine all ingredients in large slow cooker.

3. Cover. Cook on Low 6 hours.

So-Easy Spaghetti

Ruth Ann Swartzendruber
Hydro, OK

MAKES 4–6 SERVINGS

1 lb. ground beef
1/2 cup diced onions
1 pkg. dry spaghetti
 sauce mix
8-oz. can tomato sauce
3 cups tomato juice
4 oz. dry spaghetti, broken
 into 4-inch pieces

1. Brown meat and onions in skillet. Drain. Transfer to greased slow cooker.

2. Add remaining ingredients, except spaghetti.

3. Cover. Cook on Low 6–8 hours, or High 3 1/2 hours.

4. During last hour, turn to High and add spaghetti. Stir frequently to keep spaghetti from clumping together.

Louise's Vegetable Spaghetti Sauce

Louise Stackhouse/Benton, PA

MAKES 4–6 SERVINGS

6–7 fresh tomatoes, peeled
 and crushed
1 medium onion, chopped
2 green peppers, chopped
2 cloves garlic, minced
1/2 tsp. dried basil
1/2 tsp. dried oregano
1/4 tsp. salt
1/4 cup sugar
6-oz. can tomato paste,
 optional

1. Combine all ingredients in slow cooker.

2. Cover. Cook on Low 8–10 hours. If the sauce is too watery for your liking, stir in a 6-oz. can of tomato paste during the last hour of cooking.

3. Serve over cooked spaghetti or other pasta.

Joyce's Chicken Tetrazzini

Joyce Slaymaker/Strasburg, PA

MAKES 4 SERVINGS

2–3 cups diced cooked
 chicken
2 cups chicken broth
1 small onion, chopped
1/4 cup sauterne, white
 wine, or milk
1/2 cup slivered almonds
2 4-oz. cans sliced
 mushrooms, drained
10 3/4-oz. can cream of
 mushroom soup
1 lb. cooked spaghetti
grated Parmesan cheese

1. Combine all ingredients except spaghetti and cheese in slow cooker.

2. Cover. Cook on Low 6–8 hours.

3. Serve over buttered spaghetti. Sprinkle with Parmesan cheese.

variations
● Place spaghetti in large baking dish. Pour sauce in center. Sprinkle with Parmesan cheese. Broil until lightly browned.
● Add 10-oz. pkg. frozen peas to Step 1.
Darlene Raber/Wellman, IA

Dorothy's Chicken Tetrazzini

Dorothy Shank/Sterling, IL

 **MAKES 6 SERVINGS**

3–4 cups diced, cooked chicken

2 cups chicken broth

10 3/4-oz. can cream of mushroom soup

1/2 lb. fresh mushrooms, sliced

1 cup half-and-half

1 lb. cooked spaghetti

1. Combine chicken, broth, and soup in slow cooker.

2. Cover. Cook on Low 4–6 hours.

3. During last hour of cooking, stir in half-and-half.

4. Serve chicken and sauce over cooked spaghetti.

Chickenetti

Miriam Nolt/New Holland, PA
Ruth Hershey/Paradise, PA

 **MAKES 10 SERVINGS**

1 cup chicken broth

16-oz. pkg. spaghetti, cooked

4–6 cups cubed and cooked chicken, or turkey, breast

10 3/4-oz. can cream of mushroom soup, or cream of celery soup

1 cup water

1/4 cup green peppers, chopped

1/2 cup diced celery

1/2 tsp. pepper

1 medium onion, grated

1/2 lb. white, or yellow, American cheese, cubed

1. Put cup of chicken broth into very large slow cooker. Add spaghetti and meat.

2. In large bowl, combine soup and water until smooth. Stir in remaining ingredients, then pour into slow cooker.

3. Cover. Cook on Low 2–3 hours.

variations

● For a creamier dish, add a 10 3/4-oz. can cream of chicken soup to Step 2.
Arlene Miller/Hutchinson, KS
● Add 4 1/2-oz. can chopped green chilies to Step 2, for more zest.

Meat Balls and Spaghetti Sauce

Carol Sommers
Millersburg, OH

 **MAKES 6–8 SERVINGS**

Meatballs:

1 1/2 lbs. ground beef

2 eggs

1 cup bread crumbs

oil

Sauce:

28-oz. can tomato puree

6-oz. can tomato paste

10 3/4-oz. can tomato soup

1/4–1/2 cup grated Romano or Parmesan cheese

1 tsp. oil

1 garlic clove, minced

sliced mushrooms (either canned or fresh), optional

1. Combine ground beef, eggs, and bread crumbs. Form into 16 meatballs. Brown in oil in skillet.

2. Combine sauce ingredients in slow cooker. Add meatballs. Stir together gently.

3. Cover. Cook on Low 6–8 hours. Add mushrooms 1–2 hours before sauce is finished.

4. Serve over cooked spaghetti.

Chili Spaghetti

Clara Newswanger
Gordonville, PA

 MAKES 8–10 SERVINGS

1/2 cup diced onions
2 cups tomato juice
2 tsp. chili powder
1 tsp. salt
3/4 cup grated mild cheese
1 1/2 lbs. ground beef,
   browned
12-oz. dry spaghetti,
   cooked

1. Combine all ingredients in slow cooker.

2. Cover. Cook on Low 4 hours. Check mixture about halfway through the cooking time. If it's becoming dry, stir in an additional cup of tomato juice.

variations
● Add 8-oz. can sliced mushrooms to Step 1.
● Use 2 Tbsp. chili powder instead of 2 tsp. chili powder for added flavor.

Dawn's Spaghetti and Meat Sauce

Dawn Day/Westminster, CA

 MAKES 6–8 SERVINGS

1 lb. ground beef
1 Tbsp. oil, if needed
1/2 lb. mushrooms, sliced
1 medium onion, chopped
3 garlic cloves, minced
1/2 tsp. dried oregano
1/2 tsp. salt
1/4 cup grated Parmesan
   or Romano cheese
6-oz. can tomato paste
2 15-oz. cans tomato sauce
15-oz. can chopped or
   crushed tomatoes

1. Brown ground beef in skillet, in oil if needed. Reserve drippings and transfer meat to slow cooker.

2. Sauté mushrooms, onion, and garlic until onions are transparent. Add to slow cooker.

3. Add remaining ingredients to cooker. Mix well.

4. Cover. Cook on Low 6 hours.

5. Serve with pasta and garlic bread.

note
● This recipe freezes well.

Spaghetti Sauce for a Crowd

Sue Pennington
Bridgewater, VA

 MAKES 18 CUPS

1 lb. ground beef
1 lb. ground turkey
1 Tbsp. oil
5 15-oz. cans tomato sauce
3 6-oz. cans tomato paste
1 cup water
1/2 cup minced fresh
   parsley, or 3 Tbsp. dried
   parsley
1/2 cup minced fresh
   oregano, or 3 Tbsp.
   dried oregano
4 tsp. salt

1. Brown meat in oil in skillet. Place in 6-qt. slow cooker. (A 5-qt. cooker will work, but it will be filled to the brim.)

2. Add remaining ingredients. Mix together thoroughly.

3. Cover. Cook on Low 4–6 hours.

note
● Sauce can be refrigerated for a week or frozen up to 3 months.

Spaghetti Sauce with a Kick

Andrea O'Neil/Fairfield, CT

**MAKES 4–6 SERVINGS**

1 lb. ground beef
1 onion, chopped
2 28-oz. cans crushed
   tomatoes
16-oz. can tomato sauce
1 lb. Italian sausage, cut
   in chunks
3 cloves garlic, crushed
1 Tbsp. Italian seasoning
2 tsp. dried basil
red pepper flakes to taste

1. Brown beef and onions in skillet. Drain and transfer to slow cooker.

2. Add remaining ingredients.

3. Cover. Cook on Low 4–6 hours.

4. Serve over your favorite pasta.

variation
● Add 1–2 tsp. salt and 1–2 Tbsp. brown sugar or honey, if desired.

Chicken Cacciatore with Spaghetti

Phyllis Pellman Good
Lancaster, PA

**MAKES 4–5 SERVINGS**

2 onions, sliced
2 1/2–3 lbs. chicken legs
2 garlic cloves, minced
16-oz. can stewed tomatoes
8-oz. can tomato sauce
1 tsp. salt
1/4 tsp. pepper
1–2 tsp. dried oregano
1/2 tsp. dried basil
1 bay leaf
1/4 cup white wine

1. Place onions in bottom of slow cooker.

2. Lay chicken legs over onions.

3. Combine remaining ingredients. Pour over chicken.

4. Cover. Cook on Low 6–6 1/2 hours.

5. Remove bay leaf. Serve over hot buttered spaghetti, linguini, or fettucini.

Violette's Lasagna

Violette Harris Denney
Carrollton, GA

**MAKES 8 SERVINGS**

8 lasagna noodles,
   uncooked
1 lb. ground beef
1 tsp. Italian seasoning
28-oz. jar spaghetti sauce
1/3 cup water
4-oz. can sliced mushrooms
15 oz. ricotta cheese
2 cups shredded mozzarella
   cheese

1. Break noodles. Place half in bottom of greased slow cooker.

2. Brown ground beef in saucepan. Drain. Stir in Italian seasoning. Spread half over noodles in slow cooker.

3. Layer half of sauce and water, half of mushrooms, half of ricotta cheese, and half of mozzarella cheese over beef. Repeat layers.

4. Cover. Cook on Low 5 hours.

Slow Cooker Lasagna

Crystal Brunk
Singers Glen, VA

MAKES 6–8 SERVINGS

1 lb. ground beef, browned
4–5 cups spaghetti sauce, depending upon how firm or how juicy you want the finished lasagna
24-oz. container cottage cheese
1 egg
8–10 lasagna noodles, uncooked
2–3 cups mozzarella cheese

1. Combine ground beef and spaghetti sauce.

2. Combine egg and cottage cheese.

3. Layer half of the ground beef mixture, the dry noodles, the cottage cheese mixture, and the mozzarella cheese in the slow cooker. Repeat layers.

4. Cover. Cook on High 4–5 hours or on Low 6–8 hours.

Lazy Lasagna

Deborah Santiago
Lancaster, PA

MAKES 6 SERVINGS

1 lb. ground beef, browned
32-oz. jar spaghetti sauce
8-oz. bag curly-edged noodles, cooked, or lasagna noodles cut up, cooked
16-oz. carton cottage cheese
8 ozs. shredded mozzarella cheese
Parmesan cheese to taste

1. Combine beef and spaghetti sauce.

2. Combine noodles, cottage cheese, and mozzarella cheese.

3. Layer one-third of the beef mixture, followed by half the noodle mixture in slow cooker. Repeat layers, ending with beef mixture. Sprinkle with Parmesan cheese.

4. Cover. Cook on Low 3–4 hours.

5. Serve with salad and French bread.

Egg Noodle Lasagna

Anna Stoltzfus
Honey Brook, PA

MAKES 12–16 SERVINGS

6 1/2 cups wide egg noodles, cooked
3 Tbsp. butter, or margarine
2 1/4 cups spaghetti sauce
1 1/2 lbs. ground beef, browned
6 ozs. Velveeta cheese, cubed
3 cups shredded mozzarella cheese

1. Toss butter with hot noodles.

2. Spread one-fourth of spaghetti sauce in slow cooker. Layer with one-third of noodles, beef, and cheeses. Repeat layers 2 more times.

3. Cover. Cook on Low 4 hours, or until cheese is melted.

Chicken at a Whim

Colleen Heatwole/Burton, MI

MAKES 6–8 SERVINGS

6 medium-sized, boneless, skinless chicken-breast halves

1 small onion, sliced

1 cup dry white wine, chicken broth, or water

15-oz. can chicken broth

2 cups water

6-oz. can sliced black olives, with juice

1 small can artichoke hearts, with juice

5 garlic cloves, minced

1 cup dry elbow macaroni, or small shells

1 envelope dry savory garlic soup

1. Place chicken in slow cooker. Spread onion over chicken.

2. Combine remaining ingredients, except dry soup mix, and pour over chicken. Sprinkle with dry soup.

3. Cover. Cook on Low 4 1/2 hours.

Cheryl's Macaroni and Cheese

Cheryl Bartel/Hillsboro, KS

MAKES 6 SERVINGS

8 oz. dry elbow macaroni, cooked

3–4 cups (about 3/4 lb.) shredded sharp cheddar cheese, divided

13-oz. can evaporated milk

1 1/2 cups milk

2 eggs

1 tsp. salt

1/4 tsp. black pepper

chopped onion to taste

1. Combine all ingredients, except 1 cup cheese, in greased slow cooker. Sprinkle reserved cup of cheese over top.

2. Cover. Cook on Low 3–4 hours. Do not remove the lid or stir until the mixture has finished cooking.

variation

● For some extra zest, add 1/2 tsp. dry mustard when combining all ingredients. Add thin slices of cheese to top of cooker mixture.

Dorothy M. Pittman
Pickens, SC

Macaroni and Cheese

Martha Hershey/Ronks, PA

Marcia S. Myer/Manheim, PA

LeAnne Nolt/Leola, PA

Ellen Ranck/Gap, PA

Mary Sommerfeld
Lancaster, PA

Kathryn Yoder/Minot, ND

MAKES 6 SERVINGS

8-oz. pkg. dry macaroni, cooked

2 Tbsp. oil

13-oz. can evaporated milk (fat-free will work)

1 1/2 cups milk

1 tsp. salt

3 cups (about 1/2 lb.) shredded cheese: cheddar, American, Velveeta, or a combination

2–4 Tbsp. melted butter

2 Tbsp. onion, chopped fine

4 hot dogs, sliced, optional

1. In slow cooker, toss macaroni in oil. Stir in remaining ingredients except hot dogs.

2. Cover. Cook on Low 2–3 hours. Add hot dogs, if desired, and cook 1 hour longer.

Beef and Macaroni

Esther J. Yoder/Hartville, OH

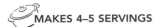
MAKES 4–5 SERVINGS

1 lb. ground beef
1 small onion, chopped
half a green pepper, chopped
1 cup cooked macaroni
1/2 tsp. dried basil
1/2 tsp. dried thyme
1 tsp. Worcestershire sauce
1 tsp. salt
10 3/4-oz. can cheddar cheese soup

1. Brown beef, onions, and green pepper in skillet. Pour off drippings and place meat and vegetables in slow cooker.

2. Combine all ingredients in cooker.

3. Cover. Cook on High 2–2 1/2 hours, stirring once or twice.

4. Serve with broccoli and applesauce.

Macaroni and Cheese

Sherry L. Lapp/Lancaster, PA

MAKES 8 SERVINGS

8-oz. pkg. elbow macaroni, cooked al dente
13-oz. can evaporated milk
1 cup whole milk
1/4 cup butter, melted
2 large eggs, slightly beaten
4 cups grated sharp cheddar cheese, divided
1/4–1/2 tsp. salt, according to your taste preferences
1/8 tsp. white pepper
1/4 cup grated Parmesan cheese

1. In slow cooker, combine lightly cooked macaroni, evaporated milk, whole milk, melted butter, eggs, 3 cups cheddar cheese, salt, and pepper.

2. Top with remaining cheddar and Parmesan cheeses.

3. Cover. Cook on Low 3 hours.

Chicken Pasta

Evelyn L. Ward/Greeley, CO

MAKES 4 SERVINGS

1 1/2-lb. boneless chicken breast
1 large zucchini, diced
1 pkg. chicken gravy mix
2 Tbsp. water
2 Tbsp. evaporated milk or cream
1 large tomato, chopped
4 cups cooked macaroni
8 ozs. smoked Gouda cheese, grated

1. Cut chicken into 1" cubes. Place in slow cooker.

2. Add zucchini, gravy mix, and water, and stir together.

3. Cover. Cook on Low 6 hours.

4. Add milk and tomato. Cook an additional 20 minutes.

5. Stir in pasta. Top with cheese. Serve immediately.

Macaroni and Cheese

Arlene Groff/Lewistown, PA

MAKES 5 SERVINGS

8 cups cooked macaroni
1 1/4 cups milk
1 lb. (1/2 block) Velveeta cheese, cubed
1/4 cup melted butter

1. Place macaroni in greased slow cooker.

2. Layer cheese over top. Pour milk and butter over all.

3. Cover. Cook on Low 4 hours, stirring once halfway through cooking time.

Macaroni and Cheese

Leona Yoder/Hartville, OH

MAKES 8–10 SERVINGS

2–3 Tbsp. butter, or margarine
1 qt. milk
1 lb. mild cheese, grated, or Velveeta cheese, cubed
1/2 tsp. salt
1/8 tsp. pepper
1 lb. macaroni, cooked al dente and rinsed

1. Melt margarine in large saucepan. Add milk. Heat slowly but do not boil.

2. When very hot, stir in cheese, salt, and pepper. Stir until cheese is melted.

3. Stir in macaroni.

4. Pour into greased slow cooker.

5. Cover. Cook on High 15 minutes, then on Low 30 minutes.

This recipe is an oven-saver. Fifty or sixty children eat this delightedly—in fact, it's one of their favorite meals—at the day school where I cook.

— • —

Slow and Easy Macaroni and Cheese

Janice Muller/Derwood, MD

MAKES 6–8 SERVINGS

1 lb. dry macaroni
1/2 cup butter or margarine
2 eggs
12-oz. can evaporated milk
10 3/4-oz. can cheddar cheese soup
1 cup milk
4 cups shredded cheddar cheese, divided
1/8 tsp. paprika

1. Cook macaroni al dente. Drain and pour hot macaroni into slow cooker.

2. Slice butter into chunks and add to macaroni. Stir until melted.

3. Combine, eggs, evaporated milk, soup, and milk. Add 3 cups cheese. Pour over macaroni and mix well.

4. Cover. Cook on Low 4 hours. Sprinkle with remaining cheese. Cook 15 minutes until cheese melts.

5. Sprinkle with paprika before serving.

Meal-in-One-Casserole

Elizabeth Yoder
Millersburg, OH

Marcella Stalter/Flanagan, IL

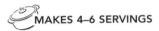

MAKES 4–6 SERVINGS

1 lb. ground beef
1 medium onion, chopped
1 medium green pepper, chopped
15 1/4-oz. can whole kernel corn, drained
4-oz. can mushrooms, drained
1 tsp. salt
1/4 tsp. pepper
11-oz. jar salsa
5 cups uncooked medium egg noodles
28-oz. can diced tomatoes, undrained
1 cup shredded cheddar cheese

1. Cook beef and onion in saucepan over medium heat until meat is no longer pink. Drain. Put in slow cooker.

2. Add green pepper, corn, mushrooms, salt, pepper, and salsa. Cover and cook on Low 3 hours.

3. After 3 hours, add noodles, cooked as directed. Top with tomatoes and cheese.

4. Cover. Cook on Low 1 more hour.

Noodle Hamburger Dish

Esther J. Yoder/Hartville, OH

MAKES 10 SERVINGS

1 1/2 lbs. ground beef, browned and drained
1 green pepper, diced
1 qt. whole tomatoes
10 3/4-oz. can cream of mushroom soup
1 large onion, diced
1 1/2 Tbsp. Worcestershire sauce
8-oz. pkg. noodles, uncooked
1 tsp. salt
1/4 tsp. pepper
1 cup shredded cheese

1. Combine all ingredients except cheese in slow cooker.

2. Cover. Cook on High 3–4 hours.

3. Sprinkle with cheese before serving.

Yum-e-setti

Elsie Schlabach
Millersburg, OH

MAKES 6–8 SERVINGS

1 1/2 lbs. ground beef, browned and drained
10 3/4-oz. can tomato soup
8-oz. pkg. wide noodles, cooked
10 3/4-oz. can cream of chicken soup
1 cup chopped celery, cooked tender
2 tsp. salt
1 lb. frozen mixed vegetables
1/2 lb. Velveeta cheese, cubed

1. Combine ground beef and tomato soup.

2. Combine chicken soup, noodles, and celery.

3. Layer beef mixture, chicken mixture, and vegetables. Sprinkle with salt. Lay cheese over top.

4. Cover. Cook on Low 2–3 hours.

variation
● For more "bite," use shredded cheddar cheese instead of cubed Velveeta.

Chicken Alfredo

Dawn M. Propst
Levittown, PA

MAKES 4–6 SERVINGS

16-oz. jar Alfredo sauce
4-6 boneless, skinless
  chicken breast halves
8 ozs. dry noodles, cooked
4-oz. can mushroom pieces
  and stems, drained
1 cup shredded mozzarella
  cheese, or 1/2 cup grated
  Parmesan cheese

1. Pour about one-third of Alfredo sauce in bottom of slow cooker.

2. Add chicken and cover with remaining sauce.

3. Cover. Cook on Low 8 hours.

4. Fifteen minutes before serving, add noodles and mushrooms, mixing well. Sprinkle top with cheese. Dish is ready to serve when cheese is melted.

5. Serve with green salad and Italian bread.

Golden Chicken and Noodles

Sue Pennington
Bridgewater, VA

MAKES 6 SERVINGS

6 boneless, skinless chicken-
  breast halves
2 10 3/4-oz. cans broccoli
  cheese soup
2 cups milk
1 small onion, chopped
1/2–1 tsp. salt
1/2–1 tsp. dried basil
1/8 tsp. pepper

1. Place chicken pieces in slow cooker.

2. Combine remaining ingredients. Pour over chicken.

3. Cover. Cook on High 1 hour. Reduce heat to Low. Cook 5–6 hours.

4. Serve over noodles.

Tuna Noodle Casserole

Leona Miller/Millersburg, OH

MAKES 6 SERVINGS

2 6 1/2-oz. cans water-
  packed tuna, drained
2 10 1/2-oz. cans cream of
  mushroom soup
1 cup milk
2 Tbsp. dried parsley
10-oz. pkg. frozen mixed
  vegetables, thawed
10-oz. pkg. noodles, cooked
  and drained
1/2 cup toasted sliced
  almonds

1. Combine tuna, soup, milk, parsley, and vegetables. Fold in noodles. Pour into greased slow cooker. Top with almonds.

2. Cover. Cook on Low 7–9 hours, or High 3–4 hours.

Tuna Noodle Casserole

Ruth Hofstetter/Versailles, MO

 **MAKES 8 SERVINGS**

2 1/2 cups dry noodles

1 tsp. salt

1/2 cup finely chopped onion

6- or 12-oz. can tuna, according to your taste preference

10 3/4-oz. can cream of mushroom soup

half a soup can of water

1/4 cup almonds, optional

1/2 cup shredded Swiss, or sharp cheddar cheese

1 cup frozen peas

1. Combine all ingredients in slow cooker, except peas.

2. Cover. Cook on High 2–3 hours or on Low 6–8 hours, stirring occasionally.

3. Twenty minutes before end of cooking time, stir in peas and reduce heat to Low if cooking on High.

Rigatoni

Susan Alexander
Baltimore, MD

 **MAKES 10 SERVINGS**

28-oz. jar spaghetti sauce

12 oz. rigatoni, cooked

1–1 1/2 lbs. ground beef, browned

3 cups shredded mozzarella cheese

1/2 lb. pepperoni slices

sliced mushrooms, optional

sliced onions, optional

1. In 4-quart slow cooker, layer half of each ingredient in order listed. Repeat.

2. Cover. Cook on Low 4–5 hours.

variation
● Use 1 lb. ground beef and 1 lb. sausage.

Slow-Cooker Pizza

Maria Folkerts/Holland, OH

Ruth Ann Swartzendruber
Hydro, OK

Arlene Wiens/Newton, KS

 **MAKES 6–8 SERVINGS**

1 1/2 lbs. ground beef, or bulk Italian sausage

1 medium onion, chopped

1 green pepper, chopped

half a box rigatoni, cooked

7-oz. jar sliced mushrooms, drained

3 oz. sliced pepperoni

16-oz. jar pizza sauce

10 oz. mozzarella cheese, shredded

10 oz. cheddar cheese, shredded

1. Brown ground beef and onions in saucepan. Drain.

2. In cooker, layer half of the following in this order: ground beef and onions, green pepper, noodles, mushrooms, pepperoni, pizza sauce, cheddar cheese, and mozzarella cheese. Repeat layers.

3. Cover. Cook on Low 3–4 hours.

note
● Keep rigatoni covered with sauce so they don't become dry and crunchy.

Pizza Rigatoni

Tina Snyder/Manheim, PA

 **MAKES 6–8 SERVINGS**

1 1/2 lbs. bulk sausage

3 cups rigatoni, lightly cooked

4 cups shredded mozzarella cheese

10 3/4-oz. can cream of mushroom soup

1 small onion, sliced

15-oz. can pizza sauce

8-oz. can pizza sauce

3 1/2-oz. pkg. sliced pepperoni

6-oz. can sliced ripe olives

1. Cook and drain sausage. Place half in 4-qt., or larger, slow cooker.

2. Layer half of pasta, cheese, soup, onion, pizza sauce, pepperoni, and olives over sausage. Repeat layers.

3. Cover. Cook on Low 4 hours.

note

● If your store doesn't carry 8-oz. cans pizza sauce, substitute an 8-oz. can tomato sauce with basil, garlic, and oregano.

Crockpot Pizza

Sharon Miller/Holmesville, OH

 **MAKES 6 SERVINGS**

1 1/2 lbs. bulk sausage

1 small onion, chopped

1-lb. pkg. pasta, or noodles, uncooked

28-oz. jar spaghetti sauce

16-oz. can tomato sauce

3/4 cup water

4-oz. can mushrooms, drained

16-oz. pkg. shredded mozzarella cheese

8-oz. pkg. pepperoni, chopped

1. Brown sausage and onion in skillet. Drain. Place one-third of mixture in cooker.

2. Layer in one-third of uncooked pasta.

3. Combine spaghetti sauce, tomato sauce, water, and mushrooms in bowl. Ladle one third of that mixture over noodles.

4. Repeat the above layers 2 more times.

5. Top with pepperoni. Top that with shredded cheese.

6. Cover. Cook on Low 6–8 hours.

Hot Dogs and Noodles

Dolores Kratz/Souderton, PA

 **MAKES 6 SERVINGS**

8-oz. pkg. medium egg noodles, cooked and drained

1 1/4 cups grated Parmesan cheese

1 cup milk

1/4 cup butter, or margarine, melted

1 Tbsp. flour

1/4 tsp. salt

1-lb. pkg. hot dogs, sliced

1/4 cup packed brown sugar

1/4 cup mayonnaise

2 Tbsp. prepared mustard

1. Place noodles, cheese, milk, butter, flour, and salt in slow cooker. Mix well.

2. Combine hot dogs with remaining ingredients. Spoon evenly over noodles.

3. Cover. Cook on Low 5–6 hours.

Chicken and Sausage Cacciatore

Joyce Kaut/Rochester, NY

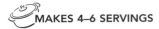
MAKES 4–6 SERVINGS

1 large green pepper, sliced in 1-inch strips
1 cup sliced mushrooms
1 medium onion, sliced in rings
1 lb. skinless, boneless chicken breasts, browned
1 lb. Italian sausage, browned
1/2 tsp. dried oregano
1/2 tsp. dried basil
1 1/2 cups Italian-style tomato sauce

1. Layer vegetables in slow cooker.

2. Top with meat.

3. Sprinkle with oregano and basil.

4. Top with tomato sauce.

5. Cover. Cook on Low 8 hours.

6. Remove cover during last 30 minutes of cooking time to allow sauce to cook-off and thicken.

7. Serve over cooked spiral pasta.

Red Beans and Pasta

Naomi E. Fast/Hesston, KS

MAKES 6–8 SERVINGS

3 15-oz. cans chicken, or vegetable, broth
1/2 tsp. ground cumin
1 Tbsp. chili powder
1 garlic clove, minced
8 ozs. uncooked spiral pasta
half a large green pepper, diced
half a large red pepper, diced
1 medium onion, diced
15-oz. can red beans, rinsed and drained
chopped fresh parsley
chopped fresh cilantro

1. Combine broth, cumin, chili powder, and garlic in slow cooker.

2. Cover. Cook on High until mixture comes to boil.

3. Add pasta, vegetables, and beans. Stir together well.

4. Cover. Cook on Low 3–4 hours.

5. Add parsley or cilantro before serving.

Company Seafood Pasta

Jennifer Yoder Sommers Harrisonburg, VA

MAKES 4–6 SERVINGS

2 cups sour cream
3 cups shredded Monterey Jack cheese
2 Tbsp. butter, or margarine, melted
1/2 lb. crabmeat, or imitation flaked crabmeat
1/8 tsp. pepper
1/2 lb. bay scallops, lightly cooked
1 lb. medium shrimp, cooked and peeled

1. Combine sour cream, cheese and butter in slow cooker.

2. Stir in remaining ingredients.

3. Cover. Cook on Low 1–2 hours.

4. Serve immediately over linguine. Garnish with fresh parsley.

Minestra Di Ceci

Jeanette Oberholtzer
Manheim, PA

 **MAKES 4–6 SERVINGS**

1 lb. dry chickpeas
1 sprig fresh rosemary
10 leaves fresh sage
2 Tbsp. salt
1–2 large garlic cloves, minced
olive oil
1 cup small dry pasta

1. Soak chickpeas in slow cooker for 8 hours in full pot of water, with rosemary, sage, and salt.

2. Drain. Remove herbs.

3. Refill slow cooker with water to 1" above peas.

4. Cover. Cook on Low 5 hours.

5. Sauté garlic in olive oil in skillet until clear.

6. Puree half of peas, with several cups of broth in blender. Return to cooker. Add garlic and oil.

7. Boil pasta until al dente, about 5 minutes. Drain. Add to beans.

8. Cover. Cook on High 30–60 minutes, or until pasta is tender and heated through, but not mushy.

Pizza Rice

Sue Hamilton/Minooka, IL

 **MAKES 6 SERVINGS**

2 cups rice, uncooked
3 cups chunky pizza sauce
2 1/2 cups water
7-oz. can mushrooms, undrained
4 oz. pepperoni, sliced
1 cup grated cheese

1. Combine rice, sauce, water, mushrooms, and pepperoni. Stir.

2. Cover. Cook on Low 10 hours, or on High 6 hours. Sprinkle with cheese before serving.

Arroz Con Queso

Nadine L. Martinitz/Salina, KS

MAKES 6–8 SERVINGS

14.5-oz. can whole tomatoes, mashed
15-oz. can Mexican style beans, undrained
1 1/2 cups uncooked long grain rice
1 cup grated Monterey Jack cheese
1 large onion, finely chopped
1 cup cottage cheese
4.25-oz. can chopped green chili peppers, drained
1 Tbsp. oil
3 garlic cloves, minced
1 tsp. salt
1 cup grated Monterey Jack cheese

1. Combine all ingredients except final cup of cheese. Pour into well greased slow cooker.

2. Cover. Cook on Low 6–9 hours.

3. Sprinkle with remaining cheese before serving.

4. Serve with salsa.

Wanda's Chicken and Rice Casserole

Wanda Roth/Napoleon, OH

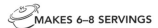

MAKES 6–8 SERVINGS

1 cup long-grain rice, uncooked
3 cups water
2 tsp. chicken bouillon granules
10 3/4-oz. can cream of chicken soup
16-oz. bag frozen broccoli
2 cups chopped, cooked chicken
1/4 tsp. garlic powder
1 tsp. onion salt
1 cup grated cheddar cheese

1. Combine all ingredients in slow cooker.

2. Cook on High 3–4 hours.

note
● If casserole is too runny, remove lid from slow cooker for 15 minutes while continuing to cook on High.

Chicken Rice Dish

Esther Porter/Minneapolis, MN

MAKES 4 SERVINGS

1 cup cooked rice
10 3/4-oz. can cream of chicken soup
1 cup chicken broth
4 chicken thighs, partially cooked
10-oz. pkg. broccoli, frozen

1. Combine rice, soup, chicken broth, and chicken thighs. Place mixture in slow cooker.

2. Cover. Cook on Low 4 hours.

3. During last hour of cooking time, stir in broccoli.

Sharon's Chicken and Rice Casserole

Sharon Anders/Alburtis, PA

MAKES 2 SERVINGS

10 3/4-oz. can cream of celery soup
2-oz. can sliced mushrooms, undrained
1/2 cup raw long grain rice
2 chicken-breast halves, skinned and boned
1 Tbsp. dry onion soup mix

1. Combine soup, mushrooms, and rice in greased slow cooker. Mix well.

2. Layer chicken breasts on top of mixture. Sprinkle with onion soup mix.

3. Cover. Cook on Low 4–6 hours.

Barbara's Chicken Rice Casserole

Barbara A. Yoder/Goshen, IN

 MAKES 6–8 SERVINGS

2 chicken bouillon cubes
2 cups hot water
1/2 cup margarine, melted
6-oz. box Uncle Ben's Long Grain and Wild Rice (Original Recipe), uncooked
4 1/2-oz. jar sliced mushrooms
10-oz. can cooked chicken

1. Dissolve bouillon in hot water.

2. Combine all ingredients, including rice seasoning packet, in slow cooker.

3. Cover. Cook on High 2 hours, or until rice is tender.

note
● To reduce salt in recipe, use 2 cups low- or no-sodium chicken broth instead of 2 chicken bouillon cubes and water.

Chicken Rice Special

Jeanne Allen/Rye, CO

 MAKES 6–8 SERVINGS

6 chicken breast halves, cooked and chopped (save 4 cups broth)
1 lb. pork, or turkey, sausage, browned
half a large sweet green pepper, chopped
1 medium onion, chopped
4 ribs celery, chopped
1 cup rice, uncooked
2-oz. pkg. dry noodle-soup mix
1/2 cup sliced almonds
1-2 oz. jar pimentos, chopped

1. Combine all ingredients except almonds and pimentos in slow cooker.

2. Top with almonds and pimentos.

3. Cover. Cook on high 4–6 hours, or until rice is done and liquid has been absorbed.

4. Stir up 1 hour before serving.

Tex-Mex Chicken and Rice

Kelly Evenson/Pittsboro, NC

 MAKES 8 SERVINGS

1 cup converted uncooked white rice
28-oz. can diced peeled tomatoes
6-oz. can tomato paste
3 cups hot water
1 pkg. dry taco seasoning mix
4 whole boneless, skinless chicken breasts, uncooked and cut into 1/2-inch cubes
2 medium onions, chopped
1 green pepper, chopped
4-oz. can diced green chilies
1 tsp. garlic powder
1/2 tsp. pepper

1. Combine all ingredients except chilies and seasonings in large slow cooker.

2. Cover. Cook on Low 4–4 1/2 hours, or until rice is tender and chicken is cooked.

3. Stir in green chilies and seasonings and serve.

4. Serve with mixed green leafy salad and refried beans.

Company Casserole

Vera Schmucker/Goshen, IN

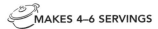

MAKES 4–6 SERVINGS

1 1/4 cups uncooked rice

1/2 cup (1 stick) butter, melted

3 cups chicken broth

3–4 cups cut-up cooked chicken breast

2 4-oz. cans sliced mushrooms, drained

1/3 cup soy sauce

12-oz. pkg. shelled frozen shrimp

8 green onions, chopped, 2 Tbsp. reserved

2/3 cup slivered almonds

1. Combine rice and butter in slow cooker. Stir to coat rice well.

2. Add remaining ingredients except almonds and 2 Tbsp. green onions.

3. Cover. Cook on Low 6–8 hours or on High 3–4 hours, until rice is tender.

4. Sprinkle almonds and green onions over top before serving.

5. Serve with green beans, tossed salad, and fruit salad.

Chicken Broccoli Rice Casserole

Gloria Julien/Gladstone, MI

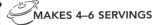

MAKES 4–6 SERVINGS

1 onion, chopped

3 Tbsp. oil

2–3 cups uncooked chicken, cut in 1-inch pieces

10 3/4-oz. can cream of chicken soup

12-oz. can evaporated milk

2 cups cubed Velveeta cheese

3 cups cooked rice

2 cups frozen broccoli cuts, thawed

1/4 tsp. pepper

4-oz. can mushrooms, drained

1. Sauté onion in oil in skillet.

2. Add chicken and sauté until no longer pink.

3. Combine all ingredients in slow cooker.

4. Cover. Cook on Low 2–3 hours.

notes
● This is an ideal dish for people who are not big meat-eaters.
● This is good carry-in for potluck or fellowship meals. I put the ingredients together the night before.

Baked Chicken and Rice

Fannie Miller/Hutchinson, KS

MAKES 10–12 SERVINGS

2 cups dry instant rice

10 3/4-oz. can cream of chicken soup

10 3/4-oz. can cream of mushroom soup

10 3/4-oz. can cream of celery soup

1/2 cup butter or margarine

1 soup can water

10 skinless chicken breast halves, or 1 chicken, cut into 10–12 pieces

1 pkg. dry onion soup mix

1. Place rice in large slow cooker.

2. Combine soups, butter, and water. Pour half over rice.

3. Lay chicken over rice. Pour remaining soup mixture over chicken.

4. Sprinkle with dry onion soup mix.

5. Cover. Cook on Low 4–6 hours, or until chicken is done but not dry, and rice is tender but not mushy.

Loretta's Spanish Rice

Loretta Krahn/Mt. Lake, MN

 MAKES 8 SERVINGS

2 lbs. ground beef,
 browned
2 medium onions, chopped
2 green peppers, chopped
28-oz. can tomatoes
8-oz. can tomato sauce
1 1/2 cups water
2 1/2 tsp. chili powder
2 tsp. salt
2 tsp. Worcestershire sauce
1 1/2 cups rice, uncooked

1. Combine all ingredients in slow cooker.

2. Cover. Cook on Low 8–10 hours, or High 6 hours.

Evie's Spanish Rice

Evie Hershey/Atglen, PA

 MAKES 10–12 SERVINGS

2 lbs. lean ground beef
2 onions, chopped
2 green peppers, chopped
1 qt. canned tomatoes
8-oz. can tomato sauce
1 cup water
2 1/2 tsp. chili powder
2 tsp. salt
2 tsp. Worcestershire sauce
1 cup converted rice,
 uncooked

1. Brown beef in skillet. Drain.

2. Combine all ingredients in slow cooker. Stir.

3. Cover. Cook on Low 7–9 hours.

Hearty Rice Casserole

Dale Peterson/Rapid City, SD

 MAKES 12–16 SERVINGS

10 3/4-oz. can cream of
 mushroom soup
10 3/4-oz. can creamy onion
 soup
10 3/4-oz. can cream of
 chicken soup
1 cup water
1 lb. ground beef, browned
1 lb. pork sausage,
 browned
1 large onion, chopped
1 large green pepper,
 chopped
1 1/2 cups long grain rice
shredded cheese, optional

1. Combine all ingredients except cheese in slow cooker. Mix well.

2. Cover. Cook on Low 6–7 hours, sprinkling with cheese during last hour, if you wish.

Hamburger Rice Casserole

Shari Mast/Harrisonburg, VA

 MAKES 6–8 SERVINGS

1/2 lb. ground beef
1 onion, chopped
1 cup diced celery
1 tsp. dried basil
1 tsp. dried oregano
10 3/4-oz. can cream of
  mushroom soup
1 soup can water
4 cups cooked rice
4-oz. can mushroom pieces,
  drained
Velveeta cheese slices

1. Brown ground beef, onion, and celery in skillet. Season with basil and oregano.

2. Combine soup and water in bowl.

3. In well greased slow cooker, layer half of rice, half of mushrooms, half of ground-beef mixture, and half of soup. Repeat layers.

4. Cover. Cook on High 4 hours.

5. Top with cheese 30 minutes before serving.

Beef and Pepper Rice

Liz Ann Yoder/Hartville, OH

 MAKES 4–6 SERVINGS

1 lb. ground beef
2 green peppers, or
  1 green and 1 red pepper,
  coarsely chopped
1 cup chopped onions
1 cup brown rice, uncooked
2 beef bouillon cubes,
  crushed
3 cups water
1 Tbsp. soy sauce

1. Brown beef in skillet. Drain.

2. Combine all ingredients in slow cooker. Mix well.

3. Cover. Cook on Low 5–6 hours or on High 3 hours, or until liquid is absorbed.

Jambalaya

Doris M. Coyle-Zipp
South Ozone Park, NY

 MAKES 5–6 SERVINGS

3 1/2–4-lb. roasting chicken,
  cut up
3 onions, diced
1 carrot, sliced
3–4 garlic cloves, minced
1 tsp. dried oregano
1 tsp. dried basil
1 tsp. salt
1/8 tsp. white pepper
14-oz. can crushed
  tomatoes
1 lb. shelled raw shrimp
2 cups cooked rice

1. Combine all ingredients except shrimp and rice in slow cooker.

2. Cover. Cook on Low 2–3 1/2 hours, or until chicken is tender.

3. Add shrimp and rice.

4. Cover. Cook on High 15–20 minutes, or until shrimp are done.

Seafood Medley

Susan Alexander
Baltimore, MD

MAKES 10–12 SERVINGS

1 lb. shrimp, peeled and
  deveined
1 lb. crabmeat
1 lb. bay scallops
2 10 3/4-oz. cans cream
  of celery soup
2 soup cans milk
2 Tbsp. butter, melted
1 tsp. Old Bay seasoning
1/4–1/2 tsp. salt
1/4 tsp. pepper

1. Layer shrimp, crab, and
scallops in slow cooker.

2. Combine soup and milk.
Pour over seafood.

3. Mix together butter and
spices and pour over top.

4. Cover. Cook on Low
3–4 hours.

5. Serve over rice or noodles.

Curried Shrimp

Charlotte Shaffer/East Earl, PA

MAKES 4–5 SERVINGS

1 small onion, chopped
2 cups cooked shrimp
1 tsp. curry powder
10 3/4-oz. can cream of
  mushroom soup
1 cup sour cream

1. Combine all ingredients
except sour cream in slow
cooker.

2. Cover. Cook on Low 4–6
hours.

3. Ten minutes before
serving, stir in sour cream.

4. Serve over rice or puff
pastry.

variation
● Add another 1/2 tsp. curry
for some added flavor.

Oriental Shrimp Casserole

Sharon Wantland
Menomonee Falls, WI

MAKES 10 SERVINGS

4 cups cooked rice
2 cups cooked or canned
  shrimp
1 cup cooked or canned
  chicken
1-lb. can (2 cups) Chinese
  vegetables
10 3/4-oz. can cream of
  celery soup
1/2 cup milk
1/2 cup chopped green
  peppers
1 Tbsp. soy sauce
can of Chinese noodles

1. Combine all ingredients
except noodles in slow
cooker.

2. Cover. Cook on Low
45 minutes.

3. Top with noodles just
before serving.

Beans

Barbecued Lentils

Sue Hamilton/Minooka, IL

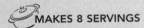 **MAKES 8 SERVINGS**

2 cups barbecue sauce
3 1/2 cups water
1 lb. dry lentils
1 pkg. vegetarian hot dogs, sliced

1. Combine all ingredients in slow cooker.

2. Cover. Cook on Low 6–8 hours.

Sausage Bean Quickie

Ellen Ranck/Gap, PA

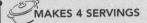 **MAKES 4 SERVINGS**

4–6 cooked brown-and-serve sausage links, cut into 1-inch pieces
2 tsp. cider vinegar
2 16-oz. cans red kidney, or baked beans, drained
7-oz. can pineapple chunks, undrained
2 tsp. brown sugar
3 Tbsp. flour

1. Combine sausage, vinegar, beans, and pineapple in slow cooker.

2. Combine brown sugar with flour. Add to slow cooker. Stir well.

3. Cover. Cook on Low 5–10 hours, or High 1–2 hours.

Barbecued Beans

Jane Steiner/Orrville, OH

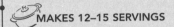 **MAKES 12–15 SERVINGS**

4 11-oz. cans pork and beans
3/4 cup brown sugar
1 tsp. dry mustard
1/2 cup ketchup
6 slices bacon, diced

1. Pour 2 cans pork and beans into slow cooker.

2. Combine brown sugar and mustard. Sprinkle half of mixture over beans.

3. Cover with remaining cans of pork and beans. Sprinkle with rest of brown sugar and mustard.

4. Layer bacon over top. Spread ketchup over all.

5. Cut through bean mixture a bit before heating.

6. Cover. Cook on Low 4 hours.

...supereasy

From-Scratch Baked Beans

Wanda Roth/Napoleon, OH

 **MAKES 6 SERVINGS**

2 1/2 cups Great Northern
   dried beans
4 cups water
1 1/2 cups tomato sauce
1/2 cup brown sugar
2 tsp. salt
1 small onion, chopped
1/2 tsp. chili powder

1. Wash and drain dry
beans. Combine beans and
water in slow cooker. Cook
on Low 8 hours, or overnight.

2. Stir in remaining
ingredients. Cook on Low
6 hours.

Pioneer Beans

Kay Magruder/Seminole, OK

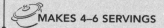 **MAKES 4–6 SERVINGS**

1 lb. dry lima beans
1 bunch green onions,
   chopped
3 beef bouillon cubes
6 cups water
1 lb. smoked sausage
1/2 tsp. garlic powder
3/4 tsp. Tabasco sauce

1. Combine all ingredients
in slow cooker. Mix well.

2. Cover. Cook on High 8–9
hours, or until beans are soft
but not mushy.

3. Serve with home-baked
bread and butter.

Linda's Baked Beans

Linda Sluiter/Schererville, IN

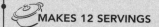 **MAKES 12 SERVINGS**

16-oz. can red kidney
   beans, drained
15 1/2-oz. can butter beans,
   drained
18-oz. jar B&M beans
1/4 lb. Velveeta cheese,
   cubed
1/2 lb. bacon, diced
1/2 cup brown sugar
1/3 cup sugar
2 dashes Worcestershire
   sauce

1. Combine all ingredients
in slow cooker.

2. Cover. Cook on Low
6 hours. Do not stir until
nearly finished cooking.

New England Baked Beans

Mary Wheatley/Mashpee, MA
Jean Butzer/Batavia, NY

 MAKES 8 SERVINGS

1 lb. dried beans—Great Northern, pea beans, or navy beans
1/4 lb. salt pork, sliced or diced
1 qt. water
1 tsp. salt
1–4 Tbsp. brown sugar, according to your preference
1/2 cup molasses
1/2–1 tsp. dry mustard, according to your preference
1/2 tsp. baking soda
1 onion, coarsely chopped
5 cups water

1. Wash beans and remove any stones or shriveled beans.

2. Meanwhile, simmer salt pork in 1 quart water in saucepan for 10 minutes. Drain. Do not reserve liquid.

3. Combine all ingredients in slow cooker.

4. Cook on High until contents come to boil. Turn to Low. Cook 14–16 hours, or until beans are tender.

Mom's New England Baked Beans

Debbie Zeida/Mashpee, MA

 MAKES 6–8 SERVINGS

3 cups dried navy beans
9 cups water
1 medium onion, chopped
1 cup ketchup
1 cup brown sugar
1 cup water
2 tsp. dry mustard
2 Tbsp. dark molasses
1 Tbsp. salt
1/4 lb. salt pork, ground or diced

1. Cook beans in water in soup pot until softened, or bring to boil, cover, and let stand for 1 1/2 hours. Drain. Pour beans into slow cooker.

2. Stir in remaining ingredients. Mix well.

3. Cover. Cook on Low 8 hours, or High 4 hours, stirring occasionally.

variation
● Use 1 lb. dried Great Northern beans instead of 3 cups navy beans.
Dorothy Miller/Gulfport, MI

Home-Baked Beans

Carolyn Baer/Conrath, WI

 MAKES 15–25 SERVINGS

2 lbs. (4 cups) dried navy, or pea, beans
1 lb. salt pork, or bacon, chopped
1 lb. (2 1/2 cups), or less, brown sugar
1-lb. 3-oz. can tomatoes
2 medium onions, chopped
2 Tbsp. prepared mustard
1/2 tsp. salt
1/2 tsp. pepper

1. Wash and pick over beans. Cover generously with water and soak overnight. Simmer in salted water until tender. Drain. Save liquid.

2. Place pork or bacon in bottom of slow cooker.

3. Mix together brown sugar, tomatoes, onions, mustard, salt, and pepper. Alternately layer sauce mixture and beans over pork.

4. Add enough reserved water to cover beans.

5. Cover. Cook on Low 8–10 hours, stirring occasionally.

note
● These beans freeze well.

Barbecued Lima Beans

Hazel L. Propst/Oxford, PA

MAKES 10 SERVINGS

1 1/2 lbs. dried lima beans
6 cups water
2 1/4 cups chopped onions
1 1/4 cups brown sugar
1 1/2 cups ketchup
13 drops Tabasco sauce
1 cup dark corn syrup
1 Tbsp. salt
1/2 lb. bacon, diced

1. Soak washed beans in water overnight. Do not drain.

2. Add onion. Bring to boil. Simmer 30–60 minutes, or until beans are tender. Drain beans, reserving liquid.

3. Combine all ingredients except bean liquid in slow cooker. Mix well. Pour in enough liquid so that beans are barely covered.

4. Cover. Cook on Low 10 hours, or High 4–6 hours. Stir occasionally.

No Meat Baked Beans

Esther Becker/Gordonville, PA

MAKES 8–10 SERVINGS

1 lb. dried navy beans
6 cups water
1 small onion, chopped
3/4 cup ketchup
3/4 cup brown sugar
3/4 cup water
1 tsp. dry mustard
2 Tbsp. dark molasses
1 tsp. salt

1. Soak beans in water overnight in large soup kettle. Cook beans in water until soft, about 1 1/2 hours. Drain, discarding bean water.

2. Mix together all ingredients in slow cooker. Mix well.

3. Cover. Cook on Low 10–12 hours.

Frances' Slow-Cooker Beans

Frances B. Musser
Newmanstown, PA

MAKES 6–8 SERVINGS

1/2 cup ketchup
1 Tbsp. prepared mustard
1/2 cup brown sugar
1 small onion, chopped
1 tsp. salt
1/4 tsp. ground ginger
1/2 cup molasses
1 lb. turkey bacon, browned and crumbled
2 1/2 lb. can Great Northern beans, drained

1. Combine all ingredients in slow cooker.

2. Cover. Cook on Low 4 hours.

Kelly's Baked Beans

Kelly Bailey
Mechanicsburg, PA

MAKES 6 SERVINGS

40-oz. can Great Northern beans, juice reserved
15 1/2-oz. can Great Northern beans, juice reserved
3/4 cup brown sugar
1/4 cup white corn syrup
1/2 cup ketchup
1/2 tsp. salt
half a medium-sized onion, chopped
8–9 slices bacon, browned and crumbled, optional

1. Drain beans overnight in colander. Save 1/4 cup liquid.

2. Mix together brown sugar, corn syrup, and ketchup. Mix well. Add salt and onion.

3. Stir in beans and pour into greased slow cooker. If beans appear dry while cooking, add some of the 1/4 cup reserved bean juice.

4. Cover. Cook on Low 6–8 hours.

Nan's Barbecued Beans

Nan Decker/Albuquerque, NM

MAKES 10–12 SERVINGS

1 lb. ground beef
1 onion, chopped
5 cups canned baked beans
2 Tbsp. cider vinegar
1 Tbsp. Worcestershire sauce
2 Tbsp. brown sugar
1/2 cup ketchup

1. Brown ground beef and onion in skillet. Drain.

2. Combine all ingredients in slow cooker.

3. Cover. Cook on Low 4–6 hours.

Roseann's Baked Beans

Roseann Wilson
Albuquerque, NM

MAKES 12 SERVINGS

2 42-oz. cans baked beans, drained
1 lb. ground beef, cooked and drained
1/2 cup barbecue sauce
1/4 cup ketchup
1 Tbsp. prepared mustard
3 strips bacon, diced
1/4 cup brown sugar
2 Tbsp. minced onion
3 strips bacon, cut in half

1. Combine all ingredients except half strips of bacon in slow cooker. Place 6 half-strips of bacon over top.

2. Cover. Cook on Low 3 hours.

Main Dish Baked Beans

Sue Pennington
Bridgewater, VA

 MAKES 6–8 MAIN-DISH
SERVINGS, OR 12–16
SIDE-DISH SERVINGS

1 lb. ground beef
28-oz. can baked beans
8-oz. can pineapple tidbits,
drained
4 1/2-oz. can sliced
mushrooms, drained
1 large onion, chopped
1 large green pepper,
chopped
1/2 cup barbecue sauce
2 Tbsp. soy sauce
1 clove garlic, minced
1/2 tsp. salt
1/4 tsp. pepper

1. Brown ground beef in
skillet. Drain. Place in slow
cooker.

2. Stir in remaining
ingredients. Mix well.

3. Cover. Cook on Low
4–8 hours, or until bubbly.
Serve in soup bowls.

Apple-Bean Pot

Charlotte Bull/Cassville, MO

 MAKES 12 SERVINGS

53-oz. can baked beans,
well drained
1 large onion, chopped
3 tart apples, peeled and
chopped
1/2 cup ketchup, or
barbecue sauce
1/2 cup firmly packed
brown sugar
1 pkg. smoky cocktail
sausages, or chopped hot
dogs, or chopped ham
chunks, optional

1. Place beans in slow
cooker.

2. Add onions and apples.
Mix well.

3. Stir in ketchup or
barbecue sauce, brown
sugar, and meat. Mix.

4. Cover. Heat on Low
3–4 hours, and then on
High 30 minutes.

Ann's Boston Baked Beans

Ann Driscoll/Albuquerque, MN

 MAKES 20 SERVINGS

1 cup raisins
2 small onions, diced
2 tart apples, diced
1 cup chili sauce
1 cup chopped ham, or
crumbled bacon
2 1-lb., 15-oz. cans baked
beans
3 tsp. dry mustard
1/2 cup sweet pickle relish

1. Mix together all
ingredients.

2. Cover. Cook on Low
6–8 hours.

"Famous" Baked Beans

Katrine Rose/Woodbridge, VA

MAKES 10 SERVINGS

1 lb. ground beef
1/4 cup minced onions
1 cup ketchup
4 15-oz. cans pork and beans
1 cup brown sugar
2 Tbsp. liquid smoke
1 Tbsp. Worcestershire sauce

1. Brown beef and onions in skillet. Drain. Spoon meat and onions into slow cooker.

2. Add remaining ingredients and stir well.

3. Cover. Cook on High 3 hours or on Low 5–6 hours.

There are many worthy baked bean recipes, but this one is both easy and absolutely delicious. The secret to this recipe is the liquid smoke. I get many requests for this recipe, and some friends have added the word "famous" to its name.

— • —

Esther's Barbecued Beans

Esther J. Yoder/Hartville, OH

MAKES 10 SERVINGS

1 lb. ground beef
1/2 cup chopped onions
1/2 tsp. salt
1/4 tsp. pepper
28-oz. can pork and beans (your favorite variety)
1/2 cup ketchup
1 Tbsp. Worcestershire sauce
1 Tbsp. vinegar
1/4 tsp. Tabasco sauce

1. Brown beef and onions together in skillet. Drain.

2. Combine all ingredients in slow cooker.

3. Cover. Cook on High 2–3 hours, stirring once or twice.

4. Serve with fresh raw vegetables and canned peaches.

note
● The flavor of these beans gets better on the second and third days.

Dollywood Cowboy Beans

Reba Rhodes/Bridgewater, VA

MAKES 8 SERVINGS

1 lb. ground beef
1 large onion, finely chopped
1 small green bell pepper, finely chopped
28-oz. can pork and beans
1 1/2 cups ketchup
1 tsp. vinegar
3 Tbsp. brown sugar
2 tsp. prepared mustard
2 tsp. salt
1 tsp. pepper

1. Brown ground beef, onion, and bell pepper in skillet. Transfer to slow cooker.

2. Combine all ingredients in slow cooker. Mix well.

3. Cover. Cook on Low 1–2 hours.

This travels well to a potluck or a picnic.

— • —

Deb's Baked Beans

Deborah Swartz/Grottoes, VA

MAKES 4–6 SERVINGS

4 slices bacon, fried and drained
2 Tbsp. reserved drippings
1/2 cup chopped onions
2 15-oz. cans pork and beans
1/2 tsp. salt, optional
2 Tbsp. brown sugar
1 Tbsp. Worcestershire sauce
1 tsp. prepared mustard

1. Fry bacon in skillet until crisp. Reserve 2 Tbsp. drippings. Crumble bacon.

2. Cook onions in bacon drippings.

3. Combine all ingredients in slow cooker.

4. Cover. Cook on High 1 1/2–2 hours.

Auntie Ginny's Baked Beans

Becky Harder/Monument, CO

MAKES 8 SERVINGS

4 slices bacon, diced
28-oz. can pork and beans
1 tsp. dark molasses
1 Tbsp. brown sugar
1 cup dates, cut up
1 medium onion, chopped

1. Partially fry bacon. Drain.

2. Combine ingredients in slow cooker.

3. Cover. Cook on Low 4–5 hours.

note
● Written down at the bottom of this recipe was this note: "Harder picnic—1974." Notations such as that one help us remember special family get-togethers or reunions. This recipe was shared almost 20 years ago as we gathered cousins and aunts together in our hometown. Today no one from our family lives in the hometown and we cousins are scattered over six states, but one way to enjoy fond memories is to record dates or events on recipes we share with each other.

Slow Cooker Kidney Beans

Jeanette Oberholtzer
Manheim, PA

MAKES 12 SERVINGS

2 30-oz. cans kidney beans, rinsed and drained
28-oz. can diced tomatoes, drained
2 medium-sized red bell peppers, chopped
1 cup ketchup
1/2 cup brown sugar
1/4 cup honey
1/4 cup molasses
1 Tbsp. Worcestershire sauce
1 tsp. dry mustard
2 medium red apples, cored, cut into pieces

1. Combine all ingredients, except apples, in slow cooker.

2. Cover. Cook on Low 4–5 hours.

3. Stir in apples.

4. Cover. Cook 2 more hours.

Tasty, meatless eating!

— ● —

Hot Bean Dish Without Meat

Jeannine Janzen/Elbing, KS

MAKES 8–10 SERVINGS

16-oz. can kidney beans, drained
15-oz. can lima beans, drained
1/4 cup vinegar
2 Tbsp. molasses
2 heaping Tbsp. brown sugar
2 Tbsp. minced onion
mustard to taste
Tabasco sauce to taste

1. Place beans in slow cooker.

2. Combine remaining ingredients. Pour over beans.

3. Cover. Cook on Low 3–4 hours.

variation
● Add 1 lb. browned ground beef to make this a meaty main dish.

Betty's Calico Beans

Betty Lahman/Elkton, VA

MAKES 6–8 SERVINGS

1 lb. ground beef, browned and drained
14 3/4-oz. can lima beans
15 1/2-oz. can pinto beans
15 1/4-oz. can corn
1/4 cup brown sugar
1 cup ketchup
1 Tbsp. vinegar
2 tsp. prepared mustard
1 medium onion, chopped

1. Combine all ingredients in slow cooker.

2. Cover. Cook on High 3–4 hours.

Baked Beans in Slow Cooker

Ruth Hershey/Paradise, PA

MAKES 12 SERVINGS

1 1/2 lbs. ground beef
1/2–1 cup chopped onions, according to your preference
3 lbs. pork and beans
1-lb. can kidney beans, drained
1 cup ketchup
1/4 cup brown sugar, packed
3 Tbsp. cider vinegar

1. Brown ground beef and onion in skillet. Drain.

2. Combine all ingredients in slow cooker. Mix well.

3. Cover. Cook on Low 4–6 hours. Stir occasionally.

Char's Calico Beans

Char Hagner/Montague, MI

 MAKES 10–12 SERVINGS

1/4 lb. bacon
1 onion, chopped
1 lb. ground beef
1/2 cup brown sugar
1/2 cup ketchup
1 Tbsp. prepared mustard
1 tsp. salt
2 15-oz. cans lima beans, drained
28-oz. can Boston baked beans
2 16-oz. cans kidney beans, drained

1. Cut bacon in pieces. Brown in skillet and drain. Brown onion with beef in skillet. Drain.

2. Combine all ingredients in slow cooker.

3. Cover. Cook on Low 6 hours.

Allen's Beans

John D. Allen/Rye, CO

 MAKES 10–12 SERVINGS

1 large onion, chopped
1 lb. ground beef, browned
15-oz. can pork and beans
15-oz. can ranch-style beans, drained
16-oz. can kidney beans, drained
1 cup ketchup
1 tsp. salt
1 Tbsp. prepared mustard
2 Tbsp. brown sugar
2 Tbsp. hickory-flavored barbecue sauce
1/2–1 lb. small smoky link sausages, optional

1. Brown ground beef and onion in skillet. Drain. Transfer to slow cooker set on High.

2. Add remaining ingredients. Mix well.

3. Reduce heat to Low and cook 4–6 hours. Use a paper towel to absorb oil that's risen to the top before stirring and serving.

Lauren's Calico Beans

Lauren Eberhard/Seneca, IL

 MAKES 12–16 SERVINGS

8 slices bacon
1 cup chopped onions
1/2 cup brown sugar
1/2 cup ketchup
2 Tbsp. vinegar
1 tsp. dry mustard
14 1/2-oz. can green beans, drained
16-oz. can kidney beans, drained
15 1/2-oz. can butter beans, drained
15 1/2-oz. can pork and beans

1. Brown bacon in saucepan, reserving drippings. Crumble bacon. Cook onions in bacon drippings. Drain.

2. Combine all ingredients in slow cooker.

3. Cover. Cook on Low 6–8 hours.

Sweet and Sour Beans

Julette Leaman
Harrisonburg, VA

MAKES 6–8 SERVINGS

10 slices bacon

4 medium onions, cut
in rings

1/2–1 cup brown sugar,
according to your
preference

1 tsp. dry mustard

1 tsp. salt

1/4 cup cider vinegar

1-lb. can green beans,
drained

2 1-lb. cans butter beans,
drained

1-lb., 11-oz. can pork and
beans

1. Brown bacon in skillet
and crumble. Drain all but
2 Tbsp. bacon drippings.
Stir in onions, brown sugar,
mustard, salt, and vinegar.
Simmer 20 minutes.

2. Combine all ingredients
in slow cooker.

3. Cover. Cook on Low
3 hours.

Mixed Slow-Cooker Beans

Carol Peachey/Lancaster, PA

MAKES 6 SERVINGS

16-oz. can kidney beans,
drained

15 1/2-oz. can baked beans

1 pint home-frozen, or 1-lb.
pkg. frozen, lima beans

1 pint home-frozen green
beans, or 1-lb. pkg.
frozen green beans

4 slices bacon, browned
and crumbled

1/2 cup ketchup

1/2 cup sugar

1/2 cup brown sugar

2 Tbsp. vinegar

salt to taste

1. Combine beans and
bacon in slow cooker.

2. Stir together remaining
ingredients. Add to beans
and mix well.

3. Cover. Cook on Low
8–10 hours.

Lizzie's California Beans

Lizzie Weaver/Ephrata, PA

MAKES 12 SERVINGS

2 medium onions, cut
in rings

1 cup brown sugar

1 tsp. dry mustard

1 tsp. salt

1/4 cup vinegar

1/3 cup ketchup

1 lb. bacon, browned
and crumbled

16-oz. can green beans,
drained

40-oz. can butter beans,
drained

2 16-oz. cans baked beans

1. In saucepan, mix together
onions, brown sugar, dry
mustard, salt, vinegar, and
ketchup. Simmer in covered
pan for 20 minutes. Add
bacon and beans.

2. Pour into slow cooker.
Cover. Cook on High 2 hours.

LeAnne's Calico Beans

LeAnne Nolt/Leola, PA

 MAKES 10 SERVINGS

1/4–1/2 lb. bacon
1 lb. ground beef
1 medium onion, chopped
2-lb. can pork and beans
1-lb. can Great Northern
   beans, drained
14 1/2-oz. can French-style
   green beans, drained
1/2 cup brown sugar
1/2 cup ketchup
1/2 tsp. salt
2 Tbsp. cider vinegar
1 Tbsp. prepared mustard

1. Brown bacon, ground beef, and onion in skillet until soft. Drain.

2. Combine all ingredients in slow cooker.

3. Cover. Cook on Low 5–6 hours, or on High 2–3 hours.

LaVerne's Baked Beans

LaVerne Olson
Willow Street, PA

 MAKES 16 SERVINGS

1/2 lb. bacon
1 medium onion, chopped
1/2 cup molasses
1/2 cup brown sugar
1/2 tsp. dry mustard
40-oz. can butter beans,
   drained
2 16-oz. cans kidney beans,
   drained
40-oz. can Great Northern
   beans, drained

1. Brown bacon and onion in skillet until bacon is crisp and crumbly. Drain.

2. Combine all ingredients in slow cooker.

3. Cover. Cook on Low 1–3 hours.

Mixed Bean Casserole

Margaret Rich
North Newton, KS

 MAKES 8 SERVINGS

3 slices bacon, cut up
2 Tbsp. grated onion
31-oz. can pork and beans
   in tomato sauce
16-oz. can kidney beans,
   drained
15-oz. can lima beans, or
   butter beans, drained
3 Tbsp. brown sugar,
   packed
1/2 tsp. dry mustard
3 Tbsp. ketchup

1. Combine all ingredients in slow cooker.

2. Cover. Cook on Low 7–8 hours.

Joan's Calico Beans

Joan Becker/Dodge City, KS

MAKES 10–12 SERVINGS

1/4–1/3 lb. bacon, diced
1/2 cup chopped onions
2 16-oz. cans pork and
  beans
15-oz. can butter beans,
  drained
16-oz. can kidney beans,
  drained
1/2 cup packed brown
  sugar
1/2 cup ketchup
1/2 tsp. salt
1 tsp. dry mustard

1. Brown bacon in skillet until crisp. Drain, reserving 2 Tbsp. drippings. Cook onion in drippings until tender. Add bacon and onion to slow cooker.

2. Stir in beans, brown sugar, ketchup, salt, and mustard. Mix well.

3. Cover. Cook on Low 4 1/2–5 1/2 hours, or on High 3–3 1/2 hours.

Barbara's Calico Beans

Barbara Kuhns
Millersburg, OH

MAKES 12 SERVINGS

1 lb. bacon, diced
1 onion, chopped
1/2 cup ketchup
1/3–1/2 cup brown sugar,
  according to taste
3 Tbsp. cider vinegar
28-oz. can pork and beans,
  drained
16-oz. can kidney beans,
  drained
16-oz. can butter beans,
  drained

1. Brown bacon in skillet. Drain, reserving 2 Tbsp. drippings. Sauté onion in bacon drippings.

2. Mix together ketchup, sugar, and vinegar.

3. Combine all ingredients in slow cooker.

4. Cover Cook on Low 3–4 hours.

Doris' Sweet-Sour Bean Trio

Doris Bachman/Putnam, IL

MAKES 6–8 LARGE
SERVINGS

4 slices bacon
1 onion, chopped
1/4 cup brown sugar
1 tsp. crushed garlic
1 tsp. salt
3 Tbsp. cider vinegar
1 tsp. dry mustard
1-lb. can lima beans,
  drained
1-lb. can baked beans,
  drained
1-lb. can kidney beans,
  drained

1. Cook bacon in skillet. Reserve 2 Tbsp. bacon drippings. Crumble bacon.

2. In slow cooker, combine bacon, bacon drippings, onion, brown sugar, garlic, salt, and vinegar. Add beans. Mix well.

3. Cover. Cook on Low 6–8 hours.

Carol's Calico Beans

Carol Sommers
Millersburg, OH

MAKES 10–12 SERVINGS

1/2 lb. bacon, or ground beef
32-oz. can pork and beans
1-lb. can green limas, drained
16-oz. can kidney beans, drained
1-lb. can whole kernel corn, drained
1 tsp. prepared mustard
2 medium onions, chopped
3/4 cup brown sugar
1 cup ketchup

1. Brown bacon or ground beef in skillet. Drain and crumble.

2. Combine beans and meat in slow cooker.

3. Combine mustard, onions, brown sugar, and ketchup. Pour over beans. Mix well.

4. Cover. Cook on Low 4–6 hours.

Ethel's Calico Beans

Ethel Mumaw/Berlin, OH

MAKES 6–8 SERVINGS

1/2 lb. ground beef
1 onion, chopped
1/2 lb. bacon, diced
1/2 cup ketchup
2 Tbsp. cider vinegar
1/2 cup brown sugar, packed
16-oz. can red kidney beans, drained
14 1/2-oz. can pork and beans, undrained
15-oz. can butter beans, drained

1. Brown ground beef, onion, and bacon in skillet. Drain.

2. Combine all ingredients in slow cooker.

3. Cover. Cook on Low 8 hours.

Mary Ellen's and Nancy's Calico Beans

Mary Ellen Wilcox/Scotia, NY
Nancy W. Huber
Green Park, PA

MAKES 12–15 SERVINGS

1/2 lb. bacon
1 lb. ground beef
2 15 1/2-oz. cans pork and beans
2 15 1/2-oz. cans butter beans, drained
2 16-oz. cans kidney beans, drained
1/2 cup sugar
1/2 cup brown sugar
1/4 cup ketchup
1 tsp. prepared mustard
1 tsp. garlic, finely chopped

1. Brown bacon in skillet and then crumble. Drain drippings. Add ground beef and brown. Drain.

2. Combine all ingredients in slow cooker.

3. Cover. Cook on Low 4–6 hours.

Variation:
● Add 1 Tbsp. liquid smoke in Step 2.

Jan Pembleton/Arlington, TX

Sara's Bean Casserole

Sara Harter Fredette
Williamsburg, MA

MAKES 6 SERVINGS

16-oz. can kidney beans, drained
2 1-lb. cans pork and beans
1 cup ketchup
1 Tbsp. Worcestershire sauce
1 tsp. salt
2 cups chopped onions
1 Tbsp. prepared mustard
1 tsp. cider vinegar

1. Combine all ingredients in slow cooker.

2. Cover. Cook on High 2 hours, or Low 4 hours.

Hamburger Beans

Joanne Kennedy
Plattsburgh, NY

MAKES 6 SERVINGS

1 lb. ground beef
1 onion, chopped
2 15-oz. cans pork and beans
15-oz. can butter beans, drained
15-oz. can kidney beans, drained
1/2 tsp. garlic powder
1 cup ketchup
3/4 cup molasses
1/2 cup brown sugar

1. Brown ground beef and onion in skillet. Drain and transfer beef and onion into slow cooker.

2. Add remaining ingredients. Mix well.

3. Cover. Cook on Low 6–7 hours.

Cowboy Beans

Sharon Timpe / Mequon, WI

MAKES 10–12 SERVINGS

6 slices bacon, cut in pieces
1/2 cup onions, chopped
1 garlic clove, minced
16-oz. can baked beans
16-oz. can kidney beans, drained
15-oz. can butter beans or pinto beans, drained
2 Tbsp. dill pickle relish or chopped dill pickles
1/3 cup chili sauce or ketchup
2 tsp. Worcestershire sauce
1/2 cup brown sugar
1/8 tsp. hot pepper sauce, optional

1. Lightly brown bacon, onions, and garlic in skillet. Drain.

2. Combine all ingredients in slow cooker. Mix well.

3. Cover. Cook on Low 5–7 hours or High 3–4 hours.

Trio Bean Casserole

Stacy Schmucker Stoltzfus
Enola, PA

 MAKES 4–6 SERVINGS

16-oz. can kidney beans, drained
16-oz. can green beans, drained
16-oz. can pork and beans with tomato sauce
1/2 cup chopped onions
1/2 cup brown sugar
1/2 cup ketchup
1 Tbsp. vinegar
1 tsp. prepared mustard
1 lb. bacon, fried and crumbled, or 1 lb. cooked ham, cubed
1 Tbsp. barbecue sauce

1. Combine all ingredients in slow cooker. Stir well.

2. Cover. Cook on High 2 hours or Low 3–4 hours.

Dawn's Special Beans

Dawn Day/Westminster, CA

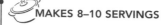 MAKES 8–10 SERVINGS

16-oz. can kidney beans
16-oz. can small white beans
16-oz. can butter beans
16-oz. can small red beans
1 cup chopped onions
2 tsp. dry mustard
1/2 tsp. hickory-smoke flavoring
1/2 cup dark brown sugar
1/2 cup honey
1 cup barbecue sauce
2 Tbsp. apple cider vinegar

1. Combine all ingredients in slow cooker.

2. Cover. Cook on Low 6 hours.

3. Serve with hot dogs, hamburgers, and any other picnic food. These beans are also great for a potluck.

note:
● If you like soupy beans, do not drain the beans before adding them to the cooker. If you prefer a drier outcome, drain all beans before pouring into cooker.

Refried Beans with Bacon

Arlene Wengerd
Millersburg, OH

 MAKES 8 SERVINGS

2 cups dried red, or pinto, beans
6 cups water
2 garlic cloves, minced
1 large tomato, peeled, seeded, and chopped, or 1 pint tomato juice
1 tsp. salt
1/2 lb. bacon
shredded cheese

1. Combine beans, water, garlic, tomato, and salt in slow cooker.

2. Cover. Cook on High 5 hours, stirring occasionally. When the beans become soft, drain off some liquid.

3. While the beans cook, brown bacon in skillet. Drain, reserving drippings. Crumble bacon. Add half of bacon and 3 Tbsp. drippings to beans. Stir.

4. Mash or puree beans with a food processor. Fry the mashed bean mixture in the remaining bacon drippings. Add more salt to taste.

5. To serve, sprinkle the remaining bacon and shredded cheese on top.

New Mexico Pinto Beans

John D. Allen/Rye, CO

MAKES 8–10 SERVINGS

2 1/2 cups dried pinto beans

3 qts. water

1/2 cup ham, or salt pork, diced, or a small ham shank

2 garlic cloves, crushed

1 tsp. crushed red chili peppers, optional

salt to taste

pepper to taste

1. Sort beans. Discard pebbles, shriveled beans, and floaters. Wash beans under running water. Place in saucepan, cover with 3 quarts water, and soak overnight.

2. Drain beans and discard soaking water. Pour beans into slow cooker. Cover with fresh water.

3. Add meat, garlic, chili, salt, and pepper. Cook on Low 6–10 hours, or until beans are soft.

Red Beans and Rice

Margaret A. Moffitt
Bartlett, TN

MAKES 8–10 SERVINGS

1-lb. pkg. dried red beans

water

salt pork, ham hocks, or sausage, cut into small chunks

2 tsp. salt

1 tsp. pepper

3–4 cups water

6-oz. can tomato paste

8-oz. can tomato sauce

4 garlic cloves, minced

1. Soak beans for 8 hours. Drain. Discard soaking water.

2. Mix together all ingredients in slow cooker.

3. Cover. Cook on Low 10–12 hours, or until beans are soft. Serve over rice.

variation
● Use canned red kidney beans. Cook 1 hour on High and then 3 hours on Low.

note
● These beans freeze well.

New Orleans Red Beans

Cheri Jantzen/Houston, TX

MAKES 6 SERVINGS

2 cups dried kidney beans

5 cups water

2 Tbsp. bacon drippings

1/2 lb. hot sausage, cut in small pieces

2 onions, chopped

2 cloves garlic, minced

1 tsp. salt

1. Wash and sort beans. In saucepan, combine beans and water. Boil 2 minutes. Remove from heat. Soak 1 hour.

2. Heat bacon drippings in skillet. Add sausage and brown slowly. Add onions and garlic and sauté until tender.

3. Combine all ingredients, including the bean water, in slow cooker.

4. Cover. Cook on Low 8–10 hours. During last 20 minutes of cooking, stir frequently and mash lightly with spoon.

5. Serve over hot cooked white rice.

Sausage Bean Casserole

Juanita Marner
Shipshewana, IN

**MAKES 8 SERVINGS**

1 lb. ground pork sausage
1/2 cup chopped onions
1/2 cup chopped green
 peppers
1 lb. cooked speckled
 butter beans
2 cups diced canned
 tomatoes
1/2 cup tomato sauce
1/4 tsp. salt
1/8 tsp. pepper

1. Brown sausage, onions, and green peppers in saucepan.

2. Combine all ingredients in slow cooker.

3. Cover. Cook on High 2 hours, or Low 4 hours.

Cajun Sausage and Beans

Melanie Thrower
McPherson, KS

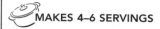**MAKES 4–6 SERVINGS**

1 lb. smoked sausage, sliced
 into 1/4-inch pieces
16-oz. can red beans
16-oz. can crushed
 tomatoes with green
 chilies
1 cup chopped celery
half an onion, chopped
2 Tbsp. Italian seasoning
Tabasco sauce to taste

1. Combine all ingredients in slow cooker.

2. Cover. Cook on Low 8 hours.

3. Serve over rice or as a thick zesty soup.

Black Beans with Ham

Colleen Heatwole/Burton, MI

**MAKES 8–10 SERVINGS**

4 cups dry black beans
1–2 cups diced ham
1 tsp. salt, optional
1 tsp. cumin
1/2–1 cup minced onion
2 garlic cloves, minced
3 bay leaves
1 qt. diced tomatoes
1 Tbsp. brown sugar

1. Cover black beans with water and soak for 8 hours, or overnight. Drain and pour beans into slow cooker.

2. Add all remaining ingredients and stir well. Cover with water.

3. Cover cooker. Cook on Low 10–12 hours.

4. Serve over rice.

This is our favorite black bean recipe. We make it frequently in the winter.

— • —

Side Dishes

Baked Sweet Potatoes

Shari Mast/Harrisonburg, VA

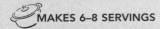MAKES 6–8 SERVINGS

6–8 medium-sized sweet potatoes

1. Scrub and prick sweet potatoes with fork. Wrap each in tin foil and arrange in slow cooker.

2. Cover. Cook on Low 6–8 hours or High 4–5 hours, or until each potato is soft.

3. Remove from foil and serve with butter and salt.

Baked Potatoes

Valerie Hertzler
Weyers Cave, VA
Carol Peachey/Lancaster, PA
Janet L. Roggie/Lowville, NY

Potatoes

1. Prick potatoes with fork and wrap in foil.

2. Cover. Do not add water. Cook on High 2 1/2–4 hours, or Low 8–10 hours.

Baked Potatoes

Lucille Metzler/Wellsboro, PA
Elizabeth Yutzy/Wauseon, OH
Glenda S. Weaver
Manheim, PA
Mary Jane Musser
Manheim, PA
Esther Becker/Gordonville, PA

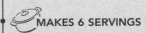MAKES 6 SERVINGS

6 medium baking potatoes
butter, or margarine

1. Prick potatoes with fork. Rub each with either butter or margarine. Place in slow cooker.

2. Cover. Cook on High 3–5 hours, or Low 6–10 hours.

...**supereasy**

Slow-Cooker Potatoes

Arlene Wiens/Newton, KS

MAKES 8 SERVINGS

32-oz. pkg. frozen hash
brown potatoes
2 10 3/4-oz. cans cheddar
cheese soup
2.8-oz. can French-fried
onion rings

1. Combine all ingredients
in greased slow cooker.

2. Cover. Cook on Low 7–8
hours.

Creamy Red Potatoes

Mrs. J. E. Barthold
Bethlehem, PA

MAKES 4–6 SERVINGS

2 lbs. small red potatoes,
quartered
8-oz. pkg. cream cheese,
softened
10 3/4-oz. can cream of
potato soup
1 envelope dry Ranch salad
dressing mix

1. Place potatoes in slow
cooker.

2. Beat together cream
cheese, soup, and salad
dressing mix. Stir into
potatoes.

3. Cover. Cook on Low
8 hours, or until potatoes
are tender.

Scalloped Potatoes

Zona Mae Bontrager
Kokomo, IN

MAKES 10 SERVINGS

5-oz. box scalloped
potatoes
5.25-oz. box au gratin
potatoes
6 hot dogs, sliced, or 1 cup
cubed precooked ham
1/4 tsp. pepper, optional

1. Mix both potatoes per
package instructions.
Combine in slow cooker.

2. Cover. Cook on High
30 minutes.

3. Add meat. Reduce heat
to Low and cook on Low
for 4–5 hours.

I often fix this for church
dinners, and I always bring
home an empty slow cooker.
The children love it with
hot dogs. A quick dish to
prepare and forget.

— • —

Corn on the Cob

Donna Conto/Saylorsburg, PA

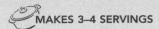 MAKES 3–4 SERVINGS

6–8 ears of corn (in husk)
1/2 cup water

1. Remove silk from corn, as much as possible, but leave husks on.

2. Cut off ends of corn so ears can stand in the cooker.

3. Add water.

4. Cover. Cook on Low 2–3 hours.

Corn Pudding

Barbara A. Yoder/Goshen, IN

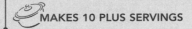 MAKES 10 PLUS SERVINGS

2 10-oz. cans whole kernel corn with juice
2 1-lb. cans creamed corn
2 boxes corn muffin mix
1 stick (1/4 lb.) margarine
8-oz. box sour cream

1. Combine all ingredients in slow cooker.

2. Cover. Heat on Low 2–3 hours until thickened and set.

Caramelized Onions

Mrs. J.E. Barthold
Bethlehem, PA

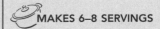 MAKES 6–8 SERVINGS

6–8 large Vidalia or other sweet onions
4 Tbsp. butter, or margarine
10-oz. can chicken, or vegetable, broth

1. Peel onions. Remove stems and root ends. Place in slow cooker.

2. Pour butter and broth over.

3. Cook on Low 12 hours.

note
● Serve as a side dish, or use onions and liquid to flavor soups or stews, or as topping for pizza.

...supereasy

Acorn Squash

Valerie Hertzler
Weyers Cave, VA

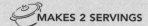 **MAKES 2 SERVINGS**

1 acorn squash
salt
cinnamon
butter

1. Place whole, rinsed squash in slow cooker.

2. Cover. Cook on Low 8–10 hours.

3. Split and remove seeds. Sprinkle each half with salt and cinnamon, dot with butter, and serve.

Doris' Broccoli and Cauliflower with Cheese

Doris G. Herr/Manheim, PA

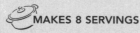 **MAKES 8 SERVINGS**

1 lb. frozen cauliflower
2 10-oz. pkgs. frozen broccoli
1/2 cup water
2 cups shredded cheddar cheese

1. Place cauliflower and broccoli in slow cooker.

2. Add water. Top with cheese.

3. Cook on Low 1 1/2–3 hours, depending upon how crunchy or soft you want the vegetables.

Creamy Cheesy Bean Casserole

Martha Hershey/Ronks, PA

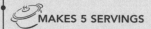 **MAKES 5 SERVINGS**

16-oz. bag frozen green beans, cooked
3/4 cup milk
1 cup grated American cheese
2 slices bread, crumbled

1. Place beans in slow cooker.

2. Combine milk and cheese in saucepan. Heat, stirring continually, until cheese melts. Fold in bread cubes and pour mixture over beans.

3. Cover. Heat on High 2 hours.

variation

● Use 15-oz. container of Cheez Whiz instead of making cheese sauce. Mix crumbled bread into Cheez Whiz and pour over beans. Proceed with Step 3.

Slow-Cooker Rice

Dorothy Horst/Tiskilwa, IL

MAKES 10 SERVINGS

1 Tbsp. butter
4 cups converted long
   grain rice, uncooked
10 cups water
4 tsp. salt

1. Pour rice, water, and salt into greased slow cooker.

2. Cover. Cook on High 2–3 hours, or until rice is tender, but not overcooked. Stir occasionally.

Southwest Cranberries

Bernita Boyts
Shawnee Mission, KS

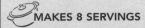MAKES 8 SERVINGS

16-oz. can whole berry
   cranberry sauce
10 1/2-oz. jar jalapeño jelly
2 Tbsp. chopped fresh
   cilantro

1. Combine ingredients in slow cooker.

2. Cover. Cook on Low 2–3 hours.

3. Cool. Serve at room temperature.

4. Serve these spicy cranberries as a side dish or as a marinade for poultry or pork.

Very Special Spinach

Jeanette Oberholtzer
Manheim, PA

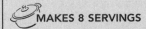MAKES 8 SERVINGS

3 10-oz. boxes frozen
   spinach, thawed and
   drained
2 cups cottage cheese
1 1/2 cups grated cheddar
   cheese
3 eggs
1/4 cup flour
1 tsp. salt
1/2 cup butter, or
   margarine, melted

1. Mix together all ingredients.

2. Pour into slow cooker.

3. Cook on High 1 hour. Reduce heat to Low and cook 4 more hours.

Spinach Casserole

Ann Bender/Ft. Defiance, VA

 **MAKES 6 SERVINGS**

2 10-oz. pkgs. frozen spinach, thawed and drained
2 cups white sauce, or cottage cheese
1/4 cup butter, cubed
1 1/4 cups American cheese, cut into squares
2 eggs, beaten
1/4 cup flour
1 tsp. salt
1 clove garlic, or 1/4 tsp. garlic power

1. Combine all ingredients. Mix well. Pour into greased slow cooker.

2. Cover. Cook on High 1 hour. Reduce heat to Low and cook 4–5 hours.

Orange Glazed Carrots

Cyndie Marrara
Port Matilda, PA

 **MAKES 6 SERVINGS**

32-oz. (2 lbs.) pkg. baby carrots
1/2 cup packed brown sugar
1/2 cup orange juice
3 Tbsp. butter, or margarine
3/4 tsp. cinnamon
1/4 tsp. nutmeg
2 Tbsp. cornstarch
1/4 cup water

1. Combine all ingredients except cornstarch and water in slow cooker.

2. Cover. Cook on Low 3–4 hours until carrots are tender crisp.

3. Put carrots in serving dish and keep warm, reserving cooking juices. Put reserved juices in small saucepan. Bring to boil.

4. Mix cornstarch and water in small bowl until blended. Add to juices. Boil one minute or until thickened, stirring constantly.

5. Pour over carrots and serve.

Glazed Root Vegetable Medley

Teena Wagner/Waterloo, ON

 **MAKES 6 SERVINGS**

2 medium parsnips
4 medium carrots
1 turnip, about 4 1/2 inches around
1/2 cup water
1 tsp. salt
1/2 cup sugar
3 Tbsp. butter
1/2 tsp. salt

1. Clean and peel vegetables. Cut in 1-inch pieces.

2. Dissolve salt in water in saucepan. Add vegetables and boil for 10 minutes. Drain, reserving 1/2 cup liquid.

3. Place vegetables in slow cooker. Add liquid.

4. Stir in sugar, butter, and salt.

5. Cover. Cook on Low 3 hours.

Stewed Tomatoes

Michelle Showalter
Bridgewater, VA

MAKES 10–12 SERVINGS

2 qts. canned tomatoes
1/3 cup sugar
1 1/2 tsp. salt
dash of pepper
3 Tbsp. butter
2 cups bread cubes

1. Place tomatoes in slow cooker.

2. Sprinkle with sugar, salt, and pepper.

3. Lightly toast bread cubes in melted butter. Spread over tomatoes.

4. Cover. Cook on High 3–4 hours.

variation
● If you prefer bread that is less moist and soft, add bread cubes 15 minutes before serving and continue cooking without lid.

Stuffed Mushrooms

Melanie L. Thrower
McPherson, KS

MAKES 4–6 SERVINGS

8–10 large mushrooms
1/4 tsp. minced garlic
1 Tbsp. oil
dash of salt
dash of pepper
dash of cayenne pepper
1/4 cup grated Monterey Jack cheese

1. Remove stems from mushrooms and dice.

2. Heat oil in skillet. Sauté diced stems with garlic until softened. Remove skillet from heat.

3. Stir in seasonings and cheese. Stuff into mushroom shells. Place in slow cooker.

4. Cover. Heat on Low 2–4 hours.

variations
● Add 1 Tbsp. minced onion to Step 2.
● Use Monterey Jack cheese with jalapeños.

Julia's Broccoli and Cauliflower with Cheese

Julia Lapp/New Holland, PA

MAKES 6 SERVINGS

5 cups raw broccoli and cauliflower
1/4 cup water
2 Tbsp. butter, or margarine
2 Tbsp. flour
1/2 tsp. salt
1 cup milk
1 cup shredded cheddar cheese

1. Cook broccoli and cauliflower in saucepan in water, until just crispy tender. Set aside.

2. Make white sauce by melting the butter in another pan over Low heat. Blend in flour and salt. Add milk all at once. Cook quickly, stirring constantly until mixture thickens and bubbles. Add cheese. Stir until melted and smooth.

3. Combine vegetables and sauce in slow cooker. Mix well.

4. Cook on Low 1 1/2 hours.

variation
● Substitute green beans and carrots or other vegetables for broccoli and cauliflower.

Golden Cauliflower

Carol Peachey/Lancaster, PA

 **MAKES 4–6 SERVINGS**

2 10-oz. pkgs. frozen
   cauliflower, thawed
8-oz. jar cheese sauce
4 slices bacon, crisply
   browned and crumbled

1. Place cauliflower in slow cooker.

2. Pour cheese over top. Top with bacon.

3. Cover. Cook on High 1 1/2 hours and then reduce to Low for an additional 2 hours. Or cook only on Low 4–5 hours.

Broccoli Cheese Casserole

Janie Steele/Moore, OK

 **MAKES 8–10 SERVINGS**

10-oz. pkg. frozen chopped
   broccoli, thawed
1 cup cooked rice
1/4 cup chopped celery
10 3/4-oz. can cream of
   chicken soup
4-oz. jar cheese sauce
4-oz. can mushrooms,
   optional
1/8 tsp. garlic powder
1/8 tsp. pepper
1/4–1/2 tsp. salt

1. Mix together all ingredients in slow cooker.

2. Cook on Low 1 1/2 hours, or until heated through.

Sweet-Sour Cabbage

Irma H. Schoen/Windsor, CT

 **MAKES 6 SERVINGS**

1 medium-sized head red,
   or green, cabbage,
   shredded
2 onions, chopped
4 tart apples, pared,
   quartered
1/2 cup raisins
1/4 cup lemon juice
1/4 cup cider, or apple juice
3 Tbsp. honey
1 Tbsp. caraway seeds
1/8 tsp. allspice
1/2 tsp. salt

1. Combine all ingredients in slow cooker.

2. Cook on High 3–5 hours, depending upon how crunchy or soft you want the cabbage and onions.

Bavarian Cabbage

Joyce Shackelford
Green Bay, WI

MAKES 4–8 SERVINGS, DEPENDING UPON THE SIZE OF THE CABBAGE HEAD

1 small head red cabbage, sliced
1 medium onion, chopped
3 tart apples, cored and quartered
2 tsp. salt
1 cup hot water
2 Tbsp. sugar
1/3 cup vinegar
3 Tbsp. bacon drippings

1. Place all ingredients in slow cooker in order listed.

2. Cover. Cook on Low 8 hours, or High 3 hours. Stir well before serving.

variation
● Add 6 slices bacon, browned until crisp and crumbled.
Jean M. Butzer/Batavia, NY

Cabbage Casserole

Edwina Stoltzfus/Narvon, PA

MAKES 6 SERVINGS

1 large head cabbage, chopped
2 cups water
1 Tbsp. salt
1/3 cup butter
1/4 cup flour
1/2–1 tsp. salt
1/4 tsp. pepper
1 1/3 cups milk
1 1/3 cups shredded cheddar cheese

1. Cook cabbage in saucepan in boiling water and salt for 5 minutes. Drain. Place in slow cooker.

2. In saucepan, melt butter. Stir in flour, salt, and pepper. Add milk, stirring constantly on Low heat for 5 minutes. Remove from heat. Stir in cheese. Pour over cabbage.

3. Cover. Cook on Low 4–5 hours.

variation
● Replace cabbage with cauliflower.

Broccoli Casserole

Dorothy Van Deest
Memphis, TN

MAKES 4–6 SERVINGS

10-oz. pkg. frozen chopped broccoli
6 eggs, beaten
24-oz. carton small-curd cottage cheese
6 Tbsp. flour
8 ozs. mild cheese of your choice, diced
1/4 cup butter, melted
2 green onions, chopped
salt to taste

1. Place frozen broccoli in colander. Run cold water over it until it thaws. Separate into pieces. Drain well.

2. Combine remaining ingredients in large bowl and mix until well blended. Stir in broccoli. Pour into greased slow cooker.

3. Cover. Cook on High 1 hour. Stir well, then resume cooking on Low 2–4 hours.

Quick Broccoli Fix

Willard E. Roth/Elkhart, IN

**MAKES 6 SERVINGS**

1 lb. fresh or frozen broccoli, cut up
10 3/4-oz. can cream of mushroom soup
1/2 cup mayonnaise
1/2 cup plain yogurt
1/2 lb. sliced fresh mushrooms
1 cup shredded cheddar cheese, divided
1 cup crushed saltine crackers
sliced almonds, optional

1. Microwave broccoli for 3 minutes. Place in greased slow cooker.

2. Combine soup, mayonnaise, yogurt, mushrooms, and 1/2 cup cheese. Pour over broccoli.

3. Cover. Cook on Low 5–6 hours.

4. Top with remaining cheese and crackers for last half hour of cooking time.

5. Top with sliced almonds, for a special touch, before serving.

Broccoli and Rice Casserole

Deborah Swartz/Grottoes, VA

**MAKES 4–6 SERVINGS**

1 lb. chopped broccoli, fresh or frozen, thawed
1 medium onion, chopped
1/4 cup butter, or margarine
1 cup minute rice, or 1 1/2 cups cooked rice
10 3/4-oz. can cream of chicken or mushroom soup
1/4 cup milk
1 1/3 cups Velveeta cheese, cubed, or cheddar cheese, shredded
1 tsp. salt

1. Cook broccoli for 5 minutes in saucepan in boiling water. Drain and set aside.

2. Sauté onion in butter in saucepan until tender. Add to broccoli.

3. Combine remaining ingredients. Add to broccoli mixture. Pour into greased slow cooker.

4. Cover. Cook on Low 3–4 hours.

Barbecued Green Beans

Arlene Wengerd
Millersburg, OH

**MAKES 4–6 SERVINGS**

1 lb. bacon
1/4 cup chopped onions
3/4 cup ketchup
1/2 cup brown sugar
3 tsp. Worcestershire sauce
3/4 tsp. salt
4 cups green beans

1. Brown bacon in skillet until crisp and then break into pieces. Reserve 2 Tbsp. bacon drippings.

2. Sauté onions in bacon drippings.

3. Combine ketchup, brown sugar, Worcestershire sauce, and salt. Stir into bacon and onions.

4. Pour mixture over green beans and mix lightly.

5. Pour into slow cooker and cook on High 3–4 hours, or on Low 6–8 hours.

Dutch Green Beans

Edwina Stoltzfus/Narvon, PA

MAKES 4–6 SERVINGS

1/2 lb. bacon, or ham chunks
4 medium onions, sliced
2 qts. fresh, frozen, or canned, green beans
4 cups canned stewed tomatoes, or diced fresh tomatoes
1/2–3/4 tsp. salt
1/4 tsp. pepper

1. Brown bacon until crisp in skillet. Drain, reserving 2 Tbsp. drippings. Crumble bacon into small pieces.

2. Sauté onions in bacon drippings.

3. Combine all ingredients in slow cooker.

4. Cover. Cook on Low 4 1/2 hours.

Easy Flavor-Filled Green Beans

Paula Showalter
Weyers Cave, VA

MAKES 10 SERVINGS

2 qts. green beans, drained
1/3 cup chopped onions
4-oz. can mushrooms, drained
2 Tbsp. brown sugar
3 Tbsp. butter
pepper to taste

1. Combine beans, onions, and mushrooms in slow cooker.

2. Sprinkle with brown sugar.

3. Dot with butter.

4. Sprinkle with pepper.

5. Cover. Cook on High 3–4 hours. Stir just before serving.

Green Bean Casserole

Brenda S. Burkholder
Port Republic, VA

MAKES 6–8 SERVINGS

1 qt. cooked green beans
1/2 tsp. sugar
10 3/4-oz. can cream of mushroom soup
3/4 cup grated cheddar cheese

1. Combine ingredients in slow cooker.

2. Cover. Cook on Low 3–4 hours.

> If I ask my husband what to make for a company meal, he quite frequently asks for these beans.

— • —

Green Bean Casserole

Mary Sommerfeld
Lancaster, PA

 **MAKES 6 SERVINGS**

2 lbs. fresh green beans, cut up, or 4 10-oz. pkgs. frozen beans
10 3/4-oz. can cream of mushroom soup
3-oz. can French-fried onion rings
1 cup grated cheddar cheese
8-oz. can water chestnuts, thinly sliced
slivered almonds, optional
salt to taste
pepper to taste
1 cup water

1. In slow cooker, layer one-third of ingredients, except water, in order given. Repeat 2 times, saving a few onion rings for top.

2. Pour water into slow cooker.

3. Cover. Cook on High 4–5 hours or on Low 8–10 hours. Sprinkle reserved onion rings on top 20 minutes before serving.

Green Bean Casserole

Jane Meiser/Harrisonburg, VA

 **MAKES 4–5 SERVINGS**

14 1/2-oz. can green beans, drained
3 1/2-oz. can French fried onions
1 cup grated cheddar cheese
8-oz. can water chestnuts, drained
10 3/4-oz. can cream of chicken soup
1/4 cup white wine or water
1/2 tsp. curry powder
1/4 tsp. pepper

1. Alternate layers of half the beans, half the onions, half the cheese, and half the water chestnuts in slow cooker. Repeat.

2. Combine remaining ingredients. Pour over vegetables in slow cooker.

3. Cover. Cook on Low 6–7 hours or High 3–4 hours.

Green Bean Casserole

Vicki Dinkel
Sharon Springs, KS

 **MAKES 9–11 SERVINGS**

3 10-oz. pkgs. frozen, cut green beans
2 10 1/2-oz. cans cheddar cheese soup
1/2 cup water
1/4 cup chopped green onions
4-oz. can sliced mushrooms, drained
8-oz. can water chestnuts, drained and sliced (optional)
1/2 cup slivered almonds
1 tsp. salt
1/4 tsp. pepper

1. Combine all ingredients in lightly greased slow cooker. Mix well.

2. Cover. Cook on Low 8–10 hours or on High 3–4 hours.

Au Gratin Green Beans

Donna Lantgen/Rapid City, SD

MAKES 8 SERVINGS

2 16-oz. cans green beans, drained
1/4 cup diced onions
1/2 cup cubed Velveeta cheese
1/4 cup evaporated milk
1 tsp. flour
1/2 tsp. salt
dash of pepper

1. Combine all ingredients in slow cooker.

2. Cover. Cook on Low 4 hours.

3. Garnish with sliced almonds at serving time, if you wish.

Green Bean Casserole

Darla Sathre/Baxter, MN

MAKES 8 SERVINGS

4 14 1/2-oz. cans French-style green beans, drained
2 10 3/4-oz. cans cream of celery soup
6-oz. can French-fried onion rings
2 cups shredded cheddar cheese
2 tsp. dried basil
5-oz. can evaporated milk

1. In greased slow cooker, layer half of each ingredient, except milk, in order given. Repeat. Pour milk over all.

2. Cover. Cook on Low 6–10 hours.

Zucchini Special

Louise Stackhouse/Benten, PA

MAKES 4 SERVINGS

1 medium to large zucchini, peeled and sliced
1 medium onion, sliced
1 qt. stewed tomatoes with juice, or 2 14 1/2-oz. cans stewed tomatoes with juice
1/4 tsp. salt
1 tsp. dried basil
8 oz. mozzarella cheese, shredded

1. Layer zucchini, onion, and tomatoes in slow cooker.

2. Sprinkle with salt, basil, and cheese.

3. Cover. Cook on Low 6–8 hours.

Squash Casserole

Sharon Anders/Alburtis, PA

MAKES 4–6 SERVINGS

2 lbs. yellow summer squash, or zucchini, thinly sliced (about 6 cups)

half a medium onion, chopped

1 cup peeled, shredded carrot

10 3/4-oz. can condensed cream of chicken soup

1 cup sour cream

1/4 cup flour

8-oz. pkg. seasoned stuffing crumbs

1/2 cup butter, or margarine, melted

1. Combine squash, onion, carrots, and soup.

2. Mix together sour cream and flour. Stir into vegetables.

3. Toss stuffing mix with butter. Spread half in bottom of slow cooker. Add vegetable mixture. Top with remaining crumbs.

4. Cover. Cook on Low 7–9 hours.

Squash Medley

Evelyn Page/Riverton, WY

MAKES 8 SERVINGS

8 summer squash, each about 4 inches long, thinly sliced

1/2 tsp. salt

2 tomatoes, peeled and chopped

1/4 cup sliced green onions

half a small sweet green pepper, chopped

1 chicken bouillon cube

1/4 cup hot water

4 slices bacon, fried and crumbled

1/4 cup fine dry bread crumbs

1. Sprinkle squash with salt.

2. In slow cooker, layer half the squash, tomatoes, onions, and pepper. Repeat layers.

3. Dissolve bouillon in hot water. Pour into slow cooker.

4. Top with bacon. Sprinkle bread crumbs over top.

5. Cover. Cook on Low 4–6 hours.

variation

● For a sweeter touch, sprinkle 1 Tbsp. brown sugar over half the layered vegetables. Repeat over second half of layered vegetables.

Baked Acorn Squash

Dale Peterson/Rapid City, SD

MAKES 4 SERVINGS

2 acorn squash

2/3 cup cracker crumbs

1/2 cup coarsely chopped pecans

1/3 cup butter, or margarine, melted

4 Tbsp. brown sugar

1/2 tsp. salt

1/4 tsp. ground nutmeg

2 Tbsp. orange juice

1. Cut squash in half. Remove seeds.

2. Combine remaining ingredients. Spoon into squash halves. Place squash in slow cooker.

3. Cover. Cook on Low 5–6 hours, or until squash is tender.

Apple Walnut Squash

Michele Ruvola/Selden, NY

 **MAKES 4 SERVINGS**

1/4 cup water
2 small acorn squash
1/4 cup packed brown sugar
1/4 cup butter, melted
3 Tbsp. apple juice
1 1/2 tsp. ground cinnamon
1/4 tsp. salt
1 cup toasted walnuts
1 apple, chopped

1. Pour water into slow cooker.

2. Cut squash crosswise in half. Remove seeds. Place in slow cooker, cut sides up.

3. Combine brown sugar, butter, apple juice, cinnamon, and salt. Spoon into squash.

4. Cover. Cook on High 3–4 hours, or until squash is tender.

5. Combine walnuts and chopped apple. Add to center of squash and mix with sauce to serve.

6. Serve with a pork dish.

Cheesy Corn

Tina Snyder/Manheim, PA
Jeannine Janzen/Elbing, KS
Nadine Martinitz/Salina, KS

 **MAKES 10 SERVINGS**

3 16-oz. pkgs. frozen corn
8-oz. pkg. cream cheese, cubed
1/4 cup butter, cubed
3 Tbsp. water
3 Tbsp. milk
2 Tbsp. sugar
6 slices American cheese, cut into squares

1. Combine all ingredients in slow cooker. Mix well.

2. Cover. Cook on Low 4 hours, or until heated through and the cheese is melted.

Super Creamed Corn

Ruth Ann Penner
Hillsboro, KS

Alix Nancy Botsford
Seminole, OK

 **MAKES 8-12 SERVINGS**

2–3 lbs. frozen corn
8-oz. pkg. cream cheese, cubed
1/4 cup butter, or margarine, melted
2–3 Tbsp. sugar, or honey
2–3 Tbsp. water, optional

1. Combine ingredients in slow cooker.

2. Cover. Cook on Low 4 hours.

3. Serve with meat loaf, turkey, or hamburgers.

A great addition to a holiday that is easy and requires no last-minute preparation. It also frees the stove and oven for other food preparation.

— • —

Corn Pudding

Lizzie Weaver/Ephrata, PA

 MAKES 3–4 SERVINGS

2 eggs, beaten slightly
1/4 cup sugar
1 tsp. salt
1/8 tsp. pepper
2 Tbsp. melted butter
2 Tbsp. flour
1/2 cup milk
16-oz. can cream-style corn

1. Combine all ingredients except corn. Pour into slow cooker.

2. Add corn. Mix well.

3. Cover. Cook on Low 4 hours.

variation
● Add 1/2 cup grated cheese to Step 2.
Brenda S. Burkholder
Port Republic, VA

This recipe frees your oven space for other dishes. It's perfect, too, for Sunday lunch if you've been gone all morning.

— ● —

Baked Corn

Velma Stauffer/Akron, PA

 MAKES 8 SERVINGS

1 qt. corn, frozen or fresh
2 eggs, beaten
1 tsp. salt
1 cup milk
1/8 tsp. pepper
2 tsp. oil
3 Tbsp. sugar
3 Tbsp. flour

1. Combine all ingredients well. Pour into greased slow cooker.

2. Cover. Cook on High 3 hours and then on Low 45 minutes.

note
● If you use home-grown sweet corn, you could reduce the amount of sugar.

Scalloped Corn

Rebecca Plank Leichty
Harrisonburg, VA

 MAKES 6 SERVINGS

2 eggs
10 3/4-oz. can cream of celery soup
2/3 cup unseasoned bread crumbs
2 cups whole-kernel corn, drained, or cream-style corn
1 tsp. minced onion
1/4–1/2 tsp. salt, according to your taste preference
1/8 tsp. pepper
1 Tbsp. sugar
2 Tbsp. melted butter

1. Beat eggs with fork. Add soup and bread crumbs. Mix well.

2. Add remaining ingredients and mix thoroughly. Pour into greased slow cooker.

3. Cover. Cook on High 3 hours or on Low 6 hours.

Scalloped Corn and Celery

Darla Sathre/Baxter, MN

MAKES 8 SERVINGS

2 16-oz. cans whole-kernel corn, drained
2 16-oz. cans cream-style corn
2 cups chopped celery
40 saltine crackers, crushed
1/8–1/4 tsp. pepper
2 Tbsp. butter
12-oz. can evaporated milk

1. Layer in greased slow cooker, half of whole-kernel corn, cream-style corn, celery, crackers, pepper, and butter. Repeat. Pour milk over all.

2. Cover. Cook on Low 8–12 hours.

Baked Corn and Noodles

Ruth Hershey/Paradise, PA

MAKES 6 SERVINGS

3 cups noodles, cooked al dente
2 cups fresh or frozen corn, thawed
3/4 cup grated cheddar cheese, or cubed Velveeta cheese
1 egg, beaten
1/2 cup butter, melted
1/2 tsp. salt

1. Combine all ingredients in slow cooker.

2. Cover. Cook on Low 6–8 hours or on High 3–4 hours.

Mexican Corn

Betty K. Drescher
Quakertown, PA

MAKES 8–10 SERVINGS

2 10-oz. pkgs. frozen corn, partially thawed
4-oz. jar chopped pimentos
1/3 cup chopped green peppers
1/3 cup water
1 tsp. salt
1/4 tsp. pepper
1/2 tsp. paprika
1/2 tsp. chili powder

1. Combine all ingredients in slow cooker.

2. Cover. Cook on High 45 minutes, then on Low 2–4 hours. Stir occasionally.

variation
● For more fire, add 1/3 cup salsa to the ingredients, and increase the amounts of pepper, paprika, and chili powder to match your taste.

Confetti Scalloped Corn

Rhoda Atzeff/Harrisburg, PA

 **MAKES 6–8 SERVINGS**

2 eggs, beaten
1 cup sour cream
1/4 cup butter or margarine, melted
1 small onion, finely chopped, or 2 Tbsp. dried chopped onion
11-oz. can Mexicorn, drained
14-oz. can cream-style corn
2–3 Tbsp. green jalapeño salsa, regular salsa, or chopped green chilies
8 1/2-oz. pkg. cornbread mix

1. Combine all ingredients. Pour into lightly greased slow cooker.

2. Cover. Bake on High 2–2 1/2 hours, or until corn is fully cooked.

Cheesy Hominy

Michelle Showalter
Bridgewater, VA

 **MAKES 12–14 SERVINGS**

2 cups cracked hominy
6 cups water
2 Tbsp. flour
1 1/2 cups milk
4 cups sharp cheddar cheese, grated
1–2 tsp. salt
1/4 tsp. pepper
4 Tbsp. butter

1. Combine hominy and water in 5–6 qt. slow cooker.

2. Cover. Cook on High 3–4 hours or on Low 6–8 hours.

3. Stir in remaining ingredients.

4. Cover. Cook 30–60 minutes.

Cheesy Hominy is a nice change if you're tired of the same old thing. It's wonderful with ham, slices of bacon, or meatballs. Add a green vegetable and you have a lovely meal. Hominy is available at bulk-food stores.

— • —

Southwest Posole

Becky Harder/Monument, CO

 **MAKES 6 SERVINGS**

2 12-oz. pkgs. dry posole
1 garlic clove, minced
2 14-oz. cans vegetable or chicken broth
2 10-oz. cans Rotel Mexican diced tomatoes
4-oz. can diced green chilies, optional
salt to taste

1. Soak posole for 4–8 hours. Drain water.

2. Combine ingredients in slow cooker.

3. Cover. Cook on High 3 hours; then turn to Low for 2 hours.

4. Serve with enchiladas, black beans, Spanish rice, and chopped lettuce with black olives and tomatoes.

note
● Dry posole can be found in the Mexican food department of the grocery store. If you cannot find dry posole, you can used canned hominy and skip to Step 2.

Candied Sweet Potatoes

Julie Weaver/Reinholds, PA

 MAKES 8 SERVINGS

6–8 medium sweet potatoes
1/2 tsp. salt
1/4 cup butter, or margarine, melted
20-oz. can crushed pineapples, undrained
1/4 cup brown sugar
1 tsp. nutmeg
1 tsp. cinnamon

1. Cook sweet potatoes until soft. Peel. Slice and place in slow cooker.

2. Combine remaining ingredients. Pour over sweet potatoes.

3. Cover. Cook on High 4 hours.

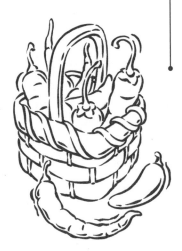

Glazed Sweet Potatoes

Martha Hershey/Ronks, PA

 MAKES 8 SERVINGS

10 medium-sized sweet potatoes
1/2 cup butter, melted
1/4 cup brown sugar
1/2 cup orange juice
1/2 tsp. salt

1. Cook sweet potatoes until just soft. Peel and cut in half.

2. Combine remaining ingredients. Pour over potatoes.

3. Cover. Cook on High 2 1/2–3 hours, or until tender but not mushy.

note
● The sweet potatoes can be cooked and peeled ahead of time, and frozen in a single layer. Defrost before putting in slow cooker. These are great to serve with Thanksgiving dinner.

Sweet Potato Casserole

Jean Butzer/Batavia, NY

 MAKES 8 SERVINGS

2 29-oz. cans sweet potatoes, drained and mashed
1/3 cup (5 1/3 Tbsp.) butter, melted
2 Tbsp. sugar
2 Tbsp. brown sugar
1 Tbsp. orange juice
2 eggs, beaten
1/2 cup milk
1/3 cup chopped pecans
1/3 cup brown sugar
2 Tbsp. flour
2 tsp. butter, melted

1. Combine sweet potatoes, 1/3 cup butter, 2 Tbsp. sugar, and 2 Tbsp. brown sugar.

2. Beat in orange juice, eggs, and milk. Transfer to greased slow cooker.

3. Combine pecans, 1/3 cup brown sugar, flour, and 2 tsp. butter. Spread over sweet potatoes.

4. Cover. Cook on High 3–4 hours.

Orange Yams

Gladys Longacre
Susquehanna, PA

 MAKES 6–8 SERVINGS

40-oz. can yams, drained
2 apples, cored, peeled, thinly sliced
3 Tbsp. butter, melted
2 tsp. orange zest
1 cup orange juice
2 Tbsp. cornstarch
1/2 cup brown sugar
1 tsp. salt
dash of ground cinnamon and/or nutmeg

1. Place yams and apples in slow cooker.

2. Add butter and orange zest.

3. Combine remaining ingredients and pour over yams.

4. Cover. Cook on High 1 hour and on Low 2 hours, or until apples are tender.

variation
● Substitute 6–8 medium-sized cooked sweet potatoes, or approximately 4 cups cubed butternut squash, for yams.

Apples n' Yams

Rebecca Plank Leichty
Harrisonburg, VA

 MAKES 8–10 SERVINGS

1 Tbsp. lemon juice or lemonade
6 apples, peeled and sliced
6 large yams or sweet potatoes, peeled and thinly sliced
1/4 cup apple juice
1 Tbsp. butter, melted

1. Toss sliced apples and yams in lemon juice.

2. Combine apple juice and butter. Pour over apples and sweet potatoes. Pour into greased slow cooker.

3. Cover. Cook on High 4 hours or Low 6 hours.

This is a tasty vegetable dish to add to a meal when serving children. The apples smell wonderful when cooking and truly moisten the potatoes when served together. It is a well-rounded and easy way to serve sweet potatoes.

— ● —

Sweet Potatoes with Applesauce

Judi Manos/West Islip, NY

 MAKES 6–8 SERVINGS

6 medium-sized sweet potatoes, or yams
1 1/2 cups applesauce
2/3 cup packed brown sugar
3 Tbsp. butter, melted
1 tsp. ground cinnamon
1/2 cup chopped toasted nuts

1. Peel sweet potatoes and cut into 1/2" cubes. Place in slow cooker.

2. Combine remaining ingredients, except nuts. Spoon over potatoes.

3. Cover. Cook on Low 6–7 hours or until potatoes are very tender.

4. Sprinkle with nuts.

variation
● If you prefer a less sweet dish, cut the sugar back to 1/3 cup.

Barbecued Black Beans with Sweet Potatoes

Barbara Jean Fabel
Wausau, WI

 MAKES 4–6 SERVINGS

4 large sweet potatoes, peeled and cut into
8 chunks each
15-oz. can black beans, rinsed and drained
1 medium onion, diced
2 ribs celery, sliced
9 ozs. Sweet Baby Ray's Barbecue Sauce

1. Place sweet potatoes in slow cooker.

2. Combine remaining ingredients. Pour over sweet potatoes.

3. Cover. Cook on High 2–3 hours, or on Low 4 hours.

Pizza Potatoes

Margaret Wenger Johnson
Keezletown, VA

 MAKES 4–6 SERVINGS

6 medium potatoes, sliced
1 large onion, thinly sliced
2 Tbsp. olive oil
2 cups grated mozzarella cheese
2 oz. sliced pepperoni
1 tsp. salt
8-oz. can pizza sauce

1. Sauté potato and onion slices in oil in skillet until onions appear transparent. Drain well.

2. In slow cooker, combine potatoes, onions, cheese, pepperoni, and salt.

3. Pour pizza sauce over top.

4. Cover. Cook on Low 6–10 hours, or until potatoes are soft.

German Potato Salad

Lauren Eberhard/Seneca, IL

 MAKES 8 SERVINGS

6 slices bacon
3/4 cup chopped onions
10 3/4-oz. can cream of chicken soup
1/4 cup water
2 Tbsp. cider vinegar
1/2 tsp. sugar
pepper to taste
4 cups parboiled, cubed potatoes
parsley

1. Brown bacon in skillet and then crumble. Reserve 2 Tbsp. bacon drippings. Sauté onions in drippings.

2. Blend together soup, water, vinegar, sugar, and pepper. Add bacon and onions. Mix well.

3. Add potatoes and parsley. Mix well. Pour into slow cooker.

4. Cover. Cook on Low 4 hours.

5. Serve warm or at room temperature.

Saucy Scalloped Potatoes

Sue Pennington
Bridgewater, VA

 MAKES 4–6 SERVINGS

4 cups peeled, thinly sliced potatoes
10 3/4-oz. can cream of celery, or mushroom, soup
12-oz. can evaporated milk
1 large onion, sliced
2 Tbsp. butter, or margarine
1/2 tsp. salt
1/4 tsp. pepper
1 1/2 cups chopped, fully cooked ham

1. Combine potatoes, soup, evaporated milk, onion, butter, salt, and pepper in slow cooker. Mix well.

2. Cover. Cook on High 1 hour. Stir in ham. Reduce to Low. Cook 6–8 hours, or until potatoes are tender.

Creamy Hash Browns

Judy Buller/Bluffton, OH
Elaine Patton
West Middletown, PA
Melissa Raber/Millersburg, OH

 MAKES 14 SERVINGS

2-lb. pkg. frozen, cubed hash brown potatoes
2 cups cubed or shredded American cheese
1 pint (2 cups) sour cream
10 3/4-oz. can cream of celery soup
10 3/4-oz. can cream of chicken soup
1/2 lb. sliced bacon, cooked and crumbled
1 medium onion, chopped
1/4 cup margarine, melted
1/4 tsp. pepper

1. Place potatoes in slow cooker. Combine remaining ingredients and pour over potatoes. Mix well.

2. Cover. Cook on Low 4–5 hours, or until potatoes are tender.

Cheese and Potato Bake

Ann Gouinlock/Alexander, NY

 MAKES 8 SERVINGS

2-lb. bag frozen hash browns
10 3/4-oz. can cheddar cheese soup
10 3/4-oz. can cream of chicken soup
1 cup milk
2.8-oz. can French-fried onion rings
1/2 cup grated cheddar cheese

1. Combine hash browns, soups, and milk in slow cooker. Mix well.

2. Top with half can of onion rings.

3. Cover. Cook on Low 6–8 hours. Sprinkle with cheddar cheese and remaining onion rings about 1 hour before serving.

Cheesy Hash Brown Potatoes

Clarice Williams/Fairbank, IA

MAKES 6–8 SERVINGS

2 10 3/4-oz. cans cheddar cheese soup
1 1/3 cups buttermilk
2 Tbsp. butter, or margarine, melted
1/2 tsp. seasoned salt
1/4 tsp. garlic powder
1/4 tsp. pepper
2-lb. pkg. frozen, cubed hash brown potatoes
1/4 cup grated Parmesan cheese
1 tsp. paprika

1. Combine soup, buttermilk, butter, seasoned salt, garlic powder, and pepper in slow cooker. Mix well.

2. Stir in hash browns. Sprinkle with Parmesan cheese and paprika.

3. Cover. Cook on Low 4–4 1/2 hours, or until potatoes are tender.

Slow-Cooker Cheese Potatoes

Bernice M. Wagner
Dodge City, KS

Marilyn Yoder/Archbold, OH

MAKES 6 SERVINGS

2-lb. pkg. frozen hash browns
10 3/4-oz. can cream of potato soup
10 3/4-oz. can cream of mushroom soup
8 oz. (2 cups) shredded cheddar cheese
1 cup grated Parmesan cheese
1 pint sour cream

1. Mix together all ingredients in slow cooker.

2. Cover. Cook on Low 7 hours.

Scalloped Taters

Sara Wilson/Blairstown, MD

MAKES 6–8 SERVINGS

1/2 cup melted margarine
1/4 cup dried onions
16-oz. pkg. frozen hash brown potatoes
10 3/4-oz. can cream of chicken soup
1 1/2 cups milk
1 cup shredded cheddar cheese
1/8 tsp. black pepper
1 cup crushed cornflakes, divided

1. Stir together margarine, onions, potatoes, soup, milk, cheese, pepper, and 1/2 cup cornflakes. Pour into greased slow cooker. Top with remaining cornflakes.

2. Cover. Cook on High 3–4 hours.

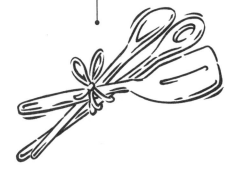

Slow-Cooker Cottage Potatoes

Marjora Miller/Archbold, OH

 **MAKES 10–12 SERVINGS**

2 lbs. frozen hash brown potatoes
1 pint sour cream
10 3/4-oz. can cream of chicken soup
dash of pepper
2 cups Velveeta cheese, cubed
1/2 cup chopped onions
3/4 tsp. salt
1/4 tsp. pepper

1. Combine all ingredients except potatoes in large bowl. Then fold in potatoes. Spoon into slow cooker.

2. Cover. Cook on High 1 1/2 hours, and then on Low 2 1/2 hours.

Cheesy Potatoes

Darla Sathre/Baxter, MN

 **MAKES 6 SERVINGS**

2-lb. pkg. frozen hash browns, partly thawed
2 10 3/4-oz.cans cheddar cheese soup
12-oz. can evaporated milk
2.8-oz. can French-fried onion rings
salt to taste
pepper to taste

1. Combine all ingredients. Pour into greased slow cooker.

2. Cover. Cook on Low 6–8 hours, or on High 3–4 hours.

Au Gratin Hash Brown Potatoes

Penny Blosser
Beavercreek, OH

 **MAKES 12 SERVINGS**

2 lb.-pkg. frozen hash brown potatoes, thawed
1 small onion, diced
1 stick butter, melted
16-oz. container French onion dip
16-oz. jar Cheez Whiz, heated

1. Place hash browns in slow cooker.

2. Combine onion, butter, dip, and Cheez Whiz. Pour over hash browns. Mix well.

3. Cover. Cook on Low 4–6 hours, or High 2–3 hours. (Use the greater number of hours if potatoes are frozen.)

Garlic Mashed Potatoes

Katrine Rose/Woodbridge, VA

MAKES 6 SERVINGS

2 lbs. baking potatoes, unpeeled and cut into 1/2-inch cubes
1/4 cup water
3 Tbsp. butter, sliced
1 tsp. salt
3/4 tsp. garlic powder
1/4 tsp. black pepper
1 cup milk

1. Combine all ingredients, except milk, in slow cooker. Toss to combine.

2. Cover. Cook on Low 7 hours, or on High 4 hours.

3. Add milk to potatoes during last 30 minutes of cooking time.

4. Mash potatoes with potato masher or electric mixer until fairly smooth.

Creamy Mashed Potatoes

Brenda S. Burkholder
Port Republic, VA

MAKES 10–12 SERVINGS

2 tsp. salt
6 Tbsp. (3/4 stick) butter, melted
2 1/4 cups milk
6 7/8 cups potato flakes
6 cups water
1 cup sour cream
4–5 ozs. (approximately half of a large pkg.) cream cheese, softened

1. Combine first five ingredients as directed on potato box.

2. Whip cream cheese with electric mixer until creamy. Blend in sour cream.

3. Fold potatoes into cheese and sour cream. Beat well. Place in slow cooker.

4. Cover. Cook on Low 3–5 hours.

Sunday Dinner Potatoes

Ruth Ann Penner
Hillsboro, KS

MAKES 8 SERVINGS

4 cups cooked, sliced potatoes
1/3 cup margarine
1/4 cup flour
2 cups milk
1 tsp. salt
pepper to taste
1 tsp. onion powder

1. Place potatoes in slow cooker.

2. Melt butter in small skillet. Add flour and stir. Slowly add milk, stirring constantly.

3. Add salt, pepper, and onion powder. When smooth and thickened, pour over potatoes.

4. Cover. Cook on High 2–3 hours or Low 4–5 hours.

Onion Potatoes

Donna Lantgen/Rapid City, SD

MAKES 6 SERVINGS

6 medium potatoes, diced
1/3 cup olive oil
1 pkg. dry onion soup mix

1. Combine potatoes and olive oil in plastic bag. Shake well.

2. Add onion soup mix. Shake well.

3. Pour into slow cooker.

4. Cover. Cook on Low 6 hours or High 3 hours.

variation
● Add more zest to the potatoes by stirring in 1 small onion, chopped; 1 bell pepper, chopped; 1/2 tsp. salt; and 1/4 tsp. black pepper, after pouring the potatoes into the slow cooker. Continue with Step 4.

Potatoes Perfect

Naomi Ressler
Harrisonburg, VA

MAKES 4–6 SERVINGS

1/4 lb. bacon, diced and browned until crisp
2 medium-sized onions, thinly sliced
6–8 medium-sized potatoes, thinly sliced
1/2 lb. cheddar cheese, thinly sliced
salt to taste
pepper to taste
2–4 Tbsp. butter, or margarine

1. Layer half of bacon, onions, potatoes, and cheese in greased slow cooker. Season to taste.

2. Dot with butter. Repeat layers.

3. Cover. Cook on Low 8–10 hours or on High 3–4 hours, or until potatoes are soft.

Hash Brown Potato Casserole

Michelle Strite/Goshen, IN

MAKES 8–10 SERVINGS

26-oz. pkg. frozen shredded hash browns
3 Tbsp. oil
2 cups chopped ham, optional
2 10 3/4-oz. cans cream of potato soup
1/2 cup grated Parmesan cheese
16-oz. container sour cream
8 ozs. shredded cheddar cheese

1. Brown hash browns in oil in skillet. Transfer to slow cooker.

2. Add remaining ingredients and stir well.

3. Cover. Cook on Low 3 hours.

Shredded Potatoes with Canadian Bacon

Carol Eberly/Harrisonburg, VA

MAKES 8 SERVING

32-oz. bag frozen hash browns
6–8 thin slices of Canadian bacon, or fully cooked ham
1 cup shredded sharp cheese
2 cups shredded mild cheddar cheese
3/4 cup chopped onions
salt to taste
pepper to taste
10 3/4-oz. can cream of mushroom soup
10 3/4-oz. can cream of chicken soup

1. Layer half of potatoes, meat, cheeses, and onions in slow cooker. Season with salt and pepper. Repeat layers.

2. Combine soups. Pour over top.

3. Cover. Cook on Low 5 hours.

> We used this, minus the meat, for our daughter's wedding reception. We made 12 slow-cookers-full. We put it together the night before, put it in the refrigerator, and got up at 4 a.m. to plug in the cookers. They were ready for lunch.

— • —

Hot German Potato Salad

Judi Manos/West Islip, NY

MAKES 6 SERVINGS

5 medium-sized potatoes, cut 1/4 inch thick
1 large onion, chopped
1/3 cup water
1/3 cup vinegar
2 Tbsp. flour
2 Tbsp. sugar
1 tsp. salt
1/2 tsp. celery seed
1/4 tsp. pepper
4 slices bacon, cooked crisp and crumbled chopped fresh parsley

1. Combine potatoes and onions in slow cooker.

2. Combine remaining ingredients, except bacon and parsley. Pour over potatoes.

3. Cover. Cook on Low 8–10 hours.

4. Stir in bacon and parsley.

5. Serve warm or at room temperature with grilled bratwurst or Polish sausage, dilled pickles, pickled beets, and apples.

Risi Bisi (Peas and Rice)

Cyndie Marrara
Port Matilda, PA

MAKES 6 SERVINGS

1 1/2 cups converted long grain white rice, uncooked
3/4 cup chopped onions
2 garlic cloves, minced
2 14 1/2-oz. cans reduced-sodium chicken broth
1/3 cup water
3/4 tsp. Italian seasoning
1/2 tsp. dried basil leaves
1/2 cup frozen baby peas, thawed
1/4 cup grated Parmesan cheese

1. Combine rice, onions, and garlic in slow cooker.

2. In saucepan, mix together chicken broth and water. Bring to boil. Add Italian seasoning and basil leaves. Stir into rice mixture.

3. Cover. Cook on Low 2–3 hours, or until liquid is absorbed.

4. Stir in peas. Cover. Cook 30 minutes. Stir in cheese.

Green Rice Casserole

Ruth Hofstetter
Versailles, MO

 MAKES 6 SERVINGS

1 1/3 cups evaporated milk
2 Tbsp. vegetable oil
3 eggs
one-fourth of a small onion, minced
half a small carrot, minced, optional
2 cups minced fresh parsley, or 10-oz. pkg. frozen chopped spinach, thawed and drained
2 tsp. salt
1/4 tsp. pepper
1 cup shredded sharp cheese
3 cups cooked long grain rice

1. Beat together milk, oil, and eggs until well combined.

2. Stir in remaining ingredients. Mix well. Pour into greased slow cooker.

3. Cover. Cook on High 1 hour. Stir. Reduce heat to Low and cook 4–6 hours.

Fruited Wild Rice with Pecans

Dottie Schmidt
Kansas City, MO

 MAKES 4 SERVINGS

1/2 cup chopped onions
2 Tbsp. margarine
6-oz. pkg. long-grain and wild rice
seasoning packet from wild rice pkg.
1 1/2 cups hot water
2/3 cup apple juice
1 large tart apple, chopped
1/4 cup raisins
1/4 cup coarsely chopped pecans

1. Combine all ingredients except pecans in greased slow cooker.

2. Cover. Cook on High 2–2 1/2 hours.

3. Stir in pecans. Serve.

Wild Rice

Ruth S. Weaver/Reinholds, PA

 MAKES 4–5 SERVINGS

1 cup wild rice, or wild rice mixture, uncooked
1/2 cup sliced mushrooms
1/2 cup diced onions
1/2 cup diced green, or red, peppers
1 Tbsp. oil
1/2 tsp. salt
1/4 tsp. pepper
2 1/2 cups chicken broth

1. Layer rice and vegetables in slow cooker. Pour oil, salt, and pepper over vegetables. Stir.

2. Heat chicken broth. Pour over ingredients in slow cooker.

3. Cover. Cook on High 2 1/2–3 hours, or until rice is soft and liquid is absorbed.

Easy Olive Bake

Jean Robinson
Cinnaminson, NJ

MAKES 8 SERVINGS

1 cup uncooked rice
2 medium onions, chopped
1/2 cup butter, or
    margarine, melted
2 cups stewed tomatoes
2 cups water
1 cup black olives,
    quartered
1/2–3/4 tsp. salt
1/2 tsp. chili powder
1 Tbsp. Worcestershire
    sauce
4-oz. can mushrooms with
    juice
1/2 cup grated cheese

1. Wash and drain rice.
Place in slow cooker.

2. Add remaining ingredients
except cheese. Mix well.

3. Cover. Cook on High
1 hour, then on Low 2 hours,
or until rice is tender but
not mushy.

4. Add cheese before
serving.

5. This is a good
accompaniment to
baked ham.

Mild Dressing

Jane Steiner/Orrville, OH

MAKES 6 SERVINGS

16-oz. loaf homemade
    white bread
2 eggs, beaten
1/2 cup celery
1/4 cup diced onions
3/4 tsp. salt
1/2 tsp. pepper
giblets, cooked and cut
    up fine
milk

1. Set bread slices out to
dry the day before using.
Cut into small cubes.

2. Combine all ingredients
except milk.

3. Moisten mixture with
enough milk to make bread
cubes soft but not soggy.

4. Pour into greased slow
cooker. Cook on Low 3 1/2
hours, stirring every hour.
When stirring, add a small
amount of milk to sides of
cooker—if needed—to keep
dressing moist and to
prevent sticking.

Slow Cooker Stuffing with Poultry

Pat Unternahrer/Wayland, IA

MAKES 18 SERVINGS

1 large loaf dried bread,
    cubed
1 1/2–2 cups chopped
    cooked turkey, or chicken,
    meat & giblets
1 large onion, chopped
3 ribs celery with leaves,
    chopped
1/2 cup butter, melted
4 cups chicken broth
1 Tbsp. poultry seasoning
1 tsp. salt
4 eggs, beaten
1/2 tsp. pepper

1. Mix together all
ingredients. Pour into slow
cooker.

2. Cover and cook on High
1 hour, then reduce to Low
6–8 hours.

Slow-Cooker Dressing

Helen King/Fairbank, IA

**MAKES 10–12 SERVINGS**

14–15 cups bread cubes
3 cups chopped celery
1 1/2 cups chopped onions
1 1/2 tsp. sage
1 tsp. salt
1/2 tsp. pepper
1 1/2 cups or more chicken broth (enough to moisten the bread)
1/4–1 cup melted butter, or margarine (enough to flavor the bread)

1. Combine all ingredients but butter. Mix well. Toss with butter.

2. Spoon into slow cooker. Cook on Low 4–5 hours.

Comforting Chicken Stuffing

Ruth Liebelt/Rapid City, SD
Esther J. Yoder/Hartville, OH

**MAKES 4–6 SERVINGS**

2 6-oz. boxes stuffing mix
1–2 cups cooked, diced chicken
10 3/4-oz. can cream of chicken soup
1/3 cup water, or milk
1/2 tsp. salt, optional
1/8–1/4 tsp. pepper, optional
4 Tbsp. (1/4 cup) butter, or margarine, melted, optional

1. Prepare stuffing mix per package instructions. Spread in bottom of greased slow cooker.

2. Combine chicken, soup, water, and seasonings, if desired. Spread over stuffing. Top with melted butter, if you want.

3. Cover. Cook on Low 4–6 hours or on High 2 1/2–3 hours. Loosen edges once or twice, or at least just before serving.

4. Delicious served with cole slaw and mixed fruit.

Chicken Dressing

Lydia A. Yoder/London, ON

**MAKES 20 SERVINGS**

3/4 cup butter, or margarine
1 cup chopped onions
2 cups chopped celery
2 Tbsp. parsley flakes
1 1/2 tsp. salt
1/2 tsp. pepper
3 1/2–4 cups chicken broth
12–14 cups dried bread cubes
4 cups cut-up chicken
2 eggs, beaten
1 tsp. baking powder

1. Sauté onion and celery in butter in skillet.

2. Combine seasonings and broth. Mix with bread cubes in large bowl.

3. Fold in chicken and sautéed onions and celery.

4. Add eggs and baking powder.

5. Lightly pack into large slow cooker.

6. Cover. Cook on Low 3–4 hours.

7. Serve with turkey or chicken, mashed potatoes, a vegetable, and lettuce salad.

note
● The longer the dressing cooks, the drier it will become.

Poultry Stuffing

Evelyn L. Ward/Greeley, CO

MAKES 8 SERVINGS

1 cup butter, melted
2 cups chopped celery
1/2 cup chopped onions
1 tsp. poultry seasoning
1/2 tsp. sage
1 tsp. salt
2 eggs, beaten
4 cups chicken broth
12 cups fresh bread crumbs, slightly dried

1. Combine everything but crumbs. Mix well. Add crumbs. Stir to blend.

2. Place in 5- or 6-qt. lightly greased slow cooker.

3. Cover. Cook on High 45 minutes, then on Low 4–6 hours.

Mashed Potato Filling

Betty K. Drescher
Quakertown, PA

MAKES 8–10 SERVINGS

1/2 cup diced onions
1 cup diced celery
1/2 cup butter
2 1/2 cups milk
4 large eggs, beaten
8 ozs. bread cubes
4 cups mashed potatoes
1 1/2 tsp. salt
1/4 tsp. pepper

1. Sauté onions and celery in butter in skillet for 5–10 minutes, or until vegetables are tender.

2. Combine onions and celery, milk, and eggs. Pour over bread cubes. Mix lightly to absorb liquid.

3. Stir in potatoes and seasonings. Pour into greased slow cooker.

4. Cover. Cook on Low 4 hours.

variation
● For more flavor, add the packet of seasoning from the bread cube package in Step 3.

Healthy Whole Wheat Bread

Esther Becker/Gordonville, PA

MAKES 8 SERVINGS

2 cups warm reconstituted powdered milk
2 Tbsp. vegetable oil
1/4 cup honey, or brown sugar
3/4 tsp. salt
1 pkg. yeast
2 1/2 cups whole wheat flour
1 1/4 cups white flour

1. Mix together milk, oil, honey or brown sugar, salt, yeast, and half the flour in electric mixer bowl. Beat with mixer for 2 minutes. Add remaining flour. Mix well.

2. Place dough in well-greased bread or cake pan that will fit into your cooker. Cover with greased tin foil. Let stand for 5 minutes. Place in slow cooker.

3. Cover cooker and bake on High 2 1/2–3 hours. Remove pan and uncover. Let stand for 5 minutes. Serve warm.

Corn Bread From Scratch

Dorothy M. Van Deest
Memphis, TN

 MAKES 6 SERVINGS

1 1/4 cups flour
3/4 cup yellow cornmeal
1/4 cup sugar
4 1/2 tsp. baking powder
1 tsp. salt
1 egg, slightly beaten
1 cup milk
1/3 cup melted butter, or oil

1. In mixing bowl sift together flour, cornmeal, sugar, baking powder, and salt. Make a well in the center.

2. Pour egg, milk, and butter into well. Mix into the dry mixture until just moistened.

3. Pour mixture into a greased 2-quart mold. Cover with a plate. Place on a trivet or rack in the bottom of slow cooker.

4. Cover. Cook on High 2–3 hours.

Broccoli Corn Bread

Winifred Ewy/Newton, KS

 MAKES 8 SERVINGS

1 stick margarine, melted
10-oz. pkg. chopped broccoli, cooked and drained
1 onion, chopped
1 box corn bread mix
4 eggs, well beaten
8 oz. cottage cheese
1 1/4 tsp. salt

1. Combine all ingredients. Mix well.

2. Pour into greased slow cooker. Cook on Low 6 hours, or until toothpick inserted in center comes out clean.

3. Serve like spoon bread, or invert the pot, remove bread, and cut into wedges.

Cornbread Casserole

Arlene Groff/Lewistown, PA

MAKES 8 SERVINGS

1 qt. whole-kernel corn
1 qt. creamed corn
1 pkg. corn muffin mix
1 egg
2 Tbsp. butter
1/4 tsp. garlic powder
2 Tbsp. sugar
1/4 cup milk
1/2 tsp. salt
1/4 tsp. pepper

1. Combine ingredients in greased slow cooker.

2. Cover. Cook on Low 3 1/2–4 hours, stirring once halfway through.

Desserts

Dried Fruit

Janet Roggie/Lowville, NY

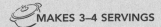**MAKES 3–4 SERVINGS**

2 cups mixed dried fruit
1/4 cup water

1. Place dried fruit in slow cooker. Add water.

2. Cover. Cook on Low 4–8 hours.

3. Serve warm with a spoonful of sour cream on each individual serving and a dash of ground nutmeg.

Rhubarb Sauce

Esther Porter/Minneapolis, MN

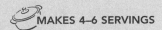**MAKES 4–6 SERVINGS**

1 1/2 lbs. rhubarb
1/8 tsp. salt
1/2 cup water
1/2–2/3 cup sugar

1. Cut rhubarb into 1/2-inch slices.

2. Combine all ingredients in slow cooker. Cook on Low 4–5 hours.

3. Serve chilled.

variation
● Add 1 pint sliced strawberries about 30 minutes before removing from heat.

Golden Fruit Compote

Cindy Krestynick
Glen Lyon, PA
Judi Manos/West Islip, NY

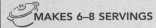**MAKES 6–8 SERVINGS**

1-lb. 13-oz. can peach, or pear, slices, undrained
1/2 cup dried apricots
1/4 cup golden raisins
1/8 tsp. cinnamon
1/8 tsp. nutmeg
3/4 cup orange juice

1. Combine undrained peach or pear slices, apricots, raisins, cinnamon, and nutmeg in slow cooker. Stir in orange juice. Completely immerse fruit in liquid.

2. Cover and cook on Low 6–8 hours.

3. Serve cold with angel food or pound cake, or ice cream. Serve warm as a side dish in the main meal.

variation
● If you prefer a thicker compote, mix together 2 Tbsp. cornstarch and 1/4 cup cold water until smooth. Stir into hot fruit 15 minutes before end of cooking time. Stir until absorbed in juice.

Hot Fruit Compote

Sue Williams/Gulfport, MS

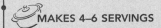**MAKES 4–6 SERVINGS**

1 lb. dried prunes
1 1/3 cups dried apricots
13 1/2-oz. can pineapple chunks, undrained
1-lb. can pitted dark sweet cherries, undrained
1/4 cup dry white wine
2 cups water
1 cup sugar

1. Mix together all ingredients in slow cooker.

2. Cover and cook on Low 7–8 hours, or High 3–4 hours.

3. Serve warm.

...supereasy

Baked Apples

Donna Lantgen/Rapid City, SD

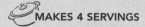
MAKES 4 SERVINGS

4 baking apples, cored
  and unpeeled
1 tsp. cinnamon
1/4 cup brown sugar
4 Tbsp. butter

1. Place apples in slow cooker.

2. Combine cinnamon and brown sugar. Stuff into apples.

3. Top each apple with 1 Tbsp. butter.

4. Cover. Cook on Low 4–5 hours.

5. Delicious as a side dish served warm, or as a topping for waffles, pancakes, or ice cream.

Dolores' Apple Butter

Dolores Metzler
Mechanicsburg, PA

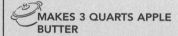
MAKES 3 QUARTS APPLE BUTTER

3 quarts unsweetened
  applesauce
3 cups sugar (or sweeten
  to taste)
2 tsp. cinnamon
1 tsp., or less, ground
  cloves

1. Combine all ingredients in large slow cooker.

2. Cover. Cook on High 8–10 hours. Remove lid during last 4 hours. Stir occasionally.

Ann's Apple Butter

Ann Bender/Ft. Defiance, VA

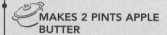
MAKES 2 PINTS APPLE BUTTER

7 cups unsweetened
  applesauce
2–3 cups sugar, depending
  upon the sweetness of
  the applesauce and your
  own preference
2 tsp. cinnamon
1 tsp. ground nutmeg
1/4 tsp. allspice

1. Combine all ingredients in slow cooker.

2. Put a layer of paper towels under lid to prevent condensation from dripping into apple butter. Cook on High 8–10 hours. Remove lid during last hour. Stir occasionally.

variation
● Use canned peaches, pears, or apricots in place of applesauce.

Marilyn's Slow-Cooker Apple Butter

Marilyn Yoder/Archbold, OH

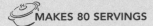
MAKES 80 SERVINGS

2 qts. unsweetened applesauce
2–4 cups sugar, depending upon sweetness of applesauce and your preference
1/2 tsp. ground cloves
2 Tbsp. lemon juice
1/4 heaping cup red hot candies

1. Combine all ingredients in slow cooker.

2. Vent lid. Cook on Low 8–10 hours, stirring about every hour. Apple butter thickens as it cooks, so cook longer to make it thicker.

Anna's Slow-Cooker Apple Butter

Anna Musser/Manheim, PA

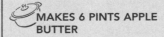
MAKES 6 PINTS APPLE BUTTER

1 cup cider, or apple juice
2 1/2 quarts unsweetened applesauce
2–3 cups sugar, depending upon the sweetness of the applesauce and your own preference
1 tsp. vinegar
1 tsp. cinnamon
1/2 tsp. allspice

1. Boil cider until 1/2 cup remains.

2. Combine all ingredients in slow cooker.

3. Cover. Cook on High 12–16 hours, until apple butter has cooked down to half the original amount. Put in containers and freeze.

Lilli's Apple Butter

Lilli Peters/Dodge City, KS

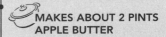
MAKES ABOUT 2 PINTS APPLE BUTTER

7 cups unsweetened applesauce
2 cups apple cider
1 1/2 cups honey
1 tsp. cinnamon
1/2 tsp. ground cloves
1/2 tsp. allspice

1. Combine all ingredients in slow cooker. Mix well with whisk.

2. Cook on Low 14–15 hours.

...supereasy

Slow-Cooker Tapioca

Nancy W. Huber
Green Park, PA

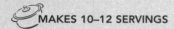
MAKES 10–12 SERVINGS

2 quarts milk
1 cup small pearl tapioca
1 to 1 1/2 cups sugar
4 eggs, beaten
1 tsp. vanilla
whipped cream, or fruit
 of choice, optional

1. Combine milk, tapioca, and sugar in slow cooker. Cook on High 3 hours.

2. Mix together eggs, vanilla, and a little hot milk from slow cooker. Add to slow cooker. Cook on High 20 more minutes. Chill.

3. Serve with whipped cream or fruit.

Peach or Pineapple Upside Down Cake

Vera M. Kuhns
Harrisonburg, VA

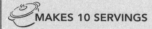
MAKES 10 SERVINGS

1/2 cup butter or
 margarine, melted
1 cup brown sugar
1 medium-sized can
 pineapple slices, drained,
 reserving juice
6–8 maraschino cherries
1 box yellow cake mix

1. Combine butter and brown sugar. Spread over bottom of well greased cooker.

2. Add pineapple slices and place cherries in the center of each one.

3. Prepare cake according to package directions, using pineapple juice for part of liquid. Spoon cake batter into cooker over top fruit.

4. Cover cooker with 2 tea towels and then with its own lid. Cook on High 1 hour, and then on Low 3–4 hours.

5. Allow cake to cool for 10 minutes. Then run knife around edge and invert cake onto large platter.

Dump Cake

Janice Muller/Derwood, MD

MAKES 8–10 SERVINGS

20-oz. can crushed
 pineapple
21-oz. can blueberry, or
 cherry, pie filling
18 1/2-oz. pkg. yellow cake
 mix
cinnamon
1/2 cup butter, or
 margarine,
1 cup chopped nuts

1. Grease bottom and sides of slow cooker.

2. Spread layers of pineapple, blueberry pie filling, and dry cake mix. Be careful not to mix the layers.

3. Sprinkle with cinnamon.

4. Top with thin layers of butter chunks and nuts.

5. Cover. Cook on High 2–3 hours.

6. Serve with vanilla ice cream.

variation
● Use a pkg. of spice cake mix and apple pie filling.

Old-Fashioned Rice Pudding

Ann Bender/Fort Defiance, VA
Gladys M. High/Ephrata, PA
Mrs. Don Martins/Fairbank, IA

 MAKES 6 SERVINGS

2 1/2 cups cooked rice
1 1/2 cups evaporated milk (or scalded milk)
2/3 cup brown, or white, sugar
3 Tbsp. soft butter
2 tsp. vanilla
1/2–1 tsp. nutmeg
3 eggs, beaten
1/2–1 cup raisins

1. Mix together all ingredients. Pour into lightly greased slow cooker.

2. Cover and cook on High 2 hours, or on Low 4–6 hours. Stir after first hour.

3. Serve warm or cold.

Ann's Rice Pudding

Ann Sunday McDowell
Newtown, PA

 MAKES 6–8 SERVINGS

1 cup uncooked, long grain white rice
3 cups milk
3 Tbsp. butter
1/2 tsp. salt
3/4 cup sugar
3 eggs, beaten
1/2 tsp. freshly ground nutmeg
1 tsp. vanilla

1. Cook rice according to package directions.

2. Mix together all ingredients in greased 1 1/2-qt. casserole dish. Cover with greased foil and set inside slow cooker. Add 1 cup water to slow cooker (around the outside of the casserole).

3. Cover and cook on High 2 hours.

Dolores' Rice Pudding

Dolores Metzler
Mechanicsburg, PA

 MAKES 8–10 SERVINGS

1 cup white uncooked rice
1 cup sugar
8 cups milk
3 eggs
1 1/2 cups milk
2 tsp. vanilla
1/4 tsp. salt
nutmeg, or cinnamon

1. In slow cooker, mix together rice, sugar, and 8 cups milk.

2. Cook on High 3 hours.

3. Beat together, eggs, 1 1/2 cups milk, vanilla, and salt. Add to slow cooker. Stir.

4. Cook on High 25–30 minutes.

5. Sprinkle with nutmeg or cinnamon. Serve warm.

Rice Pudding

Vera Schmucker/Goshen, IN

 MAKES 4–6 SERVINGS

2 1/2 cups cooked rice
1 1/2 cups evaporated milk,
  or scalded milk
2/3 cup sugar
2 tsp. butter, or margarine,
  melted
1/2–1 tsp. ground nutmeg
whipped cream
maraschino cherries

1. Combine all ingredients.
Pour into lightly greased
slow cooker.

2. Cover. Cook on High
2 hours or on Low 4–6
hours. Stir after first hour.

3. Serve topped with
whipped cream and
maraschino cherries.

Old-Fashioned Rice Pudding

Ann Bender/Fort Defiance, VA

 MAKES 6 SERVINGS

2 1/2 cups cooked rice
1 1/2 cups whole milk
2/3 cup brown sugar
3 eggs, beaten
3 Tbsp. butter, melted
2 tsp. vanilla
1/2 tsp. ground nutmeg
1/2 tsp. ground cinnamon
1/2 cup raisins

1. Mix together all
ingredients. Pour into a
lightly greased slow cooker.

2. Cover and cook on High
1–2 hours, or on Low 4–6
hours. Stir once during last
30 minutes.

3. Serve warm or cold.

Custard Rice Pudding

Iva Schmidt/Fergus Falls, MN

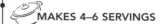 MAKES 4–6 SERVINGS

1/4 cup rice, uncooked
2 eggs
1/3 cup sugar
1/4 tsp. salt
1/2 tsp. vanilla
1 1/2 cups milk
1/3 cup raisins
nutmeg, or cinnamon
2 cups water

1. Cook rice according to
package directions.

2. Beat together eggs, sugar,
salt, vanilla, and milk. Stir
in rice and raisins.

3. Put in 1-quart baking
dish that will fit into your
slow cooker. Sprinkle with
nutmeg or cinnamon.

4. Cover with foil and set
on metal trivet or a canning
jar ring in bottom of slow
cooker. Pour water around
casserole.

5. Cover cooker. Cook on
High 2–2 1/2 hours, or
until set.

6. Serve warm or cold.

Slow-Cooker Rice Pudding

Dede Peterson/Rapid City, SD

 MAKES 5 SERVINGS

1 pkg. vanilla cook-and-serve pudding mix
1 cup cooked white rice
1 cup raisins
1 tsp. cinnamon
2 tsp. vanilla
3 cups half-and-half or milk

1. Combine ingredients in slow cooker.

2. Cover. Cook on Low 3–4 hours.

Chocolate Rice Pudding

Michele Ruvola/Selden, NY

 MAKES 4 SERVINGS

4 cups cooked white rice
3/4 cup sugar
1/4 cup baking cocoa powder
3 Tbsp. butter, melted
1 tsp. vanilla
2 12-oz. cans evaporated milk
whipped cream
sliced toasted almonds
maraschino cherries

1. Combine first 6 ingredients in greased slow cooker.

2. Cover. Cook on Low 2 1/2–3 1/2 hours, or until liquid is absorbed.

3. Serve warm or chilled. Top individual servings with a dollop of whipped cream, sliced toasted almonds, and a maraschino cherry.

Tapioca Salad

Karen Ashworth
Duenweg, MO

 MAKES 10–12 SERVINGS

10 Tbsp. large pearl tapioca
1/2 cup sugar to taste
dash salt
4 cups water
1 cup grapes, cut in half
1 cup crushed pineapple
1 cup whipped cream

1. Mix together tapioca, sugar, salt, and water in slow cooker.

2. Cook on High 3 hours, or until tapioca pearls are almost translucent.

3. Cool thoroughly in refrigerator.

4. Stir in remaining ingredients. Serve cold.

variation
● Add 1 small can mandarin oranges, drained, when adding rest of fruit.

Deluxe Tapioca Pudding

Michelle Showalter
Bridgewater, VA

 **MAKES 16 SERVINGS**

2 qts. milk
3/4 cup dry small pearl
  tapioca
1 1/2 cups sugar
4 eggs, beaten
2 tsp. vanilla
3–4 cups whipped cream, or
  frozen whipped topping,
  thawed
chocolate candy bar

1. Combine milk, tapioca, and sugar in slow cooker.

2. Cook on High 3 hours.

3. Add a little of the hot milk to the eggs. Stir. Whisk eggs into milk mixture. Add vanilla.

4. Cover. Cook on High 20–30 minutes.

5. Cool. Chill in refrigerator. When fully chilled, beat with hand mixer to fluff the pudding.

6. Stir in whipped cream or whipped topping. Garnish with chopped candy bar.

Blushing Apple Tapioca

Julie Weaver/Reinholds, PA

 **MAKES 8–10 SERVINGS**

8–10 tart apples
1/2 cup sugar
4 Tbsp. minute tapioca
4 Tbsp. red cinnamon candy
1/2 cup water
whipped topping, optional

1. Pare and core apples. Cut into eighths lengthwise and place in slow cooker.

2. Mix together sugar, tapioca, candy, and water. Pour over apples.

3. Cook on High 3–4 hours.

4. Serve hot or cold. Top with whipped cream.

Slow Cooker Pumpkin Pie Pudding

Joette Droz/Kalona, IA

 **MAKES 4–6 SERVINGS**

15-oz. can solid pack
  pumpkin
12-oz. can evaporated milk
3/4 cup sugar
1/2 cup buttermilk baking
  mix
2 eggs, beaten
2 Tbsp. melted butter, or
  margarine
1 Tbsp. pumpkin pie spice
2 tsp. Vanilla
whipped cream

1. Mix together all ingredients except whipped cream. Pour into greased slow cooker.

2. Cover and cook on Low 6–7 hours, or until thermometer reads 160°F.

3. Serve in bowls topped with whipped cream.

Simple Bread Pudding

Melanie L. Thrower
McPherson, KS

MAKES 6–8 SERVINGS

6–8 slices of bread, cubed
2 cups milk
2 eggs
1/4 cup sugar
1 tsp. ground cinnamon
1 tsp. vanilla

Sauce:
6-oz. can concentrated
    grape juice
1 Tbsp. cornstarch

1. Place bread in slow cooker.

2. Whisk together milk, eggs, sugar, cinnamon, and vanilla. Pour over bread.

3. Cover. Cook on High 2–2 1/2 hours, or until mixture is set.

4. Combine cornstarch and concentrated juice in saucepan. Heat until boiling, stirring constantly, until sauce is thickened. Serve drizzled over bread pudding.

5. This is a fine dessert with a cold salad main dish.

Home-Style Bread Pudding

Lizzie Weaver/Ephrata, PA

MAKES 4–6 SERVINGS

2 eggs, beaten
2 1/4 cups milk
1/2 tsp. cinnamon
1/4 tsp. salt
1/2 cup brown sugar
1 tsp. vanilla
2 cups 1-inch bread cubes
1/2 cup raisins or dates

1. Combine all ingredients in bowl. Pour into slow cooker baking insert. Cover baking insert. Place on metal rack (or rubber jar ring) in bottom of slow cooker.

2. Pour 1/2 cup hot water into cooker.

3. Cover slow cooker. Cook on High 2–3 hours.

4. Serve pudding warm or cold topped with cherry pie filling and whipped topping.

Apple-Nut Bread Pudding

Ruth Ann Hoover
New Holland, PA

MAKES 6–8 SERVINGS

8 slices raisin bread, cubed
2–3 medium-sized tart
    apples, peeled and sliced
1 cup chopped pecans,
    toasted
1 cup sugar
1 tsp. ground cinnamon
1/2 tsp. ground nutmeg
3 eggs, lightly beaten
2 cups half-and-half
1/4 cup apple juice
1/4 cup butter, or
    margarine, melted

1. Place bread cubes, apples, and pecans in greased slow cooker and mix together gently.

2. Combine sugar, cinnamon, and nutmeg. Add remaining ingredients. Mix well. Pour over bread mixture.

3. Cover. Cook on Low 3–4 hours, or until knife inserted in center comes out clean.

4. Serve with ice cream.

Baked Apples with Raisins

Vera Schmucker/Goshen, IN

Connie B. Weaver
Bethlehem, PA

MAKES 6–8 SERVINGS

6–8 medium-sized baking
  apples, cored
2 Tbsp. raisins
1/4 cup sugar
1 tsp. cinnamon
1 Tbsp. butter
1/2 cup water

1. Remove top inch of peel
from each apple.

2. Mix together raisins and
sugar. Spoon into center of
apples.

3. Sprinkle with additional
sugar and dot with butter.

4. Place apples in slow
cooker. Add water. Cover
and cook on Low 7–9 hours,
or on High 2 1/2–3 1/2
hours.

Raisin Nut-Stuffed Apples

Margaret Rich
North Newton, KS

MAKES 6 SERVINGS

6 baking apples, cored
2 Tbsp. butter, or
  margarine, melted
1/4 cup packed brown
  sugar
3/4 cup raisins
3 Tbsp. chopped walnuts
1/2 cup water

1. Peel a strip around apple
about one-third of the way
below the stem end to
prevent splitting.

2. Mix together butter
and brown sugar. Stir in
raisins and walnuts. Stuff
into apple cavities.

3. Place apples in slow
cooker. Add water.

4. Cover and cook on Low
6–8 hours.

Nut-Filled Baked Apples

Joyce Cox/Port Angeles, WA

MAKES 8 SERVINGS

1 cup nuts of your choice,
  ground
1/4 cup (packed) brown
  sugar
1/2 tsp. cinnamon
1 egg, beaten
8 medium baking apples,
  kept whole, but cored
1 cup sugar
1/3 cup water
2 Tbsp. butter
1/2 cup water

1. Mix together nuts, brown
sugar, cinnamon, and egg.
Place apples on rack in
large, rectangular slow
cooker. Spoon nut-sugar
mixture into apples until
they are two-thirds full.

2. In saucepan, combine
sugar, 1/3 cup water, and
butter. Stir over medium
heat until sugar dissolves.
Pour into apples until their
cavities are filled.

3. Add 1/2 cup water to
slow cooker around apples.

4. Cover and cook on Low
8–10 hours, or on High 3–4
hours. Serve warm. Top with
whipped cream, ice cream,
or frozen yogurt, if desired.

Cranberry Baked Apples

Judi Manos/West Islip, NY

MAKES 4 SERVINGS

4 large cooking apples
1/3 cup packed brown
  sugar
1/4 cup dried cranberries
1/2 cup cran-apple juice
  cocktail
2 Tbsp. butter, melted
1/2 tsp. ground cinnamon
1/4 tsp. ground nutmeg
chopped nuts, optional

1. Core apples. Fill centers with brown sugar and cranberries. Place in slow cooker.

2. Combine cran-apple juice and butter. Pour over apples.

3. Sprinkle with cinnamon and nutmeg.

4. Cover. Cook on Low 4–6 hours.

5. To serve, spoon sauce over apples and sprinkle with nuts.

6. This is a great accompaniment to vanilla ice cream.

Caramel Apples

Elaine Patton
West Middletown, PA

Rhonda Lee Schmidt
Scranton, PA

Renee Shirk/Mount Joy, PA

MAKES 4 SERVINGS

4 very large tart apples,
  cored
1/2 cup apple juice
8 Tbsp. brown sugar
12 hot cinnamon candies
4 Tbsp. butter, or margarine
8 caramel candies
1/4 tsp. ground cinnamon
whipped cream

1. Remove 1/2-inch-wide strip of peel off the top of each apple and place apples in slow cooker.

2. Pour apple juice over apples.

3. Fill the center of each apple with 2 Tbsp. brown sugar, 3 hot cinnamon candies, 1 Tbsp. butter, or margarine, and 2 caramel candies. Sprinkle with cinnamon.

4. Cover and cook on Low 4–6 hours, or until tender.

5. Serve hot with whipped cream.

Caramel Apples

Becky Harder/Monument, CO

Jeanette Oberholtzer
Manheim, PA

MAKES 8–10 SERVINGS

2 14-oz. bags of caramels
1/4 cup water
8–10 medium apples
sticks
waxed paper
granulated sugar

1. Combine caramels and water in slow cooker.

2. Cover. Cook on High for 1–1 1/2 hours, stirring every 5 minutes.

3. Wash and dry apples. Insert a stick into stem end of each apple. Turn cooker to Low. Dip apple into hot caramel, turning to coat entire surface.

4. Holding apple above cooker, scrape off excess accumulation of caramel from bottom of apple.

5. Dip bottom of caramel-coated apple in granulated sugar to keep it from sticking. Place apple on greased waxed paper to cool.

Apple Caramel Dessert

Jeanette Oberholtzer
Manheim, PA

MAKES 7 SERVINGS

2 medium apples, peeled, cored, and cut in wedges
1/2 cup apple juice
7 ozs. caramel candy
1 tsp. vanilla
1/8 tsp. ground cardamom
1/2 tsp. ground cinnamon
1/3 cup creamy peanut butter
7 slices angel food cake
1 qt. vanilla ice cream

1. Combine apple juice, caramel candies, vanilla, and spices. Place in slow cooker.

2. Drop peanut butter, 1 tsp. at a time, into slow cooker. Stir.

3. Add apple wedges.

4. Cover. Cook on Low 5 hours.

5. Stir well.

6. Cover. Then cook 1 more hour on Low.

7. Serve 1/3 cup warm mixture over each slice of angel food cake and top with ice cream.

Spiced Apples

Michelle Showalter
Bridgewater, VA

MAKES 8–10 SERVINGS

2 qts. peeled, sliced apples
2 1/2 cups water
1/4 cup cinnamon candy
1/2–3/4 cup sugar, according to your taste preference
1/3 cup Therm-flo or Clearjell
1/2 tsp. ground cinnamon
1/8 tsp. salt
1/8 tsp ground nutmeg

1. Place apples in slow cooker.

2. Combine remaining ingredients and stir until thickening agent dissolves. Pour over apples.

3. Cover. Cook on High 3 hours.

4. Serve hot with your main meal, or chill and serve with whipped cream and chopped pecans, or as a topping for ice cream, or as a base for apple crisp.

Hot Curried Fruit Compote

Cathy Boshart/Lebanon, PA

MAKES 12 SERVINGS

1-lb. can peach halves
1-lb. can pear halves
1-lb. can apricot halves
1-lb. can pineapple chunks
4 medium bananas, sliced
15 maraschino cherries
1/3 cup walnut halves
1/3 cup margarine
2/3 cup brown sugar
1/2 tsp. curry powder (or to taste)

1. Drain fruit. Pour canned fruit into slow cooker. Add bananas.

2. Scatter cherries and walnuts on top.

3. In skillet, melt margarine. Mix in sugar and curry powder. Pour over fruit.

4. Cook on Low 2 hours.

5. Serve hot as a side dish to beef, pork, or poultry; serve warm as a dessert; or serve cold as a topping for ice cream.

Fruit Medley

Angeline Lang/Greeley, CO

MAKES 6–8 SERVINGS

1 1/2 lbs. mixed dried fruit
2 1/2 cups water
1 cup sugar
1 Tbsp. honey
peel of half a lemon, cut
  into thin strips
1/8 tsp. nutmeg
1 cinnamon stick
3 Tbsp. cornstarch
1/4 cup cold water
1/4 cup Cointreau

1. Place dried fruit in slow cooker. Pour in water.

2. Stir in sugar, honey, lemon peel, nutmeg, and cinnamon.

3. Cover and cook on Low 2–3 hours. Turn cooker to High.

4. Mix cornstarch into water until smooth. Stir into fruit mixture. Cook on High 10 minutes, or until thickened.

5. Stir in Cointreau.

6. Serve warm or chilled. Serve as a side dish with the main course, as a dessert on its own, or as a topping for ice cream.

Quick Yummy Peaches

Willard E. Roth/Elkhart, IN

MAKES 6 SERVINGS

1/3 cup buttermilk baking
  mix
2/3 cup dry quick oats
1/2 cup brown sugar
1 tsp. cinnamon
4 cups sliced peaches
  (canned or fresh)
1/2 cup peach juice, or
  water

1. Mix together baking mix, oats, brown sugar, and cinnamon in greased slow cooker.

2. Stir in peaches and peach juice.

3. Cook on Low for at least 5 hours. (If you like a drier cobbler, remove lid for last 15–30 minutes of cooking.)

4. Serve with frozen yogurt or ice cream.

Scalloped Pineapples

Shirley Hinh/Wayland, IA

MAKES 8 SERVINGS

2 cups sugar
3 eggs
3/4 cup butter, melted
3/4 cup milk
1 large can crushed
  pineapple, drained
8 slices bread (crusts
  removed), cubed

1. Mix together all ingredients in slow cooker.

2. Cook on High 2 hours. Reduce heat to Low and cook 1 more hour.

3. Delicious served as a side dish to ham or poultry, or as a dessert served warm or cold. Eat hot or chilled with vanilla ice cream or frozen yogurt.

Hot Fruit Salad

Sharon Miller
Holmesville, OH

MAKES 16 SERVINGS

25-oz. jar chunky
    applesauce
21-oz. can cherry pie filling
20-oz. can pineapple chunks
15 1/2-oz. can sliced
    peaches
15 1/2-oz. can apricot
    halves
11-oz. can mandarin
    oranges
1/2 cup packed brown
    sugar
1 tsp. ground cinnamon

1. Combine fruit in slow
cooker, stirring gently.

2. Combine brown sugar
and cinnamon. Sprinkle over
mixture.

3. Cover. Bake on Low 3–4
hours.

variation
● If you prefer a less sweet
dish, reduce amount of brown
sugar to 1/4 cup, or to 2 Tbsp.

Baked Fruit

Paula Showalter
Weyers Cave, VA

MAKES 8–10 SERVINGS

4 cups sliced peaches,
    drained
4 cups sliced apples
2 cups crushed pineapple,
    drained
1 1/2 tsp. ground cinnamon
1/2 tsp. ground nutmeg
1 1/2 cups sugar
2 Tbsp. cornstarch

1. Combine fruit in slow
cooker.

2. Sprinkle with spices.

3. Combine sugar and
cornstarch. Add to fruit.
Mix well.

4. Cover. Cook on High
2 hours or Low 4 hours.

5. Serve as a side dish with
the main meal, or as a
topping for vanilla ice cream.

Curried Fruit

Jane Meiser/Harrisonburg, VA

MAKES 8–10 SERVINGS

1 can peaches, undrained
1 can apricots, undrained
1 can pears, undrained
1 large can pineapple
    chunks, undrained
1 can black cherries,
    undrained
1/2 cup brown sugar
1 tsp. curry powder
3–4 Tbsp. quick-cooking
    tapioca, depending upon
    how thickened you'd like
    the finished dish to be
butter, or margarine,
    optional

1. Combine fruit. Let stand
for at least 2 hours, or up to
8, to allow flavors to blend.
Drain. Place in slow cooker.

2. Add remaining
ingredients. Mix well. Top
with butter, if you want.

3. Cover. Cook on Low
8–10 hours.

4. Serve warm or at room
temperature.

Slow-Cooker Spoon Peaches

Jeanette Oberholtzer
Manheim, PA

 MAKES 6 SERVINGS

1/3 cup sugar
1/2 cup brown sugar
3/4 cup buttermilk baking
  mix
2 eggs
2 tsp. vanilla
2 tsp. butter, or margarine,
  melted
half a 12-oz. can evaporated
  milk
2 cups mashed peaches,
  fresh, frozen, or canned
  (if canned, drain slightly)
3/4 tsp. cinnamon

1. Combine sugar, brown sugar, and baking mix.

2. Add eggs and vanilla. Mix well.

3. Add margarine and milk. Mix well.

4. Add peaches and cinnamon. Mix well. Pour into greased slow cooker.

5. Cover. Cook on Low 6–8 hours.

6. Serve warm with whipped cream or vanilla ice cream.

This is a great warm dessert
for a cold winter evening.

— • —

Zesty Pears

Barbara Walker/Sturgis, SD

 MAKES 6 SERVINGS

6 fresh pears
1/2 cup raisins
1/4 cup brown sugar
1 tsp. grated lemon peel
1/4 cup brandy
1/2 cup sauterne wine
1/2 cup macaroon crumbs

1. Peel and core pears. Cut into thin slices.

2. Combine raisins, sugar, and lemon peel. Layer alternately with pear slices in slow cooker.

3. Pour brandy and wine over top.

4. Cover. Cook on Low 4–6 hours.

5. Spoon into serving dishes. Cool. Sprinkle with macaroons. Serve plain or topped with sour cream.

Spiced Applesauce

Judi Manos/West Islip, NY

 MAKES 6 CUPS

12 cups pared, cored, thinly
  sliced, cooking apples
1/2 cup sugar
1/2 tsp. cinnamon
1 cup water
1 Tbsp. lemon juice
freshly grated nutmeg,
  optional

1. Place apples in slow cooker.

2. Combine sugar and cinnamon. Mix with apples. Stir in water and lemon juice, and nutmeg, if desired.

3. Cover. Cook on Low 5–7 hours, or High 2 1/2–3 1/2 hours.

4. Stir for a chunky sauce. Serve hot or cold.

Chunky Applesauce

Joan Becker/Dodge City, KS

Rosanne Hankins
Stevensville, MD

 MAKES 8–10 SERVINGS

8 apples, peeled, cored, and cut into chunks or slices (6 cups)
1 tsp. cinnamon
1/2 cup water
1/2–1 cup sugar, or cinnamon red hot candies

1. Combine all ingredients in slow cooker.

2. Cook on Low 8–10 hours, or High 3–4 hours.

Applesauce

Charmaine Caesar
Lancaster, PA

 MAKES 4 CUPS

10 medium Winesap, or Golden Delicious, cooking apples
1/2 cup water
3/4 cup sugar
cinnamon, optional

1. Core, peel, and thinly slice apples.

2. Combine all ingredients in slow cooker.

3. Cover. Cook on Low 5 hours.

4. Stir until well blended. If you want a smooth sauce, put through blender or mix with a hand mixer. Cool and serve.

Wagon Master Apple-Cherry Sauce

Sharon Timpe/Mequon, WI

 MAKES 12–15 SERVINGS

2 21-oz. cans apple pie filling
2–3 cups frozen tart red cherries
1 Tbsp. butter or margarine
1/2 tsp. ground cinnamon
1/2 tsp. ground nutmeg
1/8 tsp. ground ginger
1/8 tsp. ground cloves

1. Combine all ingredients in slow cooker.

2. Cover. Heat on Low 3–4 hours, until hot and bubbly. Stir occasionally.

3. Serve warm over vanilla ice cream, pudding, pound cake, or shortcake biscuits. Top with whipped cream.

Rhonda's Apple Butter

Rhonda Burgoon
Collingswood, NJ

 **MAKES ABOUT 2 PINTS APPLE BUTTER**

4 lbs. apples
2 tsp. cinnamon
1/2 tsp. ground cloves

1. Peel, core, and slice apples. Place in slow cooker.

2. Cover. Cook on High 2–3 hours. Reduce to Low and cook 8 hours. Apples should be a rich brown and be cooked down by half.

3. Stir in spices. Cook on High 2–3 hours with lid off. Stir until smooth.

4. Pour into freezer containers and freeze, or into sterilized jars and seal.

Shirley's Apple Butter

Shirley Sears/Tiskilwa, IL

MAKES 6–10 PINTS APPLE BUTTER

4 qts. finely chopped tart apples
2 3/4 cups sugar
2 3/4 tsp. cinnamon
1/4 tsp. ground cloves
1/8 tsp. salt

1. Pour apples into slow cooker.

2. Combine remaining ingredients. Drizzle over apples.

3. Cover. Cook on High 3 hours, stirring well with a large spoon every hour. Reduce heat to Low and cook 10–12 hours, until butter becomes thick and dark in color. Stir occasionally with strong wire whisk for smooth butter.

4. Freeze or pour into sterilized jars and seal.

Kelly's Apple Butter

Kelly Evenson/Pittsboro, NC

MAKES 4–5 PINTS APPLE BUTTER

4 lbs. cooking apples
2 cups cider
3 cups sugar
2 tsp. cinnamon
1 tsp. ground cloves, optional
1/8 tsp. allspice

1. Stem, core, and quarter apples. Do not peel.

2. Combine apples and cider in large slow cooker.

3. Cover. Cook on Low 10 hours.

4. Stir in sugar and spices. Continue cooking 1 hour. Remove from heat and cool thoroughly. Blend to mix in skins.

5. Freeze in pint containers, or pour into hot sterilized jars and seal.

Charlotte's Apple Butter

Charlotte Fry/St. Charles, MO

MAKES 5 PINTS APPLE BUTTER

3 quarts Jonathan, or
   Winesap, apples
2 cups apple cider
2 1/2 cups sugar
1 tsp. star anise, optional
2 Tbsp. lemon juice
2 sticks cinnamon

1. Peel, core, and chop apples. Combine with apple cider in large slow cooker.

2. Cover. Cook on Low 10–12 hours.

3. Stir in sugar, star anise, lemon juice, and stick cinnamon.

4. Cover. Cook on High 2 hours. Stir. Remove lid and cook on High 2–4 hours more, until thickened.

5. Pour into sterilized jars and seal.

Peach or Apricot Butter

Charlotte Shaffer/East Earl, PA

MAKES 6 8-OZ. JARS BUTTER

4 1-lb. 13-oz. cans peaches,
   or apricots
2 3/4–3 cups sugar
2 tsp. cinnamon
1 tsp. ground cloves

1. Drain fruit. Remove pits. Puree in blender. Pour into slow cooker.

2. Stir in remaining ingredients.

3. Cover. Cook on High 8–10 hours. Remove cover during last half of cooking. Stir occasionally.

note
● Spread on bread, or use as a topping for ice cream or toasted pound cake.

Pear Butter

Dorothy Miller/Gulfport, MI

MAKES 6 PINTS PEAR BUTTER

8 cups pear sauce
3 cups brown sugar
1 Tbsp. lemon juice
1 Tbsp. cinnamon

1. Combine all ingredients in slow cooker.

2. Cover. Cook on High 10–12 hours.

note
● To make pear sauce, peel, core, and slice 12 large pears. Place in slow cooker with 3/4 cup water. Cover and cook on Low 8–10 hours, or until very soft. Stir to blend.

Pear Butter

Betty Moore/Plano, IL

MAKES 2–3 PINTS

10 large pears (about 4 lbs.)
1 cup orange juice
2 1/2 cups sugar
1 tsp. ground cinnamon
1 tsp. ground cloves
1/2 tsp. ground allspice

1. Peel and quarter pears. Place in slow cooker.

2. Cover. Cook on Low 10–12 hours. Drain and then discard liquid.

3. Mash or puree pears. Add remaining ingredients. Mix well and return to slow cooker.

4. Cover. Cook on High 1 hour.

5. Place in hot sterile jars and seal. Process in hot water bath for 10 minutes. Allow to cool undisturbed for 24 hours.

Strawberry Rhubarb Sauce

Tina Snyder/Manheim, PA

MAKES 6–8 SERVINGS

6 cups chopped rhubarb
1 cup sugar
1 cinnamon stick
1/2 cup white grape juice
2 cups sliced strawberries

1. Place rhubarb in slow cooker. Pour sugar over rhubarb. Add cinnamon stick and grape juice. Stir well.

2. Cover and cook on Low 5–6 hours, or until rhubarb is tender.

3. Stir in strawberries. Cook 1 hour longer.

4. Remove cinnamon stick. Chill.

5. Serve over cake or ice cream.

Lemon Pudding Cake

Jean Butzer/Batavia, NY

MAKES 5–6 SERVINGS

3 eggs, separated
1 tsp. grated lemon peel
1/4 cup lemon juice
3 Tbsp. melted butter
1 1/2 cups milk
3/4 cup sugar
1/4 cup flour
1/8 tsp. salt

1. Beat eggs whites until stiff peaks form. Set aside.

2. Beat eggs yolks. Blend in lemon peel, lemon juice, butter, and milk.

3. In separate bowl, combine sugar, flour, and salt. Add to egg-lemon mixture, beating until smooth.

4. Fold into beaten egg whites.

5. Spoon into slow cooker.

6. Cover and cook on High 2–3 hours.

7. Serve with spoon from cooker.

Apple Cake

Esther Becker/Gordonville, PA
Wanda S. Curtin
Bradenton, FL

 MAKES 8–10 SERVINGS

2 cups sugar
1 cup oil
2 eggs
1 tsp. vanilla
2 cups chopped apples
2 cups flour
1 tsp. salt
1 tsp. baking soda
1 tsp. nutmeg
1 cup chopped walnuts,
  or pecans

1. Beat together sugar, oil, and eggs. Add vanilla.

2. Add apples. Mix well.

3. Sift together flour, salt, baking soda, and nutmeg. Add dry ingredients and nuts to apple mixture. Stir well.

4. Pour batter into greased and floured bread or cake pan that fits into your slow cooker. Cover with pan's lid, or greased tin foil. Place pan in slow cooker. Cover cooker.

5. Bake on High 3 1/2–4 hours. Let cake stand in pan for 5 minutes after removing from slow cooker.

6. Remove cake from pan, slice, and serve.

Apple Peanut Crumble

Phyllis Attig/Reynolds, IL
Joan Becker/Dodge City, KS
Pam Hochstedler/Kalona, IA

 MAKES 4–5 SERVINGS

4–5 cooking apples, peeled
  and sliced
2/3 cup packed brown
  sugar
1/2 cup flour
1/2 cup quick-cooking dry
  oats
1/2 tsp. cinnamon
1/4–1/2 tsp. nutmeg
1/3 cup butter, softened
2 Tbsp. peanut butter
ice cream, or whipped
  cream

1. Place apple slices in slow cooker.

2. Combine brown sugar, flour, oats, cinnamon, and nutmeg.

3. Cut in butter and peanut butter. Sprinkle over apples.

4. Cover cooker and cook on Low 5–6 hours.

5. Serve warm or cold, plain or with ice cream or whipped cream.

Harvey Wallbanger Cake

Roseann Wilson
Albuquerque, NM

 MAKES 8 SERVINGS

Cake:
16-oz. pkg. pound cake mix
1/3 cup vanilla instant
  pudding (reserve rest of
  pudding from 3-oz. pkg.
  for glaze)
1/4 cup salad oil
3 eggs
2 Tbsp. Galliano liqueur
2/3 cup orange juice

Glaze:
remaining pudding mix
2/3 cup orange juice
1 Tbsp. Galliano liqueur

1. Mix together all ingredients for cake. Beat for 3 minutes. Pour batter into greased and floured bread or cake pan that will fit into your slow cooker. Cover pan.

2. Bake in covered slow cooker on High 2 1/2–3 1/2 hours.

3. Invert cake onto serving platter.

4. Mix together glaze ingredients. Spoon over cake.

Cherry Delight

Anna Musser/Manheim, PA

Marianne J. Troyer
Millersburg, OH

MAKES 10–12 SERVINGS

21-oz. can cherry pie filling
1 pkg. yellow cake mix
1/2 cup butter, melted
1/3 cup walnuts, optional

1. Place pie filling in greased slow cooker.

2. Combine dry cake mix and butter (mixture will be crumbly). Sprinkle over filling. Sprinkle with walnuts.

3. Cover and cook on Low 4 hours, or on High 2 hours.

4. Allow to cool, then serve in bowls with dips of ice cream.

note
● For a less rich, less sweet dessert, use only half the cake mix and only 1/4 cup butter, melted.

Self-Frosting Fudge Cake

Mary Puterbaugh/Elwood, IN

MAKES 8–10 SERVINGS

2 1/2 cups of 18 1/2-oz. pkg. chocolate fudge pudding cake mix
2 eggs
3/4 cup water
3 Tbsp. oil
1/3 cup pecan halves
1/4 cup chocolate syrup
1/4 cup warm water
3 Tbsp. sugar

1. Combine cake mix, eggs, 3/4 cup water, and oil in electric mixer bowl. Beat 2 minutes.

2. Pour into greased and floured bread or cake pan that will fit into your slow cooker.

3. Sprinkle nuts over mixture.

4. Blend together chocolate syrup, 1/4 cup water, and sugar. Spoon over batter.

5. Cover. Bake on High 2–3 hours.

6. Serve warm from slow cooker.

Chocolate Pudding Cake

Lee Ann Hazlett/Freeport, IL

Della Yoder/Kalona, IA

MAKES 10–12 SERVINGS

18 1/2-oz. pkg. chocolate cake mix
3.9-oz. pkg. instant chocolate pudding mix
2 cups (16 oz.) sour cream
4 eggs
1 cup water
3/4 cup oil
1 cup (6 oz.) semisweet chocolate chips
whipped cream, or ice cream, optional

1. Combine cake mix, pudding mix, sour cream, eggs, water, and oil in electric mixer bowl. Beat on medium speed for 2 minutes. Stir in chocolate chips.

2. Pour into greased slow cooker. Cover and cook on Low 6–7 hours, or on High 3–4 hours, or until toothpick inserted near center comes out with moist crumbs.

3. Serve with whipped cream or ice cream.

No Fat Apple Cake

Sue Hamilton/Minooka, IL

 MAKES 8 SERVINGS

1 cup flour
1 cup sugar
2 tsp. baking powder
1 tsp. ground cinnamon
1/4 tsp. salt
4 medium-sized cooking apples, chopped
2 eggs, beaten
2 tsp. vanilla

1. Combine flour, sugar, baking powder, cinnamon, and salt.

2. Add apples, stirring lightly to coat.

3. Combine eggs and vanilla. Add to apple mixture. Stir until just moistened. Spoon into lightly greased slow cooker.

4. Cover. Bake on High 2 1/2–3 hours.

5. Serve warm. Top with frozen whipped topping, thawed, or ice cream and a sprinkle of cinnamon.

variation
● Stir 1/2 cup broken English or black walnuts, or 1/2 cup raisins, into Step 2.

Chocolate Peanut Butter Cake

Ruth Ann Gingerich
New Holland, PA

 MAKES 6–8 SERVINGS

2 cups (half a package) milk chocolate cake mix
1/2 cup water
6 Tbsp. peanut butter
2 eggs
1/2 cup chopped nuts

1. Combine all ingredients. Beat 2 minutes in electric mixer.

2. Pour into greased and floured 3-lb. shortening can. Place can in slow cooker.

3. Cover top of can with 8 paper towels.

4. Cover cooker. Bake on High 2–3 hours.

5. Allow to cool for 10 minutes. Run knife around edge and invert cake onto serving plate. Cool completely before slicing and serving.

Banana Loaf

Sue Hamilton/Minooka, IL

 MAKES 6–8 SERVINGS

3 very ripe bananas
1/2 cup margarine, softened
2 eggs
1 tsp. vanilla
1 cup sugar
1 cup flour
1 tsp. baking soda

1. Combine all ingredients in an electric mixing bowl. Beat 2 minutes or until well blended. Pour into well greased 2-lb. coffee can.

2. Place can in slow cooker. Cover can with 6 layers of paper towels between cooker lid and bread.

3. Cover cooker. Bake on High 2–2 1/2 hours, or until toothpick inserted in center comes out clean. Cool 15 minutes before removing from pan.

Chocolate Fondue

Eleanor J. Ferriera
North Chelmsford, MA

MAKES 6 SERVINGS

1 pkg. (8 squares) semisweet chocolate
4-oz. pkg. sweet cooking chocolate
3/4 cup sweetened condensed milk
1/4 cup sugar
2 Tbsp. kirsch
fresh cherries with stems
squares of sponge cake

1. Break both chocolates into pieces and place in cooker. Set cooker to High and stir chocolate constantly until it melts.

2. Turn cooker to Low and stir in milk and sugar. Stir until thoroughly blended.

3. Stir in kirsch. Cover and cook on Low until fondue comes to a very gentle simmer.

4. Bring fondue to table, along with cherries and sponge cake squares to dip into it.

Chocolate Fondue

Vera Schmucker/Goshen, IN
Vicki Dinkel
Sharon Springs, KS

MAKES 8–10 SERVINGS

1 Tbsp. butter
16 1-oz. chocolate candy bars with almonds, broken
30 large marshmallows
1 1/3 cups milk, divided

1. Grease slow cooker with butter. Turn to High for 10 minutes.

2. Add chocolate, marshmallows, and 1/3 cup milk.

3. Cover. Turn to Low. Stir after 30 minutes; then continue cooking for another 30 minutes, or until melted and smooth.

4. Gradually add additional milk.

5. Cover. Cook on Low 2–6 hours.

6. Bring the cooker to the table, along with cubes of angel food cake, strawberries, chunks of pineapple, bananas, apples, and oranges, and pretzels for dipping.

Seven Layer Bars

Mary W. Stauffer/Ephrata, PA

MAKES 6–8 SERVINGS

1/4 cup melted butter
1/2 cup graham cracker crumbs
1/2 cup chocolate chips
1/2 cup butterscotch chips
1/2 cup flaked coconut
1/2 cup chopped nuts
1/2 cup sweetened condensed milk

1. Layer ingredients in a bread or cake pan that fits in your slow cooker, in the order listed. Do not stir.

2. Cover and bake on High 2–3 hours, or until firm. Remove pan and uncover. Let stand 5 minutes.

3. Unmold carefully on plate and cool.

Easy Chocolate Clusters

Marcella Stalter/Flanagan, IL

MAKES 3 1/2 DOZEN CLUSTERS

2 lbs. white coating chocolate, broken into small pieces
2 cups (12 oz.) semisweet chocolate chips
4-oz. pkg. sweet German chocolate
24-oz. jar roasted peanuts

1. Combine coating chocolate, chocolate chips, and German chocolate. Cover and cook on High 1 hour. Reduce heat to Low and cook 1 hour longer, or until chocolate is melted, stirring every 15 minutes.

2. Stir in peanuts. Mix well.

3. Drop by teaspoonfuls onto waxed paper. Let stand until set. Store at room temperature.

Apple Crisp

Michelle Strite/Goshen, IN

MAKES 6–8 SERVINGS

1 qt. canned apple pie filling, or
  2/3 cup sugar
  1 1/4 cups water
  3 Tbsp. cornstarch
  4 cups sliced, peeled apples
  1/2 tsp. ground cinnamon
  1/4 tsp. ground allspice
3/4 cup quick oatmeal
1/2 cup brown sugar
1/2 cup flour
1/4 cup butter, or margarine, at room temperature

1. Place pie filling in slow cooker. If not using prepared filling, combine 2/3 cup sugar, water, cornstarch, apples, cinnamon, and allspice. Place in cooker.

2. Combine remaining ingredients until crumbly. Sprinkle over apple filling.

3. Cover. Cook on Low 2–3 hours.

Applescotch Crisp

Mary Jane Musser
Manheim, PA

MAKES 6 SERVINGS

4 cups cooking apples, peeled and sliced
2/3 cup brown sugar
1/2 cup flour
1/2 cup quick-cooking oats
3 1/2-oz. pkg. cook-n-serve butterscotch pudding mix
1 tsp. ground cinnamon
1/2 cup cold butter, or margarine

1. Place apples in slow cooker.

2. Combine remaining ingredients. Cut in butter until mixture resembles coarse crumbs. Sprinkle over apples.

3. Cover. Cook on Low 5–6 hours.

4. Serve with ice cream.

variation
● For a less-sweet dish, use only 1/4 cup brown sugar.

Beverages

Hot Spiced Cider

Elva Evers/North English, IA

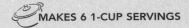
MAKES 6 1-CUP SERVINGS

12-oz. can frozen apple
juice
3 3-inch cinnamon sticks
6 whole cloves

1. Combine all ingredients
in slow cooker.

2. Cover and simmer on
Low 4 hours.

3. Remove cinnamon and
cloves before serving.

variation
● Omit the cinnamon and
cloves. Use 1/4 cup fresh or
dried mint tea leaves instead.

Hot Apple Cider

Joan Rosenberger
Stephens City, VA

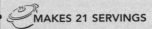
MAKES 21 SERVINGS

4 qts. cider
4 sticks cinnamon
2 tsp. whole cloves

1. Combine ingredients in
6-qt. slow cooker.

2. Cover. Cook on High
2 hours. Turn to Low and
simmer until ready to serve.

Red Hot Apple Cider

Allison Ingels/Maynard, IA

MAKES 16 SERVINGS

1 gallon apple cider, or
apple juice
1 1/4 cups cinnamon candy
hearts
4–5 cinnamon sticks

1. Combine ingredients in
slow cooker.

2. Cover. Cook on Low
1 1/2–2 hours.

3. Serve hot with a
cinnamon stick in each cup.

Our family enjoys this recipe
on cold winter evenings
and especially Christmas Eve.
The smell creates a very
relaxing atmosphere.

— ● —

...supereasy

Apple-Honey Tea

Jeanne Allen/Rye, CO

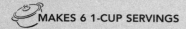

MAKES 6 1-CUP SERVINGS

12-oz. can frozen apple
  juice/cider concentrate
2 Tbsp. instant tea powder
1 Tbsp. honey
1/2 tsp. ground cinnamon

1. Reconstitute the apple
juice/cider concentrate
according to package
directions. Pour into slow
cooker.

2. Add tea powder, honey,
and cinnamon. Stir to blend.

3. Heat on Low 1–2 hours.
Stir well before serving since
cinnamon tends to settle on
bottom.

Josie's Hot Cranberry Punch

Josie Bollman/Maumee, OH

MAKES 6 1-CUP SERVINGS

32-oz. bottle cranberry juice
2 sticks cinnamon
6-oz. can frozen lemonade
12-oz. can frozen orange
  juice

1. Mix together all
ingredients in slow cooker.

2. Cook on High 3–4 hours.

Spicy Hot Cider

Marcia S. Myer/Manheim, PA

MAKES 16 SERVINGS

1 gallon cider
4 cinnamon sticks
2 Tbsp. ground allspice
1/2 cup brown sugar

1. Combine all ingredients
in slow cooker.

2. Cover. Cook on Low
3 hours.

Spiced Cider

Mary Puterbaugh/Elwood, IN

MAKES 12 1-CUP SERVINGS

12 whole cloves
1/2 gallon apple cider
2/3 cup red hot candies
1/4 cup dry orange drink mix.
1 qt. water

1. Place cloves in cheesecloth bag or tea ball.

2. Combine all ingredients in slow cooker.

3. Cover. Cook on Low 3–4 hours.

4. Serve hot from cooker during fall, or on Halloween.

Matthew's Hot Mulled Cider

Shirley Unternahrer Hinh
Wayland, IA

MAKES 12 SERVINGS

2 qts. apple cider
1/4–1/2 cup brown sugar, according to your taste preference
1/2 tsp. vanilla
1 cinnamon stick
4 cloves

1. Combine ingredients in slow cooker.

2. Cover. Cook on Low 5 hours. Stir.

Our kids just tried hot mulled cider for the first time this past Christmas. They loved it. It's fun to try new old things.

— • —

Hot Cider

Ilene Bontrager/Arlington, KS

MAKES 18–20 1-CUP SERVINGS

1 gallon cider
1 qt. cranberry juice
5–6 cinnamon sticks
2 tsp. whole cloves
1/2 tsp. ginger
1 whole orange, sliced

1. Combine cider and cranberry juice in slow cooker.

2. Place cinnamon sticks and cloves in cheesecloth bag and add to slow cooker. Stir in ginger.

3. Heat on High 5–6 hours.

4. Float orange slices on top before serving.

Hot Mulled Cider

Phyllis Attig/Reynolds, IL
Jean Butzer/Batavia, NY
Doris G. Herr/Manheim, PA
Mary E. Martin/Goshen, IN
Leona Miller/Millersburg, OH
Marjora Miller/Archbold, OH
Janet L. Roggie/Lowville, NY
Shirley Sears/Tiskilwa, IL
Charlotte Shaffer/East Earl, PA
Berenice M. Wagner
Dodge City, KS
Connie B. Weaver
Bethlehem, PA
Maryann Westerberg
Rosamond, CA
Carole Whaling
New Tripoli, PA

 MAKES 8 1-CUP SERVINGS

1/4–1/2 cup brown sugar
2 quarts apple cider
1 tsp. whole allspice
1 1/2 tsp. whole cloves
2 cinnamon sticks
2 oranges sliced, with peels

1. Combine brown sugar and cider in slow cooker.

2. Put spices in tea strainer or tie in cheesecloth. Add to slow cooker. Stir in orange slices.

3. Cover and simmer on Low 2–8 hours.

Cider Snap

Cathy Boshart/Lebanon, PA

 MAKES 12–16 SERVINGS

2 qts. apple cider, or apple juice
4 Tbsp. red cinnamon candies
at least 16 apple slices
at least 16 cinnamon sticks

1. Combine cider and cinnamon candies in slow cooker.

2. Cover. Cook on High for 2 hours until candies dissolve and cider is hot.

3. Ladle into mugs and serve with apple slice floaters and cinnamon stick stirrers.

This is a cold-winter-night luxury. Make it in the morning and keep it on Low throughout the day so its good fragrance can fill the house.

— • —

Yummy Hot Cider

Char Hagner/Montague, MI

MAKES 10–11 1-CUP SERVINGS

3 3-inch sticks cinnamon
2 tsp. whole cloves
1 tsp. whole nutmeg, or 1/2 tsp. ground nutmeg
1/2 gallon apple cider
1 cup sugar
2 cups orange juice
1/2 cup lemon juice

1. Tie spices in cheesecloth or tea strainer and place in slow cooker.

2. Add apple cider and sugar, stirring well.

3. Cover. Simmer on Low 1 hour. Remove spices and stir in orange juice and lemon juice. Continue heating 1 more hour. Serve cider from cooker, set on Low.

Great Mulled Cider

Charlotte Shaffer/East Earl, PA

Barbara Sparks
Glen Burnie, MD

MAKES 8–10 1-CUP
SERVINGS

2 qts. apple cider
1/2 cup frozen orange juice
   concentrate
1/2 cup brown sugar
1/2 tsp. ground allspice, or
   1 tsp. whole allspice
1 1/2 tsp. whole cloves
2 cinnamon sticks
orange slices

1. Tie all whole spices
in cheesecloth bag, then
combine all ingredients in
slow cooker.

2. Cover and simmer on
Low 3 hours.

Holiday Wassail

Dolores S. Kratz
Souderton, PA

MAKES 8 1-CUP SERVINGS

16-oz. can apricot halves,
   undrained
4 cups unsweetened
   pineapple juice
2 cups apple cider
1 cup orange juice
18 whole cloves
6 3 1/2-inch cinnamon
   sticks, broken

1. In blender or food
processor, blend apricots
and liquid until smooth.

2. Place cloves and
cinnamon sticks in
cheesecloth bag.

3. Put all ingredients in
slow cooker. Cook on Low
3–4 hours. Serve hot.

Maple Mulled Cider

Leesa Lesenski/Wheately, MA

MAKES 8–10 SERVINGS

1/2 gallon cider
3–4 cinnamon sticks
2 tsp. whole cloves
2 tsp. whole allspice
1–2 Tbsp. orange juice
   concentrate, optional
1–2 Tbsp. maple syrup,
   optional

1. Combine ingredients in
slow cooker.

2. Cover. Heat on Low for
2 hours. Serve warm.

Serve at Halloween,
Christmas caroling, or
sledding parties.
— • —

Hot Spicy Cider for a Crowd

Lydia A. Yoder/London, OH

MAKES 32 SERVINGS

1 gallon apple cider
1 cup sugar
2 tsp. ground cloves
2 tsp. ground allspice
2 3-inch-long cinnamon sticks
2 oranges studded with cloves

1. Combine all ingredients in slow cooker.

2. Cover. Cook on Low 5–6 hours or on High 2–3 hours.

variation

● You can replace apple cider with apple juice, especially if cider is out of season, and 1/4 cup orange juice for the oranges.

Orange Cider Punch

Naomi Ressler
Harrisonburg, VA

MAKES 9–12 6-OZ. SERVINGS

1 cup sugar
2 cinnamon sticks
1 tsp. whole nutmeg
2 cups apple cider, or apple juice
6 cups orange juice
fresh orange

1. Combine ingredients in slow cooker.

2. Cover. Cook on Low 4–10 hours or High 2–3 hours.

3. Float thin slices of an orange in cooker before serving.

Fruity Wassail

Kelly Evenson/Pittsboro, NC

MAKES 20 CUPS

6 cups apple cider
1 cinnamon stick
1/4 tsp. ground nutmeg
1/4 cup honey
3 Tbsp. lemon juice
1 tsp. grated lemon rind
46-oz. can pineapple juice

1. Combine ingredients in slow cooker.

2. Cover. Cook on Low 1–2 hours.

3. Serve warm from slow cooker.

variation

● Use 3 cups cranberry juice and reduce the amount of pineapple juice by 3 cups, to add more color and to change the flavor of the wassail.

Holiday Spice Punch

Maryland Massey
Millington, MD

MAKES 10 1-CUP SERVINGS

2 qts. apple cider
2 cups cranberry juice
2 Tbsp. mixed whole spices
—allspice, cloves, coriander, and ginger
2 3-inch cinnamon sticks, broken
lemon, or orange, slices studded with whole cloves

1. Pour cider and juice into slow cooker. Place mixed spices in muslin bag or tea ball. Add to juice.

2. Cover and simmer on Low 2 hours.

3. Float cinnamon sticks and fruit slices in individual mugs as you serve.

Hot Cranberry-Apple Punch

Barbara Sparks
Glen Burnie, MD

Shirley Thieszen/Larkin, KS

MAKES 10–11 1-CUP SERVINGS

4 1/2 cups cranberry juice
6 cups apple juice
1/4 cup + 1 Tbsp. brown sugar
1/4 tsp. salt
3 cinnamon sticks
1 tsp. whole cloves

1. Pour juices into slow cooker. Mix in brown sugar and salt. Stir until sugar is dissolved.

2. Tie cinnamon sticks and cloves in cheesecloth and drop into liquid.

3. Cover. Simmer on High 2 hours. Remove spice bag. Keep warm on Low.

Hot Cranberry Cider

Kristi See/Weskan, KS

MAKES 10–12 SERVINGS

2 qts. apple cider, or apple juice
1 pt. cranberry juice
1/2–3/4 cup sugar, according to your taste preference
2 cinnamon sticks
1 tsp. whole allspice
1 orange, studded with whole cloves

1. Put all ingredients in slow cooker.

2. Cover. Cook on High 1 hour, then on Low 4–8 hours. Serve warm.

3. Serve with finger foods.

note:
● To garnish wassail with an orange, insert 10–12 1/2"-long whole cloves halfway into orange. Place studded orange in flat baking pan with 1/4 cup water. Bake at 325° for 30 minutes. Just before serving, float orange on top of wassail.

I come from a family of eight children, and every Christmas we all get together. We eat dinner, and then set around playing games and drinking Hot Cranberry Cider.

— ● —

Spiced Wassail

Dorothy Horst/Tiskilwa, IL

MAKES 10–11 1-CUP SERVINGS

2 32-oz. jars cranberry juice
2 cups water
6-oz. can frozen orange
   juice concentrate
3 3-inch cinnamon sticks
3 whole cloves

1. Combine all ingredients in 5-quart slow cooker.

2. Cover and cook on Low 2–8 hours.

variation
● Use small candy canes as stir sticks in individual cups during the holiday season.

note
● This is a refreshing cold drink to serve over ice on a hot day.

Hot Cranberry Punch

Marianne Troyer
Millersburg, OH

MAKES 13–14 1-CUP SERVINGS

2 qts. hot water
1 1/2 cups sugar
1 qt. cranberry juice
3/4 cup orange juice
1/4 cup lemon juice
12 whole cloves, optional
1/2 cup red hot candies

1. Combine water, sugar, and juices. Stir until sugar is dissolved.

2. Place cloves in double thickness of cheesecloth and tie with string. Add to slow cooker.

3. Add cinnamon candies.

4. Cover and cook on Low 2–3 hours, or until heated thoroughly.

5. Remove spice bag before serving.

Hot Fruit Punch

Karen Stoltzfus/Alto, MI

MAKES 10 1-CUP SERVINGS

1 qt. cranberry juice
3 cups water
6-oz. can frozen orange
   juice concentrate, thawed
10-oz. pkg. frozen red
   raspberries, thawed
2 oranges, sliced
6 sticks cinnamon
12 whole allspice

1. Combine all ingredients in slow cooker.

2. Heat on High 1 hour, or until hot. Turn to Low while serving.

Punch

Kathy Hertzler/Lancaster, PA

MAKES 12 1-CUP
SERVINGS

1 tsp. whole cloves
5 cups pineapple juice
5 cups cranberry juice
2 1/4 cups water
1/2 cup brown sugar
2 cinnamon sticks
1/4 tsp. salt

1. Place cloves in small cheesecloth bag or tea ball.

2. Mix together all ingredients in slow cooker.

3. Cook on Low 6 hours. Remove cloves. Serve hot.

Christmas Wassail

Dottie Schmidt
Kansas City, MO

MAKES 6–8 SERVINGS

2 cups cranberry juice
3 1/4 cups hot water
1/3 cup sugar
6-oz. can lemonade concentrate
1 stick cinnamon
5 whole cloves
2 oranges, cut in thin slices

1. Combine all ingredients except oranges in slow cooker. Stir until sugar is dissolved.

2. Cover. Cook on High 1 hour. Strain out spices.

3. Serve hot with an orange slice floating in each cup.

Hot Buttered Lemonade

Janie Steele/Moore, OK

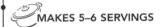
MAKES 5–6 SERVINGS

4 1/2 cups water
3/4 cup sugar
1 1/2 tsp. grated lemon peel
3/4 cup lemon juice
2 Tbsp. butter
6 cinnamon sticks

1. Combine water, sugar, lemon peel, lemon juice, and butter in slow cooker.

2. Cover. Cook on High for 2 1/2 hours, or until well heated through.

3. Serve very hot with a cinnamon stick in each mug.

Carolers Hot Chocolate

Pat Unternahrer/Wayland, IA

 MAKES 12–14 1-CUP SERVINGS

10 cups milk
3/4 cup sugar
3/4 cup cocoa, or hot chocolate mix
1/2 tsp. salt
2 cups hot water
marshmallows

1. Measure milk into slow cooker. Turn on High.

2. Mix together sugar, salt, and cocoa in heavy pan. Add hot water. Stir and boil 3 minutes, stirring often.

3. Pour into milk. Cook on High 2–2 1/2 hours.

Hot Chocolate

Colleen Heatwole/Burton, MI

MAKES 10–12 SERVINGS

8 cups water
3 cups dried milk
1/3 cup non-dairy coffee creamer
1 cup instant hot chocolate mix (the kind you mix with milk, not water)
marshmallows

1. Pour water into slow cooker.

2. Gradually stir in dried milk until blended.

3. Cover and cook on High 2–3 hours, or until milk is hot.

4. Stir in coffee creamer and hot chocolate mix.

5. Turn on Low until serving time, up to 3–4 hours.

6. Serve in mugs topped with marshmallows.

Almond Tea

Frances Schrag/Newton, KS

MAKES 12 1-CUP SERVINGS

10 cups boiling water
1 Tbsp. instant tea
2/3 cup lemon juice
1 cup sugar
1 tsp. vanilla
1 tsp. almond extract

1. Mix together all ingredients in slow cooker.

2. Turn to High and heat thoroughly (about 1 hour). Turn to Low while serving.

Johnny Appleseed Tea

Sheila Plock/Boalsburg, PA

MAKES 8–9 CUPS

2 qts. water, divided
6 tea bags of your favorite flavor
6 ozs. frozen apple juice, thawed
1/4 cup, plus 2 Tbsp., firmly packed brown sugar

1. Bring 1 quart water to boil. Add tea bags. Remove from heat. Cover and let steep 5 minutes. Pour into slow cooker.

2. Add remaining ingredients and mix well.

3. Cover. Heat on Low until hot. Continue on Low while serving from slow cooker.

I serve this wonderful hot beverage with cookies at our Open House Tea and Cookies afternoon, which I host at Christmas-time for friends and neighbors.

— • —

Home-Style Tomato Juice

Jean Butzer/Batavia, NY

MAKES 4–5 1-CUP SERVINGS

10–12 large tomatoes
1 tsp. salt
1 tsp. seasoned salt
1/4 tsp. pepper
1 Tbsp. sugar

1. Wash and drain tomatoes. Remove cores and blossom ends. Place in slow cooker.

2. Cover and cook on Low 4–6 hours, or until tomatoes are soft.

3. Press through sieve or food mill.

4. Stir in seasonings. Chill.

Wine-Cranberry Punch

C. J. Slagle/Roann, IN

MAKES 8 1-CUP SERVINGS

1 pint cranberry juice cocktail
1 cup water
3/4 cup sugar
2 sticks cinnamon
6 whole cloves
4/5 qt. burgundy wine
1 lemon, sliced thin

1. Combine ingredients in slow cooker.

2. Heat on Low 1–2 hours. Strain and serve hot.

3. Keep hot and serve from slow cooker set on lowest setting.

Kate's Mulled Cider/Wine

Mitzi McGlynchey
Downingtown, PA

MAKES 8–10 1-CUP
SERVINGS

1/2 tsp. whole cloves
1/2 tsp. whole allspice
1/2 gallon apple cider, or
   red burgundy wine
2 3-inch cinnamon sticks
1 tsp. ground nutmeg
orange slices, optional
cinnamon sticks, optional

1. Place cloves and allspice
in cheesecloth bag or tea ball.

2. Combine spices, apple
cider or wine, 2 cinnamon
sticks, and nutmeg in slow
cooker.

3. Cook on High 1 hour.
Reduce heat, and simmer
2–3 hours.

4. Garnish individual
servings with orange slices
or cinnamon sticks.

Mulled Wine

Julie McKenzie
Punxsutawney, PA

MAKES 8 1-CUP SERVINGS

1/2 cup sugar
1 1/2 cups boiling water
half a lemon, sliced thin
3 cinnamon sticks
3 whole cloves
1 bottle red dinner wine
   (burgundy or claret)

1. Dissolve sugar in boiling
water in saucepan.

2. Add remaining
ingredients.

3. Pour into slow cooker.
Heat on Low for at least
1 hour, until wine is hot.
Do not boil.

4. Serve from cooker into
mugs.

Deep Red Apple Cider

Judi Manos/West Islip, NY

MAKES 8–9 SERVINGS

5 cups apple cider
3 cups dry red wine
1/4 cup brown sugar
1/2 tsp. whole cloves
1/4 tsp. whole allspice
1 stick cinnamon

1. Combine all ingredients
in slow cooker.

2. Cover. Cook on Low
3–4 hours.

3. Remove cloves, allspice,
and cinnamon before
serving.

variation
● You can use 8 cups apple
cider and no red wine.

Index

A

About the Authors

PHYLLIS PELLMAN GOOD and DAWN J. RANCK collaborated on the highly successful *Fix-It and Forget-It™ Cookbook,* which was the country's topselling cookbook and appeared for months on *The New York Times* bestseller list. They also collaborated on the follow-up volume *Fix-It and Forget-It™ Recipes for Entertaining.*

Phyllis has been part of many cookbook projects, authoring *The Best of Amish Cooking* and *The Festival Cookbook,* and co-authoring *Recipes from Central Market, Favorite Recipes with Herbs, The Best of Mennonite Fellowship Meals,* and *From Amish and Mennonite Kitchens.*

Phyllis and her husband, Merle, live in Lancaster, Pennsylvania, and are co-directors of The People's Place, a heritage interpretation center in the Lancaster County village of Intercourse, Pennsylvania.

Dawn has been a convinced slow-cooker user for years. She and her many friends have been lining up their various-sized cookers on their kitchen counters before they set off each morning—and coming home to richly flavored full dinners.

Dawn, who lives in Harrisonburg, Virginia, is the co-author of *A Quilter's Christmas Cookbook* and *Favorite Recipes with Herbs.*

Lazy Day Cookin' metric conversion charts

Baking Pan Sizes

U.S.	Metric
8 x 1 1/2-inch round baking pan	20 x 4 cm-cake tin
9 x 1 1/2-inch round baking pan	23 x 3.5-cm cake tin
11 x 7 x 1 1/2-inch baking pan	28 x 18 x 4-cm baking tin
13 x 9 x 2-inch baking pan	30 x 20 x 3-cm baking tin
2-quart rectangular baking dish	30 x 20 x 3-cm baking tin
15 x 10 x 1-inch baking pan	30 x 25 x 2-cm baking tin (Swiss roll tin)
9-inch pie plate	22 x 4- or 23 x 4-cm pie plate
7- or 8-inch springform pan	18- or 20-cm springform or loose-bottom tin
9 x 5 x 3-inch loaf pan	23 x13-7-cm or 2-pound narrow loaf tin
1 1/2-quart casserole	1.5-liter casserole
2-quart casserole	2-liter casserole

Cooking Equivalents U.S., U.K./Australia   *All numbers have been rounded.*

Volume

U.S.	U.K./Australia
1/8 teaspoon = 0.5 ml	
1/4 teaspoon = 1 ml	
1/2 teaspoon = 2 ml	
1 teaspoon = 5 ml	
1 tablespoon = 1 tablespoon	
1/4 cup = 2 tablespoons = 2 fluid ounces = 60 ml	
1/3 cup = 1/4 cup = 3 fluid ounces = 90 ml	
1/2 cup = 1/3 cup = 4 fluid ounces = 120 ml	
1 cup = 3/4 cup = 8 fluid ounces = 240 ml	
1 1/4 cups = 1 cup	
2 cups = 1 pint	
1 quart = 1 liter – 3 tablespoons	
1 gallon = 4 liters – 1 1/2 cups	

Weight

U.S.	U.K./Australia
1/4 ounce = 7 grams	
1/2 ounce = 14 grams	
3/4 ounce = 21 grams	
1 ounce = 28 grams	
8 ounces = 1/2 pound = 225 grams	
12 ounces = 3/4 pound = 341 grams	
16 ounces = 1 pound = 454 grams	
35 ounces = 2.2 pounds = 1 kilogram	

AN AMERICAN DEATH

AN
AMERICAN
DEATH

THE TRUE STORY OF
THE ASSASSINATION OF
DR. MARTIN LUTHER KING, JR.
AND THE GREATEST MANHUNT
OF OUR TIME

By GEROLD FRANK

———◆———

DOUBLEDAY & COMPANY, INC.
GARDEN CITY, NEW YORK

PHOTO CREDITS

New York *Daily News* Photo: 1
Jim McKnight, Memphis *Commercial-Appeal*: 25 and 28
Barney Sellers, Memphis *Commercial-Appeal*: 5, 6 and 26
Jim Sherin, Memphis *Commercial-Appeal*: 30
United Press International: 11, 13, 16, 17, 18, 19, 21, 27 and 29
Wide World Photos: 2, 3, 4, 24 and 31
Bob Williams, Memphis *Commercial-Appeal*: 8, 9, 12 and 14
Ernest C. Withers: 7

Again, and always:
For Lillian

CONTENTS

A NOTE TO THE READER

An American Death is the product of nearly four years of research and writing. It is an attempt to present the true story of the assassination of Dr. Martin Luther King, Jr., the search for his murderer or murderers, and the subsequent conviction of James Earl Ray as his assassin.

In preparing this book, I have sought to find the facts in an event grievously clouded by rumor and suspicion growing out of the confusion surrounding the assassinations of President Kennedy and Senator Robert F. Kennedy, and intensified by what was to many the shockingly swift hearing at which Ray pleaded guilty and was sentenced to ninety-nine years in prison.

Dr. King was fatally shot in Memphis on April 4, 1968. I began my work immediately thereafter. What appears in the following pages is based not only upon my own research in Memphis, elsewhere in the country, and abroad, including many hundreds of hours of personal interviews with virtually everyone in the case; it is also based upon the actual records—police and court records, medical and psychological reports, transcripts and tapes of interrogations on the scene, some beginning almost before the echoes of the murder bullet ceased reverberating in the courtyard of the Lorraine Motel. I have also had access to the private diaries kept by many of the principals in the case, as well as the benefit of extensive investigative reports.

As a result, *An American Death* draws on original sources which represent, I believe, one of the most complete documentations ever brought together in a criminal investigation in our time.

In addition to the research of the facts, I have attempted to immerse myself in other aspects of this puzzling event in American history. As I have sought to learn as much as possible about Dr. King from his closest friends and associates, so I have sought to learn as much as possible about a far less known, less visible figure—James Earl Ray. I have spent hours with members of his family, his father, uncle, brothers, sister; with his schoolmates, friends and criminal associates. I have haunted the places of his childhood, have visited the house in which he was born, the school he attended, the towns in which he grew up, and have interviewed at length the police who arrested him through the years, the guards who watched him in prison, the prosecutors who brought him to trial, the lawyers who defended him, the jurors who convicted him, the judge who sentenced him—as well as those attorneys who still seek to reverse the plea of guilty he made in a Memphis courtroom the morning of March 10, 1969—his forty-first birthday.

It is important for us to know the truth about the assassination of Dr. King, who murdered him, why he was murdered, and what actually took place from beginning to end. We want to know this, if not for the sake of our own sanity in a world where the bizarre all too often becomes the commonplace, then at least in the hope that, by knowing and understanding it, perhaps in some way—still unfathomable to us—we can help prevent such things in the days to come.

GEROLD FRANK

AN AMERICAN DEATH

"It is clear that in the criminal two mental forces are fighting for supremacy. One tries to wipe out all traces of the crime, the other proclaims the deed and the doer to the whole world."

Theodor Reik, *The Compulsion to Confess*

Prologue

It was very hot, the summer before, when the fear struck.

Later there were those in Memphis who would compare what happened—sadly, and with a bitter sense that they had been given an omen in light of the tragedy to come later—with the tulip mania which swept Holland in the seventeenth century. Then a frenzy—the Dutch called it a "fury"—spread through the country, an aberration in which matter-of-fact Dutch citizens imagined such a scarcity of tulips that the price of tulip bulbs rose to incredible heights. Fortunes were made and lost as speculators gambled wildly in the flower market of Amsterdam. Diamonds seemed no less precious. Then, suddenly, the fever vanished, the market collapsed, and all was as it had been before. Why tulips, and why a scarcity, and why the hysteria? No one really knew.

So in Memphis, Tennessee, that summer of 1967. Despite its exotic name, Memphis is essentially staid and prosaic, far more like a Dutch town than the Egyptian capital of antiquity for which it is named. It breathes the languid air of the old South, an air of many generations of respectability and propriety, of son succeeding father and grandson succeeding son as planter, farmer, merchant, lawyer, white-collar worker.

"The Place of Good Abode" has been the Memphis slogan for years, and it has repeatedly won the Quiet City award.* Though

* Memphis differs from many Southern cities because of an almost monolithic white population. Once cosmopolitan, in the 1870's two yellow fever epidemics virtually decimated the city. The Germans, Jews, and Irish able to do so fled. The city lost its charter and became only a taxing district. It began to be rebuilt some

today nearly 40 per cent of the city's 600,000 population is black, the Negroes had always known their place, and there had been no major racial dispute in Memphis since 1866, when there were race riots between the Irish and Negroes in the wake of the Civil War.

There should have been no reason for the fear.

But it came, in the hot days of June 1967, a fear of black rioting— a growing conviction that, despite every denial by the authorities, one of the meekest, most compliant black communities in the nation was about to explode, triggered by an invasion of angry blacks from the rest of troubled America, monstrously armed and intent to burn, loot, and destroy.

All spring, to be sure, there had been unrest and bloodshed elsewhere between black and white—in Newark, Milwaukee, New York. Negroes had rioted in Nashville in April, and a few days later in Louisville and in Montgomery, and Cleveland, Ohio, the same week. In May black students had been killed and wounded in Jackson, Mississippi. In June there had been trouble in Tampa, Cincinnati, Atlanta. . . . Memphis, the fear grew, would not escape.

By mid June one heard the word along Beale Street, in the heart of the black ghetto, and in the white suburbs, that Stokely Carmichael, who had been preaching "Burn, Baby, Burn!" was about to arrive in town, and that H. Rap Brown, who had been haranguing Negroes up North to wage guerrilla war on the whites, was bound for Memphis too. One read the warnings in John Birch Society pamphlets found under front doors.

Memphis is a weekend town with Friday, payday, ushering in a faster, more excited tempo. By some contagion of fear, everyone knew that the first target date would be Friday night, June 23, and the place: the Memphis Fairgrounds, where the park commissioners allowed integrated dancing. Prepared for the worst, the city's two newspapers, the *Commercial-Appeal* and the *Press-Scimitar*, sent reporters and photographers to the scene. Their cars ringed the fairgrounds, walkie-talkies and radios ready. In the dark, too, waited

---

twenty years later by a migration from neighboring farm areas of Arkansas, Mississippi, and Missouri—people rural to the core, conservative, fundamentalist. Today's white residents are mainly their descendants. The blacks, too, who helped populate the ravaged city came from farms and plantations. Add to this the heavy hand for the first five decades of this century of "Boss Crump"—E. H. Crump, who ran Memphis and smothered initiative of both creative whites and blacks, so that young people who might have given leadership were either rendered impotent or simply got on the Illinois Central and went to St. Louis, Chicago, and other cities.

Memphis' police TAC units—Tactical Action Cruisers—four armed men to a car, three cars to a squad.

The dance went off uneventfully. There was no trouble.

Again, as Friday, June 30 approached, the pressure grew. The same inexplicable sense of impending disaster hung over the city. Again, nothing happened. The apprehension rose sharply when a black youth was wounded in a grocery holdup (the police later said they were mistaken, the boy was absolved, but the damage had been done) and by the first weekend in July, the fear had focused; one heard the same story whispered at cocktail parties and at wedding receptions. In a barn two miles—or was it twenty miles south or north of Memphis—black militants were building up a terrifying arsenal of rifles, pistols, machine guns, hand grenades, waiting for the signal. It was an SNCC* barn, with three armored cars waiting and machine guns hanging from the rafters, and they were poised to move on downtown Memphis. No, it was a Black Panther house, not outside the city but in the heart of black Memphis, where now no white man went after dark save at his own risk. The Negroes grew alarmed as well. The Rev. James Lawson, a leader of the black community, led a delegation of black ministers to meet with Police Director Claude Armour. "We'd like to find these places because we've heard they're supposed to exist, but we can't find them," he told Armour. Armour, whose father had been police director before him, ordered the Internal Security Division of the Memphis Police to join black volunteers in a street-by-street search for the hideouts. They could find no barn, no house, no weapons.†

Then one July afternoon, white housewives were on their phones and the awful word flashed from house to house. The mutilated body of an eleven-year-old white boy had been found in the restroom at the Public Gardens. Police rushed to the scene. There was nothing there. No body was ever found. No white boy was reported missing. But the rumor persisted. *They're hiding it, they're afraid to tell us. . . .*

Now there were runs on gunshops. In one thirty minute period the York Arms Company on South Main Street sold three revolvers, an automatic pistol, and a shotgun to white buyers. In West Memphis, Arkansas, just across the bridge, in the parking lot of the largest gun

* Student Non-Violent Coordinating Committee.

† One did not easily allay these rumors. They reached Attorney General Ramsey Clark in Washington. FBI agents made their own investigation in Memphis, even taking to helicopters in an attempt to find the stakeouts. All in vain.

dealer in the state, fourteen out of sixteen cars carried Tennessee license plates.

What brought this all about? No one was quite sure. Perhaps part of it was the heat and the growing drought that accompanied it. Day after day above ninety degree temperature and no rain. It became almost unbearable as July wore on—a strange, oppressive, atmospheric heaviness that drained one's energy and left one irritable and quarrelsome, and somehow frustrated, wanting to lash out without reason. Veterans of World War II campaigns in the Middle East compared it to the *khamsin*, the enervating desert wind that sweeps over the Arab lands, making men wretched and beside themselves, so that the time of the *khamsin* is a time of wife-beating and street violence and even murder. Memphis had no public bars where liquor was served. Drinking was done at home. One thought of the poor whites, the blue-collar workers sitting on their small porches suffering through the mounting heat, drinking their cold beer, perspiring and tormented by visions of rampaging Negroes, building fury upon fury as they exchanged rumor and wild surmise and assured each other they'd be ready. . . . *Goddammit, I hate to see it. Man, you blind? Them big black bucks in the Cadillac, from New York, that's where they're from. Joey saw them drive by his shop. Come to make trouble. The Niggers is stirred up and sompins gonna happen. You bet your ass sompins gonna happen and I gotta twelve-gauge says nothin's gonna happen near me!*

Simultaneously, in a kind of counterpoint, the poor blacks, sitting in the heavy, debilitating heat of the Memphis ghettos, drinking their warm cheap wine, perspiring and building up their own rage. . . . *All I do is take out my troubles in wine. Wine goes down your throat, out of your pores goes all your troubles. White man causes me to be drinkin' this wine. That's one of my troubles. I'm livin' in a no-good low rent housing, rats as big as cats runnin' me out of bed. I smell of sweat and liquor. Man, I've had it, I've had it. We gonna pay Whitey back. . . .*

The front pages of the two newspapers did not help. Frightening photographs of the riots erupting in Newark on July 12 (TWENTY-THREE DEAD!) and a few days later in Detroit (FORTY-THREE DEAD!). Memphis was so edgy that when a Negro woman being arrested for disorderly conduct screamed for help, an angry crowd gathered, half a dozen police cars with rifles converged on the scene, and a black-white confrontation was averted only by the arrival of Mayor William Ingram himself. He managed to calm the crowd and tempers subsided with no one hurt. But by Thursday morning, July 27, all the rumors seemed to meet in a pyramid. As the hours passed, the city was smothered in one overwhelming rumor. The blacks are rioting!

City officials were forced to go on radio and TV. No, the city was not in flames. No, there was no curfew. Newspapers kept busy sending reporters from place to place to check reports that appeared to be virtually all fantasy. No, five cars had not been overturned on Main Street. A bus was not ablaze on South Second Street. Shops had not been bombed on South Third. Negroes were not marching to burn down City Hall. Police radios crackled with dozens of "Signal H" calls from headquarters, which meant that the officer radioed was asked to call his home. Invariably it was a wife or mother wanting to know if he was all right, because he was in the center of the trouble, wasn't he; and how could he lie and say nothing was happening just because he didn't want her to get upset? At the heart of Memphis communications, in the cafeteria of the Memphis Publishing Company, publisher of both newspapers, frightening stories were dispensed with every cup of coffee. "Say, I heard that out at Crump and Lamar they got the cops hemmed in . . . snipers, too. Six hurt." A reporter would shake his head wearily. "Look, we got the police radio. If they had anybody in trouble out there, we'd know it." And the answer. "Hell you would—they're suppressing it. They don't want the people to know. Only makes it worse."

There were minor occurrences, the small bits of violence every city knows. Molotov cocktails were thrown into two small establishments, a Mexican restaurant and a sundries shop. There was a wailing of sirens and a rush of TAC units, but the only damage was minor smoke damage. Then an alarm from a pawnshop. Someone had thrown a brick through the window and made off with a guitar.

Yet the panic mounted. Groups of white men would approach police cars. "They gonna riot, eh? Well, let 'em start it, we'll finish it." The police reassured them. "We got no riot, and if it comes, we can handle it." White storekeepers, particularly liquor shops, hired armed guards. The tension grew until on Thursday afternoon Mayor Ingram telephoned Governor Buford Ellington in Nashville. Three thousand state National Guardsmen were on a two-week summer tour at nearby Camp Shelby in Mississippi. Would the governor send them into Memphis, simply as a precaution?

They began pouring into the city as dusk fell, and the sight of the long caravans of trucks rumbling through the night, bristling with armed men in uniform, seemed only to confirm everyone's fear.

Memphis trembled.

Mayor Ingram took to the radio again: "No riots or violence will be tolerated." Police Director Armour told a news conference: "There is no imminent danger. What we're concerned about is that rumors of violence might lead to violence." But it was no secret that the National Guard was bivouacked about the circumference of the city.

The men slept in their tents, rifles at their sides, ate canned food, and waited.

So it stood that Thursday night, a city tense, terrified, all but paralyzed with fear, refusing to believe, waiting for the explosion. . . .

Any moment now. Any moment. A single incident could set it off. . . .

And then the rains came.

The first drops fell in the night, and they grew larger and more frequent with flashes of lightning and peals of thunder. And Friday dawned under a sky so black, so lowering, that even at midday it was still dark as twilight. The rains came down in earnest, until at dusk the heavens opened up and a full-scale cloudburst and thunderstorm struck Memphis. The city was deluged.

The heat broke sharply. The tension vanished as suddenly and inexplicably as it had begun weeks before. It rained all night, and the next day, cooling the men and the land, and when it had ended, Memphis was as it had been before. On radio and TV an announcer said with obvious relief and a kind of embarrassed chuckle, "The Day of the Rumor has passed."

They had thought, in Memphis, their time had come, and they were wrong.

They had, of course, been given an omen. But they did not know it.

Assassination

CHAPTER I

In March 1968, eight months after the Day of the Rumor, Dr. Martin Luther King, Jr., came to Memphis. It was in response to an invitation—indeed, more than an invitation, almost an entreaty—and he was not at first particularly eager to do so. He was in the midst of planning his Poor People's Campaign. This, which he hoped would mark a watershed in the civil rights struggle, would marshal the poor, taken from all parts of the United States, for a march upon Washington "to move the conscience of the Congress," to demand decent jobs and decent income. The Government had the resources to end poverty and to end racism, Dr. King maintained, and it had failed. This would be an attempt to force it to action.

The plans, which he had first announced in December 1967, were far-reaching, the most massive nonviolent demonstration in the history of the nation. King and his colleagues in the Southern Christian Leadership Conference, the organization of black ministers which he led, had been working on them for some time. Memphis would be an interruption. Moreover, the invitation came at a most difficult time. The past year—and especially the spring of 1968—had been in many ways a painful period for Dr. King. There had been endless arguments between himself and his advisers as to the wisdom of his Washington march. Both the NAACP and the National Urban League were not happy about it. Bayard Rustin, long a father figure to King (and the man who had organized the triumphant March on Washington in 1963, climaxed by Dr. King's famous "I Have a Dream" speech) had said he would not support it. Dr. King had also separated himself from many supporters by his attacks on the Vietnam war and his insistence on linking peace abroad with the civil rights struggle at home. This was unpopular with such prestigious black leaders as Dr. Ralph Bunche, Senator Edward Brook, Jr., Roy Wilkins, Whitney Young, who not only thought this unwise but also warned him that he was diluting his strength by taking on an unpopular, misunderstood cause. With black power growing, with such men as Stokely Carmichael and H. Rap Brown eloquent in the hustings, Dr. King had been attacked as an Uncle Tom, a tool of Whitey.

He had even been booed in Chicago when he spoke of non-violence. . . . His Poor People's Campaign, his March on Washington *had* to succeed, in one blow to confound his critics and reassert all he stood for, had built his life upon, and for which he had won the Nobel Peace Prize.

Memphis would indeed be an interruption, and yet he went. A number of reasons persuaded him, among them his need to hold a strategy meeting of the Southern Christian Leadership Conference Executive Committee, the call upon him by Negro leaders in Memphis to lend his strength to a strike of 1300 sanitation workers, nearly all black, and, in the end, his realization that in this strike he had, in microcosm, the Poor People's Campaign itself.

The trouble in Memphis had been brewing for years. To the black garbage and sewer workers, it seemed that all the disabilities of the Negro were concentrated in their lot. In a city known for its low wages, they had one of the lowest-paying jobs, and one scorned by everyone else. There was no job security, no insurance. The leather tubs in which they hauled the garbage on their shoulders were old and leaky, causing painful skin blisters. Warned not to lunch in cafés lest they drink beer and become intoxicated, the men ate in the street. They had no facilities for either washing or personal comfort, and if they used a field or ravine, white residents made outraged calls to the police. Whites also objected if they took refuge from Memphis' torrential rains on their porches. They had a specified number of streets to complete in their seven-to-three-o'clock day, and if they were eight or ten houses short by quitting time, they had to continue work without overtime pay or be docked.

Memphis had never been a strong union town, for the white laborer refused to think of himself as part of the working class: that was the role of the Negro. As a consequence, their first attempts at unionization, in 1963, failed, the city simply firing several of the leaders for "incompetence." Trying again in 1966, the garbage and sewer workers ultimately managed to win a charter by the American Federation of State, County and Municipal Employees, and as Local 1733—virtually all black—issued demands for higher wages and better working conditions. The city not only refused to recognize them but went into court and obtained an injunction forbidding any strike by municipal employees.

The situation only grew more intolerable as time went on. The breaking point could not be far off. On February 1, 1968, two crew members, trapped in a heavy rain and with all other shelter off limits to them, took refuge in the barrel of their garbage truck, a huge cylinder with a powerful steel mechanism that compressed the garbage into tightly packed bales. By some accident, a shovel was dislodged, short-circuiting the machinery. The two men, unable to climb out, were crushed to death. Horrible as the tragedy was, it was compounded by the discovery that there was neither workmen's compensation nor any other benefits for their families.

A few days later, again on a rainy day, twenty-two black workers were told to go out and work or go home without pay. They went home. But their supervisors, nearly all white, were permitted to wait in the barns until the rain stopped. They remained there, some playing cards, and when the rain ended, they were put to work and paid for the full day.

The black workers protested. At the end of the week each found two hours' pay in his envelope. The following Monday, February 12, Lincoln's birthday, they walked off their jobs. They were undoubtedly encouraged by the successful nine-day strike just carried off by New York's sanitation workers. Nonetheless, what no one believed they would dare in Memphis they had done. The men struck. Local 1733, all Negro garbage collectors and sewer workers, demanded a fifty-cent raise in pay, a contract which would meet their grievances, and a dues checkoff—all of which were refused.

The course of the strike might have gone differently, and Martin Luther King might never have found himself in Memphis, had someone other than Henry Loeb III been mayor at this time. No account of what led to Dr. King's presence in Memphis can be understood without considering Loeb. A ruggedly handsome man in his forties, standing six feet five with the build of an All-American football player, Loeb was a commanding presence. Though he came from a wealthy Jewish family which owned one of the largest laundry-drycleaning businesses in Memphis, he had been confirmed in the Episcopal Church shortly after being sworn in as mayor on January 1, 1968—five weeks before the strike began.

Loeb had gone to Andover and then to Brown University. During World War II he had been a PT boat skipper and was proud of it. (In 1960, during a previous term as mayor, he welcomed John F. Kennedy to Memphis to make a campaign speech, but made it clear he did not do so because he admired Kennedy or his politics, but because Kennedy, too, had been a PT boat captain.)

A proud, opinionated man, he combined truculence and stubbornness.* It did not help that the industry with which his family was
long involved was one of the lowest-paid in the country. Although his
friends did not consider Loeb a racist, he had grown up in the
Southern plantation tradition; and his approach to Negroes, though
in his own eyes conscientiously impartial, was: let them trust him to
know what was best for them, and he'd see that they were taken care
of. But Memphis blacks considered him the enemy. In the mayoralty
election, forty-nine out of every fifty voted against him. The white
voters elected him.

Now, when the garbage issue rose, his anti-Negro reputation,
coupled with his obduracy, lessened the likelihood of a quick settlement. He refused to give any quarter. A strike of municipal employees was illegal; grievances would not be discussed until the men
returned to work; he would not permit a dues checkoff because that
meant official recognition of the union.

Loeb did not know it, but almost overnight he was to find himself
in a confrontation with the Rev. James M. Lawson, Jr., pastor of the
Centenary Methodist Church, to which many of the strikers belonged, and a long-time friend of Dr. King.

The two men could not have been more different in their approach
and their strategy. A vigorous, eloquent man of forty, Lawson had
worked with Dr. King and the SCLC for many years. He was a
controversial figure to the white community, but admittedly the most
influential of the black leaders. He had been involved in civil rights
since his student days at Baldwin-Wallace College in Berea, Ohio,
and had come to Memphis in 1962 after a colorful career in which
protest had played an important part. He had spent thirteen months
in federal prison for refusing to fight in the Korean War. He had served
for three years as a missionary in India, where he became a disciple
of Gandhi. In 1960 he had been expelled from the Vanderbilt
Divinity School for organizing lunch-counter sit-ins in Nashville. He
had helped organize the Student Non-Violent Coordinating Committee and had attended workshops on nonviolence in half a dozen
countries. When Dr. King led the successful Montgomery bus boycott in 1956, Lawson read about it on the front page of *The Times*

---

* Friends tell how Loeb, en route overseas in World War II (he was then an
ensign) had dinner in New York with a multimillionaire maternal uncle, whose
favorite nephew he was. They became involved in so bitter an argument over a
minor family matter that the uncle changed his will and left his fortune to Loeb's
younger brother, William, now owner and manager of the family business.

of Nagpur, India, where he was teaching school. Months later, back in the States, he met King. The two, both the same age, both ministers and sons of ministers, and both advocates of nonviolence, became close friends.

On Sunday, February 18, in an attempt to ameliorate a growingly difficult situation, Lawson and the Rev. H. Ralph Jackson, pastor of the African Methodist Church, called a meeting under the aegis of the Memphis Ministers Association. Since the strike had begun the Monday before, the town had been building to a crisis. On Tuesday international officers of the union began arriving to lend their support. On Wednesday Loeb laid down an ultimatum: anyone who did not return to work the next day would be fired. "The garbage is going to be picked up," he asserted.

On Thursday he carried out his threat and began hiring nonunion workers, some from out of town; next day he hired more. The garbage trucks moved, but now they were escorted, front and rear, by armed police cars—this after a group of black strikers threatened a new garbage crew with a pistol, and a newly hired white man threw a rifle to his shoulders and ordered them off.* If the racial overtones had been muted until now, by the end of this first week they were beginning to be heard. The NAACP in Memphis supported the strike and threatened a mass call-in to tie up telephones in City Hall, in police and fire stations, unless Mayor Loeb negotiated with the strikers.

But though the Ministers Association had called the meeting, Loeb refused to talk directly to the local's representatives.

The event that more than any other united the black community behind the strike came at a City Council meeting on February 23. It had been announced that the council's Public Works Committee, after a long hearing of grievances, would recommend at this meeting recognition of the union and a dues checkoff—the two principal issues. It would mean victory for the men.

But these recommendations never reached the floor. While nearly a thousand strikers and their supporters listened in dismay, the council announced that it had met earlier that day in executive session and voted that the strike was an "administrative matter"—and therefore back in the hands of Mayor Loeb. Then the council promptly adjourned.

* There were reports that the city was able to release police for the job because the governor had ordered the Tennessee National Guard to take over police duties in downtown Memphis. This infuriated the black strikers who saw it as evidence that the white leadership was joining ranks to break the strike.

The reaction was furious. Strike leaders immediately called for a protest march down Main Street to Mason Temple, strike headquarters. There were violent speeches. T. O. Jones, president of the local, attacked the police. "I'm going to march . . . they'll have to break my head to stop me!" The men poured out of the meeting bound for the first really defiant Negro march in Memphis history. Police ordered them to march only on the right side of the street. The parade began, men four abreast.

It got into trouble after about four blocks. Here there was confusion as to what happened. Half a dozen men began rocking a police car, charging that police cars had been crowding them to the curb, and this one had run over a woman's foot. Tempers exploded. The police, many with blue riot helmets and gas masks, and armed with mace, the new antiriot chemical irritant, jumped out of their cars.

There were cries of "Mace! Let 'em have mace!" The police dashed about, macing right and left. Among those temporarily blinded were Rev. Lawson, Rev. Jackson, and several other black ministers in clerical garb, who accused the police of deliberately squirting them in the face with the chemical.

For the black community, the macing was the catalyst that united the Negro forces in the city. To many, it was the moment that a labor dispute became a racial struggle. That night, strike leaders, who now included ministers, union officials, and leaders of a hitherto fragmented black constituency ranging from the NAACP to the black militants, appointed a strategy committee. Lawson was elected chairman, Jackson vice-chairman, and Jesse Epps, international union representative, an adviser. The committee immediately went into an all-night session and next day presented a five-point program to a meeting of 150 ministers for their approval and that of their congregations.

The five points were:

1. A boycott of all stores in downtown Memphis.

2. A boycott of all businesses carrying the Loeb name.

3. Two daily marches through downtown Memphis from Mason Temple to City Hall and back, a distance of two miles, the first at 2 P.M. for strikers, families, and supporters, the second at 4:30 P.M. for students.

4. Fund-raising campaigns in every church.

5. Nightly church rallies.

The ministers read the plan to their congregations that weekend. It was enthusiastically accepted. The battle lines were drawn, the campaign went into full gear. It was no secret that much of the strategy had to be attributed to Lawson.

It was Lawson a few days later who proposed that they suggest to his colleagues that they invite national figures to Memphis each week to address large mass meetings and bring country-wide attention to their cause. If, as they maintained, local newspapers, radio, and television were giving them a minimum of attention, a national figure not only would bring wide coverage but inspire the strikers.

On his desk Lawson had jotted down such names as Father Groppi, the militant white priest of Milwaukee; Roy Wilkins, head of the NAACP; Bayard Rustin, of the Philip Randolph Foundation; Whitney Young, of the National Urban League; Dr. King, and many others. Rustin and Wilkins, the first to be invited, agreed to speak on March 14. Lawson approached Wilkins first as leader of the most prestigious Negro organization in the country, for if Dr. King had been invited to deliver the opening blow, the strategy committee might find it difficult to get Wilkins.

Not until the end of February did Lawson extend an invitation to Dr. King. Reluctant though King was to take the time for even one speech, he was able to work it out. He had an all-day meeting of his SCLC Executive Committee scheduled for March 18 in Jackson, Mississippi, he told Lawson. He would shift it to Memphis, leave the meeting only long enough to make his speech and return to it immediately afterward. He was pressed. The March on Washington was scheduled for April 22.*

At one point it appeared that he might not be needed. On Friday, March 1, a series of round-the-clock strike conferences began between ministers, councilmen, and union leaders. Some of Loeb's closest friends were persuaded to appeal to him, until he agreed to send a letter on March 4 to Jesse Epps, outlining the city's maximum concessions. It was less than the strikers demanded, but it would be acceptable. A *Commercial-Appeal* reporter wrote a story carefully worded so as not to injure Loeb's pride, but someone had forgotten

---

* The plan was to gather three thousand poor people—two hundred from ten cities and five rural areas—who would be trained in nonviolent techniques. They would include blacks, Puerto Ricans, whites, Indians, Mexicans, the poverty-stricken and deprived, those who worked and yet were unable to earn minimal wages. They would go by caravan to Washington and pitch tents and live in them. Each day delegations would call upon government departments to present demands involving "jobs, income and a decent life." The three thousand would be the vanguard of many more who would come to the scene as needed and remain until they achieved a response from the Government.

to cue in the editor who wrote the headline. The story appeared under the words LOEB MAY OFFER COMPROMISE.

Loeb, furious at any suggestion that he was capitulating, refused to sign the letter that had already been drafted.

Had the headline read, UNION MAY OFFER COMPROMISE, the strike might have ended. Now the situation was back where it had started.

On March 17 Lawson telephoned King to give him a last-minute briefing before he arrived in Memphis the next day. He found him in Los Angeles. He had addressed the California Democratic State Council in nearby Anaheim the night before. "Martin," Lawson said, "do you know you'll most likely be talking to ten thousand people?" King said, impressed, "No, I didn't know that." Lawson knew he suspected him of exaggeration. Such figures were unknown with black audiences. No city in the South had a Negro-owned hall capable of holding such a crowd. Through all the civil rights campaigns in the past, small rallies had to be held simultaneously at various churches and halls, and speakers exhausted themselves hurrying from one to the other.

Next evening King arrived shortly after seven o'clock. Lawson and Epps drove out to pick him up. On their way they passed Mason Temple. It was already packed, with people outside pushing to get in. "Let's tease Martin," Lawson suggested. "Say to him, did I tell him he'd speak to ten thousand? Tell him I made a mistake."

Now as they were walking from the airport to their car, Epps said, "Dr. King, did Jim tell you yesterday you'd be speaking to ten thousand?" "Yes," said King soberly. "I didn't realize the place was so big—"

"Well, he made a mistake," Epps said lugubriously. King's face fell. His friends knew that he dearly loved to speak before large audiences. His greatest speeches had been made before enormous crowds. "Yes, he made a mistake," Epps went on. "Seems like you're going to speak to fifteen thousand."

King laughed. "You fellows must really have something going here."

When King spoke that night, it was before a tumultuous crowd that so packed the hall that some listeners actually sat on the rafters under the roof. On the platform by his side were three shining new garbage pails. By the time the evening was over, nearly five thousand dollars in contributions had been dropped into them. King spoke standing under an enormous white banner that read, NOT BY MIGHT, NOT BY POWER, SAITH THE LORD OF HOSTS, BUT BY MY SPIRIT.

Touched by what went on, he had rarely been in better form, and time and again the audience rose to shout and applaud. He sat down to the congratulations of those on the platform, particularly the ministers leading the strike. Lawson turned to him enthusiastically. "Martin, we're having daily marches. Why don't you come back and lead a big march? You see how they receive you. It would be terrific!" Rev. Jackson added, "Martin, you remember when Meredith fell . . ." In June 1966, James Meredith, the Negro student who first integrated the University of Mississippi four years earlier, had undertaken to walk alone from Memphis to Jackson, Mississippi, nearly two hundred miles, to encourage black voter registration and to demonstrate that a black man could walk unafraid through the deep South. He had just crossed the state line when a white sniper, hiding in the bushes along the road, brought him down with a buckshot blast. He had been taken to a Memphis hospital. King had immediately flown to Memphis and talked to Lawson, Jackson, and the others. Meredith's walk couldn't be permitted to end in this fashion. "We need a few folk to continue the march into Mississippi," King told them. Would they march with him? The Memphis ministers had gone down together to the spot where Meredith fell and joined King and other black leaders in a march which grew from thirty persons to several hundred.

He needed them then: they needed him now.

They had still another argument, a powerful one. They knew he was leaving immediately to tour the poorest parts of Mississippi building support for his Washington march. Now, they argued, he saw how valuable he was in their struggle in Memphis. Were not these people before him the poor? Were not these black garbage workers so inspired by him what his Poor People's Campaign was all about? If he led a march of the Memphis poor, it could be the first phase of his campaign and a perfect introduction to the march on Washington. "Begin the Poor People's Campaign right here in Memphis!" King, basking in the warmth and emotion generated by his speech, checked with his aides. They, too, had been impressed by the spirit in Memphis. Yes, he would come back. Sitting on the platform, he pulled out his little black appointment book and decided he could return the following Friday, March 22.

Moments later he stood on the podium again to say, "I want to tell you that I am coming back to Memphis on Friday. I want all of you to stay home from work that day. I want a tremendous work stoppage, and all of you, your families and children, will join me and I will lead you in a march through the center of Memphis."

The Memphis ministers were delighted. They mobilized and organized for the twenty-second, the day Memphis would literally be paralyzed. But about four o'clock of the afternoon of the twenty-first, snow began to fall—an unseasonable snow. Lawson looked out his study window, thinking, *Those are awfully big flakes, but they're bound to melt.* Snow is rare in Memphis, and it is even rarer for snow to remain long. It snowed the rest of that day however, and through the night. By 6 A.M. snow a foot deep covered Memphis. At 7 A.M. Lawson telephoned King, who had been scheduled to arrive on a 9 A.M. flight. They would have to call everything off. The snow was already too deep for a march. They agreed on a new date—the following Thursday, March 28.

When the snow ended, seventeen inches covered the streets. It was the second biggest snowfall in Memphis history. The city had no snow clearance equipment. Autos were snowbound, thousands could not get to work, schools and offices were closed. Downtown Memphis was deserted. "Martin got his work stoppage," the black community said. "The Lord done heard him."

For both blacks and whites, the big day now was the twenty-eighth —the blacks mounting a massive campaign, united as they had never been before; the whites, outraged, apprehensive, waiting.

CHAPTER II

There were reasons why King's presence in Memphis, coupled with what was, after all, the sort of unglamorous municipal strike that dozens of cities had endured at one time or another, should have so agitated the city.

One was, of course, the traumatic scare of the year before, all the more frightening because it seemed half fantasy yet half retribution. But there was another reason. It stemmed from Dr. King's remarkable effectiveness with his black constituents and the realization that his appearance could usher in a new chapter in black-white relations in the city. He had brought nonviolence to its highest pitch in the United States. In 1955 as a young minister just two years out of the seminary, he had found himself pressed into service as leader of the Montgomery bus strike. Historians were later to say that, although others had taken the initiative in the Montgomery struggle, Dr. King was elected chairman because he was a newcomer, had no enemies, and so could rally all segments of the black community behind him. Nonetheless, given the opportunity, he used it magnificently. A new Moses had come to Zion.

From then on his record had been remarkable. As he had once said to a friend, "They expect me to do miracles," and through the years he seemed able to do them. The bus boycott led to the outlawing of segregation by the U. S. Supreme Court in 1956. In the spring of 1963 his leadership in Birmingham led to the important Public Accommodation Bill. In 1965 came Selma and the Voting Rights Bill. And in 1968 the Housing Legislation Bill—each a tremendous step forward in the Negro struggle.

What King had done was to discover an untapped source of power, that generated by moving people into the street, the power of confrontation. That is, making people visible to their government and dramatizing, by their physical presence, their complaints, their demands, their recitation on the scene of injustices suffered. It brought to public attention, and to all in authority, that here was a problem, and that something must be done about it. And he could move people into the street, not only because he could inspire, but because he began with a tremendous asset. This was the remarkably close communication between the black Baptist minister and his congregation. The black Baptist minister played a unique role. More than any other clergyman, he maintained an intimate personal relationship with each member of his congregation—at once social worker, family consultant, father confessor, present in virtually every crisis in the lives of his parishioners—birth, confirmation, marriage, illness, death. He was not only a spiritual leader, but in many instances his parishioners' only link to the world of power and authority outside. In the South, many members of black congregations can neither read nor write. The road to their hearts and minds is the spoken word. If, therefore, in addition to his special role in their lives, their minister was also an eloquent man, his influence became extraordinary. Virtually all Negroes in the South attend church. This meant that each minister spoke to from five hundred to several thousand persons at a time. The ministers together represented tremendous power. Thus the SCLC, which King formed in 1957, and of which he was president, a loosely bound association, mainly of black Baptist ministers, might in numbers be small, less than twoscore, but in terms of the numbers each man represented, and could move in one direction or another, its influence was not to be underestimated.

To see this power individually at work, one had only to visit a Negro Baptist church on a Sunday morning. There one saw what miracles of emotional purgation and community unity were achieved, and how a great preacher could move his audience, as if it were one, and bring it almost to a pitch of ecstasy.

Until Dr. King's advent, the fight for equal treatment for blacks had been waged mainly through legislation and the ballot. The great Negro civil rights organizations, particularly the NAACP, founded five years after the turn of the century, and the National Urban League, founded five years later, played and continued to play a giant role. But Dr. King felt that the formula so successful through the years—one test case, one litigant, and after years of waiting, a ruling that might or might not be observed—was no longer sufficient. Under the pressure of the times the people were too impatient. They would not wait. They were the audience to which he addressed himself. The poor and the illiterate had virtually no political or economic power. They were not likely to call upon their congressmen or write letters to the editor, or make their demands felt effectively in other ways. The courts were remote—and frightening—to them. But they possessed their bodies and their voices, their ability to become visible in the mass, and when Dr. King called upon them to come into the streets and march, or sing, or chant—they felt they participated, they were at least *doing* something.

Above and beyond this, he had changed the psyche of black people. In their own words, long before "Black is beautiful" became current, "Dr. King made us feel it, he gave us a different, a prouder, image of ourselves." And they saw that the vast, faceless establishment they had always feared and resented, which they had never been able to grasp, or cope with, or influence, *was* paying attention, *was* listening.

And though Dr. King himself had never wanted this leadership role, he now had it, and he could not let go. His followers, having seen him literally work miracles, had faith that so long as he was involved in their fight for civil rights, any day—any day now—they would be able to cry out as he had promised them in his memorable speech at the Lincoln Memorial in 1963: "Free at last, free at last, thank God Almighty I'm free at last!"

This was the power he represented, and although many of those who feared his coming to Memphis might have been unable to explain precisely why, other than that they considered him a troublemaker, their fear was nonetheless deep-seated and all-pervading.

CHAPTER III

It was 9 A.M. on Thursday, March 28. He was a member of the Invaders, black and militant. He was twenty, and he stood on the steps of Clayborn Temple, where the great march was to begin. . . .

Man, the town's hot. We got a racist mayor. He says he ain't, but he is. We gotta win a victory today. This is our one chance, we got to get it! They burn down the rest of the country—they burn down Watts and Detroit and Newark; man, we got to get into this, too. The black people ain't takin' this no more, specially here in the South, where everybody thinks black people is just shit. . . .

But hell, a march like this is no good. White people waitin' for us to come runnin' down these streets so they can start killin' us off. They're tired of us . . . they goin' make an example of us Niggers here in Memphis. "You can't do this crap down here, you can do it in California and all those places up North, but boy, you don't do it down here. . . ."

9:30 A.M. Now sun's gettin' hot. People fillin' the streets. Look at all those high-school kids, they sayin'—Man, this is our day, we gotta pay Whitey back, don't forget the Jews on Beale Street, we gotta get them too. . . . Look at all 'em grownups in their Easter Day clothes. What they waitin' for, a party? We got eleven schools. We got thousands at Hamilton High, at Carver. . . . How many hundreds cut classes today? . . . What they sayin' now? They sayin' police used mace on the kids at Hamilton to stop them from comin' here? Boy, we goin' fuck the town around. . . . Hey, 10:30 o'clock. It's hot, waitin' for Dr. King to get in, where is he? He due here nine o'clock. C'mon, let's go, what we waitin' for? . . . Goin' on 11:00, lots of wine drinkin' now, all these people gettin' drunker, problems gettin' worse, sun's gettin' hotter. . . . Man, I'm miserable. Size-nine feet in size-seven shoes, it gettin' hotter and hotter, we all sweatin', we ready to go. Everybody walkin' around, waitin', let's go, let's go, what we waitin' for?

Now, here at Clayborn Temple, they kind of linin' the people up, but they can't get them lined up because crowd's so big they can't go back all the way to get them in line. They shoutin' through sound truck, "CLEAR THE SIDEWALKS, PLEASE! DON'T CROWD UP HERE—GO TO THE REAR OF THE MARCH, PLEASE!" Nobody payin' heed. All of a sudden—it's sort of like a wave, a ripple or wave through the people; and who is it but Lord God Almighty, Dr. Martin Luther King, Jr. Just got off the airplane. Somebody picked him up and drove him in, just came in, got in front of the march. . . . Why, they didn't even make place for the man to come in. Car stops in front of the crowd. Crowd jams up around him, he don't look happy, so many people— he talks to Lawson, Jackson. . . . They walk off, arm in arm, Abernathy, Lawson, Jackson, in the front row, singin' "We Shall Overcome." . . .

Sun very hot. People in front of Dr. King, people behind, they walkin' on his feet. He supposed to be at head of march, ain't he? I walk side of him. People standin' on sidewalk, drinkin', watchin', marchers carryin' signs, long quarter-inch-thick sticks, lot of kids carryin' them. . . . (Hey, you could jam them sticks into anything!) Signs read I AM A MAN. . . . TO HELL WITH KING HENRY. . . . DAMN LOEB. . . . BLACK POWER IS HERE. . . .

Now kids runnin' along on sidewalk in front of march. They came to be in on the lootin', the breakin', the burnin', whatever's gonna take place. Lawson said, "We march in peace." But these kids not listenin'. The church people came to march in peace, but not these kids. They came to raise hell because the word came down, we supposed to raise hell. Man, we owe it to raise hell. . . . They dancin', shoutin', in front of the TV cameras. . . .

How many blocks we got so far? Six? Seven? Glass crashin'. Some fool kid sticks stick through window, some fool-ass cop shoots off, and then it spreads like wildfire. Cops shot a black man!

The crowd starts runnin' back from the cops. They hear, man, we burnin' down the town, and the rest of the kids, they don't know what's happenin', so they come runnin' up Beale Street, smashin' in windows, tearin' down, and the kids runnin' from the back because the cops won't let them go in front—they comin'. Now we have old folks right in the middle, jammed between kids from the back tryin' to get to the front and kids from the front tryin' to make it to the back so they won't be shot.

*Man, it's trouble! Windows bein' smashed, people runnin', old
ladies and men bein' trampled. . . . Damn it. This is what we
told them would happen! They gonna blame us. . . .*

*All these windows busted in, people runnin' out with liquor,
bolts of cloth, radios, throwin' mannikins into the street, kids of
15–16–17 runnin' down street, smashin' windows, lootin',
shoutin', singin', dancin',* YAH HOO! WE FROM CARVER HIGH SCHOOL!
GO! GO! GO! *. . . Cops runnin' after them with billy clubs
swingin'. . . .*

*There's Lawson, shoutin' on bullhorn, tryin' to turn people
around:* "GO BACK TO THE TEMPLE, GO BACK! THE OTHER PEOPLE
HAVE BROKEN OUT AND ARE RIOTIN'! YOU CAN ONLY GET HURT,
PLEASE, GO BACK TO THE TEMPLE!"

*Two nice good-lookin' black brothers standin' corner Her-
nando and Beale. Owners standin' in window of liquor shop
lookin' at marchers comin' back . . . These two boys standin'
back to window, talkin'. There's a great big stone lyin' where
curb broke off. All of a sudden one of the brothers picks it up,
turns around and throws that stone through window. Big crash!
I see lil frightened face that lil cracker, then kid just takes stick
and pushes in rest of jagged edges of glass, people runnin',
they see that window, they clean that window out one, two,
three! Nothin' left, all bottles gone! They carryin' it by armload
between fingers, balanced on head, two fifths fall from arms of
one man. He stops, falls to pavement, flicks finger through it to
mouth, cryin', "Lord, I lost this drink," looks up, sees cop comin',
runs.*

*Law's movin' in now! Law's all over place! Seal off this street,
then that. They got cordon across Main Street. Now police runnin', shotguns on one shoulder, submachine guns hangin' from
other. . . . One o'clock, maybe later now, kid standin' on sidewalk, sayin', "I'm a spectator, don't hit me." Minute cop goes by,
bam! Somethin's thrown at fool cop. He turns around, nobody
there, just bunch of little girls. . . . Police sprayin' mace on
kids. Police shoutin', "Get back into the house." I say, "Officer."
"Move on," he tells me. "Officer . . ." "Move on," and he sprays
me. . . .*

*When I come to I'm tryin' to find my eyesight. Mace makes
you feel your head's goin' to explode any minute, grows hotter
and hotter, don't bother your eyes so much, they sting and water,
but it gets into your brain, mustard plaster inside your head. It's*

throbbin' and expandin', your skull can't contain it, it's goin' to pop. Was it mace? Was I hit over the head with a billy club?

Oh, man. They shouldn't had the march! They shouldn't had!

The day had begun badly.

It dawned hot and uncomfortable and seemed to grow hotter by the minute. Dr. King was scheduled to arrive at nine o'clock, but the plane that brought him from New York, where he had been on a fund-raising tour with Harry Belafonte, the entertainer, was an hour and a half late. The crowd grew impatient. It massed about Clayborn Temple, the rallying point, and overflowed on the sidewalks. There were a great many high-school students who had cut classes for the day. They had already been in trouble with the police at Hamilton and Carver High Schools, virtually all black. The students were excitable. There appeared to be several older youths whom Rev. Lawson, chief marshal of the parade, had never seen in strike sessions or, for that matter, in civil rights demonstrations. He became suspicious when a marshal told him, "There's a fellow with an Afro haircut standing on another man's shoulders and directing the crowd." Lawson hurried over to the youth. "Look," he said sharply, "if you're not going to march the way we are, you leave!" The other stopped his haranguing, jumped down, argued vehemently for a moment, then walked away. There were others with INVADERS printed on the backs of their jackets. They were a group of black militants who had been working among high-school students. Lawson had been having difficulties with them in planning strategy. Two had been on his steering committee, but they had wanted to run off directions for making Molotov cocktails on the church mimeographing machine— their tactics were anything but nonviolent. Finally he had ousted them. In the crowd, too, Lawson discovered later, were professional thieves, pickpockets, and shoplifters. The downtown boycott had been ruinous to them. With scarcely any Negroes going into the shops, anyone that did appear was conspicuous and watched.* They were unable to ply their trade.

King's car did not arrive until nearly eleven o'clock. It was mobbed

* Lawson checked photographs of those he hadn't recognized and found persons later identified by merchants as "Beale Street Professionals." It was alleged that they had already chosen certain stores to raid, when violence broke out, so they could replenish their supplies of clothing, electronic equipment, and liquor for sale to fences. The entire illicit industry had been paralyzed by the boycott.

before it could reach the temple, and King never had a chance to be taken inside and briefed. Instead, Lawson and Rev. Jackson, assistant marshal, helped surround the car to protect King from the press of people trying to reach out and touch him.

Lawson stuck his head through the side window. "Martin, I think you should move on and we'll call you where to meet us, once we get the crowd settled." The people were milling about; youths were waving aloft signs atop long thick staves. Other youths were chanting, GO! GO! GO! At the temple a group of the Invaders had been standing, waiting warily. One announced, minutes before King's car arrived, "We are leaving. We want you all to know, the Invaders are leaving." They had left.

Dr. King was prepared to wait, as Lawson had suggested, but one of his aides came out of the car. "Look, Jim, marches are always hard to get started. We've had this before. Once Doc gets out and starts moving, it'll all settle down. Let's start walking."

With that, Dr. King and the others got out. King linked arms with Rev. Ralph Abernathy, his second-in-command, and Bishop B. Julian Smith of the Methodist Episcopal Church, and they started off, singing "We Shall Overcome." It was 11:06. People were in front of them; the street behind was thick with humanity as far as the eye could see. Lawson hurried ahead, walking with Assistant Police Chief Henry Lux, who carried a bullhorn. Blue-helmeted police in their squad cars had taken up strategic positions on adjacent streets, deliberately out of sight so as not to incite the crowd. The sidewalks were jammed with people moving ahead of the march. At Second and Main, the street into which the parade was to turn on its way from Beale Street to City Hall, Lawson heard what sounded like breaking glass. It was behind him, on Beale. He told two marshals to race back and direct people off the sidewalks and away from the store windows, assuming that pressure had made the glass buckle.

Meanwhile, King and Abernathy had been walking, uncomfortably, on the heels of those in front of them. This was not the way it should be. Then they both heard the sound of shattering glass. King asked, "What was that?" They listened again—it was unmistakable. Abernathy said, "Looks like there's trouble back there." King, still walking, arms linked with the others, was suddenly jostled from the rear. The noise of breaking glass was louder. "We can't have that!" he exclaimed. "Get Jim Lawson—tell him to turn the march around!"

At this moment they saw Lawson, who had almost fought his way through to get to them. He was carrying the bullhorn he had borrowed from Lux. "Martin, you've got to leave—they're starting to break windows up ahead, the police are there." He was panting. "I don't know who's causing the trouble or how the police will react, but you've got to get away from here."

Now all of them were hurrying forward, propelled from behind. The Rev. Bernard Lee, King's secretary and bodyguard, cast about quickly. They were beginning to be in the very eye of the hurricane. Just ahead of them a white Pontiac was crossing Main Street, a black woman at the wheel. Lee ran to the car: "Madam, this is Dr. King—we need your car." In a moment King and Abernathy were in the back seat, and Lee had taken the wheel. Motorcycle policemen immediately surrounded the car. One policeman said, "Dr. King, we've got to get you out of here—where are you staying?" Though King and Abernathy usually stayed at the Negro-owned Lorraine Motel, union aides had reserved a room for them at the Peabody Hotel, downtown, because union leaders were staying there. But it was impossible now to reach the Peabody without cutting through the center of the march, which at this point was completely disorganized, in near chaos, with shouting black youths running on the sidewalk, using the staves that earlier bore the signs, to smash show windows. King and Abernathy just had time to glimpse police, many in gas masks, others with riot guns, bearing down on the disorder, then found their police escort conducting them to the Rivermont, a luxury motel on the Mississippi, some distance from the scene. They were taken upstairs to the eighth floor and registered in a large suite.*

Dr. King was in near despair. Before the day was over, a seventeen-year-old black youth had been fatally shot by police, sixty other blacks had been clubbed, nearly three hundred more had been arrested. The governor had ordered four thousand federal troops to the scene, and Mayor Loeb had declared Memphis in a state of emergency and imposed a 7 P.M. to 5 A.M. curfew. The police, at points as hysterical as those who rioted, had beaten looters, demonstrators, innocent bystanders with equal energy. There had been pitched battles between police and black high-school students who threw bricks and bottles, shouting, "Black power!" and chanting their "Go! Go! Go!" as they raced back and forth.

A deeply distressed Lawson visited King in his suite later that

* The police choice of the Rivermont was to plague King. Many assumed mistakenly that he and Abernathy had originally made reservations to stay there, preferring to live away from the black ghetto, and King was sharply criticized. Actually, he had never been at the Rivermont before.

afternoon. He had done his best to halt the disorder, rushing along the line of marchers, shouting through the bullhorn, "Don't panic! We're calling the march back to the Temple. Turn around, walk back the way you came!" He had seen the looters and window breakers on the sidewalk, not in the march, and ahead of the march. He had seen the high-school kids and others he did not know throwing bottles at the police, taunting them. And he had seen the police, using their tear gas and mace and clubs indiscriminately on marchers and nonmarchers—there was no time to choose. There was too much fear and fury. Fear that the time bomb they had waited for so tensely the summer before was exploding at last.

It was a terrible denouement to this day, so long looked forward to, to this march which King led but which, at the beginning, had never been contemplated. All they had wanted from Martin Luther King, Jr., at the beginning was for him to come to Memphis to speak and inspire. Now it had led to this, and to an aftermath of news stories and editorials throughout the country, infinitely painful to Memphis, to its black community, and, above all, to Martin Luther King and nonviolence.*

Lawson found King, somber and discouraged, resting in bed. He lay characteristically in his underwear, the covers pulled up to his chin, propped up, one hand behind his head, talking with first one delegation, then another. One thing he was sure of: he must return to Memphis for another march. It had to be peaceful. The entire Poor People's Campaign depended on it. "If we don't have a peaceful march in Memphis, no Washington." Shaken though he was, he was firm. "No Memphis, no Washington." Lawson, Abernathy, the Rev. Andrew Young, King's executive director, and the others immediately issued a statement denying the stories that he had fled, and emphasizing that the troublemakers were mainly those outside the march.

Before Lawson and the others arrived at the Rivermont, when King, Abernathy, and Bernard Lee were alone, King had been as despondent as these two close friends had ever seen him. He had seemed almost in shock to some who had watched him as he got into the car that took him and the others from the march. That a march he led ended in violence was awful enough, but that it did so on the eve of Washington—this was intolerable. "We live in a sick coun-

---

* The Memphis *Commercial-Appeal* had a cartoon showing a terrified King fleeing from the scene with a caption, "Chicken-a-la-King."

try," he said to Abernathy, as they reviewed what had happened. "I just don't know. Maybe we just have to admit that the day of violence is here, and maybe we have to just give up and let violence take its course. The nation won't listen to our voice—maybe it'll heed the voice of violence." He was not despairing of nonviolence as a technique; he believed it was the only weapon Negroes could use to achieve first-class citizenship. But it had become so discouraging and it was difficult, too, to control the young black militants who were frustrated. He could understand their impatience, their almost unbearable desire to act. "Maybe," he thought aloud, "we ought to let these people have their way. Just ride it out."

Abernathy could give him little comfort. He suggested that King telephone an old friend on whose judgment he relied—Stanley Levison, an attorney in New York. Levison, when he was reached, tried to raise his spirits. Yes, he'd seen it all on the evening news. Only a small minority was troublesome. The vast majority had marched in order. They had been nonviolent. Perhaps eight thousand marchers had shown discipline; perhaps fifty had lost their heads. King replied slowly and heavily. "Yes, Stanley, but we'll never be able to get that story through."

Andy Young, too, upon whom King counted greatly, tried to comfort him. Violence, he said, was too deeply rooted in American life for either the SCLC, as an organization, or for him singlehandedly to reverse the trend. King was not responsible for this. But King, like Gandhi, whom he so much admired, took the onus upon himself. Gandhi had felt responsible for the Hindu-Moslem riots; so King blamed himself for what had happened.

Black militancy troubled him deeply. To him militancy was the measure of the force behind an idea; but militancy behind a negative idea meant self-destruction. He was concerned with his inability to cope with his own people, his fear that the movement might collapse because of his own organization's reaction to black militancy—what appeared to be their growing, pragmatic acceptance of it. This was why he was on the verge of giving up, of retreating for a while. I hear this insane talk about me, he would complain—we are going to blow up the enemy, we will fight from rooftop to rooftop in the ghetto. . . . This is fantasy, this is a death wish, he would say. How did this relate to achieving civil rights, to the job of getting black and white people to live together? The blacks were a minority. For a minority to turn to violence, which would also be the weapon of the majority, was suicide. Not to speak of the fact that violence induced violence and spread it, while nonviolence could break the terrible chain of cause and effect. Yet violence—not nonviolence—was growing stronger.

So he brooded this bitter night.

Later he roused himself enough to call his wife, Coretta, in Atlanta to say he was unhurt. He was so exhausted that he fell asleep a few minutes later, though it was then only after 9 P.M. He did not waken until nearly ten o'clock the next morning. Then his spirits seemed almost magically restored. The press was downstairs, clamoring for a conference. They must have one, he told Abernathy, and he was ready. "I have my moments of despair, but you see, I get out of them," he said. He began to dress.

There was a knock on the door. Abernathy went to open it. There stood three black youths in sandals and moccasins, one almost six feet six inches tall, a striking figure. "We are with the Invaders," he said. Could they see Dr. King?

"Come in," said Abernathy. He and Martin had been told that the Invaders were behind the breakup of the march. The youths introduced themselves soberly. The tall one was Charles Cabbage, twenty-three, a 1967 graduate of Morehouse College in Atlanta, Dr. King's alma mater. He had a degree in political science and had been hired earlier by Lawson to help organize teen-agers in the Memphis antipoverty movement. He was particularly popular among black high-school students. The others were Calvin Taylor and Charles Carrington, both in their twenties, the eyes of the latter invisible behind large opaque sunglasses.

Would they have some breakfast? Abernathy asked. They politely declined. Dr. King had sent out word he wanted to talk to some of the Invaders, Abernathy went on; had they come in answer to that summons? No, they said, they had met this morning and decided to call on Dr. King and explain what had happened.

Abernathy told them how distressed Dr. King was. "He doesn't understand," he said. "Who are the Invaders? Why would they want to disrupt the march?"

"Wait a minute," said Cabbage sharply. He and his companions were seated on chairs facing Abernathy. "We didn't disrupt your march. You can't make us the scapegoat." He spoke challengingly. They had deliberately left at 10:30 A.M. before the march started, because they expected trouble. They were not responsible for what happened. They warned that the black people in Memphis were too worked up to carry off a peaceful march. The black establishment—

Jackson, Lawson, and the others—had refused to include them in their strategy committee, had refused to listen to their warnings.

Abernathy said, "We aren't saying that you caused the trouble, but everybody else is saying so. If you didn't do it, who did?"

"The people," Cabbage replied just as Dr. King walked into the room. He was buttoning his shirt. He had heard Abernathy's question and Cabbage's reply. He looked first at Cabbage, and Cabbage dropped his head. He looked at Taylor and Carrington, and they too seemed to slump. They had blamed what happened on "the people" and Dr. King's glance seemed to say, "You don't tell that lie to me."

But he greeted them only with "Good morning," and Abernathy rose and introduced them. "I was just telling them, Martin, how distressed you were over the incidents in the march. We were trying to get at the root of what caused the trouble. They say they did not, but everybody says they did."

"Yes," said Dr. King. "That's one of the things I wanted to talk to you about. But go ahead, Ralph." Dr. King left the room to finish dressing, and the moment he did so the Invaders found themselves straightening up. One was to recall, "What he did to me just by walking in and looking at me! Like you met God and you knew you were wrong, Baby, and nowhere to hide. When he looked at me, I started admitting to myself, 'Yeah, we had something to do with it.' But when he left the room, all reality came back and we were right where we were before. We felt we could deal with Abernathy. We thought, You could talk to this cat."

When King returned a few minutes later, he took a seat on the sofa and asked quietly, "Who disrupted the march?"

Cabbage replied obliquely. "The black ministers led you into a trap. They assured you that everything was fine, Dr. King. They didn't tell you there was a potential for trouble here. This has been going on all along—a leadership struggle."

King said, "I didn't know this." He added, "Cabbage, why didn't you tell me this? If for no other reason than that you're a Morehouse man. We are brothers. Why didn't *you* tell me?"

"Dr. King, I tried to get to you to tell you but they wouldn't let me."

"Well, you should have come and let me know," Dr. King said. "I would have got you to me."

Cabbage protested. "How was I going to get to you when they

wouldn't even let you know we existed?" It was the only time he
raised his voice.

Dr. King said, "Cabbage, that is no excuse," and Cabbage, a tall
man who looked more than anything else like a Watusi warrior,
scared of no man, bowed his head again.

Dr. King asked, "Who are the Invaders? What have you done?"
Cabbage told him something of their history. Four of them had
organized the group in the summer of 1967, taking their name from
the popular TV program of the time. Their purpose was to uplift
the black man, economically, socially, and politically, by whatever
means necessary. They had many plans. One envisaged the creation
of black-owned, black-operated co-operatives. They had brought
along some mimeographed material, and King looked through it.
"Does this mean violence?" he asked deliberately. "As you know, I
don't believe in violence."

Cabbage did not answer the question. He could only have answered it in the affirmative. The Invaders had done considerable
"hog work"—groundwork—among Memphis black high-school students. They had taught militancy, had taught them how to make
Molotov cocktails, had taught them how to cope with the police. In
the black ghettos of Memphis they had tried to teach the older gen-
eration why Whitey was the enemy. They had been making their
plans in expectancy of disturbances in the summer of 1968. This was
what they were preparing for, a hot, violent summer, ending in victory. But with the sudden sanitation strike, the angers and hos-
tilities they had been nurturing to play a role later had taken fire
now, instead, and in the march led by Dr. King. They insisted they
had warned the black establishment: You are making two mistakes
in this march. First, you've preyed on these people's imaginations,
they're overly frustrated, ready to do anything; and second, you have
our people, a bunch of impatient high-school kids, and once they
get started, we're not too sure whether they're going to hear us when
we yell, "Stop!"

And, Cabbage ventured, Dr. King too was at fault. He had failed
to send staff members into Memphis to help plan the march.

King turned to Abernathy. "I noted when I got to the Temple
that these people were crowding around me, Ralph. People marching
on the sidewalk. It seemed unorganized. I had second thoughts about
leading it then, but I had promised—" He stopped.

Cabbage asked, would the SCLC give them funds for their social
program? King explained that the SCLC was not a wealthy organi-

zation, but he would try to find help for them. He emphasized again, he would not condone violence. And he must return to Memphis. People were saying now that he could not lead a peaceful march in Washington. "Memphis is a good chance for me to show that I can," he said soberly. This was why he was so depressed over what had happened. "Now Cabbage, what can you do to see that it doesn't happen again? I'm going to tell Jim Lawson to include you in the strategy sessions and hear what you have to say. But you must promise we won't have trouble again. You've got to co-operate."

Cabbage demurred. He could not guarantee such control. "These are the people . . . I can't do anything with them," he began.

King interrupted him sharply. "No, you don't talk to me about 'these are the people.' You are the influence here, Cabbage, and if you don't have any say over these people, you don't have any right to be in this room because you can't speak for anybody but Charles Cabbage."

Cabbage had no reply. The meeting broke up a few minutes later. It was noon. King had his press conference waiting, and he had to return to Atlanta. He would lead the second march a week from today, Friday, April 5. Meanwhile, he had an important staff meeting tomorrow, Saturday, at his church, and on Sunday he had been invited to Washington to preach at Washington Cathedral. On Monday he would send two or three aides into Memphis, to prepare for the march, and on Tuesday or Wednesday, he and Abernathy would be back in Memphis. He promised he would see Cabbage then.

He and Abernathy returned to Atlanta that afternoon on the three o'clock plane.

CHAPTER IV

Two days before, on Wednesday, March 27, in Birmingham, Alabama, 244 miles from Memphis, a customer walked into a popular arms shop, the Gun Rack, and asked Clyde Manasco, the clerk, "Could I see some of your Remington .243 rifles, please?" It was about 1:30 P.M. The stranger, wearing shell-rimmed glasses, appeared to be in his early thirties, with dark hair, something of a receding forehead, and a sharp nose. Manasco remembered him. He'd been in the shop before. His particular interest appeared to be the speed and trajectory of bullets. Manasco's employer, Quentin Davis, had tried to answer some of his questions, too—what rifle would give the flattest and longest trajectory? How far would a bullet drop at one hundred yards? At two hundred yards? What rifle would he recommend for accuracy? He had even asked for a gun so new the shop hadn't yet received it—a Browning automatic .264, which had been written up in gun magazines. Davis had concluded that the man wanted a rifle that would fire a bullet with the least amount of drop for a considerable distance.

Manasco tried to help him now. The man had been interested in telescopic sights, too, and had asked if he had any literature on the subject he could take home with him. Manasco had given him a ballistics chart, a booklet, "Winchester-Western, 1968, Sporting Arms and Ammunition," and another on Redfield scopes. He seemed a rather difficult customer. Manasco recalled the other day trying to hand him a rifle, but the man made no move to take it. He simply looked at it, and Manasco, feeling foolish, had to put it back on the rack.

Now, however, he appeared ready to make his purchase. Unfortunately, the shop had no .243's in stock. Manasco tried to sell him a Remington 30.06. "No, it's too expensive," the man said. He thanked him, got into a white car parked at the curb, and drove away.

Shortly after noon Friday, March 29, about the time Dr. King was holding his press conference in Memphis before flying back to Atlanta, John Kopp, manager of the firearms department of the Long-

Lewis Hardware store in Bessemer, a town about ten miles from Birmingham, was approached by a customer who asked about high-powered rifles. He was about thirty or so, wearing black shell-rimmed glasses, with a pale complexion and a thin nose.

"Would you like to see a 30.30?" Kopp asked. "No, I don't think that's powerful enough," the other said. "Have you got a .243 or a .308 or a 30.06?" How much were they? How accurate was a 30.06? How many inches would a bullet drop at one hundred yards? At two hundred yards? Had he any scopes, and how long would it take to mount one on a rifle? Kopp told him about two days, because he sent his rifles to Birmingham for the work.

Was there any other place in the neighborhood that might have high-powered rifles? Kopp told him about a pawnshop across the street.

The man thanked him, and as he was leaving he glanced up at a moose head on the wall. "That's a nice trophy," he said with a quick, one-sided smile. "I once tried to bring down a moose but I missed."

Kopp looked after him. It was hard to imagine him out hunting moose, he thought. He was no outdoor man. He looked as though he'd never been in the sun. He might even be sick, he was so pale. Maybe he's an insurance salesman, or the type that goes into libraries and reads up on guns, Kopp thought, and he put him out of his mind.

Two hours later, at the Aeromarine Supply Company, just across the road from Birmingham's municipal airport, John DeShazo, twenty-five, a gun enthusiast, was leaning against the counter when a man walked in and began looking at the various weapons on display.

DeShazo might not have noticed him had he not been trying to mark time waiting for his good friend, Don Wood, son of the shop's owner, to return from lunch, and had not the man somehow appeared so out of place in such a shop. Aeromarine had one of the largest stocks of rifles, shotguns, pistols, ammunition and hunting equipment in the South. Its advertisements appeared in all Birmingham newspapers. This man with his pale face, his black shell-rimmed spectacles, his proper white shirt and dark tie and black wing-tip shoes, looked more like an accountant than an outdoor type. His eyes behind the glasses were blue, and he had a long thin nose. He was wearing a wrinkled brown business suit which looked as though he had been driving in it for some time. Perhaps, thought DeShazo idly, he was some kind of a salesman.

The man finally approached the clerk on duty, Hugh Baker. De-Shazo, having nothing better to do, watched as the customer asked diffidently to look at a Remington Gamemaster, .243 caliber. It was clear almost at once that he could not know much about guns by the way he examined the rifle when Baker showed it to him. After a moment, he asked to see one or two others, and finally decided on the .243.

"Have you got a scope to fit this?" he asked. DeShazo had been thinking, He's not from around here. The accent was Midwestern rather than Southern. Baker showed the customer a 2×7 power Red-field variable scope. The two discussed price for a moment. The man nodded, and Baker set to work attaching the scope to the barrel.

While the stranger waited, DeShazo strolled over and struck up a conversation with him. DeShazo was an ardent member of the National Rifle Association. He had been somewhat on the defensive in recent months because of attacks on the NRA and the increasing agitation to change the gun laws and limit an American's right to bear arms. This man not only didn't seem to belong in this shop, buying a powerful rifle of this sort, but he was getting a scope put on it, which meant he planned some serious shooting. "You've really got quite a gun there," DeShazo said to him with a smile, to soften his next words. "You'll have to learn how to use it."

The stranger gave him an embarrassed, one-sided grin, which seemed to appear and disappear for no special reason. He explained that his brother—or his brother-in-law—in Wisconsin had invited him to go deer hunting with him. DeShazo smelled alcohol on the man's breath, but he was not drunk. He had been thinking, the man said, of buying a rifle for some time, and now that he was finally able to, he wanted to get "a good one."

"Well, you have it there," said DeShazo, and, glancing at his watch, decided that he'd see Don Wood some other time. He left, thinking, *That guy obviously doesn't know a damn thing about guns. He's got no business buying a rifle.* He thought, giving his imagination free reign, *He's the kind of a fellow who buys a rifle probably to kill his wife and gives guns a bad name.* And, feeling indignant despite himself, he went on his way.

The stranger completed his purchase, buying a box of cartridges to fit the rifle, scrawled his name, Harvey Lowmyer, across the purchase slip, gave his address, 1807 South Eleventh Street, Birmingham, paid his bill, and left. But toward five o'clock he telephoned the shop. This time he spoke to Don Wood. He had bought a Rem-

ington .243 there earlier, and twenty rounds of ammunition. Since
then he'd spoken with his brother, who told him he'd got the wrong
gun—he should have gotten a heavier rifle, a Remington 30.06.
Would they make the exchange? "Yes," said Wood. The 30.06 would
cost more, of course. That was all right, said Lowmyer. "Well," said
Wood, "we're just about to close now." Could he come in tomorrow?

At 9 A.M. Saturday Lowmyer returned with the rifle. Wood told
him he'd transfer the scope to the 30.06, but since Saturday was a
busy day, he wouldn't have it ready for him until three o'clock. When
Lowmyer came back, Wood had to pack the rifle in a Browning carton, because the protruding scope made it too large for the box in
which it came. As he exchanged the ammunition, Wood asked curiously, "Why didn't you want the .243? It's big enough to bring
down any deer in Alabama." The .243 was an extremely powerful
weapon, a so-called "varmint" gun that virtually disintegrated the
target. It could all but decapitate a small animal.

"I want it to hunt in Wisconsin," Lowmyer said mildly. Wisconsin,
to be sure, had bigger game than Alabama, and if Lowmyer or his
brother wanted an even more powerful gun—with a 30.06 under
proper conditions a man could bring down a deer at 500 yards—
that was their business. Lowmyer took his package, got into a white
Mustang parked across the street, and drove away.

Early Monday morning, April 1, in Atlanta, a man wearing shell-
rimmed glasses, with a receding forehead and a long nose, brought
his laundry into the Piedmont Laundry at 1168 Peachtree Street.
Mrs. Estelle Peters, the manager, remembered him. He was obviously
a bachelor, or else divorced, and almost compulsively neat, as indicated by his laundry and his careful instructions; nothing starched,
everything to be neatly folded and packaged when he picked it up.
This time his wash consisted only of four undershirts, three pairs of
shorts, one pair of socks, and one washcloth. With it he brought a
jacket and a pair of slacks to be pressed. She wrote on the laundry
slip, "No starch and folded," and his name and address: Eric S. Galt,
113 Fourteenth Street. She remembered the name because he had to
spell it for her. She later recalled writing the address because it was
just around the corner of Fourteenth and Peachtree, a rather incon-
gruous neighborhood for the gentleman, for it was the heart of Atlanta's small but intense hippie district. Mr. Galt, with his neat
clothes, his proper haircut, his narrow dark tie and white button-

down shirts, and his almost prissy attention to detail seemed anything but a hippie.

No. 113 Fourteenth Street was a faded green and white rooming house. Behind it a white Mustang was parked in a small gravel-covered lot. The car had no license plate in front, but had a red and white 1968 Alabama tag in the rear. Two Mexican tourist stickers, stamped October 1967, had been pasted on the windshield. The car had caused some annoyance to neighbors because it was always parked diagonally, across three parallel parking spaces, so that others had difficulty finding places for their cars.

Had anyone been observing the stretch of U.S. Highway 78 between Birmingham and Memphis on Wednesday afternoon, April 3—Highway 78 leads from Atlanta some 155 miles to Birmingham, and from Birmingham some 244 miles to Memphis—he would have seen a white Mustang with a red and white plate in the rear turning off the highway into a dirt road. It stopped at a secluded spot. The driver emerged, opened a long cardboard box he had in the trunk, and brought out a rifle. Then he walked off the road into a glen hidden by trees and, aiming carefully through a telescopic sight fixed on the barrel, fired about a dozen shots. He was obviously trying his skill at various distances on such objects as tree branches, leaves and rocks. Then he returned to his car, packed his rifle in its box, drove back to Highway 78, and continued on toward Memphis.

The night of April 3 at 7:20 P.M., the white Mustang with the red and white rear tag stopped in front of the New Rebel Motel at 3466 Lamar Avenue—the continuation of Highway 78—just within the Memphis city line. The clerk, Henrietta Hagemaster, registered the driver in Room 34. He filled out the slip, writing down the number of his license plate and signing his name: Eric S. Galt.

At 10 P.M. Ivan Webb, the night clerk, came on duty. He saw the white Mustang parked in front of Room 34, which was brightly lit behind the drapes. At midnight, the lights were still on in the room. At 4 A.M. they still burned brightly. Mr. Galt, thought Webb, could not be doing much sleeping this night.

CHAPTER V

It was early evening, Wednesday, April 3.

Martin Luther King lay lounging on the bed in Room 307 of the Lorraine Motel, in Memphis, his shoes off, cradling a telephone and talking earnestly. "Now *Marion*," he was saying, sadly, rebukingly, "if *only* you'd *understand.* If *only* you'd come over to *my* side—"

He was debating, as he had been doing for nearly two weeks now, now from Los Angeles, now from Atlanta, now from Memphis, with Marion Logan in New York—Mrs. Arthur Logan—an officer and top fund raiser for the SCLC. The Logans—Dr. Logan, a physician, was one of Harlem's outstanding civic leaders and former chairman of HARYOU, an antipoverty agency—were family friends of the Kings, and Mrs. Logan had accompanied the Kings and Abernathys to Sweden in 1964 when Dr. King received the Nobel Peace Prize. He had considerable respect for her judgment.

Their conversation was the latest in a series that began after she had sent him, with a copy to every SCLC board member, a long memorandum, dated March 8, 1968, analyzing his Poor People's Campaign and concluding strongly that he must cancel the march on Washington.

Dr. King had taken this hard. It was bad enough that Bayard Rustin was not only against it, but had written him a letter as early as January 29 warning him that he questioned whether the SCLC could "maintain control" of the march; but that Marion Logan should have written a memo along the same lines and sent it to the board members served only, as he saw it, to encourage those rebelling against him. He had been trying to convince her to change her mind, as if, were that to happen, it would exorcise his own doubts. He had used every stratagem, every weapon in his arsenal of persuasion to make her recant. Mrs. Logan had asserted in her memo that the march would fail "to move the conscience" of the Congress, as he had proclaimed. Indeed, it would actually increase congressional resistance to black people's demands. Rather than help elect sympathetic legislators, it would help elect their enemies. Washington in the spring of 1968, after the long, hot, violent summer of 1967, was a far different city, she emphasized, from what it was in August of 1963, when he led a quarter of a million people on a triumphant march and climaxed it with his historic, "I Have a Dream" speech at the Lincoln Memorial.

Not only did she question the political value of his march, but she, too, warned that it could end in violence—a tragedy for black people and a personal disaster for him. He might not have more than three thousand poor marching at any one time, but Washington had said it was prepared to place ten thousand federal troops in the streets. She had written in her memo, "I can't imagine a situation more inflammable."*

Now, on the telephone, he still argued with her. "If only you'd under*stand*," he was saying. "If *only* you'd see it *my* way." She could not, she said again and again, only to hear him say sadly, "Marion, how could you *do* this to me?" She told him finally, "No matter how terrible a hurt you put on me by talking to me like this, by making me feel so terrible for telling you what I really believe and what you know is true, I won't change my mind, Martin."

"But I thought all this time you *loved* me, Marion," he returned, and she, "Now Martin, don't play dirty. That hasn't got anything to do with it." She knew this gambit. He had used it before, making it appear that not logic but lack of faith in him led her to differ with him. "If I didn't love you, I wouldn't have written all this, I wouldn't have tried to put this thing together. Martin, the hours I've spent agonizing, the sleepless nights I've walked the floor, thinking this out—"

They had talked in precisely this fashion, Martin, she, and her husband, Arthur, when Martin unexpectedly dropped in on them little more than a week before. It was Monday night, March 25, and he had come to New York to speak and then embark on his grueling fund-raising tour with Belafonte, before flying to Memphis for the disastrous march three days later. The front doorbell of the Logans' brownstone in Manhattan's upper West Side rang about 8 P.M., and Mrs. Logan had called into the house phone, "Who is it?" and the unmistakable voice came back, "It's Martin," and she had pressed the buzzer and hurried out to look down the stairs and

* Interestingly enough, Mrs. Logan knew nothing of Rustin's warning. Neither she nor he knew that Dr. King suspected they had joined together against him, that Rustin had put her up to writing the memo and then sending it to all the others to undercut any support he might have; that he felt he was being betrayed by two of his dearest friends. It only added to his depression.

there, trudging up the steps was Martin and his secretary-bodyguard, the Rev. Bernard Lee. Once upstairs he had loosened his tie, taken off his coat and shoes, flung himself onto a favorite sofa, put his feet on a coffee table, and begun to talk, nonstop. They had stayed up almost all night debating the issue. He could not take the advice of those who opposed it. There had always been those who warned him against this or that action. But—"If I'd have listened to them, there wouldn't have *been* a Birm-ing-ham, there wouldn't have *been* a Selma-Mont-gom-ery, if I'd have listened to *them,* we'd not have *any-thing!* We'd never have *had* a *move-ment,* Marion. Of *all* people, I never thought I'd have to *explain* this to you." And he pressed her, hard, mercilessly, to recant.

She sat silent. She had determined she would sit there and take it like a beating, but Arthur interrupted. "Martin," he said sternly, "why don't you let her alone? She won't do what you want. And Martin, look at her! She's lost twenty-three pounds, she's told you she hasn't been able to sleep or eat over this thing—"

Martin paused in mid-sentence and looked at her as if seeing her for the first time. "Yes," he said solicitously, "you *don't* look well, Marion." And then, again, "You see, Marion, if you did *right* by me, you wouldn't be *feeling* so bad—" And he was off on the subject again.

He could not stop talking. He had asked for vodka and orange juice when he came in. Now lounging, now sitting up, talking, talking, he sipped steadily from his glass, which he asked to be refilled repeatedly, and that night he drank almost a fifth of vodka and orange juice. The Logans had stayed up with him many a night before, talking the hours through, and they had never seen him drink this much. It was a strange evening that lasted almost until dawn, and Martin seemed to go through three or four different changes of personality as it went on: now tense, like a coiled spring, ready to explode, now gentle, measured, appearing completely relaxed but betraying his anxiety by a habit he had at such times—his right hand clenched into a fist, his thumb inside the cocoon of his fingers and, as he talked, slowly rubbing thumb against fingers, ceaselessly.

They knew how exhausted he was. This past year he had gone at an almost suicidal pace, sleeping only a few hours a night, almost compulsively keeping awake as though he felt sleep was taking up time he could not afford to lose. He was becoming more and more nervous. Even when Arthur, who was his physician when he was in

New York, gave him sleeping pills when he stayed overnight at the Logans', he could not sleep. He would swallow two or three, but remain up, talking; then complain, "These-pills-don't-work-Marion," and she would say, "They're not working because you keep talking, Martin. Go to sleep." He would go to his room for a little while, and then wander out and say again, "They're not working," and take another pill—and still remain awake.

So it had been that long Monday night more than a week ago when he visited them, and they argued through the night about the Poor People's Campaign, and there had been no resolution then, either.

Now, on the telephone, talking to him in Memphis this Wednesday, April 3, she found herself saying suddenly, "If you don't get out of there, you're going to get yourself killed, Martin." She did not mean it in precisely those words. But she and Arthur, watching the news on TV when he led the march the Thursday before, had seen its violent breakup, and it had frightened her. The sight of Martin, arms linked with fellow ministers at the head of the parade, behind him the sound of shattering glass, the rising shriek of police sirens, and his face as she had never seen it before—dazed, helpless, "almost like a zombie," she was to say later—shocked with disbelief that this was happening, that this could happen to him. . . . It was a sight she would never forget. She feared for him. So she had said, "If you don't get out of there, you're going to get yourself killed, Martin."

He had replied to her slowly, almost despondently, "Marion, I've been trying to tell you, darling, I'm ready to die."

She retorted, "Martin, did it ever occur to you that we're not ready to let you go? Martin, you're not making sense!"

The conversation ended a few minutes afterward on the same unhappy note. When she hung up, she was to remember later, she recalled the night in Oslo after he had accepted the Nobel prize. The day before he and Coretta had been received by King Olaf V of Norway, and now Dr. King sat in his hotel room, with a group of them, looking at the gold medal in his hand. He had said, "It's a long road from Montgomery to Oslo." Then, thoughtfully, yet with a puckish note, "Here I am with the Nobel Peace Prize. This is about as high as you can go. There's nothing left for me to do." Bernard Lee spoke up chidingly, "Leader, don't talk like that, you sound like you think you're gonna die, or something." King said, "I told you I'm gonna die . . . I'm gonna die young. All the great die young."

Marion demanded, "Like who?" King looked at her, still in his puckish mood. "Jesus. Joan of Arc. John Kennedy." "Oh, Martin!" she had said. She recalled it now, almost with a shiver.

In Room 307* at the motel, Dr. King put in another call to New York—this time to the Rev. Wyatt Tee Walker. Dr. Walker, one of his earliest associates, had been his executive director in the early SCLC days, and on the Sunday preceding Dr. King had installed him as pastor of the Canaan Baptist Church, in Harlem. But Dr. Walker was not in, and what Dr. King might have said to him—or what advice or reassurance he might have sought from him—would never be known.

For Dr. King, it had been a long and difficult day since he and Abernathy had boarded their plane in Atlanta at 7 A.M. that morning. They had remained at the loading gate for nearly an hour, then heard the pilot's voice: "Ladies and gentlemen, I want to apologize for the delay. But today we have on board Dr. Martin Luther King, Jr., and we have to be very careful—we had the plane guarded all night—and we have been checking people's luggage. Now that everything's clear, we are preparing for takeoff."

Martin had laughed and turned to Ralph: "In all my flights I've never had a pilot say that. If I'm going to be killed, it looks like he's trying to make it only too plain to me."

When they arrived in Memphis at 10:33, Dr. King held a brief press conference at the airport. Yes, they were going ahead with their march—they were moving it from Friday, April 5, to Monday, April 8, in expectation of supporters coming from all parts of the country. Perhaps as many as six thousand, to make it a major nonviolent demonstration. This had been at the suggestion of Bayard Rustin, who hoped to enlist outstanding union leaders to take part. Then Rev. Lawson had picked them up and driven them to the Lorraine Motel. Martin sat in the front seat between the driver and Lawson; on the way they stopped for a red light. As they waited, a huge black hearse pulled up alongside them and the driver, a black man, leaned out. "Reverend Lawson," he said, "will you introduce me to

---

* When possible, Dr. King made and received personal calls in rooms other than that in which he was registered, on the assumption that his calls might be tapped by the FBI. There had been charges that one of his confidants, who was said to have written some of his speeches, was a member of the Communist Party. This had been repeatedly denied. That the Bureau had tapped some of Dr. King's conversations was later verified amid allegations that tapes involving indiscretions in his private life had been played for newspaper columnists and others.

Dr. King? I've never had the honor." Lawson introduced King to Robert Lewis, Memphis' best known black undertaker. When they drove on, Martin could only smile ruefully at Abernathy: this, after their experience on the plane! At the Lorraine they were checked into Room 306. This was the motel's VIP room, a thirteen-dollar-a-day twin-bedded room almost in the center of the balcony, over-looking the courtyard and the swimming pool. Photographers snapped him standing there, on the balcony, in front of the door with the numerals 306 showing behind him.

A few minutes after noon he was driven to Lawson's church, the Centenary Methodist Church, to meet with local black ministers and discuss ways to avoid last Thursday's debacle. He learned that Mayor Loeb had obtained a temporary injunction in Federal Court banning their march, and that federal marshals would arrive presently to serve the order on him. But he could not wait for them—he had a lunch scheduled with Cabbage and his Invaders back at the motel.

At lunch with them, later, he promised he would try to obtain a grant in Washington for their co-operatives: in turn, they must pledge nonviolence in the march. For a little while James Laue, of the Justice Department's Community Relations Service,* joined them. Laue, a white man, had come from Washington a few days before to prepare for the Poor People's Campaign. In the past the CRS had helped as liaison between the SCLC and the police. Laue, too, was staying at the Lorraine, so he could have easier access to the SCLC staff. But after a few minutes, when it became obvious to him that the Invaders were unhappy at the presence of a white man, he left the table.

At this point Dr. King was called into the courtyard. Two U.S. marshals had arrived. Surrounded by his colleagues, he accepted the summons but would fight it, he said. Moments later he met in his room with a group of six local lawyers, headed by Lucius Burch, generally recognized as Memphis' outstanding attorney. Burch, a member of the American Civil Liberties Union and a man of fierce independence, had been retained by the NAACP Legal Defense Fund in New York to help fight the injunction in Dr. King's behalf. He had never met him before. A dry, incisive man, he asked one basic question: "Are you irrevocably committed to this march?"

Dr. King replied, "Yes."

---

* The CRS was set up by the Civil Rights Act of 1964 to help resolve disputes "relating to discriminatory practices based on race, color or national origin."

"Very well," said Burch. They would begin immediately to prepare their case, working through the night if necessary so they could appear tomorrow in Federal Court and attempt to lift the injunction.

"You're the lawyer," said Dr. King, smiling. "I'm the client."

They left, and he began to preside at the first of a series of staff meetings that were to last through most of the day.

About this hour, a Negro detective named Ed Redditt parked his car in front of Fire Station No. 2 at 484 South Main Street, on the edge of black Memphis. The building of white brick, with vast expanses of glass and aluminum, was newly constructed and the Fire Department's pride. Redditt, who was in a business suit, walked briskly inside, past the clublike lounge with its beige drapes, its Ping-Pong tables and checkerboards and large color TV, its coffee and soft drink machines, past the gleaming red fire engine polished like some gargantuan toy, past the white-tiled men's room into a large, high-ceilinged rear locker room, perhaps thirty by thirty feet.

He came to a stop before the rear door, which had a glass panel in the upper part and opened onto an iron staircase leading ten steps down to Mulberry Street, just behind. Gray metal lockers stood on either side of the door, above them small windows. The front entrance of the station on South Main was at street level, but in the rear, because of a sharp drop in the terrain, it was about eight feet above the street. A retaining wall had been built here, supporting a grassy embankment.

Redditt carried a newspaper and a pair of binoculars. He tore off an inside page and, using a scissors, cut out two narrow slits in the center, each perhaps half an inch by three inches, then Scotch-taped the page over the glass panel in the door so that the cutouts were at eye level. He peered through. Satisfied with what he saw, he fixed the binoculars to his eyes.

He had a perfect, uninterrupted view of the front of the Lorraine Hotel and Motel, about 150 feet away. The hotel, an old, boxlike structure, fronted on Mulberry Street, and was to his left. Attached to it, on the right, but set back perhaps fifty feet, was the long rectangular two-story modern motel. The paved setback area was used as a courtyard; cars were parked there immediately in front of the motel, and people were moving about. A small swimming pool had been built between the parking area and the street, protected from viewers by a six-foot-high fence. From his vantage point Redditt saw everything clearly; the row of rooms at ground level, each with its picture window, and narrow door, the pale green doors numbered 200 to 218, and immediately above an identical row, a balcony runway in front of them, the rooms numbered 300 to 318. The numbers were polished brass and gleamed in the sun. He could see the two metal stairways to the balcony, one to the left, the other to the right. He could see all the activity in the courtyard.

Redditt produced a notebook from his pocket and began jotting down what he saw. He noted names of persons coming and going, license plate numbers of cars arriving and departing, and the exact time. He was doing this an hour later when a tall slim Negro joined him. This was Patrolman W. B. Richmond. The two were a team. They knew virtually every black personality in Memphis and many from out of town. They were on special surveillance duty: their assignment, to keep their eyes on Martin Luther King, Jr., as long as he was in Memphis, both in King's interest and in the city's. For the last month or so they had been keeping tab on strike activities. This morning they had been officially detached from this duty and sent to Memphis airport to observe Dr. King's arrival. They were to report who picked him up, where he went, whom he saw. They had followed him to the Lorraine Motel, then from the Lorraine to the Centenary Methodist Church, where he attended the ministers' meeting. While Richmond waited outside, so he could report when Dr. King emerged, and finally report that he was back at his motel, Redditt had set up their surveillance post at the rear door of the fire station.

Dr. King had not asked for police protection. In the early years he had accepted it reluctantly. More recently he had deliberately refused it. He disliked being trailed by squad cars, disliked having them parked outside a private home he might be visiting. Not only was it embarrassing for him and his hosts, but he felt it inconsistent for an advocate of nonviolence to use weapons of violence even for defense of his own life.* Nonetheless, now in Memphis, he was protected, but surreptitiously; unmarked police cars, detectives in plainclothes, and the like. Nearly forty men had been assigned to this security detail, day and night, by the new Police Director, Frank Holloman. Holloman had been an FBI agent for a quarter of a cen-

---

* In the first days of the Montgomery bus boycott in 1955, he allowed armed guards to protect his home and family. But within weeks he concluded that he could not in conscience denounce violence and yet permit its potential use to protect him, and thereafter he refused to have guns in his house or travel with armed bodyguards.

tury, the last eight of them in charge of J. Edgar Hoover's office in Washington. The entrances and exits of the Lorraine Motel, of the Centenary Methodist Church, of every building in which Dr. King found himself, were secretly guarded every moment he was in them, and Holloman's Internal Security Division, a miniature FBI, was kept informed of King's movements. Memphis was still in the state of emergency that had been declared in the wake of Thursday's trouble. Dr. King was not only a highly controversial figure—a number of threats had been phoned in against his life, especially after he had announced he would return to Memphis for a second march— but he also seemed deliberately inviting danger by meeting with the local black militants, the Invaders, on his earlier visits. Indeed, it was known that some of them were also staying at the Lorraine to-day, down the balcony from Dr. King.

Redditt and Richmond compared notes. Redditt checked what he had jotted down:

2:15 P.M. Dr. King returned to motel in Lawson's car, followed by white Cadillac driven by Solomon Jones with unknown male colored in front seat.

2:30. Federal marshals arrived at motel. Dr. King and several aides served papers in courtyard. Approximately 30 minutes after this, meeting held in Room 306 by Dr. King and aides, and Lucius Burch and other attorneys.

Redditt turned to Richmond. "Nothing going on right now," he said. Dr. King was in his room, Room 306. Looking through his binoculars, Richmond noted that several Invaders were going in and out of Rooms 315 and 316. He put down their names. As he watched, the door to Room 309, to the left of Dr. King's room, opened, and a Negro with an Afro haircut emerged. Redditt identified him as Joseph Louw, a South African documentary photographer.

Richmond wrote in his notebook:

4:30. Invaders left Rooms 315–316 and went into hotel area. They include Charles Cabbage, Richard Cabbage, Joe Banks, and John B. Smith.

4:32. Dr. King left his room and went into Room 307.

4:50. About nine male coloreds and one female colored entered Room 316. Following this, there was seen quite a bit of drinking from room to room, and they had ice and Coca Cola sent up to their rooms. View from Fire Station window is very good.

Having gone back to Room 306 after his telephone calls, Dr. King continued to preside at the endless staff meeting. Reports had to be heard from Rev. James Bevel, Rev. James Orange, and others he had sent to Memphis days before to conduct workshops on nonviolence, especially among the high-school students who caused the earlier trouble.

It had been a hot, oppressive day. There had been repeated tornado warnings on the radio. At 7:30 a violent thunderstorm struck. The rain poured down. The wind whistled through the telephone wires. The radio continued to predict wretched weather and dangerous storms. There would be a small crowd at Mason Temple tonight for the rally. He was scheduled to address it and he did not look forward to speaking.

He turned to Abernathy, sitting beside him. Would he go in his place? He was suffering from a cold he had caught during the New York tour. It had brought laryngitis in its wake. His colleagues knew he had been sleeping badly for some time now, and that sleeping pills had not always helped, nor the nightcaps to which he was turning more and more. He had confided to one friend that he had been struggling with insomnia for months. "I can't sleep," he had said. "I fall off, and I wake up suddenly, in fear . . ." Fear, unfocused fear, the sense of impending doom . . .

Abernathy said, "Oh, Martin, don't send me. Send someone else." He was tired.

But Martin shook his head. "Ralph, I want you to go over." Dr. Abernathy agreed and left the meeting.

At their post, watching through their binoculars, Redditt and Richmond had been adding to their dossier. Various male coloreds were leaving and arriving at the motel. At 6:30 Redditt had called in: how long were they to remain? They were told they would be relieved in a few minutes by two other members of the Internal Security Division. They would resume their surveillance of the motel tomorrow at 10 A.M. Meanwhile, they were to go to Mason Temple. Dr. King was scheduled to address a rally there at 7:30 P.M.

They left at 6:40.

When Abernathy arrived at Mason Temple, it was well after eight o'clock. The rain was pelting down. There were less than two thousand persons in the huge vaulted hall. All were seated downstairs, and when he appeared they rose and applauded wildly. He knew at once this was for Martin. For invariably when Abernathy arrived at a rally, Martin would come into sight some steps behind him. This was whom they were applauding—not him.

He made his way to the platform. He was sure, he told the audience over the drumming of rain on the metal roof, that they had braved this weather to hear Dr. King, not Dr. Abernathy. He would see that they were not disappointed. He asked to be taken to the nearest telephone, in the vestibule, and there he called Room 306. "Martin, you've got to come over," he said. "There's not many people—less than two thousand—but they're so warm, so enthusiastic for you. . . ."

Martin said, "Well, you don't have to talk that way to me. You know if you say come, I'll come."

When Martin hung up he said to the others, "I'll just make an appearance, speak a few minutes, and come right back and go to bed."

As soon as the crowd caught sight of him entering the hall some minutes later, they leaped to their feet. Those on the platform gave him a standing ovation as he mounted the half-dozen wooden steps. Lawson, as chairman of the evening, had been using the time to take up a collection and to hear reports from the various strike committees. He thought Martin looked his usual tired self, even more so, perhaps. If he appeared placid, it was part of the man's serenity. One rarely saw him agitated, even in crises. He shook hands all around and took his seat next to Abernathy in the front row on stage.

Abernathy and he understood each other. They were nearly always the last to speak at rallies. When the meeting had lasted a long time and they were yet to be called upon, Martin would say soberly, "Ralph, let me speak first. I'm going to be very brief. Then you fire them up, make the real stirring speech." If the audience had been cold, if it had sat all but benumbed, Martin would say, "Ralph, you speak first and wake them up. They're sleeping. Wake them up." These were Martin's gambits, played with apparent innocence. He had the prerogative to use them as he wished, and Abernathy would not gainsay him.

Lawson came over. "Who will speak first?"

Abernathy spoke up. "I will." He had taken the choice away from Martin, though he knew he would undoubtedly have preferred to speak first and get it over with. He was a little surprised at himself.

But Martin said nothing. Abernathy assumed this was because he had been willing to go in his stead originally.

Abernathy went to the podium. In front of him the 1500 or 2000 persons seated together seemed small in the huge auditorium, an island surrounded by empty seats; above them, the huge semicircular balcony yawned emptily. The building easily held ten thousand. Yet one did not feel one was in a nearly empty hall. Perhaps because they were seated shoulder to shoulder; perhaps because of the storm raging outside, it seemed cozy, intimate, familial.

"So often we take our leaders for granted," Abernathy began. "We never introduce them. We try to dispense with some sort of short introduction. Tonight, I'm going to introduce Dr. King with all the rights and honors he's entitled to." He had no idea, nor could he explain later, why he chose this moment, this night, to deliver what became a eulogy. His introduction took nearly half an hour. He would not be hurried. He began with Martin's birth in Atlanta on January 15, 1929. The man came from the loins of Baptist preachers. "His daddy is a preacher, his granddaddy was a preacher, his uncle was a preacher, his brother is a preacher—and of course, his dearest friend and other brother is one of the world's greatest preachers."

In the laughter, he went on to tell of Martin's schooling, listing the colleges he attended, citing all his degrees and honors in order, up to and including his Nobel Peace Prize. And finally he presented Dr. Martin Luther King, Jr.

When Abernathy sat down, one of the ministers leaned toward him. "We thought you weren't going to make a speech. Didn't you say they came to hear Martin?" Abernathy laughed. "I don't know, it just happened."

Martin began easily. As he listened to Dr. Abernathy's introduction, "I thought of myself and I wondered, Who is he talking about?" and in the laughter paid tribute to Abernathy "as the best friend I have in the world," and then to the leaders of their struggle, here in Memphis.

Important things were taking place today, he said. If he were standing at the beginning of time "and the Almighty said to me, 'Martin Luther King, which age would you like to live in?'" he would pass by all the great historic periods in man's history. He would pass by Egypt and "God's children in their magnificent trek through the wilderness on toward the Promised Land," he would pass by Greece, Rome, the Renaissance, the time of Abraham Lincoln, Franklin D. Roosevelt. . . . "Strangely enough, I would turn to the Almighty and say, 'If you allow me to live just a few years in the second half of the twentieth century, I will be happy.'" That, he said, "is a strange statement to make because the world is all messed up. The nation is sick. . . . But I know, somehow, that only when it is dark enough can you see the stars. And I see God working in this period of the twentieth century in a way that men, in some strange way, are responding—something is happening in our world." The issue he said, was no longer a choice "between violence and nonviolence—it's nonviolence or nonexistence!"

In the applause he spoke of the sanitation strike. It was important to keep attention on the problem, not on "a little violence . . . I read the articles in the press. They very seldom get around to mentioning the fact that one thousand three hundred sanitation workers are on strike and that Memphis is not being fair to them, and that Mayor Loeb is in dire need of a doctor. . . ."

He paused, as the laughter and applause broke over the hall, with a rumble of thunder from the storm outside.

"Now, we're going to march again and we've got to march again, in order to put the issue where it is supposed to be. . . . I call upon you to be with us when we go out Monday." He was going into court tomorrow morning to fight the injunction. Meanwhile they must go out and tell their neighbors not to buy in the stores, to maintain the boycott, to keep united until they reached victory. He wanted to thank God, he said, for allowing him to be in Memphis with them.

He told of his attempted assassination in New York in 1958. He was in a Harlem department store autographing the first book he'd ever written, when a black woman came up. "The only question I heard from her was, 'Are you Martin Luther King?' And I was looking down writing, and I said, 'Yes.' The next minute I felt something beating on my chest. Before I knew it I had been stabbed by this demented woman. I was rushed to Harlem Hospital. It was a dark Saturday afternoon and that blade had gone through, and the X-rays revealed that the tip of the blade was on the edge of my aorta, the main artery, and once that's punctured, you drown in your own blood—that's the end of you."

In a great hush he went on: "It came out in the New York *Times* the next morning that if I had sneezed, I would have died."

From the audience, fervent cries and hallelujahs.

He had received hundreds of letters of congratulation on his escape from death, he said. From world dignitaries, from the President and Vice President of the United States, but the letter he would always remember was one from a young girl who was a student at White Plains High School in New York. She had written: "Dear Dr. King: I'm a ninth-grade student, and while it should not matter, I would like to mention that I am a white girl. I read in the paper of your misfortune and of your suffering. And I read that if you had sneezed, you would have died. And I'm simply writing you to say that I'm so happy you didn't sneeze!"

Amid the laughter and the amens, he picked up the theme, his voice rising higher as he went on: "I, too, am happy that I didn't sneeze. Because if I had sneezed, I would not have been around here in 1960 when students all over the South started sitting-in at lunch counters. . . . If I had sneezed, I wouldn't have been there in 1963 when the black people of Birmingham, Alabama, aroused the conscience of this nation and brought into being the Civil Rights Bill. If I had sneezed, I wouldn't have had a chance later that year, in August, to try to tell America about a dream that I had had. If I had sneezed, I wouldn't have been down in Selma, Alabama, to see the great movement there. If I had sneezed, I wouldn't have been in Memphis to see a community rally around those brothers and sisters who are suffering. I'm *so* happy I didn't sneeze."

He went on. "And they were telling me, now it doesn't matter now." There was a new, reflective note in his voice. "It really doesn't matter now. I left Atlanta this morning." He told the story of the pilot's announcement. . . . "And then I got into Memphis."

He paused, and the crowd laughed. "And *some* began to talk about the threats that were out, of what would happen to me from some of our sick white brothers. . . . Well, I don't know what *will* happen now. We've got some difficult days ahead. But it really doesn't matter with me now." He paused a moment, and said, his voice almost breaking as it rose, "Because I've been to the *mountaintop!*" His voice trembled on the word.

There was tremendous applause, mingling with the rumble of thunder outside and the crackle of lightning. And as he continued, these sounds, crashing and reverberating in the distance, played a strange, moving obbligato to his words:

"And I don't mind," he was saying. "Like anybody I would like to *live* . . . a long life; longevity has its place." He sounded cool, reasonable now, stating what any reasonable man would wish to say and feel. "But I'm not *concerned* about that now. . . ." His voice began to rise. "I just want to do God's *will!*" He was carrying his audience with him. "And *He's* allowed me to go up to the mountain. . . ."

His voice continued rising, its cadences greater, more rolling. "And I've looked over—and I've *see-een* . . ." He lingered on the word, his voice high-pitched, tremolo-like, the high singing voice of a violin, it pierced one, "the—*Promised Land.*" Cheers and applause, and cries from the audience. "I may not get there with you, but I want you to *know, tonight,* that *we-as-a-people-will-get-to-the-Promised Land!*" Each word intense and high, and building up again, after a pause in a quick rush, a torrent of words: "So I'm happy tonight I'm not worried about *anything* I'm not fearing *any* man!" To a crescendo that swept everything before it: "Mine eyes have *seen the glo*-ry of the *com*-ing of the *Lord!*"

It was like a crash of cymbals, a testament, a defiance, a triumph. It electrified the audience.

He wheeled about, took three steps and all but fell into the arms of Abernathy, who helped him into his seat. He seemed utterly exhausted.

There was tumult. The audience seemed to leap in its seats. It seemed incredible that there were only two thousand persons. The reverberations of the applause, mingling with the crashing thunder outside, and the rolling drumming on the roof made it appear that the great vaulted hall was jammed with cheering and weeping thousands.

Among those who surrounded him, shaking his hand, congratulating him, was the Rev. James Lawson. During part of Dr. King's speech Lawson had been busy with his chores. As he was chairman, people were bringing him memos; he had numerous telephone calls to make. He had left the platform while Abernathy was introducing Dr. King, to go into the vestibule to use the only phone, which Abernathy had used earlier to summon Martin. When Lawson returned some minutes later, Martin had just begun. Lawson slipped into the rear of the room to the back steps leading to the platform, out of sight of the audience. He sat on a step, holding his knee in his clasped hands, listening.

As Martin spoke of the threats against his life, Lawson thought, *I never heard him speak exactly like this before. He's talked about such things in private meetings, never at mass meetings.* Lawson knew nothing of Martin's conversation a few hours before with Marion Logan. He could not know that Martin's speech echoed what he had said to her—he was ready to die, he was ready to die. Beside Martin's weariness, Lawson had observed something else, however. The storm was rattling the huge ventilation shutters while

Abernathy had been introducing Martin. The exhaust fans were enormous. When they were not on, the shutters were closed. But the wind outside was blowing them open, making a bang! bang! bang! With each bang Martin had looked around, nervously. Others had noted this too. They had thought, *Martin is awfully jumpy.* Lawson told an assistant to switch on the fans so they would blow outward and stop rattling.

As Martin continued to talk, Lawson felt himself caught up in his words. He stole out into the audience so he could see him better. Martin was speaking with deep feeling, and one was aware of this. Often when he spoke his face seemed impassive, however eloquent and fiery his words, but here the muscles of his face worked, the stress of great emotion showed in his face as well as in his words. When he spoke his eyes were focused far off, above the heads of the crowd; and now and then he turned his head to one side, as if listening, speculatively, thoughtfully, expectantly, to his own words, measuring them as if he himself were hearing them for the first time. This was not the Martin Luther King of "I have a dream," declaiming shining words, well thought out, before a vast audience. It was a man talking under the stress of deep emotion, as though to himself, listening to himself as he revealed aloud the possibility of his own death. And somehow over his words lay a penumbra of almost chilling certainty, as though he knew of what he spoke. A mood of mystery on the one hand, of revelation, knowing and expecting this to be done to him, and, on the other, of a great and profound commitment which only death could halt.

Lawson gripped his hand fervently. "A great speech, Doc. Just great!"

King responded warmly but wearily. A moment later he and Andy Young were led out of the hall by the side entrance. A car awaited them and they were driven to the nearby Minimum Salary Building, union headquarters. A strategy meeting by strike leaders was to be held there in a few minutes, although it was now nearly 11 P.M. While Young went up to talk to union officials, Dr. King remained in the car, parked in front of the building. He was sitting in the front seat, on the right.

Standing on the front porch of the building was James Laue, the Community Relations representative. He had been deeply moved by King's speech and had left as soon as it was over. Now, when the Rev. Young came downstairs again, he spoke briefly with him. The rain had subsided; only a few drops fell in the quiet, dark night.

"Do you and Martin plan to go to the meeting?" Laue asked.

Young doubted it. "Martin's very tired and we have a lot of work to do," he said. They wanted to meet tonight with Judge Ben Hooks, a Negro leader in Memphis. And in the morning, there was the hearing on the injunction in Federal Judge Bailey Brown's courtroom. Martin might attend the hearing, but if not, Young would represent him.

Laue and Young stood silent for a moment. Laue suddenly realized, with a prickling of the skin of his forehead, that the two of them, a white man and a black man, and he the only white man there —were standing directly under the porch light. The city was tense: hate literature was being slipped under hundreds of white doorways. The White Citizens Councils had been holding an emergency membership drive, waiving all entrance fees; the Ku Klux Klan had warned that if King marched it would march too. . . . Suppose a white man wanted to take a shot at both of them, at Andy and him, standing under this light: they were vulnerable. He knew that a white man was rarely seen in this neighborhood, and especially never after dark. That cabdrivers, if asked by a white man to be taken to this area, would invariably turn in their seat and stare at him, suspicious and hostile. . . . He looked at Dr. King, sitting in the car, waiting. The man sat there so silently, so watchfully, looking off to the right, seeming to scan the dark houses, the dark street up ahead. Laue knew that King had been showing a growing consciousness of danger. More than once aides had remarked that he would suddenly glance about him, as if awaiting the inevitable bullet from the dark.

Moments later, Young had joined King, and they had left for the home of Judge Ben Hooks.

CHAPTER VI

One P.M. Thursday, April 4. In Room 306, Dr. King and Dr. Abernathy were waiting for lunch to be brought in.

All morning there had been staff meetings on strategy and tactics. In the midst of these, a delegation of four Invaders called on Dr. King. They had been conferring for hours in Room 316.

Dr. King suspended his meeting to hear them. They presented a series of "We Demands," among them one for a tremendous sum of money, several hundred thousand dollars, for their social program. Dr. King was indignant: this was an escalation of his promise to help. "If you come to me this way, I can't speak to you," he told them sternly. "Let's try to work this out, see how we can get your program funded, but I will not listen to demands." They had left crestfallen. They had no money to pay their motel bill, and finally it was paid by SCLC, and they were told to check out.* Later Dr. King told his colleagues he would not condone anyone on their staff who believed in violence. Cabbage, who had been helping as a volunteer worker, would have to be dismissed. He was even more blunt: anybody in the room now who couldn't live with nonviolence could leave at once. He had made his position clear. The staff meetings had been successful, the members had drifted off to their various assignments, and now Dr. King and Abernathy, the president and vice president of the SCLC, had a few minutes to themselves.

Martin wondered aloud: what was happening in the federal court hearing? Andy Young had gone there to represent him, but they had not heard from him all morning.

They had both ordered fried catfish for lunch. It was a Memphis delicacy because the fish were pulled fresh each morning from the Mississippi. The waitress who served them, however, was confused. First she arrived with only one salad. Martin, quite hungry, took a couple of spoonfuls, then waited. She came again, this time bringing Martin a double order of catfish and Ralph only his salad. "You all

---

* Hosea Williams was particularly outraged. "What are we doing, letting them meet there all day and conspire against us?" he demanded. He was also furious because the Invaders had forwarded their restaurant tabs to the SCLC for payment.

really can't get these orders right, can you?" Abernathy said, not unkindly. "You didn't bring me my fish."

Martin said, "That's all right, Ralph. You and I can eat together." And they ate from the one plate.

After lunch Ralph stretched out on his bed and, almost while talking, fell asleep. They had been up until dawn this morning. There had been the emotional rally last night, and Martin's moving speech. They had gone from there to have a bite at the home of Judge Hooks, remaining until long after 3 A.M., talking strike strategy. When they returned to the Lorraine, there were new arrivals—the Rev. A. D. King, Dr. King's younger brother, Mrs. Georgia Davis, of Louisville, a Kentucky state senator and member of the SCLC board, and King's administrative assistant, Mrs. Lucy Ward. Neither Martin nor Ralph had gotten more than a few hours' sleep.

When Ralph woke from his nap, it was nearly four o'clock, and he was alone.

The phone rang. "David," came Martin's voice. "Michael," Ralph responded. "Where are you?" David was Ralph's first name, as Michael was Martin's, and the two men when the mood was on them and they were alone would use these in a more intimate sense.

"I'm down here in A.D.'s room," Dr. King replied. "Come on down here—we're all in Room 201." Ralph did so. Martin was in excellent spirits. "We were just talking to Mother, we talked a long time, over an hour," he said. "I was just dialing her when A.D. walked in. She was so happy, she's always happy when A.D.'s with me. She doesn't often have a chance to talk to us both together." They had played tricks on her—Martin pretending he was A.D. and A.D. pretending he was Martin, taking turns talking to her, confusing her completely, and it had been all laughter and affection. It had been wonderful. Earlier he had made calls to Dora McDonald, his secretary in Atlanta, checking his plans and schedules, and to Harry Wachtel, one of his attorneys in New York.

His spirits were sustained all afternoon, as others filtered in, among them Hosea Williams, Bernard Lee, Jim Bevel. He was completely relaxed, lounging on the bed, his collar open, his tie loosened, his shoes off, now and then sinking into an easy chair and flinging one stockinged foot over the side.

Shortly after 4:30 P.M. Andy Young came in. Court had adjourned, he said, and the lawyers were now closeted in the judge's chambers. Almost as soon as he walked in, Ralph exclaimed, as if in great surprise, "Well, look who's here!" With that, he unexpectedly grabbed

Andy in a bear hug and wrestled him down on the other bed. As if at a signal, the others jumped Andy and, despite his shouts and squirming, held him down, and each time he tried to rise they pushed him down again, pinning him by his wrists and ankles. Now Martin was bending over him, demanding in a fierce voice, "You think you can always go off on your own? How many times must we tell you, you got to call in, man! You got to let Leader know what's going on!"

Andy tried to rise, but his strength was gone in laughter, and Martin shoved him back again. "You know, Ralph and I were going to call you in court, pull you right out of that room and bawl you out. Now we going teach you a lesson!" And they pummeled him and tickled him and wrestled with him and for a while Martin and A.D. wrestled each other, as they used to as boys. It was a general roughhouse and clowning, now on the bed, now on the floor, until everyone, out of breath and exhausted, called it quits.

Then for a while it was like a reception, with friends and visitors crowding in, until at five o'clock someone said, "Let's get the news." They tuned in the local news. King sat engrossed, watching as the screen showed a brief film clip of his speech the night before and his voice, trembling with emotion, filled Room 201 and the crowd's roar of applause sealed it off. At 5:30 Walter Cronkite came on. A moment later Chauncey Eskridge, King's personal lawyer, walked in. "Hi, Chauncey," Martin greeted him. "Tell me what happened in the chambers, and what you expect the judge'll do, because I want to test what you say against what Cronkite says." Eskridge briefed him swiftly. It was clear that Judge Brown would lift the stay order, but with certain restrictions, principally how many marchers could walk abreast and what route they'd take. Mayor Loeb, Police Director Holloman, and Sheriff William N. Morris, Jr., had sat in the rear of the courtroom as official observers, but the session had gone quietly.

They watched a few minutes more. King jumped to his feet. "I've got to go up and get dressed, and we'll all go out to dinner. Come on, Ralph." The two left and went up the stairs to their room. It was twenty minutes to six.

About two hours earlier, around 3:15 P.M., Mrs. Bessie Brewer, manager of a rooming house at 418½–422½ South Main Street, one block north of Fire House Station No. 2, in a seedy area of pawnshops and secondhand stores on the edge of black Memphis, was going over her accounts when there was a knock on the door of Room 2, which she used as an office.

Mrs. Brewer, a plump, matter-of-fact woman in her thirties, wearing faded blue jeans, a man's rumpled checkered shirt, her hair in rollers and a handkerchief about her head, rose and opened the door as far as the chain would allow—about two inches. Standing in the hall landing facing her was a slender man who appeared to be in his early thirties. She noticed that his eyes were blue, he had dark hair and a sharp nose, and wore a neatly pressed dark suit. "Do you have a room to rent?" he asked through the door. His manner was pleasant, and a kind of tentative smile—or was it a smirk?—twisted the right corner of his mouth. Mrs. Brewer was always to remember the smile because it seemed not to belong there—as though he were trying to smile for no reason.

Thinking, *gosh, this man doesn't belong here*, she unlatched the door. Mrs. Brewer, whose husband worked at a factory during the day, had taken over managing the place with its less than a dozen roomers about three weeks before. With the exception of Mrs. Jessie Ledbetter, a widow of uncertain age who was a deaf-mute, and Charles and Grace Stephens, a middle-aged couple living as common-law man and wife, her tenants were all elderly men, some of them alcoholic, either on welfare or piecing out meager pensions with whatever odd jobs they could find. She had been accustomed to see them shuffle about, bleary-eyed and unshaven in undershirts and filthy trousers. What was this man doing here, with his neatly pressed suit and white shirt and tie?

Aloud she asked, "By the day or week?" By the week, the man said.

Mrs. Brewer had several rooms available. Nos. 418½ and 422½ were adjacent, run-down two-story brick buildings, with stores on the ground level. The rooming house occupied the second floor of both buildings, connected by a covered passageway that had been broken through between them. Thus it consisted of two wings, each with its stairs, one at 422½, the stairs up which the stranger obviously had come (her office was right off the landing at the head of the stairs), and the other, an open staircase to the left or north of it, between the two buildings, at 418½. She had ten apartments in the south wing, six in the north. She led the stranger down the hall of her wing to Room 8, a kitchenette apartment. "This would be ten dollars by the week," she said. He looked in but did not enter. "I don't need a stove or a refrigerator," he said mildly. "I won't be doing any cooking. I was thinking more of a sleeping room."

"The only vacant sleeping room I have is 5B in the other wing," Mrs. Brewer said. "It's $8.50 by the week." The man said nothing, so she led him through the passageway with its broken mortar to 418½, the north wing. On their left, as they entered the other building, was the stairway down to the street. To their right was a long hall, with yellow-green linoleum on the floor and a single fifty-watt bulb screwed in the ceiling. The dim illumination was aided by a skylight, but at the rear end of the hall daylight appeared. Mrs. Brewer led him down the hall to Room 5B, on the right, almost to the end. It had a padlock on the door. She removed it and pushed the door open. The doorknob was missing, in its stead a wire coat hanger had been thrust through the aperture and the hooked part twisted to serve as a handle.

Again the man stuck his head in. He saw the single window with its tattered shade and green and gold floral plastic curtains, the sagging metal bed with a mattress awry on top of the open springs, the ancient, boarded-up fireplace with a portable gas heater in front of it, the faded greasy red sofa with an equally greasy red pillow on it, the bare, fly-specked light bulb hanging from the center of the cracked ceiling. "This will be fine," he said. He seemed impervious to the room's appearance, as he was to the strong odor of pine disinfectant permeating the building. Where was the bathroom?

Mrs. Brewer pointed to it, directly in front of them at the end of the hall. The door, on which was clumsily painted in red "Toilet & Bath," was open. The daylight they had seen from the other end of the hall came from a window in the bathroom. She said, "Everyone around here is usually quiet, but this guy next to you"—she indicated 6B, the room next to his and adjacent to the bathroom—"he usually drinks."

"Oh, I take a beer once in a while myself," the man said, the same odd smile on his face. He looked into the room again.

As if her pointing had been a signal, the door of 6B opened. Charles Stephens, a sad-looking man with a high domed forehead, appeared. He was wearing a white T-shirt, khaki slacks, and bedroom slippers and carried a wrench. Seeing the stranger, he hesitated, then said gruffly to Mrs. Brewer, "I've got the tank working." "All right, Charlie," she said, and he retreated into his room and shut the door. The stranger had not turned to look at him.

Mrs. Brewer led the way back to her office, talking to her new roomer as he walked behind her. She was not too comfortable. The smile so like a sneer bothered her. She couldn't understand what he could be smiling at, or sneering at. She felt vaguely that it might be something about her, and since any silence seemed menacing, she made conversation. "It's O.K. if you drink, so long as you stay in your room and keep quiet." He said, behind her, "I won't be using the room in the daytime, just at night."

In the office he dug his right hand into his pocket. She noticed his jacket was so short he didn't have to push it back to reach his pocket, and brought out a crisp twenty-dollar bill, snapping it sharply in both hands as a bank teller might to make sure two bills weren't stuck together before giving it to her. She wrote out a receipt. What was the name? "John Willard," he said. She gave him his change and he left. Later she remembered he had said nothing about the padlock on the door. Tenants usually asked how they would lock the room when they were out and she would then give them the padlock for payment of a small deposit. But Willard had not said anything. She remembered, too, that he had no luggage, but she assumed he would bring that later.

As he turned to go, Uncle Bertie Reeves, a retired hotel clerk, in his seventies, emerged from Room 5, down the hall from Mrs. Brewer's office. He saw the back of Mr. Willard's head as the latter turned down the passageway to his room in the other wing.

Toward four o'clock the new roomer rapidly descended the open staircase of 418½ to the street. Almost where he emerged a white Mustang was parked at the curb in front of Jim's Grill, at 418 South Main Street. It had an Alabama red and white rear license plate. He got into it and drove half a dozen blocks to the York Arms Company —the same shop that had done such a land-office business during the scare of the summer before.

He parked and entered. Ralph Carpenter, thirty-four, the salesman behind the counter, approached him. "Can I help you?"

"I'd like a pair of field glasses," Willard said. It was an old-fashioned term for binoculars. The man can't be too familiar with them, Carpenter thought. He said, "I have a pair around ninety dollars and one for two hundred."

"That's a little too expensive," Willard said, and turned to go.

"Wait a minute," said Carpenter. He thought he might have a cheaper pair in the window. He brought them out. Willard put them to his eyes, turning to look out the front door with them. "Do they come with instructions?" he asked. Carpenter said, "Oh, you really don't need much instructions. Just set them and regulate them to your own eyes."

Willard handed the binoculars back, saying nothing. Carpenter wasn't sure whether the man wanted to buy them or not. "They're not a cheap pair of glasses made in Japan, you know," he ventured. "They're Bushnell, which is a good name in glasses."

Still Willard was silent, so Carpenter proceeded to calculate the sales tax on a pad and said, "That'll be forty-one dollars and fifty-five cents, tax included." Willard reached into his right trouser pocket and pulled out some neatly folded bills and gave Carpenter two twenties and a one-dollar bill. Carpenter glimpsed more twenties, and thought, unhappily, he'd have to break a twenty for fifty-five cents, and he didn't have the change, but Willard then carefully produced from his left pocket two quarters and five pennies, which he dropped, one at a time, into Carpenter's hand. Carpenter went back to the cash register to ring up the money, but Willard, instead of following him, edged toward the door, waiting there, and Carpenter, after wrapping the purchase, had to walk over to him with the package. "Thanks, we certainly appreciate your business, come again," he said. Willard mumbled something unintelligible and walked out.

Carpenter looked after him. Later he recalled that he thought, *If this fellow'd go out in the sun, he'd take a tan easily*. He remembered that the man's black hair (or brown with oil on it) was combed straight back, he wore a dark suit, white shirt with a dark tie, tied with a long knot slightly off center. That was all he could remember.

Willard drove back to the rooming house. The space he had had before, directly in front of Jim's Grill, was now occupied by another car. He had to park his white Mustang a few doors farther south just beyond Canipe's Amusement Company at 424. He turned off the motor but did not get out. He remained seated behind the wheel, motionless. There was little traffic in the street. He sat, immobile, looking straight ahead.

Across the street, in the office of the Seabrook Paint and Wallpaper Company, at 421 South Main, Mrs. Elizabeth Copeland was standing at the window, looking into the street. She had quit work at 4:30, about fifteen minutes ago, and was waiting for her husband to call for her. She saw the white car drive up and park just south of Canipe's, and the driver sitting there, as if waiting. Peggy Jane Hurley's husband, Charles, usually came at this time to pick Peggy up. She called out, "Peggy, your husband is here for you." Mrs. Hurley came to the window and shook her head. "No, it's not Charles— we've got a Falcon. That's a Mustang."

A moment later, Mrs. Frances Thompson, the bookkeeper, who had been waiting for her daughter, saw her drive up and hurried outside. She had seen the white Mustang too. As they drove away, she looked curiously at its occupant. He was dark-haired, he wore a dark suit, and he still sat motionless behind the wheel. He did not glance at them as they drove by.

Some minutes after that Charles Hurley drove up and parked just behind the Mustang. Peggy Jane saw him through the window and came out and got into the car. Hurley had noticed the rear license plate of the Mustang. He was to remember it as an Arkansas plate, because Arkansas, like Alabama, had red and white plates. A young white man was sitting behind the wheel. He paid no attention to them as they pulled around him and drove off.

Not until sometime after five o'clock did Willard bestir himself. He got out of the car, opened the rear trunk, and brought out a bundle wrapped in a green and yellow bedspread. He put this under his arm and with the York Arms Company bag in his hand, he walked by Canipe's window at 424 with its sign, "Used Records, 45 RPM, 25¢," past the stairs at 422½ up which he had gone to ask Mrs. Brewer for a room, past the shop next to it, "Cohen & Co.," at 422, until he came to the left-hand stairs, the stairs he had come down, the stairs of 418½, just before "Jim's Grill," at 418 with its sign, "Plate Lunch Special: Sausages, eggs, toast, grits, coffee, 62¢." He went up the stairs.

No one saw him go into Room 5B. The knobless door opened and closed silently behind him. It had a sliding bolt on the inside and he slipped it shut. A hand-lettered sign thumbtacked on the inside of the door read, NO DRINKING, NO SMOKING IN BED ALLOWED. Below it hung a calendar showing January 1968. He placed the bundle and bag on the bed. A small chest of four drawers that someone had painted white, with a mirror in a wooden frame on top, stood in front of the window that faced the companion building, 422½, over the space of about ten feet that separated the two buildings. He pushed the chest to the other side of the room, then raised the window about two and a half feet.

It was a pleasant day. Scarcely any air came in to disturb the tattered shade or the torn plastic curtains. He rolled the shade up and pushed the curtains to one side, resting them on the top of the mantel, so the window was left clear. A wooden chair stood near the bed. He pulled it to one side of the window, opened the bag, and removed the binoculars from their case, and, sitting on the chair, put them to his eyes and looked out the window. He could see between the two buildings diagonally to the Lorraine Motel, some two hundred feet away, on the other side of Mulberry Street, which ran in front of the motel and in the rear of the rooming house. But he could not see all of the motel: he would have to lean out of the window to see the full front of it, as well as the courtyard with its parked cars and people.

After a moment he left his room and crossed the hall five strides to the bathroom. The door had no lock but had a hook on the inside. He latched it. He was in a rectangular green-walled room, stained and peeling with time and neglect. As he stood at the door, facing the window at the other end, along the right wall in order were the toilet, a gas heater, and a small sink with an ornately framed but battered mirror hanging over it; opposite it, on the left wall, in the same order, a shower stall, and an ancient pockmarked tub with lion claw-foot legs, a metal soap stand hanging on two bent rusty wires on the wall side, in it a small two-inch blob of soap, sickly white like the underside of a fish. A single bulb with a dangling pull cord was screwed into the ceiling socket. If he stepped into the tub and turned slightly to his right, he could look out the window and have a direct, uninterrupted view of the motel. A few trees were growing in the backyard of the rooming house, but their foliage was sparse.

There was considerable activity in the courtyard. Willard, watching through the binoculars, kept his eyes on what he saw. The two hundred feet, thanks to the seven-power glasses, dwindled to less than ten yards. Everything that went on in the courtyard—and on the second level or balcony of the motel—was brought within a stone's throw from him.

He stood there, watching.

At the post at the back door of the fire station a block to the south on South Main Street, Patrolman Richmond also had his binoculars trained on the Lorraine Motel. He and Redditt had come on duty at 10 A.M. as scheduled. Their visit to Mason Temple the night before, to watch King while he spoke, had been an abortive one. They had found it necessary to leave before he arrived. As they sat quietly to one side in the audience, a black clergyman came up to them. He'd heard, he said coldly, that they had been at the fire station all afternoon, "using binoculars, spying." He said, "I really wish you weren't here. This is not the place for you." The young people in the audience were already on their mettle; he did not want any trouble. As the two men sat there, they saw some in the audience staring at them. At the moment the Rev. Lawson was speaking, accusing the police of brutality in last Thursday's march, charging specifically that they had shot down in cold blood the seventeen-year-old black youth who had been killed that day. Richmond and Redditt feared Lawson might point them out in the audience, and decided it would be best to leave, and they had done so shortly before nine o'clock.

Nothing eventful had happened so far this morning. They watched. King was holding meetings in Room 306. At one point four Invaders had marched into King's room and, after some time, had emerged and returned slowly to their own rooms at the end of the balcony.

Shortly after noon, however, there had been an interruption in their own work. A fireman came into the locker room, looking for Redditt. There was a lady on the phone who wanted to talk to him, he said. Redditt went into the lounge and was directed to a phone on the wall. The woman's voice was hard. "You are doing the black people wrong, and the black people are going to do you and yours wrong." The receiver clicked, but Redditt thought he recognized the voice. The morning before when they were at the airport observing Dr. King's arrival, a Negro woman had walked up to Redditt and stuck her finger in his face. "I'm going to get you if I have to shoot you myself," she had said grimly. This could be the same woman.

Redditt was not easily frightened, but he had to reveal the telephone threat to his superiors. Police Director Holloman acted quickly. He had also gotten a private report, from his own Internal Security Division, that persons were on their way to Memphis to kill Redditt, not at his post but somewhere else. Under the circumstances, nothing was too bizarre to be disbelieved. Holloman sent a police escort to bring Redditt to police headquarters, where he told him he was arranging to move him and his family immediately to a motel under an assumed name. Redditt protested. He preferred to remain with his family in his own house. He was sent home with a police detail assigned to guard him day and night.

Richmond, alone, stayed at his post and continued his surveillance. The threats today, their forced departure from the Mason Temple last night were unnerving, but they were part of the job. He jotted down names and times as the afternoon wore on. At 5:40 he noted that Dr. King and Rev. Abernathy, who had been visiting for some time in Room 201 with other "male coloreds," suddenly emerged and almost gaily hurried up the zigzag steps to their room, Room 306, on the second level.

CHAPTER VII

In Room 306, Dr. King was standing in the bathroom in trousers and undershirt, preparing to shave. Dr. Abernathy, who had already shaved and dressed, lay in his shirt sleeves resting on top of one of the two beds. Dr. King used a powerful depilatory called Magic Shave Powder. It was used mainly by orthodox Jews, who are forbidden to have a razor touch their skin, and by men who, like Dr. King, had heavy beards and whose active public life required them to appear clean-shaven at all times. Magic Shave Powder had a dreadful, sulfurous odor, more like rotten eggs than anything else, but it did appear to have its own magic properties; it gave one a very close, long-lasting shave.

Dr. King was busy with his task. First he had to make a thick paste of powder and hot water in a cup, and when it was the right consistency, apply it to his face with a spatula, like so much clay, then allow it to dry and harden for some minutes, then scrape it off with the edge of the spatula.

Dr. Abernathy could scarcely endure the odor, but it was a cross he had borne for some time. To escape it, he got off the bed and took a chair at the opposite end of the room, near the front picture window with its green and orange drapes. He was trying to come to a decision. Dr. King had pushed the Poor People's March from April 22 to April 29. It meant a conflict of dates for Dr. Abernathy. "Martin," he finally called out, "do you know the revival in my church begins April 29? What am I going to do?"

Dr. King emerged, patting his face with a towel. Who had Abernathy invited to speak at the revival? Abernathy told him—one of their colleagues, a masterful speaker whom he'd chosen because he himself was too busy to promote the event, and he could count on a first-rate orator to ensure a large crowd anyway.

"Can't you have it a week earlier?" Dr. King suggested. "Don't start on the twenty-ninth, start a week earlier."

He'd thought of that, said Abernathy, but his guest speaker couldn't come that day.

"Well, I'll just have to make him come to you," Dr. King said. But if that was impossible . . . The two men began discussing it. Perhaps, said Abernathy, he'd invite the Rev. Lutrelle Long of the African Methodist Church in New Orleans. He would be a splendid drawing card.

"Good idea," said Dr. King. "I know Lutrelle. Let's get him on the phone and I'll talk to him." But Rev. Long was not in, his secretary said. "Let me talk to her, I think I know her," Dr. King said. He introduced himself. "You tell Lutrelle to do this for Ralph and come on that Sunday," he said with finality, and hung up.

There was a knock on the door. It was the Rev. Samuel B. Kyles—Billy Kyles—a tall, slim, enthusiastic black man in his thirties who was pastor of the Monumental Baptist Church in Memphis. He was to be their host at a soul food dinner at his home tonight, before the rally. Dr. King appreciated getting away from eating in restaurants. It meant constant interruption and signing of autographs and his food invariably grew cold. There was nothing he enjoyed as much as soul food, and especially among friends and at a friend's home. The day before, at their ministers' meeting in Jim Lawson's church, Kyles had said to him, "My wife's got dinner for tomorrow night and we'd love to have you come." Kyles had recently moved into an enormous fourteen-room house; and this could be in the nature of a housewarming. Dr. King could bring along as many persons as he liked—up to twelve or fifteen.

"Great! What time do you want us?" he had asked, and Kyles said, "Five o'clock." He and his wife Gwen had planned it for six o'clock, but you always moved up the time with Dr. King. The man was so busy he never caught up with his schedule. Telling him five made it reasonably sure he might show up by seven.

Ralph Abernathy, still concerned about the program at his church, turned to Kyles. "Why don't you do my revival?" he asked. But Kyles thought he might be preaching in Columbus, Ohio, that day.

"Wouldn't you want to come to Atlanta?" Dr. King asked. He had removed a white drip-dry shirt from a hanger and was putting it on. "Anybody'd rather come to Atlanta than go to Columbus." He tried to button the collar, but it was too tight. He finally gave up.

Kyles grinned. "Hey, Doc, you getting fat."

"I am that," said Dr. King ruefully. He turned to Abernathy. "Do I have another shirt here?"

Dr. Abernathy looked glum. "Yes, but you mean I washed that shirt for you this morning and you not going to put it on?"

Dr. King's voice had a note of helpless protest, like that of a small boy. "But I can't button it, Ralph."

"O.K.," said Ralph. "Take it off."

Abernathy found another shirt for King, but he was still thinking of his revival. "Man," he said, "you know, I got a good church. Those people are really good to me." He was always so busy, he had been away so much on SCLC business, and they always put up with him.

"You sure have," King agreed. "You know, talk about churches . . . You haven't seen anything like my dad's. Ebenezer's a great, great place. Dad is really something—he's really a great guy. He was a young man when he came from the country to Atlanta. He walked down Auburn Avenue, he saw this big church, and he met the pastor. Later he met the pastor's daughter." He laughed. "He started coming to Ebenezer to court Mother, and not only did he get Mother, but he also got the church! All three! Got the church, he became the pastor, and he married the pastor's daughter!" He shook his head admiringly. "Dad's still steppin'—" He was full of his father, the more so since the long talk he and A.D. had had with their mother.

Kyles said, "Yes, you remember when we were in Miami—" This had been in mid-February, at the SCLC staff meeting at which they'd completed their plans and set the date for the Poor People's March. "You remember, he came up and said, 'All right now, you young preachers go to bed, when you get as old as me, you can't do nothin' but go to bed.' And we said, 'Yeah, Dad, we watchin' you, we don't know what you doin' when you go to bed!' "

They all laughed, and their preachers' banter went on. Kyles remembered another conversation in Miami. They had all been sitting together in a hotel room, and had begun talking about threats against King's life. Kyles had asked, "Doc, when were you most frightened?" King thought for a moment. "I can remember twice. First was when the three civil rights workers were killed in Philadelphia, Mississippi*—we went in there and we held a rally in the church. We were on the platform and all had to bow our heads and close our eyes—" He paused and turned to Abernathy. "Ralph, who was praying, you or me?" Abernathy answered, "You were praying, Martin." King went on: "I bowed my head in prayer, closed my eyes and I said, 'O Lord,

---

* On June 21, 1964, Andrew Goodman and Michael Schwerner, white students from New York, and James Chaney, a black youth from Philadelphia, Mississippi, disappeared after an arrest for speeding in that city. On August 4 their bullet-marked bodies were found buried in an earthen dam not far away.

the killers of these boys may even be in the range of my voice,' and this big burly deputy sheriff standing just behind us with his arms folded said, and I could hear him, 'You're damn right they are!' " Everyone laughed. "I went on praying, and I just visualized myself being shot in that position." The second time that he was really afraid, he said, was in 1966, when he marched in Chicago. They marched by a long row of trees; and "From those trees I expected any moment someone to shoot. But Billy—you learn to live with it. I'd like to. I enjoy living." He thought for a moment. "They want me from the left, they want me from the right, they want me from the middle." He smiled ruefully. "What chance have I got?"

He seemed to be in no hurry now. "Tell me, Billy," he went on, "what happened here to bring the Negroes together like this? I've never seen anything quite like it before."

He had been tremendously impressed by the spirit in Memphis, the sense of solidarity among all the Negroes, middle-class and poor, when he spoke on March 18. Everyone had said the day of the big marches and big rallies was over. Yet here, in Memphis, surely no stronghold of black unity, brought together by this strike of garbage and sewer workers, nearly fifteen thousand Negroes had jammed into a place that usually held ten thousand. Extra chairs had to be brought in; it was impossible to move through the aisles, they were so packed. To what was this enthusiasm due?

Kyles explained that one of the things that had happened here was that preachers were involved who had never been involved before, and consequently their congregations knew the issues and had taken them up. "Everyone can identify with the garbage man," he said. "He's got the job nobody wants, he's the lowest on the ladder, and he's so terribly underpaid and abused . . . It just makes everything so clear cut; I guess it just caught fire, Doc."

King agreed. Certainly the thing to do was to keep up this magnificent spirit. After a moment, he began looking about him, muttering, "Where *is* my tie? Somebody's moved my tie."

Abernathy stood up. "Look, let's go—we want to get going there and eat those filets mignons." He pronounced it with an exaggerated French accent. "Feel-ay meen-yuns." Kyles laughed. Abernathy was putting him on. He knew he wasn't getting steak, he was getting genuine soul food, pigs' knuckles and fried pigs' feet and turnip greens and pot liquor, all the parts of beef and pork and vegetables, the gristle and bones with meat still on them, the water in which the meat and vegetables had been cooked, all the residue and leftovers and unwanted that the white master threw away but were good enough for the darkies in the kitchen.

Martin was repeating, "Now, where *is* my tie? Somebody's moved my tie!" He glanced about him suspiciously. Were they pulling a trick on Leader? Had they hidden his tie out of sheer orneriness?

Abernathy spoke up chidingly. "Martin," he said, "why don't you just look down at that chair."

"Oh," said King. "I thought somebody took it on me." It was a narrow brown tie, with one blue and one tan diagonal stripe in the center, and as he put it on, his good humor returned. "Billy," he said, "we're not going to get real soul food at your house. Gwen's just too pretty to cook soul food—she can't cook it."

"Who can't cook soul food?" Kyles retorted. "Man, all I gotta say, you better hurry, we're going to be late."

"Oh no," said Dr. King. He was very deliberate, carefully primping before the dresser mirror as he fixed a silver tiepin in place. "You told me five, and Ralph called the house and Gwen said six. You trying to trick us. Dinner will be served at six, so we're not late. Now, we going to take A.D. and Chauncey, is that all right?"

Kyles said, "Sure, sure, we have plenty of food."

King, still refusing to be hurried: "I want to warn you, Billy. You be like one preacher we went to in Atlanta, he had a great big house too, and he talked about all the wonderful food he'd give us, but when we got there, he had ham, and no meat on the ham—and Kool-Aid! Not even sweet." King looked stern. "Now, we go over to your place and you have anything like that, you tell me right now and we going to order our own food somewhere else."

Kyles bantered with him. "You just get ready, Doc, you just get ready and don't worry about what we going to have. . . ." It was a relief to see Martin in so expansive a mood; good-natured, teasing, the exact opposite of yesterday. There were tremendous pressures upon him. The dire warnings against the Poor People's Campaign, the attacks upon his leadership, the violent mood of the black ghetto, his controversial stand on the Vietnam war, the apparent lack of will of his country to respond to the crisis upon it, and his own very personal problems—the tapping of his telephone, the hostility of J. Edgar Hoover, the omnipresent threat that at some ultimate triumph, when it would be most damaging, most humiliating, there would be blared out some episode in his private life which might exist in the private life of any public man but which, because of the public's deification of him, would be intolerable to support, and would be used in an attempt to destroy him. He had steeled himself against this possibility, as his intimates knew, and religious and civil rights leaders, both black and white, had even prepared a provisional stategy to use if King was thus attacked. But the concerns upon him, public and private, were overwhelming. One could understand his alternate states of depression and optimism.

But today he seemed to have drawn new sustenance from the deep recesses of his spirit. He had carried through a series of important staff meetings. Despite objections and doubts, he had laid down the law, reasserting his determination that they would have their Washington march, that they were going to depend upon, and preach, and fulfill, no matter what the provocation, the substance and philosophy of nonviolence. From now on they would be even more pure in their portrayal of it, for they were the only ones now who resolutely held to it as a tactic. They would keep the Poor People's Campaign nonviolent, and prove they could. The black power advocates, the Stokely Carmichaels and H. Rap Browns, the Adam Clayton Powells who said he was finished, who said Martin "Loser" King's day was past—they were wrong. He had come across a watershed and he was in good spirits. His mood explained the wrestling and roughhousing in A.D.'s room a little while ago.

It was a few minutes before six. Dr. King, stuffing in his shirttails, walked out on the balcony and stood at the railing to greet those in the courtyard just below. The white Cadillac limousine which belonged to the R. S. Lewis & Sons Funeral Home, and which had been placed at his beck and call for as long as he was in Memphis, waited directly below him. Standing by it was its driver, Solomon Jones, Jr., a short, stocky man who had been loaned to him at the same time to fetch and take him where he wished. Standing there in the courtyard below, as though arranged in a tableau, were his close friends and associates and comrades in arms, and each was forever to remember exactly where he stood and what he saw and how he felt in the minutes that were yet to come.

Beyond Solomon Jones, who was standing, hat in hand, at the left front wheel, was the Rev. Andrew Young, his chief lieutenant, at the right rear wheel; at the left rear wheel, Chauncey Eskridge, his attorney, and a little behind him, the Rev. James Bevel, another lieutenant, and not far away, still another, the Rev. Hosea Williams —each bright, sharp, eloquent, dedicated. How many battles were they veterans of together, how many struggles had they fought through, how much insult, humiliation, ignominy had they endured;

how much depth of emotion and inspiration reaching to ecstasy had they shared; how many shattering disappointments and unbelievable triumphs . . . Like him, they had glimpsed the Promised Land and had stood, trembling, on its edge . . .

At this moment Kyles came out of the room and joined Dr. King on the balcony, greeting those below. "Hi, Chauncey," he said. "When did you get here?" Eskridge, an older man, faultlessly dressed and distinguished in appearance, had arrived at eleven o'clock that morning from Nashville, where he had been counseling another client, Mahalia Jackson, the singer. He had walked in on Dr. King, who told him, "Chauncey, drop your bags right here and get down to court. They're waiting for you." Eskridge had spent most of the day in federal court, joining Burch and the other lawyers fighting the injunction against the march. Dr. King said, standing on the balcony, "Chauncey, tell Jesse to get ready, he's going to dinner with us."

This had meaning only for a few among those who heard it. Not only were black leaders outside the SCLC doubtful about the Poor People's March; among his staff, Jesse Jackson and Jim Bevel were two who also questioned the effectiveness of a confrontation with the Government. They had been debating this in meetings for weeks. "Where is our leverage?" they wanted to know. "We've got to force somebody into a dialogue—how do we do it? If the Government doesn't respond, what do we do? If nonviolence fails and we bring all these people to Washington full of hope, and nothing happens— what then?" The Saturday before, March 30, they had argued it for hours at a meeting in Dr. King's study in Ebenezer Baptist Church, although it had all been agreed to, voted upon, and passed even a month before at their Miami meeting. Yet here, as late as Saturday, March 30, Jesse and Jim, two of his most effective men, were still fighting it. "I don't even know how to preach people into the Poor People's Campaign," Bevel had complained. On the heels of Marion Logan's memo, with its gnawing suggestion that Rustin and she were conspiring against him, on the heels of the disastrous breakup of Thursday's march with its even more gnawing suggestion that perhaps they were right, it was almost too much to cope with. To top it off now, his staff was even questioning whether he should return to Memphis. After the meeting, as they were going down the steps of the church, Jesse behind him, Jesse had said, insistently, as if to continue the debate, "Doc," and King had whirled around on the steps and said in utter exasperation, "Jesse, don't bother me. It may be that you want to carve your own niche in society. Go ahead and carve it. But for God's sake don't bother me."

Those who heard this had never known Martin to speak so harshly before, and particularly to Jesse, who, only twenty-six, was one of his most promising aides, and for whom he had considerable respect. But he had been very upset during the meeting; he had obviously not been himself. At one point he had actually walked out. "I can't take it anymore," he had said to Abernathy, who had followed him out of the room. Seeing Abernathy's concern, he had added, "Don't worry. I'll be all right." But he left. After an hour or so, when they had all agreed once again, for the final time, that yes, he should go ahead with the march on Washington, and yes, he should go ahead with Memphis before that, he had come back into the meeting, and all ended well. They had separated, then, Jesse and Jim Bevel leaving at once for Memphis to start a series of nonviolent workshops with the young people so Thursday's disaster would not be repeated. Dr. King had not seen Jesse since. Now, here in Memphis, having put all that behind him, the invitation to dinner was Martin's overture of conciliation. He called down to Jones, "Solomon, start the car. I'll be down in two minutes," and walked back into Room 306. "Ralph, let's go," he said. "We'll put on our coats."

"Just a minute," said Abernathy. "I want to put on some after-shave." The only thing that compensated for the awful odor of Martin's Magic Shave Powder was the pleasing fragrance of his Aramis lotion, and Abernathy borrowed lavishly from it with no sense of guilt. The bottle was in Martin's shaving kit open on a table near the door.

"O.K. I'll wait for you on the balcony," King said, and walked out.

The Rev. Jesse Jackson, casual in brown slacks and matching brown turtleneck, was descending the zigzag metal staircase to the court-yard. Eskridge called up to him, "Doc says you're to come along with us—you ought to get dressed."

Jesse continued down the steps. "I am dressed," he said. "You can't be dressed with a turtleneck shirt on," said Eskridge. "Yes, I am," said Jesse, imperturbably, now in the courtyard and walking toward him. "Well," said Eskridge, shaking his head, "the president will hear about this as soon as he comes out."

Martin emerged from his room, pulling on both lapels of his jacket to ensure a trim shoulder line—it was a habit with him—and stood on the balcony where he had been standing a moment before. He caught sight of Jesse in the courtyard and called down, "Jesse, I want you to come to dinner with me."

The Rev. Kyles, standing at his right on the balcony, said, "Doc, you don't know what you're talking about. Jesse took care of himself long before you did. He got himself invited!" King laughed. In the room Abernathy, hearing the conversation, called out to King, "Tell him the whole band can't go, it makes the number too large." He was referring to the Breadbasket Band, which had come from Chicago to play at the meeting tonight. The band had become nationally known for its appearances at Jesse's Breadbasket Rallies in Chicago.

King said to Jesse, echoing Abernathy, "Better not bring the whole band, it'll be too many." Jesse, looking up at him, nodded and said, indicating a man standing with him, "Doc, this is Ben Branch. Ben used to live in Memphis. He plays in our band." King said, "Oh yes, he's my man. How are you, Ben?" Branch, who was both bandleader and soloist, waved. "Hello, Doc, glad to see you."

King leaned forward, both hands on the balcony railing. "Ben, I want you to sing for me tonight. I want you to do that song 'Precious Lord.' Sing it rea-eal pretty!"

Branch laughed. "I sure will, Doc."

Solomon Jones had started the car moments before. He called up, "It's getting cool out, Dr. King. I think you'll need a coat."

"O.K.," said King. He began to straighten up. Kyles, on the balcony about ten feet away to his right, turned to him. "Doc, I'm going to get my car—I can carry five or six with me," and turned back to walk toward the stairs. He had taken about five steps when he heard a loud muffled sound, like a car backfiring. He looked over the railing into the courtyard. What he saw made no sense. Jim Bevel had fallen to his knees, his hands over his face. Andy Young was crouched down, then up, others were hiding behind the big Cadillac. Kyles turned around in time to see Dr. King's body, in profile—just half of him, because he was partly hidden by a little setback in the balcony—falling backward. For a moment Kyles was shocked into immobility, then he rushed to where King had fallen. He lay in a pool of blood, his left hand flung up and back, his right hand crooked and outstretched. The right side of his jaw was torn away. The tie, the brown, blue, and tan tie he had made such a fuss about, was snipped in two just below the knot. It had been sheered off cleanly. His feet were against the rail, his left shoe under it, his right pressed against it, and the space was not enough for his body to stretch out, so that his knees were slightly raised. His head moved a little, from left to right.

Somehow Kyles found himself in Room 306, shouting and screaming into the telephone, trying vainly to raise the operator, and he was beating his head against the wall, again and again, as she did not answer, as nothing happened to prevent what had happened.

In Room 306, Abernathy had been standing before the dresser mirror, the fragrant lotion cool in both palms, in the act of lifting his cupped hands to his face, when he heard the firecracker. He jumped, involuntarily. Firecracker? Was someone shooting? He turned and looked out the door and saw Martin's shoes and he thought, *He's taken cover, they're shooting, maybe I ought to take cover, the door's wide open, and I'm standing only a few feet from it.* Then he heard, "Oh, Lord!"—a deep groan, sepulchral as the grave, from the courtyard below. He ran out on the balcony.

To his left, Martin lay on his back where he had fallen, into the setback. He lay diagonally across the balcony, his head near the left corner of the setback. Blood was pumping from a hole in his right jaw. "Oh, my God, Martin's been shot!" he exclaimed. He knelt and looked into Martin's face and he saw that he was frightened. He patted him on his left cheek, the uninjured side, until he got his attention. The frightened eyes turned toward him. "Martin, Martin, this is Ralph. Do you hear me? This is Ralph." The fear vanished from Martin's face and Martin was staring at him. "Don't be afraid, it's going to be all right." Martin attempted to say something—his mouth moved, but the words did not come. His eyes did not leave Ralph's and Abernathy got the impression that Martin was communicating with him with his eyes, that he was saying—did he actually hear the words or did he think them, feel them, *apprehend* them?— that he was saying, in his measured way, "Ralph, I told you so. It has happened. Now I depend on you because you're the only person I can depend on."

Then Abernathy was conscious that others were there. Kneeling beside Martin, he saw a white man in shirt sleeves, wearing shell-rimmed glasses, hurrying toward him, crouching, keeping low, holding a towel in his outstretched hand. When he reached Martin he cradled his head in the towel so that part of it lay loosely on the wound, covering it. At the same time Andy Young was there. The white man said, "My God, take his pulse. Do you feel anything?" Andy fell to his knees, holding Martin's right wrist. "Yes, I do—I do." Then a man in uniform was there. A policeman? There had been no police in sight. Now and then a patrol car had driven slowly by on Mulberry Street, its men watchful, but there had been no police about, in the courtyard or in the motel. How could this man have come there so quickly? And how was it that the courtyard below was suddenly full of uniformed men, helmeted men, armed men, pistols waving—where had they all come from? "Where was he hit?" the policeman asked. He repeated it. Abernathy lifted the towel and at the same time Martin stirred. Abernathy and the policeman said almost in the same breath, "Don't move! Don't move!"

In the courtyard below, amid the turmoil, Solomon Jones wheeled in the direction from which the shot came—from across Mulberry Street. He ran toward Mulberry Street. He thought he saw a man jump from behind the bushes on the other side of Mulberry, his back toward him. The man had something fitting close around his shoulders, white, like a hood—a small man—he was moving very fast, going away from him, toward Main Street. Solomon Jones was beside himself. He ran back into the courtyard, leaped into the car, and, motor roaring, drove at breakneck speed for twenty feet, jammed on the brake, threw it into reverse, backed up wildly the same distance, jammed on the brake again, and, helpless, turned off the ignition and leaped out of the car and stood there, trembling.

In Room 306 Billy Kyles had thrown himself across the bed and was pounding his fists against the covers. He began to scream. "Oh, Jesus! Oh, Jesus!" Abernathy rose and moved inside. "Now Billy, cut that out!" he said heavily. "Don't do that. Get an ambulance." Kyles managed to compose himself. He had been trying, but the telephone was dead, everything had gone wrong. Then he saw a policeman outside the door and shouted, "Call an ambulance on your radio, I can't raise the operator." The other replied, as from a great distance, "It's on its way."

Kyles, now in control of himself, began giving orders—someone to telephone Coretta, others to notify the hospital—then hurriedly pulled the orange-colored spread from one of the twin beds and dashed out to cover Martin. With so much loss of blood, a chill might prove fatal. He and Abernathy bent over King. Abernathy touched him on the cheek. "Martin, can you hear me? Are you in pain?" Martin's eyes were moving strangely, but he did not reply.

Kyles looked at him. It seemed to him that Martin's complexion, as he lay there, had subtly changed color. His face seemed flushed as with a glow. The sun was just setting. Was it the reflection of the setting sun? He remembered as a youth that when his father died his face had taken on the same roseate quality. His father's death, so long ago, and the death of the man before him were all one and all part of this unbelievable, apocalyptical moment; tag ends of thoughts, of words and labels, surged through Billy Kyles's mind: Calvary, the sun sinking in the west, all passion spent. . . .

He stood there, looking down on Dr. King, and he could not stop his tears.

Minutes before, in Room 309, three doors to the left of Dr. King's room, around the setback in the balcony, a tall lithe Negro with huge black eyes and an Afro haircut had been pacing back and forth. He was Joseph Louw, a documentary photographer for the Public Broadcast Library who was making a film on the Poor People's Campaign. Louw was an intense, brilliant young South African who had come to the United States five years before, as winner of a Columbia University scholarship. He had been following Dr. King and documenting the campaign as it unfolded.

Now, in the late afternoon, he felt strangely uneasy. Something impended, he was not sure. The night before, just as dusk was falling, he had come out on the balcony to get some air. It had been a hot, oppressive day, with rumblings of the storm about to break. A spring cold front was moving into the area, and the radio had warned repeatedly that Memphis was under a tornado watch. Dusk had fallen suddenly, too suddenly, as though one were in the tropics. Now lightning played in the sky, and in the distance the heavy clouds were banked in fantastic forms, a huge patchwork canvas of black and gray. A sharp breeze came up; one knew it was raining a tropical storm far out there, but no drops had fallen here yet.

The door of Room 306 had opened and Dr. King emerged. He was in shirt sleeves. He moved to the balcony railing in front of his door and stood there a moment, breathing deeply. He saw Louw and Louw said, "Hello, Doc." Dr. King nodded to him. Then a streak of brilliant lightning shot across the distant sky, seeming to rivet its way through the black clouds, followed by a mighty clap of thunder that shook the building. "Oh, wow!" Louw exclaimed. "Hey, Doc, now we really see who's boss!"

Dr. King said something like, "Yes, we do," stretched slowly, almost sensually, looking up at the sky, then turned and went back into his room.

Now, the next day, Louw was somehow troubled. After the great thunderstorm of the night before, the day had dawned bleakly; yet nature was trying to smile. Azaleas were coming out in bloom; a wintry April sun shone, and as the day progressed, it grew warmer, though the air was cool. For some reason it seemed too much trouble to think. It was like a day in a tale told by Camus: the same sense of man's helplessness, of nature pressing menacingly upon him. Louw felt almost overcome, becalmed. His thoughts trailed off into silence. By early afternoon it was even too much of an effort to try to organize his thinking. He felt disassociated as the hours moved on.

Well after four o'clock he forced himself to go out to a late lunch. He had been waiting to check Dr. King's program with him. Since the march had been moved up to Monday, April 8, King would probably remain in Memphis only long enough now to learn how the court ruled on the injunction. He was scheduled to preach at Ebenezer in Atlanta on Sunday. Louw wanted to know if he could take his cameras and equipment into the church; could he go on to the King residence later that day to document his life at home with Coretta and the children . . . ? But Dr. King had been busy with staff meetings. It was difficult to get a moment with him.

At five o'clock Louw jumped up from the table. He simply had to find Dr. King. He prowled about the motel for nearly half an hour, but the man was nowhere to be found. Not knowing quite what to do, he went back to his room and put in a telephone call to a girl friend in New York. The Huntley-Brinkley news show had just come on—it was 5:30 P.M. in Memphis, 6:30 in New York—and Louw, turning the sound down, watched absently while he talked on the phone. The girl's voice came to him: why was he calling her in the middle of the dinner hour?

"I don't know, myself," he said. "I'm feeling so restless. I just called —can't I call?" he demanded querulously. He added, "It's very tense down here." As the conversation went on, the strain to be civil became too much. He said abruptly, "I'll call you later," and hung up. She was so far away from everything going on here in Memphis. Everyone was far away. They could know nothing of the sense of impending violent confrontation—black against white, Dr. King against the black militants—Louw had talked with the Invaders, they were giving Dr. King a bad time, they wanted money, they were in touch with Beale Street types, they were making life difficult for Jim Bevel and Hosea Williams, who'd been assigned to cool them. . . . Nobody outside Memphis could know what was in the air here, especially the KKK's warning that it would hold a countermarch if King insisted on his march. At the court hearing Police Director Holloman had testified (so the radio reported earlier) that he had inside information of the Klan's plans. He could not prevent violence if both King and the Klan marched. "It could be worse than Watts or Detroit," he had warned. But Dr. King had been firm. His lawyers were fighting the injunction, but if they lost he was prepared to march anyway. They had not let dogs or water hoses turn them around in Birmingham, and "We aren't going to let any injunction turn us around in Memphis."

Louw paced back and forth. Even the weather was unsettling. He heard Chet Huntley's voice: "Tornadoes and thunderstorms swept through six states today. They killed at least thirteen people and injured over a hundred. The storm also caused flash floods which left hundreds homeless or isolated in Illinois, Kentucky, and Tennessee. . . ."

It was six o'clock. The news was over. Louw switched off the set, walked toward the door, when he heard a sound like a bolt of lightning striking. It seemed to shake the motel, as the loud clap of thunder had done the night before. It sounded: OOOOOOOHHHHH! —an atom bomb of sound that struck, then pulled back, creating a vacuum that waited to be filled, and then was filled by a screaming rush of air that exploded into a tremendous peal of sound. Louw knew he had heard a shot and then the reverberation of the shot.

He pulled open his door and leaned out gingerly, automatically looking toward the right. He saw Dr. King, no more than fifteen feet away, in the act of falling backward, slowly, infinitely slowly, as if in a dream sequence. Something had struck him, and whatever struck him hit him with incredible force on the right side of his body, because it swung him around to the right, jolting him, his back to Louw now, he was falling slowly, coming down, backward, his left hand still reaching out for the railing as he toppled back into the setback.

Louw rushed toward him. Now time played tricks. Could it have been more than five seconds—ten seconds—between the moment he saw Dr. King fall and the moment he was standing over the wounded man? But Dr. Abernathy was already there, kneeling beside him, and

Dr. King's mouth still seemed to be forming the exclamation "Oh!" It was a terrifying moment.

Louw stared. King's right jaw spurted blood. As from afar he heard a shout, "They shot Dr. King!"—and then, tumbling hollowly in his ears his own words, he did not know whether he thought them or moaned them, *O God, they killed him, how could they, they killed the one guy who really can stop all this violence, look how he is dying, he is dying right here.* . . .

He found himself backing away from Dr. King like a man retreating from the unspeakable and unbearable, backing away until he reached his room. *The man who's shooting is still out there, he can shoot us.* . . . He backed into his room, keeping his face to the unknown (it would be terrible to be shot in the back) thinking, *If I had a gun I could go out and get whoever it is, but all I've got to shoot with is my camera.* . . . The fear had gone. He had put one of his cameras in the drawer of his dresser and he tore open the drawer with the frenzied gesture of a man unable to wait to get his hands on a gun, seized his camera, and rushed out on the balcony, holding it to his eye, turning it in every direction, shooting everything he could. He pointed his camera—if only it were a gun—into the distance from where the bullet must have come, perhaps he could get the assassin himself in his lens! If only it were a gun . . . ! A gun! Then he wheeled to the right and photographed the scene for history, for ever after. Dr. Abernathy, Rev. Andrew Young, all who stood on the balcony at that moment, Dr. King bleeding at their feet, their arms outstretched, pointing, answering the question, pointing in the direction from which death had come.

In Room 215, below, Earl Caldwell, a black reporter from the New York *Times*, had been watching Huntley and Brinkley too. Like Louw, he was in a nervous state. He had been trying vainly to get a call through to his office in New York. He had a 6 P.M. deadline for the first edition, and he wanted to dictate a story into the recorder in New York reporting the events so far today. It was warm in his room and he had removed his trousers, and in shorts and socks was sitting on the edge of his bed, waiting impatiently for the motel operator to call him as soon as she had a line. All outgoing calls went through the motel switchboard. The Lorraine had only two long-distance lines and with King and his staff in residence these were continuously busy.

Caldwell's nervousness stemmed not only from his own difficulties.

An almost palpable sense of apprehension seemed to fill the motel. His editors in New York doubted strongly that King would defy the injunction. And Caldwell could not rid himself of the fear that something terrible might happen to Dr. King. Frequently through the long day he had glimpsed police cars slowly cruising by. They were obviously keeping the motel under surveillance. Caldwell thought, *How funny, they're watching us as if someone here is going to do something. What could anyone here do?*

The afternoon before Caldwell had emerged from his room to see Dr. King walking down to a telephone booth not far from the zigzag iron steps leading to the balcony. *Just think*, went through his mind, *a famous person like him walking down here alone—you'd think there'd be a big crowd. If he were walking on Fifth Avenue, hundreds of people would be following him, photographers would be taking photographs of him.* . . . The thought came to him: *Nobody's guarding him. He's just walking there.* . . .

Suddenly Caldwell jumped. A sharp report, like a shot, echoed outside. He ran to the door, pushed aside the curtain that hung there, and peeked out. He saw a shattered Coca-Cola bottle on the concrete of the courtyard, a man picking up the pieces from the splash of brown liquid. A maid had been delivering food on the balcony, the bottle had rolled off her tray and crashed below. Caldwell pulled back in relief. Why should he have thought it a shot? Probably the sight of King walking unprotected the day before had triggered the subliminal fear that someone, some sniper, might pick him off. . . .

It was getting closer to six o'clock, his deadline. Nearly seven in New York. He couldn't possibly make it now. Almost desperate, he tried the operator again. Still no lines available. It was too late anyway. He thought, why hadn't he tried that pay station outside. He'd simply have to miss the first edition. He'd certainly make the final edition. That deadline was 11 P.M., hours away.

The Huntley-Brinkley show was going off. Caldwell walked to the door to close it. Something of a chill had come into the air. From the TV he heard the familiar words, "Good night for NBC News," and then the opening strains of music presaging a commercial. He had turned away from the door toward the screen when a tremendous blast shook the building. It sounded like a giant firecracker. He ran to the door, pulling it open. He remembered later messing with the curtain again, and seeing through it vaguely, as in a phantasmagoria, the shapes of people acting crazy in the courtyard outside: jumping down, crouching, jumping up again—a strange wild dance of demented men and women. He thought, *Oh man, people playing with a firecracker. That's not even funny*. He was nervous because he had missed his deadline, he'd been on the *Times* for little more than a year now and he didn't want to miss deadlines, and he was still shaken by the bottle incident and his own overreaction to it, and now this . . . a Goddam firecracker!

He was aware of voices outside, but they did not subside. They rose, and now people were yelling, and now the voices merged into a wail, a great lamentation. He thought, *They've bombed the motel*. That was it, a bomb! It was not a sharp crack, like a firecracker. It was a blast sound reverberating.

He ran out in his shorts, then ran back, like a man in a nightmare, moving yet not moving, then out again, among the people still acting crazily in the courtyard. He looked up at the balcony and two trousered legs were visible on the edge. *King*, he thought. *I knew it!*

He raced back into the room, grabbed his trousers and raincoat and a sheet of paper and a pencil, and ran out again. A crowd of uniformed men was racing toward him, bearing down on him as if they had been hiding in the bushes across the way, on the other side of Mulberry Street. *Oh my God, it's the police, they're shooting at him*. Now they were all about, police, uniformed men, some in blue shirts, some in helmets, others with shotguns. One seized his arm and shouted in his face, "Where'd the shot come from?" Caldwell was so outraged he could not speak. The man released him and grabbed someone else. Caldwell, freed, rushed up the zigzag steps, taking them three at a time, his raincoat floating behind him, to where Dr. King lay. Dr. Abernathy knelt beside him; a large towel was on Dr. King's face, but it lay loosely in folds and Caldwell could see the wound. It was enormous, a hole as big as a man's fist had been torn in the lower right jaw, and the blood, instead of flowing as blood does when you cut your hand, seemed heavy, like crimson molasses, and was horridly stacking up upon itself. He heard Abernathy repeating, "Martin! Martin!" What he would never forget were Dr. King's eyes: twisting around strangely as if they were independent of each other, then slowly closing as he watched; but before they closed their color subtly changing, and lens and iris no longer distinct but one merging slowly into the other. The left eye was closed, now, but the right one would not. It remained open just enough to show the bottom of the right pupil. King's mouth was partly open, frozen in the moment of the scream that never came. Caldwell stared, horror-struck. He was certain King was dead.

All at once he realized: the story! Martin Luther King had been shot! Murdered! He wheeled around, rushed down the steps to the telephone that Dr. King had used the day before. He found a coin, and got through to New York almost instantly, and he dictated his terrible story over the sounds in the courtyard, of women screaming, of voices wailing, of someone shouting hoarsely again and again, "The police shot him!" of sharp commands, "Call the ambulance!" and "Get back, get back!" the merged sound of cars roaring to a stop, tires squealing, the clatter of men's heels on the concrete courtyard. He was telling his story now, even as Dr. King lay on the balcony; telling it not to an inanimate recorder but to a sentient, living human being in New York who was asking quick questions, uttering oaths under his breath, gasps of shock and sympathy and alarm. . . . *They'd shot Dr. King. How could he live with a wound like that? Oh, God . . .*

When he paused a moment, he heard a low muttering nearby. It was the Rev. James Bevel. He was wandering about aimlessly, now a few steps in this direction, now a few in that, talking to himself, his head down. "Murder . . . Murder . . . ! Doc said that wasn't the way." Shaking his head, muttering to himself. "And look what happens . . ." Then Caldwell recognized another voice—Jesse Jackson's voice—lamenting to someone, to the world itself. "We were all standing below him, and he was standing up there in front of us. . . ." And then Bevel again, in a kind of contrapuntal elegy of grief. "You knew he'd never be old . . . You couldn't think of Doc as an old man . . ." Then, silence, and Bevel again, muttering to himself, "It ended as it had to end. It was written that way."

Caldwell, taking a breath before dictating again, thought confusedly, *It's true, it's like a review you have read of a play and now you see the play. . . .*

Across Mulberry Street at his post in the fire station locker room, Patrolman Richmond, binoculars to his eyes, had been dutifully noting down what he saw at the Lorraine. At 5:50 he heard voices behind him in the station lounge—a TAC force, three police cars, four men to a car, had just pulled up outside. The group, led by Lieutenant J. E. Ghormley, had stopped for a rest break. While the driver of the lead car remained behind the wheel to monitor the police radio in case of emergency, the others flocked into the station. They had just completed their daily patrol of the afternoon march of strikers and students from Clayborn Temple up Main Street to City Hall and back again, and this was their first rest stop since before the march. Richmond heard their banter as he jotted down:

5:51 P.M. Doors of Room 316 and 317 open. Nine Invaders seen gathering up their belongings, bringing them downstairs and putting them into trunk of light blue Mustang. Car leaves motel going East.

5:56 P.M. Dr. King, in shirt sleeves, comes out of Room 306, stands on balcony. Rev. Kyles comes out of Room 306, they talk between themselves, then Dr. King goes back into room. Rev. Kyles stays on balcony, talking to male coloreds in courtyard below.

5:59. Dr. King walks out of room onto balcony again, he's wearing jacket now. He stands near railing, talking to coloreds below. Rev. Kyles on balcony to his right, also talking to people below.

A fireman, Lieutenant George Loenneke, came into the locker room to get a pack of cigarettes. Richmond looked away from his binoculars for a moment. "Dr. King's fixing to go out," he said. "I guess he's going to supper."

"Hey, I'd like to see him," said Loenneke. "Last time I saw him was when he made that Meredith walk into Mississippi." He walked to the rear door and peered through the other peephole in the paper. He saw Dr. King leaning against the railing of the balcony, both hands on the railing, talking animatedly with those below, who were looking up at him. In the lounge the clock on the wall showed 6:01.

The two men heard a sharp report, like two boards struck smartly together. Then in a shocked, unbelieving voice Loenneke gasped, "He's been shot."

Richmond, eyes glued to his glasses, stood transfixed. He saw it all clearly: Dr. King falling backward, his hands shooting up as if to grab his head, then landing heavily on his back.

A number of things happened almost simultaneously.

Loenneke raced out of the locker room, through the men's room and the engine room into the lounge, shouting, "Dr. King's been shot!" and sprinted out the side door and around to the rear toward the eight-foot drop to Mulberry Street. Richmond grabbed the direct line to police headquarters and blurted out, "Something's happened to King—he fell backward and grabbed his head and he's down and not trying to get up!" One of the firemen, Charles Stone, who had wandered into the rear room and clambered atop a locker to look through the small window above it, leaped down and raced through the station, adding his cries, "Dr. King's been shot!" Fire Captain

Carthel Weeden, in command of the station, picked up a direct line to the radio dispatcher at Fire Headquarters seven miles away, demanding an ambulance at once to the Lorraine Motel. An ambulance in Fire Station No. 3, five blocks from the Lorraine, shot out seconds later.* The eleven TAC men—one was drinking a Coca-Cola, another was telephoning his wife, who'd just returned from the hospital with a new baby, a third was at the coffee machine lifting a paper cup of coffee to his lips, others were watching the news on TV—bolted like one out of the side door and raced around to the rear, on Loenneke's heels. When some came to the drop, they halted, wheeled around and ran back to Main Street and north on Main Street to Huling and down Huling to Mulberry, to the motel. The others leaped the eight feet to the sidewalk of Mulberry Street, some falling and scrambling to their feet again and ran pell-mell toward the motel, pistols in their hands.

In their vanguard was Sheriff's Deputy William DuFour, a trim, athletic man of thirty-five. He dashed across the street and burst into the courtyard and took the zigzag steps to the balcony three at a time. It was Dr. King. He lay on his back, a towel over the right side of his face. A heavy-set Negro was kneeling beside him.

"Where's he been hit?" DuFour demanded. The other looked up at him wordlessly, then lifted the towel. DuFour was shocked. A hole the size of a man's fist seemed literally to have exploded at the right jaw line. The muscles of Dr. King's face twitched. DuFour cried out, "Dr. King, don't move!"

DuFour saw people milling about in Room 306 directly in front of him, a Negro screaming into the telephone, another circling aimlessly in the room. Now the ambulance was in the courtyard below, and he was helping lift Dr. King's surprisingly heavy body onto the stretcher, helping carry it—unexpectedly, a white man was at his side helping carry it too—down the awkward sharp turn in the stairs until they reached the courtyard.

They put the stretcher on the concrete. Dr. King looked suddenly small and helpless lying there. Someone pulled open the back doors of the ambulance, and they lifted the stretcher and pushed it into the

---

* The order for the ambulance was given at 6:04, it arrived at the Lorraine at 6:06, was on its way to St. Joseph's Hospital at 6:09. The driver, J. W. Walton, shouted on a two-way radio, "Give me the lights," and radio dispatcher R. G. Spencer pressed a switch at Fire Headquarters which turned all lights on north and south streets green, and all others red. It allowed Walton to speed without pause direct to the hospital.

back. The heavy-set Negro climbed in and sat there, holding Dr. King's right hand in both of his, still saying nothing. An attendant on Dr. King's left had placed an oxygen mask over the injured man's face and was holding it in place, the doors shut, and with a scream of sirens the ambulance pulled away followed immediately by a big white Cadillac.

DuFour stood there, Dr. King's blood staining red his gray whipcord puttees and the tops of his leather boots.

Eskridge, in the courtyard, had seen it all. He had run up and helped Andy Young and DuFour and Jim Laue lift Dr. King upon the stretcher and carry him down and get him into the ambulance. Then he had pushed Abernathy into the rear of the ambulance and shut the doors. He and Andy Young leaped into the Cadillac and Solomon Jones started the car. "Follow the ambulance," Eskridge ordered. Bernard Lee jumped in next to Jones, and then they were on the way to the hospital.

Andy Young thought how Martin had been turning himself inside out! Worrying, almost beside himself worrying, was he doing the right thing? He had been wrestling so with himself. And now they had taken him. He never thought Martin would go alone. They would all go; Rev. Young thought, all at the same time. There would be a bomb, a mass assassination to wipe them all out, wipe out the entire Martin Luther King movement in one blow. . . . So many threats in Selma and in Montgomery! So many times the police had to work out routes for them, time and again sending them down this street, around that one, so they would not pass by high buildings. "We can never make these completely secure," the police said.

And here, where they really never quite expected it, they had taken him on the balcony of a Negro motel, in the midst of his friends, surrounded by armed police at every turn. . . .

In the limousine following the ambulance, Chauncey Eskridge found his mind working with admirable clearness. To him, standing in the courtyard, the shot sounded like a sharp "ping" behind him, to the left. He had looked there and seen nothing. He turned to the balcony again, and there was Dr. King on his back; with that everything came to a jarring halt for some ten seconds, when he saw Ralph emerge from the room and heard him exclaim, "Oh, my God, Martin's been shot!" Then everything was jerked back into motion.

Somebody on the balcony shouted, "The shots are coming from there." Eskridge saw him point across the courtyard and looked in that direction. He saw the back of a decrepit two-story red brick building about two hundred feet across the street and a window on the second floor partly open; below it was the backyard of the building, thick with brambled bushes. Had the shot come from the window or the bushes below? He rushed out of the motel driveway into Huling Street and looked both ways. Nothing. No one on foot, no one walking or running, except to his right about half a block away an auto disappearing in the opposite direction.

Unexpectedly several police jumped over a retaining wall to his left. "Where did that shot come from?" one demanded. Eskridge pointed to where they'd jumped down, whereupon they ran back toward Main Street.

A squad car came from the right and squealed to a stop. Three policemen leaped out. "Where'd the shot come from?"

Again Eskridge pointed in the direction of the building and the bushes.

Then he ran back into the courtyard, and the ambulance was there. He had somehow helped organize matters and was in Solomon Jones's limousine following the ambulance to the hospital, trying to put into order the terrible event he had seen.

Eskridge's relationship with King was different from that of the others. He was not a fellow minister, he was not one of the SCLC staff; he was the older man, a legal adviser and financial counselor, and he had seen Martin grow and mature through the years. A few years before, Eskridge, then a bachelor living in a large apartment in Chicago, had often been King's host. Whenever King came to Chicago, he stayed with him. Others might deify Martin, but to Chauncey he was a young, ardent lover of life, a deeply spiritual man who was equally deeply human, a man of both worlds, with a sense of humor and a puckish approach to his intimates completely unknown to outsiders. Because he was held in such awe by much of the outside world, it was difficult for him ever to relax save with three or four friends. Only to them would he reveal his inner feelings, and only they knew his effectiveness as president of the SCLC, his skill as a handler of men.

Eskridge remembered how King worked with his SCLC staff. He was like a man driving a team of wild stallions; each sparked ideas, each was vigorous, freewheeling, forever going off on his own crusades. They were both his power and his problem, for often as he had to contend with outsiders who could not go along with what instinctively he knew was right, he also had to contend with his own lieutenants. He could not, he would not confront them. He sought to achieve his way by indirection, a skillful combination of rebuke, humor, and ruefulness enormously effective with the kind of proud free souls with which he had to deal. His habit was to wait until they were all together, and then pace the floor, not in the same room but within earshot. He would talk aloud to himself, imitating a famous black preacher, the late Rev. C. L. Flankin, who had been known for "whooping"—a form of public speaking in which the speaker builds skillfully, his voice rising higher and higher, bringing his audience to a higher and higher pitch of emotion until he reaches an unbearable climax—and his audience, reaching it at the same moment, is almost shattered by the intensity of its reaction.

King would walk the floor, and the others heard him: "Lord, I don't know what I'm going to do, because I don't have no friends. . . . Come and get me, Lord, because I have no friends. Lord, look at my lawyer. He's supposed to help me and he's not helping me. . . ." With rising voice: "Look at Jim Bevel, I looked for Jim today and he was nowhere to be found. Ohhhh, Lord, look at that Andrew Young. He's letting his hair grow, he's trying to look like them hippies, he don't know he's giving me a bad image. . . ." He would walk from one room to the other, his voice growing higher, his lamentation deeper: "I put my trust in my lawyer . . . he came an hour late to court . . . I looked for Bernard Lee to take a message . . . and Lord, he's out getting himself all slicked up . . . Who can I depend upon, O Lord!"

The ambulance had turned into a driveway; it had stopped; they were wheeling Dr. King into a long deep corridor to the emergency room. Eskridge followed and found himself in a small room where he sat and waited.

He had always known Martin's life was limited. In the fall of 1966 the Chicago police took Eskridge aside to give him a composite sketch of a Negro who they said was determined to kill Dr. King. The man was half crazed with the idea that King was a false Messiah, leading his people to disaster, and that it was his mission on earth to do away with him. Chauncey still had the photograph in his desk drawer. He had never found the man. King knew of these threats. Going from city to city, he was invariably met by police on arrival to tell him of the latest threats, to offer him escort and protection. He knew that in any crowd he addressed plainclothesmen were on hand —just in case. The menace was always there. He had to accept it, uncomfortable though it was.

There had been the July night a few summers ago when Chauncey had accompanied him to Winnetka, a North Shore suburb of Chicago, where King was to speak at 8 P.M. to a meeting on the village green. As they approached they saw one lone spotlight over the high platform; it would place the speaker under it in brilliant light, but the audience would be in pitch darkness.

King stopped for a moment. "Good God," he said huskily, "do I have to stand out there in that light?"

"You can't go out there, Martin," Eskridge said. "We can't see anything."

At this moment someone came up to them. "Dr. King, the people are waiting."

There was nothing to be done. Dr. King tugged characteristically at his lapels, to straighten the lines of his jacket, and walked out into the spotlight. For the next forty-five minutes he spoke into a sea of black. For Eskridge it seemed an eternity as he waited on the side for the bullet to come out of the darkness.

So, too, Dr. King had felt. When he left the platform, he said almost breathlessly, "Man, let's get out of here."

At the SCLC meeting in Miami only a few weeks ago police had posted guards in the corridor outside Martin's room at the Sheraton Four Ambassadors Hotel. One evening they had actually pleaded with him not to leave the hotel to make an address in Miami Beach. They simply did not want him to go out this night. He remained in the hotel. He could only assume they had something more alarming than the usual threats.

Now King lay in the emergency room, and they were fighting to save his life. Andy had said he felt a pulse. Eskridge thought, *If he lives, he will never be the same. I have seen that wound. He will never be able to speak again.*

Martin had always been afraid they would take his life. His greatest fear was that "a black brother might do it." So Malcolm X had died, at the hands of his own people. But whether it came from black or white, Martin knew it would come suddenly and violently. To Eskridge, as to others, he had said, "I'll never live to be forty. I'll never make it."

Would he live? Could he live?

CHAPTER VIII

They stood side by side, the Rev. Ralph Abernathy and the Rev. Bernard Lee in the emergency room, their backs against the wall. They would not budge. The nurses bustled about the small, brilliantly lit room—it could not be more than twelve by fifteen feet—telling them to leave, going away and returning to repeat, to plead, "You really must go." But they would not. They stood, two silent black men, hands clasped before them, backs against the wall, immovable as stone, while the doctors worked over Martin Luther King, Jr., as a huge fluorescent light beat down on him from the stark white ceiling and against the pale green walls strange machines with dials and flickering lights on orange screens had a life of their own.

Dr. Abernathy mused. To escape the awful horror of this moment, he found his mind going back and vivid pictures flooding into it. One of the last trips he and Martin had taken, only two weeks before, had been to Marks, Mississippi, the poorest black area in the country, part of their people-to-people tour in the deep South to mobilize for Washington. Martin heard the stories of the very poor—they had no jobs, no income, and when he asked how they survived, they said they ate plums from the plum trees, whatever they could beg from their neighbors, and whatever they could find, and whenever they could kill a rabbit. The children were thin and huge-eyed and uncomplaining. Martin listened to them with tears in his eyes. He said, "Ralph, we must take these people to Washington. Take them just as they are." He had said, "We are going to go to Washington. We have a grievance."

Before that, in late February, Martin's doctors had ordered him to take a rest. A vacation, even if it was only for a week, was imperative. Martin had suggested Acapulco, because Abernathy had never been to Mexico, rather than Jamaica, which was usually their first choice because black people were in charge there and they always enjoyed themselves. So they had agreed on Acapulco. On the Atlanta–Dallas leg of the trip, Martin had gotten into an argument with a white Southerner sitting across the aisle. He turned out to be a segregationist from North Carolina. It was unlike Martin to get into a personal confrontation. But Martin had attacked segregation, telling the man that he and his people would march on Washington and practice civil disobedience against the Government to make it see what it must do. When they landed in Dallas, the Southerner said, parting, "Well, sir, I certainly hope you'll be successful because this may be the last chance for nonviolence."

As the two of them walked down the ramp, Martin said, with a curiously relieved air, "I don't play with them anymore, Ralph. I tell them like it is. I don't mind making my position clear and I don't care who it offends because I must stand up for what I think is right."

They had a two-hour stopover in Dallas. "I want to take you to the restaurant here," Martin said, and they had dined leisurely together, Martin very much the host. They had both always liked the haberdashery in the Dallas terminal and they spent some time there. Ralph stood admiring a tie he had taken off the rack. Martin came up. "You really like that one?" "Yes, Martin." "Very well, you may have that one. Here—" and Martin had taken out his wallet and given Ralph his American Express credit card. "Ralph, pick out another one for me and four or five for yourself." He turned to the saleswoman. "Madam, put them all on my card." Then he had gone to make a long-distance call and Dr. Abernathy like a small boy choosing toys to delight himself, picked out some forty dollars' worth of ties. Gifts from Martin Luther King.

They had gone on to Acapulco. On the way Martin told him about one of the spectacles for which the town was known—the native boys making their dangerous high, arching dives from the steep cliffs into the Pacific. "I want you to have that experience, Ralph," he said. They had had dinner that night, and then wandered through the brightly lit, colorful shops. Martin had been so solicitous of him! Everything Ralph touched, Martin said, "Give that to him." If Ralph picked up a shirt, touched a slipover sweater—anything in which he showed interest—Martin would say to the clerk, "Give that to him." They had watched the diving later and then returned to their suite at El Presidente Hotel, which rose sheer above the sea with a small white balcony that seemed poised over the waters far below.

They read in their beds, and Ralph fell asleep.

He awoke suddenly, just before dawn, to discover that Martin's bed was empty. He looked in the bathroom—he was not there. In the living room—not there. Abernathy was disturbed. Then he thought of the balcony.

There was Martin in his pajamas, standing with his back to the room, looking out to sea. Far below, Abernathy could hear the roar and hiss of the waves beating against the shore. Martin made no indication that he was aware that Abernathy had joined him, and Ralph, alarmed, asked, "Martin, what is wrong?"

Martin shook his head. "Nothing." And then slowly, "Do you see what I see?"

Abernathy looked out to sea, but saw only the darkness of slate black sky and water merging together. "Well, no, Martin. What are you talking about?"

Martin said, "I was looking at that rock."

Abernathy peered again, and, straining his eyes in the far distance, he could just make out—it might have been a trick of light—a great gray rock thrusting out of the water.

"Do you know what I'm thinking about?" Martin said.

"No—"

"I'm thinking about a hymn."

Then Ralph knew. "It must be 'Rock of Ages, cleft for me—'"

"That's it," said Martin. They were both silent for a moment. Then, without a word or suggestion to each other, they began singing the hymn—the waves crashing and breaking below them, the rock growingly visible in the distant mists as the first rays of dawn came over the horizon behind them. They sang it, softly, in unison: 'Rock of Ages/Cleft for me/Let me hide/Myself in Thee. . . .' The waves breaking below gave an awful majesty to the moment.

Then they were silent. Martin remained looking out to sea, almost remote from him. Abernathy knew how troubled he was. He thought now, as he stood against the wall of the emergency room of this hospital in Memphis, watching almost subliminally as the doctors and nurses worked over Martin lying there on the operating table, *I wanted to help him but I didn't know how to help him.* . . . He knew Martin was in agony over the Poor People's Campaign no matter how strongly he had spoken to the man on the plane. He knew he suffered anguish because not only nonviolence, upon which he had based his strength and his life, was in question, but his own leadership. They had been together in so many battles since that day fifteen years before when they first met in Montgomery, where he was pastor of the First Baptist Church and welcomed the unknown new pastor of the Dexter Avenue Baptist Church, Martin Luther King, Jr., better known for his father's name than for his own. They had been two young ardent black Baptist preachers in their twenties, with the whole world—however hostile—before them. They had been inseparable since then. Martin would never go into any movement, any action, without him. Indeed, he had never gone to jail without Ralph going at his side and sharing his imprisonment. He would never advance an idea to his staff without discussing it first with him. But now, Ralph knew that Martin felt the terrible fear of the leader who may be leading his people into quicksand, whose ego had been assailed and who was no longer sure that his reading of the future was right, had to be right. Abernathy thought, torture upon torture in this unbearable moment, *I wanted to help him but I didn't know how to help him.* . . .

He was brought suddenly back to the present. A man in a white coat, his hands and arms in rubber gloves, was standing before him, saying words. "Are you his friend?" he was asking. "Are you his friend?"

Rev. Lee said, "This is Dr. Abernathy."

"Oh yes." The doctor spoke gently. "It would be the mercy of God if he did pass, because the spine is severed and there has been awful brain damage." He turned and indicated a tall bespectacled man in a white coat leaning over the table. "You see that man working there now—he is a neurosurgeon. He is doing everything he can."

Then time elapsed again, and Dr. Abernathy saw the man who had been pointed out as a neurosurgeon lay down his instruments and leave the room. He saw the doctor who had talked to him walk away from the operating table and come toward him again. "What they are doing now is to go another step," he said. "Every human life is important, but there are certain people whose lives are more important than others, and we take these extra steps, but—it's about all." He returned to the operating table again. Moments later, he shook his head and left the table and approached them for the final time.

"Dr. Abernathy, I am not going to make any statement to the press other than that he passed at a certain hour. I'll leave all the other statements to you."

He went out of the room.

Dr. Abernathy and the Rev. Bernard Lee approached the table. At one side of the room two nurses were doing things to the machines with their dials and screens, but no one was at the table. Dr. King lay on his back, unseeing, his face up to the light; directly before him, high on the wall before him, was a small silver crucifix. Had Dr. King been able to open his eyes and see, that would have been the first thing he would have seen—the tiny silver figure of Jesus on the cross looking down on him, and above the bowed head, the black letters IMRI.

The doctors who had worked on Dr. King had done so with such speed that there had been no time to disrobe him. The jacket of his black silk suit had been cut away on the right side, as well as his white shirt and the T-shirt underneath it, and all tucked under his back. His chest was bare. The wound at the jaw was enormous, but now the two men saw that it extended downward almost one inch below the collar bone. It was even worse than they had realized.

Silently Dr. Abernathy took from Dr. King's left coat pocket everything that was there—his checkbook and some papers. The Rev. Lee took from the left trouser pocket all that was in it. They did not touch the right side because this was the side of the body that the doctors had worked upon. Dr. Abernathy and the Rev. Bernard Lee were not relatives, but they did not want anyone telling them that they could not have these possessions, and at the same time they did not want anything taken from the body by others. They had not wished to approach the table before lest the doctors think they were trying to see the wound or seeking to fault them for not doing more.

Then the two men left the table with its body and walked into a small anteroom where the Rev. Andrew Young was sitting, his head in his hands. Outside Chauncey Eskridge waited. He had caught a glimpse of the wound when the towel fell away for a moment and could not bring himself to go into the emergency room.

Dr. Abernathy silently opened the door and beckoned to Chauncey to come into the room to join the three of them. Then he closed the door and said, "Now Martin is gone from us. Now we are alone." It was impossible to measure the grief in his voice.

Eskridge said, "Ralph, you now have to become our leader. You now are our leader. The television people are waiting outside. We know Coretta is on her way here. We are going to take you in front of the TV cameras and you say your say, and then we'll go to the airport and wait for Coretta."

Dr. Abernathy said nothing, but extended his arms in a wide, embracing gesture, and the three others wordlessly came within them and each man had his arms about the other and they hugged each other and all wept, their faces together, the four alone in the room. "Let us pray together," Dr. Abernathy said, and he led them in a short prayer: "We pray for the soul of Martin Luther King, Jr. May God in His infinite mercy bless him and keep his memory alive forever."

Then it was silent save for the distant sound of police sirens some-where in the city outside. In the silence, Eskridge again was the first to speak. His voice was firm. "We're ready now," he said. He and Andy Young each took Ralph by the arm, and they helped him out the door into the tumult of the TV cameras and the reporters. The powerful floodlights burst full upon them. The two men pushed Ralph gently forward into the cameras and stepped aside, and Aber-nathy said into the cameras what was necessary to say. Then the four men continued out the door into a waiting car and the police gave them an escort to the airport.

It was 7:25 P.M.

In his car, driving away from the hospital a few minutes later, Dr. Rufas Brown, a second-year resident in surgery at St. Joseph's Hos-pital, tried to organize his thoughts.

He had been the first doctor—the resident on emergency duty—to reach Dr. King. He had heard the intercom sound urgently, "Dr. Brown—emergency room!" shortly after six o'clock, while he was in the basement cafeteria having a coffee, and he had dashed upstairs and down long corridors and into the emergency room, where a nurse clutched his sleeve: "Oh, it's Dr. Martin Luther King!"

Dr. Brown, a white man, had grown up in Houlka, Mississippi, a town of some five hundred, and had practiced several years in the Mississippi Delta. He was not impressed by the patient's identity, but he hurried to the table and helped the nurses cut away the man's blood-encrusted clothes on the right side. He saw two black men standing against the wall and wondered why they were allowed to remain there, but the man on the table required all his attention. He needed an airway to breathe: the air was not getting to his lungs. Dr. Brown called for a tracheotomy tray, saw that the vital fluids were established, ordered the patient hooked up to a cardiograph machine and a monitor, and began the tracheotomy; and as he did so, other doctors came hurrying in. Dr. Brown had no hesitancy as to how to proceed. It was a clear trauma case, every resuscitation measure had to be attempted, the treatment was distinctly indicated.

He saw the wound. The bullet had struck with terrific force. There was still a heartbeat, a fairly strong one, as the orange screen of the monitor showed—a white jagged line, like vertical lightning, appear-ing and disappearing—but the bullet had passed through the chest and severed the spinal cord, and the patient responded to nothing.

For the next thirty minutes, with nearly a dozen doctors working

over Dr. King, everything that could be thought of was done. They
monitored all the systems; all were going simultaneously. He was supported as completely as any man could be supported. The neurosurgeon was there, the general surgeon, the chest surgeon, the lung
specialist, the kidney specialist, and as the minutes ticked on, those
working over the patient realized in a kind of delayed reaction who
this man was, and they redoubled their efforts. Each specialist was
there, men who could work miracles with every organ of the human
body, but the man who lay on the table simply possessed no viable
organs. A machine was breathing for him, life was being maintained
in him artificially, and though the heart was beating on its own, this
man was dead.

Slowly the cardiogram faded out; the orange screen was undisturbed; the needle on the moving tape of the cardiograph was motionless. The chief surgeon drew back, pulled off his gloves, and
walked away. Dr. Brown moved away too, with the others, and as he
passed by the cardiograph machine, he tore off the tape showing the
last zigzaggings of Dr. King's heartbeat, and then the final flat line of
death, and put it in his pocket. He thought, *King is nothing special
to me. I did as much for him as I would do for anyone.* He thought,
walking away, getting into his car, *I'll keep the tape for my children.*

CHAPTER IX

It might be said that the search for Dr. King's assassin began almost with the shot itself. When the TAC squad rushed out of the fire station, Lieutenant Ghormley, in command, was one of those who stopped short at the embankment in the rear and did not leap down to Mulberry Street. One glance told him the motel was well covered; his men were racing toward it as fast as their legs would take them. But the gunman! Just as Redditt and Richmond could see King clearly from their post at the rear door of the fire station, so a sniper would have been able to pick off King from the rear of any other building on Main Street. Ghormley, pistol in hand, dashed back to Main Street and looked swiftly in both directions, hoping to see someone running with a gun. He saw nothing. It was like magic—a street swept clean, nothing moving, no man or vehicle. Hell, thought Ghormley, running down Main Street toward Huling on his way to the Lorraine, a guy would only have to run fifty yards and he'd have a street he could turn into, east or west.

He stopped short in front of Canipe's. The entrance was at a diagonal from the front show window so that it created a triangular setback. In front of the plate glass door, in the shadows, he made out a bundle. A dirty green bedspread had been thrown over what appeared to be a blue suitcase, next to it a long cardboard box from which protruded—it was unmistakable—five or six inches of the business end of a rifle—cold blue-green steel. Ghormley planted himself in the doorway and called headquarters on his walkie-talkie and told them what he had found. He was ordered to guard the bundle until Captain Jewell G. Ray of the Internal Security Division, who was already on his way, arrived.

At this moment the door of Canipe's unexpectedly opened and a white man emerged. Ghormley was taken aback. He had thought the shop closed. It was after six o'clock, when most shops were closed. But also the play of light was such that the windows, grimy with dirt, appeared opaque, even deserted. Perhaps whoever dropped the bundle also thought the place was closed. The man who emerged was Guy Canipe, owner of the shop. Behind him Ghormley saw the frightened faces of two Negroes. "You see who put this down?" Ghormley demanded, pointing to the bundle with his gun.

Canipe said hurriedly, yes, he saw him. "A white man, a little under six feet, pretty well dressed, dark-headed, no hat, wearing a dark suit." He blurted it out in one breath. "He just came by the door, dropped the stuff—I heard the thud, that's what made me look up just in time to see his back, walking away, going south—" Canipe gestured to his left. He'd been sitting at his desk in the back of the store while his two Negro customers had been playing secondhand records on his jukebox. When he heard the thud and looked up and through the plate glass of the door, he saw the man walking away. He thought, *Somebody's given me a present.* A year ago a drunk left a TV set in the doorway. He opened the door and walked out on the sidewalk to see what happened to the man, but he had vanished. Just at that moment a white Mustang, maybe 1966 or 1967, which had been parked south of his place suddenly pulled away. "He sure burned leather." There was only one man in it—the driver. He couldn't say if the driver was the man he'd seen walking away, but the man certainly wasn't anywhere in sight. Canipe turned around and stared at the bundle in his doorway. At first it looked like the back-seat cushion of a car with a blanket thrown over it. Then he saw the blue barrel of the rifle extending from the box, under the blanket, pointing at him. At that point his two customers, who'd also seen the man walking away, began to come out, but Canipe pushed them back and went inside, shutting the door quickly. "Stay back, there's going to be trouble," he said. He had just seen Ghormley suddenly come into sight, revolver drawn, bearing down on him.

Ghormley immediately related this information to headquarters. Seconds later—it was 6:08—Memphis police broadcast the first alarm for King's assailant—"Suspect described as young white male, well-dressed, believed in late model white Mustang, going north on Main from scene of shooting."

Meanwhile, Captain Ray and Lieutenant Jim Papia had raced to the fire station, talked briefly to a shaken Richmond, and sprinted down Main Street to come upon Ghormley, pistol in hand, standing guard over the bundle. "The guy dropped this," he said.

Captain Ray knelt down and looked at the bundle. A green and brown blanket or bedspread covered much of the cardboard box, and under it he could see part of a blue zippered bag. He took a pencil from his breast pocket and with it gingerly lifted the edge of the lid of the box, which had the word BROWNING on it. He peered inside. The rifle was there, no doubt of it, with a telescopic sight on it and beside it a box of shells.

Lieutenant Papia had taken this moment to dash up the nearest stairs, of 422½. There was a landing at the head of the stairs, and a short passageway to the left into the adjoining building. He ran through it and found himself making a sharp right into a long hall. At the other end a tall man with a high-domed forehead in a T-shirt and khaki slacks and a short plump woman in a gay print were standing in front of the door of one of the rooms. When he came nearer he saw the woman gesticulating excitedly, mouthing words but making only inchoate sounds.

"Did you hear a shot?" Papia demanded. The woman—he realized belatedly that she must be a deaf-mute—apparently read his lips, for she pointed to the bathroom at the end of the corridor. The man said in a gravelly voice, "I heard what sounded like a shot come from the bathroom. A white man moved in today and I saw him run out just after I heard the shot." He pointed to 5B. "He ran out of there."

The door was open. Papia walked in. What struck him was that there was nothing in the room—no luggage, nothing. On the floor was a short black leather strap. A second one, with a metal buckle, was on the couch. The bed had not been slept in, but it was indented on the left side, the side nearest the door, as if someone had just been sitting there. The single window was three-quarters open. The curtains had been pushed to one side to rest atop an adjacent mantelpiece; a straight-backed chair was placed at a corner of the window, so one sitting there could get a view of the Lorraine Motel.

Just then Captain Ray, who had ordered the bundle downstairs guarded by three men till Homicide got on the scene, hurried into the room. "Looks like this man was sitting there watching through the window," Papia told him. "Doesn't look like a good angle to shoot from, though." The two went into the corridor and into the bathroom. Here the window was pushed open from the bottom about four inches. Papia tried to move it, but it was jammed. Whoever had pushed it up had done so violently and left it that way. There had been a screen on the outside. Papia saw it on the grass below as he looked down. Then he looked across to the motel. "Yeah," he said. "He could get a good shot from here."

Both men stared at a palm print on the wall above the tub—a man's palm print, from the size of it. There were unmistakable scuff marks of shoes in the tub. Someone had stepped into that tub and stood there. Papia put his own palm over the print, not touching it because Homicide would have to dust it and lift it. Obviously the man stepped into the tub putting out his hand to steady himself against the wall, had shoved the window up so sharply that it jammed; had pushed his rifle through, knocking away the screen, and, standing in the tub, rifle resting on the window sill, had drawn his sights on Dr. King some two hundred feet away. If one stood in the tub, placed his feet in the scuff marks, and looked out the window, one *had* to look directly at the balcony of the Lorraine, directly at Room 306, Dr. King's room, the room in front of which he stood when the bullet struck him.

Captain Ray had been searching the tub and the floor for a spent shell. He found nothing. He turned to Charles Stephens, the tenant of 6B, who was now standing in the hall, looking in. What had he seen? A great deal, it appeared. About three-thirty he had heard Mrs. Brewer's voice just outside his door. He had been tinkering with the hot water heater. It was in his kitchen but served the entire building, and he had finally managed to get it to work. He opened his door to see Mrs. Brewer talking to a man in a dark suit in front of 5B, spoke to her briefly, and closed the door. He assumed the stranger—he'd seen only his left profile—took the room, because later he heard sounds like someone moving furniture around in it. Two or three times in the next hour or so he heard footsteps going from 5B past his door to the bathroom, then returning. The first time the man stayed only a few minutes, the toilet flushed and he went back to his room. The second time he remained slightly longer, but the toilet was not flushed. The third time he remained for a long time. Stephens was sitting at his kitchen table, pushed against the common wall that separated his kitchen from the bathroom, working on a portable radio. After about half an hour, Willie Anschutz, who lived in 4B, knocked on his door.

"Who in hell is staying in the bathroom so long?" Anschutz demanded. Stephens opened his door long enough to say, "It's the new roomer in 5B," and closed it again. He didn't get along too well with Anschutz and kept his conversation with him to a minimum.

The bathroom was much on Stephens' mind. The wall separating his kitchen from the bathroom was of thin plywood and he always heard everything that went on in there. It was a nuisance. Secondly, Mrs. Stephens, as he called her, was in bed—he had brought her home from the hospital only Monday after surgery for female trouble, and he frequently had to help her from the bed to the bathroom. Once or twice he tried to get in, but it was latched from the inside.

Around six o'clock he was working on the radio when he heard a shot. Stephens had served in Italy in World War II, and had been badly wounded. As he was to say later, "I got my head caved in, my neck broke, my chest caved in, my back broke, bullets still in my left leg. I know a shot when I hear one." This sounded like a German .88. It was very loud and from the bathroom. Since Anschutz's knock on his door, he realized he had not heard the toilet flushed or any footsteps going back to Room 5B. Subconsciously he had been waiting for a signal that the bathroom was free. Suddenly he heard shouts and screams from the rear. He jumped up and looked out his kitchen window—the glass was broken—the cries came from the courtyard of the Lorraine, which was full of people milling around. He heard Anschutz's voice just outside his door: "Charlie, come here!" He jerked the door open and stepped out in time to see the new roomer —the man in the dark suit—going around the corner of the end of the hall leading to the stairs. He was carrying something in his right hand, about three feet long, maybe six inches thick, wrapped in what looked like a newspaper. Then he disappeared around the turn. Stephens wheeled around, saw Anschutz in the bathroom peering out the window, and ran back to his kitchen window to look out again. Under the window, in the yard below, a helmeted policeman waved his revolver at him and shouted up, "Get back from that window!" Stephens backed away and sat down in his chair. From her bed Mrs. Stephens was asking weakly, "What is it? What's happening?" Then, suddenly, the place seemed full of policemen and when Stephens asked, "What happened?" someone said, "Martin Luther King was shot." Stephens hadn't even known King was at the Lorraine.

Stephens could not know that his two glimpses of the roomer in 5B would change the course of his life for the next year and more, and make his sad, long face known throughout the world as the state's key witness in the assassination of Martin Luther King, Jr.

Willie Anschutz had been in his room with Mrs. Ledbetter, the deaf-mute, sharing Cokes and cookies as they watched a movie on his TV, when he heard the shot. He sat for a moment, not quite knowing what to do, then went to his door and opened it just as the roomer in 5B hurried out of his room and went by him carrying something wrapped in a cloth in his right hand. "Hey, that sounded like a shot," Anschutz said. "Yeah, it was a shot," said the other, fling-ing the words over his shoulder as he went by, meanwhile holding his left hand up so that Anschutz never did get a good look at his face.

Captain Ray, making notes, asked, "Where's the landlord?" Mrs. Ledbetter, who had been hovering by, plucked his sleeve and led him back down the hall through the connecting passageway to the other wing and pointed to the door of Room 2. Captain Ray knocked. "Open up," he said loudly. "It's the police."

There was the sound of a bolt being drawn, and the door swung open to reveal a man and woman, who stared at him apprehensively. They identified themselves—Mr. and Mrs. Frank Brewer. She was the landlady.

"Who rented that center room in the other part of the building?" Captain Ray asked.

Mrs. Brewer rustled in a bureau drawer. She was nervous. She and Frank, who had come home from work a little before, had just fin-ished supper. She was washing the dishes and he was watching "Raw-hide" on TV, his shoes off, his bedroom slippers beside them, when they heard a sharp noise. "What was that—a shot?" asked Mrs. Brewer. Then they heard screams from the Lorraine Motel area in the rear. Frank took time to put on his slippers and they ran into the hall. They heard a shrill voice from the rear. "Oh, God, help me." Frank ran to the back door. It was kept locked because drunks and winos often slept in the yard and were always coming up the back steps, either for handouts or to steal what they could—and it took about twenty seconds to get the door open. He stepped out on the back landing. The yard below was swarming with policemen and firemen. One policeman brandished his revolver at him. "Get back into the house and lock the door!" As Frank started back, another at the foot of the steps shouted, "The shot came from there—" point-ing toward the northeast corner of the rooming house. Not knowing precisely what had happened, confused by the screaming and wailing from the Lorraine, the Brewers—she had gotten as far as the rear door—ran back toward their room, almost colliding with Willie An-schutz in the hall. "Hey," he said excitedly, "looks like your new roomer ran down the stairs with a gun."

Mrs. Brewer hastened to Room 5B. It was empty, the dresser that had been in front of the window had been moved, the chair put in its place. She glanced into the bathroom. Someone had pushed the

window open from the bottom. She ran back to her room and she
and Frank bolted the door and had been sitting there, minding their
own business, until now.

Mrs. Brewer, explaining all this, found what she was looking for—
her receipt book. She opened it to a stub showing she had written out
a receipt for $8.50 for one week's rent, for Room 5B, to one John
Willard.

When was this? Captain Ray asked.

Just a little while ago—maybe around three-thirty or so.

Who was Mr. Willard, and would she begin at the beginning and
tell everything she knew?

Downstairs, Lloyd Jowers, owner of Jim's Grill, had heard the shot
as he sat behind his cash register in the front of the restaurant, but
thought a pan had crashed in the kitchen. He went back to investigate. Then he heard the wailing from the motel, and suddenly his
front door burst open and a deputy was there, waving a revolver and
shouting, "Everybody sit down—put your hands on the table—don't
move!" Jowers had driven up in his white Cadillac at 3:50 P.M., only
to find a white Mustang in his usual parking place in front of the
restaurant. Cursing under his breath, he pulled his car directly behind it, bumpers almost touching, so he would not be too close to a
fire hydrant behind him. He noticed that the Mustang had a red and
white back license plate. Later, some time after the shot—it was about
6:15—when he was permitted to stand with customers at his front
window, looking out, he realized that the Mustang was no longer
there. He had not seen it leave. Several customers who had come in
just before six o'clock said they'd seen a white Mustang parked down
the street, to the south, the other side of Canipe's place. Could it
have been the same car? Or had there been two white Mustangs
parked on South Main Street, one about sixty feet behind the other?

In Canipe's shop his two customers, Bernell Finley, forty, and Ju-
lius Graham, twenty-two, were about to put a record on the turn-
table when they heard a thud. They looked out the window. Finley
saw a man walking away, hurriedly, to the left; he went to the door,
saw a bundle, opened the door, heard tires squeal, and a white Mustang shot by him, going to the right. Graham saw a man walk swiftly
by, drop a package, and continue on, to the left; he saw only his back
as he passed the doorway. Seconds later a white Mustang sped by, to
the right. Then Canipe, who had gone out to see who had dropped
the bundle, was coming back into the shop, pushing them both back

from the door, saying, "Stay back, there's going to be trouble." Then the police were there, brandishing their revolvers.

In Room 5B of the rooming house, Inspector N. E. Zachary, chief of Homicide, moved carefully about while his men dusted for fingerprints on the dresser, the chair, the walls, and took with them the two straps, the pillows, the bed sheets, the blanket to make chemical tests on them. They took sweepings from the floor. They found particles of dried grass, undoubtedly brought in on the shoes of Mr. Willard. Room 5B had been empty for nearly three weeks. The last tenant, a Commodore Stewart, had died there, and the room had been thoroughly cleaned by the businesslike Mrs. Brewer. One would have to assume that anything that had not been there before had been brought in by Mr. Willard. The man, then, had not been walking on pavement alone—could he have been walking about in the backyard, checking out vantage points from which to shoot? Inspector Zachary's men also found two square wooden kitchen matches in front of the sofa, and a similar match, unburned but its head missing, in front of the fireplace. Zachary moved into the bathroom. His men dusted the palm print on the wall, gathered the dirt and dust and mud that were the scuff marks in the tub. He examined the window sill. It was rotted and battered by the years, but he made out in the middle of the sill an indentation shaped like a tiny half moon. It could be the mark on the soft wood left by a hard object, like the barrel of a rifle. He sent a man downstairs to Canipe's to borrow a handsaw, a hammer, and a screwdriver. Five minutes later he had removed the center section of the sill and it was on its way to Homicide Headquarters, where it would join the rifle and the rest of the bundle of evidence that was now in a small locked storeroom, guarded by a policeman, awaiting examination.

The search for the murderer—or murderers—of Martin Luther King was already under way.

CHAPTER X

At Memphis Airport, Abernathy and the others waited for Coretta King.

Then word came to them that she had canceled her plans to fly to Memphis from Atlanta this night. She had been home earlier in the evening when she received a telephone call from Jesse Jackson, the first to get through to her from Memphis. "Doc just got shot," he said. "Take the first plane here." And he added, "He was shot in the shoulder."

She turned on the TV and began to dress. A moment later the announcer's voice: Dr. King had been shot in the head. She faltered for a moment, then continued to dress. Then another call from Memphis. It was Andy Young, calling from the pay station phone just outside the emergency room of St. Joseph's Hospital: Martin was in critical condition. He had been shot in the neck. But he was not dead. He repeated it. He was not dead.

Little by little she was being prepared. But, of course, she had been prepared for a long time.

She managed to get dressed, and with close friends at her side she was driven to the airport by Mayor Ivan Allen, of Atlanta, who had hurried to her house. There she heard herself paged, and saw Dora McDonald, Dr. King's long-time secretary, running toward her, and she knew, when she saw her, that her husband was dead. Mayor Allen confirmed the terrible news a moment later. She had turned back, then, and the mayor had taken her home to her four children. She would fly to Memphis tomorrow morning to pick up her husband's body and bring it back to Atlanta for burial.

A policeman touched Abernathy on the shoulder. Dr. Jerry Francisco, the medical examiner, wished to see him at once about performing an autopsy. Forty-five minutes later the two men met in the laboratory of the John Gaston Hospital, the Memphis morgue, where Dr. Francisco had his office. Dr. King's body lay in an adjoining room, where it had been brought from St. Joseph's Hospital.

Dr. Francisco, solid, bespectacled, his blond hair crew-cut, explained that he had already been on the telephone with Attorney

General Phil Canale, chief prosecuting officer of Shelby County, who would have to prepare the murder case against the assassin—or assassins—when and if captured. He and General Canale had agreed that everything must be done to avoid the confusion that marked President Kennedy's assassination: the questions as to the exact cause of death, the number of bullets that struck him, the nature of the injury. There was still a doubt in the minds of some Americans whether the wound in President Kennedy's throat was made by a bullet entering or exiting. There would always be those who maintained that John Kennedy had been shot simultaneously by at least two gunmen, firing from different vantage points.

An autopsy would answer many questions, Dr. Francisco explained. What did the bullet strike? How long before striking and injury? Was there any other possible cause of death? What was the precise direction taken by the bullet as it entered the body? From this it could be possible to ascertain the point from which the bullet came. (Dr. King's assassination already had its Grassy Knoll equivalent. Not only had Solomon Jones said he saw a man in a white hood running from the bushes below the bathroom window, but one Harold "Cornbread" Carter, an elderly one-time football star well known in neighborhood bars, had told police he was sitting drinking wine in the bushes at six o'clock when a man with a rifle suddenly appeared, fired once at King and then fled, going by him so close "he kicked gravel on me.") Was there anything medically that could have been done for Dr. King that was not done? (Attorney General Ramsey Clark in Washington had already received reports that Dr. King had been permitted to bleed to death.) Could some other bullet have gone through the same hole in Dr. King's jaw?

Only an autopsy could resolve these questions.

While awaiting Abernathy's arrival from the airport, Dr. Francisco had made a preliminary examination and told Canale of his findings: a gunshot wound through the face, passing through the chin into the chest, the bullet coming to rest just under the skin of the back. Canale had asked, "Can you say without question that this bullet was the cause of death?" On the basis of preliminary study, the answer was yes. Could he recover the bullet? Yes, Dr. Francisco said. He could feel it with his fingers.

In order to perform the autopsy, the medical examiner now told Abernathy, he must obtain permission from next of kin—from Coretta King. The autopsy should be done as soon as possible. Could Abernathy get Mrs. King's authorization by phone?

At eight o'clock Abernathy called Mrs. King in Atlanta. When she came to the phone, calm, self-contained, he put Dr. Francisco on an extension and they held a three-way conversation. Mrs. King sounded composed but anxious, as she listened to the reasons for the autopsy. Dr. Francisco had heard that Dr. King had resigned himself to the possibility of assassination. Obviously he must have prepared his family as well. It explained in part his widow's self-control.

When they hung up, Dr. Francisco had one more duty for Dr. Abernathy and the Rev. Andrew Young, who had accompanied him back from the airport. "I must have witnesses," he said. "You must attest that it is Dr. King in the next room."

The two men followed him into the next room—the morgue where Dr. King's body lay on a table. Abernathy approached the table and put his hand gently on Dr. King's cheek, the cheek he had touched when they were on the balcony immediately after King fell. "Yes, that's him," he said, and turned away and left.

For the next two hours, while an FBI agent and Lieutenant Jim Hamby of Memphis Homicide watched, and a second agent maintained vigil outside the door, Dr. Francisco and two assistants carried out their duties. In Dallas, though the autopsy on President Kennedy had not been done ineptly, there had been extraordinary confusion. To top it off, the original autopsy notes had been burned. Dr. Francisco therefore worked with extreme care; photographing, measuring, documenting, identifying. The nose of the bullet had been deformed, because it had struck Dr. King's jaw and spine, but whether it had been so mutilated that it could not be matched to the bore of the rifle could only be determined in the laboratory—if the rifle found at Canipe's was the murder weapon. Dr. Francisco ascertained the path of the bullet. It came from above, downward, but since Dr. King had been bending when it struck, the medical examiner could not abstract the path to establish without doubt the exact point from which it came. The wound was so large, and the body bending even slightly could alter the angle considerably. Dr. Francisco concluded that it could have come from the roof of one of the buildings, or from the windows immediately below. When he extracted the bullet, he photographed it, then scratched on it "252"—the number of Dr. King's autopsy—placed it in a manila envelope, and gave it to Lieutenant Hamby, who took it at once to Memphis FBI headquarters, where it would join the other evidence and be flown by courier that night to Washington. It was not a dumdum bullet, as had already been mistakenly reported: it did not spread or explode on impact. The enormous wound had been caused by the explosion of air outward as the high-velocity bullet struck.

Dr. Francisco determined that Dr. King had died from the bullet wound. No heart attack, no stroke. Death was practically instantaneous. It depended on how one described death, for there were really two kinds of death—somatic and cellular. The first was that point in time in which the body failed to function as a unit. The second, that point in time when the last cell died. Obviously, cell death occurred much later than somatic death. The doctors in the emergency room had found a pulse. Some functioning existed, but as an organized, intact unit that one would identify as a living human being—no. One would have to say that Dr. King had died almost instantly.

As Dr. Francisco worked over the body, he noticed almost directly above Dr. King's heart a faint scar in the shape of the cross. It was puzzling; to the lay observer, it might take on almost an eerie symbolism—a thin line down the center of the chest about six inches, a second line crossing it and extending to the right about eight inches. Dr. Francisco simply noted these in his report. He could not know their significance. When Dr. King had been almost fatally stabbed by the demented woman in Harlem nearly ten years before, the surgeon had found it necessary to remove two ribs in order to get at the tip of the blade, so perilously near the aorta. Because Dr. King was a minister, and, knowing that the scar would be permanent, he thought it was "somehow appropriate" to make the incision in the shape of the cross, as he told Coretta King sometime later.

It was eleven o'clock before Dr. Francisco had finished dictating his notes in great detail* and an assistant telephoned the R. S. Lewis Funeral Home. Dr. King's body was ready to be taken for embalming—a task that would demand great skill in preparation because of

---

* His concluding paragraph read: "Death was the result of a gunshot wound to the chin and neck with a total transsection of the lower cervical and upper thoracic spinal cord and other structure in the neck. The direction of the wounding was from front to back, above downward and from right to left. The severing of the spinal cord at this level and to this extent was a wound that was fatal very shortly after its occurrence." Had Dr. King by some miracle lived, aside from the massive brain damage, he would have been paralyzed, save for his arms, from the chest down.

the size and prominence of the wound, for lying in state for brief services before being taken to Atlanta for the funeral on Tuesday.

A little while before, a heavy-set middle-aged Negro arrived at the Lorraine Motel. After showing his credentials to the police on duty, he was allowed to enter the courtyard. He slowly climbed the motel steps and walked along the balcony until he came to Room 306. Martin Luther King's blood had congealed in a huge clot, almost covering the setback where he fell.

The man was Ernest Withers, a photographer on Beale Street, who with his camera had recorded most of the important moments in the civil rights struggle in the South. Since 1954 he had been photographing Dr. King: in Montgomery during the bus strike; in Washington during the great march of 1963; in Selma in 1965 during the march; in Little Rock during the integration of Negro students. He had photographed Dr. King arriving at Memphis airport yesterday morning, he had photographed him as U.S. marshals served the restraining order on him in the courtyard yesterday afternoon, and he had photographed him as he spoke last night in Mason Temple. Tomorrow morning, after the embalmer had done his work, he would photograph Martin Luther King in death.

He stared at the blood. It looked uncannily like a silhouette of Dr. King, in jagged profile, head, neck, and shoulders—but a damaged, ravaged silhouette, as though it were a wooden target in a much-used rifle range. But it was recognizable. One actually saw the shape of head, indentation of eyes, the nose, the shoulders. This was the mark his head and shoulders might have left had he emerged from his room, all bloody, as in an unbelievable nightmare, and fallen on his left side.

Withers pushed open the door to Room 306. The night maid was tearfully tidying up the room. "Is there a pill bottle in the medicine cabinet?" he asked. She found two for him. He emptied them of their contents. They were cold tablets. Then he returned to the balcony and, using a piece of cardboard, carefully scooped up enough blood to fill them both. One bottle bore the label of the 4th Street Drug Store, in Jackson, Mississippi, owned by Dr. Aaron Henry, President of the Mississippi State NAACP. How strange, how ironic, Withers thought, that this bottle in which Dr. Henry or someone in his shop had put cold capsules for Dr. King now held his blood.

Withers left the motel and drove back to his studio. Here and there were the debris and charred ashes of shops that had already been looted and burned in reaction to the assassination. On the walls of Withers' studio were photographs he had taken through the years: of George Lee, murdered May 7, 1955, lying in his coffin; of Herbert Lee, murdered July 15, 1961, lying in his coffin; of Medgar Evers, murdered June 12, 1963, lying in his coffin; of Malcolm X, murdered February 21, 1965, lying in his coffin; and soon to be joined by a photograph of Martin Luther King, Jr., murdered April 4, 1968, lying in his coffin. Withers carefully wrapped the two small bottles in tinfoil and placed them far back on a shelf in his refrigerator. He had no idea whether he was doing something right or wrong, something permissible or something unpermissible. It was Martin Luther King's lifeblood he kept, it was a keepsake, it was the awful, the sacred remembrance.

It was an hour after midnight, Friday. Memphis was a ghost city. No traffic moved, save armed patrol cars and military carriers. Curfew had been declared at 7:30 P.M., and at that hour strange scenes had taken place. In some restaurants diners rose in the middle of their meal and left. In others, the owner went from table to table: "We're closing up. We think you'd better leave at once and get to your homes." Cars sped by quickly. Buses moved rapidly to their destinations. The streets were swept clear of cars, people, any living thing. Shops grew dark. The city was black.

One saw lights in houses go out, one by one, plunging them into darkness, for lit windows might become inviting targets for snipers and roving bands. Driving by, one might see here and there a faint blue glow seeping from the edge of windows: the entire family huddled in one room before their television, blinds drawn, watching, listening, terrified. High over the rooftops a police helicopter floated, its brilliant blue searchlight eerily bathing the streets below like some Martian space machine.

It was a night of rioting, fire bombing, looting. By midnight eighty persons had been arrested, nearly thirty injured, and at one period firemen from one station were answering calls one every three minutes. Three artillery battalions had been put to work in the city, nine patrols of sixteen men each were on duty, and everywhere the National Guard, their troops ringing the city.

An emergency meeting was in process in Room 306 of the Lorraine Motel. It was 1 A.M. The easy chair in which Dr. King had lounged earlier that day was empty. Dr. Abernathy and the staff members of

SCLC were arranged about the room. All had been questioned by police: in the hours before midnight they had been taken by police escort to headquarters, placed in separate interrogation rooms, and dictated to stenographers what they knew; then a police escort had returned them to the motel.

They had met to determine: What now? The problems facing the SCLC were those of survival. How would they go on without Dr. King? What should they tell the black people of America? Which way must they go now?

There had been a long silence when they first assembled. Then the Rev. James Bevel rose. "Why are we so despondent?" he demanded. "We have our leader. Ralph is our leader. I loved Jesus, and I loved King as much as I loved Jesus—and in many instances I loved him more. But he's dead now, and he isn't coming back, and Ralph's our leader." He turned to the Rev. Abernathy, who sat immobile, a man stricken. "Ralph, we're behind you. Just lead. Tell us what to do."

Everyone remembered the meetings at which Dr. King had said that, if anything should happen to him, he wanted Abernathy to succeed him.

Dr. Abernathy, after a moment, slowly rose and took Dr. King's chair, and the meeting began. The first order of business was the unanimous decision to go forward with the Poor People's Campaign. The march on Washington would be held as Dr. King wanted it to be held. The second was Dr. King's funeral. Everything would wait on Mrs. King's approval, but there had been a number of offers of private planes to take Dr. King's body back to Atlanta, and it was decided to accept that of Senator Robert Kennedy. It was agreed that there would be private services for the family and members of SCLC at the Ebenezer Baptist Church, where Dr. King's father was now sole pastor, and where the father would now preach over his son's coffin. There would be public services later the same day at Morehouse College, also in Atlanta, the school which Dr. King entered at fifteen and from which he was graduated at the age of nineteen. As his friends knew, had fate ordained otherwise, he would have been content to spend the remainder of his life as president of Morehouse College.

The meeting lasted through the night. Before it ended a request was telephoned to the Memphis police; would protection be afforded to Dr. Abernathy, the new president of the Southern Christian Leadership Conference? Two plainclothesmen were waiting outside Room 306 when the meeting broke up. They accompanied him to his new room, Room 201, the room in which—was it only a few hours ago?—he and Martin and Andy and A.D. had wrestled together, and skylarked, and played pranks on each other. They guarded the room as he slept there—waking in fits and starts—in what remained of the night.

Outside the John Gaston Hospital, where Dr. King's body lay in the morgue, a reporter shivered slightly as he waited. It had become chilly in the night. He kept vigil perhaps twenty feet from the huge double steel doors leading to the basement laboratory which was Dr. Francisco's province.

The great doors, each twice as high as a man, with a huge sliding bolt across them, were at the end of a descending circular cement driveway. They were illuminated by a solitary grill-encased bulb. To the reporter, twenty-two-year-old Gregory Jaynes, for whom this was his first experience with violent death, the scene was like something out of an old Sherlock Holmes film laid in the menacing East India dock section of London—frightening, eerie, evocative. Not far from him, in the shadows, two policemen stood silent guard.

Along the descending driveway to the doors was a paved ramp, down which wheel chairs could be pushed. An iron rail ran along the graduated wall for the sick and invalided who needed its support.

Just before midnight a limousine had drawn up and parked to one side. As Jaynes watched, four black men emerged. They identified themselves to the two policemen in soft, strained voices: the Rev. Ralph Abernathy, the Rev. Andrew Young, the Rev. Jesse Jackson, the Rev. Bernard Lee. They went inside, remained about twenty minutes, then emerged as silently as they had entered. They had paid their last respects to the body of Dr. King before it would be removed to the funeral home.

Now it was silent. Somewhere a church bell chimed the quarter after one o'clock.

A moment later a black hearse emerged from the dark streets, turned, and slowly backed down the driveway to come to a halt before the giant doors. The huge bolt slipped free and the doors swung open. Two men in white jackets wheeled a gleaming aluminum table forward, on it a figure under a white sheet. The rear doors of the hearse were opened, the two men pushed the table until it touched the hearse, the body on the stretcher was pushed swiftly inside, the doors closed. One attendant had come from the front seat to supervise the transfer of the body, then he closed the rear doors, nimbly hurried about to the front, and climbed into the seat next to the driver. When he closed the door on his side, it made a muffled bang. The hearse drove off.

Greg Jaynes got into his little car and followed it. As he trailed the hearse through the deserted, curfew-silent streets, he thought, *How alone this man is now. All his life he had followers, he was always surrounded by people, admiring, worshiping, hating, people he did not even know. Now he rode alone, with two funeral home attendants. None of his aides was here, none of his companions.* This journey, which Jaynes was to remember because he was its only witness, was a journey Martin Luther King took alone.

The hearse turned off Union Avenue, one of Memphis' principal thoroughfares, into Beale Street, in the heart of the black ghetto. This was the scene of the rioting the week before, when the march King led ended in disaster. The hearse slipped like a black shadow down the street identified with Negro songs and music, with joy and zest of life, silently, without an escort, without a police car, without a band, without the sirens and the cheering, waving spectators. It passed the shattered window of a looted store. It passed another window, boarded up. Jaynes thought, wondering whether such thoughts were not banal, sentimental, yet they *were* what he was thinking. *This man, of whom not a single Negro in the country could say he had not heard, was so alone in this final hour, moving alone through the black heartland of Tennessee, and in all this city and in all this country, I, a white guy who never gave him a second thought, I'm the only one to follow him. . . .*

Hunt

CHAPTER XI

In the huge domed office of the Attorney General of the United States, in Washington, D.C., Ramsey Clark was presiding at his regular Thursday-evening staff meeting. It was April 4, 1968. The meeting had begun as usual at 5:30 P.M., and though the agenda dealt mainly with the Crime Control Act and the Gun Bill, upon which Clark had done considerable work,* Dr. King was very much in his thoughts.

Just two hours earlier he had received a call from a worried Governor Buford Ellington in Nashville. The governor had been notified that, if King carried out his march in Memphis, the KKK would march at the same time. If Clark had to federalize the Tennessee National Guard, Ellington hoped he would do it as late as possible. The Guard had been on duty for a considerable time now. Since the city had taken out a federal writ, U.S. marshals would have to police King's march; but there were not enough marshals in the entire country—perhaps seven hundred in all—to cope with the situation building up in Memphis. Ellington wondered, might there not be some other way out than to federalize his overworked Guard? The question was in the back of Clark's mind as the meeting went on.

Shortly after seven o'clock his secretary put through an emergency call. Jim Laue was calling from Memphis, she said tensely; he wanted to talk to the General because Dr. King had been shot. . . .

Seconds later Laue was telling the story to him. He had just helped lift Dr. King onto the stretcher. The ambulance had already left. "How bad is it?" Clark demanded. It looked very serious, said Laue. He described the wound. He had been one of the first on the scene, because his room, 308, was just two doors from Dr. King's. He had heard what sounded like a cherry bomb, he had looked out to see Dr. King on his back, he had rushed there with a towel—bad, very bad.

* Moments after Clark called his meeting to order, in the Senate building not far away, both bills were rejected by the Senate Judiciary Committee. Ironically enough, Senator Dodd (D. of Connecticut), sponsor of one of the bills, demanded during the angry debate: "How many more people have got to be assassinated in this country?"

"Anybody see anything?" Clark asked, meaning had anyone seen the sniper? No, Laue said.

For Clark, it was a tragic reprise. Nearly five years before, he had been in his office on a lower floor in this building when he heard of the shot in Dallas. He had raced upstairs to this room, then the office of Attorney General Robert Kennedy. Kennedy was in Virginia that afternoon, and Clark, with the others, waited those terrible moments until the final, awful word. It was a dreadful replay—to wait, once again, on life or death, in the same room.

The Attorney General slowly walked into the small private corner office he preferred and put in a call for the White House. As he waited, he wrote down on the shorthand pad he usually had with him:

7:10 P.M. Eight minutes ago Dr. King was shot. Gaping hole in right side of jaw. One shot from a distance of 50–60 yards back of Main Street. Lorraine Hotel & Motel. Laue—Room 308.

Now he had the President on the phone. Johnson was engaged in a fury of activity after his surprise announcement four days ago that he would not run again. He was to leave for California tonight to meet former President Eisenhower, then go on to Honolulu for a conference on Vietnam with U.S. officials he had summoned from Saigon. Clark's call reached him as he was talking with Llewellyn E. Thompson, Jr., U. S. Ambassador to Moscow, whom he had also called back to discuss Vietnam.

Clark reported tersely what had happened. It was too early to know if the wound was fatal: he would keep him informed. After the first shocked questions, the President told him to put every available FBI man on the case. They spoke briefly: one matter was Johnson's travel plans. Ought he go to the Coast and Honolulu? They agreed they would wait developments.

Clark hung up to call Cartha D. DeLoach, assistant director of the FBI, at his home, and ordered a complete investigation, sparing no expense. He made one specific request: an agent should be posted outside the door of the hospital emergency room where doctors were working over Dr. King. Clark wanted no repetition of the chaos and misinformation in Dallas.

The Attorney General had known and respected King. In the Selma–Montgomery march Clark, then a special assistant to President Johnson, had been sent down to co-ordinate the Federal task force on the scene. He had worked hand in hand for days with Dr.

King and his SCLC aides, and he had shared with King the almost palpable fear that King would be assassinated on that march. Minutes before King had led his marchers down Dexter Avenue to the state capitol, Clark, in an unidentified car, had ridden up and down the broad avenue, trying to check points where a sniper might have concealed himself. Clark had a premonition, a very strong premonition, that it would happen there . . .

But he had little time to think of this: he was on the phone without respite. To notify Vice President Humphrey, to check with Governor Ellington in Nashville, to caution him on moving the Guard into the city—the sight of trucks full of armed men might panic the whites into thinking the blacks were tearing down Memphis.

At 8:05 came the call he dreaded. It was DeLoach. Dr. Fred Gioia, one of the physicians in the emergency room, had been overheard to say that Dr. King was dead. "The bullet severed all prominent nerves at the base of the skull." Ten minutes later, DeLoach again. It was true. Dr. King was officially dead as of 8:11 P.M. New York time, 7:11 P.M. Memphis time, as reported by the Memphis police radio.*

Clark picked up his phone and notified President Johnson.

By this time the huge room on the fifth floor of the Justice Building had become a command post. Extra phones were being installed: every man had been pressed into service. The nation's reaction began to be reflected in the tape literally torn from the teletype machines in the newsroom downstairs and rushed up to Clark. As the evening wore on the more important messages came orally: no one took the time to get them typed. Meanwhile, interpretations of what was taking place across the country came flowing down to Clark from Intelligence on the floor above.

The pace of events quickened. DeLoach kept Clark informed not only of disorders as they broke out in the various cities but also of developments in the manhunt. Clark directed that copies of every FBI report were to be sent immediately to him.† He was endlessly on the phone with Secretary of Defense Clifford, Labor Secretary

---

* Actually, Dr. King was pronounced dead at 7:05 P.M. Memphis time, by Dr. Jerome Barrasso, surgeon on duty at St. Joseph's Hospital—one of ten physicians and surgeons who worked over Dr. King.

† He also requested to see all the evidence—an unusual request, because ordinarily the Attorney General finds it impossible to be so involved in any one investigation. For a long time Clark was to hold daily conferences with FBI personnel and make repeated visits to the Crime Laboratory to examine new evidence as it arrived.

Wirtz, with Presidential Assistant Joseph Califano to discuss the wording of a statement on Dr. King's death for Mr. Johnson. He called the White House a second time, to brief the President on the situation in the country: Johnson wanted to know, ought he go to the Democratic fund-raising dinner tonight at the Shoreham? Clark counseled no, and added, "I would also not go to California tonight —I'd wait until tomorrow."

A report from Police Director Holloman in Memphis: "Matters getting critical—they're shooting at police cars. We have general looting." Rioters had even fired on low-flying police helicopters. A call from John Doar in New York, former chief of the Civil Rights Division: he'd heard that the mayor of Memphis had ordered police to shoot out streetlights. The two men agreed "We can't have people shooting around like that, for obvious reasons." A report from downtown Washington: Stokely Carmichael was at the corner of Fourteenth and U streets addressing an unruly crowd. There was a dispute as to whether he was shouting, "Go get your guns" or simply, "Go home." 10:11: from Raleigh, "Crowd out of control." 10:35: from Nashville, fifty persons rioting at Fisk University, a Negro institution. 10:50: from Mayor Washington: twelve to fourteen stores in the capital had been vandalized; he feared a march on the White House. Later, a telephone conversation with Governor Agnew of Maryland, who was having trouble with students at Bowie State College, a predominately Negro school. Clark counseled him to be extremely light-handed. He must realize how emotional the blacks were at this moment. But Agnew told him he had already closed down the school.

Eleven o'clock. Three hours had passed, and the nation's shock was coming to the Attorney General in private and public reports. Hundreds of thousands of men and women were reacting desperately, in many instances, almost uncontrollably. It came to him from every corner of the country, more intense where King was known and had worked, less intensely elsewhere. Some wept; some just came out of their houses and stood in the streets, not knowing what to do. Some began to smash windows and loot. They were striking out in every direction, angry, frustrated, helpless. Riots had taken place in the United States before, but this was a different phenomenon, Clark thought. Usually a riot began in one specific place, in response to one small incident. Here, everyone was reacting to a national trauma.

At 11:20 he discussed with Califano and others what could be done to ease the mounting tension. Ought they to hold a national funeral in Washington with the Presidential candidates attending? They finally vetoed this, for it would concentrate human resources in one place when they were needed in others. Ought Clark himself to fly down to Memphis?

When he hung up, it was with a conviction that, if ever a murderer had to be found swiftly, it was in this instance. If the Government failed to find the killer or killers of Martin Luther King, Jr., the impact on black America would be overwhelming. The black community would question whether the Government really tried*—and whether the white power structure might not itself be involved in the assassination. People had to know that everything that could be done was being done. Clark thought, Suppose it *was* a conspiracy? How would they ever find the guilty man? Would not his co-conspirators do away with him lest he betray them if caught? Or might they not set him up in some country where he would be safe, with whom the United States had no extradition treaty. . . .

The Attorney General pored over the reports flowing across his desk.

The news came suddenly to many people. It found Vice President Humphrey addressing a Democratic meeting in Washington, which was immediately adjourned by Senator Edmund Muskie, chairman of the Democratic Senatorial Campaign Committee. It found Senator Eugene McCarthy in San Francisco, Senator Robert Kennedy in Indianapolis,† Duke Ellington backstage at Carnegie Hall. In city after city the news changed the rhythm of people and events. In Nashville, in a supermarket in the black area, the owner turned up the radio after the first flash. Store traffic continued quietly; everyone knew Dr. King had been shot, and everyone waited. Then the message came. He was dead. It was greeted by a giant exhalation of despair, an immense groan that rose until it seemed to fill the place. One

---

* J. Edgar Hoover's antipathy toward Dr. King was well known. In 1964 he had called him "the most notorious liar in the country," after King was quoted as saying Southern FBI agents did not effectively respond to civil rights violations because of their Southern bias. Clark himself later revealed that, during his tenure as Attorney General, Hoover had repeatedly asked authorization to put a tap on Dr. King's phone, the last request being made only two days before his assassination. Clark said he always had refused permission. But King's phone had been tapped.

† Senator Kennedy told a rally, "For those of you who are black and are tempted to be filled with hatred and resentment against the injustice of such an act—against all white people, I would only say that I can also feel in my heart the same kind of feeling—a member of my family was killed, but he was killed by a white man."

man slammed his fist against the counter; some women began to cry; but in minutes all who were in the store, as if moved by the same signal at the same time, began to walk out silently, saying nothing to each other, each going in his own direction.

In Chicago, at a small bar the news led to a stunned silence, then a buzz of voices. At one table four white men began to joke about it. At a nearby table three students, two boys and a girl, began to sing softly, "We Shall Overcome." Other tables took it up. Presently it seemed that everyone there was singing in unison. The four men rose and left.

In New Orleans, Matt Herron, a thirty-six-year-old photographer-investigator, who had shared a jail sentence with the Rev. William Sloane Coffin, Jr., for trying to integrate a Maryland amusement park, heard the radio report at dinner. King had been wounded. "That's false," Herron said to his wife. "They'd have made sure he was dead." He began packing to go to Memphis to make his own investigation. He had similarly flown to Dallas in 1963 and had concluded that President Kennedy had been murdered on orders that came from the highest levels of the American industrial-military complex, in order to change U.S. foreign policy. In recent months he had given considerable information to District Attorney Garrison of New Orleans, in the latter's case against Clay Shaw, indicted for conspiracy in President Kennedy's murder. Within the hour Herron was on a plane to Memphis.

In Jackson, Mississippi, the telephone rang in the home of Charles Evers, whose brother Medgar had been murdered in 1963. Was this Mr. Evers? a voice asked. When he said yes—"We just killed that black son-of-a-bitch Martin Luther King and you're next!"—and a triumphant bang of the receiver. The telephone continued to ring at intervals thereafter. Each time Evers picked it up he heard laughter, and then the click of the receiver.

In New Haven a man put in a call for Sheriff Morris in Memphis. He sobbed over the telephone. Could the sheriff get Dr. Abernathy to announce over nationwide television that he—he gave his name— a white man, was a friend of the Negro people and had always been? Steadily overseas calls came into Morris's office: from London, Sydney, Belgrade, Oslo—who had done it, who was suspected, what would happen now? The Dallas *Morning News* called. Was there any reason to believe the killer came from Dallas?

In Washington, in the Justice Building, it was 2 A.M. when Ramsey Clark telephoned President Johnson again. He had decided he must go to Memphis, he said. The President agreed. He would alert the Air Force to place a White House jet at his disposal. Clark called J. Edgar Hoover. He was going to Memphis, he told him; he wanted a top FBI man to accompany him there—DeLoach—and he wanted DeLoach to know every detail of the hunt for King's murderer so that he could keep him, Clark, informed. DeLoach had not wanted to go without Hoover's authorization. Hoover gave it.

They took off just before dawn from Andrews Air Force Base. With them were Roger Wilkins, Director of Community Relations of the Justice Department, who was black; Cliff Alexander, Deputy Special Counsel to the President, also black; and Cliff Sessions, the Justice Department's Public Information officer.

Clark had chosen his men carefully. He counted on Jim Laue and other Community Relations aides in Memphis to help avoid friction. The men he was taking with him could negotiate with the community, work with the strike leaders, help siphon off anger and frustration. DeLoach, third ranking official of the Bureau, would coordinate FBI work on the scene with Robert Jensen, agent in charge, Memphis. It was desperately important for the Government to do everything possible to establish contact with Memphis officials, the police, the black leadership, the strikers, churchmen, state legislators. . . .

As their plane bore through the dawn, Clark and DeLoach were in constant communication with FBI headquarters. The bundle of evidence dropped in Canipe's doorway was already at the FBI Crime Laboratory, two floors above Clark's office. It had been flown from Memphis by an FBI agent who had been met at Washington airport by an armed escort: he had arrived at the Justice Building at 5:15 A.M.—about the time Clark and his party were taking off. A team of FBI specialists, roused from their beds shortly after midnight, had been waiting for it. The rifle, through its serial number, had already been traced to the shop that sold it—the Aeromarine Supply Company, in Birmingham; Don Wood and DeShazo were presently to tell about the diffident man with the shell-rimmed glasses and long nose named Harvey Lowmyer, who bought a powerful hunting rifle on March 29 only to exchange it the next day for an even more powerful one after talking with his brother.* The binoculars had been

* The FBI worked with astonishing speed. At 10 A.M. Friday, shortly after Clark landed in Memphis, Don Wood was telling what he knew to Bureau men. The Birmingham address Lowmyer gave turned out to be false.

traced by Memphis police to the York Arms Company, a few blocks down Main Street from Mrs. Brewer's rooming house. The bullet Dr. Francisco extracted from Dr. King's body was already being examined to see if it came from the rifle, as was the section of bathroom window sill to see if the depression on it had been made by the barrel of the rifle, and everything found in Canipe's doorway as well as everything taken from Room 5B of the rooming house was being studied microscopically and chemically for prints, human hair, cloth fibers, and anything else that could lead to the identity of the mysterious Mr. Willard.

None of these details was revealed to the press, not only for the usual security reasons—the more so after the awful debacle in Dallas—but also because of the volatile emotions aroused by the case with all its racial overtones. As a matter of fact, the FBI hunt for Dr. King's killer or killers was conducted with a secrecy rarely before known. It was to characterize every development in a search which became the most massive, far-reaching and expensive manhunt in history, enlisting more than 3500 agents as well as the police of a dozen countries and in the end costing more than a million dollars.

The secrecy was imperative. Witnesses were fearful of their lives. They were not reassured when the FBI somberly warned them all to be silent—not to speak about what they saw, heard, or knew save with their own lawyers or with members of law enforcement agencies. Every leak was to be avoided: the less the murderer, or those associated with him, knew of how much the FBI knew, the better. In the months to come newspapermen were to find themselves against a wall of silence. Police and FBI response was invariably, "No comment." United Press International, one of the two major news services in the country, was to write at the end of the first week, "Sources which normally provided guidance in critical investigations say they have never seen such secrecy . . . this secrecy, sources indicate, comes from beyond the FBI, beyond the Justice Department —from the White House."

To this report, involving the highest office in the land, the FBI reaction was, as to all else, "No comment." When a frustrated editor finally demanded, "Who ordered the 'No comment'?" the reply was "No comment." Thus, every rumor fell on fertile soil and, whether true or false, flourished without correction. Inevitably it heightened the growing conviction that the country was faced by a mystery of overwhelming and frightening proportions.

This problem was to haunt Clark from the moment he stepped off the plane in Memphis shortly before 8 A.M. Friday morning. He arrived in a cordoned-off airport resembling an armed camp. The curfew-ridden night had been hideous with its lootings, fires, and bloodcurdling rumors of black vengeance. Hundreds of helmeted police, sheriff's deputies, and National Guardsmen with bayonets at the ready, with sawed-off shotguns and billy clubs, were on duty, and spectators were held behind ropes. The fact that virtually all the armed men were white, and virtually all those held behind lines were black, only made the situation more abrasive. All flags were flying at half staff, following a proclamation by Mayor Loeb that Friday, Saturday, and Sunday were to be "days of mourning."

Nearly a hundred reporters and television cameramen were on the scene, awaiting the arrival of Mrs. King and her four children from Atlanta aboard an Electra Jet chartered for her by Senator Robert Kennedy. Mrs. King would take her husband's body back with her to Atlanta for the funeral on Tuesday. The hearse bringing the body from the Lewis Funeral Home was expected almost at the same time.

Into this tense arena the Attorney General unexpectedly landed. The press immediately surrounded him and he was forced to hold an impromptu news conference on the field. He was confident, he said then, that they would find the assassin soon. The man had left behind an unusually large amount of physical evidence. Leads from this had already taken the Bureau into several states. No, he said in reply to a question, they had no indication that this was a conspiracy, and in reply to another, "All of our evidence at this time indicates that it was a single person who committed this criminal act."

Clark knew the risk in making such a statement so soon. Whatever he might say beyond "No comment" would be attacked as premature. As one reporter was to say later, "Here we are, Dr. King's body is hardly cold and the Attorney General drops in from Washington, D.C., to tell us there's no conspiracy." This was, of course, unfair to Clark. He had said only that they had no evidence of conspiracy. Nonetheless his words were seen as an attempt by a panic-stricken Administration to quash the idea of a plot. But Clark felt it was his duty at such an emotional time to give the public whatever could safely be given it so long as he did not jeopardize the investigation or impair the rights of anyone who might later be charged.

He went into Memphis for a full day of conferences with only a brief interlude later in the morning when he returned to the airport to visit Mrs. King in her plane to express the sorrow and concern of President Johnson and the nation.* As the afternoon wore on, reports of growing rioting throughout the country made him cut his trip short, and just before five o'clock he and DeLoach flew back to the capital. Both felt that the case would be solved soon, for rarely had there been so much evidence found immediately after a major crime.

In a euphoric moment DeLoach bet Clark a bottle of sherry that the murderer would be captured within twenty-four hours—"by 5 P.M. Saturday, Central Standard Time." Clark had not made a dozen wagers in his life, but this was one he wanted to lose.

He would never forget that return flight. A northwest breeze blew, their plane came in toward the capital from the south, and fifteen miles before they saw the city they saw the smoke of burning Washington. Clark asked the pilot to circle low over the city, and he did so twice. The Attorney General had known Washington from childhood: his father, Tom Clark, had been a lawyer in the Department of Justice, rising through Assistant Attorney General to Attorney General and finally to Supreme Court Justice. Ramsey Clark had been nine years old when he first started school in Washington. Now he saw the fires spreading all over the city—a tragic, unbelievable sight. Then he was in his office, to continue working there through Friday night, Saturday, Saturday night, and much of Sunday. In those nearly ninety-six hours after Dr. King's assassination, he was able to steal less than five hours of sleep.

Behind him, in Memphis, he left reporters who, even as they had dutifully written down his words—we have no evidence of a conspiracy—would not believe them.

There were simply too many unanswered questions.

They were to be asked repeatedly, not only by reporters but by the country at large, in the days that followed—as on Monday, April 8, the memorial march in honor of Dr. King took place in Memphis, with Coretta King in her husband's place at its head, carried off, as Dr. King would have wished, peacefully and without violence; and as his funeral was held the next day in Atlanta with hundreds of thousands of persons, the known and the unknown headed by Vice President Humphrey representing President Johnson, following a mule-drawn farm wagon carrying Dr. King's coffin

---

* A memorial service had been held in Washington Cathedral that morning attended by the President, Cabinet members, and thousands of mourners.

for four miles through the streets of Atlanta before burial in South View Cemetery. The questions still hung poised as disturbances throughout the country subsided, leaving a terrible toll: riots in 125 cities, thirty persons killed, scores of persons injured, damage estimated in the thirty millions and more.

What the nation wanted to know was, if it *was* a conspiracy, who engineered it? Within twenty-four hours after the murder, the reward for information leading to the arrest and conviction of whoever was responsible had reached $100,000.* And if it was not a conspiracy, how explain the crime? What kind of a man would have attempted to kill Dr. King in so inept and dangerous a fashion? How could such a man, working alone, escape, with scores of police on the scene within minutes—really seconds—of the shot? How could he have disappeared, car and all, with all the alarms out for him, with every radio and TV alerting people to be on the lookout for a white Mustang?

Dr. King had been shot at 6:01 P.M. By 6:02 police were converging on the scene. By 6:08 the police radio had already broadcast an alert for a young white man driving a white Mustang. How could a white Mustang disappear without someone seeing it? Even more, how could so clumsy a murderer have escaped unless he had help?

If one examined the murder, one had to conclude that it *was* done in an incredibly careless fashion. The assassin took enormous risks—and they were unnecessary. King was a highly visible man, and an easy target. A sniper had innumerable opportunities to pick him off from any roof or window overlooking the main streets down which he so often led marchers. Time and again he stood unprotected on speakers' platforms, in church pulpits; no Secret Service men shielded him on his arrivals and departures at his home, his office, the countless churches and halls where he spoke.

Considering all these options, why should his killer choose to carry a weapon as conspicuous as a big game rifle down the hall of a rooming house at six o'clock of a weekday—an hour when most tenants would be in their rooms, having just returned from work—and into a bathroom whose only exit was the door by which he entered?

Why would he lock himself in there (this, in a house whose tenants were mainly winos, beer drinkers, and alcoholics, so that the bathroom was in constant demand) and deliberately fire his weapon

---

* The Memphis *Commercial-Appeal* offered $25,000; Scripps-Howard Newspapers (owner of both the *Commercial-Appeal* and the Memphis *Press-Scimitar*), $25,000 and the Memphis City Council, $50,000.

from there? He could hardly have chosen a more public place. And why had he loaded his rifle with only one cartridge? Only one spent shell had been found in the chamber of the gun. What sniper would not have fully loaded his weapon in case his first shots missed?

Add to this that after firing his rifle—he must have known the sound would reverberate like a thunderclap throughout the building —he would have to fling open the door, making himself visible to anyone who might pop his head out to see what had happened, retrace his steps, carrying his rifle down the same narrow hall, then down a long staircase into a street still busy with home-going workers. The rooming house was in the heart of a factory area. Add, too, the fact that Jim's Grill, on the ground floor, at the very point he would emerge from the staircase, was always crowded at this hour with men who'd dropped in for a beer and a turn at shuffleboard before going home to dinner.

It was hard to believe that anyone with the intelligence to trail his victim to the balcony of Room 306 of the Lorraine and the skill to carry off the deed with a single bullet would have chosen such a dangerous sniper's nest.

Yet Dr. King's murderer did.

That he succeeded, both in the act and the escape, meant he was either an amateur with incredibly good luck or a professional killer carrying out a plan so sophisticated that only an elaborate conspiracy could explain it.

Again, how account for the evidence dropped so conveniently— for the police—in Canipe's doorway? Why would a fleeing assassin take the murder weapon with him? Why not drop it out the bathroom window into the bushes below? Or shove it under the tub? To be seen emerging with it from the bathroom immediately after the shot, to be caught with it on the street below—this would be tantamount to a confession. And, once having taken the risk of fleeing with the evidence, why drop it in Canipe's doorway? Another two steps and he could have tossed the entire incriminating bundle over a nine-foot wooden billboard sign just beyond Canipe's. It would have landed in a clump of weeds, where it might have remained undiscovered for some time, giving the murderer that much more margin for escape.

In short, how account for a murderer deliberately presenting the police with the very evidence they would need to convict him?

Unless he *meant* to drop the evidence under the noses of the police.

Unless the shot did not come from the bathroom window, and was not fired by the mysterious John Willard, and the bundle seized so swiftly and being examined so diligently in Washington by the FBI had nothing to do with King's death—had been dropped in the doorway, indeed, to send everyone off on a false trail.

CHAPTER XII

If one throws a handful of small stones into the air and allows them to fall on a carpet, when they come to rest they form a discernible pattern—if one looks for it. One can discover relationships between the various stones. These two rows are parallel, these three form a right angle, this small one lies precisely equidistant between two large ones.

It is, of course, all accidental.

But unless one knows how the stones came to be there, it is easy to accept a statement that they have been deliberately arranged on the carpet.

So it was with the assassination of Martin Luther King, Jr., and the ofttimes puzzling and inexplicable events which served to confuse the story.

From the very first, the search for the murderer—or murderers— was overwhelmed by developments which might have been conceived by a mystery writer to bedevil his readers. Whether Dr. King's assassination was conspiratorial, as virtually everyone was convinced even after the Attorney General of the United States declared the evidence so far indicated it was not, it would still be a long time before each of the events would be explained to everyone's satisfaction. President Kennedy's assassination five years before, the fatal shooting before millions of TV watchers of Lee Harvey Oswald by Jack Ruby, the unanswered questions all the more compelling because they could never be completely answered—all this was to throw a penumbra of doubt over nearly every fact developed in the King assassination and what followed. Forever afterward the element of human imagination, intensified by fear, prejudice, wishful thinking or simple naïveté, would becloud the story. What was rumor became fact, what was fantasy became truth, what was coincidence or accident became proof of Machiavellian cunning. All of it pointed, had to point, to a conspiracy, and it is worth following these events as they unfolded to know what really happened.

A few minutes before six o'clock, April 4, Jim Killpatrick, night city editor of the Memphis *Commercial-Appeal*, eased himself into the chair behind the city desk. At arm's length a small radio, which monitored all police broadcasts, chattered softly, and he listened almost absently as he checked his assignment schedule. High on the day's sheet was the notation that Dr. King was to speak at the strikers' rally that evening. Word of King's emotional speech last night, in which he seemed to forecast his own death and say that he was prepared for it, was all over town. Tonight's speech could mean trouble if, in the same mood, he declared that he would march no matter what happened—KKK or not. Killpatrick circled the notation. Mayor Loeb, he knew, had gone into federal court to ban the march because a federal order would not only bar Memphis citizens but also out-of-towners from marching, and there had been talk that as many as six thousand men and women would pour into town to take part; and it was more politic, anyway, to shift the responsibility for the whole thing to the Federal Government.

Killpatrick cast about for whom to assign to cover the speech, when the police dispatcher's voice, until now droning routine orders, suddenly rasped, "TAC Nine and Ten—we have a report King has been shot at the Lorraine."

Killpatrick's first feeling was one of emptiness. He thought, *This can't be.* And, in the back of his mind, a gnawing: *Had the man a premonition? Or had he gotten word of a plot to kill him, here in Memphis?* Automatically Killpatrick's eye went to the large clock on the wall: 6:03. Then he sprang into action, shouting at reporters to rush to the Lorraine, assigning others to call all major hospitals, then turning up the police monitor to hear the minute by minute bulletins:

6:04 VERIFIED. KING SHOT. TAC UNITS ELEVEN AND EIGHTEEN DISPATCHED.

6:05 YOU ARE TO FORM RING AROUND THE MOTEL. RING AROUND THE MOTEL. TAC UNITS RESPONDING. PERMIT NO PEDESTRIAN TRAFFIC IN VICINITY OF MOTEL.

6:05 HAVE INFORMATION SHOT CAME FROM BRICK BUILDING EAST OF LORRAINE HOTEL. ALL TAC UNITS SEAL AREA OFF COMPLETELY. GOT ANY DESCRIPTION? STAND BY.

6:06 TAC UNIT REPORTS WEAPON FOUND. [This came from Lt. Ghormley's first report on his walkie-talkie—the bundle in front of Canipe's.]

6:08 YOUNG WHITE MALE, WELL DRESSED, RAN SOUTH FROM 424 SOUTH MAIN . . . HAVE INFORMATION SUBJECT MAY BE IN LATE MODEL WHITE MUSTANG, NORTH ON MAIN . . . [This was, of course, based on Canipe's description as given to Ghormley.]

6:09 AMBULANCE WITH KING ON WAY TO ST. JOSEPH'S HOSPITAL.

6:10 ENTIRE AREA SEALED OFF.

Then, at 6:15: HOSPITAL ADVISES KING CRITICAL CONDITION.

In the first eight minutes after the shooting, virtually every top police and FBI official had converged on the motel. Inspector Zachary, chief of Homicide, had been taking statements from witnesses in connection with the Negro boy killed by police in the wake of the March 28 troubles.* He immediately drove to the Lorraine, leaving one man to answer phones. All police cruisers in the vicinity converged on the motel. John Carlisle and E. L. Hutchinson, Jr., investigators from Attorney General Phil Canale's office, also hurried to the scene, as did FBI Agent in Charge Robert Jensen, after alerting the FBI in Washington.†

Police Director Holloman, who had spent much of the last hour dealing with Detective Redditt and the threats against Redditt's life, heard the bulletin and could only gasp, "My God, not this!" He had been trying to cool the waters, he was to say later, and they had been struck by a tornado. His police force was underhanded: he should have had at least 1400 men even in ordinary times, but there were less than 900 working twelve-hour shifts with no days off, covering the two daily marches, protecting the strikers as well as the

---

* The boy, Larry Payne, who had been caught looting, had been fatally shot after police trapped him in the basement of a housing project. His friends said he emerged unarmed. The police report said he was armed with a butcher knife. The policeman who shot him was later tried and exonerated.

† The Bureau has an emergency procedure in such cases. The moment King was reported shot, Memphis Homicide notified Jensen. Within seconds Jensen had notified the FBI communications center in Washington: the message went out simultaneously to Hoover and other top FBI officials. Similarly, Ramsey Clark's call to President Johnson automatically alerted the U. S. Secret Service.

garbage collectors hired by Mayor Loeb, guarding the nightly rallies, meeting the sporadic outbreaks of violence—and this in a racially-tense city still in a state of emergency after the street riots of March 28. They had a major strike on their hands, and now, in the midst of it, they had the shooting—perhaps the murder—of one of the most important and controversial figures in the entire black-white complex. He began to marshal every force he had.

Wild rumors spread. The first news service bulletin had Dr. King shot while sitting in the front seat of an automobile parked in front of the Lorraine Motel. Military Intelligence reported that a caravan of seven cars, full of armed black militants belonging to RAM—the Revolutionary Action Movement—had just left Louisville, Kentucky, headed for Memphis. Reports came of frantic traffic tie-ups; it was the home-going hour, but white drivers were afraid to go through the Negro sections of the city, and this made travel particularly difficult as people tried to get off the streets before the riots broke because it was almost impossible to go from one part of Memphis to another without driving through a black area. Reporters landing at Memphis Airport immediately after the murder found only a few drivers— and those were black—prepared to take them into the city. White cabdrivers refused, certain that the Negroes would attack any white man on sight.

At police headquarters officials were in a dilemma. They had broadcast word that a suspect was believed to have fled in a white Mustang. But they had no proof that the driver seen by Canipe and his two customers was actually the man. Had they been sure, they would have issued an all-points bulletin, which would have blanketed not only Tennessee but surrounding states. Even then it would have been impossible to block off every possible escape. Memphis is at the confluence of Tennessee, Arkansas, and Mississippi. Distances to the neighboring states are short. By 6:11 the driver could have been in Arkansas, by 6:16, in Mississippi. Twenty minutes later, dusk would have fallen and the man would be swallowed up in darkness. In addition to the obvious routes, there was a veritable labyrinth of dirt roads in the area, in any one of which the man could hide.

To add to the difficulties, the search was complicated by police bulletins reporting at least three white Mustangs, going off in different directions at about the same time.*

* Ford dealers estimated there were some four hundred white Mustangs in the Memphis area. This was bad enough, but some drivers of white Mustangs, hearing the alarm on their radios, immediately began racing homeward, to get off the

After the flurry of reports dealing with the shooting and King's critical condition, at 6:25 P.M. the police dispatcher reported that a white Mustang was driving north on Danny Thomas Boulevard, at a high rate of speed, headed toward Highway 51—which leads south—a natural route for escape into Mississippi. A police car was in pursuit.

Two minutes later a second white Mustang was halted at the corner of Chelsea and Watkins—miles from the first. It proved a false alarm. At 6:36 the car racing down Thomas was caught. The driver turned out to be a physician who was answering an emergency call. But a minute before, the dispatcher reported that Police Car 160 was reporting a wild chase, in which a driver with a Citizens' Band radio in his car was pursuing "a white male responsible for the shooting" speeding ahead of him in a white Mustang.

In Memphis police cars cannot communicate by radio with each other: each reports to the police dispatcher, who then relays the message to all other police cars. Thus, only the dispatcher's end of his conversation with Car 160 could be heard, but it was a confusing series of reports. The pursuing driver was now racing seventy-five miles an hour, eighty, eighty-five, trying to draw near enough to take down the license number, but when the murder car reached almost one hundred miles an hour, someone in it suddenly turned and began firing back at the pursuer. . . .

Suddenly the reports stopped. There was no explanation.

Car 160 denied it had been in a chase. Neither the FBI nor the police would say more.

One had to know that shortly before 6:30 P.M. a twenty-four-year-old man who shall be called Bob Whitney, was driving home in his car, which was equipped with a CB radio. He was one of about three thousand enthusiastic CB'ers in Memphis who used this two-way private communications system for business and pleasure. They were allowed a number of shortwave channels and could usually call only their homes, or "base," or another mobile operator. They could not communicate on police channels.

A bus passed and Whitney heard a boy shout out the window, "They shot Dr. King!" He switched on his regulation radio. Yes, it had just happened: an alarm was out for a white man who fled in a white Mustang. A moment later a young, excited voice broke in on

_____

streets as fast as possible. Others saw them, thought their speed suspicious—this must be the man!—and alerted police, so that the hunt was thrown into even greater disorder.

Whitney's CB set, which he had also turned on: "Can someone give me a landline to the police?"

This was CB language for, "Can someone telephone the police for me?"

Usually at this late hour Whitney heard only the day's tag-end conversations, a man asking his wife if he should pick up anything at the grocery, a repairman asking if there were any other jobs before quitting for the day.

He listened. As he expected, another CB'er replied from his home base: "I'll give you a landline—what do you want to note?"

The voice came back, "I'm chasing the white Mustang with the man in it that shot King!"

At this moment the static became overwhelming. The other repeatedly asked for the message to be repeated. Whitney saw a police car halted at a red light in front of him. He broke in: "Station that's chasing the white Mustang, I've got a squad car ahead of me. Stand by and I'll relay your message."

"Ten-four!" came the crisp answer—CB code for "affirmative." Whoever was sending was an experienced operator.*

Whitney sped forward and came to a halt with squealing brakes in the middle of the street, alongside the police car. A lieutenant was behind the wheel, a patrolman next to him. Whitney blurted, "I've got a guy on my radio that says he's chasing the car with the man in it who shot King." The lieutenant looked at him strangely; the patrolman jumped out, opened the door to Whitney's car and slipped in beside him with a curt "Pull up over there," pointing to a parking lot. Whitney did so, to find the police car almost upon him so he could not get out. The driver maneuvered so they were side by side. "What's going on?" he demanded. He introduced himself as Lieutenant Bradshaw. When Whitney told him, he said, "See if you can get him back."

"Station that's chasing the white Mustang—" Whitney spoke into his microphone. "I've got the police—"

The excited voice was clear: "I'm chasing him—he's going eastbound on Summer, just east of Parkway, at a high rate of speed—"

Whitney had turned up his receiver so Lieutenant Bradshaw could hear the voice and relay the information on his police radio to the

* Ten-one: "Very poor reception." Ten-two: "Good reception." Ten-one hundred: "Going to the bathroom." CB'ers sign themselves often anonymously, using such names as the Kentucky Colonel, Applejack, Hog-Caller, Geronimo, Big Joe, etc., although FCC rules require them to use assigned call letters.

dispatcher, but Bradshaw found it difficult to make out the words and Whitney had to repeat them: "He's on top of the Summer Avenue viaduct . . . going out Summer, across Highland, east on Highland, crossing to National, National out Jackson—" Each time Bradshaw repeated Whitney's words to the dispatcher, who in turn broadcast the substance to all police cars.

Prompted by Bradshaw, Whitney asked his informant, "What kind of a car are you driving, so police can identify you?"

"A 1966 blue Pontiac," was the answer. Then: "That Mustang is going seventy-five miles an hour!" There was a barrage of static. Whitney, unable to hear clearly, appealed to other CB'ers: "Anybody listening who can copy him, please pass the message on to me so I can pass it on to the police—they're with me."

Out of the noise came a man's gruff voice: "Let the guy go—he may be the one that shot King. Give him a chance to get out of town!"

Lieutenant Bradshaw ignored the interruption. "Ask him if he can get the license number."

Whitney repeated the question. Now he heard his informant, hurriedly: "No, I can't get close enough to him—" Then: "There's three white men in the car. . . ." Then, an exclamation: "One man leaned out with a rifle—" His voice rose. "He's shooting at me—he's hit my windshield!" But he was continuing to follow the car, he said. Now they had reached Stage Road and Austin Pey Highway. "The Mustang went through a red light doing more than one hundred miles an hour—"

A moment later Bradshaw spoke up sharply: "There's something not right here!" The police dispatcher, who had been faithfully rebroadcasting Bradshaw's relay, had just broken in with information. "We have a patrol car sitting at that intersection—there's been no car like that going through—and nothing at that speed," he said. He looked hard at Whitney.

The latter bent back to his microphone. "Can you give me a better description of your location? A police car at that intersection says he didn't come through—"

There was no answer. Again Whitney tried to raise him. No reply. Whoever it was had stopped sending.

In the silence Lieutenant Bradshaw and Whitney sat, each in their cars, looking at each other. For Bradshaw the question was, is this fellow Whitney part of the conspiracy? As for Whitney, he was thinking frantically. At no time had the signal strength changed. It should have grown weaker as the sender drew farther away. Not only that: if the man was going one hundred miles an hour in pursuit of the Mustang, the wind would have folded his antenna far back, causing his signal to drop sharply. It had not. Suddenly Whitney realized that the sender must have halted his car long before—*if he had been in a car at all*—and been broadcasting the last minutes from a stationary position.

Was the whole thing a hoax? Or was it deadly serious, an accomplice using a pirate radio station carefully set up to go into action at this moment to mislead the pursuers? And why did his informant say he was in a 1966 blue Pontiac? Was it because Sheriff Morris's car, well known about town, was a 1966 blue Pontiac? To taunt the police? Or to make them more convinced of the authenticity of the messages on the assumption that Sheriff Morris himself was pursuing the man?

Neither Lieutenant Bradshaw nor Whitney could know what confusion had resulted from the chase. The dispatcher had broadcast the reports to all police cars. They had been heard, as well, by newspapers, television and radio stations, all of whom routinely monitored police calls. By this time not only Memphis but the entire country knew of the chase, a chase which—perhaps—had never taken place.*

Who had wanted to pull the hunt for Dr. King's assailant—at 6:48 P.M., when the mysterious informant stopped broadcasting, King had not yet been reported dead—to the northeast corner of Memphis, when the logical direction for anyone wanting to get out of Memphis fast would be to the southeast? Squad cars sent in pursuit had found themselves at least six miles from the route anyone in his right mind would have taken.

It could be a hoax. Two years before, a CB'er had broadcast a frenzied appeal: his car had overturned, he was pinned under it, he was losing consciousness. . . . An army of cars had spent hours searching for him, all in vain, because nothing of the sort had occurred. Someone had simply parked his car on a side road and broadcast a wild story.

On the other hand, many Klan members were CB operators. Robert M. Shelton of Tuscaloosa, Alabama, Imperial Wizard of the

---

* Memphis police even went so far as to alert every glass-repair shop in the city to be on the lookout for a blue Pontiac with a bullet-shattered windshield. None showed up.

United Klans of America, which had units in eighteen states, communicated with members by means of Citizens' Band radios.* And the Klan *had* been threatening trouble. . . .

Who had done this? Whitney, grilled by police for long hours that night, had no answer—nor had the police, until much later.

* In 1965, Grady Mars, then chief of the Security Guard for the United Klans of North Carolina, told an interviewer: "Some of my Captains can put a hundred armed Klansmen at a given point within one hour's notice. . . . All our cars are equipped with CB radios and with our Relay Stations I can talk to any Unit in the state and get a message out to them even while I'm driving along the road." From *Assassination and Political Violence: A Report to The National Commission of the Causes and Prevention of Violence,* by James F. Kirkham, Sheldon G. Levy, and William J. Croatty. Bantam Books, 1970.

CHAPTER XIII

It was late Friday, April 5.

Attorney General Clark and Assistant FBI Director DeLoach had left, the widow of Dr. King, with Rev. Abernathy and the top leadership of the SCLC had flown back with Dr. King's body to Atlanta, an intense police alert lay over a distraught city, and in a small office on the third floor of Memphis Police Headquarters two men sat behind locked doors studying a detailed list of the evidence that had been dropped in Canipe's doorway.

With the exception of two items, everything was now at the FBI Crime Laboratory in Washington, but here Inspector Zachary, of Homicide, in charge of the murder investigation by Memphis police, and John Carlisle, chief investigator of the Shelby County Attorney General's office, were trying to learn what they could.

The evidence, as Inspector Zachary had itemized it:

First, the two articles he kept—a white T-shirt, size 42–44, and a pair of gray and white Paisley shorts, size 34, with laundry mark 02B–6, black letters imprinted on white tape, fixed to each. The shorts had been darned in the crotch seam in two places with brown thread.

One green and brown bedspread, herringbone design, that had been wrapped around a Browning Mauser Rifle box and a fifteen by twenty inch blue zipper plastic overnight bag.

In the box had been found:

1 Remington Gamemaster Rifle, Model 760, 30.06 caliber, on it a Redfield 2×7 telescopic sight

1 pair Bushnell "Banner" 7×35 binoculars; 1 gray paper bag, "York Arms Co." printed on it

1 .30-caliber metal-jacketed "soft point" Remington Peters bullet

1 cartridge case of that size, taken from the rifle, with no other cartridges in it

1 Peters cartridge box containing nine 30.06 cartridges

In the overnight bag were:

The first section of the Memphis *Commercial-Appeal*, for April 4, 1968*

 1 plastic bottle of Mennen's after-shave lotion

 2 unopened twelve-ounce cans of Schlitz beer, brewing date 3/15/68 on bottom, with Mississippi tax impressions

 1 No. 20 brown paper bag, in which beer had been carried, with name HOMESTEAD printed on it

 1 six-transistor portable radio, No. 00416 scratched on side

 1 can of Right Guard spray deodorant

 1 package of Dial soap

 1 bar Cashmere soap, 1 bar Palmolive (both hotel size)

 1 partial roll toilet tissue

 1 can Gillette rapid-shave cream

 1 tube Brylcreem Hair Lotion

 1 bottle Bufferin tablets

 1 hairbrush; 1 white handkerchief

 1 bottle of One-a-Day Vitamins

 1 tube Head & Shoulders Shampoo

 1 can Kiwi brown shoe polish

 1 pair flatnose duckbill pliers, name ROMAGE HARDWARE stamped on handle

 1 tack hammer

Inspector Zachary was a hardheaded, practical man, for more than twenty years a law-enforcement officer, and a graduate of the FBI Academy. He worked closely on homicides with Carlisle, who had a reputation as a relentless pursuer of facts. Zachary, sober, taciturn, keeping his opinions to himself, had been the first to take possession of the evidence the night before. He had ordered it photographed as it was found, in Canipe's doorway, before anyone had touched it; then had it carefully taken to police headquarters. At 10 P.M. he had told FBI Agent in Charge Jensen, "We have some evidence you ought to see," and he and Carlisle had led Jensen to this room, in front of which a policeman stood guard. Once the men were inside the room, Zachary had taken a clothes hanger from a closet and used the hook to unzip the zipper that extended three-fourths the

* The lead article, Column 1, Page 1, had the headline: KING CHALLENGES COURT RESTRAINT. VOWS TO MARCH. BUT U.S. ATTORNEY SAYS BAN TO BE ENFORCED EVEN IF TROOPS NEEDED. The story described Dr. King's acceptance of the summons brought to him in the courtyard of the Lorraine Motel, and his declaration that he would fight it.

way around the overnight bag, and then gingerly pushed its walls apart so they could look inside.

Zachary had then given all but the underwear to Jensen, who had one of his men fly with it to Washington. Zachary kept the underwear to check out the laundry mark. Fingerprints were almost impossible to lift from cloth; and while the FBI was processing everything else, Memphis police were doggedly making the rounds of every laundry in the Memphis area. The FBI was similarly checking laundries throughout the country.

At the same time hundreds of police and agents were checking hotels, motels, and rooming houses for a white man with a white Mustang who might have stayed there. Before the FBI was finished with its search for the killer, the day-to-day reports from its agents and foreign police would mount to more than five thousand pages. But as of this early date, what could be learned about the mysterious John Willard that would help in finding him?

A little, perhaps. The darned shorts suggested something about the man. He must have darned them himself. No laundry would have used brown thread on gray and white shorts; and the sewing was clumsy. Only a very frugal man would go to the trouble of darning shorts—after all, how much could a new pair cost? Perhaps he was even too cheap to buy a spool of white thread to darn them with. It suggested, too, a man who did not expect to have much to do with women. Perhaps this was farfetched, but a man who anticipated intimacies with a woman would hardly be found in underwear which made him look slightly ridiculous.

The toilet tissue suggested frugality too, as well as a way of life. Who would carry toilet tissue with him save a man who stayed at rooming houses so skid-row in character that they might lack even that convenience.

As for the hair cream, the after-shave lotion, the deodorant, the shampoo so well known for its claim that it prevented "telltale dandruff," the soap so well known for its claim that it gave "round the clock protection"—this pointed to a man insecure about his person, who doused and sprayed and perfumed himself lest he offend. The shoe polish added to this intimation of frugality and attention to respectability. The Bufferin tablets, the vitamin pills, the soap saved from motel bathrooms—each added one more detail to the picture of a man prim, economical, concerned about himself, his health, his appearance, and perhaps under some kind of a strain—at least, sufficiently troubled by headaches to keep headache tablets on hand.

Such Sherlock Holmes attempts to create a man from his possessions might be unscientific, but they could give one some kind of a lead on John Willard. One had a fairly good idea of his age and general appearance: five feet ten or so, larger proportionately in the body than in the waist. Size 34 shorts should fit a man weighing nearer 125 pounds than the 160–75 ascribed to John Willard and Harvey Lowmyer. The T-shirt was size 42–44—generally too large about the chest for a man wearing 34 shorts. Could the shorts belong to somebody else? An accomplice? Or was it simply that Mr. Willard-Lowmyer liked to wear his shorts snug? This would explain the need for repeated darnings of the crotch. Whatever the case, the man they were hunting was in his thirties, dark hair, receding hairline, blue eyes, sometimes shell-rimmed glasses, sometimes sunglasses, long, sharp nose, lopsided or twisted smile (probably as much nerves as smile), conservative clothes, no hat, soft-spoken, even retiring in manner—was *shy* the word? (Don Wood remembered him as "timid")—and driving a late model white Mustang.

But who was he? Where was the white Mustang? How had he vanished so quickly? One had to be dubious about the theories already current: that a huge moving van waited for Willard around the corner of the rooming house and he simply drove his Mustang up a portable ramp into it and so was transported out of Memphis. Or that he managed to reach one of the many private airfields about the city—West Memphis, for example, abounded in them (this would explain reports of white Mustangs going in every direction except south, the logical one)—drove the car into a garage where it was immediately painted another color while he was spirited away in a plane.

If he had been helped, who helped him? The problem was not only to reconstruct the killer from the evidence left behind but also to reconstruct his movements, to learn about every person with whom he had contact.

What now got underway might have been set up by a Hollywood mystery film director. A huge dragnet spread across the United States as agents combed tax rolls, union lists, telegram senders, safety-deposit box holders, hospital lists, parole files, the signers of all money orders bought in the Southern United States for a Harvey Lowmyer or a John Willard. Meanwhile others were tracing each item of the evidence to where it would lead.

First, the duckbill pliers.

A call to the National Retail Hardware Association in Indianapolis brought the information that a Romage Hardware—the name stamped on the handle—was listed in Los Angeles, at 5542 Hollywood Boulevard.

On Saturday, April 6, armed with a sketch of Willard and a photograph of the pliers, an agent walked into Romage Hardware. The sketch meant nothing to Tom Ware, the manager, but he recalled the pliers. On October 10, 1966, his records showed, he purchased a shipment of seconds at a good price, stamped his store's name on them, and dropped them into a large bargain barrel near the entrance.

Someone had bought them from the barrel between October 10, 1966 and April 4, 1968.

This was of doubtful help, but it was a lead. That someone might be the murderer or an accomplice, or an innocent man who later sold them to the murderer or his accomplice. They could have been lost, and then found by the murderer or his accomplice. Other hardware merchants might have bought or sold them. . . . Who was to know in how many ways the pliers might have gotten into the possession of John Willard? The proliferation of possibilities was staggering.

Every known customer of Romage was checked, as was every plumber, carpenter, electrician, and handyman in the neighborhood. At some point in the last eighteen months the murderer of Martin Luther King, Jr., or someone linked to him had purchased these pliers at Romage Hardware in Hollywood.

The search for the laundry mark went on simultaneously. Inspector Zachary and his men had completely exhausted the Memphis area. It was most frustrating. The white tape, with 02B–6 in black— the o partially clipped out, apparently through a fault of the marking machine—had been fixed onto the inside of the T-shirt and the outside of the shorts. It turned out to be a Thermo-Seal Tape, made by a small appliance manufactured by the Textile Marking Machine Co., of Syracuse, N.Y. The company knew to which laundries it had sold its appliances, but had no record of those which might have been resold. Nonetheless, by Sunday, virtually every laundry throughout the South with a Textile Marking machine had been checked— and the machine producing this tape had not been found.

That Sunday afternoon, April 7, in the office of a gas station in Somerville, Tennessee, a small town some forty miles from Memphis, Baxton Bryant, executive director of the Tennessee Council on Human Relations, a biracial civil rights organization, was in earnest conversation with a Negro couple, Mr. and Mrs. John McFerren. Bryant was a big-boned, effervescent Methodist minister in his early fifties, who had spent much time working behind the scenes in an attempt to mediate the garbage strike. McFerren, who owned a thriving shopping center, had telephoned him that morning in his Nashville home, inviting him to Somerville to address a luncheon meeting. Under ordinary circumstances Bryant would be inclined to accept: McFerren was an energetic civil rights leader. He had helped register black voters; he had organized Negroes in the early 1960's to fight a boycott called by the racist White Citizens Councils; his life had been threatened, his insurance canceled, and several times he had been blacklisted by local white wholesalers, which had forced him to go on long, expensive trips to buy supplies. Nonetheless, because of his diligence, he had been able to build a one-pump gas station into a $70,000-a-year business.

But what made Bryant accept at once was the urgency in McFerren's voice. When Bryant arrived in Somerville it was as he surmised: McFerren had used the invitation as a ruse (in case their phones were tapped) to bring him there to hear an extraordinary tale. Now, his wife at his side, he told Bryant the following story.

He had driven his truck into Memphis the Thursday before—April 4—to make the rounds of produce houses. About 5 P.M. he was in the last of these establishments. He was well enough known so he could go about choosing his purchases without a salesman. Returning to his truck, parked at the loading dock, he passed a small office on the ground floor and heard a man's voice, raised emphatically: "Hell no, you're not going to get your pay until you do the job. You do the job, then you get your pay."

McFerren glanced into the office. Two white men were there, their backs to him; one stood near the desk; the other, a man whom he recognized, was sitting at the desk, talking into the telephone. McFerren walked on but not before the man said sharply, "You can shoot the son-of-a-bitch on the balcony!" McFerren heard the bang of the receiver.

Shocked, he halted, standing off to one side in the corridor. After a moment the telephone rang; a pause, then McFerren heard the second man say, "It's him again," and once more the first man's voice, clearly and angrily: "Hell, no, don't bring your ass back around this place. Don't come here." A pause again. Then, sharply: "No, you can pick up the five thousand bucks from my brother in New Orleans." A few more words, which McFerren could not make out, and he hung up.

McFerren hurried out to his truck. He did not know what to make of the conversation. He drove back to Somerville, arriving after six o'clock. He was unloading his purchases some minutes later, when his wife excitedly telephoned him from their house. There was a rumor that Dr. Martin Luther King had been shot in Memphis. It was all over the neighborhood. He had been shot at three o'clock.

"Oh, he couldn't have," McFerren blurted out, hardly realizing what he was saying. "I heard them talking at five."

Then, he told Bryant, the import struck him. He turned on his radio and learned the truth—that King had been shot at 6:01, an hour after the conversation. He went to his wife at once and told her of his experience in Memphis. For the next two days and nights they were greatly agitated. Should he report it? *He had overheard the actual plotters!* Dare he tell it? What would happen if he, a black man, made this accusation against two white men? The man he had recognized was a well-known Italian-American businessman; he had several brothers, mainly in the same business. . . . McFerren was terrified. Was the Mafia involved? Hadn't he had enough trouble? Yet how could he remain silent if indeed he had overheard one of the men who plotted the murder of Dr. King?

Bryant questioned him closely. He knew the businessman, knew also that there was at least one brother who was a well-known figure in New Orleans. More, he had heard of a cousin—a priest—who reportedly performed many religious ceremonies, such as baptisms, weddings, funerals, for Mafia families. Everything seemed to fall into dreadful place.

Was McFerren telling the truth? Could this be a complete fabrication? But the story could boomerang so dangerously—why in heaven's name would he invent anything like this? Granted that he distrusted most white men, that he might overreact, that he was capable of great excitement—but he was honest, and Bryant had yet to catch him in an outright lie. One thing, too, Bryant was sure of: John McFerren would never say anything that would hurt his business.

And because this story could affect his business, because it might not only put McFerren and his family in great physical danger but also ruin him by setting the entire industry against him and closing off all his supply sources, Bryant concluded that it had to be true.

"John, we have to share this with the FBI," he said. McFerren shook his head: he feared for his life. Bryant promised that he would guarantee that his identity would be kept secret by the FBI. And if his name did become known, he and his family would have complete protection.

Reluctantly McFerren agreed.

That night Bryant drove to Memphis, reaching town shortly after ten o'clock. He took a room at the Peabody Hotel and immediately telephoned Police Director Holloman at his home. He had something he had to discuss with him in person. He would not talk about it on the phone.

Couldn't it wait until morning, Holloman asked? He was in bed. He had been up for thirty-six consecutive hours after the shooting, and tomorrow, April 8, would be a tense day. It was the Monday that Dr. King had planned to lead his march. Now his widow would lead it as a memorial to him. All day black and white personalities had been arriving in Memphis from all parts of the country. Their security and the city's security bore heavily on him.

But Bryant did not think it could wait, and Holloman dressed and drove into town. Just before midnight they met in his office at police headquarters. Shortly after, summoned by Holloman, Inspector Zachary and FBI Agent O. B. Johnson arrived.

The three listened to Bryant's story. Could he produce McFerren? At once?

Because he knew the man was fearful of using the telephone, and would have to be persuaded to come to Memphis, at 1 A.M. Bryant drove back the forty miles to Somerville, managed to convince a trembling McFerren to get out of bed, and brought him back to Memphis. At 3 A.M., while armored cars patrolled the city, still under curfew, Inspector Zachary and Johnson began their interrogation of McFerren in Bryant's room at the Peabody. Also present was David Kaywood, an attorney who was chairman of the Memphis branch of the American Civil Liberties Union.

It was nearly 5 A.M. Monday when they had finished. Zachary and Johnson had taped McFerren's story in minute detail, had him sketch the office in which he had seen the two men, down to its furnishings, the position of the men, and where he himself had stood in the corridor, listening.

They would check it all out.

Three days later, on the morning of April 11—a day, as will be seen, in which many paths were to converge—Bryant was given word that the FBI believed that the telephone call, if overheard, was not related to Dr. King's assassination. However, they would continue their investigation.*

Bryant suspended judgment. Were they telling him this knowing that it might get back to the conspirators and allow them to think McFerren's story had been dismissed as fantasy or paranoia or hysteria, and so perhaps lead those involved to drop their guard? Bryant didn't know. He waited.

The night before, Wednesday, April 10, in a quiet apartment not many miles from the Peabody Hotel, where McFerren had been questioned, an equally puzzling scene took place. Russell X. Thompson, a courtly, forty-one-year-old criminal lawyer known for handling most of the murder cases in Memphis, was sitting over a late coffee with his wife, when the telephone rang. It was just after ten o'clock. Usually the Thompsons would be out of an evening—their eighteen-year-old son, Russell, Jr., had been killed in Korea seven months before, and they had kept intensely busy lest their grief overcome them—but because of the curfew they had remained at home.

Was this Mr. Thompson, the attorney? The man's voice at the other end had definitely a Western twang: "I just flew in from Chicago, sir, and I'd like to talk with you."

Had his caller been referred to him by anyone, the lawyer asked.

"Well, sir, you're very well known in the circles I know in Chicago," said the voice, and added, "I also have friends in the Brownsville area." Thompson's mind began to work. Not long before he had successfully defended a Negro murder suspect in Covington, Tennessee. The man had come from Chicago, and part of Thompson's fee had been paid by the NAACP Legal Defense Fund, set up to help defray legal costs in civil rights cases in which the NAACP was interested. The reference to Brownsville—that was something else again. Brownsville, Texas, had a certain notoriety as the headquarters of Doyle Ellington, State Grand Dragon of the Ku Klux Klan. And not long before, Thompson had successfully defended a Browns-

---

* One phase they did not tell him. A check had located an Italian-American family in New Orleans. Several brothers lived there: one lived in Memphis. Some days before the assassination one of the brothers in New Orleans made a surreptitious telephone call to his brother in Memphis, going outside his office and home to make it. Had it something to do with the plot McFerren said he overheard? The call was traced and proved to be harmless: the man needed money and called his brother for a loan, and had not wished his wife or office associates to know about it.

ville man charged with first-degree murder who had turned out to be a member of the Klan.

Since his caller apparently didn't care to be more specific, Thompson asked, "What do you want to talk to me about?"

"It's something very private, sir, and I'd like to meet with you."

"All right," said Thompson. "If you can come to my office first thing tomorrow morning, I'll see you."

"I certainly appreciate that," said the other. Then he asked unexpectedly, "What time does your secretary get in?"

When he was told, about nine o'clock, he asked if he might drop in before that hour. "I don't care for anyone to see me."

Very well, said Thompson, who had had his share of odd clients. "I'll be in at eight, sharp. Can you tell me what this pertains to, generally?"

"It pertains to murder," was the reply. "I'll be there at eight." He hung up.

Thompson turned to his wife. A nut? Not until he had hung up did it occur to him that the caller had not given his name.

He had hardly sat down at his desk a few minutes after eight the next morning when his phone rang. He recognized the voice. "Mr. Thompson, I'm the one who talked to you last night. Are you alone?"

Thompson assured him he was. "I'll be right over," said the other, and within a minute (he must have telephoned from the booth in the lobby) a slender, broad-shouldered, light-haired man, about six feet tall, wearing a sombrero, strode in. He appeared to be about thirty-five. Thompson rose and introduced himself. His caller shook hands but did not give his name, and sank into a chair in front of Thompson's desk.

He had come, he began without preface, on behalf of "another person." Who? asked Thompson. "Well, let's just call him my roommate." "What do you mean, roommate?" "Well, not an actual roommate. He's one of several fellows who roomed with me in Denver."

Thompson waited. His caller drummed his fingers gently on his knee. Thompson noted the nails were manicured. "The party responsible for Dr. King's death is my roommate." He said it quietly, with no particular emphasis.

Thompson thought, *My God! Either I have got a nut or he's not a nut and he's talking about himself, and the man who killed King is sitting in this chair in front of me.* Then skepticism assailed him. After every major crime there were always psychotics eager to claim credit for it. He said casually, "Do you mind if I make a few notes?"

He pulled a yellow legal pad toward him. "Why are you telling me this? Do you want me to defend this man?"

Not necessarily, the other said. His roommate—"Let's call him Pete, which isn't his name"—was still in Memphis. He had not been apprehended. If Pete were caught, however, would Thompson be available to defend him?

Thompson said slowly, "I'd have to make my decision at that time, depending on the situation then."

Would he require a retainer? That, too, would depend upon the circumstances then, Thompson said. As they talked, the lawyer made his notes. The man before him—"You can call me Tony—Tony Benevitas—and that isn't my name, either"—wore a dark blue pin-striped suit, a blue button-down shirt with buttoned sleeves, and a neat maroon, small-figured foulard tie. He had removed his hat and Thompson saw that his hair was brushed up in a kind of pompadour. He was well dressed and self-possessed. Benevitas, the lawyer thought. Wasn't that Spanish for Good Life, a kind of salutation? Why did he choose that?

Had Thompson been reading the newspaper accounts, his caller was asking. "I can tell you, they're all wrong," he said. Anyone would know, for example, "that only a damn fool would take a shot at King from that rooming house." It could be done, of course, but the branches of the trees growing in the yard could deflect the bullet, and it was a crazy risk—firing from a second-floor bathroom at the end of a corridor. Only a damn fool would put himself in a situation where he could be trapped so easily.

Since this had troubled Thompson too, he listened with increased interest. "How much of this do you want to explain to me," he asked.

"That shot didn't come from the window in that rooming house, the bathroom window—I can tell you that," Tony said with authority. "It came from the wall behind the rooming house." *Well,* thought Thompson, *this is like the grassy knoll in the Kennedy assassination.** There were bushes there, Tony went on. Pete fired from the wall, then jumped down and ran unnoticed in the confusion—so many others, police, sheriff's deputies, firemen, and the like, were running out of the fire station where they'd stopped for a rest break—all

---

* The conclusion of the Warren Commission that President John Kennedy was killed on November 22, 1963, by a bullet fired from a sixth-floor window of the Texas School Book Depository building in Dallas has been disputed by those who believed the shot came from a grassy knoll in front of the President's car as it moved past Dealey Plaza.

these people were rushing about and in all that excitement and disorder Pete got away easily. "He had a motorbike stashed on a side street and was out of the area in less than a minute." Pete used a .30-caliber Savage rifle at a distance of thirty yards. The FBI would get nowhere with its ballistic examinations. The bullet that killed King could never be traced to the rifle firing it because Pete had disassembled the weapon and melted the barrel down.

"Are you prepared to tell me why he shot Dr. King?" Thompson asked.

"He's a professional hired gunman," Tony said.

Thompson looked at him. "Are you the man?" he demanded bluntly.

The other remained imperturbable. "No, Mr. Thompson. I'm telling you that it was my roommate."

Thompson jotted down: *shows no sign of emotional problems: is consistent, doesn't sound paranoid: cool, casual, low key.*

His visitor took out a pack of cigarettes and stuck one in his mouth. On Thompson's desk was a ceramic bowl filled with match pads, his name imprinted in gold: they had been a gift from his wife. "Would you give me a light?" Tony asked. Thompson handed him one of the pads, but the latter made no move to reach for it. Instead he said, "Would you mind striking the match?" and when Thompson did so, Tony leaned forward, cigarette in mouth, so Thompson could light it. "Why didn't you take the matches?" Thompson couldn't help asking. "Why did you have me light it for you?"

"I don't want to leave my prints anywhere in your office," Tony said with a smile. "If I'd have kept the matches they could be traced to you. If I'd given them back, you'd have my prints."

He never took chances, he said. He was a professional gunman too. He knew "all the tricks." He never carried anything in his pockets to identify him. There were no labels on his clothes. He never drove a car, lest a minor traffic violation put him in the hands of the police. He was always armed: he carried his gun in the small of his back, beneath his belt: he could get it as quickly as at his hip; and his jacket covered it without a suspicious bulge. He stood up, turned around, and lifted his jacket. A tiny automatic, in a holster suspended by shoulder straps, was nestled in the lower small of his back. Thompson had never seen anything like that before. "Even when they frisk you," Tony explained, "they usually skip you there. Cops divide the body into three parts for searching—top right, top left and bottom. They pat you up and down both sides and check your crotch, but not the small of your back."

He sat down again. "Let me show you something else," he said.
"I always wear long sleeves. I can have tattoos or not, as I please." He
unbuttoned his left shirt cuff to show the capital letters T and S
intertwined, tattooed on the inside of his arm just above the wrist.
Then, as Thompson watched, he rubbed his thumb vigorously over
the tattoo; slowly it began to slough off, until nothing remained.
Tony smiled. "You'd have to know how to erase something like this,"
he said. "Drives the cops wild when it comes to identifying a guy."

Thompson stared at him, nonplused.

Tony was asking, now, how could he make contact with local Klan
leaders.

Thompson said he didn't know who that would be. His caller was
now apparently in a conversational mood—his home was in New
Orleans, but he had been living in Denver lately—and went on to
say that he "hated Niggers," and that since he was a gun for hire, he
might as well make money out of it. He had built up this hate, he
explained, because a couple he knew in New Orleans had been shot
dead by one, and he knew of white girls who had been raped by them.
He had in mind, he said, killing certain black troublemakers, particularly Stokely Carmichael, and he thought it a good idea, therefore,
to get in touch with KKK leaders. He might go on to Brownsville,
he said, where there were some pretty important Klansmen.

Thompson listened in silence. Tony rose. He put out his hand.
"You may never hear from me again—or I may call you next week or
next month, Mr. Thompson."

The lawyer said carefully, "I understand that we are still talking
about the murder of Dr. Martin Luther King, Jr. That is why you
would get in touch with me?"

"Yes, that's right. On behalf of my roommate."

He remained standing, and Thompson realized that he was waiting
for him to open the door to the outer office; that Tony had touched
nothing in the room so far, and was not about to touch the door-
knob now.

Thompson opened the door—his secretary, Adele, had come in a
few minutes before—and closed it quickly. Tony said, in a low voice,
"That's all right. I know how to handle it." Then he spoke up:
"Thanks, Mr. Thompson, we've had a most pleasant conversation.
You'll probably be hearing from me tomorrow." With that he walked
casually by Adele and out the open front door.

Thompson's office associate was former Mayor Ingram, who had
been in office during the scare of the year before. When Ingram
arrived a few minutes later, Thompson immediately closeted himself

with him and told him about his visitor. "I don't think I'm dealing with a nut," he said. He needed Ingram's advice. The greatest manhunt in history was underway: the entire country was still in a state of emotional shock, fearful of conspiracy and fearful, too, of what awful facts might lie behind it: one had to move carefully. Much like John McFerren a few days before, he posed the question: ought he tell the authorities?

Tony had come to him as a lawyer, and the attorney-client relationship, a privileged relationship, was one which Thompson, a conscientious man, held sacred. What a client revealed to his attorney must not be divulged. On the other hand, it could be argued that the man was not really his client. He had approached him on behalf of someone else. If, indeed, Tony knew the assassin . . . bizarre though Tony Benevitas was, with his disappearing tattoos, his revolver behind his back, and his blood-chilling small talk—who else but someone like him would be likely to be the intimate of a professional killer? You wouldn't expect a banker or Boy Scout leader to walk into your office and announce that his roommate killed a man. If Tony did know the murderer's identity—if perhaps he was the murderer himself—wasn't Thompson's duty as a citizen more compelling than that as a lawyer, and should he not immediately inform the police?

Ingram's counsel was to do so. If Tony should later appear and ask Thompson to take the case, he would disqualify himself.

That afternoon, Thursday, April 11, at three o'clock, Thompson told his story to two men whom he had asked to come to his office—Inspector Zachary, who three days earlier had listened to McFerren's story, and William Lawrence of the Memphis FBI.

Thompson told what happened in painstaking detail, doing his best to recall every word, every gesture. So that he would have a complete record of what might become a controversial issue, he taped the session with Zachary and Lawrence—his recital and their questions and his answers.

After the session was over, they requested him to keep secret all that had taken place. If Tony approached him again, he was to notify them.

Thompson, too, waited for developments.

Just before noon that day, April 11, Rev. James M. Latimer, pastor of the Cumberland Presbyterian Church in Memphis, and his friend, Rev. John Baltensperger, were seated in a rear booth at Jim's Steak

House, a well-known businessman's restaurant. They were there in answer to a telephone call received an hour earlier by Rev. Latimer from a man who said pleadingly, "I need spiritual help, Pastor—can I see you right away?" Latimer had made the appointment for noon and had asked his colleague to come with him. Past experience had taught him the wisdom of this.

Now they were waiting for the stranger. He arrived five minutes late—a white man, about six feet tall, slim, wearing tight dark trousers and a sport jacket, a blue shirt with two-button sleeves, and a Paisley tie with matching handkerchief in his breast pocket. He was wearing dark-tinted glasses.

He introduced himself as J. Christ Bonnevecche, and this was the story he told, quite nervously, repeatedly taking off and putting on his glasses.

On Thursday, April 4, just a week ago, he had been in St. Louis, where he was employed as a runner for the Mafia. He was making a delivery in a briefcase in which, he had been told, was $300,000 in counterfeit American Express traveler's checks. How the next event came about—whether he had been drinking, or taken drugs, or what —was not too clear, but: "I was rolled by two colored men who grabbed my briefcase, and got away. I called New York and told my contact there what had happened. He said, 'Come up with that money in twenty-four hours, or else!' I was scared for my life. I got on the first bus that left town and it took me to Poplar Bluff, Missouri. I stayed there until yesterday. Then I decided I'd come to Memphis because somebody once told me this is the only city in the country that has never done business with the Mafia, so I thought they might have trouble locating me here."

He wanted some kind of solace and comfort from them.

The two ministers had listened in amazement. Rev. Latimer questioned him cautiously. What were his plans now?

Mr. Bonnevecche said, "I think I'm going to Brownsville, Texas, because I know a man there who will help me hide. I once served time with him in Leavenworth." He had been sent to Leavenworth, he said, to take a drug cure. He pulled up his right sleeve to show the ministers a scar on the inside of his elbow—the result of constant mainlining, he said.

When he pulled up his sleeve, the Rev. Baltensperger saw several tattoos on his arm. One appeared to be a capital T over a capital J. "Does that mean anything?" he asked Bonnevecche. "It's the Mafia death sign," the other said.

Suddenly, as if remembering, Bonnevecche pulled out his billfold. "I have one of those counterfeit checks left," he said, and extracted what appeared to be a regulation fifty-dollar American Express check. Neither name nor date had been filled in. He gave it to Rev. Baltensperger as a souvenir. He produced another billfold and exhibited several credit cards, each with a different name. "The Mafia gave me these so I can travel under assumed names—besides, no place can trail me, because I never use the same card twice in the same town."

The three talked awhile longer, then moved on to Robilio's, another popular restaurant. Bonnevecche appeared restless. He said he was half Italian, half French, that he spoke eight languages. At this point the ministers felt they might venture to ask him: Did you kill Dr. King?

He shook his head vigorously. "No, I didn't do it but I know who did, how much he was paid, and who paid him." When they pressed him, he finally said the killer was a man named Nick; a well-known fraternal order, he said, had paid Nick twenty thousand dollars for the job. He did not say why they wanted Dr. King killed. Nick, he said, was dark-complected and came to Memphis disguised as a black man with the help of theatrical makeup. He had circulated among the black population and so knew that King was staying at the Lorraine, in Room 306, and when he would emerge from the room and appear on the balcony. Then he removed his makeup, shot King, and left town. Bonnevecche refused to say how Nick had gotten out of Memphis, nor would he say where he was now or whether he knew where he was.

He changed the subject. He himself had been involved in numerous murders, he said. To avoid detection, he had had his fingertips removed by surgery. He showed his fingers to the ministers. The tips appeared to be perfectly smooth, with no whorls or patterns visible.

The ministers pressed him to give himself up to the police and tell them everything he knew. Bonnevecche said he could not do this, but he gave them the name and address of a woman friend in North Carolina. Would they tell her they had seen him, that he was in good health, and that he had accepted Jesus as his Saviour?

Then he asked to be taken to the Greyhound Bus Station so he could go on to Brownsville. They drove him to the station. He took a bag out of a locker. He told them he had just checked out of a six-dollar-a-day room in the nearby Tennessee Hotel.

Then, bag in hand, he walked away, out of their sight.

The two ministers later told their story to Inspector Zachary. The man had admitted being a drug addict. Was he still? Was his story the fantasy of a confused, dope-crazed mind? Usually, Rev. Latimer observed, when he was called upon for spiritual help, at some point before the interview ended the visitor would ask for financial help. This man had not asked for money.

Inspector Zachary pondered the curious information he had now received from both Russell Thompson and the ministers. The only conclusion he and his colleagues could come to was that Tony Benevitas and J. Christ Bonnevecche were one. The man had called on Thompson in the morning, then changed his clothes, added the tinted glasses and kept his noon appointment with the ministers. The tattoos he had exhibited must be the same. Thompson had read them as T and S, the ministers, as T and J. He must have had the same design on each arm. Tony had shown Thompson his on the left arm and, as Thompson watched, erased it; therefore Bonnevecche had shown the ministers his right arm. And were not both Tony and Bonnevecche bound for Brownsville, Texas? And finally, wasn't Bonnevecche most probably "Buon Vecchio"—Good Old Man, or Good Life—a rough Italian approximation of Benevitas?

As Zachary had reported to Baxton Bryant and to Russell Thompson, he now reported to the two ministers: it would be checked out.* Wild, wild, wild! he thought. He might have been more concerned had he not received word—almost minutes after he returned from Thompson's office—that the hunt for the laundry mark was over. It had been traced to Los Angeles, to the Home Service Laundry at 5880 Hollywood Boulevard—two blocks from Romage Hardware, where the pliers had been bought!

Their man—King's killer—had been, perhaps still was, in Hollywood.

And they knew his name—Eric Starvo Galt.

* Within a few days Zachary had complete reports from the sheriff at Brownsville. The town had less than fifteen thousand population—small enough so a stranger would be noticed if he tried to contact any well-known citizens. An exhaustive check failed to disclose anyone resembling the man, with or without his tinted glasses. The FBI ran a check of its files as well: no name or alias such as Benevitas or Bonnevecche was found.

CHAPTER XIV

Since April 4 a hundred and one trails had been followed. All at once, within a period of hours on this April 11, they converged.

In Los Angeles, agents had shown the laundry mark to Mrs. Lucy Pinela, manager of Home Service. It was theirs, she said. Esther Neita, an employee, identified it as one she herself affixed to shorts and T-shirts. She pointed to the o from which a little arc was missing—that was her machine. Besides, other laundries fixed the tapes on the inside of men's shorts, where they would be out of sight. Home Service put them on the outside to indicate the item was not to be starched. More, she could even pinpoint when she had done this pair. She had begun using the machine on March 4; on March 18 Mrs. Pinela told her to stop using it on shorts. Therefore, she had processed this pair between March 4 and March 18.

Mrs. Pinela's records showed that 02B–6 had been assigned to a Mr. Eric S. Galt, who had been bringing his laundry in for at least three months.

Eric Galt, whoever he was, the man who dropped the bundle in front of Canipe's, had taken his laundry into a shop on Hollywood Boulevard in Los Angeles between March 4 and March 18. He had wandered into a hardware store two blocks away on the same street and picked up a pair of duckbill pliers from a bargain barrel—perhaps around the same time.

Dr. Martin Luther King, Jr., had been in Los Angeles March 16 and 17. He had spoken Saturday, March 16, before the California Democratic State Council in Anaheim, an hour's drive away. The following day, Sunday, he had preached at the Second Baptist Church in Los Angeles.*

Had Galt been on his trail then?

Eric Galt had shot King, if one was to believe the evidence on hand. Eric Galt, alias John Willard, Eric Galt, alias Harvey Lowmyer.

But who was Eric Galt?

* It will be remembered that Rev. Lawson had spoken to Dr. King by telephone that day, giving him a last-minute briefing on the situation in Memphis, where he was to speak the next night.

Did a man named Eric Galt exist? Or was this simply one more alias for the mysterious man with the sharp nose and the crooked, nervous smile?

As if to taunt them, the name came from Atlanta, too.

In that city, almost a stone's throw from the golden dome of the state's capitol, is a low-cost housing project, Capitol Homes, made up of two-story red-roofed brick apartment houses separated by cement parking areas. Early Friday morning, April 5, Mrs. John H. Riley, in Apartment 492, looked out her back window to see a white car parked in the small space at the side of her building. It stuck in her mind because none of the neighbors had a car like that—low slung, sporty, expensive-looking.

She mentioned it to her thirteen-year-old son Johnny, as he was leaving for school. Johnny, who had been excited by automobiles since he was five, looked it over carefully. It was a Mustang; its white-walled tires were dirty, so it must have been driven a long way. It had a 1968 Alabama plate in back, there were two Mexican tourist stickers on the windshield, and when he peered inside (as he was to say later) he made out red mud on the driver's side, and what appeared to be ashes all over the floor, as if the driver knocked his cigar or cigarette against the ashtray. He reported to his mother and went off to school.

Later a neighbor dropped in to join Mrs. Riley in a cup of coffee. The two women talked about Dr. King's murder in Memphis the night before, and the big funeral the papers said would be held in Atlanta. Her neighbor said, "They're looking for a man who escaped in a white Mustang." Mrs. Riley, sipping her coffee, nodded toward her window. "It's sitting right out there," she said dryly.

Both women laughed. Toward evening the car was still there. By that time several neighbors had talked about it too. In Apartment 550, Mrs. Mary Bridges had seen the car arrive. She was getting her daughter off to school when the driver pulled up to the left of her door, then backed his car into the parking space. She saw him get out—a dark-haired man—and, his back to her, walk across the lot and disappear. He was about thirty or thirty-five, wearing a navy blue suit and white shirt. She surmised he was an insurance salesman. (Only later did it occur to her that he had *backed* into the parking space. Nearly everybody drove in and backed out when they left. The police were to point out that the driver, having the one license plate in the rear, obviously backed in so the plate would not be visible to passers-by.)

In Apartment 490 around the corner Mrs. Lucy Cayton had also just sent her children off to school. She was sweeping her front stoop—which meant it was nearly nine o'clock, because she was methodical, beginning her house cleaning at the same time each morning—when she looked up to see a dark-haired, hatless man walking toward her from the parking lot, carrying a black notebook with a slip of white paper showing. She did not see him come out of a car —when she looked up, he was walking in her direction. She could not remember his features but he was "nice-looking." He stopped for a moment, seemed to hesitate, than went on toward Memorial Drive, the main street. She, too, thought he could be an insurance salesman starting to call on prospects in the neighborhood.

In Apartment 551, next door to Mrs. Bridges, Mrs. Ernest Payne was at breakfast when the white car drove up. She and her husband watched as a dark-haired man emerged from it with a little black book in his hands, spent a moment or two locking the door, then walked away.

When the man had not returned for the car that evening, and it was there the next day, and the day after that, it became a prime subject of conversation. Mrs. Riley was to say later, "That car kept me awake a whole week."

On Tuesday, April 9, when Dr. King's funeral was held, she wanted to telephone the FBI, but there was so much excitement in town, so many marching black people, that she decided against it. That night she heard a late news report. The search had spread to Mexico, after the Mexican consul in Memphis said that a white man with a sharp nose, who resembled the sketch in the Memphis newspaper* had obtained a Mexican travel card on April 3—the day before Dr. King's murder. *Mexico!* Mrs. Riley thought, *The white Mustang outside her window had Mexican stickers on it.*

She spent another sleepless night and on Wednesday at dinnertime finally telephoned the FBI. "A car just like the one they're looking for is sitting out in the lot," she told them. Alabama license. Mexican stickers . . .

At the FBI a man listened courteously, then asked if she'd called the local authorities. No, said Mrs. Riley, she thought the FBI was

---

* The Memphis *Commercial-Appeal* carried an "artist's conception" based on the descriptions given by those who had seen Willard.

the logical place to call. He told her to contact the police. Mrs. Riley hung up, indignant, but she telephoned the Atlanta police. That night two policemen appeared, studied the car, and left. Next morning, April 11, however, FBI agents were all about the car and shortly after it was towed away.

A quick police check had disclosed that it was registered in the name of Eric S. Galt, 2608 South Highland Avenue, Birmingham. The name Galt meant nothing to Atlanta police, but it meant a great deal to the FBI. A day before, two agents checking motels in the Memphis area for anyone recalling a white man with a white Mustang, came on the New Rebel Motel. The hotel clerk, Mrs. Hagemaster, remembered the man with the white Mustang and found the registration slip he had filled out: Eric S. Galt, 2608 South Highland Avenue, Birmingham. He had checked in about 7:15 P.M. Wednesday, April 3, the night before Dr. King's murder. He must have left before 1 P.M. April 4—check-out time—or he would have been charged for another night. And later that afternoon he had shown up in his white Mustang at Mrs. Brewer's rooming house on South Main Street.

An Eric Galt of 2608 South Highland Avenue, Birmingham, with a white Mustang was in Memphis the morning of the murder: the same man in the same car abandoned in Atlanta the day after the murder.

This was, indeed, the missing car hunted in all fifty states and Mexico.

On Thursday, April 11, the same day that the laundry mark was traced to Los Angeles, the Mustang was exhaustively examined: trunk, glove compartment, ashtray, what was vacuumed from seats and floor, even the scrapings from under the fenders—all of which was flown that night to Washington to join the other evidence.

The car turned out to be a treasure trove.

In the back seat they found a white sheet. This caused a certain amount of consternation because Solomon Jones, King's chauffeur, had told of seeing a white man flee from the bushes behind the rooming house immediately after the shooting—a small white man (the size 34 shorts found in the bundle dropped at Canipe's could belong to him) who appeared to have a white hood—this white sheet?—about his head.

Then a pair of olive green shorts, again size 34: two halves of Styrofoam packing material, such as is used to pack new cameras; a beige cotton rug, a black sport shirt, a blue sweat shirt, a pair of brown socks, a left beach sandal, a camera shutter. Pasted inside the left front door was a sticker showing that the car had been serviced in garages off Hollywood Boulevard, Los Angeles, on February 13 and again a week later; and the garage records, obtained immediately by teletype, showed the service had been ordered by "E. Galt."

So Galt was still tied to the Mustang and had spent considerable time in the Hollywood area. The laundry mark placed him there between March 4 and 18; the service records put him there in February, a month before; and Mrs. Pinela said he had been her customer for three months, which placed him there from mid-December at least.

Now the search concentrated in Birmingham and Los Angeles. No. 2608 South Highland Avenue, Birmingham, turned out to be a boardinghouse. Peter Cherpes, the elderly owner, remembered Galt as a seaman who stayed there from August to October 1967 and while there bought a used white Mustang. Cherpes himself had driven Galt to the license bureau because the man wanted an Alabama license but was afraid to drive the car before he got it. "The police might stop me," he had said. Galt told Cherpes he worked in shipyards in Pascagoula, Mississippi, and was on a vacation. He had no visitors, kept strictly to himself, and annoyed the help by waiting each morning until all the other boarders had eaten before showing up for breakfast.

A check of the Mustang's previous registration showed the name of William D. Paisley, Sr., a Birmingham lumber executive. He had advertised on August 27, to sell the car for $1,995. A man named Eric Galt telephoned him about the ad, came up by cab, let Mr. Paisley and his teen-age son drive him around the block—he refused to drive it himself because he had no license and didn't want to risk being stopped by the police—and bought the car, giving Paisley two thousand dollars in cash the next morning in the doorway of a downtown bank. To young Paisley's questions, he said he was divorced, that he worked as a merchant seaman on barges between St. Louis and New Orleans, and that he had considerable cash "because you have to have a lot of money when you work on a barge—no place to spend it."

In Los Angeles the garage records gave Galt's address as 1535 North Serrano Street, around the corner of Hollywood Boulevard. The landlady remembered him: he had stayed there in a hundred-dollar-a-month apartment from November 19 to January 21, a quiet man who said he was a salesman. He wore sunglasses, drove a white sports car, had no visitors, and prepared his meals in his room. She had trouble with him at first because he haggled over paying an additional ten dollars a month for gas and electricity, but finally agreed to do so. He also had a telephone installed a few days after he moved in.

Post-office records showed that Galt, when he left 1535 North Serrano Street, moved to the St. Francis Hotel, a few blocks away. He checked out there on March 17, little more than seven weeks later, giving his forwarding address as general delivery, Atlanta, Georgia. And there, in Dr. King's home town, his trail vanished.

At this point one could pinpoint the tight little world in which the economical, enigmatic, and retiring Galt operated in the period just before Dr. King's murder—living off Hollywood Boulevard, taking his laundry, buying his hardware, servicing his car, and, when he moved, remaining still in the same neighborhood.

Meanwhile, at the FBI Laboratory in Washington, the contents of the white Mustang were filling out the story. Microscopic slides of fibers found in the trunk proved to be the same as the fibers found on the pillow and sheets in Room 5B of the Memphis rooming house. The same fibers were found on the sweat shirt, the jacket, and in sweepings taken from the floor of the car. Even more, hair taken from the hairbrush in the bundle found in Canipe's doorway turned out to be similar to hair found on the various items in the Mustang.

Clearly, the man who was in Room 5B in Memphis was the man who abandoned the Mustang in Atlanta. Furthermore, a comparison of Galt's handwriting on the New Rebel Motel registration slip and that of Harvey Lowmyer on the rifle purchase slip at Aeromarine Supply in Birmingham showed that they were by the same man.

The chain binding Willard to Galt and Galt to the murder was being drawn tighter and tighter.

But who—and where, if he was alive—was Eric Starvo Galt?

Had the name a symbolic meaning? Starvo was a strange name. Virtually hundreds of Galts had now been questioned in the United States and not one had been found with Starvo as a given or family name.* The villain in one of the most popular James Bond detective stories, *On Her Majesty's Secret Service*, who was involved in "a most diabolical plot for murder on a mass scale" was named Ernst Stavro Blofeld. Starvo? Stavro? A faithful reading of all James Bond books threw no light on the subject. Ayn Rand, the novelist, founder of a

---

* A Galt family in Birmingham supplied a book-length family history covering several generations of Galts in the United States. It was of no help.

philosophy called "objectivism," which maintained that "the only moral purpose" to life was to achieve one's own happiness, to be selfish, to live for oneself, in her best-selling book *Atlas Shrugged,* used the name John Galt for her hero. Throughout her pages the question was repeatedly posed: "Who is John Galt?"

None of this seemed to have any relevance.

So the FBI and the police labored, and checked, seeking an invisible man.

CHAPTER XV

Of course Eric Starvo Galt existed. He was quite visible.

Marie Martin could tell them about him. As could her cousin, Charlie Stein.

Marie was a cocktail waitress in the Sultan Room, the bar of the St. Francis Hotel, Galt's last address before he left for Atlanta, abandoned his white Mustang there, and vanished. She was a dark-eyed woman in her thirties, with a saucy face under a jet black wig, and she had been one of the first to notice the stranger who began to frequent the Sultan Room as early as the December before, a quiet man who sat by himself, drinking orange juice and vodka, speaking to no one and by his curtness discouraging anyone from speaking to him. Marie came from New Orleans. She had been an exotic dancer, she had married three times, and she smiled easily and often, and one evening as she passed him—he was in his thirties too, dark haired, with blue eyes and a sharp nose—he said unexpectedly, "Can I buy you a drink?" He said it so softly, so hesitantly, that she was not sure that he'd spoken to her, but she nodded—and their friendship began. She had been curious about him because strangers were not often seen in the bar, which was patronized mainly by elderly guests of the hotel. When she was not too busy, she sat with him.

Often when he was not at the Sultan Room, he could be found two blocks away at the Rabbit's Foot Club, at 5623 Hollywood Boulevard, sitting over his vodka and orange juice, alone there as at the Sultan Room.

He had just come up from Mexico, he told Marie Martin, and had taken a room on North Serrano Street, not far away from the Sultan Room. He'd owned a bar in Mexico, which he recently sold to his Mexican partner. Now and then he used Spanish phrases. She reminded him, he said, of a girl he'd known in Guadalajara. He did not smoke, though he admitted he'd once tried marijuana, but it did nothing for him. He liked Mexico, he liked bullfighting, but not cockfighting, which he thought too cruel.

A few afternoons later—it was Thursday, December 14—her cousin, Rita Stein, who resembled her, dark-eyed and curvaceous, dropped into the bar. Marie introduced them. "This is Mr.—" She looked at him. He had never told her his name. "Galt," he said. "Eric Galt." The two women began to talk animatedly, Galt listening, somewhat ill-at-ease. He had a habit of pulling on his right earlobe and smiling a kind of crooked smile, as though he'd just heard a private joke.

Marie turned to him. "Rita's got a problem," she said. "Her two girls are living with her mother in New Orleans and they're going to put the kids into a children's home unless she brings them back here. We've been looking for a ride to New Orleans—" She threw a roguish glance at Galt, and said, half jokingly, "You wouldn't drive me down to pick them up, would you?"

Galt seemed to consider it seriously. "Well, maybe I would."

"You would?" The girls were delighted. Rita said, "You've got to meet my brother Charlie. He'd go with you and help you drive." Galt didn't seem to take this adversely, and Rita hurried away, saying she'd be back soon.

She went home to a white frame house at 5666 Franklin Avenue, a few blocks away, where she lived with Charlie and her two smaller children, whom she had kept with her in Los Angeles. Charlie was baby-sitting for her at the time. He was a hippie and cut a striking figure: a huge man, over six feet, weighing nearly 240 pounds, he had darting black eyes, a full black beard and mustache, and was bald save for a few long locks of black hair that came curling behind his ears. He walked about in sandals and beads, and often lay on the grass at night behind the house searching for flying saucers. He also, according to stories his mother in New Orleans told her friends, talked to trees, because the Creator must have placed them on earth for a purpose. He gave his profession as songwriter, but there were many strings to his bow. He had been a professional boxer, garage operator, a car salesman, he played chess, he had owned a bar in New Orleans, he had worked as a bouncer in a New Orleans strip tease show, he had been married and divorced, and was currently working out psychic approaches to life. Rita looked upon him indulgently. He had once tried to cure Marie of arthritis. He had placed his hand on her knee and after a brief trance told her to remove her panties, which he buried in a hole he dug in the backyard. At the end of three days, her pain would be gone, he told her. As it turned out, the pain did vanish. Rita could only assume her brother was sensitive to things she did not always see and hear. He knew they'd been asking around about getting a ride to New Orleans: breathlessly Rita told him about their good luck. "We met a guy in the Sultan Room who's willing to drive down, you've got to meet him." And she hurried back to make sure Galt wouldn't leave.

Charlie showed up at the bar half an hour later. He saw Rita and Marie at the far end, talking to a man seated on one of the stools. Marie introduced them. "Charlie, this is Eric—he's been nice enough to say he'll drive you to New Orleans to pick up the kids."

The stranger gave Stein a limp hand. Stein, as he was to recall later, felt strong antivibrations from the man. He decided the girls must have given Galt the idea that Galt would be driving Marie or Rita down to New Orleans, and now here he was, showing up—a big, hairy ape. The man couldn't be too happy about it.

Nonetheless they discussed the trip. Charlie was quite prepared to go down—he'd like to see his mother, and his young son. Could Galt leave tomorrow morning, Friday? It would give them the weekend to drive. Galt said yes. He had some business of his own to transact in New Orleans. He'd pick Stein up at 10 A.M.

After Stein left, Galt turned to Marie. She had not seen him like this before. His face was white. "If this is a setup, I'll kill him!" He almost stumbled over the words. "I have a gun. If he tries to pull anything on the trip—"

"Oh, Eric, it's not a setup," Marie said gaily. She didn't believe him. He was such a quiet, mild man. "It's like I said—if Rita doesn't get her girls back, they go into a children's home." She spoke vaguely of in-law trouble.

Promptly at ten next morning Galt picked up Marie at the St. Francis, where she had a room, and drove her to the Steins'. Marie added something new to the plans when she saw her cousins. Eric, she said, had set up a condition before he'd drive Charlie to New Orleans: he wanted them all to register for George Wallace, who was running for President. If they did that, Galt would pay the expenses of the trip, as well. As she explained this, Galt stood to one side, silent, with his cryptic smile.

"Sure," said Stein. Politics was no big deal to him. Did Galt want them to do it now, before they left on the trip? Galt nodded. They all got into Galt's car—Stein, Marie, and Rita—and he drove them to the Voter Registration Office of the American Independent Party, in North Hollywood. On the way he said, "I just want you to register so Wallace will have enough signatures to get his name on the California ticket." The California primaries, he explained, were to be held in June.

Once at party headquarters, Galt watched as the three registered.

Stein thought, *This fellow must be a politician, he seems to know his way around here.* As Stein bent over to sign, Charlotte Rivett, deputy registrar, a short, gray-haired woman with thick glasses, showed him where to put his name. "God bless you for registering for Mr. Wallace," she said fervently. Stein signed and looked at her coldly. "What's God got to do with it?" he demanded. She looked at his beard and beads and turned away.

Galt, meanwhile, was wandering about the room, glancing at the Wallace literature on the tables. Stein helped himself from a coffee urn and growled that the coffee wasn't hot enough. Mrs. Rivett glared at him. She was to remember him later with great distaste.

Then Galt drove them back to Stein's home. Stein packed and put his bag in the back of the Mustang, next to a blue suitcase. He also noticed a Kodak camera box in the trunk. Marie had a box of clothes she wanted dropped off at her mother's house in New Orleans. She gave Galt the name and address.

It was noon, Friday, December 15, 1967, when the two men got on their way. They made their first stop for gas in Arizona, then drove through the night, taking turns at the wheel. At one point Stein said, "Eric, I'm certainly grateful to you for what you're doing. It's a real favor to the girls."

"I'm not doing any favor—I've got business in New Orleans," Galt replied. He was going to see friends he'd known in Mexico. He mentioned a name—it sounded Italian to Stein, but he could not be sure. It wasn't always easy to understand Galt—he either swallowed his words or spoke so rapidly that half of them were undistinguishable.

Early Saturday Galt was driving through considerable snow, and Stein, dozing, awoke with a jolt. The car had skidded off the road and into a field, fetching up against a wire fence. Later, in El Paso, Galt stopped at a gas station and bought a used tire for four dollars to replace one that was threadbare. Stein thought, *You'd think a guy with so much money wouldn't have such worn tires on his car and when he bought one, he'd buy a new one.* . . .

That night, with Galt driving and Stein again dozing, the car stopped. Stein woke. They were in a gas station. He saw Galt, standing in a telephone booth, the light shining down on him, talking intently into the mouthpiece. Two or three times before Galt had used the phone at gas stops, but only for a moment. Apparently he'd been unable to reach whoever he was calling. This time though he evidently had his party. Stein assumed he was talking to the man he was to see in New Orleans.

Generally their conversation was limited. Galt was not one to answer questions, and Stein did not want to press him. Clearly, however, Galt wanted Stein to remember his name. Once Stein asked, absently, "What did you say your last name was?" and Galt, annoyed, replied, "It's Galt—Eric—Starvo—Galt. Galt!" He said it clearly and sharply. Stein thought, *He's no Eric. He's too country.* He wondered, was the name phony? Was the man trying to build up a fictitious identity? And he wasn't sure how much to believe Galt's story of owning a bar in Mexico, either. Galt's few Spanish phrases were touristy—he should certainly know more Spanish. He had told Stein he was paying five hundred dollars for dancing lessons. *Dancing lessons!* Stein thought, *The man can't even walk straight.* He lumbered across a room like a farmer. Now and then Stein felt he was getting the same bad antivibrations as when he first met him. But he was growing interested in the man. Galt ate only hamburgers, ordering them "with everything on it." He drank enormous quantities of beer, often while driving, holding the wheel with one hand, a can in the other. He had the radio constantly turned on to country and Western music. He used large quantities of cream on his hair. He had no hat, no raincoat, no glasses. He told Stein he'd bought the Mustang from a friend, and had done a lot of traveling in it. He had trouble driving through Negro areas because of the Alabama license. "Once they threw tomatoes at me," he said.

They arrived in New Orleans on Sunday, December 17. Stein delivered the box of clothing, then drove to his mother's house in the French quarter. It was just after noon. "Come in and meet my mother," Stein said. If Galt wanted to, he was welcome to stay with them. No, said Galt. He'd like to get to a motel, he wanted to change his clothes. So Stein drove about until they found the Provincial Motel, not far away from his mother's house, at 1024 Chartres Street.

Again Galt made him feel he wanted him to remember his name. Stein drove the Mustang into a passageway between the front and rear court of the motel and sat in the car while Galt went into the office and registered. Galt gave his name to the clerk in so loud a voice—Eric Starvo Galt!—that Stein heard it in the car. Why should he do that? It wasn't likely that the clerk was deaf. Whatever the case, Galt emerged, drove Stein back to his mother's house, and took off.

By six next evening Stein had heard nothing from Galt, and began to fear that Galt might return to Los Angeles without him. He telephoned him at the Provincial, inviting him to join him at the home of his married sister, Mrs. Marie Lee. Galt presently drove up, parked, and walked up a path to the front porch, where Stein and his sister were sitting. "Eric," Stein said, "say hello to Marie." Mrs. Lee said, "Glad to know you," but Galt said nothing. He leaned against the porch post like an embarrassed schoolboy and stared at his feet. He did not even meet her eyes, so that later when she tried to remember his appearance, she realized she had never had a full view of his face. A moment or so later she had to leave. Galt bobbed his head in acknowledgment that they'd met, still looking down. Then he said to Stein, "I saw you and the two boys earlier in front of the Trade Mart Building. I was having a beer at a bar." Stein had taken a walk downtown that afternoon with his son, Charles, Jr., and Charles's schoolmate. Galt had undoubtedly seen whoever it was he'd been trying to contact by telephone on the way down. As if to confirm what he was thinking, Galt said, "I saw the people I had business with. You ready to go back?"

This last surprised Stein. The earliest they'd planned to go back had been Wednesday. "Why don't we stay overnight?" Charlie asked. "I want to check on the weather—we don't want to start back to L.A. in a snowstorm." Actually, he wanted to see friends and to rest. All right, said Galt neither enthusiastically nor unenthusiastically, and presently he left, with the understanding that they would start back the next day.

Tuesday afternoon, when Galt came to pick up Stein, one of Charlie's friends, Tony Carvelho, was there. He'd been a bartender in Marie's Lounge, which Stein had operated in New Orleans a few years before. Charlie had fascinated Tony by talking about his new cosmic philosophy which involved people from other planets arriving on earth in space ships. Finally Tony asked about the trip. How'd he find this fellow so willing to drive him down? "The Creator provided for me," said Stein. He spoke highly of Galt. The man didn't let him pay a penny on the trip down, which was fine, because he, Charlie, only had about thirty dollars on him. Tony offered to loan him money, "Nope, I'm no longer interested in material wealth," Charlie said. "Only in cosmic philosophy." He had been working on Galt on the way down, he said, and was almost on the verge of converting him. "But I've got to overcome a mental block in the man. I'll do it on the return trip."

That afternoon Charlie and Galt with the two small girls left for Los Angeles. They drove almost nonstop, arriving in Los Angeles on Thursday, December 21.

All this was carefully told the FBI men, but beyond this Marie and the Steins had little more to say. Marie saw Galt on and off over the next few months. In January at her suggestion he moved from North Serrano Street to the St. Francis, where she stayed. It would be more economical, she pointed out—eighty-five a month instead of one hundred dollars—and if he came in late he wouldn't have neighbors to contend with.

On St. Valentine's Day he traded his console TV for her portable Zenith—he was planning a trip, he explained, and the portable was better to travel with. He gave her twenty dollars in addition. He invited her into his room that day—it was the only time she'd been in it, she said, and she made emphatically clear that she had never been more than a friend to Eric Galt—but on this occasion she saw a girly-type magazine on a dresser, with nude pictures in it. She was surprised, because once, laughingly, she'd shown him an ad in the Los Angeles *Free Press*, an underground publication, reading, "Wanted, passionate man. Send photo." He had reddened like a young boy. She had discovered something else interesting about him. He was a weight lifter. One morning he'd knocked at her door and asked if he might leave a set of barbells in front of her door. She said yes, through the door, not even bothering to get out of bed. Later in the day he telephoned her and she asked him for money for taking care of the weights. The management had been annoyed and she'd gone to some trouble to store them. He told her he was broke—he was waiting for money from his brother, he said—but he left her ten one-dollar bills in an envelope at the desk downstairs. She learned too that he was taking bartending lessons: he asked her if he could put down her name, and that of her cousins, as reference. She had said yes, of course. He wasn't very good even after he'd finished the course. She had to loan him a book of drink recipes. But she never, really, learned anything personal about him.

At the Rabbit's Foot Club, Galt was remembered, too—particularly because he got into arguments, something that never occurred at the Sultan Room. One night, according to bartender Jim Morison, Galt was talking with a girl, Pat Goodsell, sitting at the bar several stools away from him. The customers at the Rabbit's Foot were younger, vaguely show business types, in contrast to the more sedate patrons of the Sultan Room. They knew of Galt as a man from Alabama (his white Mustang with its Alabama plate was always parked outside) who usually minded his own business. However, once before, he had gotten into a vehement argument with Morison, who supported Robert Kennedy for President while Galt was a Wallace man. On this occasion Patty berated Galt for the way Negroes were treated in Alabama. "Negroes are good people, why don't you give them their rights?" she demanded. Galt suddenly grabbed her arm, pulled her off the stool, and tried to drag her out the door, saying something like, "If you love Niggers so much, I'll drop you off in Watts and we'll see how you like it there!" Other customers separated them.

Such was the information gained at the Sultan Room and Rabbit's Foot Club, and such was the story unfolded by Marie and particularly by Charlie Stein. Certain highly significant things had been learned about Galt. He was touchy about Negroes; he supported Wallace; he had "done business" with persons in New Orleans, probably in the Trade Mart area.

Charlie Stein had spent more time with Galt than anyone else. But a man who hunted flying saucers and talked to trees might be a dubious source. Perhaps Stein and Galt had been involved in drug traffic. Could they have driven to New Orleans to obtain drugs? Stein denied it indignantly. "I wouldn't have talked to you in the first place if I was involved in anything illegal with Galt," he said in an injured voice. "I know a dopehead when I see one, and Galt isn't a user of hard drugs. He could have been a pillhead but I never saw him take any. Once or twice when we were driving he looked a little droopy, but it could've been lack of sleep." Nor was Stein clear as to what Galt actually had said on the trip. He was to see a man in New Orleans "whose name sounded Italian." New Orleans, again and again! The telephone call McFerren said he overheard purportedly sent the killer to New Orleans to get his five-thousand-dollar fee for the deed. Tony Benevitas, who said his roommate killed King, told Attorney Russell Thompson in Memphis that he himself came from New Orleans; and hadn't Lee Harvey Oswald also lived in New Orleans . . . ? A thousand and one possibilities assailed the hunters.

But dancing schools and bartending schools?

Yet it was through this last tip by Marie that Eric Galt's real identity was uncovered—that he turned out to be one James Earl Ray, thirty-nine, an escaped convict from Missouri State Penitentiary, Jefferson City, Missouri, where he had been serving twenty years for armed robbery. He had escaped April 23, 1967.

The revelation came with surprising suddenness on April 19, 1968.

Two days before, Ramsey Clark had announced that the FBI sought Eric Starvo Galt on a federal fugitive warrant growing out of Dr. King's murder. Based on what Galt had said when he bought the rifle, the warrant charged Galt "and an individual whom he alleged to be his brother," with entering into a conspiracy to violate Dr. King's civil rights,"* which continued "until on or about April 5, 1968"; and "in furtherance of this conspiracy," Galt bought a rifle in Birmingham on or about March 30, 1968. The hunted man owned a 1966 white Mustang which had been bought in Birmingham on August 30, 1967, and found abandoned in Atlanta on April 11, 1968; between those dates it had been driven some nineteen thousand miles, including trips to Los Angeles, Birmingham, and Mexico, as well as Memphis and Atlanta.

Then, only forty-eight hours later, came the new announcement with the man's true identity. It showed three photographs of James Earl Ray, one front, one profile—both taken in 1960—and one facing front, taken in 1968, with the words under it, "Eyes drawn by artist." There was no explanation of this.

Below the black letters CRIMINAL RECORD: "Ray has been convicted of burglary, robbery, forging U.S. postal money orders, armed robbery and operating a motor vehicle without owner's consent." Under CAUTION, the warning: RAY IS SOUGHT IN CONNECTION WITH A MURDER WHEREIN THE VICTIM WAS SHOT. CONSIDERED ARMED AND EXTREMELY DANGEROUS.

What had happened was that Galt's remark to Stein that he took dancing lessons had led to the National Dance Studio in Long Beach. He had been a student there from December 5, 1967, to February 12, 1968. The girls who taught him were vague about him; he was silent, spoke only when spoken to, never attempted to date a teacher, was impossibly awkward on the floor, and once said something about having owned a bar in Mexico. Given the bartending school tip, it

---

* Murder is not a federal charge, but the civil rights provision has sharp teeth in it: "If two or more persons conspire to injure, oppress, threaten or intimidate any citizen in the free exercise or enjoyment of any right or privilege secured to him by the Constitution . . . they shall be fined not more than $10,000, or imprisoned not more than ten years, or both; and if death results, they shall be subject to imprisonment for any term of years, or for life." 18, U. S. Code, Chapter 13, Section 241.

was easy to find the International School of Bartending, on Sunset Boulevard, not far from the St. Francis. Tomas Reyes Lau, the director, a dapper little man with a pencil-thin mustache and a Latin-American accent, remembered Galt. The man enrolled January 19, paying $220 for the six weeks' course. He told Lau he was a chef in the merchant marine and often had to serve cocktails, and wanted to become expert at it. He had graduated March 2, and though Lau had offered to obtain a bartending job for him he had turned it down.

As Lau looked through his records, trying to recall more about the man—Galt had the sort of face which simply vanished from your memory—agents studied the photographs on the walls of Lau's office. One showed Lau and a man in the black jacket and bow tie of a bartender—a man with a long nose and receding hairline. The two stood side by side, facing the camera, Lau beaming, holding the man's right elbow proprietorially, the other standing awkwardly, feet planted slightly apart, clutching a diploma in front of him, and his eyes tightly shut—as if he had deliberately closed them a moment before the picture was taken. His black bow tie was askew, the jacket obviously too small for him, and his lips were tightly compressed as though he was not enjoying himself.

Acting on a hunch, the agent asked, "That wouldn't be Mr. Galt with you?" pointing to the photograph. Lau looked. Yes, of course it was. He was delighted he could be of help. "I loaned him the jacket and tie, so we'd have a nice picture of how he looked as a bartender. He didn't want to pose at first, but I told him all our graduates do this."

Even as the FBI seized their greatest prize so far—the first photograph of their mysterious quarry*—an important new lead appeared. An examination of all money orders cashed in the Los Angeles area produced several bought at the Bank of America by an Eric S. Galt, made out to the Locksmithing Institute, of Bloomfield, New Jersey. The institute's records showed that Galt had been receiving lessons by mail—how to make keys, pick locks, and the like† beginning in

---

* Within twelve hours Donald Wood of Aeromarine Supply, who had exchanged the rifle for Lowmyer, had chosen Galt's photograph out of those of eight men shown him, as being that of Harvey Lowmyer.

† The full course, costing $199.50, comprised thirty-two lessons and assured the student that he would quickly "acquire the skills that make it possible for you to open any lock without a key." Galt signed a statement that he had never been convicted of burglary or similar crimes, and pledged himself "never to use my knowledge to aid or commit a crime."

Montreal, Canada, on July 17, 1967. His latest lesson—only a few days before—had been sent to him at 113 Fourteenth Street, Atlanta —again, Dr. King's city, and the city in which the white Mustang had been found!

Agents descended on that address to find it a weather-beaten rooming house in the heart of Atlanta's small hippie district. Surreptitiously they learned that Galt still had a room there, No. 2, on the ground floor. Was he hiding in it even now, thinking no one would dream of looking for King's murderer only blocks from King's home? They set up a twenty-four-hour surveillance, but no one resembling Galt entered or left. They dared not ask questions at the place, lest this alert him; nor could they obtain a search warrant, for that might set the press on their trail. Under orders from De-Loach in Washington, two agents disguised themselves as hippies and rented a room from James Garner, the owner. They turned down several until he showed them one adjoining No. 2, with a connecting door between. They put their ears to the door: no sound from the room. They tried the door: it was padlocked on the other side. An agent telephoned DeLoach for instructions.

"Take the door off the hinges but get in there," DeLoach ordered.

They found the room empty. There was a small cot, a battered table, and a dresser. The room opened onto a tiny storeroom, which had a desk in it, on the desk a portable Zenith TV. A pamphlet, "What Is the Birch Society?" lay nearby. This seemed to have some significance in view of Galt's reported support of Governor Wallace, which suggested he was a conservative in politics. But in a dresser drawer they came upon an exciting find: a map of Atlanta with four places circled in pencil: the home of Martin Luther King, Jr.; the Ebenezer Baptist Church; the SCLC offices; and the Capitol Homes Housing Project, where the white Mustang had been abandoned.

This was of tremendous significance, not only because it was proof, if it was Galt's map, that he had been stalking King (who had been in and out of Atlanta during the time Galt was there), but also because the map showed a clear left fingerprint. This would greatly help the FBI in its attempt to find Galt's true identity—if the man's prints were on record.

There were other maps like the first, the kind obtained at gas stations, of Los Angeles, Birmingham, Mexico, Texas, and Oklahoma, and a booklet "Your Opportunities in Locksmithing," published by the Locksmithing Institute.

In another drawer they found typical Galt possessions—it was obvious the man traveled like a pack rat—a box of Nabisco crackers, a can of Carnation milk, a can of instant coffee, sugar, an electric cup water heater, a bottle of French salad dressing, a plastic package of lima beans which needed only to be dropped into boiling water, a tin of ground pepper.

The agents slipped out of the room and replaced the door. That night, Easter night, two agents formally visited Garner. Again they found one more man who had brushed shoulders with Galt and had little to tell. Galt, neatly dressed, and proper enough to have been a preacher, had knocked on Garner's door Sunday, March 24, wanting a single room. Because No. 2 was small, Garner told him he could have use of the adjoining storage room. "Fine," Galt had said, "I got a TV in my car. I can put it on the desk there." He paid $10.50 rent in advance, parked his white Mustang behind the house, and went about his business. Garner saw him only once after that—the following Friday, March 29, when they passed in the hall. Galt said then, "I may as well pay you for another week," and did so.

On the following Friday, April 5 (this would be the morning after King's murder), Garner came into Galt's room to change the linen. He found a note on the bed, printed with a ball-point pen on a rectangular piece of cardboard such as laundries use in shirts: "Had to leave for Birmingham. Left TV. Will pick up soon."

The agents placed photographs of half a dozen men on the table. Was his roomer any of these?

Garner picked one. "If this isn't the guy, it's his twin brother."

It was the bartending school photograph of Eric Starvo Galt.

The agents flew the maps and other items to Washington. The Atlanta map proved all important. The left thumbprint was legible. The FBI had never revealed that though they had been able to lift twenty-six prints from the evidence flown from Memphis, only three could be used for identification—a latent print on the rifle, one on the telescopic sight, and one on the binoculars. There were prints on the after-shave lotion bottle, one on a beer can, and one on the April 4 *Commercial-Appeal*, but these were blurred.

In order to find Galt's identity, it was necessary to match his prints against nearly two hundred million. This procedure could be telescoped by eliminating prints of women, of men over fifty, and further shortened by checking only those of white men under fifty wanted by the police. In this last category alone there were fifty-three thousand sets of prints.

The FBI specialists began matching prints at 9:30 A.M. April 18, under the direction of George Bonebrake, who had looked through his magnifying glass at the first print on the binoculars at dawn Friday, April 5, less than twelve hours after King's murder. Now he and his men worked through the night.

At 9:15 A.M., April 19, they had gone through 699 cards. The seven hundredth card before them bore prints that matched. The name on the card was James Earl Ray. On it, too, was a rundown of his criminal record, from his birth in Alton, Illinois, on March 10, 1928, through a dozen petty crimes and arrests and prison terms to his escape from Missouri State Penitentiary on April 23, 1967. It added up to a small-time burglar and holdup man—hardly the type of man likely to commit deliberate murder.

Now, minutes passed while all available fingerprints of James Earl Ray were wirephotoed from various police stations and prisons where they were on record. There had to be no doubt.

And there was no doubt. J. Edgar Hoover announced, "Galt and Ray are identical."

The brief summary of Ray's history showed he had dropped out of school in the tenth grade and had been a drifter since. His first burglary conviction—for stealing a typewriter—had led to ninety days in the Los Angeles County Jail. Then, convicted of armed robbery in Chicago in 1952, aged twenty-four—he had held up a cabdriver—and served two years in the state prisons at Joliet, Illinois, and Pontiac, Illinois. Convicted of forging U.S. postal money orders in Hannibal, Missouri, in 1955, aged twenty-seven—three years in Leavenworth Penitentiary. Convicted of robbing a St. Louis supermarket in 1959, aged thirty-one, he and James Owens, also an ex-convict, had gotten $190 at gunpoint—and sentenced under the habitual criminal act to twenty years in Missouri State Penitentiary, from where he had escaped nearly a year ago after two attempts that failed.

A day later the FBI announced that Ray had been added to the Bureau's "Ten Most Wanted Fugitives" to give the widest possible dissemination of his photograph and description. He had a small scar on the center of his forehead, and another on the palm of his right hand. He had served from 1946 to 1948 in the U. S. Army, mainly in Germany, once receiving a three-month sentence for drunkenness and breaking arrest, and had left the Army with a general discharge "due to ineptness and lack of adaptability for military service."

They had his name, his history, his fingerprints. They should zero in on him swiftly. In Washington there was a collective sigh of relief.

CHAPTER XVI

Now, at once, an extraordinary task began. It was to learn everything possible about James Earl Ray. Hundreds of FBI agents were sent about the country to question every person who could be found who had ever known him. Some of those they questioned co-operated. Some refused, fearing a terrible vengeance. Some obviously lied, particularly members of his family, who though apparently remote from each other were far more closely knit than first appeared; and particularly convicts who had known him. Everything a fellow prisoner said was suspect. One could not know what private scores were being settled, or what special privileges were being sought by telling the authorities what one thought they wanted to hear.

Within hours of learning that Galt was Ray, the agents had traced down James Gerald Ray, his father, now known as Jerry Rayns. It was done in greatest secrecy. To the world, the elder Ray had died long ago. As early as 1946, James Earl Ray, aged seventeen, wrote next to his father's name on his enlistment application, "Dead." His two brothers, John and Jerry, also reported him dead each time they gave their histories. But he was unmistakably alive, a small, wiry man of sixty-nine, a one-time auto mechanic, used-car salesman, railroad hand, and carnival fighter, living alone with his dog on a farm south of Center, Missouri. When agents found him he became upset. If people learned that Ray was his son, the Negroes might burn down his place.

Yes, nine children had been born of his marriage with Lucille Maher. She'd become an alcoholic, and they had separated long ago, in 1952. Anyway, he'd had little contact with the family—saw none of them these sixteen years, except his daughter Carol, who lived in St. Louis, not too far away, and came up weekends with groceries for him. But the others—he knew nothing about John's and Jerry's whereabouts. There was another daughter, Melba, but he hardly ever heard from her—she had mental trouble. Franklin had been killed in an accident in Quincy in 1958, there'd been a little girl, Marjorie, who'd burned to death when she was six, Max and Susy had been given away for adoption after he and his wife separated. He had no idea of what had become of them.

He knew nothing of this King trouble until Carol called him the night before to say the newspapers said Jim was involved. If Jim came to see him and he failed to report it, he was warned, he could be charged with harboring a fugitive—a federal offense with heavy penalties. Rayns had a prison record—he'd served time for larceny as a young man—and he wanted no trouble with the law now. "No, no," he said. "I'm afraid of him. I've barred my doors." He had a shotgun and a pistol on the premises.

The agents visited him the next day—the second of many visits. The records showed that he and Lucille had not separated but that he had gone off long before with another woman; that Lucille, once a pretty, buxom girl, had begun to drink and the family, living in a red light district on a street on which there were more than a dozen brothels, began to fall apart, so that by 1955 five of the children had become wards of the court, the three youngest taken from their mother despite her frantic protests and put into a Catholic orphanage; and by 1961 Lucille, in a pitiable state, arrested repeatedly for drunkenness, for disorderly conduct, for loitering at bars, was dead of acute alcoholism; that Franklin had not died in 1958 but in 1963, when, aged eighteen, he drove a car off the Quincy Memorial Bridge, drowning himself and an eighteen-year-old girl companion. Jerry Rayns had paid for the funeral, which became a family reunion— all except James Earl Ray, who was in prison—and so Rayns had seen some of his children as recently as five years ago. Had he remembered anymore today, they asked?

No, he said, but he had been thinking. If Jim killed King, he certainly didn't plan it himself. He wasn't that smart. He remembered the boy as very shy, no close friends, never went out with girls, tight with money, wouldn't trust banks, so his grandmother, Mrs. Mary Katherine Maher, of Alton, Illinois, kept his money for him. He remembered seeing Jim around 1943, when Jim lived with his grandmother. The boy worked the next year or two, Rayns heard, in a shoe factory, then lost his job and enlisted in the Army and was sent to Germany. He'd saved something like $1400 by that time, which his grandmother held for him until he got out; and he came out of the Army with something like $4000. Jim made a buck stretch a long way.

The agents looked about them. This farm of his—how large was it? Forty-six acres, said Rayns. When had he bought it? Where did he get the money? Rayns bristled. Did they think that if Jim killed that colored fella, he'd turned over some of the loot he got for it to him? Rayns said pugnaciously he bought the farm last September with the help of a loan from Carol. He had seen it listed in a bank foreclosure sale, appraised at $8000, but it could probably be bought for $3000, he'd been told, so he went to the sale, "and I was able to pick it up for $2600." He had sold a small shack that he owned in St. Louis, took $700 of the proceeds, Carol loaned him $1900 from her savings —and that was where the money came from.

They found Carol Jean Pepper, his daughter, her husband, Albert, and their two small boys in their comfortable, old-fashioned, two-story house in a suburb of St. Louis. Carol, dark-haired, solidly built, matter of fact, made clear at once that like her father she had heard nothing from Jim for years. "I only met him three or four times in my life," she said. They had to remember that she was thirteen years younger. She was twenty-seven now, and when Jim came out of the Army in January 1949, she was only eight years old. She remembered how happy her mother was that Jim was home. She saw him again in 1957, when she was sixteen and living with her father in St. Louis. Even then she had only brief encounters with her big brother, usually on the street. The last time she saw him was at least ten years ago. Her husband, whom she married eight years ago, had never even met Jim.

Yes, she had loaned money to her father to buy the farm. She and Albert bought this house, too—for ten thousand dollars, which they were able to do, thanks to a small down payment. They both worked hard, saved every penny—Albert for an engineering company, earning three dollars an hour, plus overtime, she as a teacher's aid in a Catholic Head Start program, earning sixty dollars a week. She'd always had one paying job or another since their marriage.

The same day, Friday, April 19, they found the second sister, Melba Marie Ryan, a plump, round-faced woman of twenty-nine wearing faded brown dungarees, her light brown hair cut short and bound with a scarf. They could not question her. She was hysterical in her tiny one-dollar-a-day room at the Virginia Hotel, a run-down rooming house overlooking the train sheds in Quincy. They knew her history. She had been hospitalized as a mental patient several times, she was known as a religious fanatic, she had been arrested often for disorderly conduct and drunkenness. She had never married, she lived alone, spending much of her time in the large square hotel lobby watching TV. Eight months before, she had been arrested marching through the streets carrying a seven-foot-high wooden cross, which she had made of four-by-fours and painted red, white, and blue. On another occasion she had gone down the street with a four-by-four, smashing show windows. When they asked her why, she said, "God told me to do it."

The agents returned the next day when she had calmed down. Today the radio had reported that her brother had been put on the FBI's "Ten Most Wanted Fugitives" list. She could not get over it. She was able to choose him from half a dozen photographs of men shown her. She, too, said, "I only saw him two or three times in my life."

The last time had been about ten years ago, when he was living with them for a few months in a St. Louis boardinghouse her mother ran. The family's real name was Ray, she said, but when they moved from Ewing to Quincy in 1944, her mother changed it to Ryan, since the children were going to St. Boniface's Catholic School and she thought Ryan sounded more Catholic than Ray. They'd used all kinds of names: Ray, Ryan, Raines, Raynes, Rayns.

As for Jim—all she could remember was that when she saw him last he said he might go back to Germany. He liked it there. Maybe he was there now.

She had little more to tell. She lived on a disability pension; all her bills were taken care of. She had never written Jim in prison, he had never written her, she had never visited him.

While agents were questioning Melba, others were interrogating John Larry Ray, James's brother, three years younger, and generally recognized as the head of the family. He was a huskier, more muscular edition of the James Earl Ray shown on the FBI photograph, with the same long nose, the same receding hairline. He was behind the bar of his tavern, the Grapevine, in St. Louis, and joined them in their car, which they parked down the street and in which they conducted interviews whenever possible. "What's all the excitement about?" he asked roughly. "It's only a Nigger. If you thought he'd killed a white man you wouldn't be here." He had the same one-sided smile, at once sardonic and bitter. "King should've been killed ten years ago." He spoke rapidly but with a small impediment in his speech, an inability to pronounce his r's.

Did he know where Jim was now? He shook his head. When had

he seen him last? "Either two or four years ago," he said vaguely, when he visited him at Missouri State Penitentiary. He wasn't certain of the date because before that he hadn't seen Jim for some nineteen or twenty years—back around 1949, when Jim was discharged from the Army and visited the family in Quincy. In all the time Jim had been in jail, he, John, had not visited him more than two or three times.

He was down on the prison records, however, as visiting him on April 22—the day before he broke out. The records showed he had visited him eight times in all: once in 1962, three times in 1963, three in 1966, and the last visit in 1967.

John took this calmly. "I don't really remember when I visited him last. I had a visitor's permit and it was issued to either John or Jerry Ray. Maybe my brother Jerry visited him that day. I don't remember." He grinned his sardonic smile. "Maybe he visited him the other times, too."

John had no reason to co-operate with the law. He had served seven years—from his twentieth to his twenty-eighth year—in Menard Penitentiary, Illinois, and, with the same easy interchange of names, he had been there as John Ryan. As a felon, he could not obtain a liquor license, so when he opened the Grapevine four months ago, the license was taken out in his sister Carol's name. He'd worked before at all kinds of jobs—bartender, bus-station attendant, golf-course attendant. He had sent small amounts of money to Jim, too—no more than three or four dollars at a time, for candy and odds and ends at the commissary—because Jim had done the same for him when he was in Menard. He did not tell the agents that since Jim was twenty-one the only times he had seen him had been when Jim was in jail.

That reminded him, he said, that he did visit Jim in 1960. His visits were never more than half an hour. "Jim is closemouthed. We talked mainly about his welfare." On his last visit—maybe he did visit him in 1967—Jim, who kept up with all the news, said that the former German army officer, Ian Smith, was doing a good job as prime minister running Rhodesia. "It was just a passing comment," John said, with his grin.*

---

* The month before, the Ian Smith government had condemned three black men to death for murder. Queen Elizabeth had commuted their sentences to life imprisonment, but Smith had defied the Queen and hanged the three. Rhodesia, a one-time British colony, had broken away from Britain in 1965 after Britain refused to grant it independence because of its stringent white supremacy policies.

1. Dr. Martin Luther King, Jr., moments after a demented black woman stabbed him with a letter opener while he was autographing copies of his book, *Stride Toward Freedom*, in a Harlem department store on September 20, 1958. The letter opener can be seen in his upper chest, near his tie.

2. Oslo, December 10, 1964: Dr. King contemplating the Nobel Peace Prize gold medal.

3. Dr. King congratulated in Amsterdam on October 20, 1965, by Queen Juliana of The Netherlands after he received an honorary Doctor of Social Science degree from Amsterdam's Free University. At left is Queen Juliana's husband, Prince Bernhard, who also received an honorary degree.

4. Locking arms with Rev. Ralph Abernathy (right) and Bishop B. Julian Smith (left), Dr. King leads the ill-fated civil rights march of March 28, 1968, in Memphis.

5. (Left) April 3, 1968: the morning before the assassination. Dr. King, preceded by Rev. Abernathy, as they entered Room 306 at the Lorraine Motel, Memphis. Following Dr. King is Rev. James M. Lawson, Jr., whose invitation brought King to Memphis.

6. (Right) Shortly after noon, April 3: in the courtyard of the Lorraine. Dr. King being served with the injunction barring his march by Marshal Cato Ellis. Others, left to right: Rev. Abernathy: Rev. Andrew Young; Rev. James Orange; Rev. Bernard Lee.

7. Moments after the assassination, the Rev. Samuel B. Kyles and Ben Branch being interviewed at the Lorraine Motel.

8. (Left) The killer's room. Room 5B at 422½ South Main Street, Memphis, occupied by James Earl Ray. He kept watch on Dr. King, waiting for him to appear on the balcony of the Lorraine Motel, visible from the open window. Ray placed the chair there and lifted and pushed to one side the drapes so as not to obstruct his view.

9. (Right) The murder bathroom in the Memphis rooming house. Ray dashed into the bathroom from Room 5B, stood in the tub, and, resting his rifle on the window sill, fired the fatal shot at Dr. King as the latter stood, clearly visible, on the balcony of the Lorraine Motel, 203 feet away.

10. The rear of 422½ South Main Street (left) and its adjoining building, showing the small bathroom window—fourth from the right—from which Ray fired the fatal shot. Frank Brewer, husband of the building manager, came out on the landing atop the wooden steps of 422½ a moment after the shot, to be ordered back into the building by police who were already on the scene.

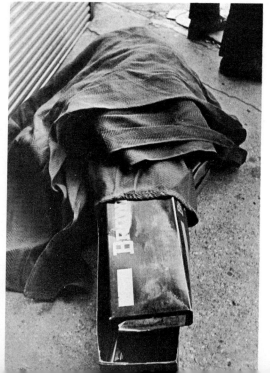

11. The bundle of evidence dropped by Ray in the doorway of Canipe's Amusement Company. The box, with word "Browning" on it, contained the murder rifle. Partly covering it is the bedspread Ray traveled with.

12. A few minutes after Dr. King was shot, police standing guard in the doorway of the Canipe Amusement Company. Immediately to the left is the door to the stairs leading up to the rooming house; to the left of No. 422 is the stairway down which Ray fled after the shot.

13. This is what Ray saw from the window of the bathroom. The Lorraine Hotel and Motel—the motel to the right, with men standing on the balcony in front of Room 306 at the spot Dr. King was struck by the bullet.

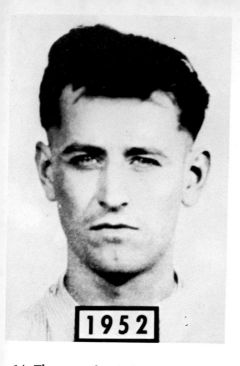

1952

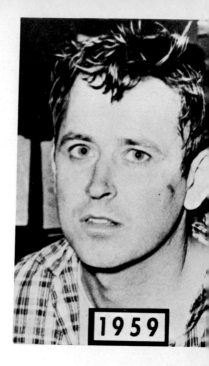

1959

14. The many faces of James Earl Ray. The four photographs were taken at variou
prisons in which he was incarcerated.

1960

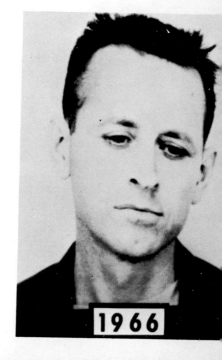

1966

15. James Earl Ray, above, as he looked when he entered Missouri State Penitentiary in September 1960, to serve a twenty-year term, escaping April 23, 1967. Below, photo taken when he graduated on March 2, 1968, from the International School of Bartending, Los Angeles, a month before killing Dr. King. Ray had closed his eyes when the shutter snapped: an FBI artist, to help identification, painted in the eyes.

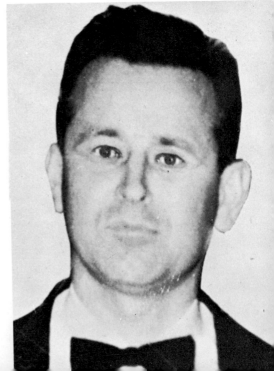

16. Ray's passport photograph, taken in Toronto on April 11, 1968, just before he assumed the name Ramon George Sneyd. The protruding tip of his nose had been removed by surgery five weeks before. He dyed his hair black and wore shell-rimmed glasses to help disguise himself further.

7. Three residents of Toronto whose names James Earl Ray (far right) used before and ter the assassination. Ray assumed the name Eric Starvo Galt prior to the assassination, variation of Eric St. Vincent Galt, a businessman (second left); Paul Bridgman, an lucator (far left) in Toronto; and Ramon George Sneyd, a policeman (second right) for s passport. All four men are similar in height, weight, and coloring and look approxi- ately the same age.

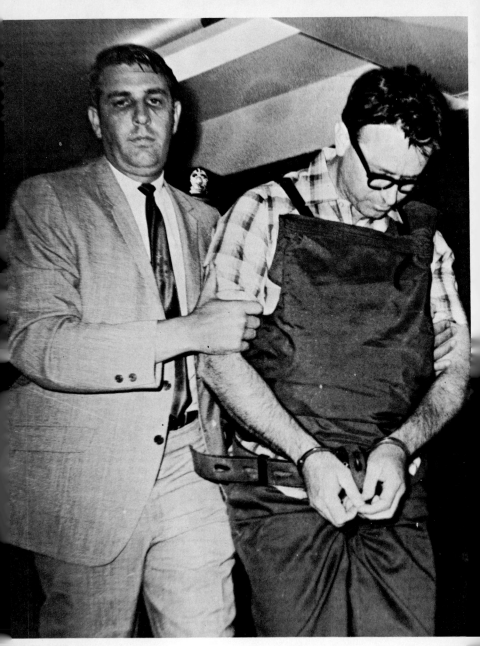

18. Sheriff William N. Morris, Jr., bringing Ray, hands manacled to belt, and protected by bulletproof apron, into Shelby County Jail, Memphis, Tennessee, before dawn July 19, 1968, after Ray's extradition from London.

9. Charles Q. Stephens, the state's chief witness. Stephens saw Ray when he rented
oom 5B in the Memphis rooming house—Stephens and his common-law wife occupied
oom 6B—and also saw him as he fled from the bathroom after shooting Dr. King.

20. James Earl Ray, aged 14, snapped in 1942 in front of Terrill's Filling Station and Cafe, in Ewing, Missouri. Ray is in the white sweater. Standing with him is his friend, Robey Peacock. The others are Charles Peacock, Robey's brother, and Mrs. Carrie Terrill.

21. Photograph of the first eight grades, Ewing School, 1938. Ray, just turned ten and small for his age, is last boy in third row with tousled hair and wide smile. He was in the third grade. Robey Peacock is at his right. Carlisle Washburn, today Ewing postmaster, is last boy on right, bottom row.

22. In the basement of this wooden house in Alton, Illinois, on March 10, 1928, James Earl Ray was born. His maternal grandmother, Mrs. Mary Katherine Maher, who lived here, gave Ray's parents two basement rooms where they waited for the baby, their firstborn, to arrive.

23. Left to right (front): Renfro Hays, private detective; Arthur J. Hanes, Jr., and Arthur J. Hanes, Sr., Ray's first attorneys. Taken in front of Shelby County Criminal Court building, which also houses the Shelby County Jail, where Ray was kept.

24. The prosecution in Memphis: left to right: Assistant Attorney General James C. Beasley; Attorney General Phil M. Canale, Jr., in charge of the state's case; Executive Assistant Attorney General Robert K. Dwyer.

25. Criminal Court Judge W. Preston Battle, Jr., presiding judge in the James Earl Ray case. Judge Battle died of a heart attack on March 31, 1969, three weeks after Ray pleaded guilty and accepted a ninety-nine-year sentence in his court.

26. Left to right: Attorney Percy Foreman of Houston, with author Gerold Frank, taken in Memphis on November 12, 1968, the day Foreman succeeded Arthur J. Hanes, Sr., as Ray's defense counsel.

27. Rev. James L. Bevel, one of Dr. King's top aides, who on January 19, 1969, announced that Ray was innocent of Dr. King's murder and offered to defend him without a fee.

28. Left to right: Jerry Ray, James Earl Ray's brother; J. B. Stoner, attorney and organizer for the National States Rights Party, who succeeded Foreman as defense counsel for Ray, and by whom Jerry Ray was later employed.

29. John Larry Ray, brother of James Earl Ray. John Ray was sentenced in 1971 to eighteen years in Leavenworth Penitentiary, for bank robbery.

There was no point in the agents hanging around his tavern. Jim wouldn't show up here. He knew the law kept tab on every relative, every friend, every ex-con who might know Jim. Jim was nobody's fool. He, John, didn't believe he killed King, but if he did, it was for a lot of money. Unless he was crazy.

"He was O.K. until he came back from Germany," John said. He didn't want to work anymore. John had heard Jim began using narcotics in the Army. Or maybe something else happened to make him act crazy. "If he killed King, he was crazy or he was well paid for it. If he was crazy, he wouldn't contact any of us. And if he was paid to do it, he wouldn't contact us either because he wouldn't need any help. And if he *was* paid—" John shook his head. "They're sooner or later going to kill him." He added, "But why should he kill King, even for a lot of money? He could always pick up money easy by robbing—that's why he was in jail in the first place."

He did not tell them that a few days before when he passed a newsstand and saw a sketch on the front page of the St. Louis *Post-Dispatch* of Eric Starvo Galt, wanted for the murder of King, through his mind flashed, *It looks like Jimmy—could be.* Today at noon Jerry had called him from Chicago. "You know who they're looking for in the King murder?"

John said, "You don't have to tell me. You wouldn't be calling me if it wasn't Jimmy."

John remembered that the night before King was killed the man was all over the TV. John listened to him making his speech down in Memphis about going to the mountaintop and not being afraid to die, and he thought, *He's going to get killed. This is probably the day he's going to get it.* He, himself, had no use for the man. But he never thought, he said later, that his own brother would be the suspect.

They found Jerry Ray in his room at the Sportsman's Country Club in Northbrook, a Chicago suburb, where he worked as a greens' keeper. At thirty-two he was a younger, darker edition of the man on the FBI flyer. He had just gotten into bed when he heard the report on his bedside radio that Eric Starvo Galt was really James Earl Ray. He had got up and dressed and sat on the edge of the bed, waiting for them. He knew the FBI would come, and soon.

Thirty minutes later there was a knock on his door and when he opened it, two agents were standing there. "Come in," he said resignedly, and sat on the edge of the bed again and submitted to their questions. No, he hadn't seen Jim since he visited him in prison in 1966. No, Jim couldn't have killed King. They could check Jim's record—he never fired a gun, never pistol-whipped anyone, never slapped anyone around. That wasn't Jim's style. And Jim had nothing against Negroes. Why, neither he nor his brothers had ever really known a Negro until one moved next door to them when he was about fourteen. There were no Negroes in Ewing. You had to go ten miles down the road to another town to see one. Maybe somebody hired Jim for a great deal of money—if he was the one that did it. But if Jim had done it, no one would ever know. He'd never talk. That was a family trait—none of the Rays talked.

Jerry, like his brothers and his father, had a prison record. At one time Jerry and John—and their uncle Earl Ray—were in Menard Prison, Illinois, together. Earl, who had a long prison record, was convicted of assault with intent to kill, after throwing acid in his wife's face. Jerry, a school dropout at fourteen, went to reform school, later worked as a factory hand, and at nineteen, was sent to Menard after he and three friends robbed a tavern. He went to jail under the name Jerry Ryan. After parole a year later, he'd held up a gas station and returned to Menard for two more years. Since then he had not been in any trouble. John helped him find this job. He'd been here for three years, the longest stretch so far.

Juvenile court and welfare records helped fill out the picture. Within forty-eight hours after Ray's identification all of the children had been questioned, save two, Max and Susy, who had been adopted and had different names. Max, now seventeen, was retarded; he had spent time in an institution for the feeble-minded. Susy, who would be celebrating her twenty-first birthday this week while the most intensive manhunt in history was underway for her brother, had been the only one in the family to complete high school. She was a girl with some spirit. At twelve she had run away from the orphanage and had been found living with her grandmother. She was a go-go dancer, now, in Chicago. Neither she nor Max knew anything about James Earl Ray, and neither they nor he would have known the other had they met on the street.

By the end of the first week virtually every inmate of Leavenworth, of Pontiac, and of Missouri State Penitentiary had been questioned. The best picture of Ray came from Walter Rife, an ex-convict who had known him since both were fourteen. Rife owned the restaurant in the Virginia Hotel, in Quincy, where Melba lived. Rife had been seized with Ray in 1955 for cashing stolen U.S. postal money orders, and both had served time at Leavenworth. Because Ray was charged with stealing and cashing, and Rife only with cashing, Rife got out in 1957, a few months before Ray. That was the last time he had seen him. They had played together as boys when Jim used to come from Ewing to visit his uncle Earl, in Quincy. Jim had great respect for his uncle, who was a gang leader and tough.

Rife could not believe Ray killed King, although he knew he hated Negroes intensely. He never knew why. To Daniel Greene of *The National Observer*, the first reporter to reach Rife, Rife said, "Jim Ray was prejudiced. He was prejudiced to the point that he hated to see a colored person breathe. You could gather from his conversation that if it was up to him, there wouldn't be any colored people— they'd either be shipped back to Africa or be disposed of in some way."

Ray was, according to Rife, first and last a professional thief who would "steal anything and everything he could get his hands on," who would burglarize shops and get rid of stolen goods through a fence in Peoria, Illinois. Rife knew that Ray broke into houses, taking anything he could sell; that he pulled armed stickups, burglarized safes, rolled drunks for money, that he was a surprisingly strong man (always exercising with weights, doing push-ups and handstands) and a dangerous and dirty street fighter, winning by any means. But, Rife repeated, he knew Ray as a thief, not a murderer, a man who had a gun now and didn't have one the next day, who might buy or hock or trade one, but always a thief, a man who kept to himself, who liked to roam about the country on his own, a man who was closemouthed, never talking about himself or his family. The whole Ray outfit was remarkably tight-lipped.

Rife looked at the agents. If they wanted proof of it—only today he'd learned that Melba Marie, who ate all her meals in his place, was Ray's sister. He had known Ray off and on for twenty-six years, they'd played ball together as kids, they'd swum together, they'd gone on beer binges together, they'd knocked about the country together, they'd robbed together and been jailed together—and he had never known that Melba, whom he knew as well as if she'd been part of his own family, was Jimmy Ray's sister.

CHAPTER XVII

May 1. May 10. May 25.
They hunted James Earl Ray.
And in vain.

The last glimpse anyone had had of him was shortly before 9 A.M. Friday, April 5—the morning after the murder—when the housewives of Capitol Homes in Atlanta had seen the dark-haired man in the blue suit emerge from the white Mustang, lock the door, and walk away. He had walked into invisibility.

The Justice Department did not wish to admit it, but the trail was cold. Confusing alarms filled the air. Eric Starvo Galt could not be James Earl Ray. They were different in age, appearance, personality. One was sophisticated, outgoing, a Wallace supporter, a racist, an enthusiastic dancer, an habitué of hippie neighborhoods—the other a shy, inarticulate hillbilly, a loner, a humorless, nonpolitical, inverted sociopath. Inside stories multiplied. Raymond Curtis, who had been a fellow prisoner at Missouri State Penitentiary, said that he and Ray were in the exercise yard when they learned of President Kennedy's assassination. Ray said, "Somebody made a pretty penny from that," and added bitterly, "I'm always inside when something big like that comes up."

Not long after that he and Ray overheard a new prisoner say that a million-dollar price had been put on Martin Luther King's head by a Southern "Businessmen's Association." Ray remarked with a grim smile, "I'll collect it." On the wall of a telephone booth at the St. Francis Hotel in Hollywood, where Ray, as Galt, stayed, reporters found pencil doodlings which looked like, "Down with Mexicans and Niggers and Martin Luther Coon." Louis Lomax, a well-known black journalist, rented a white Mustang and with Charlie Stein retraced the trip Stein and Ray had taken to New Orleans in December. In a series of syndicated articles, Lomax asserted unequivocally that Ray's telephone calls en route had been to the mysterious "industrialist" in New Orleans, and that Ray had met the man there at least twice "in the Trade Mart area."

In Memphis tips of every kind poured into Inspector Zachary's Homicide Division. Three nights after the murder, a Memphis housewife, listening on her shortwave radio in the kitchen while doing the supper dishes, tuned in a ship-to-shore conversation dealing with a "Mr. Galt, who wanted to leave the ship at Memphis and go south." Amid scores of letters and telephone calls from persons who insisted they saw the wanted man furtively riding a bus, or speeding by in a white Mustang with red and white license plates, was a woman, who shall be known here as Mrs. Frederic Myers, calling from a small Tennessee town. She was in tears. Her husband, a salesman whose territory covered several Southern states, was near a nervous breakdown because he had overheard (and was certain he was seen overhearing) five men in a men's room at a truck stop near Lebanon, Tennessee, plotting to kill Dr. King. He had been sitting in one of the stalls when the men came in. They had glanced under the three-quarter doors but had not seen his feet because he had the habit of sitting with his legs up, his feet propped against the door. They had talked freely, then, thinking themselves alone. When they walked out, he had hurried after them a moment too soon. One man happened to turn around and saw him, and looked at him suspiciously, as if to say, "Where did you come from?" This had been March 29, the morning after King's march in Memphis ended in a riot. On April 5, the day after King's murder, her husband's car had been broken into. Nothing had been taken but he found a small pocket calendar, which he'd left on the seat, tucked into the recess area of his speedometer. When he extracted it he saw that someone had clipped words from a newspaper and pasted them on the calendar so they read IF YOU GO TO THE POLICE OR FBI YOU WILL BE KILLED. When Ray's photograph appeared in the papers on April 19, her husband was absolutely terrified: Ray, he told her, looked like one of the five men. Now her husband was somewhere on the road, convinced he was being followed, telephoning her every few hours and so agitated he dared not tell her from where he was calling. Could the police help? Especially since five months before King's assassination her husband had told her he'd learned in Baton Rouge that a group of wealthy businessmen "were taking up a big collection to get King killed." In a strange upsetting way, the rumors, however bizarre, seemed to turn upon themselves, one strengthening the other. Why should Frederic Myers, a salesman passing through Baton Rouge, Louisiana, hear almost the same account as Raymond Curtis, a prisoner in Missouri State Penitentiary?

From the Royal Canadian Mounted Police came two startling reports. On April 23, Samuel Marshall, assistant manager of Loblaw's Groceteria—a supermarket in Toronto—had almost collided with a hatless, dark-haired man who unexpectedly emerged from a back room. Only employees were allowed there, because a winding stairway in the rear of the room led directly to the office safe. "Can I do anything for you?" he asked the stranger warily. The latter, a man about 5' 10", wearing a small-checked jacket and slacks, seemed taken aback for a moment, then said, "I'm looking for a job." He had had two years' experience in a grocery in Mexico, just below the border, he said. Marshall said he had part-time work available, but the other wanted only full-time, and when Emerson Benns, the manager, approached, the stranger edged toward the door and was gone a minute later. Benns hurried after him in time to see him run half a block to a corner bank and stand inside, watching Benns through the large plate-glass window. When the manager emerged from his shop, the other darted out a side door of the bank, jumped on a trolley, and vanished. Next day Marshall opened his copy of *Newsweek* magazine and saw Ray's photograph. "That's the man," he exclaimed, and immediately called the police. But Ray—if it was Ray—was nowhere to be found.

Even more troubling was a confidential report from the night manager of the Sheraton-Mt. Royal Hotel in Montreal. About 10 P.M. on the evening of May 9, a woman guest from California who was staying on the fourth floor of the huge hotel noticed a piece of folded yellow paper crumpled on the corridor carpet on her way to the elevators. She had seen it lying there earlier, around four o'clock. This time, because it was still there, she picked it up. The paper had been wrapped around a miniature matchbox with the inscription "St. Moritz-on-the-Park," which intrigued her because she had once stayed at the New York hotel. Almost automatically she unfolded the paper, which was yellow onion skin of memo pad size, and suddenly the name Martin Luther King leaped at her. There, across the top, printed in block letters in black ink, she read:

THINGS TO DO

Below them:

    1. Martin Luther King, Jr.
    2. Rap Brown
    3. Stokely Carmichael

But what horrified her was that the name of Martin Luther King, Jr., had a sharp slashing line drawn through it—crossing him off the list.

She immediately told the night manager. He surmised that the note and matches had been dropped on the hallway floor by a cleaning maid while she was transferring wastepaper taken from the wastebaskets in each room from her cleaning cart to the refuse closet on the floor. This meant they originally must have been tossed into a wastebasket in one of the 131 rooms on the floor. A secret investigation began. Every guest on the floor was checked; the trash in the refuse closets on all eight floors was examined for anything else that might be found. Registration cards for everyone who had been staying in the hotel—this meant more than a thousand rooms—on the night of May 8 were examined for anyone who might have put down his home address in printing similar to that on the note; even guests who had attended a large banquet on May 7 were checked out. Every piece of hotel stationery—memo pads, envelopes, "This Week in Montreal," even room service menus and all of the literature usually found in hotel rooms—was examined, down to the desk blotters in each room, on the assumption that the writer must have written other notes or memos and unknowingly left the impression of his ball-point pen behind him. Nothing helpful was found. In New York the management of the St. Moritz said that certainly the matchbox was theirs, that they were available only at their hotel. The hunters grew excited. Not many persons could have been guests at both hotels in recent days; a simple rundown of their registration cards should narrow the search to a few people. Then it was learned that the St. Moritz was the client of a large advertising agency which always kept a supply of matchboxes on hand for publicity purposes. The memo writer might have picked one up anywhere. There was gloom again.

As day followed day, the rumors of conspiracy only grew. They flourished in the press. The country's black community was almost unanimously convinced of it: Dr. King's associates thought so too. Dr. Abernathy, struggling with Resurrection City, the city of tents he and his followers had erected in Washington, D.C., to house the thousands of poor people he had led into the capital, believed it was a conspiracy, as did Dr. King's widow. By mid-May, Ramsey Clark, in a TV interview, admitted that the FBI could not rule out the possibility that King's killer might have been hired by foreign agents. Had foreign intelligence seized Ray and placed him in some country beyond U.S. extradition, so that he would never be brought to justice, the full story never known, all the anguish of the Lee Harvey Oswald case repeated again? Was he in Cuba, perhaps? New Orleans, so often mentioned, could be a jumping-off place for Cuba. The city of New Orleans had been gone over with a fine-tooth comb. The Trade Mart area, where Charlie Stein said Ray had told him he'd seen him with the two boys, and where Louis Lomax said Ray had conferred with the mysterious industrialist, had been sifted through almost microscopically, reputed Mafia leaders questioned, every underground contact alerted—but no trace of Ray or anyone resembling him, and no trace of the industrialist.

Or—and this was even more troubling in its way—was Ray dead? Had black militants done away with him? Had rivalry between the Negro leadership led to Ray's act and to his disposal lest he betray those who hired him? There was an even wilder surmise. Was King's assassination a crime of passion? A jealous husband who had ordered King done away with because of his attentions to his wife, and then had the killer done away with to protect himself?

To those hunting Ray, this was a delicate matter. Dr. King, as the most charismatic black leader in the nation, was a man admired and literally pursued by women wherever he went, and he was known to be responsive to feminine beauty. In the hysteria following his death, it was recalled that six weeks before the assassination a black informant had tipped off the FBI to an alleged affair between King and a beautiful black woman, wife of a prominent black man on the West Coast, and had wondered whether the most ancient of reasons might be behind the murder. The FBI checked it out, and concluded that the affair, if true, had nothing to do with King's death. But, to set at rest for himself this disturbing possibility, a newspaper columnist accompanied by an agent called upon the husband, interviewed him frankly and at length, and obtained his permission to speak separately to his wife, assuming she would see them. After interviewing the husband, the visitors were convinced that it was sheerest fantasy to imagine that he had hired a killer. The wife had no hesitancy in seeing them, and although it was true, she said, that Dr. King telephoned her every Wednesday night, she indignantly denied anything more than a friendship.

By the latter part of May the conviction that Ray *was* dead hung like a cloud over Ramsey Clark's office. Police experience indicated that, if a murderer was not caught in the first week, he might never be caught. Ray could well be dead. His fellow conspirators had destroyed him because he had been too clumsy, had left behind too much evidence, his identification had been too easy—the FBI was all over the United States, Mexico, and half a dozen European countries with his photograph and fingerprints—they simply had been forced to get rid of him, because he was too much of a danger to them at large.

Time and again Clark's office was electrified by the discovery of an unidentified body that might have been Ray. In May the bullet-ridden body of a white man of Ray's age and height had been found buried in the sand of a beach in Puerto Vallarta, Mexico. Because of the Mexican tourist stickers on the white Mustang, the FBI had asked Mexican police to investigate. Ray, as Galt, had been in Puerto Vallarta in November 1967, just before going to Los Angeles. He had spent several weeks there, much of it in the company of prostitutes, and information on what he had been doing there was still being gathered by the Mexican Federal Police. Why could he not have fled there after the murder to escape whatever fate was pursuing him, and why could he not have been trailed to Mexico and murdered? The Bureau sent an expert to Puerto Vallarta to take fingerprints from the body. It was almost decomposed, the skin of the fingers dry and shrunken. Fluid had to be injected to puff them up sufficiently to take prints. They did not match Ray's.

A few days later another man's body, similar in size and age, was found in a shallow grave in Pottsville, Pennsylvania. There were four bullet holes in it; in addition, lime had been poured over the body—this, tests indicated, within the last month or so. Again, tense hours passed before Ray's dental records were obtained and the body determined not to be his.

The search so far had been the most intensive in history. There were days when 1500 agents were simultaneously working on the case, following the proliferating leads, although a total of more than 3000 were enlisted in the case at one time or another. Because Ray had subscribed to a hippie publication in Los Angeles, and because he had chosen to live at Garner's rooming house in the hippie section of Atlanta, agents dressed like hippies circulated in these areas in every major city in the United States, hoping to come upon his trail. There was no clue too minor to follow. During his periods of freedom, Ray had always driven a used car of one make or another. Agents went back twenty years to check out each of them—the original salesman, the first owner and each subsequent owner, in hope of getting a line on Ray or his whereabouts. In vain.

Dead—or out of the country. He had once said that if he ever got out he'd hide away below the border. But now new evidence came to light revealing that he had considered South Africa. On May 9, Joseph Acord, an official of the American Southern African Council, in Washington, D.C., going through his files on another matter, came upon a letter signed Eric S. Galt. The name, now so much in the news, startled him. He had completely forgotten his brief correspondence with the man five months earlier. He read the letter over, misspellings and all. Dated December 28, 1967, it read:

> Dear Sir: I recently read an article in the L.A. Times on your council. The local John Birch Society provided me with your address. My reason for writing is that I am considering immigrating to Rhodesia. However there are a couple of legal questions involved.
>
> 1. The U. S. Government will not issue a passport for travel to Rhodesia.
>
> 2. Would their be any way to enter Rhodesia legally (from the Rhodesian Government point of view?)
>
> I would appreciate any information you could give me on the above subject or any other information on Rhodesia.
>
> Sincerely,
> Eric S. Galt
> 1535 N. Serrano
> Los Angeles, Cal.

Acord had sent a form letter in reply that the council did not handle such matters. Now he immediately forwarded the letter to the FBI. Rhodesia! The place seemed to fascinate Ray. Hadn't John Ray mentioned, in his sardonic fashion, that when he visited his brother the day before he broke out of Missouri State Penitentiary, Jim had spoken approvingly of the way Ian Smith "was running Rhodesia"?

If Ray had gone to Europe, or to some country in South Africa, how would he have done it? He would need a forged passport and other identification. At Missouri State Penitentiary, Canada was known as the easiest country in which to obtain such a passport. All one needed was five dollars, someone to sign as your guarantor—that is, swear he knew you at least two years—and a baptismal certificate. These were available, as well as guarantors, in the Rue Notre Dame neighborhood in Montreal. You made contact through a floater or a prostitute, who would show you where to buy your certificate for about fifty dollars. And Ray had been in Montreal. On July 28, 1967, three months after he escaped from prison, as Eric Starvo Galt he had first sent off his application for mail-order locksmithing lessons from a Montreal address—*an apartment house at 2589 Rue Notre Dame, E.* He had lived there evidently, for several weeks, before showing up in August in Birmingham, at Cherpes' boardinghouse. This was, of course, before King's murder, but here, as recently as April 23—after the murder—was the episode in Loblaw's Groceteria, in Toronto, not to mention the mysterious onion-skin memo found in the Sheraton-Mt. Royal in Montreal. Even if one discounted the latter as a sick joke—a murderer or his accomplice would hardly be likely to write such incriminating memos and leave them around* —one had to consider the grocery incident. One could never be too sure of such identification, made after the fact. But Ray's criminal history showed a definite pattern of robbing and holding up grocery stores.

Ray could have been in Canada *after* King's murder.

Routinely the FBI and the Royal Canadian Mounted Police at the FBI's request had been searching through recent passport applications for someone under some other name who might be Ray. There had been no success in the United States, though more than ten thousand passport applications, with their attached photographs, had been examined. Since early May a task force of a dozen constables had been secretly engaged in the same task at the External Affairs Passport Division Office in Ottawa, where, working at night after all employees had left, and armed with magnifying glasses and Ray's photograph, they were going through some 230,000 photos accompanying passport applications made since Ray escaped from prison on April 23, 1967.

They worked steadily, night after night.

On May 20, a twenty-one-year-old constable suddenly paused over a photograph. "This looks like the party would look if he wore glasses." None of Ray's photographs showed him wearing glasses. He had no need for them: in prison his eyesight had tested 20–20—perfect. If it was Ray, the glasses were there as disguise. The photo was attached to the passport application of one Ramon George Sneyd, thirty-five, a native of Toronto. With it was a copy of his birth certificate. Behind the professorial shell-rimmed glasses, Sneyd stared unsmilingly at the photographer, his lips in a thin line. His face was fuller than Ray's but the left ear protruded noticeably and was set lower on the face, as was Ray's. The nose appeared slightly shorter. This could be due to the angle at which the photograph was taken. Sneyd was far neater than Ray, but all of Ray's photographs were

---

* Those hunting Ray were to think twice about this, only shortly after, when the diaries of Sirhan Sirhan, the accused assassin of Senator Robert F. Kennedy, were found with scribbled notes, "Kennedy must die."

either prison mug shots or photos taken immediately after arrest, showing him dirty and unkempt, or the uncomfortable bartending photo, on which an FBI artist had had to paint the eyes. Sneyd also looked far more substantial than Ray, in white button-down shirt, dark knit tie and inconspicuous patterned sports jacket. But—there was the telltale ear, the receding hairline, the sharpness of nose and chin, and the passport was recent: it had been issued on April 24 and sent on that date to Sneyd, care of the Kennedy Travel Bureau, in Toronto.

The RCMP quickly found Ramon George Sneyd. He turned out to be a Toronto policeman who had been on the force for the last fourteen years. When he arrived for questioning by Detective Sergeant Marsh, it was immediately apparent that he was not the man on the passport photo. *But a description of Ray would have fitted him.* His eyebrows were heavier, but he was similar in size, weight, and even cast of features.

Marsh gave him only the most meager information. After all, he might be an accomplice. "Mr. Sneyd," he began, "on April 4 a killing took place in Memphis, Tennessee. The American authorities are seeking a suspect. That suspect later took up residence here, in Toronto, under the name Ramon George Sneyd. What, if anything, can you tell us about this?"

Sneyd, perplexed, had something to say. Around May 1 he had received a telephone call from a stranger who asked him, "Is this Mr. Sneyd?" He replied, "Yes." "He wanted to know if I'd lost my passport—he said he was with the passport division and was making a routine check. I said, 'You've got the wrong Mr. Sneyd.' But he asked me again, wasn't I George Sneyd born in Toronto on October 8, 1932? I said 'Yes, but there must be some mistake. I've never had a passport.'" The man said, apologetically, obviously it was a mistake, thanked him, and hung up.

Marsh listened noncommittally. "When this suspect applied for a passport in your name, Mr. Sneyd," he said, "he wrote down both your father's name and your mother's maiden name. How could a stranger know this?" Might Sneyd have given out the information? Sneyd shook his head. "Could someone else have given it out?" His wife, perhaps? Again Sneyd said no. He'd been married before, but there was no friction between his first wife and himself, and, as for the present Mrs. Sneyd, "She doesn't know my mother's maiden name."

Sneyd was permitted to go, a highly puzzled man, and the passport application was forwarded to the FBI Crime Laboratory in Washington. The handwriting was immediately compared, not with Ray's, but with his signature as Eric Starvo Galt, because both aliases had capital S's and G's which allowed a minute comparison. No question of it: the bogus Sneyd was James Earl Ray. The capital S beginning the name Sneyd was identical to a capital S beginning the name Starvo; the G of George was identical to the G of Galt. Ray, inept bungler, third-rate robber, petty criminal and all, was either far more ingenious than he'd been given credit for, or he must have had help.

In the next four days the RCMP backtracked on Ray's movements in Canada, beginning with the Kennedy Travel Bureau in Toronto. One door then opened into another. They discovered that Ray had arrived in Toronto on April 8, four days after King's murder, and had borrowed two new identities—not only that of Sneyd, but also that of one Paul Edward Bridgman, also thirty-five, a consultant at the Toronto Board of Education, under whose name Ray had lived in a rooming house his first two weeks in Toronto—and *who also looked like him.* Even more astonishing, they discovered a third Toronto citizen, Eric St. Vincent Galt, fifty-three, a plant official for the Union Carbide Company, who signed his middle initials "St. V." drawing tiny circles instead of periods, so that it could be read "Starvo"—Eric Starvo Galt. *And Galt also looked like Ray!* Same size, same height, same cast of features. Although Galt was older than Ray, he could have easily passed for a man ten or twelve years younger. Bridgman, Sneyd, and Galt all lived within walking distance of each other in the same suburb, Scarborough. None knew the others, although Galt and Bridgman had a mutual acquaintance. Bridgman, too, had been telephoned within the last month by a man in the passport division who asked if he had applied for a passport. Bridgman said he had one about eight years ago, and the voice said apologetically that it was evidently a clerical mixup, thanked him, and hung up. Galt had not been telephoned by anyone but was the best known of the three, having a name as a sportsman. Articles had been written about him in several small publications, with his photograph and his easily misread signature under it. He so much resembled Ray—even to the small scars on his forehead and right palm—that when the FBI's first circulars appeared with the detailed physical description of the wanted man, a friend turned to him and said, "Pretty close, isn't it?" He had not been surprised to learn that the RCMP had questioned his employers when the name had first appeared, but he had been cleared since he had been at his job at the plant when King was shot in Memphis.*

The RCMP was certain now they had a conspiracy. A spokesman said, "He didn't come cold into the city. There was organized help of some kind." In some fashion someone had been able to find three Toronto citizens resembling Ray—it was noted that all three had receding hairlines, in addition to all the other points of resemblance—in some fashion had obtained private family data and made all this information available to Ray. The police pushed on to learn that the Kennedy Travel Bureau sold the bogus Sneyd a BOAC excursion ticket to London and booked him on a flight that left May 6. BOAC promptly reported that the Toronto–London section of the ticket had been used, but the return portion was still out. Ray, as Sneyd, had flown to London, then, some three weeks ago; was still in England, perhaps, or elsewhere—perhaps Rhodesia.

An all-ports warning was secretly issued by Scotland Yard. This meant that every airport, every seaport, every means of exit and entry in the British Isles was alerted. Scotland Yard agents were primed with Ray's photograph and description. But only those at the top knew the real reason he was wanted. The others were told that Sneyd, traveling on a Canadian passport, had violated the alien immigration act. If apprehended, he was to be held for questioning by Detective Chief Superintendent Thomas Butler—head of Scotland Yard's famed Flying Squad, who had broken the London–Glasgow mail train robbery of 1963—or Chief Inspector Kenneth Thompson.

Four days later, on Saturday, June 8, a hatless man in a beige raincoat wearing shell-rimmed spectacles, with dark hair and a thin nose, ambled unconcernedly toward the passport desk at Heathrow Airport, London. It was 11:15 A.M. He was bound for Brussels aboard British European Airways Flight 466 scheduled to leave at 11:50. He opened his raincoat and extracted a dark blue passport from his billfold, which he carried in his inside breast pocket, and handed it to the clerk, Immigration Officer Kenneth Human. Human glanced through it. It was a Canadian passport, issued by the Canadian Embassy in Lisbon, Portugal, on May 16, in the name of Ramon George Sneyd, born in Toronto. Human checked the details, almost automatically comparing the photograph with the man

---

* To add to the mystery, police discovered a John Willard in Toronto, who was, like Ray, slender, dark-haired, thirty-ish and five feet ten–eleven inches.

in front of him, noting age, height, color of eyes—it was in perfect order. But when the man had pulled the passport from his billfold, Human noticed a second Canadian passport in it. "May I see that, too?" he asked. It turned out to be identical to the first, save that it had been issued in Ottawa, on April 24, but the name under the same photograph was Ramon George Sneya, and the passport had been canceled. Human asked, "Why are these names different?" The traveler replied that they had made a mistake in Canada, spelling his name wrong, but he'd had no time to get it corrected before leaving Canada. He'd been in Lisbon a few weeks ago and took it to the Canadian Embassy there, who said they could not correct it but would cancel it and issue a new one, and they had done so.

He had hardly finished his explanation when he felt a gentle tap on his shoulder. He turned to see a slim young man with a typical small British clipped mustache, blue eyes, and a courteous smile on his face. "I say, old fellow," the young man was saying, "would you mind stepping over here for a moment? I'd like to have a word with you."

Human, his face impassive, returned the two passports to the traveler, who obediently followed the other to a nearby room. "I am Detective Sergeant Philip Birch," said the latter. As if from nowhere two policemen seemed to materialize. "May I see those passports, please?"

Given them, Birch glanced through them, excused himself, and went into an adjacent office. He was one of the few Scotland Yard men briefed on Ray, and had recognized him almost instantly from his photographs as he approached the passport desk. Now he telephoned Scotland Yard. Detective Chief Superintendent Butler and Inspector Thompson left immediately for the airport, and Birch returned to Ray, who was sitting stolidly in a chair.

Birch asked politely, "Would you mind if I searched you?" Ray stood up unprotestingly and Birch in a moment had extracted from Ray's back right pocket a .38 revolver, its handle tightly wrapped in black electrician's tape. Birch opened it and spun the barrel. It was fully loaded, a bullet in each of the five chambers: the guard had been released: one had only to squeeze the trigger to shoot.

Why was he carrying this gun?

Ray said, "Well, I'm going to Africa. I thought I might need it." The crooked smile, like a tic, appeared and disappeared. "You know how things are there—"

Birch did not ask why he was carrying a loaded gun if he did not expect to need it until he reached Africa. He only said, politely, as before: "I have reason to believe you have committed an arrestable offense." Ray said nothing, obviously still unconcerned. Carrying a gun without a permit was not a particularly heinous offense anywhere. Birch handed the pistol over to one of the policemen and continued searching Ray. In his wallet he found a British European Airways one-way tourist ticket, London to Brussels; the return stub of a BOAC excursion ticket, tourist class, Toronto–London–Toronto. In his jacket pocket he found a blank key, a South African airline timetable with a pencil checkmark against a flight to Salisbury, Rhodesia; a clipping from the London *Daily Mail* advertising cheap flights to South Africa; a leaflet describing rifle-silencing equipment; and an air claim luggage ticket for one suitcase.

Shortly after 1 P.M. Butler and Thompson arrived. Birch met them in an anteroom, reported what had happened, and gave them the two passports and the .38 with its taped handle. The inspectors studied the weapon. Such tape, rough and sticky to the touch, was usually used to wrap the grip of fancy pearl-handled revolvers, so they would not be too slippery to hold. But this was a regulation snub-nosed .38—a Japanese-made Liberty Chief revolver—with a stock pistol handle made of checkered walnut so that it would not slip in the hand. The tape could be there for only one reason—so Ray could unwind it and use it to tape the weapon to the inside of his leg, a trick of professional gunmen to avoid discovery if unexpectedly stopped and searched on the street. But he had not carried it taped to his leg: he had it ready for instant action. It occurred to both men that it was lucky for Birch that he did not try to arrest Ray at gunpoint, and that Ray had no idea that this was more than a routine passport checkup.

They entered the room where Ray waited. Butler, ruddy-faced and precise, addressed him formally. "We are police officers. I understand you have in your possession two passports—"

Ray interrupted him. "I can't understand why I'm here." There was indignation in his voice.

Butler continued imperturbably, "—in the names of Sneyd and Sneya. What is your name, sir?"

Ray subsided. "My name is Sneyd."

Butler tapped the passports. "Both of these passports show that you are a Canadian citizen born in Toronto on October 8, 1932. Are these details correct?"

Yes, of course they were, said Ray somewhat impatiently.

Butler produced the gun, from which he had removed the bullets.

"This .38 revolver with five rounds of ammunition in its chambers was found in your hip pocket when you were first questioned." He held it in his palm. "Is this your gun?"

Yes, it was his gun, Ray said.

Butler's questioning was soft-voiced, exact, and extremely courteous. "Would you like to tell us, Mr. Sneyd, why you are carrying a gun at all?"

"I was going to Brussels," Ray said.

Butler looked at him. Since Ray apparently was not about to say more, Butler pursued his question. "Why should you want to take a gun to Brussels?"

"Well," said Ray, seeming to stumble over his words. "I'm really thinking of going on to Rhodesia and things aren't too good there just now."

Butler listened gravely. Then he said, "In this country one has to have a firearms certificate to own a gun—even to have ammunition in one's possession. Have you a firearms certificate issued by the competent authority?"

No, said Ray, shaking his head. He was frank, a man not too perturbed. "I haven't got a certificate."

Butler looked unhappy. "I must inform you, Mr. Sneyd, that you are under arrest for possession of a gun without a permit. I must also caution you that anything you may say may be held against you." They would have to take him into custody. A man had been sent to retrieve his bag from the Brussels-bound plane. Meanwhile, he must accompany the police.

Guards surrounded Ray and he was taken to Cannon Bow Police Station, attached to the ancient Cannon Bow Court. There, after fingerprinting, he was placed in a cell with an armed guard.

Two hours later Butler and Thompson entered his cell. Ray, who had been seated on a bench, rose as the heavy door swung open. Once more Butler was all formality. "As a result of inquiries we have made, we have very good reason to believe that you are not a Canadian citizen but an American."

Ray said after a moment, in an almost offhand manner, "Oh well, yes, I am."

Butler went on in the same tone of voice: "I now believe your name is not Sneyd but James Earl Ray, also known as Eric Starvo Galt, and other names, and that you are wanted in the United States for serious criminal offenses including murder in which a firearm was used."

As word followed word relentlessly, Ray seemed paralyzed, his face frozen. Suddenly, as though all strength had drained from him, he slumped down on the bench behind him and put his head in his hands. "Oh, God!" he exclaimed. Then: "I feel so trapped."

Butler looked down on him and said, not ungently, "I should caution you again—anything you say may be held against you."

Ray did not even look up. "Yes," his voice came dully. "I shouldn't say anything more now." And, after a pause, almost to himself, "I can't think right."

They left him then.

He had not known it before, but he knew it now: the extraordinary and unparalleled 411-day run of James Earl Ray, alias Eric Starvo Galt, alias Harvey Lowmyer, alias John Willard, alias Paul Bridgman, alias Ramon George Sneyd, had ended.

Trial

CHAPTER XVIII

At Brixton Prison, across the Thames from the heart of London, Michael Eugene, solicitor appointed by the court to represent Ramon George Sneyd, otherwise James Earl Ray, the accused slayer of Dr. Martin Luther King, Jr., was having his first interview with the prisoner.

It was 3 P.M. Monday, June 10.

Outside, at every corner, they were hawking newspapers with giant black banners telling of Ray's arraignment that morning in Bow Street Court on charges of illegal possession of a firearm and possessing a falsified passport, and on the same front pages, like a sinister counterpoint, dispatches from the United States on the aftermath of Senator Robert F. Kennedy's funeral two days before. Another story told of the arrival in London of Assistant Attorney General Fred Vinson, Jr., who had flown in yesterday from Washington, had attended Ray's brief, two-minute hearing that morning, and was reported to have interviewed him in his cell.

Eugene, a stocky, scholarly, thirty-two-year-old lawyer who specialized in criminal cases, was associated with the firm of Michael Dresden & Company. He had not anticipated being called into the Ray case. His office was only two blocks from the Bow Street Court, and when he read that Ray would appear there Monday morning, curiosity had brought him to the courthouse in hope of seeing the man. Eugene had been walking down a hall when suddenly a group of eight or ten men appeared at the end of the corridor leading from the jail, walking briskly. In the middle of the group, carried along almost involuntarily, was a slim, bespectacled man of pale complexion, dressed in an open-necked blue sport shirt and sport jacket. His face was expressionless. Eugene was to remember how the group swept silently past him and, as though everything had been synchronized, as they reached the door of the courtroom, it opened and without pausing in step the group went inside, with several of its members peeling off in a sort of fighter formation as if to cover every possible point of attack.

He had a fleeting glimpse of Ray sitting on a bench in front of the prisoners' dock; then the man was completely closed in by the men who surrounded him in a circle so close-knit that no bullet could have gotten through to him.

Little more than two minutes later the courtroom door opened and the same group of men, the same pale, bespectacled man carried along in its center, emerged in the same formation and disappeared with the same swiftness down the corridor leading back to the cells.

It's like watching a film run in reverse, Eugene thought.

Two hours later he received a call from the court. Would his firm be prepared to act in Ray's behalf? They were on the list of legal firms from which the court appointed lawyers in such cases. Eugene had misgivings. The man's arrest on Saturday had electrified a London still overwhelmed by Senator Kennedy's assassination. The Kennedy family was almost as well known in England, where the elder Kennedy had been ambassador to the Court of St. James years before, as it was in the United States. Dr. King's murder had shocked the British and brought up sharp memories of President John Kennedy's assassination only five years earlier. The stories on Saturday telling of Ray's capture had shared the front pages with moving photographs of Senator Kennedy's funeral. It was an almost unbearable assault on everyone's senses, and Eugene was caught up in it. However, whatever Ray was alleged to have done, the man was entitled to legal representation. Despite his misgivings Eugene had taken the assignment.

Now, as the clock was striking three, he found himself, after an elaborate security search, ushered into a room in a section remote from other prisoners. The pale, bespectacled Ray, still dressed in the same blue sport shirt, was sitting at a table, facing the door. A policeman introduced the two and then left, locking the door behind him.

Eugene's first thought, as he sat down on the other side of the table, was, *This man doesn't fit the role. He'd be more at home behind a bank counter, or in an office filing papers.* It was immediately apparent to Eugene that Ray considered him a necessary evil. He had shaken hands coldly and unsmilingly; he seemed calm and assured, and when Eugene explained that he was there "to learn what I can and help you in any way I can," nothing in Ray's face indicated that he was ready to proffer any information.

The solicitor hurried on. "I should tell you that I am not interested in the circumstances of the assassination. My sole concern is to represent you in the extradition proceedings and in fighting the application that has been made by the United States Government."

Ray sat silent in his chair, looking at him impassively. Only the slightest twitch at one corner of his mouth indicated that he might be under more pressure than he showed.

Eugene pushed on: "If at any time you wish to tell me about yourself, or any other facts, that is entirely up to you."

This time Ray said, in his flat American voice, "Yeah."

"I shall have to take some details from you," Eugene continued, opening his briefcase. It was very difficult to achieve any rapport with the man. But he began to ask routine questions: age, place of birth, next of kin, any special requests he wished to make. Ray answered in monosyllables, then unexpectedly leaned forward and, tapping his fingers on the table for emphasis, said with surprising sharpness, "Look, they have got me mixed up with some guy called James Earl Ray. My name is Ramon George Sneyd. I don't know this Ray guy and they are trying to say that he is me. I've never met the guy in my life and I don't know anything about this. They are just trying to pin something on me that I didn't do."

Eugene, somewhat shocked by this sudden intensity—the man had seemed so passive, so indifferent to his presence—digested this for a moment. *Was this the game Ray was going to play?* Then he said circumspectly, "If you want to raise an objection based on mistaken identification, we can deal with that when we oppose the application for extradition." He could not help adding, "But if the American Government is going to continue with these proceedings, it's only reasonable to assume they have proof." When Ray said nothing, he went on, "Anyway, your real identity isn't of concern to me at this stage. I just wanted to obtain general background information and get to know you better so we can work together on your defense."

"All right," said Ray. He then spoke so rapidly and with so pronounced an American accent that Eugene found him difficult to understand. But it was clear that Ray wanted him "to get in touch right away with my brother Jerry and also with Arthur Hanes. He's a lawyer in Birmingham, Alabama."

His brother's name, he said, was Gerald Ray, and he gave Eugene his address in Chicago. Eugene marveled. *Didn't the man realize that by telling him his brother was Gerald Ray he was giving the lie to what he'd just said so emphatically—that he was Sneyd, not Ray?* But the lawyer only asked "Do you know Hanes?" Where would he get hold of him?

No, said Ray. He had never met Hanes. Hanes had never acted for him. "But I know he'll represent me and look after my interests back in the States." The assurance with which he said this—as if he *knew* that Hanes would represent him—stuck in Eugene's mind. Ray added that "I saw Hanes a couple of times on television a few years ago when he was mayor of Birmingham." Then: "I also want you to get hold of F. Lee Bailey, the Boston lawyer, and also Melvin Belli in California, and ask them whether they'd be interested in taking the case as well."

Again Eugene was taken aback. The man knew what he wanted and he wanted the best. He ventured, "Isn't it unusual for more than one lawyer to act in behalf of one defendant?" Ray had the answer, still unsmiling, "It's all right," he said. "They can all work together."

Eugene made his notes. "I understand lawyers in the States charge rather high fees," he said mildly. "A considerable amount of money is likely to be involved and they might want advances by way of security. Will this be a problem? Do you have any means?"

Ray brushed it aside. "I'm not worried about their fees. Even if it takes a hundred thousand dollars, I can raise it. They'll be taken care of. Anyway, I think they'll act for me in any case, but you just get hold of Hanes and let him sort it out." He added that he was writing to both Hanes and Bailey.

Now he moved to another subject. "There's been a pack of lies printed about Vinson seeing me—that Assistant Attorney General from the States. I mean, about him seeing me in the police station. I saw nobody." He repeated it emphatically. "I have never seen anybody. Nobody called to see me. I did not talk to Vinson. He did not talk to me. I want to make this quite clear so the people back home won't think that I've seen anybody." He tapped on the table again. "I want you to clear this up because the story is not true."

Eugene said he would look into the matter at once. Silence fell again, and after a moment or two Eugene left, saying he would call on him again. He did not know what to make of the man. Ray's certainty that Hanes would represent him, although he did not know him; that the lawyers' fees, however high, would be taken care of; his concern that "the people back home" should not think he had spoken to anybody . . . If there was any flavor to this, to the behavior of this strange, hostile, elusive man who had hoodwinked the police intelligence of half a dozen countries with such apparent ease, who had one moment denied his identity and the next confirmed it—the flavor was that of conspiracy.

Thursday afternoon, June 13, Arthur J. Hanes, Sr., was chatting with a client in his old-fashioned law office in downtown Birmingham when his secretary buzzed him. He picked up the phone. "Yes, Mary Sue?"

"Mr. Hanes," came Mary Sue's voice, almost breathless, "Mrs. Hanes is on the line and she sounds awfully excited." Then Hanes was listening to his wife. "Art, someone's calling you from London, England, and I gave them the office number—"

"London?" Hanes was puzzled.

"Art, it's about the James Earl Ray case. I'm sure it is. I've even made a bet with Mary Sue it is. You better hang up—they're probably trying to get you now."

A moment later there was the overseas operator and a cool British voice. Was this Mr. Arthur Hanes, the Mr. Hanes who had once been mayor of Birmingham?

"My name is Michael Eugene and I am associated with Michael Dresden & Company," the voice went on. "We have been appointed to act for Mr. Ramon George Sneyd, an American citizen, who has been arrested here and accused of the murder of Dr. Martin Luther King, Jr. Mr. Sneyd wants to know if you would be interested in representing him if and when he is extradited to the United States."

So it *was* about Ray! Hanes asked cautiously, "Does the man have any money to pay counsel?"

"He gave me that indication, sir," Mr. Eugene's voice came back, rising and falling as if it were actually being carried over the waves.

What did Mr. Eugene mean by "indication"? Eugene replied that he had asked Sneyd, "Do you have any means?" and Sneyd had said that, even if it took a hundred thousand dollars, he could raise the money.

"Very well," said Hanes. Would Eugene please send him a letter of confirmation. Eugene agreed and added that Sneyd was also writing him himself. The conversation ended.

Hanes had spoken calmly on the telephone, but when he hung up he discovered that his knees were trembling. He finished quickly with his client, then sat there trying to organize his thoughts. There was no reason for him to be upset. At fifty-one danger was not unknown to him. He had been a member of the U. S. Border Patrol in Texas as a young man, a PT boat commander in World War II, landing upon Japanese beaches under fire, and after the war he had spent three years as an FBI agent. But this . . . ! The thought that he might be getting involved in a mighty conspiracy—black militants,

Hanoi, Peking, Chinese Communists, American leftists, Lord knew who might be behind this—was sobering.

Then the thought struck him, *Maybe it's a hoax.* He jumped up —a dapper man in sharply creased blue suit, his white shirt with pinned collar and polka-dot blue tie, his brown hair fastidiously brushed in place—took his hat and hurried out. Twenty minutes later he was back. He had been to the library to check the London telephone directory. There was a Michael Dresden & Company, solicitors. Mary Sue was told to call them back and confirm that their Mr. Eugene had indeed called him. Her next task was to go to the Birmingham *News* office and buy every edition of the paper since April 4, 1968—the day of King's murder.

Next morning, Friday, June 14, there was a telephone call from the Birmingham Bar Association. A letter had just arrived for Hanes from Brixton Prison, London, care of the association. It was postmarked June 10, 1968—two days after Ray had been arrested. The man had chosen him quickly. Perhaps too quickly? Hanes wondered.

Inside the envelope was a smaller one sealed, with his name on it and a slip of paper bearing the words printed in ink:

"Dear Sir. Would you please forward this letter to Mr. Arthur Hanes. I don't know his address. He was mayor of Birmingham in the early 1960s. Thanks."

The letter, hand-printed in capitals and with words frequently misspelled, read:

DEAR MR. HANES. I AM WRITING THIS LETTER FROM LONDON, ENGLAND. I AM BEING HELD HERE ON A CHARGE OF PASSPORT FRAUD. ALSO I THINK FOR TENN IN THE MARTIN KING CASE. I WILL PROBABLY BE RETURNED TO THE U.S. ABOUT JUNE 17, AND WOULD LIKE TO KNOW IF YOU WOULD CONSIDER APPEARING IN MY BEHALF? SO FAR (THREE DAYS) I HAVE ONLY BEEN PERMITTED TO TALK TO POLICE AND ALSO HAVE NOT SEEN ANY PAPERS EXCEPT A HEADLINE TODAY BY ACCIDENT, STATING THAT I HAD GIVEN AN INTERVIEW TO A MR. VINSON WHICH IS FALSE. MOST OF THE THINGS THAT HAVE BEEN WRITTEN IN THE PAPERS ABOUT ME I CAN ONLY DESCRIBE AS SILLY. NATURLY I WOULD WANT YOU TO INVESTIGATE THIS NONSENSE BEFORE COMMITING YOURSELF, FOR THESE REASONS

AND OTHERS WHICH I WON'T GO INTO I THINK IT
IS IMPORTANT THAT I HAVE AN ATTORNEY UPON
ARRIVAL IN TENN. OR I WILL BE CONVICTED OF
WHATEVER CHARGE THEY FILE ON ME BEFORE I
ARRIVE THEIR.

AN ENGLISH ATTORNEY CAME TO SEE ME TODAY
AND SAID HE WOULD ALSO WRITE TO YOU. I DONT
KNOW YOUR ADDRESS IS WHY I AM SENDING THIS
LETTER TO THE BAR ASSO. THE REASON I WROTE
YOU IS I READ ONCE WHERE YOU HANDLED A CASE
SIMMILAR TO WHAT I THINK MAY BE FILED ON ME,
ALSO WHATEVER THE PAPERS MITE SAY I DONT IN-
TEND TO GIVE ANY INTERVIEWS UNTIL I HAVE
CONSULTED WITH AN ATTORNEY. IN THE EVENT
YOU CAN NOT PRACTICE IN MEMPHIS WOULD YOU
CONTACT AN ATTORNEY THEIR WHO COULD?

SINCERELY

R. G. SNEYD

P.S. AMONG THE MANY NAMES THEY HAVE ME
BOOKED UNDER IS THIS ONE SO IF YOU SHOULD
CORRESPOND USE THIS ONE, ADDRESS ON ENVE-
LOPE.

Hanes stared at the letter thoughtfully. His biggest case had been
as defense attorney in the Liuzzo murder some years before. In
March 1965 Mrs. Viola Liuzzo, a white housewife from Detroit and
a civil rights worker for Dr. King's Southern Christian Leadership
Conference, had been fatally shot while driving on the highway
between Selma and Montgomery with a nineteen-year-old Negro
youth.* The bullets had come from a car that passed her at high speed.
In it were four Klan members, one of whom was an FBI informant.
The federal indictment had charged the three with "violating the
civil rights" of Mrs. Liuzzo, the identical charge brought by the
Government against James Earl Ray—that of violating the civil rights
of Dr. King. The trial had ended in a hung jury. After the Klan's
chief counsel, Matt Murphy, also of Birmingham, had been killed in
an auto accident, Hanes had taken over and won acquittal. Ray was
considered something of a jail-house lawyer at Missouri State Peni-

---

* Mrs. Liuzzo, the mother of five, had volunteered to transport participants in
the Selma–Montgomery march back to Montgomery after the march ended. The
youth with her was to guide her to the pickup points.

tentiary, Hanes had read. He must have followed the Liuzzo case with great attention.

Hanes and his son, Art, Jr., twenty-seven, who was his law partner, spent the next twenty-four hours on the phone to see if they could find anyone who knew this man of mystery. They put out feelers to every likely organization—the Klan, the White Citizens Councils, the National States Rights Party, the American Nazi Party, the Minutemen—crackpot groups and paramilitary. But no one had ever heard of James Earl Ray.

On Saturday, Hanes organized a family detail to work with him and Art, Jr., over the weekend, going through every edition of the Birmingham *News*, clipping everything relating to Martin Luther King, Jr., and James Earl Ray. All were persons he could trust—his wife, his daughter-in-law, his wife's three sisters and their husbands. At Sunday brunch they all studied the material, and then discussed it. Unanimously they agreed the murder had to be a conspiracy. For this third-rate bungling robber and holdup man to trail King, to kill him, to escape from Memphis and elude capture for more than two months in the face of the greatest manhunt in history—he *must* have had help.

James Earl Ray could be brought to trial, but was he the man? And if he did fire the shot, was he not simply the tool of the others?

Very well. Who would want to do away with Dr. King? Who would profit most by his death? Who would be capable of carrying it off? Who could finance it?

Some possibilities were in the very air. For example, that the CIA —the Government's Central Intelligence Agency—might be behind it. Why the CIA? It had been publicly charged that Dr. King had associated with Communists, had lectured at Communist schools, that some of his speeches had been written by a friend and confidant who was a "card-carrying member of the Communist Party." Dr. King and his associates had vehemently denied this. But if it *were* true, if it were Communist sympathies that led Dr. King to attack the Vietnam war,* and if he were to use his great influence to persuade black soldiers, the mainstay of our Army in Vietnam, not to fight; if, with his international stature as a Nobel Prize winner, he were to travel to Cuba, or Red China, or the Soviet Union, to denounce the United States as a militaristic and racist nation, it could be argued that he

---

* On April 4, 1967, just a year before his death, Dr. King in a major speech in New York City had denounced the war, had declared that Negro boys were dying in numbers completely disproportionate to whites.

was so potentially dangerous that his permanent silencing was not only a strategic but a patriotic necessity.

The black militants had their reasons, too, for wanting to do away with him. Here the orientation would be quite different. Only a few days before, the New York police had seized members of a black power group known as RAM—the Revolutionary Action Movement—and charged them with plotting to murder Roy Wilkins, head of the NAACP, Whitney Young, executive director of the Urban League, and other moderate national black leaders. Why could not King's murder have been part of the same strategy, carried out by militants dedicated to the elimination of all who stood in the way of black violence and revolution?

Threading his way through the world of conspiracy and espionage, so remote to most people, was not a new endeavor for Hanes. After he resigned from the FBI, he had taken a job in late 1959 as security officer at the Hayes Aircraft Corporation, in Birmingham. He had found himself involved in the aftermath of the Bay of Pigs invasion —the ill-fated American-backed attempt to invade Cuba and overthrow Castro, in April 1961. Hayes Aircraft held government contracts dealing with the modification of secret equipment, and some of the airplane personnel used in that doomed venture had been Hayes employees or people recruited through the company. Within two hours after the invasion failed, Hanes had been called upon to make certain that the widows of four employees killed in the attempt—two pilots, a flight engineer, and a technical inspector—were warned to say nothing about their husbands' activities.

By Monday, June 17, Hanes had decided to take the case. In London events had moved swiftly. F. Lee Bailey had responded from Boston to say he would consider representing Ray if Ray was not guilty, and if he entered the case and learned Ray had, in fact, killed Dr. King, "I'll pull out at once." He added, "Dr. King was my friend and it would be unfair for me to defend him, then, because I'd be hoping that he got convicted." Melvin Belli had not responded at all. Meanwhile, Ray was to be informed in Bow Street Court tomorrow of the first-degree murder indictment voted against him on May 7 by the Shelby County Grand Jury,* and of the U.S. action to extradite him to stand trial in Memphis. Eugene also learned that it had been almost impossible to obtain police volunteers to drive Ray from

---

* Such indictments are voted secretly and not disclosed until the accused person is in custody.

his jail cell to court for his appearance—they expected an assassination attempt—perhaps a bomb thrown—the moment he came into the open.

Hanes himself had no doubt that he was dealing with a hired killer. Why should Ray have done it on his own? Why should he put his neck into a noose after escaping from jail? A man would have to be insane —or else be given a fortune for taking the risk. As Hanes said to Art, Jr., after the long weekend of family consultation, when the two, over drinks, were discussing the case: "It has to be a contract job. The guy was home free, enjoying himself. Why should he bring the lightning down on his head, if not for—" Hanes paused, and rubbed his thumb and fingers together, signifying money. How else take Ray's remark about the one hundred thousand dollars for defense? This, from a penny-ante burglar who, according to the newspaper stories stole typewriters, pulled $11.20 holdups of cabdrivers, and rifled grocery store cash registers, whose life style until now had been a step above that of a skid-row bum! And if, as Hanes had always believed, President Kennedy's death had been ordered by Castro patriots in reprisal for Kennedy's Bay of Pigs invasion, by a logical extension there was every reason to believe that Castro patriots and those friendly to the Cuban dictator—black militants, perhaps backed by Castro or even by the Chinese Communists—plotted Dr. King's murder. If they had used Ray, Hanes promised himself that Ray would not go down alone: those who backed him would go down with him.

Hanes made his plans. He sent off a letter to Sneyd—if Ray wanted to be known as Sneyd for the while, Hanes would not deny it to him—saying he would accept his defense, that he had already begun preliminary research, and that under no circumstances should Ray say anything to anyone.

Hanes knew that certain personal risks were involved. Next day when the papers were full of the news—that James Earl Ray had asked Art Hanes, Sr., of Birmingham, to defend him, and that Hanes had accepted, the threatening calls began—to his family, to Mary Sue, even to Lena, the Haneses' seventy-year-old Negro maid. Mary Sue had to be sent home from the office in tears after a gruff voice on the phone told her, "You better get your boss off this or you ain't going to have no boss." At home Mrs. Hanes picked up the telephone to hear a man's deep, deliberate voice intone, with chilling slowness: "Death . . . death . . . death," and hang up. Lena was close to hysterics. The calls to her from her own people were bitter and violent.

"You don't quit working in that house we going take care of you—"
But Hanes had made up his mind. A call to the State Department
in Washington elicited the fact that he and Art could obtain passports
there in twenty-four hours. They would fly to Washington tomorrow
and leave for London the next day. All things being equal, Ray would
most likely be extradited. The Government was powerful: they would
be out to wrap him up fast. Hanes would insist on flying back to
Memphis on the same plane with the boy, lest he be questioned on
the way without benefit of counsel. Ray was only the patsy in this
case, no more. There were much bigger fish to fry. But he had turned
to Art Hanes, and Art Hanes would see that he was protected.

CHAPTER XIX

On Thursday, June 13, a few days after Ray's arrest in London, Judge W. Preston Battle, Jr., one of Shelby County's five Criminal Courts judges, walked thoughtfully into his office in the County Courts Building in Memphis. Judge Battle, aged fifty-nine, a man of great dignity, soft-spoken and erudite, was to meet for lunch with his four colleagues and discuss what had to be done in expectation of Ray's extradition. Sooner or later the trial would be held in Memphis, and it would fall on one of them to preside—and they, as well as Memphis, had to be ready.

The city King's assassin had left behind him on April 4 in such a chaotic condition had been slowly reorganizing itself. Citizens' groups had sprung up, called, "Save Our City," and "The Memphis Search for Meaning Committee," which sought to bring about a communal soul-searching to learn why this had happened, and why it had happened in Memphis. On Sunday, April 7, several thousand had gathered at Crump Stadium in a "Memphis Cares" rally, to proclaim that this Southern city did care that Dr. King had been assassinated there, and that its citizens were determined to find some way to bring black and white together before fear and hate and mutual distrust destroyed the city altogether. And why Memphis, they wanted to know, in which Dr. King had appeared, in all, only four times in his life? Why not Atlanta, or Birmingham, or Selma, or so many other cities closely associated with him? Was there in Memphis some basic sickness that led to this thunderclap event, this terrible exclamation point of history?

All that was known was that, as in Dallas, a stranger had come into town and brought shame and horror to the city; and although many privately were not outraged by the act, all were outraged that it had been done in Memphis. Now that the accused man had been captured and would soon be returned to Memphis, the eyes of the world would be on them. They did not want the awful hippodrome that debased Dallas to take place here.

In the complex of Police Headquarters, the Criminal Courts Building, the Shelby County Jail, meetings had been going on steadily ever

since that fateful April 4. Attorney General Phil N. Canale, who
would have to prosecute James Earl Ray; Sheriff William N. Morris,
Jr., who would have to keep him safe and alive until his trial, Police
Director Frank Holloman, who would have to secure the city against
riot, insurrection, or any other possibility at that time, and all the
other officials who would be involved in what was already heralded
as "the trial of the century" had been conferring almost daily.

Judge Battle had been among those deeply concerned. He had
seen what a trial could do to a city, and, as a third-generation
Memphian, he did not want what had happened elsewhere to happen
in Memphis. They had the experience not only of Dallas, but of the
Billy Sol Estes case in Texas, the Sam Sheppard case in Cleveland.
A trial could tear a city apart. The Memphis *Commercial-Appeal*,
which articulated as few other newspapers the tone and feeling of
the city in which it was published, had already warned editorially
that "we must brace ourselves" for the difficult days ahead, and had
called on every citizen to "make a determined effort to maintain
equilibrium and sanity" when this "emotion-charged court proceeding" finally got under way.

Judge Battle had been ready to believe that the killer was dead. He
thought, *Whoever is cruel enough to hire an assassin to wait for a man
and shoot him down in cold blood would be cruel enough to execute
the gunman.* Then word had come of Ray's arrest.

Battle learned it as he lay on the sofa in his study, sadly watching on TV the slow funeral train bringing Robert Kennedy's body
from New York to Washington for burial at Arlington. The announcer broke in to say that Ray had been seized at Heathrow Airport, London, and that Coretta King had been told of the capture
of the man accused of her husband's murder as she sat in a pew in
St. Patrick's Cathedral in New York attending a high requiem mass
for Senator Kennedy. Battle thought, *Well, this is it. We've been
fooling ourselves, thinking he's dead, because we wanted to escape
the ordeal of a trial. Just a question of time before he'll be on our
doorstep—we better throw this thing into high gear.* Then he noticed
that the funeral train had stopped; tragedy upon tragedy, the crowd
had been so immense at one station that a man and a woman had
been forced out on the tracks and a train coming from the opposite
direction had run them over, killing them. Battle thought, *God, this
country is going mad over sensation. Why am I looking on this scene?
What does it all mean?* Why was he lying there, supine, a sheeplike
observer of a spectacle that had elements of madness about it?

Millions of other Americans, like himself, were watching at this moment, too, this moving, tragic, suddenly doubly dreadful emotional scene, the thousands lined up along the tracks to watch a train go by, all immersed in this, all overwhelmed—what was happening to his country? These assassinations, these killers, this hysteria . . . Sometimes he had the uncomfortable feeling that he was being manipulated, like a puppet, as if some sort of malign power were pulling the strings, making all Americans sway in unison—now in this direction, now that, now to tears, now to pity, now to violence . . . All this emotion poured upon everyone, affecting them, and they in turn affecting each other, and this repeated and echoed and reechoed . . . He thought, *How much am I being manipulated, and how much am I my own man?*

He had risen heavily from the sofa and sat down at his study desk. Judge Battle was a conscientious man. A brilliant lawyer whose early career had almost been ruined by liquor, he was a member of Alcoholics Anonymous and accustomed to its disciplines, and stern in carrying out the tasks he set for himself. One of his duties, as president of the Criminal Courts Division of the Tennessee Judicial Conference, was to see that he and his four colleagues on the bench were prepared. He began making notes that day on the legal issues that might arise once Ray was put on trial, and to look up cases which might contain precedents. He would assign these to himself and his colleagues to study. Finally, when the time came, one of their number would be chosen by lot to preside at the trial. Judge Battle did not envy whoever that would be. Such a trial could last three months or more. Ray was entitled to a fair and impartial hearing. It must be handled with painstaking care, every i dotted, every t crossed, so there would be as little chance as possible for an appeal to reverse their decision, to throw doubt on Memphis justice—and on Memphis motives. They owed it to their city—and to all the whites and blacks in the nation who would be watching them so critically, so suspiciously—to do this thing right. But they could not emerge happily no matter what resulted. If a conviction, Memphis would be accused of railroading the man for fear of black reprisal; if freed, Memphis would be accused of racism, one more Southern court letting a white man go free for murdering a black man.

Judge Battle thought, as he entered the grand jury room now where he and his colleagues had met each Thursday since that April 4 to lunch over sandwiches and coffee brought up from the snack bar downstairs, *Whoever gets the case will be denounced, threatened,*

*and abused by the press. In order to give the man a fair trial, he'll
have to end up a plain old bastard. That's all he can wind up being.
He won't be able to please anybody.*

Two floors above the grand jury room, in the opposite wing of the
building, Attorney General Canale was trying to catch a few winks
of sleep in his office. An hour after Ray had been captured Canale
was studying the Anglo-American extradition treaty. For the next
four days and nights he and his aides had worked steadily, with a few
hours out for naps, preparing the extradition papers which had to be
flown to London. It had been an arduous task. To extradite a U.S.
citizen from Great Britain, the U. S. Government had to present
sufficient evidence to convince the British authorities that it had a
bona fide case. This meant a stipulation of facts, affidavits from major
witnesses, sworn statements from experts, ranging from the medical
examiner who performed the autopsy to the FBI specialists in ballistics, fingerprinting, chemical analysis and the like, and similar
proofs. Nor could the extradited man be tried for any crime other
than that for which he was extradited. The whole thing was complicated by the fact that extradition could be refused if the accused
man could prove that his crime was political and that he sought political asylum in Great Britain, the home of the Magna Charta, where
such matters were given serious consideration. Canale and his men,
working closely with the FBI, had been able to obtain the salient
affidavits. Each night they had driven with all extra copies and notes
and burned them in the city incinerator on the outskirts of town, to
prevent them from falling into anyone else's hands. On the day
Michael Eugene telephoned Art Hanes in Birmingham, the three-
pound package of documents was on the desk of Magistrate Frank
Milton in Bow Street Court, London.

Canale, who would have to mastermind the state's case against
Ray—indeed, the United States Government's case against Ray—was
to know few hours of relaxation in the next months. A stocky, quiet,
churchgoing man with an engaging smile and an encyclopedic knowledge of Tennessee Criminal Law, he oversaw twenty trial assistants
and four special investigators, headed by his Executive Assistant Attorney General, Robert K. Dwyer, and Assistant Attorney General
James C. Beasley. This team had handled some three thousand criminal cases a year over the last ten years. It would be their duty
to bring together all the evidence against Ray, to determine whether
Ray had fellow conspirators, to prepare the state's case—against the
man or men.

Down the hall from Canale, Administrative Assistant Attorney General Lloyd A. Rhodes was collating all the unsolicited letters— wild, bizarre, threatening—received from the moment of King's murder, to see if there was any pattern as to person, city, content. Such letters were voices from the outside world. If the history of conspiracy showed anything, it showed that whoever else was involved with Ray would sooner or later make himself known.

On the second floor of the Criminal Courts Building, the office of Sheriff Bill Morris had become a command post. Relays of men came and went. As chief law-enforcement officer of Shelby County, he would be responsible for Ray's safety; and the fear of what happened in Dallas five years before hovered over him like a menacing cloud. A host of questions assailed him. If there was a conspiracy, how big was it? Who were the conspirators? Was it international, and was it a chain whose links led, as Art Hanes was being quoted as saying in London, to somewhere in Red China? Was it a gigantic arrangement that had begun with John Kennedy, then Martin Luther King, and now Robert Kennedy?

King could have been assassinated in so many other cities. The question echoed again and again, and nowhere so insistently as in the sheriff's office: Why Memphis? King was a virtual stranger in Memphis. In other cities his habits were known. He had scores of friends, he was always visible. Was it because persons in Memphis were involved? Perhaps someone in the police department? Between Holloman and himself, counting police and sheriff's deputies, they had had more than forty men watching King—and that did not include the FBI. These men knew King's movements. Perhaps someone in Morris's own official family? Someone under his very nose? Those involved in King's killing would know that if the murderer were caught he would be brought to Memphis, to the Shelby County Jail—the prisoner and responsibility of Bill Morris. Had this all been taken into account, and had King been murdered in Memphis so that the murderer would end up in Shelby County Jail, where arrangements had already been made to get him out—or kill him?

Morris thought of these things seriously. He was not one to brush off responsibility. At thirty-six, he was a tall, vigorous, handsome figure, father of four, a spellbinder on the lecture platform, a driving force behind the Jaycees, the Boy Scouts, the Little Baseball and Football Leagues. The walls of his office were hung with more than thirty plaques honoring him for civic services. He had been one of the first to prepare for Ray's return. Himself a graduate of the FBI Academy, he had already borrowed Charles Holmes, the thirty-three-year-old director of information at Memphis State University (whose president, Dr. C. C. Humphreys, was an ex-FBI man), to become his press officer for the trial. Holmes had been a top Memphis newspaperman, and it would be his duty to cope with the world of communications that would descend on Memphis—reporters, radio correspondents, columnists, commentators, TV newscasters, special writers from the ends of the earth. Memphis would be comparable to Hopewell, New Jersey, in 1935, at the Lindbergh baby kidnaping trial; to Nuremberg in 1945 at the War Crimes Trials; to Jerusalem in 1961 at the Eichmann trial. Perhaps only half a dozen times in a century was there a crime so overwhelming—with the alleged perpetrator caught alive—as to become an event in history.

But more than this, Morris's concern was with Ray himself. When Ray was seized, Morris had immediately asked the help of the U. S. Bureau of Prisons in Washington. The chief of federal prisons, J. J. Clark, had promised to come down with other experts to study Shelby County Jail and advise Morris on security. The sheriff arranged to visit a Mississippi company known to manufacture the newest type of riot control armaments and to fly to Dallas with Holmes to learn from police officials what lessons had their terrible experience—Lee Harvey Oswald shot by Jack Ruby, before the eyes of millions—taught them? At the same time Morris began interviewing his top prison personnel from whom he would choose fourteen men who would guard Ray day and night in eight-hour shifts—checking into their temperament, their family life, their financial probity, their emotional stability. Bad enough that Ray had a reputation for breaking out of jail. His guards would be under tremendous pressure. They could be offered bribes of thousands of dollars for a single photograph—one magazine had reportedly offered twenty-five thousand dollars for an exclusive photograph of Ray in jail—and anyone who could photograph Ray could shoot him. They had to be immune to every temptation. There could be nothing in their background, for example, which might make them vulnerable to blackmail—to permit a shot at Ray, to slip him poison,* or to kidnap him. To be doubly

* Hermann Goering, Hitler's chief lieutenant, cheated the hangman at Nuremberg by swallowing a cyanide pill, secreted behind a filling in a tooth, moments before guards came to take him to the gallows. They found him dead on the cell floor.

sure, Morris would have the FBI run its own careful check on them. Nothing would be overlooked.

Ray's capture was to change the rhythm and direction of other lives, as well. In Houston, Texas, the morning after his arrest, Percy Foreman, the lawyer, as was his habit rose before dawn, irritable as usual, and, while he had the first coffee of the day, read the news on the front page of the Houston *Post*. About an hour later, when he lumbered into his office in downtown Houston, he gave the paper to his secretary, Martha, with the story circled in heavy black pencil. "Clip everything on this from now on," he said. "I want to keep a file on it."

Foreman did not know James Earl Ray. But he knew that at one point or another he could expect an inquiry from a friend, or relative, of the accused. His reputation as a defense lawyer was such that nearly always, in the nation's more sensational murder cases, the ripples sooner or later washed against his office door.

Foreman's record was awesome. Of nearly one thousand accused murderers that he had defended only fifty-three had gone to prison and he had lost only one man to the executioner. He had no hesitancy in telling others that he was the greatest trial counsel in the United States. At sixty-six, he was a forbidding figure, a gray-haired, shaggy giant of a man, six feet four, weighing nearly 250 pounds, who was both a deacon of the Baptist Church and an ex-wrestler. He was unpredictable in and out of court. His moods, which changed with kaleidoscopic rapidity, ranged from enormous charm to a kind of snarling ferocity. Since a whiplash auto accident in 1962 left him with constant back pain, he slept badly, and his threshold of irritability was lower than ever. But nothing kept him from pursuing his work. He was known for warehouses crowded with possessions he had taken as fees from his various clients. He did not hide this: he gloried in it, as he gloried in the fact that he demanded tremendous fees. The more it hurt a client, he maintained, the more likely the client would take his advice. (The house in which he lived had been given him as part payment of a legal bill, and one tearful woman client accused him of cutting off her wedding ring as a down payment, using a jeweler's cutter he kept in a desk drawer for that purpose.)

Now he sat for a moment, thinking. In Tennessee, the state must convince each of the twelve jurors beyond a reasonable doubt of the guilt of the accused. If what he had read so far—the report of Harold "Cornbread" Carter that someone had fired the bullet that killed King from the bushes behind the rooming house while Carter was sitting there, drinking wine, so close to him that the assailant's feet "threw gravel on me" when he fled; and the report of Solomon Jones, Jr., King's chauffeur, that he saw a man with "something white" over his head run from the same bushes—if these stories had even the semblance of truth, the state would be in trouble.

Sitting at his desk that June morning, grimacing as a sudden movement sent a twinge of pain across his back, Percy Foreman planned how he would handle the defense if they came to him. . . .

In Hartselle, a small Alabama town, another man read about Ray's arrest with particular attention. He was William Bradford Huie, the writer. Huie had known Dr. King. Indeed, Dr. King had written the introduction to one of his books, *Three Lives for Mississippi*, which dealt with the 1961 murder of Goodman, Schwerner and Chaney in Mississippi. After his initial shock at King's death, Huie had closely followed the search for the assassin. Within a week or so of Ray's capture he read two other items: that Ray had chosen Arthur Hanes, Sr., of Birmingham, as his lawyer, and Hanes was leaving at once for London to see him; the other, that J. B. Stoner, lawyer and organizer for the anti-Semitic, anti-Negro National States Rights Party of Savannah, Georgia, had offered his legal services free to Ray.

Huie pondered these developments. He knew and understood the South. The first Huie had come to Alabama eight generations ago, and Huie, like his father and grandfather before him, had spent much time fighting the Ku Klux Klan at every level, because he considered the Klan to represent all that was backward, ignorant, and cruel in the South. As a result, more than once a procession of cars, filled with jeering white men, would slowly and ominously circle the corner ranchhouse in which he and his wife, Ruth, lived alone, and each time, Huie, a lean, compact man known as a crack shot, promptly floodlit the grounds and announced that he had Remington riot guns on every window seat and that he and Ruth were ready to use them.

Now for a moment, he toyed with a bizarre idea. Could Art Hanes be part of the operation? Had the script been written months before, waiting only to be put into effect when and if Ray was captured? How would Ray, who had spent most of the last twenty years in Missouri and Illinois jails, know about Art Hanes of Birmingham, and why, with his life at stake, would he choose this relatively obscure country lawyer to defend him? To be sure, Hanes's sympathies were no secret. His role in the Liuzzo case was on the record. And Hanes had been mayor in 1963, during Dr. King's civil rights campaign in Birmingham, when Police Commissioner "Bull" O'Connor turned fire hoses and police dogs on the black marchers. Hanes had bitterly denounced King. Had it been planned for Hanes to be hired, and was it part of his duty to get to London as soon as possible to close Ray's mouth and stop him from blurting out the truth?

But as quickly as the thought occurred to him, Huie dismissed it. He knew Hanes, and although Hanes's politics were not his, he could not believe that Art Hanes would have any part of a conspiracy.* But Stoner, a violent, fanatical and self-proclaimed racist—at eighteen he had become a Klan organizer, at twenty he had founded the Stoner Anti-Jewish Party†—posed a problem. At the moment Stoner and his group were raising money for the George Wallace campaign. His publication, *The Thunderbolt*, which went into thousands of homes, was beating the drum for Wallace. The May 1968 issue had declared, "The man who shot King was actually upholding the law of the land . . . He should be given the Congressional Medal and a large annual pension for life, plus a Presidential pardon." If Stoner and his group could capitalize on the Ray case, if they could use him as a rallying cause for racists throughout the country, still at a high pitch of anger and fear after the riots following King's death, they could raise even more money—and perhaps change the course of American history. If James Earl Ray's defense became involved with the Klan and the ultraright in the South, this could only be disastrous, Huie felt. Hanes, he knew, was not affluent. Hanes did

---

* Hanes did not know it, but several newspaper reporters had already begun researching his life and times—even to the identity of his neighbors. Since the CIA was deeply involved in the Bay of Pigs effort, it was undoubtedly the CIA that had sent Hanes to warn the widows of the pilots lost in the invasion to remain silent. The possibility, however farfetched, of CIA complicity in Dr. King's assassination, was not being overlooked by those reporters, who also strongly doubted that Ray could have chosen Hanes as his attorney on his own. Perhaps the CIA had hired Hanes?

† The purpose of his party, Stoner said in an interview, was "to make being a Jew a crime punishable by death . . . We'll just take them out and kill them." As for Negroes, "The Nigger is not a human being. He is somewhere between the white man and the ape. [He] is our enemy." All Jews and Negroes were Communists, he said, and the FBI was led and controlled by Communists. In 1964 Stoner ran for Vice President of the United States as a white supremacist on the National States Rights Party ticket.

not like Stoner, he considered him a menace, but he would need money for the defense . . . There was a real danger here.

Huie picked up the phone and called Hanes in Birmingham. He did not make contact with him until June 20, several days later, when Hanes returned his call from Washington, D.C., on the evening of his departure for London.

"I'm interested in this thing too," Huie said. From what he had read about Ray, the man was a sociopath, hostile to society, a man who had been in criminal circumstances since his twenties. Huie was convinced that Ray, true to the criminal code, would never give information to the law. Huie was prepared to take a calculated risk and offer money for the truth. He had paid money in the past to buy the truth—to the men who killed Emmett Till in Mississippi in 1955, and to KKK informers, to learn the facts for his book, *Three Lives for Mississippi*.

"The only way we're going to know what happened in the King assassination," Huie said, "is for someone like me to make a deal with your client to tell me all he can about his involvement and who helped him."

Hanes listened with interest. He made clear that, though he was gambling the cost of a round trip to London, he was not prepared "to chase around the world and defend that boy" unless he had money to do it with. He doubted that the Klan or racist politicians could raise a large amount. If defense money could be obtained by selling Ray's story to be published after the trial—that was another matter. Huie said, "I've got no illusions about trying to learn the truth from a man who has used deception all his life." Ray had rarely admitted committing any crime, even when caught red-handed. "Most of what he'll give me probably won't be true, and that's the chance I'll take." But he would check and recheck what Ray wrote him, and he should be able to get some useful leads. If Hanes, after meeting Ray and sizing him up, thought the project had possibilities, would he give Ray a letter from Huie offering Ray an advance of thirty thousand dollars to be used for defense funds, in return for Ray furnishing information to Huie—where he went, whom he saw, who gave him assistance.

Hanes agreed. He had taken Ray's talk about raising money with a grain of salt. If Ray could put his hands on large sums, he dared not: it would be taken as proof that he *had* been paid off. Ray's two brothers, John and Jerry, had set up a post-office box in Memphis asking for contributions for his defense. Only a few dollars had dribbled

in. There were considerable letters of encouragement and approval—
"God bless you! My prayers will always be with you"—and one envelope full of nude photographs of women to solace him in jail. But
of money—hardly anything.

Hanes would make up his mind about Ray. If the man would go
along, they'd get a contract worked out. As Huie planned it, Huie's
thirty-thousand-dollar advance would be collectable by him against
all earnings from the book, magazine articles, and film rights. Huie
hoped to be able to interview Ray in prison, in Memphis, but he
would immediately prepare written questions for Hanes to give Ray.
Hanes would then turn Ray's written replies over to Huie. Actually,
this would be information Hanes had to have, anyway. Proceeds
would be divided 30 per cent each to Ray and Hanes, and 40 per cent
to Huie. Ray would immediately sign over his share to Hanes, so that
Hanes would be assured, in the end, of 60 per cent.

It was all speculation, of course. One never knew how well a book
would do, or even if a book would result. But Huie's advance of
money made certain that Hanes would go ahead with what undoubtedly would be a very expensive defense.

As Huie summed it up for himself; at best, he would learn the
truth and get the story. At worst, he would have the satisfaction of
knowing that he had helped to prevent Dr. King's assassination from
becoming a political pawn used by professional racists to promote
hatred and division in the United States.

CHAPTER XX

In the chambers of Judge Percy Sellers, senior judge of the Shelby County Criminal Court, a meeting was being held under top secret conditions.

In the room were the five criminal court judges, with Judge W. Preston Battle, Jr., sitting in one corner, lost in thought. They had drawn straws a few days ago, and it had fallen on him to preside at Ray's trial. Others in the room included Attorney General Canale; Police Director Holloman; two men who had just flown down from Washington—J. J. Clark, and Ken Bounds, a top FBI official; and Dr. McCarthy DeMere, of Memphis, who had been pressed into service for what would take place shortly before dawn tomorrow.

It was 5 P.M. Thursday, July 18. Sheriff Morris had called the meeting to inform them that James Earl Ray was to be secretly spirited out of London one hour from now and flown direct to Memphis. "He will leave on a U. S. Air Force jet at midnight, London time," Morris said. "That's 6 P.M. here." The plane would land at Millington Naval Air Base, eighteen miles from Memphis. It had been a magnificent job of co-ordination by Scotland Yard and the FBI. Morris had had to determine the prevailing winds and flying time so as to insure that Ray would leave London and arrive in Memphis in darkness. The trip had been planned to bring the plane to a halt at Millington sometime before 4 A.M. Memphis time. Dawn came at 6 A.M. "We'll have more than an hour of darkness to get him here from Millington, and we should have him in his cell before daybreak."

As the sheriff spoke, they could hear the hammering outside as workmen completed placing quarter-inch steel plates, each capable of withstanding small-arms artillery, over the windows on the third floor of the jail where Ray would be kept. Everyone in the room knew why this was being done. They knew that Attorney General Canale had taken parallel measures. He had requested the Federal Aviation Agency to monitor all air traffic over the jail complex, and, fearful for the safety of witnesses once the trial began, had obtained approval for the roof of the adjoining Shelby County Office Building to be used as a helicopter pad to transport them to and from the court.

This might sound like science fiction, but neither Phil Canale nor Bill Morris was known as a man given to fantasies. If Dr. King's assassination was a conspiracy, then Morris, charged with Ray's safety, was playing chess with an invisible opponent whose strength, resources, and ingenuity were unknown. If millions of dollars had been spent, if scores of persons had been employed, if all kinds of doors had been opened, and all sorts of payoffs made, if Ray had, for example, been flown about the United States by chartered plane—if it was truly a "Man from U.N.C.L.E." operation—what might "they" not be prepared to do to silence Ray? Or to rescue him? A jet plane taking off from a private field somewhere in the South, swooping over the jail, firing a few rockets into the windows, even dropping a few bombs. . . . With a conspiracy of such magnitude, who would care if "they" killed two or three hundred other persons to obtain their objective?

Dr. King *had* been assassinated. The deed *had* been done.

They were finishing exterior security not a moment too soon.* Originally they had not expected Ray in Memphis for at least another month. Magistrate Milton had ruled on July 2 that Ray must be extradited; under British law he had fifteen days in which to appeal. But Art Hanes, who had seen his client in London, had suddenly announced that Ray would not appeal and would return to Memphis to stand trial. Ray had stood up in the British court to deny that he knew King, to deny that he bore a grudge against King, to deny that he had shot King. The British now wanted to get him—and the responsibility for keeping him alive—off their hands as soon as possible. It explained why Ray would be on his way within the hour.

Every arrangement had been made, the sheriff said, for Operation Landing, which would be carried out in absolute secrecy. Ray, riding in an armored vehicle in the center of an armed convoy, would be transported from Millington to Memphis under impregnable security conditions. The sheriff assured the meeting of this before it broke up, but even to this trusted group he would not divulge all his plans. Not even he knew the route he would take, and he would decide that at the last moment so that he could not inadvertently reveal it. He had made plans to prevent anyone from ambushing them—assuming that conspirators might have infiltrated his own staff—unless they

* By the time Sheriff Morris was finished modernizing the building and installing special electronic and security equipment, in accordance with the advice of U. S. Bureau of Prisons experts, he had spent more than $100,000 preparing Shelby County Jail for James Earl Ray's arrival.

were prepared to post an army of men on every road that fed into Memphis.

If their convoy were stopped en route, if they were attacked from ground or air, a series of actions would go into effect. If the driver of the armored car should be shot, the man next to him would take over. If *he* was incapacitated, a third would leap into the breach. Every possible contingency had been anticipated: breakdown, road block, bridge collapse, booby traps, fire bomb, assault by one or many, by helicopter, by tank, by poison gas. Every man had his orders and his emergency procedures, practiced beforehand. For on this return route, on this eighteen-mile stretch of road from Millington to Memphis, the best opportunity would be afforded to those who might want to spirit him to safety or to kill him.

The sheriff had asked Dr. DeMere to accompany him. Dr. DeMere was an unusual figure in Memphis. A wiry, energetic man in his fifties, he had been medical aide to General Patton in World War II. He was a plastic surgeon with an international reputation, a professor of law at Memphis State University Law School, medical director of the Shelby County sheriff's department, a trained police officer, and a redoubtable long-distance runner. For a number of years Sheriff Morris had required all candidates for the Sheriff's Reserves to run the mile against Dr. DeMere and accepted only those who outran him.

The sheriff had asked DeMere to be Ray's physician as long as the prisoner was in Memphis. His first task would be to examine Ray when he was turned over to the Shelby County authorities. DeMere would ride in the convoy that would pick up Ray at Millington.

At 2 A.M., Morris, DeMere, and his party moved to a police sub-station on the outskirts of Memphis, where Morris was in radio code communication with the pilot of the plane bringing Ray from London.

From Millington Naval Air Base the word came that all was quiet. Some thirty newspaper reporters, acting on a London rumor that Ray had been spirited out of prison during the night, had spent the last hours fruitlessly checking every private and commercial airfield in a fifty-mile radius of Memphis. At 9 P.M. Nick Chriss, an indefatigable reporter from the Los Angeles *Times*, had driven out to Millington and carefully examined the scene. All appeared normal. The air tower showed no unusual activity, the Officers' Club was in full swing, no area of the base had been declared off limits. Chriss left.

At 3 A.M., a reporter for the Memphis *Commercial-Appeal* made a last try. He telephoned the base. Were they expecting any more planes tonight? The officer of the day replied no. The reporter persisted: Could he speak to the commanding officer? "If it's that important I'll wake him up, but the colonel sure as hell will be sore if I get him out of bed at this hour." The reporter gave up.

Actually, the preparations for getting Ray out of London were as elaborate as those for getting him into Memphis. Assistant Attorney General Fred Vinson, Jr., had flown to London twice to oversee the extradition proceedings. The first time had been Sunday, June 9, the day after Ray had been seized. He had watched the brief arraignment next morning in Bow Street Court, sitting on the same ancient wooden bench that Charles Dickens had occupied when he took notes more than a century before. After the hearing Vinson had been taken on a tour of the fortresslike jail. He had been escorted down a long corridor outside a row of high-ceilinged, windowless cells and, peering through a long, narrow, slotlike peephole in a massive door to one of the cells, had seen Ray, who had just been returned from court. The man was seated on a wooden bench, which was also to serve as his bed. He sat, bowed, elbows on knees, his cupped hands supporting his chin, his head down, staring at the floor—the picture of a disconsolate man. Though Vinson had only a three-quarter view, he recognized him immediately by the protruding left ear. At this moment there was a small commotion elsewhere: the prisoner looked up, and Vinson had a clear view of his face. It was James Earl Ray, all right. (Vinson, on the transatlantic telephone to Ramsey Clark later that day, told him, "No question of it—he's our man.") It had been a tremendous relief to them both, for Vinson had shared with Clark the ordeal of waiting for Ray to be found, and the dread suspicion, as the days went on, that he might be dead, with everything that would mean, an intolerable reprise of Lee Harvey Oswald and the forever unanswered questions. Before Vinson left London, he had been interviewed, and to the question "Have you seen Ray?" he replied, literally, yes. The British reporters interpreted this to mean that he had interviewed Ray in his cell. This became headlines, and brought immediate charges that the U. S. Government was taking unfair advantage of Ray by questioning him without a lawyer present. Ray himself remained convinced that here was one more proof that the Justice Department and the FBI were out to lie about him.

Vinson had worked with Scotland Yard on the problem of safely transporting Ray to the States. He had checked first on chartering a commercial plane large enough to fly London–Memphis nonstop. He dared not risk making a stop en route lest Ray be the target of a rescue or assassination attempt. Only a Boeing 707 was capable of such an extended flight, and charter costs ranged from seventeen thousand dollars upward. This was prohibitive. Vinson then looked into the possibility of putting Ray, well guarded, aboard a regular commercial flight, London to New York, New York to Memphis. But this would mean not only a stopover, but also changing planes in New York—a still greater risk. He decided, finally, to ask the U. S. Air Force to fly Ray and a guard escort from London nonstop to the military airport nearest to Memphis—which was the Millington Naval Air Base.

Vinson had hoped that an Air Force jet might be available in Europe. There was none. The Air Force consequently had to fly a C-135—equivalent to a Boeing 707—from Washington, D.C., to London, with a three-man relief crew and two FBI agents familiar with the investigation. When they arrived in London, they were joined by two more agents who had attended the extradition hearings in Bow Street Court. These four, accompanied by an Air Force physician, would fly back with Ray to Memphis. The actual transfer from British to American custody took place at 11 P.M. at the prison, where Ray was given a physical examination and officially handed into the custody of the four FBI men.

He was whisked to the Royal Air Force Base at Northolt, outside London, to be put aboard the plane. Usually a C-135 or Boeing 707 carries as many as 127 persons, including crew and attendants. This plane carried the three-man relief crew and six passengers—Ray, the physician, and the four FBI men. The four last-mentioned also officially represented the States of Tennessee and Missouri and had taken custody of Ray in their names.* There would have to be another transfer in Memphis—this time from the FBI to Shelby County. Ray would be given another physical examination so that the agents could bring Washington a receipt attesting that James Earl Ray had been delivered, in good health and good condition, to Shelby County Sheriff William N. Morris, Jr.

Meanwhile, the sheriff and his group waited at the substation. As the plane approached the American coast, Morris checked with the

---

* Vinson had been in communication with the governors of Missouri and Tennessee, who had agreed to divide the expenses. They did finally take care of legal fees in London, but when confronted by a bill—sent by the U. S. Air Force to the Justice Department and forwarded by the Justice Department to the State Houses in Jefferson City and Nashville—for some seven thousand dollars in transportation costs, they balked. In the end it was paid by the U. S. Government.

pilot so that he could leave at the last moment to give the least possible notice to anyone who might be following him in order to get at Ray. To be doubly safe, the sheriff had a police van, escorted by three squad cars, waiting to roar out of the Memphis jail toward the Memphis Municipal Airport as a decoy—for the press or anyone else.

At the proper moment he signaled the decoy to leave. Five minutes later he and his party left for Millington Naval Air Base. As DeMere slipped into his place in the front seat of the armored car, next to the door, Morris gave him a wry grin. This was difficult for the sheriff, because he was in deadly earnest about his task. One had the impression that Morris would be prepared to do away with himself—commit *hara-kari* were that the sort of a thing an American did—if anything happened to Ray; that if an attack came, he would willingly throw himself in front of the prisoner to take the bullets in his own body. The sheriff was the kind of a man who would walk alone down the center of the street in *High Noon*. "Mac," he said, "there's only one weak spot in this car." He pointed to a heavy plate just at DeMere's temple. "The armor's only single thickness here." DeMere gave him an equally wry grin as they got under way.

It was a moonless night. Earlier the city had been lashed by a heavy rain, accompanied by lightning and high winds. It had begun just before sunset and subsided just before midnight. Now it was quiet and very dark.

They rode silently: First, six motorcycle policemen, then two squad cars of heavily armed guards, carrying submachine guns, then the massive, armor-plated truck in which Ray would be brought back to the jail. It had been borrowed from the Jackson, Mississippi, police, who had bought it two years before for riot control. Named "Thompson's Tank" for Mayor Allen Thompson of Jackson, it looked more like an Army tank than anything else, except for its blue and white color, the whirling red and white dome light on top, and the pair of enormous, blindingly bright spotlights in front, which could be turned in any direction. It was a monstrous vehicle, completely steeljacketed, with double steel armor, equipped with gunports and its tires protected by heavy steel flanges down to a few inches from the road. The windshield was of inch-thick bulletproof glass.

Behind Thompson's Tank came three more squad cars, two filled with sheriff's deputies, the third carrying federal marshals headed by Clark.

When the caravan arrived at Millington, the group emerged and took their place at the end of one of the runways. The lights of the

C-135 were coming into sight, blinking in the Eastern sky. DeMere glanced at his watch as the wheels touched down at the far end of the field and the plane began to taxi toward them. It was 3:48 A.M. It had hardly come to a halt before it was surrounded by the guards, placed so they faced in every direction.

Now other armed men took their positions to form a passageway to the ladder that had been wheeled to the plane. An attendant hurried to it, the door opened, and Sheriff Morris climbed the steps and went inside, a paper in his hand. He was followed by half a dozen others.

Waiting for them inside was James Earl Ray. He had been strapped and locked to a rear aisle seat during the entire flight, save for one time when he went to the lavatory and then he was accompanied by two of his guards. Now he was unstrapped and brought to his feet. He was quickly stripped of everything he wore, until he stood naked in the soft golden light of the plane's interior. He stood, head down, a surprisingly slight, slumped wretched man, his skin sickly white.

While those from Memphis stood, waiting, in the front of the plane, the Air Force physician gave Ray a quick physical examination. When he was finished, he said to the sheriff, "He's all yours."

Sheriff Morris spoke. "James Earl Ray, alias Harvey Lowmyer, alias John Willard, alias Eric Starvo Galt, alias Paul Bridgman, alias Ramon George Sneyd, will you please step three paces forward?"

Ray dutifully did so. The prisoner had crossed an invisible line which brought him into Shelby County territory. The sheriff now motioned to Dr. DeMere, and the latter opened his doctor's bag, brought forth a stethoscope, and placed it against Ray's bare chest, and listened. He brought out his blood pressure apparatus. He had him turn and thumped his back, asking him to breathe deeply. In a few minutes the swift physical examination was completed. Dr. DeMere stepped back and nodded to the sheriff.

The chief FBI man stepped forward and handed the proper documents to Sheriff Morris, saying, "I now give the person and property of James Earl Ray into the custody of Shelby County, State of Tennessee." He extended a receipt for Ray, and the sheriff solemnly signed it. Even as he did so, behind the principals a sheriff's deputy was recording the transfer on videotape, using a portable machine that the sheriff had purchased a few days before. It continued to record what went on, sight and sound, in the plane.

Now, standing at attention before Ray, who still stood, naked and slumped like a question mark, his head down, Morris formally introduced himself. He was William N. Morris, Jr., sheriff of Shelby County, Tennessee, and he was taking him into custody to stand trial on a first degree murder indictment voted by the Shelby County Grand Jury on May 7, 1968, accusing him of fatally shooting Dr. Martin Luther King, Jr., in Memphis, Tennessee, on April 4, 1968. Morris cleared his throat and began reading in a strained voice from the paper in his hand. It was a statement of Ray's rights. What the sheriff read, in essence, was that Ray had the right to remain silent; that he had the right to be represented by counsel, and the right to have counsel present at all times when he was questioned; that if he could not afford a lawyer, one would be provided for him; and that anything he said could be used against him in court.

Ray gave no sign that he heard. He kept his head down. He said nothing. Morris turned to his chief aide, Ray Nixon, who opened a small valise and drew out a pair of dark green trousers, a green plaid sport shirt, and a pair of sandals. Nixon had purchased these the day before on the pretext that they were for his brother. He also brought a bulletproof vest and a leather harness which, like an iron maiden, went around the prisoner's waist in a wide leather belt and between his legs. Attached to the belt were two small steel rings. Nixon helped Ray get dressed, placed the harness upon him, manacled his wrists, and then attached the manacles to the rings. Ray could walk, sit, and stand, but his hands, manacled to the belt, were powerless.

At this point the Medical Corps lieutenant took Dr. DeMere aside. "I'd watch this man," he said softly. "He has suicidal tendencies."

DeMere looked at him. Nothing like this had appeared in the prison psychological reports on Ray that DeMere had seen. His colleague would not amplify his statement save to say that Ray had not said a word during the entire trip. He had refused to talk, he had not responded to any civil overtures. He had kept his face averted, or looked into space, or slept. The FBI had ordered that two agents must keep Ray in view at all times. The agents took turns watching and resting, two awake, two asleep. They observed that Ray would appear to be sound asleep, then unexpectedly one eye would slowly open, stare at them, then close again. Why was he feigning sleep? The agents had other orders, too. If Ray wished to talk, they were to listen, and since they were familiar with his case, they could assess his words. But they were not to interrogate him. The subject had come up in Washington: should the agents attempt to question him on the trip? He might be stupid enough to blurt out an all-important fact. The Justice Department decided against this.

But Ray said nothing, asked for nothing, complained about nothing.

Now, his right arm grasped in a grip of steel by Morris, his left held similarly by an FBI man, Ray was almost carried down the ladder. He kept his face down. When his feet touched ground, he looked up to see a huge black man towering over him. One almost heard him gasp. This was Henry Hooper, one of Morris's deputies, a former Marine Corps boxing champion, six feet four and weighing 260 pounds, who had been stationed at the back door of the armored car. The vehicle had been backed up until it almost touched the ladder. Almost at the same moment Ray was literally lifted off his feet and swung to the rear of the truck, then they were inside, and the heavy armored doors clanked shut.

The procession left immediately, moving at high speed down the highway to Memphis, preceded by the two squad cars. Inside Thompson's Tank, Ray sat between Morris and Ken Bounds of the FBI; facing him were several guards, headed by Tennessee Safety Commissioner Gregg O'Rear. O'Rear was truly a giant of a man. He was over six feet six and at least twenty pounds heavier than Hooper; and O'Rear sat staring at Ray in a fashion which fascinated Morris, despite his anxieties. Not once during the trip did O'Rear's eyes leave Ray's face; even more astonishing, not once did O'Rear blink. Sheriff Morris watched him, unbelieving, thinking, *This is amazing, we're going to hit a bump, and O'Rear'll change expression, or blink, or look away for a second*. But never did this happen.

In the last week Morris had made trial runs over three different routes to Memphis, clocking the time, noting where he might be held up or surprised. Now, at the last moment, he chose the shortest, most direct route. He was in radio communication with the jail, sending code numbers at intervals so those at the jail could have a fix on his whereabouts and expected arrival time. To throw off the press and any others, not only had Morris sent off a decoy pickup caravan to Memphis Airport, but shortly before he was to arrive with his prisoner, a second decoy of three squad cars raced up to the jail's back entrance. The press, which had been waiting more than one hundred strong, with klieg lights, TV cameras, and the rest, in trees and every other available place, swept into frenzied action, only to subside again. Had the half-dozen men who dashed from the cars into the jail included Ray? No one was sure.

In Memphis, at the jail, they waited. The Criminal Courts Building, which contained the jail, had become a fortress. No one was permitted on the side of the street adjacent to it. On the roofs of nearby buildings, armed guards were silhouetted against the sky as they patrolled back and forth.

There was constant activity in the streets below. Police cars slowly circled the block. At midnight jailers had been seen hanging blankets over windows of cells facing the street. Shortly after 4 A.M. a dozen sheriff's deputies suddenly appeared. They augmented the guard. Helmeted men, in riot uniform, khaki shirt and trousers, black ties, black belts, they took their places on the sidewalk. They stood spaced about twenty feet apart, each man with a sawed-off shotgun cradled in his arm, a pistol on its holster on each right hip, a pair of manacles hanging from each belt at the left hip, next to it a dangling billy club. "My God," one reporter exclaimed. "It's like something out of 1984!"

Toward 4:30 A.M. several police cruisers appeared. They deliberately stopped in the center of each street intersection to block any traffic trying to approach the jail. Then, suddenly, a squad car came roaring up and pulled into the rear of the jail. A few seconds later, six motorcycles screamed into view, then two squad cars raced nearly sixty miles an hour down the empty, guarded streets to turn sharply into the jail yard, between the jail proper and the courthouse. Moments before, a huge bus had driven up and come to a halt opposite the jail door—leaving room for vehicles to pass between it and the door. The bus would act as a shield to protect against snipers if any managed to escape the heavy guard.

Then the caravan swept in with a shriek of sirens and the blue and white armored car, its dome light whirling madly, came to a halt between the bus and the jail door. Suddenly the entire scene, like a Hollywood set prepared for some ancient mass assault upon a castle, was bathed in incandescence as TV klieg lights were switched on. A stentorian voice boomed out over a loudspeaker, "Turn out those lights!" They died out and at this moment the powerful spotlights of Thompson's Tank were turned on and aimed directly at the press and spectators. The brilliant glare blinded them, but armed men, at least five deep, could be seen between the armored car and the jail entrance, but no one saw Ray and the two men who rushed him, one on either side, so swiftly that his feet did not touch the ground, from the car to the jail.

When the steel doors of Thompson's Tank opened, the first person Ray saw was a photographer, crouching in the jail entrance before him. Ray dropped his head; he could not put up his hands, manacled to his belt, to hide his face. The photographer had anticipated this: crouching, back-pedaling while he snapped furiously. Ray was whisked into an elevator to be taken up to the waiting cell block on the third floor. The photographer followed him in. Ray immediately moved into a corner of the elevator and pushed his face into it, so only his back could be seen.

The photographer placed himself so he would be first out of the elevator, then, viewfinder to his eyes, whirled about to shoot Ray as he emerged. In the viewfinder the photographer suddenly saw a huge object swooping toward him. Instinctively he fell to one side. He heard Ray's curse—the first words anyone had heard Ray utter from the moment he had been taken from his cell in London. "You son-of-a-bitch!" Ray, held so firmly by either arm, had, like a man on the parallel bars, swung his feet off the floor and viciously aimed his heels at the photographer's head. The latter had missed injury by inches.

Once inside the cell block Ray was disrobed again, and Dr. DeMere made a more thorough physical examination, the photographer taking one shot after another of him. Ray protested vehemently. Morris quieted him. "This is not for any news release: this is the Sheriff's Department photographer." Then they dressed Ray in the jail attire he would wear—shorts, T-shirt, sport shirt, denim slacks, slippers.

Sitting in his office that morning of July 19, with Ray under guard in Shelby County Jail, Attorney General Canale drew a piece of legal foolscap to him and printed the words SECURITY PRECAUTIONS—HOME across the top. Then he began writing:

1. Raise telephone line to house or bury it to prevent cutting. Get new unlisted number.

2. Put plastic glass in rear-landing storm window. Buy smoke alarm for each room in case fire bomb thrown. Put locks on all windows. Put floodlights in driveway, backyard and patio, with backyard floodlight switch in master bedroom. (See these are installed by electricians checked for security.)

3. Put in arc light fed by batteries in case current cut.

4. Get shortwave communications set from house to police station.

5. Buy rope ladder and install to reach from balcony to ground.

6. Telephones: Put visual and sound checks on each line re taps.

7. Cut down hedges and trees to give visibility to security men stationed around house.

8. Get magnetic key rings for keys for car to allow easy access to gun in glove compartment.

9. Put intercom between children's bedroom and ours.

10. New locks on all bedroom doors.

At six-thirty that evening the Attorney General met at the First Memphis Bank with four friends. Three were bankers, the fourth an insurance executive. When Canale was finished and was ready to drive home to dinner with his wife and four children, this first day in which James Earl Ray was under a Memphis roof, he had achieved the purpose of the meeting. It was the organization of a movement by friends "to create a trust fund for the benefit and education of my family in case my life is taken by anybody before, during, or after the Ray trial."

CHAPTER XXI

Had anyone, the next day, had a camera capable of photographing through many layers of iron, steel, and concrete to James Earl Ray's Block A on the third floor of Shelby County Jail, he would have seen an odd sight that Saturday morning, July 20. It was to be repeated on Sunday and Monday mornings.

Block A contained six individual cells, each with its barred door, and in front of them, an eight-foot wide corridor, or bullpen area thirty-five feet long, the whole enclosed by a latticework of heavy steel bars. The six cells, each with a metal combination toilet and washbasin, and a metal bunk attached to the back wall, were for Ray's use, so that no one could know in advance in which cell he would spend the night. At the far end of the bullpen there was a stall shower and next to it an alcove, hardly larger than the shower itself.

Here Arthur J. Hanes, Sr., his son, Art, Jr., and James Earl Ray were in conference. The three lay on their backs on the concrete floor, their heads together, whispering. The shower had been turned on, and the water poured from it loudly.

It was awkward, it was ridiculous, and anything but a dignified posture for a former mayor of Birmingham, but it was the only means Hanes knew to outwit Sheriff Morris's almost surrealistic security precautions. Morris had set up an arrangement which made Ray the most carefully guarded and monitored man in history. He was never alone, and never in darkness: two guards were in the cell block with him at all times, and one pair of eyes had always to be on him, day and night. The cell block was brilliantly lit around the clock. Hanging from the ceiling were two microphones. Outside the block, day and night, a supervisor sat, able to watch and hear Ray and the two guards through the bars, while before him a TV screen also registered, by means of two cameras, one focused on the length of the block, the other scanning its width, everything that took place in it. Even when Ray used the toilet, or showered, he was in sight of supervisor and cameras; the shower curtain might hide his nakedness, but it was made of translucent plastic so that his silhouette was visible.

Assuming that he might try the impossible—to strangle himself, to swallow poison, to injure himself—this would be seen.

Another screen and speaker had been installed in Sheriff Morris's private bar in his office two floors below. At any time of the day or night, with a turn of the switch, Morris could not only bring the entire cell block into view, but also overhear what went on in it.

As Hanes knew, these were only the basic security measures taken by the sheriff. A hundred-page instruction manual dealing only with Ray's care had been prepared with the help of the Federal Bureau of Prisons, and it had become the Bible of the fourteen men assigned to guard and tend him. But now, in order for the lawyer to have his first confidential interview with his client, to avoid the TV cameras, the microphones, the possibility that Morris himself might be sitting before the screen in his office with a lip-reading expert at his side to learn what Ray was revealing to his lawyers, Hanes had suggested they lie flat on the floor next to the shower. The sheriff had told him that the microphones were switched off when Hanes visited his client, but the lawyer was not reassured, and just in case Morris might have secretly planted bugs elsewhere, he had turned on the shower to drown out their words.

Now, at last, he was able to say to Ray, "All right, Jimmy, let's start talking. From your breakout on April 23, 1967, to June 8 when they picked you up in London."

A bushel basket could have covered their three heads as Ray began whispering his story and the two, father and son, one on each side of the accused man, listened intently.

He had planned to break out long before, and to aim for Canada for two reasons: everyone in prison knew that Canada was the easiest place to pick up false identification papers; and he had read how Lowell Birrell, a New York securities operator indicted for swindling customers out of millions, had gotten a Canadian passport and fled to Brazil, from where he could not be extradited, and lived like a millionaire until he returned to the States.

Missouri State Penitentiary officials had announced that Ray escaped by hiding in a bread box transported by truck from the prison bakery to a prison farm four miles away. They said fellow inmates had helped him, covering him with loaves and then replacing the lid on the box. On the way to the farm the truck stopped for traffic signals and Ray simply got out of the box and jumped off the rear of the truck, unseen by the driver enclosed in his cab.

"The whole story is a lie," Ray told the Haneses. He had scaled a wall to get out, using a thirteen-foot iron pole used to open and shut high windows. He had managed to get on the roof, to hide there, and then drop to safety on the other side. He had tried this before and failed, but this time he succeeded.

He knew how to handle dyes, because of his job years before in a tannery: His green prison trousers had a side telltale stripe down each leg; he dyed them black with stenciling ink. In this day of hippies with their oddly colored slacks, he was not conspicuous. He took candy bars with him and had $275 in his shoes, money he'd made by selling commissary items to other prisoners. He walked along train tracks for several nights, then caught a train to St. Louis, where a "friend"—Hanes suspected that it was his brother John, who visited him the day before he escaped—drove him to Chicago. There he bought a suit in a secondhand shop, stuffed his prison clothes in an ash can, and answered an ad for a kitchen worker in the Indian Trail Restaurant, in Winnetka, under the name of John L. Rayns. There he could be out of sight, catch his breath, and meanwhile earn more than one hundred dollars a week. There had been no great alarm out for him. Prison authorities disclosed that he was missing only several days later, after vainly searching for him inside the walls, where they'd found him before. When they did send out a notice, it offered the usual reward for the almost anonymous run-of-the-mill criminal—fifty dollars. Nobody, really, was looking for James Earl Ray.

In July, when he had some money saved up, he quit his job, bought a used Plymouth for two hundred dollars and drove to Montreal. He feared using the name John Rayns too long, and he looked for another alias. In Canada he passed a road sign indicating the town of Galt. He chose Galt for his last name, and Eric Starvo—names he had read somewhere—for his first and middle names. You always picked something odd so you could remember it. With a name like John Smith or Bill Roberts, you might become confused if suddenly stopped and questioned.

In Montreal, as Eric Starvo Galt, he leased an apartment at the Har-K Apartments, for seventy-five dollars a month, and loitered about the waterfront, letting it be known that he was looking for an I.D. He wasn't sure how he'd get it—perhaps he'd buy a seaman's papers or roll him if drunk.

Then, in a chance encounter over a beer, he met a man who changed the course of his life. He was a red-haired French Canadian sailor, about thirty-five, named Raoul. He never learned his last name. As Ray put it—his language was always proper—"After talking to him a couple of times I got the impression that he was in some sort of illicit activities. When you associate with this type of person for years, you get so you can usually tell them." At first Raoul suggested he might get him a job on a ship, but Ray told him, "I'd been in minor trouble in the U.S.," had no identification papers, and so couldn't get a job. Ray told him he had thought of going to Australia, or some other country, but couldn't for the same reason. Raoul listened sympathetically.

After several meetings at a waterfront tavern, and after learning that Ray had a car, Raoul made a proposition to him—that Ray do a series of odd—and illicit—jobs for him. It was the beginning of a remarkable relationship, Ray said, that was to direct his comings and goings until King's murder broke up their partnership, placed Ray in terrible jeopardy, and led him to end up in London in the hands of Scotland Yard for a crime he did not commit.

As the Haneses, father and son, listened, fascinated despite their discomfort on the cold, hard concrete, Ray told how for the next seven months, until April 4, 1968, he followed Raoul's orders, carrying out various small smuggling jobs with him—using his Plymouth to smuggle heroin into the United States from Canada, to smuggle jewels, rare coins, and the like between Mexico and the States (often in the tires of his car). He did this because Raoul, who seemed to know his way around, promised him an identity card, travel papers to enable him to reach a foreign country, and a nest egg of twelve thousand dollars to start a business wherever he went.

He repeated: from the July day he met Raoul in Montreal, it was Raoul who directed his movements, who told him where to go, what motels to register in, who met him at various rendezvous points in Canada, Mexico, and the United States. It was Raoul who told him to buy camera equipment and gave him the money; who told him to get rid of his Plymouth—the gears were stripped, and it was becoming useless—and buy the white Mustang in Birmingham and gave him money for it; who told him to go from Birmingham to Mexico, and met him in Mexico, and then told him to go to Los Angeles, then wrote him to come to New Orleans just before Christmas when he took Charlie Stein along. . . .

Hanes interrupted him impatiently. "Jimmy, right now I'm not concerned with all that. I'm concerned with the crucial time, which is March 29, when the rifle was bought at Aeromarine in Birmingham through April 4, 6:01 P.M., in Memphis."

O.K., said Ray. When he returned to California after his New Orleans trip in December, he was told to wait until Raoul sent for him. Raoul always wrote him care of general delivery in whatever city he was, and also had given him a New Orleans telephone number to call in case of emergency. Raoul was having trouble getting Ray his papers, but with each postponement he promised he would have them almost any day. Meanwhile, every few weeks, Raoul would give him a little more "capital" to keep going. (Ray explained that he was not too badly off; in Montreal, before meeting Raoul, he had held up a brothel, getting $1700. Brothel owners never complained to the police.) And Raoul was not ungenerous: he had given him $3000 in Birmingham to buy the Mustang and camera equipment, he had given him $2000 in Mexico, and when Ray drove down with Charlie Stein and met Raoul in New Orleans, the man had given him $500 for expenses. So he had played along with him.

In early March, Ray said, Raoul wrote him to leave Los Angeles and meet him in New Orleans on March 20. They would be bound for Atlanta, where they'd stay for a while. Ray thereupon checked out of the St. Francis Hotel, leaving a forwarding address as general delivery, Atlanta. He had signed up for mail-order locksmithing lessons, so he'd have some kind of a trade, and he didn't want to miss out on them, he explained. When he arrived in New Orleans and telephoned Raoul's number, he was given a message that Raoul had gone on to Birmingham, and he should meet him there at the Starlight Club, a rendezvous they'd used before. He got lost on the way to Birmingham, and had to spend the night of March 22 in Selma, Alabama, at the Flamingo Motel. He met Raoul in Birmingham the next day, they drove together to Atlanta, where on Sunday, March 24, they found Jimmy Garner's rooming house in the hippie section of town and Raoul told him to check in there.

They were going into a new enterprise, he told him—gunrunning. Raoul had customers interested in buying rifles to run into Mexico and perhaps Cuba. He wanted Ray to buy about ten good rifles, as well as several hundred foreign surplus weapons, which could be gotten cheaply. First, however, Ray was to purchase one rifle as a sample. Raoul would show it to his customers, who were in Memphis. If they approved, Ray would buy the rest. Raoul gave him seven hundred dollars to pay for the rifle, a scope, and ammunition, and told him to buy everything at the Aeromarine Supply Company, in Birmingham. He was to check into a Travelodge Motel there and make his purchase. Raoul and he had both studied a newspaper advertisement in which Aeromarine claimed it had the largest stock of guns in the South.

On Friday, March 29, Ray bought the stuff at Aeromarine and took it back to his motel room, where Raoul waited. Ray gave a false name when he bought the rifle, he said—Harvey Lowmyer, there was an inmate by that name in prison—because his driver's license was in the name of Galt, and if the gunrunning led to trouble, it would be wiser not to use Galt. When Raoul saw the gun, he said, "You've bought the wrong one." Ray had brought back an Aeromarine catalogue, and Raoul checked off a Remington 30.06. That was the weapon they were to show their Memphis customers. Ray telephoned Aeromarine. They would exchange it the next day, because they were closing up now. He went back Saturday morning and exchanged the rifle. "I gave them some kind of a cock-and-bull story about my brother wanting a different gun," he said.

When Raoul saw the purchase he said, fine. He had to return briefly to New Orleans. Ray was to drive to Memphis, go to a rooming house—Raoul gave him the address, 422½ South Main Street—and check in there at 3 P.M. Thursday, April 4, using the name John Willard. Raoul would meet him there. Ray followed orders, he said. He took his time driving the 244 miles to Memphis, staying at motels along the way. Once he tried out the gun, firing it several times, so he would be able to talk intelligently about it. He reached Memphis on Wednesday night, April 3, and registered around seven o'clock at the New Rebel Motel. He had difficulty next morning finding the rooming house, so he parked in a parking lot and walked about until he found the place, and rented his room from Mrs. Brewer. By now it was nearer to 3:30 P.M. than three o'clock. He placed the box with the rifle in it and his overnight bag on the bed, as well as a bedspread he carried with him which he would use if Raoul wanted him to spend the night there.

Raoul must have been watching for him, because he was no sooner in Room 5B than Raoul walked in on him. "You're twenty minutes late," he said rebukingly. "Where's the car?" Ray told him. It was at least twelve blocks away. "Get it and park it out front," Raoul told him. On the way back he was to pick up a pair of infrared binoculars. Ray had no idea what these were—he thought perhaps there were infrared lenses you attached to ordinary binoculars, so after he got his car he bought a pair of field glasses on the same street as the rooming house.

When he came upstairs with the binoculars, Raoul said, "Just put them on the bed." Ray did so, next to the Browning box with the rifle in it, and his overnight bag, which were on the bedspread he had brought up. It was now about 5:15 or 5:20.

They spoke for a few minutes. Then Raoul said, "Why don't you go downstairs and get yourself a beer?" There was a restaurant on the ground level. "I want to wash up a bit, shave and change shirts. Then I'll come on down and get you, and we'll drive around a bit, get a drink, and have something to eat."

Ray said he went downstairs to Jim's Grill, had his beer, and when, after some minutes Raoul did not show up, he left the restaurant and waited for him by the car. He was standing next to the white Mustang when suddenly he heard a shot. A moment later Raoul appeared, dashing down the stairs into the street and making for him. He was carrying something long and wrapped in his right hand, and as he passed a shop he dropped it. It was a bundle wrapped in Ray's bedspread. It opened when it fell and Ray saw the Browning box and his bag. He was about to race over to pick it all up—Raoul must have dropped it accidentally—when he saw dozens of police rushing out of a corner fire station and dashing around to the back. That frightened him, so he jumped behind the wheel. At that moment Raoul reached the car, pulled open the door, jumped in, and covered himself with a white sheet that was in the back. Ray shoved his foot hard on the accelerator and they shot away. They had gone about four blocks when he had to stop for a red light. Raoul opened the door, jumped out, flung over his shoulder, "See you in New Orleans," and vanished into the traffic.

He never saw Raoul again.

All he could think of at that moment, he said, was to get out of town, fast, and get out of the country, fast. As an escaped convict, he was in trouble. Besides, someone might tie him to Raoul and to whatever happened in that room. He dared not take the chance of going to New Orleans to see Raoul—even though the latter owed him the twelve thousand dollars he had promised him. Instead, he drove back to Atlanta, abandoned the car in a parking lot—it hurt him to do this, for it cost good money—went to his room, swiftly packed, and went by bus to Cincinnati, then Detroit, and on to Canada, to find some way to use Canada as a jumping-off place for Europe.

So Ray told of his experiences during three consecutive morning sessions Saturday, Sunday, and Monday, July 20, 21, and 22. After each session father and son returned to their hotel and Art, Jr., wrote down everything they could remember while it was still fresh in their

minds. They asked only a few basic questions looking toward what
the state might seize upon to prove motive. For example, what about
Charlie Stein's story that Ray made the trip to New Orleans just before Christmas conditional upon Charlie, his sister Rita Stein, and
Marie Martin all signing up for Wallace? That would make Ray a
strong Wallace man, perhaps a racist. . . . That had been completely
twisted, Ray said. It had been Charlie and the two girls who wanted
to sign up for Wallace, and he had simply dropped them off at Wallace headquarters, because it was near a shop where he had to buy a
tire; after he bought the tire, he drove back to pick them up. They
were still inside, so he went in to get them. That explained why he
was in Wallace headquarters, should the state produce someone to
say he had been there.

What about the anti-Negro charge—that he got into a violent argument about Negroes in the Rabbit's Foot Club in Los Angeles and
tried to drag a girl out, saying, "If you love Niggers so much, I'll drop
you off at Watts and see how you like it there."

That, too, had been twisted around. He was sitting at the bar, he
had had a few drinks, the girl was riding him about being from Alabama, that Negroes were such good people, and denouncing him for
not giving Negroes their rights, and "I may have said something
back," but he didn't want any trouble, he was an escaped convict, so
he walked out, but two men followed him outside, and jumped him.
He broke away, they kept his jacket with his car keys in the pocket,
he had to hide until he found a locksmith to open the car and start
the motor. He had never tried to drag her out the door.

What about his telephone calls en route to New Orleans to an
"industrialist" as reported by Charlie Stein. Stein was imagining
things, said Ray. He was a strange fellow, a hippie, anyway. Ray had
simply telephoned his brother Jerry at the country club he worked in
outside Winnetka to say he was O.K. and on the way back he'd telephoned his brother John in his tavern, the Grapevine, in St. Louis,
to say he was O.K. He had never told Stein anything about an industrialist. He told him only that he was going down to New Orleans to
meet some former business associates from Mexico. He knew no industrialist in New Orleans. The only person he knew there was
Raoul, who had written him to come down to see him.

Would Ray explain the locksmithing lessons, the bartending lessons, the dance lessons? "All my own idea," Ray replied. His work for
Raoul allowed him much free time. He always wanted to improve
himself. He'd worked in tanneries and bakeries and kitchens, and

locksmithing would give him another trade. As for bartending—if he succeeded in hiding out in South America—Brazil, say—or some country in which he did not know the language well, he could still get a job as a bartender. You only had to learn the names of the drinks. And the dance lessons—Ray knew he wasn't very graceful, he wasn't much of a ladies' man—women never thought too much of him—perhaps the dance lessons would help make him more successful in that field.

Very little more was asked at these first three sessions. The Haneses wanted to get a first, over-all picture as quickly as possible of the most important facts so they could begin planning their defense. They would have time to zero in on the details later.

On Sunday, after the second session, Hanes made a visit to the Lorraine Motel and the rooming house at 422½ South Main Street to see for himself the scene of the crime. It was noon of a perfect summer's day when he walked unannounced and unknown into the motel courtyard. There was noise and laughter from children in the swimming pool. Gay red and white deck chairs were all about, and the water was very blue. The pool had been covered with a gray tarpaulin that chill April day, which now seemed so long ago. Hanes stood in the courtyard where King's aides stood when he was shot, and looked up at the balcony on which King had been standing when the bullet struck him. Then he climbed the zigzag metal steps to see Room 306.

The room and the balcony before it were now enclosed in a glass and aluminum rectangular structure. On the door a large cross, covered with purple satin, had been hung. It was draped with lilies of the valley. To the left was a stone plaque, inscribed: MARTIN LUTHER KING, JR. JAN. 15, 1929–APRIL 4, 1968. FOUNDING PRESIDENT, SOUTHERN CHRISTIAN LEADERSHIP CONFERENCE. Below it, the words chiseled in the stone: "They said one to another, Behold, this dreamer cometh. Come now therefore, and let us slay him . . . and we shall see what will become of his dreams.—Gen. 37:19, 20."

The room itself had been altered. The beds on which Dr. King and Abernathy had slept had been removed, on the walls now, were photographs of Dr. King—of Dr. King in his casket, April 5, 1968, taken by Ernest Withers; of Dr. King's coffin on the mule-drawn wagon in Atlanta, April 9. In the corner a tape recorder softly played King's speeches over and over. His voice was forever in the room. In the center, under glass, was a table set for two—dinner plates, cutlery, napkins, complete even to salt and pepper shakers. A neatly typewritten card read: "These are the last dishes used by Dr. King. He had ordered a double order of catfish when Dr. Abernathy came in and said, 'Where is mine?' Dr. King said, 'I didn't order one for you, Doc; we can eat this one together.'" Under glass, too, with another card of explanation: "This is the cloth in which they wrapped Dr. King's body." It was the bedspread with which the Rev. Samuel Kyles had covered Dr. King as he lay dying on the balcony, and which had been put about his body as he was taken down to the ambulance below.

The place had become a shrine. There was a register to sign, and a box for contributions. A table was set up under the stairs each Sunday and visitors were able to buy books dealing with Dr. King, and banners and ashtrays with his portrait on them, with the legend, "I have been to the mountaintop," and other mementos of his last, fatal stay in Memphis at the Lorraine Motel.

Then Hanes walked across Mulberry Street and around the block to South Main Street, and climbed the twenty-five steps—for some reason he found himself counting them—to the second floor of Mrs. Brewer's rooming house. She had long ago left, and the place had changed ownership several times since. Room 5B had been padlocked since the murder. Hanes waited silently while a sheriff's deputy opened it for him, then glanced in swiftly but said nothing. It was a sad, desolate room, with its ragged paper hangings and pitted walls. He walked into the bathroom across the hall, and stepped into the ancient tub on its lion-paw feet and looked out the window to the balcony of the Lorraine. One could take a perfect sight on anyone standing on the balcony—particularly anyone standing in front of Room 306. Standing in the tub, Hanes went through the motions of a man with a rifle, putting it to his shoulder, and aiming out the window. Standing there, drawing a bead with an invisible rifle on the balcony two hundred feet away, he shivered involuntarily, the skin at the back of his neck prickled; it was easy enough to think of a fatal bullet going from the bathroom to the balcony, or—and this is why his skin prickled—of a bullet going from a gun held in a black man's hand standing on that balcony to strike him, standing there at the open window.

Back at his hotel he held a press conference. Reporters had been clamoring to see him. Yes, he had had a chance to have a long talk with his client. Ray was the victim "of an international Communist plot." Attorney General Clark was 100 per cent wrong. "This is a giant conspiracy and my client is being used."

Hanes was convinced of this. When he flew to London with Art, Jr., a month before to see his client for the first time, he had not been so sure. He wanted first to see Ray and size him up, as he had promised Huie. He had been unable to see Ray on that first trip. The British had refused. But on July 2, after Magistrate Milton ruled that Ray must be extradited, the U. S. State Department had notified him that he could see him. Hanes had flown back to London, and they met in Wandsworth Prison, a maximum security institution, to which Ray had been transferred, in a tiny interview room, divided by a glass partition reinforced by wire mesh, so they could see and hear but not touch each other.

Hanes had been seated in the room first, a guard standing behind his chair, and then through the glass partition he saw a door open and a man about five feet ten, with one shoulder lower than the other, walked in, so heavy-footed that he literally lumbered into the room almost off balance, long-armed, eyes darting to one side, then the other. . . .

Ray sat down in a chair facing Hanes, a massive guard took up his position immediately behind him, and the two men looked at each other. Although Ray had been icy to Michael Eugene, he appeared enormously grateful to see Hanes.

"Well, buddy," Hanes had begun with a bluff heartiness which was always effective, "it looks like you're in a little trouble back home and I'm here to see how I can help you." Ray had responded, "I'm awfully glad you came over, Mr. Hanes." He said he had protested angrily when he learned Hanes had flown to England before and had been unable to see him. Then Hanes got down to business. He advised him not to appeal the extradition ruling. "Only a guilty man fights extradition," he explained. Ray nodded; he wanted to get home, too, and take care of "this nonsense." Hanes advised him, too, to have nothing to do with Attorney J. B. Stoner, who had not only offered to defend Ray free of charge, but had telephoned Hanes in Birmingham to suggest that the National States Rights Party organize a nationwide fund-raising campaign for Ray. Hanes had refused. He warned Ray that if he allowed the case to be tagged with racism it would be taken as proof that he killed King because he hated Negroes. Ray, listening calmly and thoughtfully, nodded. He would steer clear of Stoner, he said.

Then Hanes brought up Huie's offer—a thirty-thousand-dollar advance for defense purposes. Ray, surprisingly enough, knew Huie's name. While in prison he had read in a 1956 issue of *Look* magazine an article by Huie about the Emmett Till case, how he paid four thousand dollars to two Klan members who, having been acquitted of murdering the youth, could now with legal impunity admit they had done it because Till whistled at a white woman. Ray was ready to go along with Huie's proposal.

Hanes had seen Ray about half an hour on July 5 and again the next morning. He left him with the promise that he would try to fly back with him to the States when the British extradited him.

But it had not worked out that way. Scotland Yard and the FBI had spirited Ray out of England on an Air Force jet under great secrecy, and Hanes had been forced to fly back alone by commercial plane.

Now, having seen Ray twice in London, and then for three consecutive mornings in Cell Block A in Memphis, Hanes was convinced that if Ray killed King it was as part of a plot. This boy was not insane; he was not mad enough to kill King on his own. He was alert, in touch with reality; he knew who he was, where he was, and why. He was not a hysterical type, not a defeated, broken man. Hanes had been impressed by Ray's demeanor from the first. When Hanes had seen him, at Wandsworth Prison, Ray had just come out of the ordeal of a tremendous manhunt and an accusatory hearing among enemies, apparently unscathed, in control of himself, even outraged over one aspect of his arrest. This was Detective Chief Superintendent Butler's statement that he had slumped on a bench, clapped his hands to his face and exclaimed, "Oh, God! I feel so trapped!" Nothing like that had happened, Ray had said indignantly to Hanes, speaking through the wire mesh in the wall separating them. "You might expect a ten-year-old girl to act like that, but not a grown man." He was also indignant at the stories carried by newspapers and magazines, particularly by *Life* magazine, painting his family like something out of *Tobacco Road*. . . . It wasn't true. *Why*, thought Hanes, *he's more upset about his image than he is about the murder charge. He certainly doesn't act like a guilty man.*

In fact, he had wanted Hanes to sue *Life* for libel.

It was this aspect of his client's character—the jailhouse lawyer—that intrigued Hanes during that long weekend of research in Hanes's home. In 1959 Ray and an accomplice had gone on trial for the armed robbery of a Kroger supermarket in St. Louis. The trial was nearly over when Ray tried to fire his court-appointed lawyer.

The judge refused, whereupon Ray, despite his lawyer's warning, insisted on taking the stand to testify in his own behalf. It proved disastrous. It allowed his criminal past to be brought out. It was then he received his twenty-year sentence as a habitual criminal to Missouri State Penitentiary, while his accomplice, who had pleaded guilty and kept his mouth shut, received only seven years.

But aside from this insistence on trying to outwit the law, this readiness to duel with the prosecution, Ray was a typical con, in Hanes's estimation. Wary, trusting no one, a man who refused to look you in the eye, the more noticeable because of that curiously twisted smile on one side of his mouth that went on and off, apparently sardonic, but not really so. Bill Huie would have his work cut out for him, Hanes thought. But without Huie, Ray would be in the hands of a court-appointed local lawyer and chances were that it would be a routine defense, and the world would never learn the truth about the killing of Martin Luther King, Jr.

Hanes had already outlined his defense. He would, of course, plead Ray not guilty. He felt reasonably certain that he would end, at worst, with a hung jury. Among twelve Memphis citizens, good and true, surely there must be at least one who hated King; even if the jury found Ray guilty, the single juror could insist upon some kind of compromise sentence. He might even be able to save Ray, to win an acquittal, as he won the Liuzzo case—through reasonable doubt. Hanes had been able to establish there that the first police broadcast for the murder car—the car from which came the shots that killed Mrs. Liuzzo at the wheel of her car—had been for a red Sprite; and this was not the car the suspects were alleged to have used. It had been enough of a discrepancy to cause reasonable doubt in the jury's mind, a jury of eight Negroes and four whites. . . .

What worried Hanes was, who hired the boy? Suppose it was Peking? Or Hanoi? Hanoi and the United States were even now about to meet at the negotiation table in Paris. Only Hanoi was capable of the weird logic that King's killing might help its cause in Paris by bringing about such civil disorder in the United States that this country would have no stomach for waging war abroad and would pull back its troops from Vietnam—only Hanoi might be capable of believing this, and at the same time hiring a man like Ray, with such a lackluster record as a criminal.* Yet, who else other than Peking or

* There were other reasons for considering this possibility. George Ben Edmondson, a civil engineer and a fellow prisoner at Missouri State Penitentiary, had escaped nearly two years before Ray—August 3, 1965. Hanes had learned that Ed-

Hanoi would have the elaborate, far-reaching machinery to set up the assassination, including the false radio chase, whisk Ray to Atlanta, where the Mustang was found, then Toronto, then London, then Lisbon and back to London again? Lisbon had undoubtedly been selected because Portugal, like Switzerland, allowed numbered bank accounts, so that Ray could either be paid off there or bank his money there.

How could it not be a conspiracy? Hanes thought. When he had flown alone from London to New York, and then to Memphis, after he had been refused permission to accompany Ray to the United States, it was made clear enough that in Memphis it was considered a conspiracy. For as Hanes's plane approached the city, Memphis police radioed the pilot: "Mr. Hanes is to remain on board until we take him off." When the plane arrived, two groups of police were on the field at Municipal Airport. One immediately closed the gate, so no one could come on the field; the other group, made up of about ten men, moved en masse to the rear of the plane. When all other passengers had disembarked, they came aboard. One took Hanes aside. "I don't want to alarm you but we believe an attempt may be made on your life." They took him in a caravan of police cars to the Rivermont Motel—the same luxurious motel to which Dr. King and Dr. Abernathy had been taken when their march broke up. Two detectives accompanied Hanes to his room and remained with him, insisting on answering the telephone and the door. When he walked outside, two others were seated on chairs on either side of the door. As long as he was in Memphis, his bodyguard accompanied him everywhere each time he left the Rivermont—it was a little unsettling to learn that Judge Battle, Attorney General Canale, and other principals also had been assigned bodyguards—and he was trailed by police cars wherever he went. They had followed him to the jail, and when he visited the Lorraine, they were behind him, too.

Why should Ray's accomplices want to do away with his lawyer? Perhaps they feared Ray might have revealed something to him he

mondson, who spoke German like a native, had gone to Montreal and assumed a completely new identity, obtaining a passport and a name—Alex Borman; that under that name he was given a position as chief engineer of the West German Pavilion at Expo 67. There had been rumors that Edmondson had been seen in the company of men who were allegedly Red agents. Could these men have given Ray's name to Hanoi, suggesting him as a possible tool in the assassination, the more likely because he would be the last person the authorities would suspect, since he had never been involved in a homicide before.

should not have. Hanes decided that he would carry a revolver with him at all times. But suppose there were persons ready to come forward with information valuable to the defense? If every move and word of his was being monitored by the FBI—Hanes did not doubt that his room at the Rivermont had been bugged—how could anyone ever get through to him?

That night in Memphis, Hanes went to bed with not the least doubt in his mind that Ray was a tool. Why should this man—the question repeated itself like an obsessive refrain—do it unless someone paid him for it? Ray was no Don Quixote. He was not a fighter for causes. Nothing in his sorry history, nothing in his sad life style suggested that he did anything except for what was in it for him. There was nothing ideological in his makeup. It was a perversion of common sense, contrary to all human nature, for Ray to have done it on his own. And if he had done it for a cause, if he had been identified with a movement—if, like Lee Harvey Oswald, he had distributed Castro literature and gone to the Soviet Union, or if, like Sirhan Sirhan, Robert Kennedy's accused assassin, he had been a fanatical Arab nationalist and filled his notebooks with hymns of hate against his enemies—then one would understand it. If Ray had something in his craw about killing Martin Luther King, Jr., and had to get it out of his system no matter what, why had he not crowed to the world about it? Hanes, an avowed segregationist, had had long experience with violent "Nigger haters." He knew them, Klansmen and others who bristled at the sight of a black man—men to whom antiblack violence was part of their daily thinking, daily reacting. Hanes understood such men. He recognized them and knew how they thought. James Earl Ray was not one of them. Hanes would have felt it in his bones had Ray really belonged with them. Why, Ray would not even use the word "Nigger." There were black deputies and black orderlies at Shelby County Jail; Hanes had seen them. Ray had reacted to their presence by not so much as a flicker of the eye. When he had worked at the restaurant in Winnetka, a job he had held for seven weeks as a kitchen helper, his supervisor was a black man, a difficult, even arrogant black man, known to be hard to get along with—and Ray had been able to work so well under him, so unresentfully, that he had had his pay increased twice in the first two weeks. This was not the demeanor of a man with an uncontrollable, a homicidal, hatred for Negroes.

As of the moment, Hanes was prepared to argue that Ray did not even fire the fatal bullet. Ray indicated that Raoul had done it.

He told the Haneses that he had not known what took place in the room, what the sound of the shot meant, until later, when, driving out of Memphis, he heard on his radio that King had been the victim of a sniper. . . . They would have to convince him, Hanes thought, that Ray did fire the fatal shot. He would work on that later. What concerned him was, who had hired Ray, and even as he pondered the question for the hundredth time, he wondered whether it might not be better not to know. In any event, Ray himself probably did not know. He undoubtedly had only the one contact. That was the way the chain of conspiracy was always forged: link by link, no one knowing of the link beyond or before, so that Ray, even if he talked, could at most implicate only one other.

That would be Raoul.

It would be their job to find Raoul—and, if possible and if helpful, determine whom he represented.

Before they returned to Birmingham to throw themselves into an analysis of their case, there was one more task awaiting Hanes. That was to plead Ray not guilty at his arraignment in the Memphis court. It was done before Judge Battle that Monday, July 22, in a quick, unimpressive session, noteworthy only for the extraordinary security arrangements. The thirty-eight members of the press, chosen from two hundred applications from media all over the world, were finger-printed, photographed and videotaped, so their voices would be on record. Before they could enter the courtroom they were thoroughly searched, even to the heels of their shoes (they might be hollow and contain an explosive), their neckties (a poison tablet might be concealed in the lining), their watches (one might hide some un-imaginably effective electronic device to kill Ray or blow up the court-room so he could escape). A wand was passed over their bodies to determine if they had hidden anything metallic (a gun, a knife, a bomb), and only then were they permitted to file in, a full half hour before the proceedings began. Not only they but every other per-son was rigorously searched, including even the prosecuting and de-fense attorneys, and even Judge Battle himself; and when the guards had searched everyone else, including other guards, the last two searched each other.

It would have been ridiculous were it not so deadly serious.

Then Ray, in a dark blue suit, white shirt, and narrow black tie, appeared behind Sheriff Morris—a slender man with a long-strided, lurching walk, his face down, glancing neither right nor left, his pinched nose and pale face, his posture, his walk, all giving him a hangdog look. He was followed by two watchful deputies; he sat behind the two Haneses, the deputies on either side of him, and looked straight ahead. He said nothing as Hanes, Sr., rose and said the defendant at this time would like to enter a plea of not guilty to the indictment charging him with first-degree murder; he said nothing as Judge Battle set trial for November 12, more than three months later, a date agreed upon by both sides and chosen, too, because it came after the national elections and so whatever verdict was rendered would not influence the elections. Judge Battle asked, would the state be ready by that date? Attorney General Canale rose and said yes. Would the defense be ready? Hanes rose, rubbed his hands together briskly, looked about the courtroom, and said, Yes, Your Honor, it would.

It was done as swiftly as that. Ray was ushered out into the guarded back corridor to vanish in an elevator taking him to his cell block two floors above before anyone else was permitted to leave his seat.

When the Haneses left Memphis, they took with them a "Financial Record" which Ray had prepared. He had begun writing his account, which Hanes would pass on to William Bradford Huie, in accordance with contracts signed by all three. Ray's financial record dated from his prison escape on April 23, 1967, to the day he arrived in Canada after Dr. King's murder, after, as he said, Raoul jumped out of his car and vanished, never to be seen again. It was as carefully itemized as if an accountant had drawn it up, and Hanes was to put it away gratefully for further study:

FINANCIAL RECORD
Left prison with $275.
Saved at restaurant (Winnetka) $245.   Total: $520.
After arriving in Canada first time and paying two months rent in Montreal (first and last month), I had approximately $90. Holdup of $1,700 gave me . . . . 1,790.
  Spent in Canada—$1,000 . . . . 790.
  Received from Raoul in Detroit, $750 . . . . . . 1,540.
  Received from Raoul in Birmingham, $3,000 . . . . 4,540.
  Car and photo equipment cost $2,500 . . . . . . 2,040.
  Spent in Birmingham, $1,000 . . . . 1,040.

Received from Raoul in Mexico, $2,000 . . . . . 3,040.
Spent in Mexico, $700 . . . . 2,340.
Received from Raoul in New Orleans, $500 . . . . 2,840.
Spent in California, $1,900 . . . . 940.
Left California with $940.
Received from Raoul in Birmingham, to buy
    gun, $700 . . . . 1,640.
Spent for gun, $500 . . . . 1,140.
Arrived in Canada with $1,140.

What money I spent travelling I counted as money I spent in the city I had just left, or was going to.

CHAPTER XXII

It was the first week of August 1968.

Executive Assistant Attorney General Robert K. Dwyer, the man who would try James Earl Ray in the courtroom, was sitting in his office when FBI Agent Robert Jensen walked in, carrying a heavy briefcase, a look of expectancy on his face. He unlocked the bag and brought out three five-inch loose-leaf volumes. "Here's the first of them," he said. "I miss my guess if you don't find them interesting reading."

Dwyer and his colleague, Jim Beasley, the Assistant Attorney General who would put together the proof against Ray, had been waiting for these—the reports of the FBI investigation into Ray and the assassination of Dr. King, augmented by those of the Royal Canadian Mounted Police, Scotland Yard, the Mexican and Portuguese police, and half a dozen other intelligence agencies of Europe. The moment the hunt for King's killer went beyond the borders of Tennessee, the chase had been in the FBI's hands. Inspector Zachary and his men had exhausted every investigative possibility within his province. Now they could only wait for what had been uncovered outside Tennessee.

Dwyer, accepting the volumes from Jensen, looked at him quizzically. "I want to ask you a simple question, Mr. Jensen. Was this guy Ray by himself?"

Jensen said, "Yes."

Dwyer nodded. "O.K. Now, you ask me a question, Mr. Jensen, will you? Ask me if I believe that."

Jensen smiled. "All right," he said. "Do you believe it?"

Dwyer said slowly, "No, sir. I do not. And"—he pointed out the window—"and nobody walking down that street out there believes it. I just don't believe and I just can't comprehend, from what little I know about this and from what I've read, that this fellow did it alone."

Jensen shook his head. "You start reading this," he said, "and the rest that will come to you, and then I'll drop in and ask *you* a question. All right?"

Moments later Dwyer walked into Beasley's office, which adjoined his, and told him what had happened. "Jim, you believe Ray was alone?" Beasley shook his head. No, emphatically, he did not.

"We are going to move slowly, Jim," said Dwyer. "And very carefully."

Both men had their reservations. Was the Government—the Justice Department—giving them a package deal, setting them up to become whipping boys for this conspiracy? They did not know what might lie behind this. It could go all the way up, very high, and the Administration might be trying to protect itself. Dwyer thought, *We are not going to be used down here—we're proud of our reputation.* He thought, *Maybe they're trying to unload something on us, some nondescript guy they're putting up as the lone killer, and we're going to punish him in court and the conspirators or whoever's behind this thing will go unpunished.*

Dwyer, a fiery prosecutor, who was known for his sharp cross-examination, was very much on guard. Canale would direct the prosecution, but he had told Dwyer that Dwyer would fight the case in court: Canale himself had not tried a murder case in seven years. Dwyer thought, *We're not going to be patsys for anybody. First inkling I get that they're using me, that it's going to reflect on me later, I'm getting out of this thing.* So, too, Beasley felt, and so the two men approached their task.

Before they were finished, they were to make their own investigation, traveling thousands of miles through the United States and five other countries, questioning the most important witnesses produced by the FBI and other police intelligence to determine if these were witnesses for whom they could vouch in a Memphis court, witnesses who had not been coached, who were not themselves part of the conspiracy. They would follow James Earl Ray's trail from his escape to his arrest in London, his travels and activities and associations from April 23, 1967, to June 8, 1968. They would be accompanied on this trip by John Carlisle, chief investigator of their office. Then, and only then, would they know the kind of case they had and how to handle it.

They had discussed this thoroughly with Canale. Canale had obtained from Washington a pledge that the Justice Department would keep hands off the prosecution in Memphis. Canale, Dwyer, and Beasley would be in complete charge of the case, with Washington available for consultation and guidance on any particularly abstruse questions of law.

The three men made up an almost familial team, one that had worked together through the years with the least possible friction. Canale was fifty, Dwyer forty-four, Beasley, forty-two; all three had graduated from the same law school, the Memphis State University School of Law, as had Judge Battle, who would preside. Dwyer had a quick temper and a sharp wit; Beasley, his skepticism honed by years as an insurance claims adjuster before entering the Attorney General's office, was pipe-smoking, methodical, and a superb handler of detail. As the material came in—reports from London, Acapulco, Lisbon, from Montreal, St. Louis, Los Angeles, from Missouri State Penitentiary, Leavenworth, Pontiac Prison, a total in the end of more than a million and a half words—Dwyer would read it from the point of view of the prosecutor, Beasley, from the point of view of the man who had to put it together as evidence in a court of law. Canale, supervising the entire operation, would read every word as well, and they would meet regularly to compare notes and so slowly and carefully reach their conclusion. At their side Carlisle, the top detective of the Attorney General's office, would study and analyze every fact with them, index all the exhibits, and, unencumbered by legal technicalities, keep a cold, objective eye on the maze of reports.

Beasley had set up a procedure to handle this, the most exhaustive, detailed investigation ever made into a criminal and the crime he was alleged to have carried out. On the third floor, in a room with complete electronic security, were filing cabinets, each locked with two keys, one in Beasley's possession, the other in Carlisle's. A method had to be set up to handle parallel investigations, for the FBI agents worked in pairs, not communicating with each other, so that a man in Acapulco or St. Louis might have been questioned by a dozen pairs of agents at different times. All these reports had to be collated and compared, particularly since the Bureau never evaluated its material, but simply recorded it.

As the pages came in Beasley numbered them chronologically. The first time the name of anyone who had ever known or dealt with Ray, from childhood to his capture, appeared, it was copied onto a three-by-five card, and each time it popped up again, the page number on which it appeared was jotted down next to it on the card. One name might have a dozen page references next to it. Thus, at any point, Beasley could look up everything relating, say, to Jerry Ray, who so far had been interviewed at least ten times over a five-month period by agents working in pairs (so there was always a witness) who saw him in Chicago, in Memphis, in St. Louis. Not only this but Jerry's account of a meeting with his brother John, as told to one pair of FBI agents, could be compared with John's account of the same meeting, told to another pair. The fact that different men interviewed the various subjects, unaware of what they had replied at other interviews, was helpful: no attempt was made to catch anyone in a lie, nothing anyone said was challenged, and the stories were permitted to be told in full truth—or fancy.

Beasley looked particularly for patterns of association. Did this ex-con stay at a motel that was later visited by Ray? Was either John or Jerry Ray in the same town as King at the same time? Was Ray thrown together with any person more than once?

Conspiracy—always the search for conspiracy.

They would have to systematize their search, Beasley decided. They would divide Ray's life into four parts. First, from birth, March 10, 1928, to his last imprisonment, March 1960, in Missouri State Penitentiary, from where he escaped April 23, 1967. That would cover James Earl Ray's first thirty-nine years. Perhaps from a study of his childhood, his school years, his teen-age experiences, what his schoolmates and teachers knew of him, his first crime, and on through the petty antisocial acts which made up those first thirty-nine years, one could come to some conclusion as to the kind of human being he was.

Second, a camera put on him in prison. How did he spend those years behind bars, fully one-third of his life? What could his fellow prisoners, and parole officers and psychiatrists and all the other experts assigned by society to study such a man—what had they learned about him? If he alone killed King, could the motive, or an inkling of it, be found here?

Third, put the camera on the man from the moment of his escape on April 23, 1967, to the murder of Dr. King on April 4, 1968. In those eleven months and two weeks, how did Ray live, how did he support himself, what did he do, day by day? At some point in this period Ray either decided he would kill Dr. King or he was hired to do so. Surely an examination of this time should be revealing. Nothing would be too unimportant to examine.

Fourth, Ray's activities from 6:01 P.M. April 4—when King was shot—to his capture in London at 11:15 A.M. Saturday, June 8, 1968, two months and four days later. If he had been hired, a study of this period would show whether he had been contacted by his superiors.

If he was on his own, this too would be deduced from what he did and how he did it. A hired killer would have money—the means, the necessary help, to get out of the country to safety. Those who were skilled enough to conceive the assassination, to hire Ray, to enable him to travel about the continent, to escape to Canada after the murder, to assume the identity of three living men with no one the wiser, and even to travel on the passport of one of them, to fly to London, then to Lisbon, then back to London—would be skilled enough to contact him, sooner or later. Or he would contact them. And if it became clear that everything he did he could have done alone, and indeed, did do alone—by what he wanted to do, and did, and by what he wanted to do, and could not—both by his freedom and his limitations—one should be able to reach some judgment on the question of conspiracy.

For if there was one thing certain, it was this: they would not be likely to get the truth from James Earl Ray.

They set to work, each in his locked room, reading.

CHAPTER XXIII

Early on a Sunday morning in late August, a strange drama took place in a remote field somewhere in Mississippi a few miles from the Tennessee border. Three large goats were tethered to three trees about ten feet apart. Some two hundred feet away, a heavy-set man with a shock of unruly black hair and a noticeable tic pulsing in his right cheek, repeatedly threw a rifle to his shoulder, peered down the barrel through a telescopic sight, and fired. He aimed carefully each time, but it appeared he was not shooting to kill, for after every shot the goats were obviously still alive. The terrified animals, wounded and bloody, leaped about hysterically, the bleating with its counterpart of echoing rifle fire was horrifying, but the man continued his work without pause.

He was Renfro T. Hays, private investigator, and he was involved in a cruel experiment which he hoped would help Arthur Hanes acquit James Earl Ray of the charge that he had fired the bullet that killed Dr. King. Hays was one of the best-known figures in the back streets of Memphis, familiar with criminal types, at home among winos, drunks, and drug addicts, con-men and ex-cons, and he had been hired by Art Hanes, Sr., to interview those in the neighborhood of Mrs. Brewer's rooming house, and to learn everything he could that might help the defense. Renfro, at forty-one, not only suffered from a tic but also had the habit, when he was nervous, of repeatedly opening and closing his mouth, as if gasping for air. It had proved disconcerting, particularly when he was on the witness stand testifying as to what he had learned about attempted extortion, insurance company bamboozling, or life among the Memphis underworld. No one, however, underestimated Hays; he might appear to be on the edge of asphyxiation, but his words were good words and often made surprising sense.

Renfro had already drawn up several reports casting doubt on certain of the state's key witnesses. He had learned, for example, not only that Charles Stephens, the state's chief witness, was known as "Bay Rum Charlie" in wino hangouts, but that a cabdriver named McGraw reportedly saw Stephens, half an hour before the assassination, "too drunk to walk." What could be more significant than to prove that at the time the state's principal witness swore he saw Ray dashing down the corridor, he, Stephens, was staggeringly drunk? But at the moment Renfro's experiment with the goats was the most important.

In boning up on the Warren Report on President Kennedy's assassination (which Renfro was convinced stemmed from conspiracy in high places), he had come upon the interesting fact that in the consistency of flesh and bone goats most closely approximated man. In other words, a bullet caused similar damage in a human body and in a goat's body.

Renfro had decided the best way to prove that the fatal bullet did not come from the rifle found in Canipe's doorway was to try to approximate the same type of wound, at the same distance, using the same type of rifle and ammunition. He had bought an identical Remington 30.06 and fired it about a dozen times so its condition would be comparable to the alleged murder weapon. He had bought a box of .30-caliber Peters "soft-point" bullets, identical with that used by the assassin. Then he bought three goats, at five dollars each, and tethered them to the trees on the farm of a friend.

Dr. King had been struck in the jawbone. Renfro tried to create the identical wound. But at no time did he get a hole as big as a fist. What he found, after putting each animal out of its misery, was an elongated wound. Equally important: none of the bullets had been retained by the animal's body. They had gone through flesh and bone completely: those he fired through skull and shoulder emerged out the flank. None had been flattened and mutilated as had been the bullet taken from Dr. King's body by Dr. Francisco. The bullets went through almost unscathed. Not even the biggest goat could stop a 30.06 at two hundred feet.

When he finished his grisly experiment, Renfro had a butcher cut out sections of the goats' bodies containing the wounds and store them in his freezer. With the unscathed bullets they would wait as evidence for Hanes to use when the time came.

Word had slipped out that the FBI would have difficulty matching the bullet taken from King's body to the rifle. The fine rifling impressions by which experts could match it to the bore of the rifle had been blurred too much. The state could not absolutely say that that bullet had come from that rifle.

Whether working on ballistics or other evidence, Renfro's job was to find every possible doubt, so that Hanes could exploit it. Hanes was an expert in this type of defense: clouding the facts. "I don't have to prove anything," Renfro told a friend. "I simply have to make it difficult for the state to prove beyond a reasonable doubt what it sets out to prove."

For example, there was the widely reprinted photograph taken by Joseph Louw, the South African photographer, on the motel balcony seconds after King fell. It had first appeared in *Life* magazine, showing King's lieutenants, lined up at the balcony railing, all pointing upward and to the right in answer to the question, Where did the shot come from? But one man's arm was not pointing up: that of Ben Branch, the bandleader. He had run up to the balcony a moment after King was shot. Branch, standing farthest from the camera in the photo, also had his arm out, but he was pointing down. That is, perhaps he wasn't pointing down; if you looked closely, it might be said that his right hand was down. Perhaps a moment before he had been pointing up, and at the moment the shutter clicked his arm was coming down. A moot point. But it could raise doubt, Renfro argued: it could mean that he was pointing to the bushes in the yard below the window, the bushes from which Solomon Jones, Jr., King's chauffeur, said he saw a man "with something white over his face" running a moment after the shot, the same bushes from which Harold "Cornbread" Carter had said a man fled after firing a rifle in the direction of the Lorraine.

The defense needed only two or three conflicting stories. No juror would send a man to the electric chair unless he was absolutely certain of every statement made by the prosecution. The state had to prove its charges "beyond a reasonable doubt and to a moral certainty." Surely, no Southern juror, dealing with a white man accused of shooting a troublemaking black man, could conscientiously convict him if he had the slightest doubt.

Renfro had other points to prove. He had heard that Ray, unknowingly playing the dupe, had gone into the Aeromarine Supply store in Birmingham a day before the 30.06 had been purchased. He had asked to see rifles which he was to buy for Raoul's gunrunning customers. The salesman had pointed out a 30.06 on the rack. Ray had taken it, held it for a moment to judge its heft, then replaced it on the rack and left, without buying. The next day a white man walked into the shop, gave his name as Harvey Lowmyer, and bought the very rifle Ray had handled, knowing that it bore Ray's fingerprints. *That was the rifle used in the murder and dropped at Canipe's, and that was how Ray was caught in the conspiracy.* That was how the impossible was made possible: how James Earl Ray's fingerprints could be found on a murder rifle and Ray still not be the man who fired the shot that killed King.

Take the state's witnesses—three hundred or more. In Tennessee the defense was always permitted to know the names of the prosecution witnesses and to interview them. All to the good. But Renfro had found witnesses not on the state's list, men and women who were not on it for good reason—because they would destroy the state's case! For example, one of the hospital attendants who rode with Dr. King to the hospital was reported to have told a friend that he saw three to five wounds—not only the huge one in the right jaw, big enough to put your fist in, but five or six small wounds, each the size of a dime, below it, in the neck. But when King had been treated at the hospital, a tracheotomy had been performed, so all trace of the small wounds was gone. If there had been such small wounds, King might not have been killed by the bullet allegedly coming from the bathroom window. Could two gunmen have shot him simultaneously? This had come up in President Kennedy's assassination: was the wound in his throat an exit or an entrance wound? Had Kennedy been shot from the front, too? No one could be certain because the original autopsy notes had been destroyed—highly suspicious, indeed! In King's case, there was no question whether he had been shot from front or back; the question was, where had the bullet come from? And could there have been *two* gunmen?

A second witness, not on the state's list, was a man who had been in Jim's Grill and had seen the white Mustang parked out in front. He was ready to testify that it had a loaded antenna—a Citizens' Band antenna. Could not this car have broadcast the false chase? And what about the second white Mustang some had seen: one parked in front of Jim's Grill, the other parked sixty or seventy feet behind it? And was it true, too, as Renfro had heard, that several white Mustangs had been stolen in Memphis just before the killing?

There was still a third witness, a thirty-five-year-old married woman, who would pose a problem so far as testifying, because she had been two-timing her husband, dating a fireman from Fire Station No. 2, across the street from the Lorraine. She had revealed to a confidant that her boyfriend told her that just after the shooting, an eleven-year-old colored boy ran to the fire station saying he saw a white man shooting at someone at the motel—he fired from behind the bushes above the retaining wall behind the fire station. The firemen had sat the boy on a stool in the firehouse, listened to him . . . And no one had seen him after that. The boy had simply vanished.

As for Charlie Stephens himself, Bay Rum Charlie, he was now in protective custody in Shelby County Jail, in a cell just above James Earl Ray's—a kind of poetic justice, Renfro thought. Charlie was there against his will, held in ten-thousand-dollar bond by Judge Battle, because, the state explained, he might not be on hand when the trial started. Renfro interpreted it to mean they were afraid he'd be killed by the conspirators. But Charlie had hired two lawyers to get him out. They had signed a contract with him to share the reward of one hundred thousand dollars which he expected, because it would be his testimony that would convict Ray. Renfro hoped to find the cabdriver; he was ready to believe Charlie was drunk at the time. He had checked on Charlie. The man received a one-hundred-dollar-a-month pension for his World War II injuries. The check came the first of the month and Charlie promptly cashed it and began drinking, so that he was usually drunk the first six or seven days of the month. King had been killed April 4. It all added up.

But Renfro's most important witness, to date, from whom he had obtained a sworn affidavit which was on its way to Art Hanes in Birmingham, was "Cornbread" Carter. His affidavit read:

"Statement of Harold Carter, male, white, age 66, taken on August 25, 1968, in Memphis, Shelby County, Tennessee: My name is Harold Carter. I live at 422½ S. Main St., Memphis. I have not worked for the last three years because of a stroke. On the afternoon of April 4, 1968, I was sitting out on the vacant lot behind the rooming house with Dude Wheeler and another man who works on the river. We were sitting there on some cardboard next to some bushes, watching the people over at the Lorraine Motel as there was a lot going on over there.

"Just before six o'clock Dude and the other fellow left, but Dude was supposed to come back. Then two Male Coloreds standing on the ground at the Lorraine Motel starting calling up asking for someone; to get Dr. King to the door. A man, I guess he was Dr. King, came out of the door and came to the rail and started talking to these men on the ground.

"At the same time I heard someone walking behind me from the other side of the bushes. I thought it was Dude Wheeler coming back and I didn't even look around. Then, there was a loud shot from the bushes right beside me. I looked around and saw this man running away, north. He was about my size and he must have been young because he moved fast. He had on dark clothes with a high-necked white sweater. He had a rifle or shotgun in his hand. When he got to the northwest corner of the lot, he took the stock off his gun and threw it in some bushes and put the barrel under his jacket. Then, he stepped down onto the sidewalk.

"Everyone was running to the motel then and he just walked on away from there. I got up and walked back up to the street and up to my room. Later that night the police came and took us all down to the station. I told a detective what I saw and he called me a damned liar. When they talked to me again I told them I didn't know anything. I never got around to telling them where the gun stock was.

"I have nothing to hide about this. I never saw that man before or since, that I know of. If the police had treated me like a human being I would have told them everything I know.

"I have read this statement of one and two thirds pages and it is true to the best of my knowledge. Signed, Harold Carter."

Renfro was contemplating obtaining an even more important affidavit—this from Grace Stephens, Charlie's common-law wife. He had heard that she changed her first story, about seeing nothing from her bed. Now she said that immediately after the shot she had seen—because the door of their apartment was partly ajar—a man run past their door. Charlie had not seen this because he was in the kitchen, fixing the radio. But the man she saw looked nothing like James Earl Ray. He was older, in his fifties, with iron-gray hair, stocky, wearing a plaid sport shirt under a military jacket, and he was carrying something long and wrapped in his right hand. She had not told this when first questioned, because she wanted no trouble.

This change in her story had upset the state tremendously, because only a few days before, on July 31, Grace had been suddenly taken away and committed to the Western State Hospital as "mentally ill." Charlie was in protective custody, and Grace was in a mental ward. Nobody was going to get away with that, Renfro pledged himself. He was convinced that Grace was no more mentally ill than he was, and before he was finished he would get into that hospital and obtain a sworn affidavit from Grace.

Renfro had his own theories as to the conspiracy. Ray, of course, had not done it. Renfro saw King's killing as an inside job, ordered by some of King's own associates in a struggle for power in the black establishment identified with the Democratic Administration. When the Administration learned this, it was in shock, for if it became known, they would lose the black vote, which would mean disaster in the Presidential election. "So they better find some other culprit,"

Renfro explained to a friend. "They prayed, 'God find us a white man real quick and make it him and him alone. When you get him, build a wall around him, so nobody reaches him, but let enough of a trail show so you can get after him.'"

That night Renfro wrote a long, detailed memo to Hanes in Birmingham, spelling out his progress to date.

What Renfro had to report was good news to Hanes. The goat experiment, if it stood up, was dramatic and effective; and if the affidavits also stood up, he would have no great problem to establish reasonable doubt. Hanes himself was in a state of high excitement. Twenty-four hours earlier, he and Mrs. Hanes had been entertaining friends at dinner when Hanes was called to the phone. A man named Victor Bartlett* was calling from Nashville. He spoke rapidly, with a stutter; but there was no doubt of what he was saying, "Mr. Hanes, I can put your man Ray on the street a free man. He's innocent."

Hanes said cautiously, "How do you know that?"

"Mr. Hanes," said the other, "I was an eyewitness to this thing. I saw the shooting." And before Hanes could recover, he went on, "I mean—I mean—I saw the shooting. He didn't do it. I saw the man who did."

"Why haven't you brought this forth until now?" Hanes demanded, wanting to believe, yet sure he had a psycho on the line. There was silence for a moment. "I was afraid," Bartlett said.

Hanes questioned him a few minutes longer. Then he took a gamble. Nashville is an hour and a half by air from Birmingham. Would Mr. Bartlett fly to Birmingham to see him first thing tomorrow morning if Hanes wired him the money for a round-trip ticket? Bartlett said yes and gave Hanes his address. Hanes would see him 10 A.M. tomorrow morning. He hung up.

Hanes went back to their guests, thinking, *If he's not a nut—Hell's bells, this guy was with him!* After they left, he drove downtown to the Western Union station and wired Bartlett $150.

Next morning at 7:30 A.M. Bartlett called from the airport. Hanes drove there, to find a neatly dressed man, about forty, with clear blue eyes, his dark hair neatly parted, pacing back and forth. On the half-hour drive to Hanes's office, Bartlett appeared anything but a nut, and, sitting in Hanes's office, he told his story, quite self-possessed save for his stutter which intensified when he became excited.

* Not his true name.

He gave Hanes all the data about himself so he could check up on him. He was a shoe salesman, employed in a large department store. He was divorced; he had a son in the custody of his ex-wife; he himself lived with his mother, Mrs. Helen Bartlett, at such an address, with such a telephone number.

He had been in Memphis in early April for four or five days, drinking and partying. Drink was a weakness with him, he admitted. Wednesday morning, April 3, having had only a few hours' sleep and being low in money and feeling miserable, he went to the Greyhound Bus Station to take a bus back to Nashville. Then he thought, *Well, if I move to a cheaper place, I can stay another night or two.*

He had been staying at the Peabody Hotel, *the* hotel of Memphis. He asked a cabdriver to take him to a cheap rooming house. The man drove him to 422½ South Main Street. It was about 10 A.M. Bartlett met the landlady coming down the stairs. He told her he wanted an inexpensive room. She led the way back up to a landing on the second floor, then down a corridor which seemed to lead to another building, and gave him a room on the far side.

How much was it, Hanes asked sharply.

Three dollars, said Bartlett. Hanes thought, *This checks out.* When he had visited the rooming house, he had talked with the landlady there about the rent. Ray had been charged by the week—$8.50. How much would it be by the day? Three dollars, Hanes had been told. This figure had never appeared in the newspapers.

"I'd been drinking all night, I just lay across the bed and fell asleep," Bartlett was saying. "When I came to, it must have been around 3:30 in the afternoon. I went to the bathroom at the end of the hall and on the way I met a guy in the hall. He wanted to borrow a dollar.

"I said, 'I don't have it.' I had it, but I couldn't spare it. When I got out of the bathroom, I met the guy again. He said, 'Well can you gimme a cigarette?' I gave him a cigarette and we talked a bit and he invited me into his room to have a beer with him."

He described the man. Blond, chunky, long sideburns, the ends cut so they pointed forward, about forty-eight, about five feet eight, weighing 175–80 pounds, and wearing a military jacket, white shirt, blue jeans and black square-toed Navy shoes.

Hanes stiffened involuntarily. This had to be the same man Grace Stephens said she had seen. Renfro was even now trying to obtain an affidavit from her. As Renfro understood it, she had been frightened and upset when she was first questioned—after all, she had just been brought back from the hospital after surgery—she wanted no trouble, and so she had said that the door was closed and she had seen nothing.

Hanes sat back and let Bartlett continue.

"This guy had two cans of beer—Pabst Blue Ribbon—on the table in front of him," he went on. The man drank a beer, and he drank a beer, and they sat around, talking. Bartlett looked idly about the room at one point and saw a rifle leaning against the wall in one corner, near the fireplace. He thought nothing of it: everyone hunted in Tennessee. They had been sitting there, "shooting the breeze" for he didn't know how long, when suddenly "this guy says, 'I'm going to kill that damn Martin Luther King.'" Bartlett was shocked: vaguely he remembered reading somewhere that King was in town, and then he thought, *Well, hell, probably a lot of other guys would like to do that too.*

"We finished the beers and I went downstairs—there's a grill on the ground floor—and I bought a six-pack of Pabst for $1.65 and brought it back up. We talked some more, I drank, he drank, I'd had three, he two, we were sitting on the bed and every little while he'd get up, walk to the window, and look out. All of a sudden, he was looking out the window, he jumped back, grabbed the rifle in the corner. 'There's the son-of-a-bitch now!' He just threw up that rifle and he fired that shot. He was two or three feet from me, at most. I jumped up and stuck my head out the window and it looked like King and he was falling."

What did he do then?

Bartlett began to stutter. "The guy didn't say good-by, kiss my tail, or glad to meet you—he just turned and ran out of the room with the gun. I thought, *Man, I'm scared.* I just stayed there maybe five or ten minutes, then I went down the stairs and mingled with the crowd down there and walked to the bus station and left on a Nashville bus a little after midnight." He stopped.

Hanes sat back and studied the man. *Mingled with the crowd down there?* There had been no reports of people gathered in front of 422½ South Main Street immediately after the shooting. Only the police had been swarming on the scene a minute after the shot, checking on everyone, ordering Canipe and his two customers back into Canipe's shop, ordering the patrons in Jim's Grill to stay in the restaurant, even locking the door on them. . . .Wouldn't the police have seen Bartlett? Unless the scene in front of 422½ South Main was not as the police reported it, or unless the police, in some way involved in the plot, wanted deliberately *not* to see Bartlett, as perhaps they might have deliberately wanted *not* to see the man in the military jacket dashing out a moment before. . . .

Hanes had Bartlett go carefully over his story again. He did not change it. Would he draw a sketch of the room, where he sat, where the man sat, the bathroom's position, what was in the man's room? Also the stairs, the landing, everything he could remember? Bartlett did so. It was a good representation. Bartlett certainly had been in that rooming house at one time or another. The question was, Had it been at 6:01 P.M., April 4?

Hanes called in Mary Sue and dictated Bartlett's account, as he had told it, had him read and sign it, as well as sign a statement that he had given this information voluntarily, without threats or offers of reward.

Was he prepared to come to Memphis and testify when and if needed? Yes, Bartlett said. It was probably dangerous, but he could not let an innocent man go to the chair. He had hesitated and hesitated and finally decided to come out with it. "I had to take a good stiff drink before I could call you," he admitted.

Hanes drove him to the airport and saw him board the Nashville plane. Bartlett's story differed from Ray's. The man in the military jacket didn't fit Ray's description of Raoul. But why assume that Ray was telling him the full truth? He might be covering up for reasons he could not explain now. Hanes thought, He would have to check out Bartlett, check him out well. But *if*—just *if*—this stood up . . .

Others were laboring almost as energetically to find the conspiracy. In addition to reporters and columnists making their own investigations, in Washington a Committee to Investigate Assassinations was being formed, headed by Bernard Fensterwald, Jr., about to resign as chief counsel to the Senate Subcommittee on Administrative Practice and Procedure. Fensterwald, forty-seven, a native of Nashville, was a graduate magna cum laude of Harvard, a graduate of the Harvard Law School, and had done postgraduate research at Cambridge University. He had dedicated himself "to helping unravel some of the mysteries of the several political assassinations" and was bringing together in his committee, a non-profit organization, some well-known figures—some of whom had written books denouncing the Warren Report on the President Kennedy assassination as a shameful fraud upon the public—and all of whom were concerned that the three murders—the two Kennedys and Dr. King—might be related.* They believed there had been a conspiracy in Dallas; that the full story of the Robert Kennedy assassination was yet to be known; and that James Earl Ray was either a hired gunman or a patsy and so either the tool or dupe of a conspiracy.

Several matters were to trouble Fensterwald with respect to the King assassination, one, particularly, when the name of Raoul, Ray's mysterious colleague, appeared. Fensterwald had copies of two photographs. One was a snapshot taken in Dallas on November 22, 1963, half an hour after President Kennedy's murder, showing two men crossing Dealey Plaza with an FBI agent. They had been arrested and later released. One of the two was a slender, curly-haired man with a long nose, identified as a French-Canadian, wearing a suit of French cut. The second photograph was of a man who had been identified to Fensterwald as "Skinny Ralph," one of several American soldiers of fortune "trained for invasions and/or assassinations in the Florida Keys." Fensterwald thought it possible that Skinny Ralph was also one of the two men in the snapshot—but, more important, that he could be, in reality, the elusive Raoul. If Ray were shown these photographs, would he identify Raoul, the man who had directed and duped him? Would he dare to do so? Would he be believed?

Another question perturbed Fensterwald. How many men had been arrested at London Airport on June 8, 1968? One, or two? The first news agency report had stated that Scotland Yard had seized Ray, as Ramon George Sneyd, at 6:10 A.M., en route from Lisbon; the second, that Ramon George Sneyd had been arrested at 11:15 A.M.—a man who reportedly had been hiding for weeks in London. Could there be two James Earl Rays?† If so, which one had been

---

* Those who became members of the board of directors included District Attorney Garrison of New Orleans, William Turner, a former FBI agent now with *Ramparts* magazine, Richard Sprague, a computer expert of New York, W. Lloyd Tupling, Washington representative of the Sierra Club, and John Henry Faulk, of Austin, Texas, a TV personality and writer. Among those who joined later were Fred Cook, Paris Flammond, Professor Richard Popkin and Penn Jones, writer-investigators. Ultimately the committee took office space in Washington, built up a comprehensive file of materials dealing with political assassinations and those writing and investigating in the field, and issued a newsletter.

† Fensterwald was not the only one to pose this question. There was a precedent. In World War II, British Intelligence assigned a double of General Bernard Montgomery to travel about, publicizing his activities, so as to draw attention away from the movements of the real General Montgomery. Why not, then, two

returned to the United States and now occupied Cell Block A in Shelby County Jail? Although it seemed highly speculative, it could be possible, Fensterwald thought, that the James Earl Ray in Memphis was not the James Earl Ray who escaped from Missouri State Penitentiary. The only man who *knew* Ray, and who also had seen the prisoner in Memphis, was his brother, Jerry. Now, Jerry had visited Ray the day before he escaped from the Missouri prison. Prison records had John Ray's name down, but both brothers used the same permit and Jerry was the one who visited him the most often, who was the closest member of the family to him. Jerry Ray might have excellent reasons for *not* revealing that the man in Memphis was not his brother. Certainly, the picture filtering out from Cell Block A was of an intelligent, sardonic man, alert, well read, competent, a type that hardly squared with what one read about Ray, the dropout, the inept bungler, the laughingstock criminal. And the two Sneyd passports—Fensterwald strongly doubted that story. Would the Canadian Embassy in Lisbon give a man a new passport and not pick up the old one? Sneyd, whoever he was, was traveling on *two* passports. . . . Even more, would a man moving through various countries change his passport because one letter was wrong?

Fensterwald wanted all this looked into. Someone who was not part of the Memphis establishment must obtain the photograph and fingerprints of the man in Cell Block A. The only photograph anyone had seen of him from the day he was picked up in London was the official one that Sheriff Morris issued after he had his prisoner in Memphis, and that had been unsatisfactory—the man was looking down, away from the camera. He might be the real Ray, he might not. If he was really Ray, he should be shown the Dealey Plaza photographs. He might say nothing, but his reaction might say a great deal.

Still another matter perplexed Fensterwald. If it was the genuine Ray who had been picked up in London, why was he carrying with him books on hypnotism? One was *Self-Hypnotism: the Technique and Its Use in Daily Living,* by Leslie M. LeCron; he also had *How to Cash In on Your Hidden Memory Power,* by William D. Hersey; and *Psycho-Cybernetics,* by Dr. Maxwell Maltz. These were found in his suitcase when it was retrieved from the Brussels-bound plane, according to the newspapers. What role, Fensterwald wondered, might

James Earl Rays? There were some who maintained that there were two Lee Harvey Oswalds and that the man who was shot and killed by Jack Ruby was not actually President Kennedy's assassin.

hypnotic conditioning have played in Ray's activities? A similar question had been raised, too, in the Sirhan Sirhan case. Could self-hypnosis be involved? Or posthypnotic suggestion?

Why *was* Ray carrying the books with him? From Los Angeles to New Orleans, to Atlanta, to Birmingham, to Memphis, to Toronto, to London, to Lisbon, back to London, even taking them on to Brussels. . . . Ray was not the type of man who, having once read a book, would carry it with him across the United States and even overseas.

One answer might be that they contained a code. *How to Cash In on Your Hidden Memory Power* described a code for remembering numbers by converting them into words. If Ray had taught himself such a mnemonic code, certain passages in one or the other books might be translatable into numbers which related to names, addresses, contacts, money sources—passages that would mean nothing to anyone else but carried a message for those he expected to meet in Brussels, or beyond Brussels. . . .

In the search for conspiracy, no door was too important to push open, no road too obscure or twisting, to follow. These matters and many others were to be the subject of investigation by Fensterwald and his colleagues in the days to come.

CHAPTER XXIV

Lone murderer of Dr. Martin Luther King, Jr., or dupe in the conspiracy to kill him, or member of the conspiracy to kill him, James Earl Ray rested on his cot in Block A of Shelby County Jail.

He lay on his back, asleep—perhaps not asleep. One never knew, for he could remain in this fashion for long periods of time, his eyes closed but not sleeping, lost in his own world of silence. Noise would not disturb him. The bright lights forever beating down on him did not disturb him. Arthur Hanes had complained about the lights, he had told Judge Battle that they constituted cruel and unusual punishment, and Judge Battle had ordered Sheriff Morris to provide Ray with an eye mask; but Ray had disdained it; he knew how to cope with all this. He had succeeded in filling the space, the place, the circumscribed milieu, smoothly and apparently without stress. So he had been able to make time pass through his long years behind bars. He slept, or rested, on top of the neatly made bed with its gray blanket—the bed he made himself each morning, tucking in the corners as they should be—his slippers on, his hair neatly combed, his long lanky body absolutely motionless.

His sealed and air-conditioned world was watched and controlled and recorded as no man's had ever been before, so that everything that came to him—sight, sound, physical objects—was known, measured, appraised.

Before the two guards who were always in the block with him could enter it, they were stripped nude and searched, and in the presence of the supervisor donned special denim coveralls. When they emerged after their eight-hour term of duty, they were stripped again, searched, and resumed their original clothing. Then Ray was stripped, examined, placed into a security area while the entire block was scrubbed and hosed down.

The fourteen guards so rigorously selected by Morris had specific duties. A logbook was zealously kept and logged every half hour, day and night; everything had its time and place. Their duties were to see that Ray did not harm himself, willfully or accidentally; that he did not contrive a noose, or swallow a spoon, or stab himself with a fork.

Every utensil given him was checked out and checked in, as well as the time it was taken and returned. When he asked for an aspirin, a cold tablet, a vitamin pill, it was checked out, the time given entered into the logbook, and he had to swallow it as a guard watched, then opened his mouth like a child so the guard could ascertain that he had, indeed, swallowed it and hadn't tucked it away between teeth and lip. He might hide otherwise harmless pills until he had enough to swallow at one time to cause a stomach upset and so engineer a trip to the hospital. Accomplices might then, en route to the hospital or in the hospital itself, help him escape—or kill him.

No letter sent Ray by his few approved correspondents was given him: only Xerox copies. The original might have on it a message in invisible writing. Or it might even have been soaked in poison: and Ray might deliberately or unknowingly put it in his mouth, or chew on it. When he wrote—and he spent long hours with a pencil, printing word after word of his story, or writing his jailhouse-lawyer briefs to Hanes—pencil and paper were supplied by his jailers. They bought these in different stationery shops, ostensibly for themselves; and since no one knew the identity of his guards, a secret guarded upon pain of dismissal by Sheriff Morris, there was no risk. When a medicine was prescribed by Dr. DeMere, Captain Billy Smith, the chief jailer, had it filled out in his own name at a different pharmacy each time to avoid the chance that someone might learn that it was for Ray and spike it with poison.

Ray's food, cooked in the prison kitchen, came up to him in a specially designed padlocked stainless steel box which held three trays of identical food: two for his guards, one for him, and he had first choice. No one knew which he would choose. If the idea was to poison him, the poisoner had to be prepared to kill two others with him.

The sheriff's most elaborate precaution was known as Condition Red. At Condition Red, each time the door to Cell Block A opened, a red light flashed in Morris's office and every other door in Shelby County Jail was locked shut, every prisoner and turnkey literally frozen in his tracks. In short, if there was any movement into or out of Ray's special world, there was no movement elsewhere in the jail. No chance for any diversionary trick, no emergency, no fire alarm— nothing could ever distract his guards or break his security.

The supervisor on duty outside Cell Block A, seated before the monitor on which he watched Ray, kept the log through the day and night. He reported what Ray ate and how much, and what he left untouched; what time he rose, when he napped, what time he showered, what exercise he took, what books, newspapers, and magazines he read, the content of the letters he received, of the letters he wrote, the radio and TV programs he tuned in (by means of remote control he could operate a TV set outside the bars). . . . The result was that Sheriff Morris knew everything that went on in the world of James Earl Ray. He knew what influences were playing on him from the outside and how Ray reacted to them by what he did, said, wrote, by how he slept or did not sleep.

And Ray took all this in his stride. It did not disturb him.

One of his guards was Sheriff's Deputy William DuFour, who was the first of the TAC force to reach Dr. King as he lay dying on the balcony of the Lorraine. He had found Dr. Abernathy kneeling by Dr. King, and had helped carry the fatally wounded man down to the ambulance. It was a strange coincidence that he should now find himself one of those guarding the accused assassin of Dr. King.

DuFour and his fellow guards would play hearts and gin rummy and checkers with Ray; he would watch TV with him, joke and laugh with him. He never knew quite what to make of the man. Now and then the scene he would never forget would come back to DuFour —King lying on the concrete balcony, bleeding from the enormous hole in his jaw, the arrival of the ambulance, the struggle to carry the stretcher down the zigzag steps, the sight of King lying on the stretcher in the courtyard, the lamentation and weeping all about him. . . . DuFour remembered that, after he helped lift the stretcher into the ambulance and it had left, he had been assigned to direct traffic at the corner of Huling and Mulberry. He had done so almost automatically. After he was finally relieved of duty and sent home just before dawn, he realized that King's blood had dried on his boots and puttees; and though he was utterly exhausted and it took a great deal to upset him, he had to down almost half a pint of whiskey before he calmed himself enough to go to bed. . . .

He looked at the sleeping man on his bunk. Could he be the one that did it, who was responsible for all this? This mild, uncommunicative man who seemed always under control, always agreeable, with his own pixie sense of humor? Because Ray knew how carefully he was watched, he played little tricks. Once, fussing with his slippers, he pretended surreptitiously to toss a tiny tab of leather behind the commode, only to grin when one of the guards pounced on it. One night he cut out a newspaper ad of a Caribbean cruise that was to

leave in two weeks, circled it in pencil and stuck it under his mattress
for his guards to find. A third time he told DuFour importantly, "Be
sure to let me know when it's 10:20," as though he would leave then.
He took everything in stride. When he was told a few dollars were
dribbling in for him from friends and admirers, he grinned. "Forget
it," he said. "I don't want to get messed up with Internal Revenue."
He had his pet names: Martin Lucifer King, Rancid Clark. He was
sure all the onerous jail rules had been devised by the Justice Department to harass him. Once, while looking through a magazine, he
came on an ad for a Remington 30.06 with a scope attached. DuFour
asked, "James, is that the rifle you bought?" Ray looked up, his blue
eyes wide open in innocence. "What rifle?" he asked. "I never bought
no rifle." The same issue told of a sixteen-year-old girl trap shooter
who broke ninety-nine out of one hundred. Ray said, with a sardonic
grin, "Why don't they ask her where she was April 4?" He bought both
Memphis newspapers, as well as *U.S. News & World Report, Time,*
and *Newsweek*. Some unknown admirer had sent him a gift subscrip-
tion to the New York *Times*. He read them all avidly. He pored over
civil war dispatches from Nigeria, the Biafra revolt, the political up-
risings in the Congo. He watched TV programs for hours, sometimes
news reports back to back. He never missed the Sunday night *FBI*.
He would make sarcastic, contemptuous comments as he looked
at the show—"Hell, that's the silliest thing I ever saw! No pro would
do that!" He had nothing but scorn for FBI methods. When the
sessions of the Democratic National Convention in Chicago were
shown, he sat up all night watching it. When the camera showed police clubbing demonstrators, he enjoyed it hugely. "Yah, give it to
'em!" he exclaimed. He turned to his guards. "You see that? More of
your police brutality, beating up innocent citizens." The guards
teased him in return. "James, weren't you an MP in Germany? Hell,
you're just a guard gone bad." Ray sparred with them. "No, sir, no
difference between cops and robbers except you guys are working for
the politicians." He had always expressed contempt for politicians.
DuFour thought, *He's proud to be a robber.*

Ray was fascinated to learn that DuFour had been in the TAC
force in the fire station across the street of the Lorraine. He wanted
to know how many men there were, where they were standing, what
happened when they heard the shot. DuFour kidded him. "How'd
you get past us, James? We were there in forty-five seconds. How
could you possibly get past me?"

"Well, you blew it," Ray retorted. He grinned. "If you'd of got that other guy, I wouldn't be here now and you'd probably be a lieutenant." "How'd you get out of town?" DuFour demanded.

Ray looked around him. They were all ears—the guards in the block with him, the supervisor outside—for all he knew, Sheriff Morris downstairs and maybe even J. Edgar Hoover and Ramsey Clark in Washington, on some secret extension. The quick, sardonic smile twisted his mouth. "You really want to know?" "You're damn right we want to know." A pause. "I got lost," Ray said.

Laughter. They felt he was telling the truth. The entire city looking for him, scouring the most logical streets he would take, and he, meanwhile, lost—characteristically messing it up—trapped in alleys and side streets. By the time he found himself on Highway 78, which led to Birmingham, his searchers were everywhere else. It was ridiculous. Highway 78 was well traveled and under repair; it was rush hour; time and again he found himself sitting in his car, motionless, in the long line of bumper-to-bumper traffic, waiting for it to move. For the first hundred miles he could not have averaged more than thirty-five to forty miles an hour. He had no idea where he was until he saw two Alabama state troopers standing on the side of the road—then he knew he was in Alabama.

"James, you sure got by us and you sure got by them," said DuFour. He still did not believe Ray killed King.

Had Ray attempted to engineer a trip to the hospital, he would have failed. Nothing less than catastrophe could have brought him out of Cell Block A. Dr. DeMere had prepared for every eventuality, including an emergency operation, even to shielding the floor against static electricity. If, nonetheless, Ray had to be rushed to the hospital, a telephone code had been set up to alert officials there as to their patient's identity and trigger special security measures that had already been rehearsed.

DeMere studied Ray, too. It took him several weeks to gain his confidence. When, on that hectic July morning Ray had been finally brought safely into jail, Dr. DeMere had begun preparations for a complete physical examination. Ray drew back. "I'm all right," he said sullenly. "Nothing wrong with me. I don't need no physical."

Dr. DeMere tried to explain. "You're going to be here for at least several months," he said. "I have to know if you've been on drugs." Not only had there been rumors that Ray trafficked in amphetamines at Missouri State Penitentiary, but also that he used them. Certain writers had even theorized that he could have killed King while under-going an acute but temporary paranoid psychosis brought on by an overdose, thus explaining why he could carry out so inexplicable and uncharacteristic an act. "If you have been on drugs," DeMere went on, "you're going to have withdrawal symptoms, and I have to be prepared. I want to know how much alcohol you're accustomed to, and whether you've been on sedatives—"

Ray shook his head. "I've never taken any kind of dope," he said emphatically. "I've robbed banks and things like that—but no dope."

Well, said DeMere, he'd take his word for it. If Ray was lying, he'd know soon enough. But he had to take some blood—he might have picked up hepatitis.

"Oh no," Ray said in alarm. "You're not sticking me, you don't stick me with nothing."

The physician did not insist. There would be time for that. Ray had been returned to an angry city, he was understandably fearful. This doctor could kill him with a single hypo. DeMere was uncom-fortable too. He had more access to the prisoner than anyone else—at any hour of the day or night. Though the guards checked his bag, they had no idea what drugs he brought into Cell Block A. DeMere realized that he was the greatest security risk of all. Suppose there was an effort to kill Ray. DeMere might be the man they would work through. For the first few days he went about thinking, half-seriously, *I must be careful—someone may try to brainwash me.*

By September, Ray had begun to trust him, and allowed him to take a blood sample. The man was in excellent health. He could walk on his hands the length of the block, he could do over 130 push-ups—DeMere encouraged him to exercise, because he never had a walking period outside, he never left his block save for the two or three times he was taken down the elevator into Judge Battle's courtroom for legal procedures. There was no doubt that Ray kept himself in perfect physical condition, ready to take advantage of any chance to escape. The guards told DeMere that Ray had warned them, "Anybody turns their back on me, I'm gone." But he admitted he could not break out of A Block.

Doctor and prisoner established a rapport. DeMere asked, curiously, Why had he refused to talk on the plane bringing him to Memphis? Did he know the doctor who accompanied him warned DeMere to watch him—he thought Ray had suicidal tendencies? Ray shrugged his shoulders. "Mr. Hanes told me to say nothing to nobody, so I just kept my mouth shut." *Was* the man a racist? DeMere wondered. Ray was a challenge to him. He tried to test him—to tease him about Negroes. Ray never took the bait. DeMere would casually make an anti-black observation. Ray would not react. Not so much as an understanding smile, or a quick glance of silent agreement. DeMere finally asked him bluntly how he felt about Negroes. There were reports that Ray hated them.

Ray angrily denied it. "I've lived among coloreds all my life," he said. "I don't have anything against them. It depends on the person. There's a lot of whites I don't like—it has nothing to do with color." DeMere noted Ray's use of the word "coloreds." It was not the kind of word you'd expect from a Midwestern American like Ray. It was a South African term. But he went on: How about Dr. King? I don't have anything against Dr. King, Ray said. He did not particularly like preachers, but that was their business, so long as they let him alone. Ray, it seemed to DeMere, knew little about the man he was accused of murdering, and hardly anything about his career. He showed surprise when DeMere told him a black woman tried to kill King in New York some years before, stabbing him in the chest with a letter opener. DeMere thought, *Sirhan Sirhan knows a great deal about Robert Kennedy, Lee Harvey Oswald was involved in political movements, he obviously knew much about John Kennedy—this man seems to know nothing about King.* Perhaps he was clever at dissimulating, and he was being taken in by him, but DeMere felt that Ray had no great racial feeling.

As a matter of fact, only two allegations seemed to anger him. The first, that he was a racist; the second, that he was a latent homosexual. One writer had wondered publicly whether this might not be one of Ray's problems. Ray was furious. That was a lie, he asserted. He had once refused to work in a spud room, at Missouri State—a punishment room where inmates peeled potatoes—because most of the men were homosexuals, and he had suffered even worse punishment for his stubbornness. Well, said DeMere, I didn't think so either. "After all, what about all those women you're supposed to have had—in Los Angeles, in Mexico, in Portugal?" Ray reddened. "I wish I had all the women they said I did."

Whatever Ray told DeMere, or whatever DeMere thought about the man and his case, he kept to himself. He had pledged himself this. Judge Battle, the day Ray arrived, had made sure that such a silence would be maintained by every principal in the case, by issuing unprecedented pretrial publicity restrictions. All lawyers, state and defense; all witnesses; all investigators and their legal staffs; all county employees—the police, the firemen, the sheriff and his deputies, the jailers, guards, attendants, the medical examiner, all persons in any way involved with the case—all were prohibited from being interviewed by press, radio, or TV; and if they disobeyed and did talk to the press, the reporters were prohibited from printing what they said. The penalty would be contempt of court—a fine or jail sentence, or both. Added to the silence already imposed by the FBI from the very first, it meant that the James Earl Ray case would be as hermetically sealed as possible before trial.

In the first month Judge Battle had already found Renfro Hays, several reporters, and even Art Hanes himself in contempt of court for disobeying his rules.

"I have to balance the rights of the press against the right of this man to get a fair trial," Battle said. "I am determined that this man will receive a fair trial, if humanly possible."

Judge Battle thought, what he had predicted months before was coming to pass: whoever would be saddled with the case had to end up "a plain old bastard . . . denounced, threatened, and abused by the press."

CHAPTER XXV

In his office in Birmingham, Arthur Hanes, Sr., labored far into the night, working out the prosecution and defense. He had had to dismiss what might have been a dramatic development—the eyewitness testimony of Victor Bartlett. He would not call on the man to testify. He had sent an inquiry to a lawyer in Nashville to learn what he could about his surprise witness. The two-sentence reply was devastating:

"I am enclosing a photostatic copy of Bartlett's police record in Davidson County. You will note that it shows 104 arrests for drunkenness, disorderly conduct, assault with a butcher knife, resisting an officer, loitering, false robbery report, obscene telephone calls, and other assorted offenses."

Hanes had sighed regretfully and gone on with his work. In the weeks to come he would receive a dozen other calls from men and women ready to pledge their sacred honor that they had been in an adjoining room with the killer, that they had overheard men plotting that a confidant of a confidant had disclosed an oath in high places to do away with King, that—it was astonishing how the murder of a famous figure seemed to draw, like a lamp drew moths, otherwise apparently rational citizens to confuse and bedevil the situation. And no one could sound more sincere, speak in greater accents of truth, than the sincere paranoid.

Hanes turned to the sheet before him.

What *was* the state's case? How would he answer it? He wrote it down, point by point, on the left side of the sheet. On the right side he wrote the defense rebuttal as it now stood.

1. King was killed by a rifle shot on April 4, 1968, and taken to a hospital, virtually dead on arrival. *No contest.*

2. By hearing of witnesses and triangulation studies, the shot was fired from the bathroom window at 422½ South Main Street. a. *No witnesses could be found who were absolutely certain the shot came from the bathroom. b. Most were uncertain as to where it came from. c. Some said the shot came from the bushes. d. Even to determine course bullet took by triangulation would not be absolute*

proof, because a slight change in the body angle of Dr. King would result in a great change in the location of the wound at a distance of 175 or 200 feet.

3. A 760 Remington rifle, binoculars, and a suitcase full of clothes were dropped in front of the door of the Canipe Amusement Company immediately after the shooting. *The rifle and suitcase could have been dropped by someone else before the shooting. The times given by the witnesses, Canipe and the two men in his shop, were not exact. In addition, some of the clothes found in the suitcase—the shorts—were too small to fit James Earl Ray.*

4. James Earl Ray, under alias of Eric S. Galt, spent the night of April 3 at the New Rebel Motel. (Proof: Personal identification; handwriting; fingerprints.) *No real contest. Might make something of the state threatening witnesses with jail if they talked to the defense.*

5. James Earl Ray checked into rooming house at 422½ South Main Street, midafternoon of April 4, 1968, and took room down hall from bathroom. *Might make headway cross-examining Bessie Brewer re state hiding her out, her testimony suspect because of possibility of receiving reward. Same with Charles Stephens. Could argue these witnesses cannot be believed because state allegedly threatened to send them to jail if they talked to defense; others refused to talk to defense saying they had been warned against talking by FBI.*

6. James Earl Ray bought binoculars from the York Arms Company in midafternoon of April 4, 1968. *Carpenter, the salesman, is reported to have said that he could not identify Ray as the man who bought the binoculars.*

7. Those binoculars were found in suitcase in front of Canipe's. *No contest.*

8. Those binoculars had James Earl Ray's fingerprints on the left part, near the base of the eyepiece. *Normal fingerprint cross-examination.*

9. The suitcase and clothing belonged to James Earl Ray. (Proof: the laundry marks were the same. There were matching threads in suitcase and in Mustang and in room.) *Not intrinsically incriminating. Normal cross-examination re marks, dirt, threads, etc.*

10. A white Mustang with Alabama tag fled the scene. *State witnesses not certain re tag or timing. One says white Mustang in front of Jim's Grill had a whiplash antenna (hence could broadcast—false chase?) and was gone ten minutes before King shot.*

11. A white Mustang with Alabama tag was seen left in Atlanta

the morning of April 5. *Witness to abandoned car describes someone other than James Earl Ray.*

12. That white Mustang belonged to James Earl Ray. *No contest.*

13. Threads and dirt samples from white Mustang matched those found in Memphis. *Normal weakness of threads and dirt as evidence; also we must emphasize that these things don't show who or when Mustang was near a place like Memphis. Do not prove that Mustang was in Memphis. This material could have gotten into car before.*

14. James Earl Ray's fingerprints were found in 422½ South Main Street. *Few good prints. Most not good.*

15. A shot was heard to be fired from the bathroom of 422½ approximately 6 P.M. April 4, 1968. *Only Stephens says this.*

16. Immediately thereafter James Earl Ray was seen to run from the bathroom at 422½ carrying something long in his hand. *Stephens and Anschutz say this. Dubious witnesses.*

17. The rifle found in front of Canipe's, dropped shortly after the shooting, was purchased by James Earl Ray in Birmingham on 3/29 and 3/30. *Baker, seller of rifle, can't identify Ray as purchaser; both he and Wood say buyer, if Ray, totally unfamiliar with guns and probably couldn't make shot. Also, trip back for an exchange.*

18. The rifle had only James Earl Ray's fingerprint on it. *Prints can travel. The print was isolated. Some person could have wiped it clean and missed the one print.*

19. The rifle probably fired the shot which killed King, i.e., was consistent with wound. *New rifle, hard shell—no positive identification. (We could have a field day on the theory of possibility, cross-examination.)*

20. James Earl Ray fled to Canada, then to Portugal and London. *"Accidentally" let that he was ex-con on lam, and explain flight of poor fugitive, accidentally hooked into a great manhunt this way.*

21. When apprehended, he dropped his head and said, "Oh, God, I feel so trapped!" *Belittle this, if we can't keep it out otherwise; don't blame him for feeling that way, with 6000 FBI agents on trail, etc.*

22. Ray and Galt were the same person. *No real contest, but maybe weakness will develop.*

23. Marked map of King's haunts found in Ray's room in Atlanta, with Ray's prints on it. *Can't tell who made marks, when made, whether a before or after print, or what else was within mark. Also a lot of other marked maps in Ray's belongings.*

24. Ray had expressed dislike for Negroes. *If this based on Ray's remark in bar, with girl, re Watts—Ray didn't start fight and it wasn't all bad.*

25. Ray had offered to collect bounty on King. *This based on story of convict Curtis, now in prison, and is probably unreliable. (See Warden's remarks as well as those by other cons.)*

Hanes put the sheet aside.

Now he tried the argumentation from another approach, writing busily.

CASE FOR CONCLUSION THAT RAY KILLED KING

1. Ray owned the gun found on Main Street.
2. The gun found on Main Street fired the fatal shot.
3. Ray was in the Memphis area on April 4, 1968.
4. Ray was in the rooming house on the afternoon of April 4, 1968.
5. An expended cartridge from the gun was found in the gun.
6. Ray's prints were on the gun (also scope).
7. Ray bought binoculars on 4/4/68 that were found in rooming house.
8. Ray's prints were on the binoculars.
9. Ray had expressed an interest in and willingness to kill King for money.

Conclusion: Ray killed King.

Again, on another sheet, which he headed: CASE FOR CONCLUSION THAT RAY WAS FRAMED.

1. Ray was unfamiliar with guns. (Testimony by Wood and possibly Manasco.)
2. There is no evidence of a motive. (One-man-acting-alone-theory-all-the-way.)
3. The state's main witness is lying for money and was drunk and nonseeing at the time. (Himself; McGraw, cabdriver who swears Stephens was drunk afternoon of 4/4; Jowers; perhaps Stephens' lawyers.)
4. The eyewitnesses to the shooting say a shot and a man came from the bushes. (Solomon Jones; fireman at No. 2 station; police.)
5. Ballistics are just opinion.
6. a. Ray had never been in the rooming house, nor in the Lorraine Motel, or for that matter, in Memphis. b. King's whereabouts not generally known. c. Fact shot could be made from 422½ to Lorraine is not obvious, would take preplanning and casing of the build-

ing and relationship to each other. d. No evidence of another person, is evidence pointing to him, suspiciously obvious; therefore, Ray could not have done it logistically or was it in his capability. But what evidence there is points to Ray. *One conclusion only: Ray was framed.*

Having put all this down, Hanes studied it for a considerable time. Then he concluded by heading a page OUR AFFIRMATIVE CASE:

A. BUSHMAN.

1. Solomon Jones said he saw a man with a white cloth over face who ran toward Main Street from hideout in bushes. (He fired the shot.)

2. Harold (Cornbread) Carter was in bushes drinking wine when a man jumped up, fired a shot toward the Lorraine, and kicked gravel on him as he turned and ran.

3. Firemen in Firehouse Station No. 2 must have thought the shot came from the bushes because they all ran to see into bushes who fired the shot. TAC units were all over Station No. 2 and sealed off area in seconds—no one was seen leaving area. Rooming house was not shaken down after shooting (also, Jowers heard shot from bushes).

4. Bushes since then cut down by persons unknown.

B. MOTIVE FOR SOMEONE OTHER THAN RAY, ETC.

1. Holloman said Invaders and militants had been threatening King because (a) power struggle; he too nonviolent; (b) Money, had blackmailed him before; (c) Foment violence. Extra guards in area for this reason.

2. Richmond, watching through peephole for Invaders.

3. Walter Bailey, manager of Lorraine—said Invaders were all over Lorraine.

4. Grace Stephens, Charlie Stephens, Cornbread, others in rooming house said: "Miscellaneous niggers all the time coming up to rooming house." (Even applied to Memphis Fire Department to close back stairs.)

C. CHARLIE STEPHENS.

1. Cabdriver McGraw—came to pick Charlie up about 30 minutes before shooting: Charlie was in bed too drunk to move or to haul in cab.

2. Grace: said Charlie was in kitchen and didn't go to door until man from bathroom was at end of hall, didn't see him at all.

3. Charlie denied any knowledge of shooting on several occasions, immediately afterward. See reporters, etc.

4. Charlie was most interested, along with his lawyers who would share, in the $100,000 reward he thought he could get.

D. EYEWITNESSES VARY.

1. Grace—said she saw man leave bathroom. He was short—5'7", 5'8"—and slight (approximately 125 lbs) and about 48–50, wearing plaid shirt and army jacket. (Some clothes in suitcase dropped at Canipe's—shorts—would fit man this size.)

2. Canipe—said man who dropped gun and suitcase was larger than this, and well dressed, dark suit and tie.

E. SHERIFF DEPUTIES AND TAC UNITS ALL OVER SOUTH MAIN STREET WITHIN SECONDS AFTER SHOOTING. (See Firemen, Lloyd Jowers, people in Jim's Grill.) *Chronologically no time to shoot, pack gun in gun box, get suitcase, and wind through labyrinth of 422½, throw down box and suitcase, and get into car without being seen.*

F. NO MOTIVE.

G. ROOMING HOUSE IS REMOTE—NEEDING CASING BEFOREHAND WITH KNOWLEDGE OF KING'S ITINERARY.

Reasonable doubt, thought Hanes: *so much reasonable doubt to place before a jury prepared to consider, seriously and conscientiously, reasonable doubt.*

He was sure he had himself a lawsuit.

CHAPTER XXVI

In Memphis, James Beasley, the man who had to compile the state's proof against James Earl Ray—and against his fellow conspirators, if any—sat in a triply locked room on the third floor of the Criminal Courts Building, surrounded by files containing every known fact about the man—files into which there was still coming page after page of information about him.

He was reading, as he had been for many days. Slowly, before his eyes, the first twenty years of Ray's life had begun to take shape. It was a drab and saddening story of a deprived man, a born loser— "The guy never got the breaks," Beasley was to comment to Dwyer. "He began at the bottom of the totem pole and stayed there." The city of his birth, Alton, Illinois, was a poor industrial river town of forty-five thousand, known mainly because Elijah P. Lovejoy, the abolitionist, had been killed by a mob there back in 1837, and because the final Lincoln-Douglas debate had been held there. That was its only claim to notice—save that now they would add that James Earl Ray had been born there. After James Gerald Ray and Lucille Maher were married in St. Louis on April 26, 1926—he twenty-seven, she seventeen—her parents, who lived in Alton, Illinois, had let them move in with them and stay in two rooms. There James Earl Ray was born on March 10, 1928.

He was about a year old when his parents left the Mahers and moved back to St. Louis. Marjorie was born in June 1930, John about a year later, and four years later Jerry. That year, 1935, the family moved to a farm that Lucille's mother, Grandmother Mary Katherine Maher, bought them in Ewing, across the river from Quincy, and in August 1935, seven-year-old Jim enrolled in the first grade of the Ewing public school.

As a young child, he had a history of constant bed-wetting, of troubled sleep. He "made frequent outcries in the night," the doctor's report showed. At eight he became unconscious and lay jerking and twitching for nearly half an hour, his knees drawn up to his chin. It was later believed to be an epileptic fit. At ten he woke up one morning in panic, screaming—he could not see, he was blind. It was diagnosed as an attack of hysteria.

In a poor village of blue-collar workers, in the depression, the Rays were among the poorest. Ewing, little more than a railroad crossroad with a dozen dirt streets, had a population of under four hundred. The elder Ray went by various names. He was James Gerald Ray on the marriage certificate, Beasley noted, in 1926, but by 1930 he was Jerry Raynes, and by the time he moved to Ewing he was Gerry Raines. When Jim entered school, it was as James Earl Rayns—still another spelling. When James Earl Ray suddenly burst into the news as the accused killer of Dr. King, everyone in Ewing was confused. They had not known anyone by that name. Someone finally recognized him as "little Jimmy Raines"—a lonely, silent youngster with a quick smile, wearing patched hand-me-downs made from his father's clothing. Few knew the family. Not only did they live a mile and a half out of town, but as newcomers they were objects of suspicion in Ewing, where families had roots going back several generations.

James Gerald Ray—or Jerry Rayns as he was to be known—was seldom seen. One or two of his son's schoolmates remembered him "a little drunk," weaving down the street. Nobody was sure how he supported his family—his farm, sixty-three acres bought by Grandmother Maher for six hundred dollars, was poor acreage, thin topsoil over rock, most of it better suited for grazing sheep than crops. There was a county food arrangement and regularly the Rayns, like other families, picked up their sacks of corn meal and other staples to help feed themselves and their growing family. Now and then he would show up in town with a battered ton-and-a-half hauling truck—a thin, wiry man who spoke slowly, with a strange musical slur to his words, a bantam cock of a man with a reputation as a carnival boxer and Jack-of-all-trades, wanting to know if there were any odd jobs about.

The mother, Lucille, was even more rarely seen. She was remembered as a quiet, timid girl who was almost a recluse, keeping to herself with the family in a decrepit old house lit by kerosene lamps, sleeping in beds without sheets. Ewing has harsh winters, the thermometer sometimes dropping to fifteen to twenty below zero. Now and then townspeople would take food out to the family. They would find Rayns gone, no heat in the house, and Lucille and the children all in bed together, under every blanket they could pile on themselves, trying to keep warm. Lucille was to bear five more children before her husband, always footloose, finally left her, and there were to be tragedies—one after the other.

Many in Ewing tried to draw a picture of young Jim. One schoolmate, Mike O'Brien, remembered him as a bully. "He was small for his age, but I was smaller, we got into a fight, and he kind of run over me." But Robert O. Brown, now a school instructor in St. Louis, recalled him warmly. Brown had a weakened right shoulder from polio, and more than once when he walked home from school Jim came along and silently took his books and carried them. Brown thought of him as a Huck Finn type—a painfully shy boy. It was hard to understand Jim when he talked, because he swallowed his words, or simply because he could not communicate. He was seen most of the time with three friends, who lived near him outside Ewing—the Peacock brothers, Robie and Charlie, and Gerald Hobbs. They would hunt together for possums and skunks; they were experts with the slingshot, and the rabbits and squirrels they brought home went at once on their table. They were often hungry.

They went swimming, too, in a small muddy creek. It was dirty and full of snakes, but it was their swimming hole. When they were ready to go home, all climbed up the bank at the only point where it was sandy. But not Jim. He swam down the creek about thirty feet, where he was almost out of sight, and climbed up a bank that was pure mud. He emerged, an apparition covered with brown muck, and began hurriedly scrambling into his clothes as he was. The others, who had been watching, whooped in ridicule, pounced on him, and threw him back into the water, not letting him out until he had rinsed himself off; then they forced him to climb up the sandy bank. He preferred the mud rather then expose himself—or he may have been ashamed of his tattered underwear. "None of us were rich, we were all poor," Brown said, "but somehow Jim always looked poorer than any of us. He might show up in new overalls in the morning and they'd be filthy by afternoon. He just didn't care."

His school record seemed to show the same indifference. His IQ tested at 108, and his teachers told him he could head his class if he applied himself. He never did. He remained two years in the first grade, absent a fourth of the time. He often did not have warm enough clothes for the bitterly cold winters, or shoes in good enough condition. A teacher's notes jotted down on his Personality Card in the school files when he was nine years old reads: "Attitude toward regulations: violates them all. Honesty: needs watching. Appearance: repulsive. Courtesy: seldom if ever polite." However subjective these judgments sounded to the men studying Ray as a youth, they painted a picture of the sociopath of the future—suspicious of others, resentful of authority, ill at ease in the world about him.

Ray completed the eighth grade in May 1943, when he was fifteen. Having started school a year late, he had never caught up, although in many courses he received marks of excellent. He left in disgrace. He was accused of stealing the class lunch money, about $3.50, from a box kept in the desk of his teacher, Miss Ina Kitson. Each student who ate lunch at school—Miss Kitson taught the fourth, fifth, and sixth grades in one room—brought a dime each morning. The box vanished after lunch one day, and because Ray was one of two boys who were in the room after the others had gone down to lunch, suspicion fell on him. He denied it, blaming it on Carlisle Washburn, now postmaster of Ewing, who was the other boy. Of the eighteen children in Miss Kitson's room, only Ray and Washburn went home for lunch, Ray because he had no money, and Washburn because he wanted to. Miss Kitson wrote a note to Lucille, telling her of the theft, and asking her if she thought Jimmy might bring back the box. Lucille had known nothing of it—but she found the box, the money in it, under their front porch, and promptly sent it back, with apologies, and everyone tried to forget what had happened. "Mrs. Rayns was a very honest woman," Miss Kitson said. "She didn't try to cover anything."

Six months after his schooling ended, young Ray came to Alton to live with Grandmother Maher and her son, his Uncle Bill Maher, who was a well-known painting contractor. Ray wanted to earn money. Grandmother Maher, who was to do her best to keep the Ray family together, helped him obtain a job at the International Shoe Company tannery in nearby Hartford, Illinois. He worked there for two years—1944 and 1945—the longest period he was to hold a job. He mixed dyes and began learning a skill. The foreman allowed him to sleep in a back room and gave him considerable overtime. "Why would anyone want to steal when it's so easy to make so much money regularly," he said to his uncle. But he was laid off in December 1945, because of returning war veterans, and little more than a month later he enlisted. The draft was about to take him: by enlisting he could choose his tour of duty. He wanted to see Germany. At the tannery he had been the assistant of Hans Miller, a German immigrant in his forties. Miller (which is not his real name) was an ardent Nazi who carried around a photograph of Hitler. Ray and Miller became almost inseparable, not only at work but after hours. It was an odd friendship, the sixteen-year-old boy and the older man, the more because Ray had no confidants his own age. Miller got him excited about Germany. There was a story, attested to by several employees, that Miller had been knocked down in a fight at the tannery with another worker because of his loud admiration of Hitler, his boasts about Nazi *Herrenvolk*, his talk about superior and inferior races.

The Army proved a disaster for Ray. He went off in high spirits, not yet eighteen, and found himself a driver of refrigerated trucks in the Quartermaster Corps in Nuremberg. He was in Germany, but nothing went right. He was unable to maneuver the huge trucks. Ridiculed, the butt of jokes, he was transferred to a Military Police school in Bremerhaven, only to end up a jeep driver. Here, again, he got into difficulty. He was court-martialed for being drunk in quarters and resisting arrest; he was confined to hard labor for three months with a cut in pay; he contracted gonorrhea and syphilis, he was found AWOL in town, he was demoted to the infantry, which he despised —"Everybody kicks you around there"—and in the end was discharged "for ineptness and lack of adaptability for military service," and sent home from Germany in the last days of 1948.

Beasley, a deacon of the Baptist Church, a Sunday-school teacher, paused, wondering: what had all this done to James Earl Ray? What role could Hans Miller and his enthusiasms have played in Ray's thinking? And what had been the effect of his experiences in the Army?

Who was to know what twenty-year-old James Earl Ray felt and thought about the world around him?

In his office adjoining Beasley's, Robert Dwyer was deeply immersed in an older James Earl Ray, Prisoner No. 00416 J at Missouri State Penitentiary. He was studying Ray behind bars—the man who began to find himself in jail almost as soon as he came out of the Army. "Penny ante" had been the description given Ray by Warden Harold Swensen of the Missouri prison. But a paragraph in one of the many psychological reports on Ray caught Dwyer's eye. It had been written more than thirteen years ago—July 1955—when Ray, just turned twenty-seven, entered Leavenworth Penitentiary for stealing and forging U.S. postal money orders.

The federal probation officer, Edward B. Murray, wrote a terse, sharp report. "The defendant shows absolutely no remorse at this time. He anticipates receiving a substantial sentence for the instant offense. In the writer's opinion, he is a confirmed criminal and a menace to society when in the free world." Dwyer whistled. To call a man at twenty-seven a confirmed criminal, "a menace to society," was strong language. And Murray had added, as more than one student of Ray was to echo later, "Just what motivates him to commit crime is not known."

A strange man, Dwyer thought, as he probed deeper into Ray's criminal career: full of quirks, but not to be underestimated. In March 1966, when he failed his second attempt to escape from Missouri State Penitentiary, he had been able to manage a trip to a hospital— where he would have a far better chance to break out—by claiming he could not remember trying to escape, and he heard voices at night. A court ordered a sanity hearing and Ray was sent to the State Mental Hospital in Fulton, Missouri, in September for observation.

A day after he arrived there Ray changed his complaint. No, amnesia was not his problem: he remembered everything. What he suffered from, he said, was confusion, neuritis, and anxiety. Why had he changed his ailment, Dwyer wondered? Because in the hospital Ray learned that amnesia called for shock treatment, of which he was terrified—he knew "it turned a person into a vegetable"—and he wanted none of it. The doctors, finding nothing wrong with him, returned him to prison before he had been able to work out a plan to break out of the hospital. They described him as "coherent, alert, relevant; no hallucinations; no delusions; no signs indicating a mental disease." His IQ was 105—normal. They diagnosed him as "Sociopathic personality, with anxiety and depressive features"—a routine, general description given almost every long-term prisoner. He had "a good verbal assessment of reality," they wrote, "but in the past has used bad judgement."

Ray, the jailhouse lawyer, nothing daunted, promptly asked for an outside psychiatrist, "someone not connected with the prison" to examine him. As always, he distrusted the establishment. His request was not granted, but Dr. Henry V. Guhleman, Jr., a consulting psychiatrist to the probation board with a private practice—and therefore to Ray the next best thing—examined him three months later.

He found Ray "an interesting and rather complicated individual." This hardly fitted in with the picture of the simple-minded, clownlike Ray of newspaper stories. "He reports that within the last year he has had considerable difficulties from a physical point of view, involving a number of complaints such as pain in the 'solar plexes,' 'tachcardia,' and 'intercranial tension.'" When Dr. Guhleman commented that these "were rather large words" to be used by a layman, Ray explained that "I've been reading up on the medical literature" in the prison library.

The physician wrote: "This man's basic problem revolves around what appears to be an increasingly severe obsessive compulsive trend." From time to time, Ray told him, he would be seized by overwhelming fears and had to do certain things to stave off some nameless and terrible fate. "What sort of things?" Dr. Guhleman asked. Ray replied that he felt better if he moved a glass of water back and forth on the table. He added that he used to think he suffered from cancer and other incurable diseases, but he had gotten over that. Fellow inmates, as prison officials could have told Dr. Guhleman, thought Ray a hypochondriac: now and then he would ask someone to take his pulse, and he had once asked another prisoner, who had arthritis, to let him have some of his pills. Had he arthritis? No, said Ray, "but just in case."

The psychiatrist wrote that Ray was not psychotic but "severely neurotic" and appeared to be under considerable tension. Ray, trying to diagnose his own case, wondered whether this tension might have led to his attempt to escape—this feeling, this compulsion, that he had to do something to cope with his anxiety. He was afraid, he told the physician, that this might lead to more serious trouble.

Dr. Guhleman concluded: "It is felt that he is in need of psychiatric help and that should any serious parole consideration be given, some type of psychiatric help should be considered—that is, help which he can receive on the outside during his parole period."

All this, Dwyer saw, was academic. Ray's parole was to come up for consideration in November 1967. The parole board might have given him his freedom, but it really did not matter. For in April 1967 Ray made his escape. For a man with thirteen years yet to serve, it was not the wise thing to do, to escape only months before the parole board might have opened the door for him. But this sort of thing—"bad judgement"—accompanied by an almost classic pattern of chase, capture, breakaway, and capture again—marked most of Ray's criminal career, beginning with his first jail sentence, at twenty-one, for attempted theft of a typewriter.

When Ray was discharged from the Army in December 1948, he had tried his luck at one or two jobs in Chicago, briefly attended a business-school class, played with the idea of becoming a private eye, and even began a course for private detectives. He dropped out when he concluded that the job was far less glamorous than it appeared in films. Then he worked his way to Los Angeles. The night of October 7, 1949, he was surprised in the third-floor office of the Forum Cafeteria by the assistant manager. There was a fierce struggle: Ray broke away and jumped through an open window to the fire escape. A typewriter was perched there. Ray had apparently carried it out and gone back to see what else he could take. He dashed down the three flights, the other shouting after him. When Ray reached the street a parking attendant grabbed him. Ray broke away but his bankbook and Army discharge papers fell out of a torn shirt pocket. Since there was no Los Angeles address for him, it would all have been forgotten had not Ray appeared at the same corner four days later. The attendant recognized him, called police, and Ray was arrested.

He pleaded not guilty, but on December 12 was convicted of second-degree theft and given ninety days in the county jail. Ray's not-guilty plea, Dwyer noted, set a pattern that Ray followed thereafter: at the last moment, deny everything. Years later one of Ray's lawyers said, "Ray thinks he can rearrange reality to suit himself. If he doesn't want a chair to be in a room, he wills it away. It's not there for him."

He knew nothing about a typewriter, Ray said. He had walked into the building and gone up the stairs and was sitting there when someone grabbed him and ordered him to leave. A few days later while walking down the street, he was arrested for no reason. The assistant manager accused Ray of almost breaking a chair over his head in their struggle. Ray denied it. There had been no struggle. And he had not gone into the building planning to steal anything. The probation officer asked, "Jim, if you didn't plan to steal anything, why did you go into the building?" The answer: "He was unable to give any motivation for his entering the building except 'I guess I had a few beers or something.'"

He was released in March, 1950.

On the morning of April 18, 1950, railway police pulled a young hobo from a freight train at a crossing just outside Cedar Rapids, Iowa. It was James Earl Ray, riding the rails back to Chicago. They would have sent him on his way, but they found nearly fifty silver dollars in his pocket, some still in the original paper-wrapped rolls as supplied by the bank. Obviously, these had been stolen either from a cash register or from a bank. Ray could not explain the money, so he was charged with vagrancy and thrown into jail for three weeks.

Then he was given a suspended six-month sentence and ordered to leave town.

In the early hours of May 6, 1952, back in Chicago, he hired a cab, stuck a gun against the back of the driver's head, took eleven dollars from him, jumped out and began to run. A passer-by who had seen all this—Ray, with characteristic carelessness, had pulled his hold-up as the cab stopped under a streetlight—alerted a police car. Ray was caught when a policeman's bullet forced him into a dead end alley and he tumbled through a basement window. He had superficial bullet wounds of both arms and a bleeding scalp as they clamped handcuffs on him. He looked up at the man responsible for his capture and asked in a voice half disgust, half wonderment, "What are you going to get out of this?"

Dwyer thought, *It tells a lot about the guy.*

In court Ray tried to will away the gun. It was a piece of pipe, he claimed. But he was convicted of robbery, served twenty-one months in the state penitentiary at Joliet, Illinois, and when he was let out, in the spring of 1954, went to Quincy, where he tied up with Walter Rife, the ex-convict he had known since their teen-age days. They drove about the country, carrying out odd robberies and holdups until they were arrested in Hannibal, Missouri, on March 23, 1955, charged with forging and cashing $1800 worth of U.S. postal money orders. It led to their sentencing to Leavenworth.

When Ray was released in April 1958, he had just turned thirty. He had spent six of the last nine years behind bars.

Dwyer surveyed this period. When Ray was not in jail, everything he put his hand to was petty and mostly outside the law, ranging from stripping parked cars, to sell the parts for whatever he could get, to filling half-pint bottles with cheap wine he bought by the gallon and sold at good prices to winos on Sundays when liquor stores were closed. When he was caught, he was completely unco-operative with the police. He would say as little as possible; and not only would he cling to a story that was patently untrue, but it was impossible not to know that he was lying. Police Chief Harold Riggins of Alton, who had dealt with Ray over more than a decade of troublemaking, summed him up: "He was the most reluctant, sarcastic, overbearing liar I ever saw."

Ray's twenty-year sentence to Missouri State Penitentiary from where he was finally to escape, came as the result of a botched Kroger supermarket robbery in St. Louis. He and James Owens, another ex-convict, had heard that large sums were kept overnight in the safe. It could be opened only by a key and a combination, the combination known only by the manager, the key kept by his woman assistant. Ray had his eye on a Ford sedan which he would steal. This would become their getaway car, from which they would switch to Owens' Plymouth, parked some blocks away. By the time the owner of the Ford would report his car stolen, they would have discarded it, and anyone in the supermarket who had taken down its number would have wasted his time.

They were to meet at the store at 8 A.M., October 10, 1959, walk in with the manager and his assistant as soon as they unlocked the place, and then force them at gunpoint to open the safe.

But Ray had trouble starting the Ford and arrived at the supermarket forty-five minutes late. The two men walked in, Ray put his gun on the manager, Owens used his to cow a handful of customers. Ray ordered the man to call his assistant: he did so over the public address system. Her voice came back: "I'm busy, be there in a few minutes." "Call her again," Ray ordered nervously. Again she responded, "In a few minutes, please." Ray became jittery, he and Owens seized what little they could scoop out of two cash registers—about $190—and fled. A customer drove after them, saw them switch cars, and gave police the license number of Owens' car.

Less than twenty minutes later the two were seized in Ray's rooming house. Ray grappled with the police, tried to break away, was stopped by a warning shot, lunged at one of the detectives who tried to collar him, only to be stunned by a pistol blow over his head. Subdued, he signed a confession: he had planned the whole thing, he recruited Owens for the job, gave him the revolver he used, and they had already split the proceeds.

But in court Ray repudiated the confession. It had been beat out of him, he said. He denied everything. Four customers identified him. He still willed away the entire crime. He knew nothing about a robbery. He had been in his room all day. When his court-appointed lawyer, Richard D. Schreiber, refused to let him take the stand, Ray tried to fire him and insisted on testifying on his own behalf—the episode that stuck in Art Hanes's mind.

The entire episode was worth considerable study, because it forecast the James Earl Ray of the future. Schreiber, a young attorney, explained to Ray: "Look, you have a record. You don't dare take a chance on a trial because if you're found guilty, you can be sentenced to life as a habitual criminal. You signed a confession—you can't pretend it doesn't exist. It will go into evidence and destroy you. But if you plead guilty, I can probably get you off with seven or eight years." Owens had already pleaded guilty, he pointed out.

No, said Ray. Not only did he want to go on trial, but he wanted to testify in his own defense.

"If you take the stand they'll bring out your record," Schreiber warned. "But if you don't, they can't refer to it."

Ray would not be moved. Schreiber concluded that Ray had convinced himself that if he could only get on the stand and tell his story, the jury would believe it despite his confession and the damning evidence.

The trial began on Monday. On Wednesday, the day before the summing up, Ray unexpectedly rose in court to tell Judge John C. Casey, Jr.: "I haven't been adequately represented at this trial. I don't want Mr. Schreiber to argue my case in front of the jury." He wanted to dismiss him and take over himself.

Schreiber sat at the counsel table, astonished at the denunciation. Nothing like this had been indicated by Ray, though they had disagreed about the plea. Ray obviously had read lawbooks, he'd been counseled by fellow-inmates—this was the jailhouse lawyer in action. He took the stand, and testified; he called witnesses—other roomers. But the case clearly was going against him.

When the session was over, Judge Casey spoke privately to Schreiber. "I've been watching your man," he said. "He's getting that look in his eye. I think he might make a break for it in the courtroom tomorrow." If that happened, the judge suggested, "You better duck under the table. Somebody might shoot that fellow."

Next morning as Ray was being brought to the third-floor courtroom he suddenly kicked his guard in the stomach, broke away from him, and leaped into a self-service elevator. The guard recovered in time to pull open the outside door, which halted the lift between the second and first floors. Moments later Ray, handcuffed, was led into court. The jury, which had heard his criminal record brought out by the prosecution, took twenty minutes to find him guilty, and the twenty-year sentence, as a habitual criminal, followed.

Ray first tried to break out of Missouri State Penitentiary in November 1961, little more than a year after he entered. He scaled an inside wall on a rickety ladder he made out of shelves from the bakery; it collapsed, letting him crash to the concrete floor, where he was found, dazed and bloody. The second time—in 1966—he rolled up the blankets in his bunk, arranging them with a prison cap so that when the guards came for the 9 A.M. count next morning they would think him huddled up in sleep. Then he took a thirteen-foot transom pole, fixed on its end a bakery hook used to pull bread pans from the oven, pulled himself up to a window twelve feet above his cell, cut the wire mesh over it with a wire cutter he got through barter, crawled two hundred feet along the top of an interior wall, and hid in a ventilating shaft. He planned to hide there until he thought it safe to creep out, scale another wall to the roof and drop to safety on the other side.

But Warden Swensen outwitted him. He determined that Ray must be hiding in the shaft, and stationed a guard at the point he expected him to emerge. At 12:10 A.M. March 13—twenty-seven hours later—Ray wiggled out, carefully let himself down—into the waiting arms of the guard.

Dwyer thought, *The man was never spared any humiliation.*

By now Ray had a certain notoriety as an escape artist. He was "the hideout guy" or "the mole." Some inmates said these attempts were not genuine, that Ray was shrewdly establishing a precedent so when he made a bona fide attempt prison officials would assume he was still hiding within the walls and not issue an alarm, so giving him a head start on his pursuers.

Whatever the fact, the man was a loner. He was silent, uncommunicative, according to one prisoner, a man who "didn't fool with as many as five guys" in prison. The prison barber, who cut his hair for years, said, "Anyone who says he knows James Earl Ray is a liar." Ray seemed to have no need to confide in anyone, to talk about his past or future. At most, he might make sardonic remarks while watching television: those who ran the country were out to get what they could, nobody was to be trusted, anyone worth his salt who didn't get his while the getting was good was an idiot. He spoke contemptuously about Negroes: it was Martin "Lucifer" King, and Martin Luther "Coon." He would mutter under his breath when, devouring the news magazines from beginning to end, he read about Adam Clayton Powell or Stokely Carmichael. He became furious when Negro inmates went on a sit-down strike because a guard called a black prisoner "boy." He got into a fist fight with a Negro who referred to him as "Gray" instead of "Ray," and one inmate quoted Ray as saying, of a Negro guard, "That's one Nigger that should be dead." Yet it would be difficult to conclude from this that he was more racist than anyone else in that special, angry world in which he lived at Missouri State Penitentiary.

He read avidly not only newspapers and magazines, but paperback
spy stories, murder mysteries, and detective novels. He had so
large a stock that he rented them out at twenty-five cents a reading.
He was often paid in cigarettes, and since he did not smoke, he sold
these, extending credit—four dollars to be paid for every three outstanding. Fellow inmates who dealt with him said he was insistent
on being paid back when promised: "If you owed him a nickel he'd
bug you until he got it back."

Ray also reportedly belonged to a clique of prisoners who supplied
drugs to inmates. It was a lucrative traffic. Guards were paid one hundred dollars to bring in a thousand-pill bottle of Benzedrine tablets or
amphetamines, taped to their legs or carried in small pouches tied
under their testicles. The clique sold each tablet for one dollar—a
profit of nine hundred dollars a bottle, less the cost of the tablets
outside. Two-ounce packets of amphetamine hydrochloride, a powder,
were also smuggled in, for the same payment. Each packet was
immediately cut with one ounce of powdered sugar (easily obtained
from the bakery), making three ounces of adulterated drug. This
sold for one hundred dollars a spoonful—and fifteen spoonfuls could
be gotten from every three ounces. This simple transaction netted
$1400 a packet, less the cost of it outside.

Whether Ray trafficked in drugs was a moot point, Dwyer decided.
Nothing about him suggested his participation in group activity. At
every point one put the camera on him he was alone.

One thing was certain: he never stopped scheming how to break
out, and the third and successful attempt came Sunday morning,
April 23, 1967—eleven months after his last failure.

That Sunday Ray was working in the third-floor bakery. One of his
tasks was to pack loaves of bread into a three-by-four box, to be
taken by truck to an honor farm some miles away. Each morning the
truck brought the empty box from the farm, backed up to a loading
dock, where a prisoner took the box up an elevator to the bakery.
There Ray packed it according to the farm's needs that day—a maximum of sixty loaves in four layers. The box was brought down again,
checked by the driver, checked again by a guard at the prison exit
and the truck drove out on the open road to the farm.

This Sunday both driver and guard were off. Only later did the
relief driver recall that a filled bread box already awaited him at the
loading dock. He watched as two inmates lifted it onto the truck. At
the exit the relief guard lifted the cover, saw the loaves neatly packed,
and waved him on.

Half an hour later at the farm the box was found to hold only thirty loaves, most of them so mashed they had to be fed to the chickens.

An investigation uncovered two interesting facts. Guards now recalled that they had seen Ray curling himself up into a ball in the corner of his cell. They paid little attention; the man was always doing calisthenics, push-ups, walking on his hands—now he was into yoga. But of course it was not yoga. Ray was preparing for his ordeal in the bread box.

The second fact was that the farm had ordered more bread than it needed for three days preceding; for this reason, the truck had not been sent back for more bread Sunday, which would have immediately revealed Ray's absence.

Obviously, the entire thing had been carefully planned, and Ray had been helped. Two prisoners were singled out. They denied any part in it, and there was no proof. Ray was to insist later that he got out by scaling the wall, this evidently to absolve those who helped him. Dwyer wondered, Could these two have been part of the plot against King? But if Ray was aided to escape on April 23, 1967, in order to kill King, why would he wander about the United States, Canada, and Mexico, exposing himself to capture for nearly a year before carrying out his assignment? It made no sense.

Prison authorities spoke at great length to one inmate, Walter E. Nolan, who walked daily with Ray in the exercise yard and was his closest friend. Yes, he knew Ray constantly planned escape. Nolan doubted that more than six or seven inmates had ever spoken more than thirty minutes to Ray in all the time he had been there. Ninety per cent of that conversation was how to get out, legally or illegally. Ray, he said, ordered lawbooks by mail and read them diligently. He was determined to get out, one way or another, and now he had done it. Nolan added that Ray was an incredibly suspicious man who believed that every convict was a stool pigeon. He would trust none of them. "You'll never find him by checking ex-cons," Nolan said. "Ray would run a mile if he saw one—he'd be sure the guy would turn him in."

The investigation had to halt there. On April 25, two days later—prison officials did spend forty-eight hours searching for him within the walls—a flyer was issued offering the routine reward for escaped run-of-the-mill prisoners: fifty dollars.

It must have been, for Ray, the ultimate humiliation, Dwyer thought.

CHAPTER XXVII

The man was out. What now?

Carefully Dwyer and Beasley followed his trail after he left Missouri State Penitentiary. He moved circumspectly, his only aim in the first weeks to keep out of sight. He spent the first five days putting a considerable distance between himself and the jail, walking nights, sleeping days, until he reached St. Louis, where he caught a bus for Chicago. There, as John Larry Rayns, he rented a twelve-dollar-a-week basement room at 2731 North Sheffield Avenue. He told the manager that he had been a cook on a Mississippi River barge, that he planned to go to Canada to get a job, and that his feet hurt—he was always rubbing salve on them. The manager's wife noted that he bought cooking utensils and prepared his meals in his room.

On May 3, ten days after his escape, again as Rayns, a name for which he had a Social Security number dating back to 1951, he answered an ad for a dishwasher at the Indian Trail Restaurant, in Winnetka, a suburb of Chicago. There were any number of dishwashing jobs to be had in Chicago itself, but fifteen minutes away from Winnetka by car, in Northbrook, his brother, Jerry, under the name Jerry W. Ryan, was working as a golf-course attendant.

Ray had been at the restaurant two days when Mrs. Harvey Klingeman, the owner, learned that he had kitchen experience. She promoted him to the steam table, where he worked uncomplainingly in the hottest, most uncomfortable part of the kitchen, filling orders hour after hour. She raised his salary twice in ten days. He was a model employee, he kept to himself, spoke to no one except to exchange greetings, and appeared each morning, promptly on time, a bundle of newspapers under his arm. When lunchtime came, he ate alone, his nose buried in one of the papers.

After three weeks Ray bought a 1959 Chrysler for two hundred dollars. One night a waitress asked if he would drive her home—they were going in the same direction. She said later, "He was a gentleman in every way." She had joshed him for not being married—"A young, handsome man like yourself," and he had said awkwardly, "I don't have anything to do with girls—they don't like me." But everyone seemed to like him at the Indian Trail Restaurant.

He quit his job Saturday, June 24, asking that his final check be sent to a friend, Jerry W. Ryan. The two brothers had seen each other frequently, and Jerry had even visited him at the restaurant, knocking on the back door of the kitchen to call him outside where they spoke together.

While in Chicago, Ray had written to the Canadian consul asking how he could immigrate to Canada. Before going there, he spent some time in the St. Louis-Quincy area, where many of his family lived: John in St. Louis, his sister, Carol, in a St. Louis suburb, his sister Melba in Quincy, and his father in Center, Missouri, forty miles from Quincy.

Beasley and Dwyer kept their microscope on Ray's activities:

Friday, July 14. Sold Chrysler for forty-five dollars, after it broke down, bought 1962 Plymouth at the Bundy Olds Company, East St. Louis, for two hundred dollars, under name John L. Rayns.

Monday, July 17. Drove to Montreal. Registered as John L. Rayns at the Bourgarde Motel.

Tuesday, July 18. As Eric Starvo Galt—his first use of this name— leased a seventy-five-dollar-a-month apartment at the Har-K Apartments, 2589 Notre Dame Avenue, East, Montreal. Told proprietor he worked for Expo 67.

Tuesday, July 18. Robbed Montreal supermarket, obtaining $1700.

Wednesday, July 19. Bought suit, sports attire, haberdashery, swim suit, underwear at Tip-Top Tailors, Montreal. Cost, two hundred dollars.

Friday, July 21. Ordered suit (sixty-nine dollars) from English & Scotch Woolen Company, Ltd., tailors, Montreal. This was in preparation for a week's vacation at a resort where he hoped to pick up a Canadian woman who might act as a guarantor for his passport application.

Monday, July 24. Purchased Canadian money order for nine dollars, payable to Futura Books, Inc., Inglewood, California. This was for the purchase of three sex manuals advertised in a man's magazine. One ad read:

"Dr. Kelly: A Sex Manual. Valuable for three reasons. One, it covers the entire subject of sex in marriage. Two, male and female reproductive organs; sex impulse in men vs. women; masturbation in and out of marriage; precoital stimulation; problems of sexuality; frustrated wives with case histories; sex myths; aids to penetration; oral eroticism; enlarging the penis to a maximum; assistance in overcoming premature ejaculation, etc. Original drawings."

Friday, July 28. Purchased Canadian money order for $17.50 payable to Locksmithing Institute, Plainfield, N.J. This was sent with his application as his first payment on his mail-order course.

Sunday, July 30. Left for Gray Rocks Inn, resort hotel in the nearby Laurentians, recommended by a travel bureau. Here, according to account he gave Hanes and Huie, the night before his week ended he met a Canadian divorcée from Ottawa and spent the night with her. When he learned she had a Government job, he gave up the idea of asking her to help him get a passport.

Monday, August 7. Left Gray Rocks Inn. Paid bill of $195.

Tuesday, August 15. Tried on suit at English & Scotch Woolen Company.

Friday, August 18, to Sunday, August 20; at Town & Country Hotel, Ottawa, with woman he met at Gray Rocks Inn.

Friday, August 25. In Chicago. Transferred his 1962 Plymouth to Jerry W. Ryan, otherwise Jerry Ray, his brother. Dwyer and Beasley noted this contact with his brother—one of many.

Saturday, August 26. In Birmingham, where he rented room, two meals included, for $22.50 per week, at Economy Grill & Rooms.

Ray's seven weeks in Birmingham followed the same picaresque pattern. He signed up for five Tuesday-night dancing lesssons at ten dollars for the course. The dance instructors remembered him as a silent, shy man who had nothing to do with other students and, when the music stopped, sat by himself in a corner. He bought his white Mustang and obtained his driver's license. He continued his locksmithing correspondence: he bought camera equipment—photography was one of his interests. He rented a safe deposit box, which he visited four times, each time for less than six minutes. He told Huie he got it "to hide my Rayns ID in," because he was now Galt and dared not to be found with any identification that could be traced back to Ray, the escaped convict.

On October 7, Ray drove from Birmingham to Mexico. He spent the next five weeks there. He had made money in Mexico before, smuggling contraband. A study of his Mexican stay was significant for three reasons: an anti-Negro episode; then, evidence that he was indeed smuggling marijuana and other items; and, third, indication that he was moving about as the spirit moved him, with no specific plan in mind.

On October 10 he arrived in Acapulco but remained only a few days because it was so expensive. "Everybody had their hand out," he complained later. He was in Guadalajara Sunday, October 15, treating a toothache, and arrived in Puerto Vallarta, a fishing village that became a tourist attraction after Elizabeth Taylor and Richard Burton filmed *Night of the Iguana* there. He checked in on Thursday, October 19, at the Rio Hotel, taking a $4.80-a-day single room. In the registry he wrote his profession: publisher's assistant. He had a portable typewriter with him that he had gotten by trading in his TV at a pawnshop before entering Mexico.

That evening he wandered into the Casa Suzanna, a night club and brothel, where he met a prostitute who called herself "La Chilindrina"—"The Little Trifle." He introduced himself as Eric Starvo Galt, an American writer on vacation, and spent the next several nights with her in her room on the second floor.

The following Wednesday night Irma, one of the girls in the place, observed him arrive at his usual time, around nine o'clock. By now he was an object of some interest to the girls. He was the American from Alabama who drove a racy white American sports car, which gave him a cachet of wealth to add to his importance as a literary figure.

He looked around the room for La Chilindrina, but she had gone out of town for a week. Disappointed, he invited Irma to join him for a drink. He spent that night with her in her room.

He and Irma hit it off well. He dropped in each night about the same time. They would drink together—beer and later gin—and then about midnight adjourn to her room. She told police she slept with him every night from the night they met. As far as Beasley and Dwyer could determine, this was the first really sustained intimate relationship Ray had had with any woman since his escape. As they followed his days and nights in Mexico, it was clear that he was coasting, living an aimless, relaxed life, indulging himself in women, sunning himself on the beach, making various trips to buy marijuana. He slept late each day, lunching around three o'clock at the same place— the Discothèque Café—on hamburger and Pepsi. In the first week he ordered green chili peppers with his hamburger, but later told the waiter he had been having stomach pains and a doctor warned him against hot peppers.

Irma was impressed by him, as was Rodi, the bartender at the Casa Suzanna, and they became a threesome. One Sunday he invited them to drive to nearby Mismaloya Beach, where the Taylor-Burton picture had actually been filmed. They swam, drank beer, had a seafood lunch, and then drove back to Puerto Vallarta.

Halfway home Galt stopped his car and took a Polaroid camera from the trunk. He explained that he had two shots left on the roll and wanted to photograph Irma. He asked her to sit behind the wheel, her skirts up, so that she was exposed. She fell in with the spirit of the thing, giggling—who was to know what this strange American wanted next?—so methodical in his ways, spending a hundred pesos, eight dollars, a night—no more—for their drinks, and a hundred pesos a night—no more—for her favors; and she allowed him to do as he wished. The snapshot turned out badly. He cursed under his breath and tore it up. They resumed driving. Ten minutes later he stopped again, and again photographed her according to his directions. And again, annoyed with the result, he tore it up.

Next day, Monday, he appeared at the club late. They sat together drinking, silently—there was not much they could say to each other, because her English was as bad as his Spanish—when they became aware of a noisy table nearby. Six men—four black and two white—were sitting there, laughing uproariously. Irma thought they were American sailors from a yacht that had docked in the harbor that afternoon. One black man was quite tall, a second fat, very drunk, and very loud.

Galt became angry. "I hate Niggers," he exclaimed. As Irma put it, "He said many insulting things about them." As the minutes passed, he grew angrier. She had never seen him like this, for he seemed a mild, agreeable man, though he complained constantly of headaches and tiredness. Suddenly he sprang to his feet, strode to the other table, and spoke vehemently to the fat Negro, then came back and sat at her side, muttering under his breath. Irma was extremely uncomfortable. Those at the other table stared at Galt.

Again, suddenly, Galt rose and left the room, to return about three minutes later, and sit down beside her, very grim. "Where did you go?" she asked. "To my car," he said. "Feel my pocket." She did so—he had come back with the small revolver he always carried under his seat in his car. "I'm going to kill them," he said.

At this point the tall black man approached them and spoke to Galt. Irma did not understand English well enough to know what he said. His manner suggested an attempt to soothe Galt. But Galt replied angrily. The other shrugged his shoulders, returned to his table, took his fat companion by the arm, and led him out of the place.

"Eric wanted to follow them with his pistol," Irma told the police. "But I said no, no—it is nearly ten o'clock, the police always visit us at this hour—you will be in great trouble." Galt immediately subsided, muttering something about, "I don't want anything to do with the police."

Irma did not know he was smuggling marijuana. He had devised an ingenious method of transporting contraband. He had used it before with jewels, stolen in the United States, which he would take into Mexico. On his second day in Mexico he bought a tubeless tire and an inner tube, cut a hole in the tube, dropped the jewels into the tube, then placed it into the tire. It would be invisible there. He used a slightly different method in transporting marijuana. He could stuff as much as seven pounds of loose marijuana into a tubeless tire, then place an inner tube in it, inflate it so that it held the marijuana against the inside of the tire, and place the whole on the back of his car as a spare. If customs officials should shake it, they would hear nothing.

On Friday, November 3, Galt showed up drunk at the Casa Suzanna. Irma had not seen him this intoxicated before. A photographer asked to snap them together. Galt shook his head, but Irma insisted, so Galt drunkenly put on his sunglasses and permitted the picture to be taken. Then he wanted to go to her room with her. She refused. "I do not go to bed with drunken men," she said, and left him. Galt remained at the table, drinking morosely.

She did not see him again until Monday night. He was quite sober and hurt because she had rejected him Friday. "I want to talk to you," he said, and the tone of his voice caught her attention and she sat down.

Galt, she said, asked her to marry him. She said no. She liked him but did not wish to marry. He tugged at his ear unhappily. He had been thinking of settling down in Mexico. He and Rodi, the bartender, had driven out to see a plot of land that Rodi owned. Rodi had wanted to trade it for the white Mustang. Galt had finally decided against the deal. He said to Irma that if she would not marry him he would begin to take out other girls. She was sympathetic but firm. He could do whatever he wished.

He left her table and approached La Chilindrina, who had returned some days before. No, she would not drink with him. "You better stay with Irma," she told him. Galt said, bitterly, "I'm finished with Irma," and walked out.

He moved from the Hotel Rio to the Hotel Tropicana, and began visiting the bar of the Hotel Oceana, where he struck up a friendship with Luis García, the bartender, telling him that he was a professional soldier who had come to Mexico to take it easy after nearly twenty years in the service.

Two or three times when García was finished with his duties, the two men went out, making the rounds of the night clubs. One evening, after watching the floor show at the Posada Vallarta, the town's best-known hotel, as they were driving away they saw a girl waiting at a bus stop. It was Alicia, a divorcée, who worked as a cigarette girl and photographer's aide at the hotel. The two men offered her a lift. On the way the three stopped to visit another night club—Los Lobos —where Galt drank too much, became ill, and had to go out and sit in his car until he felt better. Later he dropped García at his home and drove Alicia to her apartment.

Now she became his girl. Galt was interested in photography, she told police, and they went often to the beach, photographing each other. They spent their nights together—usually at the Hotel Las Glorias, on the road to the airport—because she could not take him to her apartment because of her children. Once more Galt tried to establish a permanent relationship with a woman. He told Alicia he was buying marijuana on his weekend trips to Yalapa, a nearby resort, and wanted her to help him. He would take her on his next trip. But first he gave her six hundred pesos—forty-eight dollars—to rent an apartment for them. Instead Alicia used the money to take her children with her on a trip to Guadalajara. Before she left she asked the bartender at the Posada Vallarta to write a note for her to the American writer.

When Galt showed up to meet her that night at the bar, he was given the note. In it Alicia begged his forgiveness for using the money for other purposes. She could not see him again. As she was to say later, she wanted nothing to do with marijuana.

A week later Galt was en route to Los Angeles.

In his spare tire he carried a full load of marijuana.

CHAPTER XXVIII

Of all the periods under scrutiny by Beasley and Dwyer, two would become all important. The first would be Ray's stay in Los Angeles from November 18, 1967, to March 17, 1968, when he left to drive south—ultimately to Memphis. The second would be the period immediately after King's death in Memphis on April 4, when Ray fled to Canada and then to England.

They concentrated on Los Angeles.

They were fascinated to observe how the man operated here—secretive, self-effacing, always trying to find a base upon which to exist. As nothing in his first months after his escape pointed to any lurking intention to assassinate Dr. King, so nothing in his first months in Los Angeles gave any such indication. Only later was a plan to show itself. His life in Los Angeles began as a continuation of Mexico—drifting, unhurried, living a make-believe life, this time not as a writer or editor but as an American businessman who after several years operating a bar in Mexico had just sold it to his Mexican partner and was now back in the States, looking around for what he might do.

In his first weeks in Los Angeles he tried to get a job. He installed a telephone in his apartment and placed two ads in the Los Angeles *Times*—one looking for restaurant work, the other for general labor. Although he received several calls, in each instance the employer required police clearance or Social Security identification, and Ray had none for the name Eric Starvo Galt.

He applied for several jobs advertised in the newspapers, but here again the lack of Social Security frustrated him. He tried to get a position as a maintenance man in a resort at Big Bear, California, as a vacuum cleaner salesman in Los Angeles: these all fell through. So did a try at the merchant marine.

Meanwhile, he was taking dancing lessons—if he found himself in a Spanish-speaking country, a knowledge of dancing would help him with women. He was also taking bartending lessons, because a job as bartender required only a skeleton knowledge of the language.

None of these attempts to get a job, as Beasley and Dwyer noted, suggested that this was a man assigned to carry out an assassination a short time later. What the two men in Memphis did discover was that Ray lied later when he asserted that it was in response to a summons from the mysterious Raoul that he drove down to New Orleans with Charlie Stein on December 15.

This revelation came through an oddly oblique fact. Ray had obtained his telephone, interestingly enough, by claiming that he was a worker in the campaign to put George Wallace on the California state ticket. It was difficult to obtain telephones, and he counted on the fact that the telephone company would act quickly lest it be accused of discriminating against Wallace supporters. His first call was to a Dr. Mark O. Freeman, a clinical psychologist. It was made at 10 A.M., Monday, November 27, the morning the phone was installed. According to Dr. Freeman's diary, the call came from a "James Earl Ray, who wanted to overcome his shyness, gain social confidence and learn self-hypnosis so he could relax, sleep and remember things better."* When the name Ray appeared, FBI agents were incredulous. He had not used his true name since his escape. Obviously, Beasley and Dwyer agreed, Ray feared that the psychologist would hypnotize him and learn it anyway.

Ray had come to see Dr. Freeman at 5 P.M. that afternoon, diffident, neatly dressed, his dark hair combed into place. He said he was single, came from East St. Louis (again the truth), was born March 10, 1928 (again the truth), had worked as a cook on a Mississippi river steamer but quit because he didn't like it (not the truth, but not important, either).

Dr. Freeman found him in excellent health: no indication of being psychotic or having any special neuroses. "I thought he was rather young and immature for his age," Dr. Freeman said: his attitude toward hypnosis was really naïve. "He actually thought you could go around looking people in the eye and hypnotize them and make them do whatever you wanted them to do."

Ray had visited him five times, an hour's session each time, at three- or four-day intervals. He saw Dr. Freeman on Thursday, December 14, from 10 to 11 A.M., and left after making an appointment to see him the following Monday at 3 P.M. But on Friday morning he telephoned Dr. Freeman to say he was going out of town and had to cancel Monday's appointment.

---

* By the time Willard had been identified as Galt and the various leads tracked down, including the Los Angeles telephone calls, the FBI knew that Galt was Ray. Had the trails been followed in a different order, they might have reached Dr. Freeman sooner and so have discovered Galt's identity sooner.

This was significant. It meant that when Ray left Dr. Freeman at 11 A.M. Thursday, he expected to see him again the following Monday. But Thursday night he met Marie Martin's cousin, Rita, and Charlie Stein, and they asked him then if he could drive to New Orleans the next morning, Friday, and he had agreed. Before picking them up Friday morning he had made his call to Dr. Freeman, canceling Monday's appointment.

If Raoul had written him days before to drive down to New Orleans on Friday, the fifteenth, why would Ray have made an appointment to see Dr. Freeman on the following Monday? He would have known then that he would be in New Orleans on Monday. This meant, simply, that Raoul had not written him.*

It was also interesting to learn that, when Ray had signed up on January 19 for his six-week bartending course, he had to pay a non-returnable cash advance of $125. If during his Los Angeles period he was, as he said, waiting for a summons at any time from Raoul, would Ray, not a generous man with money, have paid $125 in advance for a course that would require him to remain in Los Angeles the next month and a half?

Despite what Dr. Freeman had told him that one could not hypnotize a subject by looking at him, Ray continued to be deeply intrigued by hypnotism—particularly self-hypnosis. On January 4, he visited Rev. Xavier von Koss, director of the International Society of Hypnosis. Ray knew that salesmen, seeking to improve their memory, their ability to influence prospects, sometimes turned to hypnosis. It was the Rev. Koss, it was now learned, who had recommended to him the three books on hypnosis found in his luggage in London.

Ray's delving into hypnosis was not the only revealing aspect of the man to be uncovered in Los Angeles. The trail of money orders he always left behind indicated what else he had been doing on the West Coast beside taking dancing and bartending lessons and courting Marie Martin.

The outline of a new concern began to show itself in late January: suddenly his appearance became important. He began taking measures to record his appearance, to circulate it, and after circulating it, to change it.

His first step was to take a number of profile shots of himself, with

* Friday morning, before driving with Charlie Stein to New Orleans, Ray also telephoned the National Dance Studio to say he would be out of town—additional proof that he did not know until Thursday night, and his meeting with the Steins, that he was going on the trip.

his Polaroid. He selected one and had nearly a dozen copies made of it. He would use these to send out.

Then he subscribed on January 28 to a mail-telephone service called Hedgepath, costing one dollar a month. He sent out an ad to the Los Angeles *Free Press*, an underground newspaper Marie had introduced him to. The ad would have astonished her, coming from the blushing Mr. Galt:

> SINGLE, MALE, cauc. 36 yrs. 5'11. 170 lbs. Digs Fr. Cult.* Desires discreet meeting with passionate married female for mutual enjoyment and/or female for swing session. Apt furnished. Will ex photo. Write Eric S.

He gave the Hedgepath address and telephone number.

Two weeks later he answered an ad by *Swinger*, a correspondence club, which offered the names and addresses of six girls for one dollar. He wrote them, sending each a copy of his photograph. Three days later he answered another ad, sending a letter to a girl who advertised in the *Swinger*, prepared to forward his photograph to her, too. It read:

> Dear Miss: I am answering your listing in the local Swinger since I think I share most of your interests, with emphasis on Fr. Cult. And swing sessions. I've just returned from Mexico after five yrs and the few females I've met don't go for the swing parties & it takes two to swing. The same routine gets boring, don't you think? Will close till I hear from you. 5'11. I'll be 36 yrs.

In February, Ray sent off money orders for a pair of Japanese handcuffs and for sex manuals similar to those he had ordered when he had been in Canada. He also ordered a chemical substance which turned ordinary plate glass into a two-way mirror. This, with his interest in hypnotism and photography, and the relationships he sought with "swingers" could suggest endless bizarre and pornographic enterprises. Nonetheless, Beasley and Dwyer suspected that all these were secondary to a grand plan that had been slowly forming in his mind.

Now came an unusual and unexpected act—part of that plan.

On March 5 Ray visited Dr. Russell C. Hadley, a plastic surgeon in Hollywood—he had written the California Medical Association for a

* French culture.

recommendation, and Hadley's was one of several names given him—
and had the tip of his nose removed. When he got back to his apartment and while his nose was still numb from the anesthetic, he tried
to push the bridge to one side. Then, on March 17, bringing to a close
this curious period, Ray filed a change-of-address card to general delivery, Atlanta, Georgia—the home of Dr. Martin Luther King, Jr. Dr.
King that day preached in Los Angeles, before flying south, as the
newspapers reported.

On St. Valentine's Day Ray had exchanged his console TV for
Marie's portable set. Now he told her he was going off again. "To
New Orleans?" she asked. Yes, he said. Would he drop off a bundle of
clothes for her daughter there? He agreed to do so.

He drove to New Orleans, dropped off the package, then went on
to Selma, Alabama, where he spent the night of March 22 in the Flamingo Motel. Dr. King, visiting Marx and other nearby towns in behalf of his Poor People's Campaign, had been scheduled to be in
Selma March 22. Instead, he stopped in Camden, Alabama, thirty
miles away. On Sunday, March 24, Galt drove his white Mustang
into the yard of Garner's rooming house in Atlanta, in the heart of
the hippie neighborhood, and took a room there. He had a map of
Atlanta. On it he circled Dr. King's home, his church, his office at
SCLC headquarters. On Wednesday, March 27, he was in the Gun
Rack, in Birmingham, asking Clyde Manasco about hunting rifles
and the speed and drop of bullets; on the twenty-ninth, he was in the
Long-Lewis Hardware Store in Bessemer, just outside Birmingham,
asking similar questions of John Kopp, manager of the firearms de-
partment; and later that day he walked into the Aeromarine Supply
Company, in Birmingham, and bought a Remington .243 while John
DeShazo, a customer, leaning against the counter, watched him and
later engaged him in conversation. The next morning he exchanged
the .243 for a Remington 30.06—the same rifle that was dropped, with
other evidence, in the doorway of Canipe's Amusement Company on
South Main Street, Memphis, minutes after Dr. Martin Luther King,
Jr., was fatally shot on Thursday, April 4, 1968.

Ninety-six hours later Ray was in Toronto, to begin the two
months and two days of flight that would end in London on June 8
at Heathrow Airport.

It was clear to Beasley and Dwyer, as they studied Ray in this last
lap of their examination, searching constantly for the stranger's hand,
if any, that from the moment he arrived in Toronto he had one goal:

to assume the identity of a native Canadian, obtain a passport in that person's name, and go abroad, either to Rhodesia or Portuguese Angola or some preferably English-speaking country where he would be safe. Long before the plan to kill King took shape, Ray had given Rhodesia serious consideration. He liked the country. He had told his brother John when the latter visited him the day before his escape in April 1967 that he liked what Ian Smith was doing there, keeping the blacks in their place. He had written as recently as December 28 to a Rhodesian organization in Washington, D.C., asking how he could emigrate there.

His first act in Toronto was to find a room. No longer Eric Starvo Galt—he had doffed that identity when he abandoned the white Mustang—on Monday, April 8, he rapped on the door of 102 Ossington Avenue, W., in an area where many foreign born lived. A sign in the window read ROOMS TO LET. Here Mrs. Feliksa Szpakowski lived with her husband, Adam, and their nine-year-old daughter, Lydia. Ray chose a front room, with three bay windows overlooking Ossington Avenue. It cost ten dollars, it had a tinted painting of Jesus on the wall, an embroidered doily reading, "Home Sweet Home," and an old console TV in the corner.

When Dwyer, Beasley, and Carlisle called on her, in the course of their investigation, she remembered him as a good tenant. Like Mrs. Brewer in Memphis, she had wondered what so genteel-appearing a man was doing in her neighborhood. He had told her he was a real-estate salesman, but he kept mainly to his room the first days. Later in the week he began to go out. He would leave in the morning and bob his head respectfully if he passed her in the kitchen. Once, glancing out the window, she saw him walking to the nearby corner of Dundas and Ossington and wait for a trolley which went into downtown Toronto. He usually returned around lunchtime, then went out again, coming back after dinner.

She thought about him because he kept so quietly to himself. He had no visitors, he was always alone, always watching TV after dinner—she would hear the set when she passed his room with its closed door—and he read enormous numbers of newspapers. She would find them on the floor next to the bed when she came in to clean up. He ate in his room, too. She would find the cellophane wrappings of sandwiches, the plastic envelopes that had contained frozen vegetables which could be made ready for the table by being dropped into boiling water, and crumbs from the little pastries he had bought. Mrs. Szpakowski, herself an immigrant from Poland a decade before, thought it a forlorn life for one born in the New World. He looked troubled and she felt sorry for him, wondering if he could be worrying about his family. He had not given his name, and she had not asked for it because she never got American names right.

Ray had a plan to carry out in Toronto. On Monday he had visited the Central Branch of the Toronto Public Library and sat before a viewing machine (the attendant would thread the reel for him) glancing through microfilm copies of Toronto newspapers of thirty-six years ago, seeking names of men born in Toronto whose names (and birth certificates) he might use to get a passport. He knew he could pass for thirty-six instead of forty, so he looked through the birth statistics for 1932 instead of 1928. These listed birth date, father's name, and mother's maiden name—the only data required to obtain a duplicate copy of one's birth certificate. Ray wrote down several names, deliberately avoiding popular names, then checked the Toronto telephone directory for them. Among those now living in Toronto were two: Paul Edward Bridgman and Ramon George Sneyd. Both lived in the same section—Scarborough.

Ray loitered near their homes to catch a glimpse of them as they left for work each morning. Their general appearance had to be similar to his. If Bridgman, or Sneyd, turned out to be black, or short or fat, or bald, or crippled, he could be trapped if a clerk tried to check up on him. He had to be sure that a quick description over the telephone would encompass him. This meant a man of medium build, neither too fat nor too lean, about five feet nine to five feet eleven, with dark hair and generally aquiline features. Both men, he found, fit the bill. This coincidence was to be made much of, later; although on reflection, one would realize that, given a dozen Anglo-Saxon men in their middle thirties, most of them would meet such a general description.

Then on Wednesday, April 10, he wrote to the Registrar of Births in Ottawa, painstakingly printing the words and keeping his request free of all unnecessary information:

DEAR SIR: INCLOSED IS $2. FOR BIRTH CERTIFICATE. NAME: PAUL EDWARD BRIDGMAN, BORN, ONT. NOV. 10, 1932. FATHER, EDWARD G. B. BRIDGMAN: MOTHER, MAIDEN NAME, EVELYN GODDEN. THANKS, PAUL EDWARD BRIDGMAN, 102 OSSINGTON AVE., TORONTO, CAN. ONT.

The next day at noon he had passport photos taken at the Arcade Photo Studio, giving his name as Paul Bridgman. Mrs. Mabel Agnew, the manager, remembered him because he would not smile, but stared sternly through his shell-rimmed glasses into the camera.

Before he applied for a passport in Bridgman's name, he had to be sure that the man had not applied for one himself. If so, it would be on file, with his photograph, and Ray's deception would be immediately found out. Getting Bridgman on the phone—he turned out to be a teaching consultant with the Toronto Board of Education—Ray said he was with the Passport Division and wanted to know when Bridgman had last applied for a passport. "About eight years ago," Bridgman said. Why? Ray had to carry through to allay suspicion. He gave Bridgman's birth date and his parents' names, and although he had his father's middle initial wrong, the call sounded authentic, and Bridgman assumed there was, as Ray explained, a clerical mixup which he was straightening out.

But if Ray could not use Bridgman's name for a passport, he had other uses for it.

Again posing as a Passport Division employee, he telephoned Sneyd and learned that he had never had a passport. Now he had an identity he could use.

On April 16 he wrote to the registrar for Sneyd's birth certificate. As in the first note, he misspelled "Enclosed," but he changed the language slightly:

DEAR SIR: INCLOSED IS M.O. FOR TWO DOLLARS. WOULD YOU PLEASE SEND BIRTH CERTIFICATE, NAME RAMON GEORGE SNEYD, BORN OCTOBER 8, 1932. FATHER'S NAME GEORGE SNEYD, MOTHER'S NAME, MAIDEN, GLADYS MAE KILMER. THANKS. RAMON GEORGE SNEYD, 962 DUNDAS ST., W. TORONTO, ONT.

Ray could give a new address because earlier that day he had walked five blocks down Dundas to No. 962, put on his shell-rimmed glasses, and rented a room from Mrs. Sun Fung Loo. Mrs. Loo knew even less English than Mrs. Szpakowski. Ray paid her nine dollars— a week's rent in advance—and wrote "Ramon George Sneyd" on a slip of paper, pronouncing it for her several times, explaining that calls might come for him. He tried to make her understand that he was a night worker at a hospital. It was difficult because she moved busily about her kitchen with her newest baby strapped on her back while two other small children played at her feet. Ray expected to receive Sneyd's passport at Mrs. Loo's.

Now he had a place to hide out during the day without arousing comment. He would spend days at Mrs. Loo's, nights at Mrs.

Szpakowski's. Neither woman was likely to gossip about him. He had understood that, to get a passport, he had to appear at the passport bureau bringing his birth certificate and also producing a Canadian citizen who would swear he had known him at least two years. It was his plan to apply for a passport as bespectacled Ramon George Sneyd, submitting the photos he had just had taken. Then he would disguise himself by removing the glasses and using theatrical makeup (he had even considered a toupee when he was on the West Coast: Polaroid photographs of him with a hairpiece would certainly confuse the FBI) and show up again at the passport bureau as Paul Bridgman, Sneyd's friend and witness. It would be dangerous, but it had to be done, and he would go, if possible, to another clerk.

This was on his mind when he walked into the Kennedy Travel Bureau on Bloor Street on April 16—the same day he had taken the room at Mrs. Loo's—and told Lillian M. Spencer, the manager, that he would like to buy a round-trip ticket to London—a twenty-one-day excursion ticket, which was the cheapest. Had he his passport, she asked? Not yet, Ray said. Before he could add that he was about to apply for one, she said she would be glad to obtain it for him. This placed Ray in a dilemma. He could not very well stand before Miss Spencer as Sneyd, and return later, however well disguised, and claim to be Bridgman. So he said unhappily that though he had been born in Toronto, he'd been away for years, and came back only three weeks ago; he did not know if he could find anyone to vouch for him. Miss Spencer solved that, too. He had only to fill out a "Statutory Declaration in Lieu of Guarantor," swearing that he was born in Canada, and that there was no one in Toronto who knew him well enough to vouch for him because he had been in the city only three weeks. This would be notarized on the spot by her boss, Mr. Henry Moos, and mailed out next morning to Ottawa with his application and photos. If he came back in about two weeks, the passport would be ready. When did he plan to go to London?

Ray chose Monday, May 6. Miss Spencer called up and booked him on BOAC Flight 600 to London that day. When he returned to pick up his passport, she'd have his ticket, too. All he had to do now was to be vaccinated.

Greatly relieved, Ray filled out his passport application. He listed his occupation as hospital worker; the person to call in case of emergency, Mr. Paul Bridgman, 102 Ossington Avenue, W., Toronto. The top of the form had a section divided into small blank squares, one for each letter of his name. Ray filled these in with his ball-point pen—the first line of blanks for his given name, the second for his middle name and the third for his last—printing in block letters, as he always did. But he did not quite complete the bottom of the D in Sneyd, so that that letter, placed directly in the center of its small square, looked like an A. Though he signed his name at the bottom, Ramon George Sneyd, the name as printed could be read: RAMON GEORGE SNEYA.

Two days later, Thursday evening, April 18, Mrs. Szpakowski saw on the front page of the Toronto *Star* a large photograph that was vaguely familiar. Above it was the headline: FBI SAYS THERE WAS CONSPIRACY—MYSTERIOUS SEAMAN SOUGHT IN KING DEATH. Under it was the name, Eric Starvo Galt. The photo resembled her tenant for whom she felt so sorry. She told her husband about it. He laughed and said, "You're crazy."

Next morning Bridgman was gone. She found his key on the hall table and the room empty. But there on his bed was the same newspaper she had seen the night before—*open to the same photograph.* It sent a chill through her. When her husband came home, she said, nervously, "Maybe we ought to call the police." No, no, no, said her husband; and because in Europe one feared the police, and never got involved with them, she did nothing. But she recalled that a few days earlier a letter came addressed for Paul E. Bridgman. By this time she knew it was his name—he had written it down for her but she had paid little attention to it. She had told him about the letter on the table the next morning, but he had not picked it up. Now he was gone, the letter was still there. She finally gave it to the mailman.

Ray had of course moved to his room at Mrs. Loo's. As Beasley and Dwyer reconstructed it, he knew that the letter—it had a return address, 70 Lombard Street, which was the Bureau of Vital Statistics —contained the Bridgman birth certificate, that the calls most likely were from the Registrar's office, checking his name and address as Bridgman. But he no longer needed the Bridgman identification.

Now, in his daytime hideout in the home of his Chinese landlady, her husband, and their three small children, where English was hardly understood and newspapers, full of the hunt for Eric Starvo Galt, now identified as James Earl Ray, were no threat, he could wait for his passport and tickets.

But he needed money, and on Tuesday, April 23, he ventured out to look over Loblaw's Groceteria, a few blocks from Mrs. Loo's, only to be surprised in the rear, talk his way out of danger by claiming to be looking for a job, and finally be forced to make a humiliating getaway when the manager became suspicious.

He emerged again on Monday, April 29, to be vaccinated, and again on May 2 when he telephoned the Kennedy Travel Bureau, learned that his passport and tickets had arrived, and went there to pick them up. The passport was made out in the name of Ramon George Sneya. He decided to do nothing about it until he got abroad. He had one bad scare. He was in his second-floor room after returning from the travel bureau when Mrs. Loo called up to him from the foot of the stairs. A man was at the front door with a letter, asking for him. Ray would not come down: she had to come up. As she later described the scene to Dwyer, Beasley, and Carlisle, Ray's face went white: he seemed almost to tremble. Was she sure the man asked for Mr. Sneyd? What did he look like? She could only say he was a white man, he was in shirt sleeves, and he had a letter in his hand and he had clearly asked, "Is Mr. Sneyd in?" Ray refused to go downstairs and Mrs. Loo had to go down to say Mr. Sneyd was not in. The stranger did his best to explain that he found the letter, addressed to Sneyd, in a telephone booth half a block away, saw that it was opened, and, since he was so near, had returned it. She took the letter, thanked the man, and he left. Then she brought it up to Ray, who accepted it, enormously relieved. It was the envelope containing the Sneyd birth certificate. He had left it in the booth when he called the travel bureau earlier that morning.

Early Monday, May 6, Mrs. Loo found that her tenant had left. In his room was a small blue overnight bag. It held a metal strong box, six rolls of film bought in Toronto, a light meter, a jar of cold cream, a box of Band-Aids, gas station maps of Toronto, Montreal, and Canada, and three sex magazines that had been bought at a back-issue shop at cut rates—the reduced prices scrawled in black crayon on them.

Mrs. Loo put it all aside. Later, when the hue and cry broke, she took the stuff to police headquarters.

Meanwhile Ray, as Sneyd, flew to London. Aboard the plane he sat alone during the entire flight, speaking to no one. He arrived at 6:40 A.M. Tuesday. He loitered about the airport all day until he boarded a Lisbon plane at 10:55 that night, turning in the return portion of his excursion ticket for the tourist seat to Lisbon. The girl gave him a refund of about fourteen dollars and asked curiously, "How will you get back to Toronto?" Ray said, "I'll worry about that when the time comes." Again, he sat alone during the two-and-a-half-hour flight, arriving after 1 A.M. and finding his way to a third-class Lisbon hotel—the Portugal—where he was to stay for the next ten days in a back room at $1.80 a day.

Lisbon was a recruiting center for white mercenaries, and Ray sought a way to get to Africa. He had no luck. He looked for a ship to take him to Portuguese Angola, but he found one only after his eighth day, and when he tried to get a visa, he was told that would take another week; by then the ship would have sailed and he would have to wait around once more.

Perhaps, thought Beasley and Dwyer, he had come to Lisbon for a payoff. But nothing in Ray's lonely stay there could substantiate this. As in Canada, he was always by himself: no hand ever came out of the darkness toward him. The day and night clerks at the Portugal assumed he was another tourist—the man slept late, remained in his room most of the day, stayed out late, and twice tried to bring a girl to his room. When he was told this was forbidden in Portugal, he left with her and stayed out all night. He was unfriendly, never seen with a man, had no visitors, neither made nor received telephone calls, never used room service, and never tipped. The desk clerk remembered him particularly because "he walked around with his head down"—never looking anyone in the face. He visited the nearby Vienna Bar, where he sat alone, drinking beer. About midnight he would move to the Bolero, or the Bar Bohemia—all sailors' hangouts —and sit there for an hour or two, drinking beer, talking to no one. Ray, whether in a bar in Los Angeles, or Birmingham, or Atlanta, or New Orleans, or Toronto, or Montreal, or Lisbon, was always the same: always by himself. At Maxim's night club he picked up a prostitute named Gloria. She told police she spent four nights with him. What struck her was his obsession with newspapers. He bought every British and American paper he could get. She could not know he was following the international manhunt for James Earl Ray. She learned little about him. As she put it, "He could speak no Portuguese, I could speak no English, so we spoke the international language of love."

He tried various airlines. The South African Airways office gave him a timetable, but it was frustrating. He visited the South African Embassy. He asked here, too, about going to Angola to join the mercenaries, but was told no foreigner could get in without Government permission. Biafra, which had broken away from Nigeria, had an unofficial legation in Lisbon: he went there but nothing came of it.

Ray was growing short of money. If he had more money, he could wait it out until he received his visa and found another ship, if not to Angola, then somewhere else. He had his snub-nosed .38, but to attempt a holdup in a strange country whose language he did not know, whose currency confused him, made no sense. He decided to return to London. When he had passed through customs at Lisbon's Portela Airport and signed his entry card Sneyd but showed a passport with the name Sneya, he had been warned to have it corrected: he might have trouble. They advised him to go to the Canadian Embassy in Lisbon, and on Wednesday he went there. No, they had no power to correct the name, Mrs. Manuela Lopez, the consular clerk said, but if he had his birth certificate, they could cancel the passport and give him a new, corrected one. He would have to keep the canceled one with him, too, because that had the stamp showing his legal entry into Portugal. "How long will it take to get a new one?" he asked impatiently. "I'm only here for a day or so. I don't want to wait around all week for it." Mrs. Lopez helped him fill out the necessary forms and he got his new passport the next day. On Friday, May 17, he flew back to London, checking into the inexpensive Heathfield House Hotel, in an area known as "Kangaroo Valley," because so many Australians lived there.

Early Tuesday afternoon, June 4, Ian Colvin, an editorial writer on the London *Daily Telegraph*, found a note in his typewriter: "A Mr. Sneyd called, will call later." At 5 P.M. his telephone rang. "This is Ramon Sneyd," said a nervous voice. He was a Canadian, he had read Colvin's articles about mercenaries in Africa—particularly about a Major Alistair Wicks, who could put one in touch with those recruiting mercenaries for the Congo. Could he have Major Wicks's telephone number? His brother was fighting with the mercenaries in Angola and had been reported missing. Perhaps the major might help him locate him.

Colvin, who knew that Wicks had been annoyed by persons posing as volunteers who later denounced him, suggested it might be better if he gave Sneyd's number to Wicks. O.K., said Sneyd. He could be reached at the New Earls Court Hotel.

Two days later Sneyd called again. Wicks hadn't contacted him, and he wanted to tell Colvin that he had moved to the Hotel Pax. He sounded even more nervous. He had been unable to get anyone to help him, he complained. Under Colvin's questioning, he admitted that his brother was not really missing—he just hadn't heard from him for four months—but he, Sneyd, would really like to join the mer-

cenary forces. As he spoke Colvin realized that the man was not telephoning him from his room, but from a call box. Every few minutes
he heard the "beep-beep-beep" indicating another sixpence had to be
dropped, and Sneyd, who was pouring out his troubles almost nonstop, had to interrupt himself to say in an agitated voice, "Wait a
minute, please, I got to put in more money—" He would hang up and
a moment later Colvin's phone would ring, and the voice would be
there again, unnecessarily reintroducing himself, "This is Ramon
Sneyd, I was just talking to you—" This happened two or three times,
Sneyd reintroducing himself each time. Colvin explained that this
was a bad time to try to join. There were few mercenary forces left in
Africa. Brussels was the place to check out possibilities. They had an
information center there. He would mail Sneyd the name and address
of someone—he didn't have it at hand at the moment—who was in
touch with Congo affairs.

After he hung up, Colvin had second thoughts. The man's purpose,
his manner on the telephone, gave him, as he said later, an impression of "someone odd, almost unbalanced." Instead of sending the
name, he wrote Sneyd a postcard suggesting that he check the Bel-
gian Embassy.

Colvin was not the only one to be put off by Ray's manner. London for Ray had been almost as frustrating as Lisbon. After ten days
at Heathfield House—no mail, telephone calls or visitors—he had
moved on May 28 to another cheap lodgings, the New Earls Court
Hotel, a few blocks away. Here Janet Nassau, the receptionist, tried
to be of service. He told her he was trying to trace a Major Wicks he
had read about, but, she said, "he was so incoherent nobody seemed
able to help him." She remembered that on June 4 he called the *Daily
Telegraph* from a call box a few steps up from the lobby. She remembered the date because it was the same day, Tuesday—he had been
there a week—that he asked how much his bill was, because he was
going out to get the British currency.

That afternoon one of the five tellers in the Fulham branch of the
Trustee Savings Bank looked up to see a man in a blue suit, heavy
sunglasses hiding his eyes, standing in front of her window. He
pushed what appeared to be a deposit toward her, but instead of
money, it was a note. "Hand over cash." Between his fingers she saw
peeping the muzzle of a small revolver. She seized a pile of bills—it
was one hundred pounds in five-pound notes, the equivalent of $240
—and pushed them at him. He grabbed the bills and walked out, leav-

ing the note. It had James Earl Ray's fingerprints on it, which doubly alerted Scotland Yard to the fact that Ray was in London.

After he paid his bill and checked out of the New Earls Court Hotel, in case anyone might trace him, he told Miss Nassau he was going to the airport to take a plane. Instead, he wandered around in a pouring rain looking for a room elsewhere. The YWCA, which also had single rooms for men, was filled: they referred him to the Pax Hotel, a few doors away. This was a private house owned by Mrs. Anna Thomas, who let out several rooms "to paying guests." Her experience with him was similar to that of all the other hotelkeepers. Her bell rang at 5 P.M. Wednesday. She opened her door to see a man standing there in the downpour, wearing a beige raincoat, carrying a suitcase, with newspapers and books under his arm. Would she have a room for a few days? "I'm from Canada, my name's Sneyd," he said as he came in, dripping. He took the room she showed him—$3.60 for bed and breakfast—and complained of a bad headache. Had she any aspirins? She gave him several.

She brought him his breakfast tray next morning at 7:45 and knocked on the door. There was no response. She tried her key, but it was locked from the inside, the key in the door. She put the tray down on the floor in front of the room and had taken only a few steps when the door opened and Sneyd, fully dressed, took in the tray without a word and locked the door again. For the next two days he scarcely left the room except to go out for armfuls of newspapers and for food, which he ate in his room. He laundered his shirts—she saw them, hung up to dry—and it seemed to her that he must sleep in his clothes, because when she let herself into the room early the next morning, Friday, he was still in bed with his clothes on. He stayed in his room, the door locked, most of the day.

He paid his bill Saturday morning at 9:30, and that was the last she saw of him—a harassed man, rushing out of the house with his luggage, his beige raincoat flapping about his knees.

A little less than two hours later, at Heathrow Airport, as he stood at the passport desk, Detective Sergeant Birch tapped him on the shoulder.

CHAPTER XXIX

There was no doubt now in either Dwyer's or Beasley's mind. Ray had done it. Ray—like it or not—Ray alone.

These two men, for whom the investigation had been a way of life for months, who had begun by profoundly doubting it, now believed it.

O.K., they had said. *This is how he did it.* They had checked their conclusions against those of Attorney General Canale, and Chief of Homicide Zachary, and FBI Agent in Charge Jensen, and Chief Investigator Carlisle, against what they themselves had learned on their thirteen-thousand-mile trail of Ray's footsteps, from the experts like themselves who had worked on the case in half a dozen countries—and from the voluminous investigative reports, totaling over a million and a half words, surely the most exhaustive study ever made of a man and his crime.

When had Ray decided to kill King? Probably sometime in late January 1968. Nothing in his drifting, unstructured life until then suggested any target date in mind. He moved as the wind and events pushed him; he improvised his way, staying five, six weeks in one place, then another, making attempts to find a job in this place, then in that. Had he obtained any of the jobs he sought—for example, as a maintenance man in the resort in Big Bear, California, or in the merchant marine, he might well have remained in California indefinitely. Before that he might have remained in Mexico. He liked the country; he had made money easily there before. Had Irma accepted his marriage proposal—assuming that he really meant it—or had Alicia taken the apartment he asked her to rent for the two of them—he might have stayed longer, or until the urge to move on came over him.

But in late January, in Los Angeles, came the first change in the rhythm of his activities since his escape. He began to act like a man who expected sudden notoriety to descend upon him—a man who would be desperately sought by the FBI. Nothing like this had shown itself before, although he had been out of prison for more than ten months. January 1968, then, might well be when he made the decision to kill Dr. King. The murder of Dr. King would surely catapult him on the FBI's Ten Most Wanted Fugitives list—far beyond the petty, fifty-dollar-reward class. Everything he did from then on was predicated on the certainty that he would be the subject of a nation-wide manhunt, his photograph and description broadcast everywhere. This was why he took measures to change his appearance to frustrate the FBI, and deliberately to leave clues that would throw them off the track.

Thus, the elaborate mailing out of his Polaroid profile photo-graphs, not only to the girls whose names he had obtained from the Los Angeles *Free Press*, but to girls who had advertised that they wished to exchange photographs. Then, after that, the plastic sur-gery, and his own attempt to change the line of his nose. He planned to have his drooping left ear repaired, too, thus altering his two most recognizable features, but he did not get around to it. Ray knew one other fact that would help frustrate his pursuers. He was one of those persons who rarely look like their photographs. When he had been released from Leavenworth in April 1958, he so little resembled the mug shot they had taken of him when he entered less than three years earlier that the prison authorities had to fingerprint him again and compare prints to make sure they were discharging James Earl Ray.

Now, when the FBI would begin to hunt for him, the girls to whom he had sent his photographs, eager to collect the large re-ward that would be offered for him, would turn them over to the FBI, leading the Bureau to concentrate its search in California while he would be far away—somewhere in Africa—and the Bureau, to add to its difficulties, would be seeking a man whose available photographs would only confuse it.

When Ray left Los Angeles on March 17, he left for the purpose of killing Dr. King. When Ray reached Selma, Alabama, on March 22—ostensibly because he lost his way, as he told Hanes and Huie—Dr. King was speaking in nearby Marx. Ray had stalked King in Atlanta, circling on a map of Atlanta the places where King could make a tar-get—his home, his church, his office. He had stalked King in Birming-ham, as well as Atlanta and in the Selma-Marx area, but had been unable to get close enough to take a shot at him with safety, using his Japanese-made .38—*for wherever he saw Dr. King in Alabama, he saw the police, protecting him.*

It became clear to Ray, then, that he would have to shoot King from a distance, with a long-range weapon—a high-powered rifle, such as one hunted big game with. It was then that Ray began his careful research into rifles and the drop of bullets at various distances, asking questions in one gun shop after another, finally deciding on his weapon, exchanging it when he found a fault, and then, the rifle with him, following King to Memphis.

Here the police were undercover, so that King appeared to be without protection. He had refused police protection and Memphis police could not insist, as did police in other cities, for in Memphis the police had been guarding Loeb's garbage collectors and so far as the black community was concerned, were helping break the strike. They had to remain out of sight or it would be taken as a provocation, or a threat, or antagonism toward Dr. King.

Memphis police had tried to protect him. When Dr. King and Abernathy had arrived Wednesday morning, April 3, on their delayed flight from Atlanta, and the Rev. Lawson's car waited to take them from the airport, two police officers asked Lawson where he was taking Dr. King. Lawson had been evasive. Why tell the police where they were meeting and give them the chance to eavesdrop on their strike strategy? So Lawson had said vaguely, "We haven't quite made up our mind," and they had driven off. But Director Holloman's Internal Security Division—men wearing civilian clothing, driving unmarked cars—had followed them, and King was under surveillance at all times—but not by men in uniform. So the police were not conspicuous about King, and Ray was not frightened off. Memphis was perfect.

Everything Ray then did had its own explanation, however inexplicable it may have appeared at the time.

One by one Beasley and Dwyer ticked off the questions that had hounded them.

How did Ray know that King was in Room 306 of the Lorraine Motel? There was no mystery to it. That he was at the Lorraine was carried in the April 4, 1968, issue of the Memphis *Commercial-Appeal* —the very newspaper found in the bundle Ray dropped in front of Canipe's door. News photographs showed him entering Room 306.

How did Ray know that King would be on the balcony in front of his room at six o'clock that night?

He did not know it. But had King emerged at 5:30 or 6:30 or 7:30 the result would have been the same. He had to emerge through that door, opening on the balcony. There was no other exit from his room. Ray was waiting for him, watching the balcony from the window of Room 5B in Mrs. Brewer's rooming house. Had King come out in darkness, he would be as clear a target as in daylight, for the balcony was brightly illuminated at night—a bulb in its protective grille was fixed over every doorway.

How did Ray know he would have a perfect shot at King from the second-story rear window of 422½ South Main Street? He had only to drive down Mulberry Street. To his right he would see all the motel rooms, ground and balcony level. To his left, he would see the rear windows of buildings on South Main Street. He had only to drive around to the front of these buildings to come upon the sign—hanging in front of 422½ as though there for his purpose—reading, ROOMS.

The result would have been the same had King been assigned any other room in the motel. All faced the rear windows of the rooming house, and all opened either onto the balcony, on the second level, or on the courtyard, on the ground level. This, of course, did away with talk that King had been deliberately assigned a motel room facing the bathroom window of 422½ South Main Street.

Why had Ray dropped the bundle of evidence in Canipe's doorway? Two or three more strides and he could easily have tossed it over the large wooden billboard next to Canipe's shop, to fall into deep weeds out of sight. Why had he not left the rifle in the room—or shoved it under the tub—or concealed it in the dark interior of a closet? He dared not. He knew his fingerprints were on the weapon. The same was true of the binoculars and the beer cans. He had not had time to erase them. He had not even had time, in that room, to open a can of beer.

The fact was that he never expected King to appear so suddenly on the balcony. Ray had prepared himself for a long wait in Room 5B. He had taken up with him his toilet articles, his underwear (he did not sleep in pajamas), his bag, the bedspread he traveled with for use in the filthy motel rooms he frequented, and the beer. All things pointed to his planning to shoot King after nightfall—King was hardly seen during the day, always closeted in his room, holding meetings—and nightfall would have been fine. King, thanks to the illuminated balcony, would still be a perfect target, and Ray's escape would be even easier because the streets in that factory area would then be deserted.

Ray had been in no great hurry to get up to the room earlier. He had sat for some time in his parked car, doing nothing, simply looking straight ahead. He had not gone up until after five o'clock, but he knew that he had plenty of time. It would not get dark for another hour and a half or so. The sun set that day at 6:24 P.M.: that was in his newspaper too.

But once up in his room, sitting on the chair he drew up to the window so he could rest while keeping his vigil, he had seen King unexpectedly appear on the balcony in shirt sleeves and, after a moment or so, go back into his room to emerge once more, this time wearing his jacket—clearly, about to leave. Ray might not get so good a chance again. He could not shoot King from the window of his room: he would have to lean out in so awkward a position that an accurate shot would be impossible—not to mention the fact that he would be clearly visible to those at the motel and in the courtyard. Whereupon he grabbed his rifle, had time only to shove one cartridge into the chamber, and dashed into the bathroom, where he knew he had a perfect shot at King, if only he remained on the balcony long enough to allow him to draw a bead on him.

And Dr. King had obliged him. He stood on the balcony, both hands on the railing, leaning forward, talking to those below, waiting for Abernathy to finish his toilette. Ray, standing in the tub, could take his time now. He had pushed out the screen, which fell to the bushes below, rested his rifle on the sill of the open window (the barrel making its small, telltale indentation on the soft wood), aimed carefully through the telescopic sights which brought the leaning figure 203 feet away to within thirty feet, and when he had him in the very center of the cross hairs, fired. He saw King fall. Then he stepped out of the tub, unlatched the door which he had hurriedly latched after he dashed in, and was back in his room, five strides across the corridor, seconds later. There the Browning box, the overnight bag, the binoculars were on the bedspread open on the bed. He threw the rifle into its box, slamming the cover back on (in his haste not pushing the rifle completely inside, so that several inches of barrel protruded), scooped everything up in the bedspread, making a long roll of it (leaving behind the binoculars strap and the strap of the binoculars case), and hurried out, to be seen by Anschutz, emerging from his own room as Ray went by, hand up to his face so Anschutz could not get a good look at him, and, a moment later, to be seen by Stephens, who stepped out of his room in time to see Ray rounding the turn at the far end of the corridor toward the stairs leading to the street. When Ray emerged on the sidewalk of South Main Street, at 418½, he turned swiftly to his left, toward his Mustang parked fifty feet farther on. He would throw the incriminating bundle into the back of the car and get rid of it when he was safely out of town. But as he came abreast of Canipe's shop, at 424, where South Main Street curves slightly to the left, he saw around the curve, about one hundred feet ahead of him, beyond his Mustang, the three TAC police cruisers parked in the driveway of the fire station on the corner.

One more step and Ray would come into sight of anyone in the police cars, and he dared not be seen with the evidence. Canipe's recessed entrance way was at his left elbow. He thought the place closed—most shops closed at 5:30, it was now just after six o'clock—in addition, because of the angle of his view and the grime on the windows, the glass was all but opaque, so that Canipe and his two customers were invisible to Ray. Ray stepped into the entrance, which was out of sight of the firehouse driveway, dropped the bundle there, and managed to reach his car a moment later without being seen by any of the police or firemen. For those inside the firehouse, alerted by the shouts that King had been shot, rushed first toward the rear, toward the Lorraine, behind the station—not to the front, to Main Street, where they would have seen Ray making his run for the car. By the time Lieutenant Ghormley, the leader of the TAC squad and the first to reverse himself and race to Main Street, arrived there, Ray and his car were gone. Ghormley had missed Ray by a matter of seconds.

How had he managed to get out of Memphis, with all the alarms out for a white man in a white Mustang—with the road blocks, the state-wide alerts, and all the rest?

There were no road blocks. No all-points bulletin had been sent out. Other states had not been notified. The police dispatcher had reported that a suspect was believed to have fled in a white Mustang. But there was no proof that the sniper was the driver of that car. A perfectly innocent man might have parked his white Mustang on South Main Street and emerged from any one of a dozen buildings, any one of a score of shops, and driven off. Memphis police had not sent off an alarm to neighboring states. There was no fugitive warrant out for the man, there was not sufficient evidence for extradition, and Tennessee would have had to be prepared to extradite him. A contributing explanation for Ray's escape had been given by Ray himself, when he told his guards, "I got lost." It was typical of the man. If it be assumed that, because of the police dispatcher's alert, police cars were watching main highways, they would not have seen Ray. He was driving in and out of back streets, going forward and back in dead-end alleys, trying to find his way out of town, and wherever they were logically looking for him, he was not there.

Then, other questions.

Why had Ray exchanged the Remington .243 for a 30.06? The .243 was a powerful weapon, more than adequate for his purpose. Why had he returned it, running the risk of being seen twice by clerks who might have to identify him?

Ray had discovered a small imperfection—a tiny metal burr in front of the chamber, which prevented the bullet from slipping into it. Anyone who knew guns would have simply filed it down with a nail file or scraped it smooth with a pocketknife—a one minute job—and have no difficulty chambering the cartridge. But Ray only knew that the gun would not work; he wanted to make no complaint, he wanted to have no trouble, so he went the long way around, saying that his brother told him it was the wrong gun. This was unfortunate, both Dwyer and Beasley agreed, because Ray's mention of his brother had caused the FBI, in issuing its original warrant for Galt's arrest, to state that "Galt and an individual whom he alleged to be his brother, entered into a conspiracy" to violate Dr. King's civil rights. The word "conspiracy" was planted in the public mind—a word that would not vanish and would constantly haunt those seeking the truth.

How explain the false broadcast? Zachary's investigation had produced a seventeen-year-old high school student, a CB enthusiast who had a powerful sending station in the attic of his home, located in the area from which the broadcast emanated. Zachary had sent Lieutenant Hamby to the house: the youth was at school, but his mother allowed Hamby to examine the equipment. It was of professional quality, a high-powered, complete twenty-three-channel CB transceiver. But the boy, questioned later, denied making the broadcast. He was doing his homework, he said, when a friend telephoned him about 6:30 P.M. to say King had been shot. He had simply continued with his work. Dwyer and Beasley had exchanged glances: what seventeen-year-old boy, a rabid ham operator, would not have stopped whatever he was doing and dashed to his set to hear what was happening? Those who heard the broadcast described the voice as high and excited, that of a boy, not a man; in any event, there was no other sending station of comparable power in that area.

What finally made Dwyer and Beasley dismiss it as a prank, a hoax, a teen-ager's practical joke, was that the broadcast came so late. Had the conspirators sought to draw Ray's pursuers to north

Memphis while he was escaping from south Memphis, why would they wait more than half an hour before sending the police on a wild goose chase? It would have been too late to help Ray then. King was shot at 6:01, the false broadcast did not begin until 6:35. By then Ray would either have been caught or out of the city. *But the boy had not learned of King's shooting until 6:30.*

If Ray had no confederates, how was one to explain the episode of the duplicate driver's license? A man who said he was Eric Starvo Galt telephoned the auto license bureau in Montgomery, Alabama, on February 28 and asked for a duplicate driver's license to be sent to him at the Economy Grill & Rooms, in Birmingham. The twenty-five-cent license fee had been marked paid at the bureau; the license had been mailed to the boarding house, but Peter Cherpes, the owner, never saw it; so whoever paid the twenty-five-cent fee must also have picked it up from the mail on the table in the hall. But on February 28, Ray was in Los Angeles: records showed he attended his bartending class that day. Who had paid the fee and waited for the license to arrive and picked it up?

The answer was surprisingly simple. In the altercation in the Rabbit's Foot Club in Los Angeles, Ray had fled from the place, leaving his jacket in the hands of his two assailants, in it his wallet with his driver's license. He himself had telephoned the license bureau in Montgomery from Los Angeles, asked to have the duplicate mailed to him c/o the Economy Grill & Rooms, in Birmingham, and mailed the twenty-five-cent fee. The Birmingham post office, which had a change-of-address card for him, automatically forwarded it to him in Los Angeles. This was an excellent example of how the apparent proof of a confederate vanished before the fact. He had not asked for the license to be sent directly to him in Los Angeles: he particularly did not want his whereabouts to be on the records of the license bureau, always a source of police information.

What about the cigarette ashes found in his white Mustang? Ray did not smoke. This report was simply erroneous. No ashes were found. The FBI and Birmingham police had gone over the car with microscopic thoroughness—even the grime on the exhaust pipe had been scraped off for chemical analysis. And since they did not know who Galt was then, and whether or not he smoked, there was no reason for them to falsify the report.

How did Ray, a man isolated for years in prison, know how to manage all the details he had to manage, unless he was helped? The answer was that at every point clerks and the like explained procedures to him. Paisley, from whom he bought the Mustang, told him that an Alabama resident must go with him when he applied for a license, so he asked Peter Cherpes to accompany him. The technique of obtaining a false passport he learned from the experience of Benny Edmondson and many other criminals who used Canada for the same purpose. In Toronto, Miss Spencer at the Kennedy Travel Bureau took over from there, all but filling out the necessary forms for the passport, and getting them notarized, as well as booking Ray on the plane and finally delivering to him tickets and passport, and even advising him to be vaccinated; in Lisbon, customs officials told him to correct his passport, and where to do it, and at the Canadian Embassy Mrs. Lopez, like Miss Spencer, all but filled out the questionaire required to obtain a new passport.* In London, Ian Colvin of the *Daily Telegraph* briefed him on the mercenary situation and suggested that he go to Brussels. . . .

Very well. Where did Ray get the money for his travels? He told Huie and Hanes that Raoul gave him "capital" from time to time— sums adding up to nearly $7000. Ray had admitted obtaining $1700 by a robbery in Canada. By his own careful accounting, this, with Raoul's money and what he brought out of prison and saved at his restaurant job, was sufficient for him to travel as he had. If one eliminated Raoul, all that had to be accounted for was $7000. Ray was a professional holdup man and robber who for the last nine months had traveled with a .38—the revolver found on him when he was arrested in London. But to make more plausible his claim that Raoul was the source of the $7000, he had maintained that he had not bought the revolver until a few days before his arrest in London on June 8.

This was a lie. Beasley and Carlisle had traced the weapon from its manufacturer in Japan to California, to Georgia, where it had been sold to a Walter L. Spain, of Birmingham. On October 1, 1967, Spain advertised it for sale in the Birmingham *News*. Galt had answered his ad. Spain remembered him. "I want sixty-five dollars for it," he told Galt, and the latter brought out sixty-five dollars, pocketed the gun, and left. So he had traveled with it since October 1, 1967, and if he could by his own admission net $1700 from one holdup, what might he not have realized in that nine-month period

---

* Mrs. Lopez remembered: "He did not seem to be well educated. I had to give him much help."

in supermarket holdups and in who knows how many small gas-station holdups during his driving about the country? Ray should not be sold short as a holdup man: his known record was bad, but that record was based only on those robberies in which he had been caught. No one knew how many he had pulled off successfully. He had gone some nineteen thousand miles in his white Mustang; that meant many, many stops for gas on lonely roads. And no record was kept of such holdups, for the FBI investigated only those that reported losses over five thousand dollars. Ray held up a bank, too, in London, just before his capture, and that he obtained a small sum was merely the luck of the draw.

In short, all the money that Ray, the fugitive, needed on his travels he could supply himself, depending upon the risks he wanted to take. The fact was that he needed much less money to move about from the day of his escape to the day of his capture than one might think. The highly publicized manhunt, the reports, exaggerated by rumor, from Canada, Mexico, England, Portugal, even Australia and the Far East, had given everyone the picture of a man moving swiftly and effortlessly through this country and half of Europe, presumably at the cost of many thousands of dollars. Actually, save for the flight to London and Lisbon, all of Ray's travel was by car or bus, and he had remained long periods of time in one place, living in the most inexpensive lodgings.

It was Canale, who in the first week of November, in a series of discussions with Dwyer, Beasley, and Carlisle after they had returned from their investigations here and abroad, and after they had interviewed all the key witnesses themselves—it was Canale who summarized their conclusions as to this aspect of Ray and its relevance to conspiracy.

"Gentlemen," Canale began, "this was not a man being fed money by conspirators. Wherever he could, he economized. He lived like a beachcomber. When they found his white Mustang, it was full of crackers and canned food. He ate his meals in his car when he was on the road; when he stayed in motels, they were the cheapest, and he prepared and ate his meals in his rooms, buying the cheapest foods. He traveled with everything he needed, from soup and coffee heaters to condiments. He probably never ordered a full meal in a restaurant: he lived on hamburgers, candy, pizza, potato chips, and beer.

"When he was captured in London, in his pocket was an advertisement he had clipped from a newspaper advertising cheap airline rates to Africa. He went to London from Toronto on the cheapest possible excursion ticket. He darned his shorts, he accumulated soap from motels, he lived the life of a penurious, money-short man all the time. When he was seized at the airport in London, his shoes were run down almost to the point of unwearability and he had less than $125 on his person."

But not only the lack of money underwrote the nonexistence of conspirators; so did the nature of all of Ray's operations.

Again, Canale summed it up:

"Every step of the way from his escape to his capture, he himself did everything required in the preparation and carrying out of the murder. If it were a conspiracy, the actual trigger man would never be so exposed. Ray himself researched the rifle, the ammunition, the scope; he himself bought them, then exchanged them; he bought the binoculars, he bought the pistol he carried, he bought the car he drove, he took it to be serviced, he rented the rooms himself wherever he went; he bought his own clothes, made his own telephone calls; nothing was done for him, there is absolutely no evidence that anyone prepared the way for him, helped him or made anything easy for him in the commission of this crime. He himself went about picking up travel folders and information, buying the airplane tickets, applying for the passport, picking up the photographs, tickets, and passport. If it had been a conspiracy, his fellow conspirators would have kept him hidden as long as possible, so that the man who fired the fatal shot would have remained out of sight until then, a stranger, someone not easily identifiable—someone not likely to be captured and so put in jeopardy the others in the conspiracy. What conspirators would have allowed such a man to leave such a trail?"

The others agreed with him.

Had Ray had co-conspirators, Canale concluded, they would have provided him with money so that he did not have to undergo the additional risks of holdups to finance himself; and had he money, he would have remained in Lisbon (his co-conspirators would have informed him that Portugal had never signed an extradition treaty with the United States, so he was quite safe there) until he got his visa and made his way to some other haven where he knew the language. Had he money, he would be a free man today in some English-speaking country which has no extradition treaty with the United States.

There he undoubtedly would have let it be known that it was he,

James Earl Ray, who had conceived and successfully carried out the assassination of Dr. Martin Luther King, Jr.

Which was precisely what the Messrs. Canale, Dwyer, and Beasley were now determined to prove, in the trial to begin Tuesday, November 12, 1968.

They were satisfied with their case. How would the jurors, the press, and the people respond?

CHAPTER XXX

The telephone call came, as sooner or later Percy Foreman expected it to come, on Friday afternoon, November 8, as he was speaking at the Baylor University Law School in Waco, Texas. It was from his secretary to say that a letter had just arrived from James Earl Ray in Shelby County Jail, Memphis, asking if Mr. Foreman could come there at once to talk to him about becoming his attorney. Jerry Ray, James's brother, had also called from St. Louis, leaving his number.

When Foreman finished his lecture, he lumbered into the dean's office and called Jerry. Yes, Jerry knew about the letter. Jim had written it on his advice. Would Mr. Foreman come?

This was certainly a last-minute call. Ray was scheduled to go on trial on Tuesday, with Art Hanes of Birmingham as his lawyer. Yet there had been two or three nibbles before. As early as June 13, five days after Ray's arrest in London, a St. Louis *Post-Dispatch* reporter had telephoned him to say that Jerry Ray was sitting at his side and wanted to know if Mr. Foreman would represent his brother if he was extradited. After that, Jerry called him twice, and each time Foreman had explained that he could be employed only by the principal, or by a lawyer representing the defendant, and only if the latter released his first attorney. Now, Foreman said, he would go to Memphis only if both brothers accompanied him to Shelby County Jail.

Early Sunday morning Foreman flew to Memphis, where the two brothers met him and repaid him one hundred dollars for his plane fare. Then the three went to the jail. A courteous Sheriff Morris met them. Mr. Foreman could not see Ray. He was not the lawyer of record.

"Sheriff," said Foreman, "I personally don't care whether I'm admitted to talk to him or not. But the law is that if he wants me or any other lawyer he's entitled to talk to me and you're violating the law if you don't allow me to do so." Morris promptly telephoned Judge Battle at home, who told him Foreman was right.

Foreman met Ray privately in his cell a few minutes later. As Foreman described the meeting, Ray told him that Hanes, Sr., wanted him to plead guilty, but he did not want to do so; that Ray thought Hanes was representing Huie rather than him, and he wanted someone, as he put it, who would be "primarily interested in me." He was unhappy about Hanes, it was clear to Foreman, but it was also evident that Ray did not know he could change lawyers at this late hour. Ray had wanted to see Foreman to learn whether, if he should be convicted, as he expected to be, Foreman would become his lawyer to file an appeal for a new trial.

Foreman explained that hiring a new lawyer did not guarantee Ray a new trial. That depended on the original trial. Ray digested this. "Well, if I asked Judge Battle for the right to change my lawyer, would I still have to go on trial Tuesday?"

Foreman said he thought not. Ray would probably be granted a postponement.

Ray nodded. All right. He'd like to discharge Mr. Hanes. The jailer gave him a yellow legal pad and he wrote a note to Hanes, printing it, as always, painstakingly. He gave the note to Foreman, who took it down to Sheriff Morris. Morris immediately telephoned Judge Battle to learn if this, too, was proper. Yes, said the judge; a defendant had the right to change attorneys up to the very moment of the trial.

As Foreman saw it, he had no choice in the matter. The file he had kept on the Ray case had proved valuable: he knew what had taken place, he had evaluated the evidence: Ray, he thought, was a good cinch for the chair. He felt he had to take his case. Had he been called in two weeks earlier, he would have engaged a Nashville attorney to defend Ray. The logical man would be John J. Hooker, Sr., Foreman's own lawyer in Tennessee. There was no time now. This was Sunday. Tomorrow was a holiday—Veterans Day. And Ray had to go on trial Tuesday morning. Whatever had to be done had to be done now. Foreman thought, *It's me or the electric chair.* He could only assume, being a deacon of the church and a pious man, as he had assumed many times before, that the Lord had sent him to save a man's life.

Arthur Hanes learned of his dismissal the next night—Monday, the night before the trial was to begin. He and Art, Jr., and their wives drove up from Birmingham, prepared to set up housekeeping for the duration—perhaps three months—at the Rivermont Motel. They came into a city tense with excitement. One entire floor of the huge State Office Building, adjacent to the Criminal Courts Building, had been transformed into a giant communications center, with a vast telephone switchboard and some hundred thousand dollars' worth of teletype, telegraphic, TV, and other electronic equipment already installed. Hanes had brought his client a new suit, a gray single-breasted suit, to wear at the opening of his trial, as well as a white button-down shirt, a neat patterned tie, and a pair of black wing-tip shoes, a style specified by Ray. A movie star could not have been more concerned with his appearance. Ray wanted to be the glass of fashion when he faced his public. He had asked Hanes if a tailor might come to the jail to fit him. He always had trouble with ready-made clothes, because his shoulders were disproportionate to his waist, and one sloped lower than the other. Sheriff Morris had flatly refused, and Hanes had put his own jacket on Ray, measured waist and shoulders and sleeve length, pinned it about in the right places, and took it to his tailor in Birmingham and had the suit made up. He had been uncertain about the length of Ray's inseam, so he telephoned Captain Billy Smith, the chief jailer, and Smith dutifully went into Ray's cell, measured the inseam with a tape measure, and reported the figure to Hanes.

Ray had wanted, too, to be well shaved. "If they don't give me a regular razor and get a barber in here to cut my hair, I won't go into court," he had said. He had complained for weeks that the electric razor which he had to use caused a rash.

Hanes dropped Art, Jr., and the two women off at the Rivermont and drove to the jail to give Ray his new suit. He pushed his way through the score of newspapermen who were camped in the area, and went into the jail. The guard told him he would have to notify the sheriff. "Hell," said Hanes, annoyed. "Morris knows me. You know me." Well, said the guard, the sheriff always liked to know when someone visited Ray. So Hanes sat, tapping his foot impatiently, while the sheriff was telephoned. A few minutes later Morris himself appeared, a troubled look on his face. Would Hanes mind coming into his office?

There Morris without a word grimly pulled out a folded slip of paper from his breast pocket and tossed it on the table in front of Hanes. It was a Xerox copy of a letter written in ink, in an all too familiar printed script.

Dear Mr. Hanes: Due to some disagreements between me and you in regards to the handlings of my case I have decided to engage a Tennessee attorney and perhaps someone else, there-

fore I would appreciate it if you would take no further action
on my case in Memphis Tenn. Also I appreciate what you have
all ready did for me.

Sincerely,
James E. Ray.

Hanes fought to control himself. "I had an idea something like
this might happen," he said slowly. Where was the original of the
letter?

"Percy Foreman is here. He has it," said the sheriff.

Did Judge Battle know about this turn of events? Morris nodded.
Both the judge and General Canale had been informed.

At this moment the telephone rang. The sheriff answered it and
turned to Hanes. If he would pick up an extension, he would introduce him to Percy Foreman. Hanes was brief. "Mr. Foreman, I understand you have a letter." "Yes." "When will I get it?" "In court
tomorrow." Foreman added, "I expect you to co-operate, Mr. Hanes,
and to let me have your files."

Hanes responded furiously. "Foreman, you'll get my files when I
get the rest of my fee." He hung up. James Earl Ray, that conniving,
ungrateful, paranoid . . . Hanes thought, *That pin-headed son-of-a-
bitch, I'd like to be alone with him for a few minutes in that cell.*
He did not trust himself to dwell on the man.* Ray owed him twelve
thousand dollars. He wanted it.

In their hotel the Haneses discussed it. Hanes, Sr., could only admit he was not surprised. Something like this *had* been in the cards.
In late September he had examined the state's physical evidence. Tennessee was one of the states which permitted the defense to know
what evidence the prosecution possessed. He had seen the proof that
linked Ray to Galt to Lowmyer to Willard to the rifle to the bathroom from which the shot had come. Hanes had always counted on
reasonable doubt, on confusion in identification, on Renfro's affidavits clouding the testimony of the state's witnesses, on the goats'
corpses, on the stories of two white Mustangs, on the state's inability
to prove ballistically that the bullet came from the rifle found in
Canipe's doorway. But these were peripheral. When he added up

---

* "There goes two million dollars!" Hanes was to lament to a friend later. His
estimate was wildly overexaggerated. There had been talk that Carlo Ponti, the
Italian producer, was interested in the film rights.

the pros and cons, he was far less optimistic than when he first toted them up in his office.

So he had told Ray he would go to trial but could not win acquittal unless Ray made Raoul more believable to a jury. Perhaps, said Hanes, Ray wanted to plead guilty? To make a deal with the state? No, said Ray. He was pleading not guilty. Then tell me about Raoul, Hanes demanded. He gave you a telephone number to call in case of emergency—what was it? He wrote you letters—you must have kept some? Let me see them. But Ray would not answer these questions to Hanes's satisfaction. Raoul remained vague, unclear. And Raoul was Ray's whole case, his alibi, his proof that he had been the dupe of a conspiracy—yet Ray would not give Hanes the facts he needed. Ray was holding out on him—*his own lawyer*.

Their sessions had always been the same after the first, almost Keystone Kops interview on the floor of Cell Block A. The Haneses, after the usual ordeal of search, would go into Ray's block, where Ray waited, with an agenda he had prepared on legal foolscap. The man who drew up the Financial Record months before could be very methodical. They would begin taking up the subjects as Ray had listed them. Ray would sit back in his chair, teetering on the back two legs, a blue sport shirt over his white T-shirt, his shirttail out, rubbing the beginning of a paunch reflectively—a characteristic habit —while Hanes put questions to him and Ray thought about his answers. At the beginning Hanes felt the plot must center in Louisiana not only because New Orleans had figured so often in stories and rumors, but also because Ray appeared concerned only with witnesses for the state who came from Louisiana.

They would go over the names. "Might this guy hurt you if he testified?" Hanes would ask. Ray, sitting back, would say no. Well, this one? No, she was the landlady in Los Angeles. All she could say was that he cooked in his room or had left a shirt there. As they went over the names, it was obvious that most of them posed no threat to Ray—pilots to testify he flew from Toronto to London, or motel clerks to identify his registration. But Louisiana witnesses—

Here Ray would come forward sharply in his chair, and study the name. "I wish you'd talk to him, Mr. Hanes," he would say. "Get some idea of what he's got." And then, staring at another name, almost under his breath, "What could he say? I don't remember him—"

Hanes, becoming excited, would demand, "Jim, why does he trouble you? What's he got to do with what happened?"

Ray would become evasive. "I don't want to go into it now, but try to find out what he'll say, will you?"

Only as time went on did Hanes realize that Ray's concern had nothing to do with a plot in Louisiana. It was simply that Ray feared he might suffer from perjured testimony. He had not met an important Louisiana businessman in New Orleans—a rumor based on Charlie Stein's vague recollection of what he thought Ray told him—and he knew that the Louis Lomax series, claiming to know names and dates, was wildly imaginative. Ray feared the state would frame him, that Attorney General Canale might put on a witness who would say, "Yes, there is a rich businessman in New Orleans and I saw him and Galt talking together in the Trade Mart."

There could be no other reason. For if there were witnesses who could damage him, why would Ray not arm his lawyer against them? Why this evasion? Ray was only making it easier for the state to send him to the chair if there *were* such witnesses.

Time and again Hanes would press him. "No, Mr. Hanes, I can't tell you. Maybe sometime I will."

"But, Jimmy," Hanes would say, stifling an impulse to grab his client by the scruff of his neck and shake sense into him, "I'm your lawyer, damn it! I'm not the prosecutor. It's you and me and Art, Jr., against everybody—you've got to tell me! I have to know!"

Ray would refuse.

There was something perverse about the man—that was the only word. Father and son took turns questioning him, then comparing notes. It was like cat and mouse. They got the idea that Ray wanted them to find the answers themselves: he would not help them. Was this because he knew that if Hanes got him off he would have to serve out his term at Missouri State Penitentiary, and other inmates would not help him escape again if he broke the code by squealing? But what insanity to worry about that if his failure to assist his lawyers made it impossible for them to get him off? The whole thing was like an incredible put-on. While Hanes, Sr., questioned Ray, Art, Jr., would be out investigating; he would tell his father what he learned. The elder Hanes would brief Ray on this. Some days later Art, Jr., would question Ray, and Ray would blandly feed back what Art, Sr., had told him. At one point young Art exploded. "Oh, bullshit!" he exclaimed. "Pop told you that last week. What are you trying to give me?" Ray would hang his head and grin his sickly grin, like a small boy caught in a fib.

But it was where Raoul was concerned that Ray was impossible.

Each time Hanes, Sr., questioned him about Raoul, Ray would become even more evasive, and when he finally answered, he would watch the lawyer's face closely as if gauging his response to his reply. If he said something that Hanes knew was a lie and Hanes took him to task: "Look, buddy, don't tell me that. Jimmy boy, that won't help us." Ray would look guilty, shake his head, and remain silent. Once Ray gave Hanes an answer which the lawyer recognized as drawn from a speculative story written by a *Commercial-Appeal* reporter a few days before. Hanes caught him up sharply. Ray looked sheepish. "Well, it sounded good," he said lamely.

Hanes could not understand it. A conviction had been growing in his mind, strengthened with every frustrating session, that Ray was really using him as a sounding board to rehearse the testimony he would give if he took the stand, and was taking advantage of Hanes's probing to tighten his story. This would explain his untruths. If Hanes, a trained lawyer, would accept them, a jury of laymen probably would too.

Throughout it all Ray had seemed far too unconcerned, as though incapable of realizing his jeopardy. "Jimmy, you'll burn if we don't straighten that out!" Hanes would exclaim. Ray would remain unruffled. Indeed, he seemed to flourish in jail. He looked far better than when he had arrived. He joked with his guards, he slept a great deal—Sheriff Morris's logbook showed an average of eight and a half hours a night—and he ate well, ordering what he liked from the commissary. He had gained nine pounds in the first two months. Little seemed to upset him. He never spoke about the twelve thousand dollars he said Raoul promised him, and which he had never collected. In a man known in prison for "bugging" other inmates insistently to pay back as small a sum as a nickel, this was hard to fathom. Nor did he show any resentment over the fact that Raoul and the others, whoever they were, had left him to face the music alone. All this did not make sense. *This guy is playing a game with me*, Hanes had thought more and more often.

Could Ray have something going for him? Had he worked out a deal with someone in return for remaining silent for two, three years? It had not helped that Ray, asking about mail arriving for him—he was permitted to read copies of mail from only a few approved correspondents—once told him, "Better save all the mail, Mr. Hanes," adding soberly, "There may be some code in it that I'd recognize but wouldn't mean anything to you."

Nor had it reassured Hanes that Ray had recently been visited by

J. B. Stoner, whose offer to raise money for his defense Hanes had turned down at the very beginning. Ray had asked his brother Jerry to contact Stoner, and although Ray explained that he was conferring with Stoner on other civil matters—such as a libel suit Ray and his father wanted to file against *Life* magazine and other publications for their derogatory descriptions of the family—Hanes did not like it. He had given Ray an ultimatum: If Stoner comes in, I go out.

Despite his dissatisfaction, Hanes had been prepared to go to trial. He had told Ray he would not let him testify. How could this man get on that stand and allow Dwyer on cross-examination to turn him inside out? No lawyer would permit a habitual criminal to testify. His record would then become an issue. Didn't Ray realize that his pigheadedness in taking the stand back in 1959 in St. Louis led to his twenty-year term in Missouri State Penitentiary?

So they had had "disagreements" about the "handlings" of the case.

Could his dismissal, Hanes wondered, have been arranged long before? Was it possible that Art Hanes, Sr., was never destined to try this case in court? That he had been hired only because he was known as a segregationist, a lawyer who defended KKK clients, and those behind the scenes wanted to stamp King's killing as racist, hoping that it would lead to a black-white explosion and even the downfall of the Republic?

Whatever the case, Ray had gained time by hiring Foreman. What else had he gained? Whatever it was, Hanes had certainly lost. Now everyone would think his firing was part of a prearranged plan and conclude that Hanes had been in the conspiracy from the first.

Months before he all but gloated, *I have myself a lawsuit.* Now he thought angrily, *I have been had.*

Next morning in a brief hearing in Judge Battle's courtroom, Hanes withdrew as Ray's counsel and Judge Battle accepted Percy Foreman, remarking unhappily that this change came "at the eleventh hour —at the fifty-ninth second of the fifty-ninth minute," but the law permitted a defendant to choose who should represent him. A man's life was at stake. He postponed the trial until March 3, 1969, requesting Foreman to return in one month—December 12—to report his progress: this over the angry objections of Dwyer, who said such a delay was intolerable and could only help the defense.

Hanes and Ray exchanged cool greetings. Those between Hanes and Foreman were cooler still.

That afternoon the four Haneses drove back to Birmingham, Art, Sr., taking with him the suit he had had tailored for Ray. He would have it altered to fit himself. It was little enough consolation.

In his office Attorney General Canale, who was forced to accept the delay philosophically, glanced through an advance copy of a book which later appeared under the title *The James Earl Ray Hoax*, by Joechem Joesten, an American writer living in Munich, who had published many political exposés.

Joesten, one of several authors who had attacked the Warren Commission report, had written in an earlier book that President Kennedy's assassination had been a plot involving the FBI, the CIA, Dallas police, and even some of Kennedy's aides; that he had been shot from the grassy knoll and that Oswald was an innocent dupe whose rifle had been planted by police.

Dr. King's killing, Joesten's new book asserted, had similar earmarks. Ray, too, was a dupe, and his rifle had been planted in Canipe's doorway. The plotters, in New Orleans, were Southern businessmen who joined with the Klan and Wallace supporters to kill King in order "to strike fear into the hearts of the black people and deprive them of effective leadership." The conspirators had contacted Ray in Missouri State Penitentiary, hired him to act as a decoy—to lay down a false trail—and arranged his escape. To confuse the police in Memphis, there were two James Earl Rays, similar in appearance, speech, and behavior, driving two identical white Mustangs and later traveling abroad on two copies of the same false passport.

King, wrote Joesten, was actually shot from the bushes under the bathroom window, which explained the statements of Solomon Jones and "Cornbread" Carter. After the shooting the two white Mustangs went off in different directions, which explained the reports of white Mustangs seen simultaneously in opposite ends of Memphis. Then, in London, on June 8, both men were arrested under the name Sneyd, Ray at 6:10 A.M., the other man—(in reality the CIA operative who had shot President Kennedy),—at 11:15 A.M., by mistake. The FBI, unaware of the CIA's role, and embarrassed by its arrest of the CIA operative, "a man who enjoyed protection on the highest levels," immediately whisked him away to security, and the entire story revised so that the world was told that only one man, Ray, had been seized.

Thus, wrote Joesten, all the confusing stories fell into place.

Canale learned that Judge Battle, Police Director Holloman, and other principals in the case had received copies of Joesten's publication. A conspiracy which meant that the FBI, the CIA, Scotland Yard, and all the law enforcement personnel involved on both sides of the Atlantic had played a secret, shameful role and managed to keep it secret despite the most brilliant kleig lights of publicity trained on them . . . Canale found this difficult to believe. Even if such a bizarre fantasy were true, why should all those involved have done it?

Canale sent the publication down to Assistant Attorney General Rhodes for his file, which was growing larger by the day.

CHAPTER XXXI

On Wednesday afternoon, December 18, 1968, shortly after four o'clock, Hugh Stanton, Sr., dropped in on Attorney General Canale. A salty man in his seventies, vigorous and direct, he was Shelby County public defender, and six days before Judge Battle had appointed him co-counsel with Percy Foreman to help speed up the defense of James Earl Ray.

Foreman had appeared on December 12, a month after he took over Ray's case, to make the report ordered by Battle; it would be a miracle, he said, if he could be ready by March 3, as planned. He was still checking out some of the three hundred and more witnesses, whose names the state had given him. Judge Battle had set the case to April 3 and said any further delay could not be accepted. He would put Public Defender Stanton, and his son, Hugh Stanton, Jr., associated with him, at Foreman's disposal. The three had been working together furiously and Stanton had just come from a long talk with Foreman. He had asked Foreman bluntly, he told Canale, did Foreman think Ray was guilty? And Foreman had said yes. He had checked every important witness, he had seen the state's physical evidence against Ray—the case was overwhelmingly against his client. Ray had not a single alibi witness: the man had not come up with anything Foreman could use. The defense had no answer to the state's case.

Now Stanton said to Canale, whom he had known for years, as he had known his father before him, "Foreman wants to know if you'll offer Ray the possibility of his taking a guilty plea. If you do, Foreman will present the idea to Ray."

Canale doodled on the sheet of paper before him. The possibility of a guilty plea had been in everyone's mind. More than 90 per cent of all first-degree murder cases in the country were settled in this fashion. But since Ray had always maintained his innocence, any discussion seemed a waste of time.

Canale asked, "Will Ray go for it?"

"Foreman doesn't know," Stanton replied. "Neither do I." They both believed there was a chance.

Canale was in a predicament. Under Tennessee law any defendant was permitted to plead guilty to a first-degree murder charge if he accepted his punishment—usually a sentence ranging from seventy-five to ninety-nine years in prison. But to allow such a plea by James Earl Ray, what with all the talk of conspiracy, with the country's black community suspicious of a whitewash to hide the white higher-ups presumably behind Ray, and the country's white population suspecting that the South was out to railroad the man to salve its conscience. . . .

To choose a jury, Canale knew, would be a most difficult task. How could they be sure that one of the black jurors was not a militant, wildly opposed to King, convinced that he was an Uncle Tom— Nobel Prize winner, darling of white society, black glamour figure among white women. . . . As for white jurors—however carefully the state might examine them, they could still get one who so hated King that justice could not prevail. It was no secret that, as many white citizens had made clear to the prosecution, they would not hurry to convict Ray. It took only one man to cause a hung jury, requiring a new trial, and the onerous, disaster-frought ordeal to begin all over again.

And suppose Ray *were* found guilty? No one had gone to the chair in Tennessee in nearly ten years. Governor Ellington would commute it to ninety-nine years, as had been done in the past. Only the year before he had urged legislation to ban the death penalty. And they would have reached the same result as a guilty plea. And this without all the difficulties a long trial must bring—the possible riots, the polarization of an already traumatized community, the enormous expense—weeks of hearings, witnesses to be flown in from all parts of the world, to be housed, fed, protected by bodyguards. . . .

He told Stanton that he would have to take it under advisement.

Much the same concerns had gone through the mind of Stanton a few hours earlier. Foreman had visited Stanton, and had no sooner eased his enormous bulk into a chair than Stanton demanded, "Do you think this guy is guilty?"

Foreman did not hesitate. They were both veterans of the law. There was no point in playing games. "Yes, I do," he said.

He had begun believing Ray was probably guilty. He had often observed, half-humorously, half-cynically, that only the guilty came to Percy Foreman. They needed him. When he saw the state's evidence, there was little question in his mind of Ray's guilt. But he had counted, like Hanes, on reasonable doubt. The evidence supporting that, he quickly discovered, did not exist. He had questioned the few favorable witnesses that Renfro Hays had produced for Hanes, and were now turned over to him. They had simply collapsed on him. Either they denied they had said what they were quoted as saying, or else they did not want to testify. Harold "Cornbread" Carter, who said someone fired a rifle at the Lorraine from the bushes as he was sitting behind the rooming house, was a man who claimed to be sixty-six but looked well over seventy; he had a long history of heavy drinking and had suffered a stroke a few years before. A dubious witness, thought Foreman. And under his questioning, Carter had recanted. No, he wasn't sure that he could go on the stand and swear to it.

So, too, with Solomon Jones, Jr., Dr. King's chauffeur. He also backed away from his highly publicized story—the man with something white over his face fleeing from the same bushes. What with the excitement—Dr. King shot before his very eyes—maybe he saw a fireman or policeman with a pale blue crash helmet which looked like a white hood or sheet at that distance. . . . Foreman could not count on Jones. Dwyer would demolish him if he took the stand.

And even if they swore to their stories, it would mean nothing. The bullet that killed Dr. King could not have been fired from the level of the bushes.

It had taken a sharp downward course in Dr. King's body. A surveying team of city engineers had done precise triangulation studies. Dr. King was five feet seven and one-half inches tall. He was leaning over when he was shot, so that the bullet struck him at a point four feet eleven inches above the floor of the balcony on which he was standing. The bathroom window sill was 16.63 feet higher than the point at which the bullet struck Dr. King. For it to take the course it had taken in his body, it had to come from that window sill.

Any other version was beyond the bounds of logic.

This was true, too, of all the other stories: of John McFerren's overheard telephone call, of Attorney Russell X. Thompson's mysterious visitor, Tony Benevitas, of J. Christ Bonnevecche, who spoke to the two ministers, of Frederic Myers' report of men plotting King's assassination in the men's room of a truck stop in Tennessee, of the curly-haired man photographed in Dealey Plaza in Dallas just after President Kennedy's assassination who looked like Raoul as described by Ray, and turned out to be a vagrant found sleeping in a boxcar a mile from the scene of the assassination, of Victor Bartlett, with whom Art Hanes had had his disillusioning experience and who now harassed Foreman with long-distance calls from Nashville insisting he saw someone other than Ray shoot King from Room 5B, of the two white Mustangs which turned out to be the same car, Ray's car, seen by some parked in front of Jim's Grill and seen, minutes later, by others parked sixty feet down the street, of the story of the two Sneyds seized in London, which turned out to be based on simple error, of the man in a military jacket seen in Room 5B by Stephens' common-law wife, who could not have seen anything because she was in bed and could not have seen out the door, and all the rest of the mythology of plot. . . . They had fallen by the wayside upon investigation. And although it was true that the fatal bullet could not be proved ballistically to have come from the rifle because it had been mutilated when it struck King, the cartridge casing found in the rifle was the casing of such a bullet, and given the chain of events only an idiot, as Foreman put it, would say that it did not come from that rifle.

Above and beyond all else, Ray with his insistence upon Raoul . . .

Foreman had studied Ray. He had studied this curiously unprepossessing, hostile, grudge-carrying man who had grown up in a red-light district, whose father had abandoned his mother, whose mother died of acute alcoholism, a man who scarcely knew his siblings—in his last seven years in prison Jerry and John Ray had visited him little better than once a year, the others not at all—Ray's background could hardly be expected to make him anything but a distruster of his fellow man, a loner with a grievance, a habitual criminal. . . . Foreman had disdain for criminal thinking processes. Men who had spent years in prison, where all thinking was done for them, where they were not required to match wits against others for day-to-day survival—such men, he maintained, developed a softness of perception, of intellect, of reaction. The finest brain, he would say, if confined behind bars, must atrophy, as a muscle does, with disuse.

He had taken voluminous notes each time he visited Ray, questioning him at length, then after each session, returning to his hotel to read his notes and ask himself, *What will Canale, what will Dwyer, do with this?* He would jot down the questions he was certain they must ask. Then, at his next session with Ray, he would pose these questions to Ray. Session after session was in reality a rehearsal for the trial.

Foreman would fire his questions relentlessly:

"Where did you first meet Raoul? What time of day was it? Who else was in the room? Anyone sitting at the bar? Did the bartender see you? The barmaid? Is there any living soul we can bring into court to say he saw you and Raoul together—sitting together, having a beer together, eating together, walking together?"

But though Ray insisted that he had met Raoul at least twenty times and in public places—now at the Neptune Bar in Montreal, now in the Starlight Club in Birmingham, now in Garner's rooming house in Atlanta, now at the customs shed in Mexico, now in the rooming house in Memphis, at this restaurant and that coffee shop —not once had Ray been able to give him a name or the description of anyone who had seen them together, anyone who could corroborate the existence of Raoul.

Foreman would glare at Ray. This was impossible. He was experiencing the same frustration felt by Hanes. Hanes interpreted Ray's reluctance to be specific about Raoul as fear of being a squealer. Foreman looked at it more simply. Ray was evasive because there was no Raoul. Ray undoubtedly had dealt with various persons in his petty smuggling jobs, bringing packets of heroin in his car from Canada into the United States, transporting marijuana and contraband jewelry between the States and Mexico—and Raoul could be the generic term he used to designate these persons. But a Raoul, a man of flesh and blood who was intimately involved with Ray, a mysterious, well-heeled stranger who assigned him jobs and dispatched him about the continent and met him at one rendezvous after another and parceled out "capital" to him, and sent him to buy the rifle which Ray did not know was to be used to kill King—that simply did not stand up.

What particularly reinforced this conclusion for Foreman was the fact that Ray possessed a remarkable visual memory. He could diagram the interior of a bar, the exact detail of its furnishings, with extraordinary fidelity. It was close to total recall. Yet he could not recall anyone who had ever seen him with Raoul—or with anyone else.

Even more damaging: Ray had said that between five and six o'clock Thursday, April 4, after meeting Raoul in Room 5B of the Memphis rooming house, at Raoul's suggestion he had gone downstairs to Jim's Grill and had a beer while waiting for him. When Hanes had asked Ray to describe the interior of Jim's Grill, Ray had made a sketch which to Hanes's dismay bore no resemblance to it. Obviously, Ray had never been inside Jim's Grill. Hanes thereupon described it to him. Now, when Foreman, months later, questioned Ray about it, Ray, to prove he had been in the place, described it for

Foreman—and his description, as Huie was to point out to Foreman, was virtually Hanes's description, word for word. As the two Haneses had discovered earlier, Ray fed back to one what the other had told him. Now he was doing the same to Foreman.

There had to be only one explanation. Ray's story of Raoul—or of a companion, an employer, a co-conspirator—was pure fiction. It was made of whole cloth. This explained why the man had been vague when Hanes questioned him, as he had been vague when he tried to answer Huie's written questions; it explained why he floundered when Foreman bore down on him; it explained why Ray improvised his story as he went along, trying hopefully to insert here and there a fact or rumor that might help lend credence to it, even as he realized that he was not being believed, even as he was resigned to the fact that he must end in jail again. All this explained his apparent indifference to his plight as he sat in Shelby County Jail, as he held court in his air-conditioned quarters, read his newspapers and magazines, chose his TV programs, and played his cat-and-mouse games with his attorneys.

Foreman knew that one learned the truth not so much by what is said in reply to a direct question as by the manner in which the reply is given—or avoided. Psychoanalysts used this technique, seating themselves behind and to one side of the patient on the couch so they could observe his face and manner as he spoke.

Only a few days before, as Foreman pressed him sharply on a detail of his story, Ray had suddenly looked up and said, half plaintively, half challengingly, "I don't believe you believe that somebody else killed Dr. King." Foreman shot back, "Do *you* believe it?"

Ray's response was his self-conscious, one-sided smile—no denial, nothing else, a smile that had in it something smug, something contemptuous, something superior, a sense of a secret known but not to be put into words. At that moment Foreman knew that Ray, and Ray alone, had killed Dr. King.

So now, aloud, he replied to Stanton's question, "Do you think this guy is guilty?" with the words, "Yes, I do."

"Then it seems a wise thing to cop out—take a plea," Stanton said.

Foreman was doubtful. "You'll never be able to plead this case guilty," he said. What district attorney would give up a chance to star in the trial of a lifetime, particularly when he knew, as Canale must know, that he had it sewed up, he had an airtight case, he had to win—not to mention winning it from Percy Foreman. Foreman did not know if Phil Canale had political ambitions, but good Lord! With a case like this under his belt, Canale could walk right into the Statehouse. He could be governor.

Stanton said mildly, "I still think we might try to talk to him."

All right, said Foreman. "See what you can do." He would meanwhile check out more witnesses and then explore the subject with Ray. But he had little chance to do much at the time. Stanton telephoned him the day after Christmas to say that Canale was considering the idea but did not know what his decision would be. In any event, the next step must come from Ray. A day later Foreman came down with influenza, and for the next three weeks was bedridden in Houston.

When he was back on his feet, Foreman managed to obtain another delay—Judge Battle reluctantly postponed the trial to April 7—and began questioning other witnesses. In his absence Stanton had had two investigators interviewing nearly forty more, only to find they made the state's case even stronger. Those Foreman interviewed could contribute nothing that would help the defense. It was then that Foreman broached the subject of the guilty plea to Ray.

Ray would not hear of it. "No, I'd rather take my chances on a trial." And then, with a sudden nastiness which could crop up unexpectedly—the man was either arrogant, riding high with confidence, or humble and subdued—he said, "You don't know anything about this case except what you've read in the papers."

Foreman exploded. "Let me tell you, Jim, you go to trial and they'll burn your ass! They'll barbecue you!" He had harsh words for some of Ray's guards. "Don't let those jailhouse lawyers piss in your ear about how you saved the white race by killing King. I know what they're telling you—that the worst you'll get is a two-dollar fine for shooting a coon out of season. Don't you believe it. The jury will make an example of you. You'll fry, boy!"

No, said Ray doggedly. He had been studying the results of the Presidential election. In Shelby County, 70 per cent of the voters voted for either Wallace or Nixon. "I figure the jury will break down the same way, so I got a seventy–thirty chance to get off."

Not so, said Foreman. This jury would be like a blue ribbon jury—men there to do their duty. His strongest argument was based on two recent murder trials in Memphis. In one, a jury had given ninety-nine years to a girl involved in a murder which she herself had not committed; in the second, a ninety-nine-year term had been given to a naval petty officer with a perfect record. Both were cases which in other times would have brought a far lighter sentence.

Ray was stubborn. "I don't want to plead guilty. No white man ever got the chair in Tennessee for shooting a Nigger." Suppose Wallace became President in 1972. He would pardon him—might even give him the Medal of Honor. Ray grinned his sardonic smile. Even if he did get the chair, and even if Wallace never became President, and whatever President sat in the White House refused to pardon him, "It'd be twenty years before they'd execute me, and you and me would both be gone by then."

No, said Foreman wrathfully, he was misjudging the country. There was a vast difference between today and a few years ago. John Kennedy had been assassinated, Martin Luther King had been assassinated, Robert Kennedy had been assassinated. Why shouldn't they want to make an example of James Earl Ray? If he thought he had endeared himself to anyone by killing King, he was a damn fool. He put the blacks on the warpath throughout the country and he had scared the shit out of the whites, and, as for Memphis, from where the jurors would be drawn, he had torn Memphis apart and won the garbage strike for the blacks. Before he came along, the city had King and his forces on the run; the union never would have won the strike. But with King's death, Mayor Loeb and the white establishment had to back down. They hated Ray; he was the cause of all their troubles —not to mention the riots, the burnings of property, the loss of millions of dollars of business through the curfew. . . . Whites and blacks both had no use for him. Nobody was ready to hail James Earl Ray, except in his own fantasies.

"You can't deny the evidence," Foreman told him. He killed King. If he went on trial, his only defense would be that he was the tool of a conspiracy. Did Ray not realize that that put him in an even worse position than if he had killed King out of conviction? "Don't you see that to be a hired killer is more contemptible than to kill a man because you sincerely think you're doing the right thing? Do you think that jury will think better of you if you killed only for money, and were therefore available to kill anybody—including the members of that jury—rather than just a man who got rid of King because he believed he was a danger to the country?"

Ray was silent and unmoved. Clearly, the man actually believed he stood higher in the jury's estimation as a hired killer: it made him an elite professional in a world of swindlers, rapists, thugs, and burglars. There was one other factor. Ray might also think in his twisted mind that, as a hired killer, he would not be responsible for King's death; the responsibility would be on the conspirators.

Meanwhile, Canale had been wrestling with the problem of the guilty plea. The attorney general, whose father before him had been a distinguished lawyer and civic leader, was a moderate man, a devout Catholic who hated violence. He had had his fill of death in World War II, where, as an Air Corps major, he had flown many combat missions. He had been so deeply affected that when he returned he wrote a poem, *I Know, for I Was There*, which had been widely printed.* He himself had not prosecuted a murder case since 1961. He had then won a death penalty, but knew little peace of mind until the governor commuted the sentence to ninety-nine years the very morning that the man, a Negro convicted of rape and murder, was to go to the chair. Canale had asked his pastor only minutes before to offer up a mass for the repose of the man's soul.

Because in the years since Canale had been busy with administrative tasks, he had decided to direct the Ray prosecution but to leave the trying of the case to Dwyer and Beasley. Now that it was ready to go forward, he faced the complicated question of the plea.

A guilty plea meant no adversary trial. Once the agreement had been worked out between state and defense, a brief public hearing would be held at which the state would establish the corpus delicti —that Dr. King had been alive, he had been unlawfully killed, and the man before the bar was responsible. There would be no cross-examination. None was needed: the man had admitted the crime. Only if he had denied it would the state be required to prove that he had done it. Under Tennessee law, however, the state would have to outline for benefit of jury and public what it would have proved had there been a full-scale trial. The jury would then vote acceptance of the plea and the judge would sentence the man to ninety-nine years in the State Penitentiary at Nashville.

How many of the public would understand this? Canale wondered, *If this case ends without a full-dress trial, they'll think I'm trying to suppress the surfacing of a conspiracy, that we're all trying to hide something.*

The day after Stanton broached the subject to him, Canale telephoned Stephen Pollak, head of the Civil Rights Division in the Justice Department, and Robert D. Owen, his first assistant, both

* One stanza read: "I saw Death stalk across the earth/And wield his sharpened sword;/I felt his breath upon my neck,/And trudged through blood he poured."

men with whom he had checked out various questions of the law in the past. He, of course, would make the decision on the guilty plea, which would also have to have the consent of Judge Battle, but he would be interested to know the reaction of the Justice Department. The two men in Washington said they would take it up with Ramsey Clark.

Over the next two months Canale made many calls, exchanged many letters. What if this was a trick? Assuming Foreman convinced Ray to plead guilty—why should Ray agree? If he did agree, what might be going through that devious mind of his? Could this be a ploy—for example, Ray would agree to plead guilty, come into court, hear the state outline its proof, then, if the state's case appeared not as strong as feared, withdraw his plea and demand to go to trial? Ray could change his mind, no matter what he promised. He could stand up in court at the last minute and pull out. He was a last-minute man. He fired Hanes at the last minute.

Dwyer and Beasley were deeply concerned too. They knew they had a perfect case. Dwyer, particularly, had looked forward to trying it. It would crown a career of seventeen years in the attorney general's office. He thought, *Maybe this is why I spent all my years here, never left Memphis—this was waiting for me, to try the biggest lawsuit of the century against the biggest lawyer in the country.* When Hanes had been fired, and Percy Foreman had unexpectedly appeared, to be lionized by the press, lawyers, public, Dwyer had watched him walk into court. He thought, *Well, he walks, he stands, he sits—he's human, I can take him.*

Aside from his personal disappointment, the motives of both Ray and Foreman troubled him. *What about Foreman?* Canale and Dwyer knew considerably more about the celebrated attorney than he had any idea. They had studied his major cases, his behavior in court, his flamboyant stratagems, the techniques by which he had built up that extraordinary record of defending perhaps a thousand accused murderers and losing only one to the chair. They had reports from lawyers who had crossed swords with him: they had even studied tapes of his speeches before law students. They had researched Percy Foreman well. Now they could only conclude that Foreman, like them, had reached the same realization: the defense simply had no case. It was Ray and only Ray all the way through. If Foreman, with his tremendous reputation, and with all that rode on this case, not to mention the staggering sums being talked about if film rights

were sold—if Foreman thought he had the slightest chance of winning, nothing would have made him consider a guilty plea. They had
to believe in his sincerity.

Then the question rose, How would the black community in the
United States react? The King family?

On December 31, the last day of this upsetting year, Canale telephoned Harry Wachtel, a New York lawyer, who was Mrs. King's
personal attorney, to request him to ascertain her reaction should
Ray plead guilty and the state accept his plea. It was not known
whether this would happen, but there was a possibility. Wachtel said
he would take it up with the widow, as well as with Dr. King's parents,
the Rev. Abernathy, and other SCLC leaders.

On January 2, Wachtel called back. Mrs. King and Dr. King's parents were conscientiously and morally opposed to capital punishment.
Therefore, they had no objection if Ray pleaded guilty and took
ninety-nine years. If this came about, Mrs. Coretta King would issue
a statement of approval. She had reservations, to be sure. The family
and Dr. King's associates still believed that others could be involved
in the murder, but they also realized that this information probably
would not come out even were there a trial.

That was true, Canale said. He added, "I can assure you that we
have no evidence whatsoever of a conspiracy, but you can be sure
that if any evidence ever comes to us pointing to a conspiracy, I will
vigorously prosecute it. There's no statute of limitations in Tennessee
to first-degree murder." The case would never really be closed.

In the interim Pollak had called back to report that Attorney
General Clark thought that, since Tennessee allowed others in similar
cases to plead guilty, it would be inconsistent—and probably not
equal justice before the law—to refuse Ray this right. Clark felt that
in a public sense a trial would be of value, but in a legal sense the
man had the right to plead guilty and, if he chose to do so, the law
did not have the power to force him to face a trial. Pollak added
for himself: I think chances of Ray pleading guilty are pretty remote.

By the end of January, Canale had put out straws to test the wind
in as many directions as possible. Black leaders in Memphis had no
objection. Most of the Negro community felt the same. The black
man on the street had contempt, rather than hatred, for James Earl
Ray. The black citizens of Memphis did not doubt that Ray was involved, but they, too, could not believe that he had acted alone.

Canale came to his decision. If Ray changed his plea from not guilty to guilty, they would accept it but under the stiffest possible terms.

On Friday, February 21, the die was cast.

Foreman called Canale from Houston to say he had obtained a signed statement from Ray asking to be allowed to plead guilty.

"Is this a definite commitment?" Canale asked.

"Yes, he's agreed," Foreman said. He added that he had gone to St. Louis the Tuesday before, ostensibly to prosecute a lawsuit, but he had secretly visited Ray's sister, Mrs. Carol Pepper. At his request she had set up a family conference with John and Jerry Ray, and their father, Jerry Rayns, now seventy, whom she had brought in from his small farm in Center, Missouri.

Foreman had wanted to meet the family, first to determine, in case Ray insisted on going to trial, whether he could use any as witnesses to show the jury that Ray had people like their own brothers, sisters, and fathers; and, second, to point out to the family that if Jim did go to trial, he, Foreman, did not think he could save his life. The state's evidence was unanswerable. Jim was locked into the murder—absolutely nothing could be done about it. They would not have a single witness to controvert the state's evidence, unless Jim himself took the stand; and if he did, most jurors would probably consider the fact that from his twentieth year he had spent more than 75 per cent of his life behind bars, and though they might have a doubt about his guilt, at best they would send him away for life; at worst, put him in the chair.

Jim must plead guilty, accept ninety-nine years, and save his skin. It would be wise for Jim's family to let Foreman carry back that advice.

Foreman told Canale that the family had agreed on the plea,* and that he had brought this to Ray, who did not like it. Anyway, Ray didn't think that Canale would go along with a plea. Ray thought the state would insist on the chair. "But I told him, General, that you're a Christian man, and not one to let your office become bigger than you." In the end, Ray had agreed. If Ray backed out at any time, Foreman added, Ray knew what to expect: he, Foreman, would with-

---

* Ray's family—Jerry Rayns, his father; Mrs. Carol Pepper, his sister; John and Jerry Ray, his brothers—all who took part in the meeting with Foreman—were to insist later that they never advised Ray to plead guilty. The message they sent to their brother, through Foreman, they said, was for him to do what he thought best.

draw from the case, leaving Ray high and dry. Foreman added that he would do all in his power to keep Ray to the guilty plea.

Foreman meant this. He had had his fill of Ray. Since that day when he demanded of him, "Do you believe it?"—do you believe that someone else killed Dr. King—and he realized that Ray wanted to tell him that he was, indeed, the man, wanted to boast about it, and yet not tell him—since that day Ray's behavior had completely disenchanted Foreman. He had had one frustrating experience after another with him.

In mid-January, after Foreman got over his illness, a remarkable gift had fallen into his lap. The Rev. James Bevel, one of Dr. King's closest associates, the leader of the SCLC's workshops on nonviolence, had publicly announced that Ray was innocent—and that he, Bevel, could prove Ray had not killed Dr. King. He had wired Ray: I know that you are not guilty and I am prepared to come to Memphis and defend you at your trial.

It was a sensational development for the defense. Foreman was certain that Bevel, known for his mysticism, his sometimes involved analyses of the black-white struggle, yet a man who could be amazingly lucid when he wished, would probably be of little actual help. Co-operation with Bevel, however, might mean an entry with the Rev. Martin Luther King, Sr., or with Coretta King. Foreman thought he might even elicit their help in saving Ray's life, if Ray insisted on going to trial. He determined to go ahead with Bevel's suggestion only to find Ray adamantly opposed. He would have nothing to do with Bevel. He told his lawyer: if we take any favors from Niggers, we'll lose the support of all our own people. Ray meant, of course, the white people. He saw himself leading a white fight against the blacks, in Foreman's view, and feared that any contact with Bevel would destroy his support. He was almost violent on the subject. It was astonishing, Foreman thought: this man had a deep-seated, obsessive hatred for Negroes which he had managed to conceal with extraordinary success from almost everyone. It was the best kept secret of James Earl Ray. But now, when the chips were down, he could not hide it. It had been there all the time, though. When Foreman first entered the case he had wanted a Tennessee lawyer familiar with Tennessee law to sit at the defense table with him. He had told Ray in their first week that if he could hire John J. Hooker, Sr., of Nashville, the distinguished attorney who was Foreman's own lawyer in Tennessee, it would be a tremendous coup for them. Ray was enormously grateful. Fine, Mr. Foreman, he said, fine.

That had been on a Friday. When Foreman saw Ray again, on Monday, Ray said, "I don't want Hooker." Over the weekend one of his guards had told him that Hooker's son, John J. Hooker, Jr., had been a candidate for the Democratic nomination for governor of Tennessee two years before, "and he got every Nigger vote in the state." Nothing Foreman could say—"You damn fool, we're talking about saving your neck!"—would change Ray's mind.

When Ray had been in Leavenworth in the late fifties, he had been kept in the serious offenders' section, under rigorous discipline. He had worked in the kitchen and done well, however, and toward the end of his term he was offered the chance to spend the remaining year in an honor farm—a halfway house to freedom. To live there meant many privileges. Prisoners jumped at the chance. Ray refused. His prison record showed that he turned down the offer because the dormitory was integrated and he would not sleep in the same room with blacks.

Then, on the occasions when he could not control himself, when liquor made him less guarded, it showed itself again, as in Acapulco, where he was restrained from pursuing the black sailors, as in Los Angeles, where he suddenly exploded at the Rabbit's Foot Club. . . .

And now the Bevel situation.* Nonetheless, on the evening of January 23, Foreman took Bevel and Rev. William Rutherford, who had also been an aide to King, to Shelby County Jail. Ray had been so exercised by Foreman's suggestion that he had written a letter to be given Foreman when he arrived repeating that he would not have anything to do with Bevel. Foreman insisted and finally prevailed on Ray to let them speak to him, but Ray refused to allow the two black ministers in his cell block: they had to stand outside and talk to him through a two-inch screened aperture in the door, which was unsatisfactory because Ray could hardly make out Bevel's quick, impassioned words, and Ray's reluctance to talk made his monosyllabic returns almost unintelligible. Bevel told Ray that King had been killed either by business interests who feared his influence over the poor, or by political interests who feared his anti-Vietnam influence; that Ray, who obviously could not have killed King—he could not have "conceptualized" such a murder—believed in his simple-minded

---

* Not until later did Huie tell Foreman that after the guilty plea, Jerry and John Ray had said: "All his life Jimmy has been wild on two subjects. He's been wild against Niggers and he's been wild on politics. He's wild against any politician who's for Niggers, and he's wild for any politician who's against Niggers. Nobody can reason with Jimmy on the two subjects of Niggers and politics."

fashion that he had only to say in court that he had not done it to be acquitted. Bevel admitted that he was not a lawyer, but his presence at the defense table would immobilize the prosecution. What prosecutor could challenge Bevel's motives as they could Hanes, a lawyer for Klansmen, or Foreman, out to win at any price? "The white folks need a victim," he told Ray. "What you got to have is a lawyer to develop as much sentiment as the prosecution can. I can do this. Otherwise, your trial is going to be just an emotional lynching party, a war dance and a killing."

Ray's response to this was such that Foreman hastily intervened, explaining to Bevel that his client "thinks he has got the best lawyer now and doesn't feel he needs more help."

The interview was over and the two black ministers left.*

There was nothing else to be done. The man had to be pleaded guilty.

So it was arranged. Canale, for his part, felt that he actually had little option in the matter if he wanted to be absolutely fair. As Ramsey Clark had pointed out, Tennessee had always allowed a guilty plea. Canale had to give Ray equal treatment. The length of sentence, Canale told Foreman, would of course have to be the maximum—ninety-nine years. No objection, said Foreman. Nor would his client object to ninety-nine years. At such times as Ray was not telling him how to practice law, Foreman said, he was making clear to him that no matter what sentence was meted out to him, "he does not expect to serve more than two years. It doesn't make any difference to him." Ray was confident that he would either break out —or be pardoned.

Now both sides moved swiftly, but with great secrecy, toward the day of the guilty plea.

* Bevel later explained to friends that he had wanted to "sensitize" the country. "The black lawyers of the United States should have taken Ray's case and made the people understand that you can't bring one cat back by killing another: all you have then is two cats dead. If we can't do something after such a tragedy to sensitize people, leave them with a broader perspective, a broader perception, we have failed to make use of the event. People must see that killing—killing of any kind—is ridiculous. It solves nothing."

CHAPTER XXXII

In Hartselle, Alabama, William Bradford Huie, working separately, checking everything Ray had written him and all that Hanes had told him of his sessions with Ray, had come to the same conclusion even earlier: Ray killed King. He had done it alone. It was not a conspiracy.

Huie had proclaimed that it was a conspiracy, into which Ray had been drawn unknowingly, in two articles in *Look* magazine, dated November 12, and November 26. Now he would have to admit that he had made, as he put it, "a serious mistake." He would acknowledge this in his third and final article to appear after the trial, scheduled for April 7, 1969, and in the book that would appear shortly after.*

He felt unhappy about his role. He would have to bear a considerable part of the blame for promoting the idea of conspiracy. Now it would be almost impossible to shake that conviction from the minds of many people. Not that they would take his word that it was, or was not: so many *wanted* to believe that it was a conspiracy, and he had mistakenly encouraged them. There was, obviously, a profound need to believe in conspiracies. It seemed unjust, it was intolerable to accept by most people, that a great figure could so easily, so instantly be destroyed by the whim, or obsession, or delusion, of some anonymous and wretched human being suffering his own private malady and unhappiness, engaged in his own search for a place in the sun: that a Martin Luther King could be destroyed by a ne'er-do-well James Earl Ray. One wanted to believe in a world of equal cause and effect, as one had been taught in school: a world of balance in which evil was punished and good rewarded. In such a world, a great and elaborate machinery was required to eliminate a great figure. Otherwise, there was no justice in the world, there was no balance in nature.

Huie had been willing to believe there was a plot. But he could not find Raoul, as Foreman could not find Raoul, as Hanes before Foreman could not find Raoul, as the FBI and the Royal Canadian Mounted Police and the Mexican Federal Police, as the police of

* *He Slew the Dreamer,* by William Bradford Huie. Delacorte Press, 1970.

St. Louis, Chicago, Los Angeles, New Orleans, Birmingham, Atlanta, Memphis, Toronto, and Montreal could not find Raoul. Hanes and Foreman both noted that Ray's behavior when questioned about Raoul was conspicuously characteristic. It never differed. He acted as he always acted when caught in a lie—and this from childhood on. He reddened, he looked down at his feet, he squirmed in his seat, he was acutely uncomfortable—the lie was written all over him. So it had been when he was a child in Ewing, questioned by schoolteachers, a teen-ager in Alton and Quincy, questioned by police, a soldier in Germany, questioned by his superiors, a prisoner in Leavenworth and Missouri State Penitentiary, questioned by wardens and parole officers—and now it was the same when, as the celebrated guest of Shelby County Jail, he was questioned by his own lawyers. His reaction was like a tic. He could not control it. It betrayed him each time.

And if one were to suspend one's common sense—to assume that, however invisible, Raoul did exist, and had directed Ray—what was Raoul's motivation? Why should this thirty-five-year-old French-Canadian seaman, involved in smuggling and similar activities, want to kill Martin Luther King, Jr.?

Suspend one's common sense still more: assume that he wanted to kill King. Why would he have chosen as his associate James Earl Ray, a stranger he picked up on the Montreal waterfront? Why should he have chosen such a man for so delicate an assignment—to buy the rifle, to return it, to rent the room from which Dr. King would be shot? Nothing in Ray's record would give anyone confidence that he could carry out such assignments.

Now, suspend one's common sense again, to the third order. Assume that Raoul wanted to kill King and hired Ray as a decoy, a patsy. Why? Why could Raoul not have killed King without bringing Ray upon the scene? Whether or not Raoul pulled the trigger, Raoul would be just as guilty before the law. Why have a James Earl Ray there to point to him, to say, "He hired me," or, "He did it"? If Raoul was the man to kill King, he did not need James Earl Ray; he could have killed King and made a complete getaway, and there would not have been anyone named Ray to say there was a man called Raoul, to give police a description of him, or, in the event Raoul's photograph was in the FBI files, to pick it out and say, "That's the man who made me the decoy and wants me to take the rap for him." In short, why choose an inexperienced man, brief him patiently on the rifle to buy, send him back to exchange it when he bought the wrong one, tell him where to go, where to stay—when Raoul could have done it all himself, immediately, efficiently, and without a witness?

It was all utterly ridiculous, if one thought about it.

What also was disillusioning were Ray's lies. Some were harmless. If he wanted to say that he escaped by scaling a wall, so as not to implicate prisoners who helped him, if he wanted to say he robbed a brothel and not a supermarket, if he wanted to say he met a "friend" after his escape rather than his brother—these were unimportant. But Ray tried to maintain the fiction that he bought the rifle only as a sample to be shown Raoul's customers in Memphis. Why Memphis, one might ask, if the idea was to run guns to Mexico? And why a meeting in Memphis on the very day that Dr. King was shot, to discuss and look at the type of gun and a type of ammunition which were precisely the type of gun and type of ammunition used to kill Dr. King?

And the picture of Raoul dashing down the stairs of the rooming house, throwing himself into the back seat of the Mustang, then covering himself with a white sheet. . . . Why should Raoul have hidden under a white sheet? Nothing could have made him more conspicuous. But Ray had read that Solomon Jones saw a figure with something white about his head fleeing from behind the rooming house, and in some surrealistic childish corner of Ray's mind the one might justify the other.

Huie communicated with Foreman, who as Hanes's successor had also taken over Hanes's contractual obligations—and proceeds, if any —in their arrangement with Ray. There was no disagreement. Huie, too, agreed, as state and defense agreed:

Ray had done it. Difficult though it was to believe, Ray had done it. Alone.

Why?

Canale and his aides knew that they could not wrap up Ray's motives for killing King in a single, neat package. The difficulty with putting oneself in the mind of a criminal was that his logic was not as that of other men. This always hampered the hunters, asking themselves the classic question, What would I do if I were in his shoes? In Ray's case there was another element. There was something in Ray that made him do the inappropriate, the capricious, throwing the careful investigator, proceeding by logic and experience, off the trail. It explained why he had been so hard to catch.

But the idea to kill King, the focusing upon him as an object, must have been intensifying itself in the back of Ray's mind for a long time. In Missouri State Penitentiary, inmates recalled how he would snort indignantly when he read in the news magazines about Stokely Carmichael, or H. Rap Brown, or Adam Clayton Powell—or, as he called him, Martin Lucifer King. When Ray was in Birmingham in the late summer of 1967, buying his white Mustang, claiming to be a ship's worker on vacation, the name of Dr. King was never far away. The man had been a thorn in the city's side for a long time, and each time he came into the news, the local papers broke out with angry, outraged letters to the Editor. While Ray was in Birmingham the Birmingham *News* carried several such letters. One read: "It has been revealed that the FBI has unimpeachable evidence, including photographs, showing that Dr. King is now associated with a man who is the biggest money raiser in the Communist Party, and clearly is more interested in destroying the United States than he is in civil rights." There were others, all denouncing the man as a menace to the country. Ray—his entire family—were bitterly anti-Communist. Ray himself religiously read *The Thunderbolt*, the publication of the National States Rights Party, whose lawyer and organizer, J. B. Stoner, who claimed that Negroes fell somewhere between man and ape, had repeatedly offered to become Ray's defense counsel. It was *The Thunderbolt* which had dubbed King Martin Lucifer King, and which, after his assassination, declared that whoever had done it should receive the Medal of Honor and a Presidential pardon. The paper was forever linking Jews and Negroes in a world Communist plot to bastardize the white race through interracial marriage. When one considered what had been discovered about Ray's true attitude toward Negroes—the observation of his brothers that "Jimmy's been wild against Niggers all his life . . . It's a subject you can't reason with him about," and the observation of Walter Rife, the ex-convict who as a boy had played with Ray and as a man had robbed and been jailed with him, that "Jim was prejudiced to a point that he hated to see a colored person breathe . . . If it was up to him, they'd either be shipped back to Africa or disposed of in some way,"—when one considered this attitude, how much did the almost palpable fear and hatred of King wherever Ray moved and looked in Birmingham and elsewhere in the South, and in Los Angeles in the wake of the Watts riots, play on him and help slowly bring an idea to fruition?

It was not necessary for anyone to approach Ray and formally offer him a large sum of money to kill King. The urgency to strike at King and all he stood for came out of the very atmosphere in which Ray grew up and lived, particularly in his years in prison where whites were bitterly hostile toward blacks*; it came from the knowledge that somewhere in the land there must be those who would "take good care" of him if he rid the world of Martin Luther King, Jr.; and from the rumor of the million-dollar bounty awaiting the man who would do this.

However, given even such powerful motives—the promise, if not tacit, then in the very air, of enormous sums of money, and his deep hatred of Negroes, even these might not cause a man to kill. The motives for murder, the men in Memphis knew, for this murder, were not simple: racism, anti-Communism, patriotism, the yearning for status of a man doomed from birth to be last on the totem pole, the resentment of such a man for a "Nigger" who had the arrogance of fame, the admiration of white women; the private rage always held in check, seeking an object, waiting for the moment of full, triumphant, revengeful release—all these played a part. But the mystery would have to be sought deeper, in the roots of Ray's character, in the tremendous hostility of the sociopath, the man eternally suspicious, fighting for his existence against a society he saw as his enemy. Indeed, it would have been strange had Ray not become a sociopath. He had grown up in a broken home with a drunken mother, an absent father, a retarded brother, a sister who was to be committed to mental institutions—the father an ex-con, his uncle Earl an ex-con, Jerry and John, his brothers, ex-cons. In the Quincy he knew best from his 16th year on—the Quincy known as the most wide-open town on the Mississippi—the Ray house on Spring near Third Street was in a neighborhood notorious for its population of gamblers, pimps, prostitutes, thieves and dope-peddlers, where he was exposed to the worst of poverty and the worst of companions. To be ambitious there meant to be ambitious to make one's mark in crime.

* John Ray had said to a reporter, "If I hit a supermarket or rob a man on the street, that's a crime against a person or business. That guy King was an enemy of America. J. Edgar Hoover said so, didn't he? He called him a Communist . . . I rob a place and I wind up with seven to ten, and working in that hot laundry, but some Nigger rapes a white woman and gets two years and works in the kitchen. Them Niggers would always give the big pieces of meat to other Niggers and would fish out a little piece for you." Also what infuriated John and other white inmates were comments blacks made as they watched prison movies—what thrills they'd give the white actresses if they had the chance.

Above and beyond this was the fact that Ray belonged to a family always in conflict with the authorities, one that had a long-time score to settle with a society which had dismantled it, taken it apart and passed its members around to be reared by others. One could understand why Ray saw this society as his bitter enemy always tricking and duping and victimizing him, so that he had to plot shrewdly and cunningly to outwit it.

There was, too, a method in his madness when he assaulted King.

Ray was an escaped convict. If he had been picked up by the police walking harmlessly on the street, he would have had to go back to serve his thirteen unserved years, plus those years added as punishment for his escape—which, to him at forty, might well be a life sentence. He would go back, too, as the same anonymous small-time thief and holdup man for whose capture the state of Missouri offered the humiliating reward of fifty dollars. But *after* King—if he was caught, he would go back a hero, one of the FBI's "Ten Most Wanted," a peer among peers in the only world he respected and wanted respect from: to him the superior, cynically sophisticated criminal world, the only world in which he had been able to make his mark.

The electric chair, as punishment, seemed remote. Certainly, as he told Foreman, no Southern jury would send a white man to the chair for killing a "Nigger," and even if it did, no one was executed these days. There was even the possibility that King's assassination would set off a wave of such riots and violence by the "black savages"—to use *The Thunderbolt*'s favorite term for Negroes—that the outraged whites would rise in their wrath and steamroller Wallace into the White House—and then Ray would receive a pardon, which would also wipe out the sentence still hanging over him at Missouri State Penitentiary.

In short, however one examined it, Ray had almost everything to gain and nothing to lose.

And so he had acted.

On Friday, March 7, Judge Battle unexpectedly announced that he would hold a special hearing the following Monday at 9 A.M. It concerned "a development in the James Earl Ray case." The hearing had been requested by Mr. Foreman, who had asked that Ray be present in court.

Battle refused to say more. All other sources were clamped shut. But the story was everywhere, and it filled the press here and abroad. Ray would plead guilty and accept ninety-nine years. Ray would fire Foreman as he had fired Hanes. Ray would stand up in court and make a clean breast of everything, revealing the conspiracy, naming names. . . .

There was no end to the speculation. Perhaps not only the King assassination would be brought into the open, but at long last, that of President Kennedy, even Senator Kennedy. . . .

9 A.M., Monday, March 10, 1969.

James Earl Ray's forty-first birthday.

CHAPTER XXXIII

In his chambers, Judge Battle was reading the last pages of *Wigmore on Evidence*—a Bible of the law. He had set himself the task, in preparation for the Ray trial, to read most of the ten volumes, each seven hundred pages, in order to refresh himself on all the points of law that might arise.

Sitting behind his desk, reading, he had a habit of pursing his mouth, jutting out his lower lip like a boy, pouting and stubborn, as a thought occurred to him. He had a habit, too, when presiding in court, where he seemed to belong as though he had been born to the position, of looking down over his black half-rimmed glasses—a plump, somewhat roly-poly man, who with his black robe, his white shirt like a breastpiece, his chin buried in his chest, the glasses perched an inch down his nose, looked more like a penguin than anything else.

His black hair neatly brushed, parted a little to the left, one saw in the older man the face of the Harvard-Yale undergraduate in the Scott Fitzgerald days. It was that kind of a face. College albums of the turn of the century, particularly the football teams, were full of them, the hair then parted directly down the center, the wholesome, proper face.

Few knew how arduously Judge Battle had prepared for this occasion. He had taken it all on his shoulders. Canale had had the prosecution, but Battle had had both prosecution and defense to contend with, holding them both in rein, knowing that everything that took place in his court would be open to review, analysis, and constant replaying. He had said more than once, to his friends, "I'm going to have to live with this case the rest of my life."

He, too, had wrestled with the problem of the guilty plea. In Tennessee the judge was considered the thirteenth juror. He had to approve the action in his courtroom. He had to weigh the issues and their consequences. He knew the question of conspiracy agitated the country, but even were the state to refuse Ray's plea and force him to trial, who was to say that this question would be resolved? Ray most likely would not take the stand. If he did, there was no assurance that he would give any more revealing answers than to repeat, as he had from the very first, the story about Raoul.

Battle had always been deeply ashamed of the Scopes "Monkey Trial" in Dayton, Tennessee, in the 1920's. Then a precocious high-school student, he had cringed to see how Tennessee became a laughingstock throughout the country for insisting upon prosecuting a schoolteacher because he taught evolution. And so Battle had promised himself that, if he had anything to say about it, the trial of James Earl Ray for the murder of Dr. Martin Luther King, Jr., would make amends for that long-ago farce. It had explained his unprecedentedly strict rules against publicity, his holding in contempt even the defense counsel for talking out of court, his rigorous measures to ensure a proper hearing.

At the first weekly Thursday luncheon after Ray's arrest in London, when Battle and his four colleagues drew straws to see who would get the case, and Battle found it was himself, he was not surprised. He had said, "Well, it's my baby." Somehow, he had expected it. The interesting point was that, had it been given to a vote of the others, Battle would have been chosen to preside.

He had never hidden the fact of his alcoholism, which had begun in his high-school days. Despite his high grades—he was valedictorian of his high-school class and entered the university on a scholarship— he was expelled for drunkenness. Later he managed to complete his undergraduate work, attend law school, and, as a protégé of Boss Crump, become a district prosecuting attorney, then a successful criminal lawyer before his election as a criminal courts judge. He had been a good, sound jurist, running a taut court, learned in the law and scrupulously conscious of his duty and obligations. He was proud that he had not taken a drink since New Year's Day, 1945. In recent years he lectured publicly for Alcoholics Anonymous. Many times he had sat, night after night, at the bedside of other distinguished Memphians in his profession, helping them through the agony of a "cold turkey" withdrawal. As he had been helped, so he helped others, and though they might meet in court and in the law corridors, no one was the wiser. He was highly respected.

Battle was considerably taken aback when Huie entered the case. The quickness and assurance with which the writer had moved into the situation nonplused him. Huie, as he saw it, stood in a quasi-lawyer-client relationship to Ray, and although Battle did not like this arrangement, he felt helpless to do anything about it if Ray's attorney and Ray himself wished it so. Yet, he could not help speculating. Could it be possible that Ray's payment for killing King—*if* he had been hired—was via Huie-Ray-Hanes? Was this an elaborate façade created to enable Ray and his counsel to receive additional moneys that might be waiting for them? Huie had known Hanes before King's murder.

Even to allow himself to think in this fashion, Battle knew, might be outrageously unfair to Huie and to Hanes, but no one was absolutely above suspicion in so wide-ranging a case. *If* it was a conspiracy. If there was a payoff, one had to look for the money: and wherever money accrued to James Earl Ray, one had to examine the process coldly and impersonally.

Such were Judge Battle's concerns as the trial approached. Yet he did not lessen his calendar. He insisted, even while preparing for the Ray trial, upon hearing all the cases in his docket. It meant taking work home, and sometimes finding himself so involved in it, so wrought up, that he was unable to get food down until nearly eleven o'clock each night.

He could not know that in the end this case would be the death of him—and help make almost endless its legal aftermath.

CHAPTER XXXIV

Under extraordinary security precautions, the special hearing began.

The first to be allowed into the small courtroom were Jerry and John Ray: bailiffs escorted them in at 8:45 A.M. Both wore dark suits: dark-eyed, dark-haired, with aquiline faces, long thin noses and receding hairlines, they bore striking resemblance to Ray. They took seats together in the third row of the public area behind the chancel rail, and sat side by side, hands folded in their laps. Jerry, particularly, looked like some medieval Italian monk with his dark eyes gleaming in a saturnine dark face, above a white shirt which emphasized the contrast, and in a swift glance could be mistaken for a monk's white cowl. John, lighter complexioned, grimmer in the set of his mouth, looked more the man of everyday affairs. But both were somber in mood, both looked straight ahead, not even by a flicker of their eyes betraying any interest in those who filed in to take seats on either side of them, in front and behind them. They sat almost at attention. They had spent the last two days and nights under the name Ryan at the Tennessee Hotel, which occupied eight floors near the Greyhound Bus Terminal across the street from the Peabody Hotel. Across the front of the hotel was a huge sign blazing at night with electric bulbs which always spelled out a pious biblical admonition, even though some of the Tennessee's roomers were women with numerous male callers. The message was changed each week. This week's read: JESUS SAVES!

Meanwhile, the reporters and special writers fortunate enough to have seats were also filing in. By nine o'clock all were in their places —thirty-eight, as always, seated on the right side of the courtroom. They were silent, craning, noting every person who came in. Each had gone through Sheriff Morris's rigorous ritual of search. Each had, in addition, stood before a videotape machine (the same that recorded Ray's arrival and every appearance he had made in court) and stated name and publication. Each this time had been given an identity card not only with his photograph but fingerprints and each knew that in Morris's file room his voice was on record. The same procedure had been undergone by everyone—not only had Judge

Battle and the other court officers been searched, but they too had stood self-consciously before the videotape machine to identify themselves and state their purpose in the courtroom. Even before the room had been opened for the proceedings, the deputy sheriff in charge of preparing it had stood before the machine to give his name and formally announce, "This courtroom is now ready for the James Earl Ray hearing." Posterity would never have to doubt what took place in the James Earl Ray case in Memphis.

At 9:30 half a dozen aides walked in, carrying the evidence: one man with a black suitcase, another with the blue plastic overnight bag, a third with the rifle with an identifying tag on it. In front of the chancel rail were two large tables, objects on them covered with white sheets. These were mock-ups of the murder scene and the surrounding area—the rooming house at 422½ South Main Street, the Lorraine Motel and Hotel, the buildings immediately about. They were extraordinary examples of precision and detail, built to perfect scale (even to the size of the letters on the swinging sign, ROOMS, that hung in front of the entrance of the rooming house).

A moment later Ray appeared, preceded by Sheriff Morris and followed by a huge deputy. He looked paler than before. He was dressed in the same small checked blue-and-brown sport jacket and slacks, but the shell-rimmed glasses were missing. He wore a white shirt, a narrow blue tie, and it was obvious that he had been told what chair to take, for he walked directly to it in his rolling farmer's gait—as though he were walking over furrows—his eyes fixed only on it. He did not look at anyone in the courtroom, he did not look at his brothers, and, once seated, he stared straight ahead, almost as if he feared, even by accident, to catch anyone's glance. Dr. Freeman, the psychologist he had consulted in Los Angeles, said Ray actually thought one could hypnotize anyone by looking him in the eye. Could this fear explain the characteristic observed by everyone who ever dealt with Ray—his extreme reluctance to look anyone in the eye?

All were now in their places, the general audience in six rows, seven chairs to a row. No members of Dr. King's family were present. Although three seats had been offered them, they had preferred not to attend. On the left side of the room was the jury box; on the right, a row of chairs occupied by armed deputies in business suits, each of whom had his specific duties. Among those seated here was Dr. DeMere, so placed that he had an unobstructed view of James Earl Ray's face. Two deputies were to keep their eyes, as well, on

Ray at all times, prepared to shield him against attack, or to throw themselves upon him if he should suddenly go berserk. Others had been assigned to guard the principals: Judge Battle, Canale, Foreman. Others were posted so that in the event of any disturbance in the corridors outside the courtroom, they could instantly surround Ray and rush him to a place of safety. As in Operation Landing, every eventuality had been anticipated by Sheriff Morris, the possible moves worked out in advance as if it were a bizarre chess match with human beings instead of pieces.

The bailiff rose and called the court to order. Judge Battle appeared, plump in his black robe, and took his seat at the high bench. "All right," he said briskly. "I believe the only matter we have pending before us is the matter of James Earl Ray."

As Battle spoke, Foreman had been slowly rising to his feet, and stood there, waiting, a huge man, a lock of gray hair falling over his forehead, so long that it almost touched his nose. He had been jesting earlier. When he first entered and saw the mock-up, he lifted one corner of the covering sheet and looked under it, and said with a grin at the reporters watching him, "It looks like the Last Supper," but now he stood poised and silent, almost deferential, suggesting a courtier bowing, ever so slightly, to his monarch, as he began to talk. Ray, seated directly behind him, between Sheriff Morris on his right and a powerfully built deputy on his left, had his eyes fixed on Foreman's back.

"May it please the court," Foreman began in his deep rumbling voice, "in this case we have prepared, and defendant and I have signed, and Mr. Hugh Stanton, Sr., and Jr., will now sign, a petition for waiver of trial and request for acceptance of a plea of guilty—" He moved to the bench and handed up the petition to Judge Battle as a wave of small murmurs passed through the room, followed by a buzz of voices which the attendants could not silence with all their frowns and raised hands. Until the last there were some in the audience who believed that the rumors were not true, that this hearing had not been called to accept a guilty plea; rather, that Ray might fire Foreman, or make some sensational disclosure, or that Foreman would announce his withdrawal, or that Foreman, the matchless defense counsel, had found a rock upon which to wreck the juggernaut of the state's case. But no. The unbelievable was happening. James Earl Ray was pleading guilty! There would be no trial; he would not take the stand; he would not be examined and cross-examined; he would tell nothing. . . . The disappointment (and with it the growing suspicion) hung heavy over the room.

Judge Battle was all business. He looked down at Foreman over his glasses. "This is a compromise and a settlement on a plea of guilty to murder in the first degree and an agreed settlement of ninety-nine years in the penitentiary. Is that true?"

Ninety-nine years! This was longer than life imprisonment, though most persons did not know this. With life imprisonment Ray could be paroled—if parole was granted—in twelve and one half years, or in September 1981. But in Tennessee a ninety-nine-year sentence meant that one had to serve forty-eight years and seven months before parole could be considered, though those forty-eight years and seven months could be reduced, if the prisoner had a perfect record of good time and honor time, to thirty-three years. Ray, however, with his reputation as an escape artist and the likelihood that he would attempt to break out sooner or later, was not one to collect good time. All other things being equal, he was agreeing to serve almost the next half century—the rest of his life—behind bars.

Foreman nodded. "That's the agreement, Your Honor."

"All right," said Battle. "I'll have to *voir dire* Mr. Ray." He looked beyond Foreman to Ray. "James Earl Ray, stand." Ray rose, his hands loosely clasped behind him. The tip of a white note pad peeped out of his back pocket. He stood with his feet planted slightly apart, one shoulder a little lower than the other.

"Have you a lawyer to explain all your rights to you, and do you understand them?"

"Yes, sir," said Ray. His voice was soft, hardly audible to those a few rows behind him.

"Do you know you have a right to a trial by jury on a charge of murder in the first degree against you, the punishment for murder in the first degree ranging from death by electrocution to any time over twenty years?"

Ray gave a jerky nod, and Judge Battle went on, reading from a typed paper before him. His text was a clear exposition of what avenues of appeal Ray would have open to him had he pleaded not guilty, been tried, and found guilty. It spelled out as well what avenues of appeal he was now shutting off by his guilty plea. Had there been a trial, the burden of proof would have been on the State of Tennessee to "prove you guilty beyond a reasonable doubt and to a moral certainty." The decision of the jury would have to be unanimous, both as to guilt and to punishment.

"You would have the right to file a motion for a new trial addressed to the trial judge. If you lost that, you would have the right to successive appeals to the Tennessee Court of Criminal Appeal, and the Supreme Court of Tennessee, and to file a petition for review by the Supreme Court of the United States."

At this point Judge Battle, looking more like a penguin than ever, his head to one side, his chin tucked against his chest, stared over his half-rim glasses an inch down his nose at Ray:

"Do you understand that you have all of these rights?"

"Yes, sir," came Ray's almost inaudible voice.

The room was very quiet. No one was permitted to enter or leave—everyone had been warned beforehand—and all had been told not to speak with their neighbors. The usual background hum of subdued voices was absent. Everyone seemed waiting—not certain for what, now. Only one sound was heard, at precise fifteen-minute intervals. It came from the Western Union clock on the wall: a whirring, like a cuckoo clock without vocal chords, as some mysterious adjustment went on, each time, and, over the whirring, the quiet question and answer of judge and defendant:

"You are entering a plea of guilty of murder in the first degree as charged in the indictment, and you are compromising and settling your case on an agreed punishment of ninety-nine years in the state penitentiary." Judge Battle's voice was matter-of-fact. "Is this what you want to do?"

"Yes, I do," said Ray.

Judge Battle, who had labored over these questions more than a week before, to make sure that there would be no doubt or uncertainty as to the meaning of every word, repeated:

"Is this what you want to do?"

Ray: "Yes, sir."

Carefully Judge Battle went on, reading the next question, which rephrased what he had asked before, as if he were dealing with a retarded child to whom the lesson had to be endlessly repeated:

"Do you understand that you are waiving—which means giving up—a formal trial by your plea of guilty, although the laws of this state require the prosecution to present certain evidence to a jury in all cases on pleas of guilty to murder in the first degree?" Ray said nothing. "By your plea of guilty, you are also waiving your right to, one, your motion for a new trial; two, successive appeals to the Supreme Court, to the Tennessee Court of Criminal Appeals, and the

Supreme Court of Tennessee; and three, petition to review by the Supreme Court of the United States."

He looked at Ray. The defendant stood before him in exactly the same position, shoulders slightly bowed, one lower than the other, hands behind his back, clasped together—his whole posture that of a man resigned to what must befall him.

"By your plea of guilty," Judge Battle went on relentlessly, "you are also abandoning and waiving your objections and exceptions to all the motions and petitions in which the Court has heretofore ruled against you in whole or in part, among them being, one, motion to withdraw plea and quash indictment; two, motion to inspect the evidence; three, motion to remove lights and cameras from the jail . . ." The judge's voice rolled on, citing all the motions Ray and his attorneys had made since the case began eight months before, including even his request to be permitted to talk to Huie, his request to have photographs of himself made which might be sold to a magazine for money to help defray legal costs—requests which, with the others, had been turned down by Judge Battle.

The court took a long breath. "You are waiving or giving up all these rights." He paused again, pushed his spectacles up on his nose, and stared at Ray. Ray remained mute. Battle seemed convinced, finally, that the man before him understood what he was saying.

"Has anything besides this sentence of ninety-nine years in the penitentiary been promised to you to get you to plead guilty? Has anything else been promised to you by anyone?"

"No, it has not," said Ray.

"Has any pressure of any kind by anyone in any way been used on you to get you to plead guilty?"

For the first time Ray seemed uncertain of his answer. He fumbled for words for a minute, then asked, "What did you say?"

Judge Battle shifted in his chair, almost impatiently, and in a tone of voice which suggested that he was thinking in so many words, *I'm going to summarize this whole thing as clearly and bluntly as possible,* said:

"Are you pleading guilty of murder in the first degree in this case because you killed Dr. Martin Luther King under such circumstances that it would make you legally guilty of murder in the first degree under the law as explained to you by your lawyers?"

Ray's voice came: "Yes, legally, yes."

The jailhouse lawyer. A fine point. Why?

Judge Battle: "Is this plea of guilty to murder in the first degree with an agreed punishment of ninety-nine years in the state penitentiary freely, voluntarily, and understandingly made and entered by you?"

"Yes, sir."

As if to make doubly sure, reading from the sheet, Battle pursued the question in different words: "Is this plea of guilty on your part the free act of your free will made with your full knowledge and understanding of its meaning and consequences?"

"Yes, sir," Ray said doggedly.

The judge relaxed. "You may be seated," he said. He looked at Foreman. "All right, are you ready for a jury?"

Foreman was on his feet. "Yes, Your Honor."

"All right." The judge turned to the clerk of the court. "Sir, call twelve names. Pick them one at a time out of the box and call their names."

The clerk, a heavy man in a white shirt and thick glasses, put his hand in a box and picked out slips of paper, reading twelve names, and a thirteenth as alternate, and as he did so, the jurors filed in— all men, eleven white, two black—moving slowly and taking their seats in order in the jury box.

All stared at Ray. They could not keep their eyes off him. He did not so much as glance in their direction. They were the first thirteen called out of a venire of thirty that had been on call for the last three weeks. Tomorrow would have been their last day of jury duty. They knew what trial they were being called into: court officials had asked them if they had any objection to being screened as to past criminal records.

At this point Canale rose and took a few steps toward the jury to open the case for the state. For Canale, as for Judge Battle, this day was the climactic day in what had been a long ordeal. He had risen early and, accompanied by his bodyguard had gone to his family church at 8 A.M. There he had lit a candle. Sinking to his knees, he crossed himself and prayed, "Dear God, give me the courage, strength, and wisdom to know and do what is right and just." He rose, thinking, *I have done all I can. I leave the rest up to God.*

Now, in court, as the clock showed exactly 10 A.M., he began gently: "May it please the court, and gentlemen of the jury," introducing himself, his associates, the defense counsel, and other principals in the case. "Now, gentlemen," he went on, "this defendant, Mr. James Earl Ray, has a right by law to a trial by jury. He also has a right to enter a plea of guilty if he so desires. This morning Mr. Foreman, his attorney, has announced to the court that James Earl Ray desires to change his plea from not guilty to guilty." Before the jury had entered, Judge Battle had spelled out Ray's rights to him. He had questioned him in detail as to his plea, and Ray had replied, yes, his plea of guilty was made voluntarily, of his own free will. In such cases, it was his duty as prosecuting attorney, Canale said, to make a recommendation as to punishment, and he had recommended a sentence of ninety-nine years in the state penitentiary at Nashville. Each of the jurors would be asked to accept that guilty plea and that punishment. Then he explained the procedure. A number of witnesses would be called "to fill you in on certain important aspects of the case." Certain physical evidence would be introduced. Then Mr. Dwyer, assistant attorney general, would question the witnesses. Then Mr. Beasley, another assistant attorney general, would give them a "stipulation of facts that the state has gotten up which contain what the state would prove by witnesses"—facts which both the state and the defendant had agreed upon, had the case gone to trial.

"Now—" His voice took on a more urgent note, as he talked about what was in everyone's mind. "There have been rumors that Mr. James Earl Ray was a dupe in this thing, or a fall guy, or a member of a conspiracy to kill Dr. Martin Luther King, Jr. I want to state to you as your attorney general that we have no proof other than that Dr. King was killed by James Earl Ray and James Earl Ray alone—not in concert with anyone else." The prosecution, he said, had examined more than five thousand printed pages of investigation work done by "local police, by national police organizations, and by international law enforcement agencies." More than three hundred pieces of physical evidence had been studied. In addition, three men in his office, Dwyer, Beasley, and his chief investigator, John Carlisle, had made their own independent investigations, traveling thousands of miles in this country and abroad. "And I just state to you frankly that we have no evidence that there was any conspiracy involved in this." If at a later date, competent evidence was presented that other people were involved, not only his office but national law enforcement agencies would act at once to search it out and move for an indictment.

He thanked them and sat down. Canale had not been legally required to make this statement, but he felt he had to make it to help clear the air. He had no sooner taken his chair than Foreman was on his feet, moving toward the jury in his stately, courtier-like manner. "May I?" he asked with a bow. Towering over the others, he stood only a few feet from the men in the jury box, and when he spoke he addressed them directly, as if no one else was in the room. He had a yellow pad in his left hand.

"I never hoped or expected from the beginning to accomplish anything except perhaps save the defendant's life," he began. His voice, as he went on, took on a warm, confidential timbre. It had taken him a month, he said, to convince himself of the fact which the Attorney General of the United States and J. Edgar Hoover of the FBI had announced last July, and which Canale had stated to them just now: *there was no conspiracy.* "I talked with my client more than fifty hours, I would estimate," and most of that time he had cross-examined him, "checking each hour and minute" of Ray's time while he was free, and "each expenditure of money down to seventy-five cents for a shave and a haircut." And he was convinced it was not a conspiracy.

He paused and swept the lock of hair out of his eye. Perhaps the jurors were asking themselves, if there was this agreement between prosecution and defense as to Ray's guilt and punishment, why should they be there? Anglo-Saxon law demanded a public trial, he explained. They, the jurors, represented the public: they must be present, and they "must understand what is going on." They would be required to accept the guilty plea and the amount of punishment. If any felt this was contrary to his conscience, he could be excused before being sworn in. Someone else would be called to take his place.

A ninety-nine-year sentence, he pointed out, is "the extreme penalty short of one step, the death penalty." Many thought a death sentence was "worse punishment than life or ninety-nine years in the penitentiary." Foreman intimated that he did not think so. There was no punishment at all in the death penalty "except from the time the punishment is set until it is carried out." The punishment ended then.

This agreement might not have been worked out, he went on, had there not been in Memphis a judge who was humane, and a prosecuting attorney who was "not out for scalps." The jurors should know, too, that in the past anyone pleading guilty to first-degree murder in Shelby County had been permitted to do so. Equal justice was being applied here "as it would be if this was Joe Blow or John Doe instead of James Earl Ray."

Now, glancing at the pad in his hand, which listed the names of the jurors, he polled each one of them, beginning with the first juror, Amos G. Black: "Mr. Black, are you willing to effect the punishment that His Honor and General Canale and the attorneys for the defense have agreed upon in this case, ninety-nine years?"

Black answered, "Yes, sir." Foreman continued down the list, addressing each in turn, pronouncing each name carefully, hastening to correct himself if he mispronounced it and apologizing each time; he asked each the same question, sometimes rephrasing it. While he did this he looked intently into each face, as if to fix his features clearly in his mind. As each juror answered, he thanked him and moved to the next.

When he was finished with the last, a Mr. Ballard, he turned to Judge Battle. "Thank you, Your Honor."

"Do both sides accept the jury?" the court asked.

Foreman answered, "We do, Your Honor," and Canale's words were almost on top of his: "The state does, Your Honor."

Foreman, like a man with a weight off his shoulders, walked back to his chair. He was about to turn to lower himself into it, facing Ray, when Ray unexpectedly stood up, as if to speak to Foreman, whose face was about two feet away. But Ray's gaze was not on Foreman but on Judge Battle. It was apparent that he was about to make some kind of a statement: for the space of a heartbeat there was a frozen tableau—Ray, standing, facing the judge, looking past Foreman at him, going through a little nervous movement of his mouth as he prepared to speak, and Foreman, staring at him, on his face a look of mingled astonishment and expectation, his jaw dropped a little, as if he had been caught in the middle of a word.

Ray spoke, rocking a little on his feet, seeming to swallow his words so that they were not distinct, almost as though he had difficulty mustering enough breath to project them: "Your Honor, I would like to say something too, if I may."

The room buzzed, heads craned, some stood up in their seats, and even the deputies were taken unaware and made no attempt to silence the room. This was what everyone was waiting for—Ray to break open the entire case, repudiate his guilty plea, demand a trial—

Judge Battle looked down on him. "All right," he said, noncommittally. His face showed nothing.

"I don't want to change anything I have said but I don't want to add anything onto it, either." Ray managed to get the words out more distinctly this time. "The only thing I have to say, is, I don't exactly accept the theories of Mr. Clark."

Judge Battle looked puzzled. Foreman looked warily at Ray, near enough to clap a hand over his mouth, had he wished, and interjected, "Ramsey Clark."

"And Mr. Hoover," said Ray.

Judge Battle blinked. "Mr. who?"

"Mr. J. Edgar Hoover," Ray said formally, and hurried on, slurring his words. "The only thing I say, I am not—I agree to all these stipulations. I am not trying to change anything. I don't want to add something onto it."

Judge Battle squirmed in his chair.

"You don't agree with whose theories?" he demanded, a note part patience, part exasperation, in his voice.

"I mean Mr. Canale, Mr. Clark, and Mr. J. Edgar Hoover," said Ray. "I mean on the conspiracy thing." He paused, but went on doggedly. "I don't want to add something onto it that I haven't agreed to in the past."

The interchange had been rapid and not clear. But by this time Foreman understood what had happened. He broke in: "I think that what he is saying is that he doesn't think that Ramsey Clark's right or J. Edgar Hoover is right. I didn't argue them as evidence in this case. I simply stated that underwriting and backing up the opinions of General Canale, that they had made the same statement." He turned to Ray. "You're not required to agree or withdraw or anything else, Jim," he said.

Judge Battle stared at lawyer and client for a long moment. He seemed to bustle again in his seat impatiently. Then he picked up the sheet from which he had read before containing the questions and answers between him and Ray, and addressed Ray again, gesturing with the sheet as he spoke:

"There is nothing in these answers to these questions I asked you —in other words, you change none of these."

"No, sir, no, sir," said Ray quickly.

"In other words, you are pleading guilty and taking ninety-nine years." Judge Battle made it a statement, not a question. "I think the main question here that I want to ask you is this: Are you pleading guilty to murder in the first degree in this case because you killed Dr. Martin Luther King under such circumstances that would make you legally guilty of murder in the first degree under the law as explained to you by your lawyer?" He was reading from the sheet.

Ray bobbed his head up and down. "Yes, sir, make me guilty on that."

The judge pursued it: "Your answers are still the same?"

"Yes, sir," said Ray. During most of the exchange he had stood with his hands clasped behind his back, as before, only once breaking his posture to gesture when he said, "I mean on the conspiracy thing."

Judge Battle sat back in his chair. "All right, sir, that is all." That had settled it. He turned to the clerk of court. "Swear the jury."

The buzz would not die down. Why hadn't Judge Battle seized this extraordinary opportunity to question Ray about conspiracy? Why hadn't Judge Battle, knowing what was still unresolved, knowing what protests must still rise because there had not been a full-scale trial, and since Ray had opened the door to it himself, why had not Judge Battle demanded, "Mr. Ray, why don't you agree 'on the conspiracy thing'? Was there anyone else involved in this with you?"

The fact is that Judge Battle could not do this, for it would not then have been a free and voluntary plea of guilty, and it could have been overturned by the Supreme Court. The accused had to plead guilty of his own volition, without threats, without pressure. To ask such questions of Ray would constitute pressure. When Ray said he did not want to change his answers—that he was pleading guilty to murder in the first degree—Judge Battle had no recourse but to continue through the required legal procedure.

What did Ray mean when he stood up to say he did not "exactly accept" the "theories" of Canale, Clark, and J. Edgar Hoover, and what did he mean when he said, "I don't want to add something onto it that I haven't agreed to in the past"?

It was a situation that would cause great misunderstanding in the future. One had to know what had happened.

On Thursday, March 6, four days before the trial, at 11 A.M. Ray had received in his cell, and read carefully, the "Voir Dire of Defendant on Waiver and Order"—the text from which Judge Battle had read the questions and answers they had just exchanged in court. It contained every word, every question asked by Battle, and every reply to be given by Ray, beginning with Battle's words, "James Earl Ray, stand. Have you a lawyer to explain all your rights to you, and do you understand them?" then Ray's reply, "Yes, sir," then Battle's second question, "Do you know you have a right to a trial by jury on a charge of murder in the first degree against you, the punishment for murder in the first degree ranging from death by electrocution to any time over twenty years?" Then through the judge's detailed explanation of what remedies and recourses Ray was giving up, and his understanding of what he was giving up by waiving a trial, down to the last exchange, "Is this plea of guilty on your part the free act of your free will made with your full knowledge and understanding of its meaning and consequences?" with Ray replying, "Yes, sir," and even the judge's last words, "You may be seated."

In short, Judge Battle and Ray had simply recited verbatim what was on the *voir dire*. Ray had read all this in his cell Thursday, in the presence of his lawyer, Percy Foreman; it had covered two and a half pages of legal length paper, and Ray had initialed each page on the bottom left corner, then Foreman had initialed each page on the bottom right corner, and then both Ray and Foreman had signed the last page. Ray had then read the "Petition for Waiver of Trial and Request for Acceptance of Plea of Guilty," to which he also signed his name. Its last paragraph read:

"In the exercise of my own free will and choice and without any threats or pressure of any kind or promise of gain or favor from any source whatsoever, and being fully aware of the action I am taking, I do hereby in open court request the Court to accept my plea of guilty to the charges outlined herein. I hereby waive any rights I may or could have to a motion for a new trial and/or an appeal."

Even more. Ray had, at the same time, read carefully the most important document of all. This was the state's stipulation of facts which it would be prepared to prove. It consisted of fifty-five statements of fact, each of which Ray had agreed was true, beginning with his purchase of a radio at Missouri State Penitentiary the day before he escaped and concluding with his arrest and fingerprinting at the London Airport. It was actually a signed confession. Its most important statement of fact was No. 37:

"That at approximately 6:01 P.M. April 4, 1968, defendant fired a shot from the second floor bathroom in the rooming house at 422½ S. Main Street and fatally wounded Dr. Martin Luther King, Jr., who was standing on the balcony of the Lorraine Motel."*

Ray read this, initialed each page of it, and then signed it.

There was no question, then, that Ray knew exactly what he was saying when he pleaded guilty, exactly what he was admitting when he pleaded guilty, exactly to what he was agreeing.

But he stood up in court because Foreman, in his statement to the

---

* For the full stipulation see Notes, Chapter XXXIV.

jury, quoted Canale, Clark, and J. Edgar Hoover as saying there was no conspiracy. Ray thought Foreman was trying to create the impression that Ray had also agreed to these views. These were not in the papers I signed, he was saying: this is outside of what I have agreed to. It was then that Foreman explained that he had not argued these views as evidence, that what Canale and the others had said had nothing to do with what Ray had signed: they were merely opinions expressed in the courtroom. Therefore Ray did not have to agree with them, or withdraw, or do anything else.

Foreman had sized his client up correctly. Ray did not want to allow the idea of conspiracy to vanish. He clung to it because he believed that if he was seen as a man hired by conspirators, he not only had a loftier status, but was in some fashion absolved of the responsibility for the crime: he was not really guilty, only, "legally" guilty. He could not deny the murder; as he told Judge Battle, he was not retracting any of his admissions. But if he could keep conspiracy alive, the entire affair and his part in it took on a stature and a mystery far beyond an ordinary homicide. In addition, it sharply increased the sales value of his story, from which he hoped enormous sums of money would flow to enable him to make a fight for freedom at some later date. He knew that, if he ever hoped to win such freedom, it would have to be based on the belief that he was really the victim, the dupe of conspirators.

The jurors had listened to this unexpected exchange with impassive faces. Most of the time they simply stared at Ray. He continued to ignore them. If they were disappointed because this had not turned out to be a full-fledged trial, with dramatic examination and cross-examination, with a pugnacious, hot-tempered prosecutor and a fabled defense counsel crossing swords, they did not show it. One at least had wanted no part of the case. But he had a son serving in Vietnam and thought, *If he can go through that, I can go through this*. He felt that it was extremely dangerous to be a juror here: if they freed the man, someone might want to punish them; if they sent him to the chair, someone else might want to punish them. He was sure it was a conspiracy. He thought, *It takes a lot of nerve to look through a scope and kill a man, not being angry with him*. But he and the others sat, expressionless. They would play their role.

Called as the first witness by Dwyer was the Rev. Samuel Kyles, and Kyles, tall, dark, slim, entered by the same door used by Ray. He and the handful of other witnesses had been sequestered in another room and had heard none of the proceedings.

As he entered, he glanced once about, seeking Ray. It was apparent that he did not recognize him: defendant and deputies surrounding him might all have gone to the same school.

Dwyer led him through a brief biographical recital. Had Martin Luther King, Jr., been a friend of his? Yes. For how many years? About ten years. On April 4, 1968, at around six o'clock in the eve-ning, did the Rev. Kyles remember where he had been?

"I was at the Lorraine Motel in Room 306," said Kyles.

Why had he been there? He had gone to pick up Dr. King to take him to his house for a soul-food dinner, he replied. When he saw Dr. King a few minutes before six o'clock on that date, Dwyer asked, was Dr. King alive, in good health and good spirits? Yes, said Kyles.

Dwyer asked him to step down from the stand and examine the mock-up. Attendants quickly pulled off the sheets and it was seen that the roofs had been removed from the rooming house and the motel, so that one could see the burrow of rooms and corridors. Dwyer had Kyles point out Dr. King's room, then had the witness tell how Dr. King left the room, returned to get his jacket, then came out again; how the two of them stood together on the balcony for a minute or so, greeting those in the courtyard below; how he had turned and walked away from Dr. King toward the steps leading down to the courtyard, because he was taking some guests to his house; how he heard the shot, how he turned to see Dr. King falling backward into the setback of the balcony— He stopped. It was still difficult for him, now, nearly a year later.

Dwyer showed him a photograph taken from the balcony showing the rear of the rooming house, the yard and bushes below, the direction from which the shot appeared to have come. Had he looked in that direction immediately after the shot? Yes.

"Now, I'll ask you, Reverend Kyles, did you see anybody moving about over there?" Dwyer asked. No, said the witness. Foreman listened impassively. Dwyer was destroying, for the last time, the stories about men being seen in the bushes behind the rooming house. The two witnesses who claimed they had seen something had recanted, the defense knew, but Dwyer had to make the record for the public and scotch those stories once and for all.

Dwyer then showed Kyles a photograph of Dr. King taken immediately after death. The witness flinched. "Does that depict the wound you saw on Dr. King's face when you saw him the night of April 4, 1968?" Kyles said softly, yes.

Chauncey Eskridge, King's lawyer, followed Kyles on the stand. He, too, scanned the room as he walked in, to pick out Ray—and could not. As he was to say later, ironically, "I saw a room full of white men. All white men look alike, you know." He told his story briefly. Standing in the courtyard, he heard something zing past his right ear, he turned to see what it was, he turned back—to see Dr. King down on the balcony.

Had he looked in the direction of the rooming house? Yes. Had he seen anything moving? No.

Then, in succession, while the reporters took notes and the jury listened and Ray sat motionless, his eyes on the back of Foreman's neck, and his brothers sat equally immobile, eyes straight ahead, three other witnesses took the stand. First, Dr. Francisco, who performed the autopsy, to identify the bullet and testify that the path it took in Dr. King's body "was consistent" with a bullet fired downward from the bathroom window of the rooming house; then Inspector Zachary, chief of homicide, to tell of the bundle dropped at Canipe's, which he had turned over to Robert Jensen, FBI agent in charge, Memphis; and then Jensen took the stand to testify that the Bureau had traced the rifle found in the bundle to the Aeromarine Supply Company in Birmingham, that the white Mustang found abandoned in Atlanta had led agents to Los Angeles, where the pliers found in the bundle had been purchased, and where the laundry mark had been affixed to the underwear found in the bundle; and that, finally, the search had led to Mexico, to Canada, to Portugal, and to England, with the arrest finally of James Earl Ray in London.

Now the state had only to present its stipulation of fifty-five facts— the summary of proof, already read and agreed to by James Earl Ray—which would have been testified to by some seventy witnesses had there been a full-scale trial. Since the presentation of this would be detailed and lengthy—the proceedings so far had taken less than ninety minutes—Judge Battle declared a thirty-minute recess.

The reporters rushed to their telephones.

CHAPTER XXXV

Outside the courtroom, in the long corridors of the Criminal Courts Building, a furious babel of voices filled the air. The speed with which everything had occurred, the intensity of what had occurred—Ray's standing up in court, the expectation of some dramatic, earth-shaking revelation, the letdown that followed. . . . No one but the principals knew what had preceded this hearing, the weeks of negotiations between state and defense, the safeguards taken to avoid uncertainty and disillusionment in the public mind. It had not helped, for the general feeling among press and spectators was *We've been cheated*. Was this all there was to it? James Earl Ray had done it all, and all by himself, conceived it and carried it out by himself? And this was all we were ever to learn about it? Disbelief and outrage marked every face. Ray's two brothers, John and Jerry, pursued even to the men's room by reporters, kept themselves as aloof as possible under the circumstances, but the characteristic Ray smile, half-sardonic, half-resigned to the fraudulence of those in high places, appeared and disappeared. Jerry Ray had said, and repeated now, "Jimmy didn't do it. I say he didn't do it and I'll say it to my dying day." John Ray had said and repeated, "Nobody ever called Jimmy a fool. Maybe he made mistakes, but he was never a fool. He stands up there and tells them the truth, and they won't touch it."

Robert Dwyer, walking through the corridor, hearing the voices, the doubt, the anger, could only shake his head. Perhaps the stipulation Beasley had worked out so carefully—the precise, clear unfolding of the chain of evidence, forged link by forged link—would make it more believable. Yet how could one expect the outsider to understand and accept? He and Beasley and Carlisle—they, too, had had to rub their faces in it to understand and realize the truth.

Percy Foreman had gone into another room to rest. At sixty-six, this case had taken a great deal out of him. He had had an almost traumatic weekend. Word had come to Hugh Stanton, Sr., from Ray's guards that Ray was "acting up," he was "raising hell," he wanted to withdraw his guilty plea and take his chances with a trial. They'd give him life, at worst, not the chair or ninety-nine years. Foreman had flown in yesterday afternoon and gone directly to Ray's cell block and confronted him; it had taken time and skill and persuasion, but he had calmed him down. He dared not risk the chair; and as Foreman had explained so many times before, he explained again: they had no case. He went over the state's stipulation, point by point. They had no answer.

Ray had listened, sullen, depressed.

Foreman could not help feeling sorry for a man who had thrown his life away—and in the process committed murder. An astonishing thing, that the same society could produce two such dissimilar men at the same time, almost of the same age—Martin Luther King, Jr., thirty-nine, and James Earl Ray, forty—men so vastly different, one to become a Nobel Prize winner, revered throughout the world, the other to become his murderer, known only because of his terrible deed.

Foreman saw Ray as one for whom the cards had fallen wrong from the very beginning. He hated the establishment, he hated J. Edgar Hoover and Ramsey Clark and the FBI and the police. He had never forgiven Foreman himself for being a friend of former Supreme Court Justice Tom Clark, Ramsey Clark's father. When Ray heard Canale in court say there was no evidence of conspiracy when he, Ray, had been talking conspiracy all the time, when he heard his own lawyer quote as authority on the same subject the two names anathema to him—Clark and Hoover—he could not take it.

An odd, stubborn man, Ray, cynical, with a bitter sense of humor, and a man whom nearly everyone had underestimated. When Foreman returned to his seat after his opening statement in court, Ray had leaned toward him. Only Foreman heard his almost snarling words, "You seem a hell of a lot more interested in complimenting the attorney general than in saying something about me. He doesn't care if I burn, he just doesn't want to see Memphis burn." Foreman had said nothing. Just as the man had been able to make people believe he was not a racist, so he had been able to project the image of a completely nonpolitical criminal, interested only in money and nothing else. The fact was that Ray saw himself and his plight in political terms. One of the issues Foreman had had trouble with had been the fact, included in Beasley's stipulation as first written, that Ray had taken Marie Martin and the Steins to sign a petition for Wallace in Los Angeles Friday morning, December 15, before driving with Charlie Stein to New Orleans. Ray insisted that the idea of signing up for Wallace had come from them, that he had taken them to Wallace headquarters only because it was near a garage where he had to pick up a tire. Beasley had found this to be a lie. Not only had Ray obtained his telephone by claiming to be a Wallace campaign worker, but his telephone records showed that *before* he drove to pick up Marie and the Steins that morning, he had telephoned Wallace headquarters. The idea had been his, not theirs. When Ray realized that the state had this proof, he insisted that all reference to it be deleted from the stipulation before he would sign it. He wanted no political reference to be made. His brothers, whose approval of the stipulation was also obtained by the state, had also wanted no mention made of the visit to Wallace headquarters. The issue was resolved when Canale agreed not to include the episode in the stipulation but reserved the right for the state's witnesses to testify, if necessary, to the true facts.

These political considerations constantly worked in Ray's mind. One of the reasons he fired Hanes was that Foreman assured him that if he changed counsel Judge Battle would have to postpone his trial, then scheduled to be held November 12, 1968. This would mean that it most likely would be held after January 20, 1969—when Richard Nixon would be in the White House. Ray counted on a lesser emphasis on civil rights in the country, and therefore an atmosphere which he believed would be more friendly to him.

Yet despite his political awareness, his jailbird shrewdness, his cynicism, there was a striking vein of immaturity in the man, Foreman thought. After yesterday's confrontation—the trouble began when the secret of the guilty plea leaked out, and some of Ray's guards told him that he was a fool for not going to trial—and after Ray had finally made his peace with his plea, they had managed to talk quietly for a few minutes. An extraordinary exchange then took place between the man and his lawyer.

Foreman said, "Jim, now that it's all over, why did you drop the bundle in front of Canipe's? Why didn't you take it on to the car? You knew it had the rifle with your fingerprints, all the other evidence—"

Ray was in better humor now, the characteristic sardonic smile appearing and disappearing at the corner of his mouth. He looked at Foreman for a moment and said, "I suppose I could never convince you that I didn't do it—"

Foreman could only marvel. Just seventy-two hours before Ray had admitted that he killed King, he had signed three separate documents swearing to it, because he knew he could not deny the state's evidence, because even with one of the world's most skilled defense lawyers at his side, a man who would give almost everything to crown his long career with a victory in this case, he could not save himself. What kind of a childish make-believe worked in this man's mind? The kind, Foreman supposed, that could produce a Raoul to be blamed for everything, as a small child caught in mischief blames an invisible playmate he has invented.

But aloud, Foreman only said emphatically, "Not in a thousand years, boy!"

"Well," Ray said, speaking swiftly, "I thought I was going to get away. I thought I'd get to Africa and serve in one of those mercenary armies and after two or three years they wouldn't send me back."

Everyone filed back into his seat in the courtroom.

Now, for nearly an hour, Beasley outlined the state's case. He stood before the judge's bench, facing the jury, the mock-up to one side, the many sheets of the state's stipulation in his hand, the essence and detail discovered by all the men who had questioned and traced and retraced Ray's trail, the burden of all that had been done by society in its pursuit of this man from the day he broke out of Missouri State Penitentiary to his capture in London. It was a damning indictment, a relentless chain of evidence that would have strangled Ray had he not pleaded guilty.

Painstakingly Beasley took Ray step by step to his arrival in Memphis, and then, using a long rod to point out places in the mock-up, he followed Ray from the moment he knocked on Bessie Brewer's door, rented Room 5B, bought the binoculars, returned to his room, lay in wait, watching, hurried into the bathroom, and at 6:01 P.M. April 4, resting his rifle on the window sill, fired the bullet that killed Dr. King. Ray had admitted all this, but the state wanted its proof to be on the record, each fact supported by at least two different forms of evidence—evidence that could not be refuted because it was not based on fallible human memory and impression. Days before, as Beasley summed up his proof, he had told himself, *We could have woven this chain about Ray even if we hadn't a single witness to identify him face to face.* Inanimate objects spoke, and their voice was unanswerable.

They had spoken eloquently that long Friday, April 19, when Galt was found to be James Earl Ray.

By fingerprint matching, by handwriting examination, by chemical analysis, done by FBI specialists whose lives had been spent in the work, it was determined that the Lowmyer who bought the murder rifle (the fingerprints were Ray's, Lowmyer's signature on the receipt was Ray's), was the Galt who drove the white Mustang (Ray's hair was in the car, Galt's signature on the driver's license was Ray's), was the Willard who stayed in Room 5B (the fibers of Willard's bedspread were identical with the fibers found on the upholstery on the white Mustang, and with the fibers found embedded in the rug in Room 5B), was the James Earl Ray who escaped from Missouri State Penitentiary (Galt's fingerprints were Ray's), was the Bridgman who obtained the birth certificate (Bridgman's handwriting was Ray's), was the Sneyd who was arrested in London (Sneyd's fingerprints were Ray's).

So it all tied together. There was no way to refute the evidence, or break the chain. The man who fired the shot that killed Dr. King from the bathroom of 418½–422½ South Main Street, Memphis, was Lowmyer, was Willard, was Galt, was Bridgman, was Sneyd—was James Earl Ray.

So it moved swiftly to its conclusion. Beasley finished his presentation. Judge Battle, who had been sitting back, his chin on his chest, listening, sat upright. "Anything anyone wants to say at this time?" He looked at Foreman.

Foreman, who had been sitting like a Buddha, his hands placidly folded on his stomach, rose and with a courtly bow said, "No, Your Honor," and sat down again.

"All right, gentlemen," Battle said, turning to the jury. "All of you who can do as you said you could and accept this compromise and settlement on a guilty plea and the punishment of ninety-nine years in the state penitentiary, hold up your right hand."

All in the jury did so.

"I believe that's everyone," the judge said. "All right, you can have someone sign the verdict." This was to the clerk. Battle looked over his glasses at Ray. "James Earl Ray, stand." Ray rose quickly and stood as always, his head down, his hands clasped loosely behind his back. The judge's voice, though soft, carried to the farthest part of the room. "On your plea of guilty to murder in the first degree as charged in the indictment, it is the judgment of the court that you be confined for ninety-nine years in the state penitentiary. You may be seated." The words almost ran together, and Ray sat down again.

Judge Battle ruffled some papers on his desk. "Now, we've been here for some time and I don't propose to keep us here much longer," he said. "But I think that the court should make a few remarks at this place in the proceedings. The fact was recognized soon after this tragic murder took place that there was no possible conclusion to the case which would satisfy everybody. It was decided at that time that the only thing the judge could do was to try the case as nearly as possible to other like cases, and to scrupulously follow the law and his own conscience. This I have done."

He paused and looked around the room. There was a new, conversational tone to his voice as he picked up a sheet and began to read: "'Memphis has been blamed for the death of Dr. King, to me wrongfully and irrationally. Neither the decedent nor his killer lived here. Their orbits merely intersected here. The State has made out a case of first degree murder by lying in wait. Why accept any plea, say some? Why not try him for the electric chair?'" Battle seemed to bustle again in his seat—a kind of impatient shifting in his chair. "Well, I have been a judge since 1959 and I, myself, have sentenced at least seven men, maybe more, to the electric chair, and my fellow judges in this county have sentenced several others to execution, but there have been no executions of any prisoners from this county since I took the bench. All the trends in this country are in the direction of doing away with capital punishment."

He went into the question of conspiracy. "It has been established that the prosecution at this time is not in possession of enough evidence to indict anyone as a co-conspirator in this case. Of course, this is not conclusive evidence there was no conspiracy; it merely means that as of this time there is not sufficient evidence available to make out a case of probable cause. However"—he spoke slowly—"if this defendant was a member of a conspiracy to kill the decedent, no member of such a conspiracy can ever live in peace or security or lie down to pleasant dreams, because in this state there is no statute of limitations in capital cases such as this. And while it is not always the case, my thirty-five years in these criminal courts have convinced me that in the great majority of cases, Hamlet was right when he said, 'For murder, though it have no tongue, will speak with most miraculous organ.'"

Then, with a wry smile, he concluded:

"None of us know what the future will bring. I submit that up to now, we have not done too badly for a 'decadent river town.'" This was a reference to an article in *Time* magazine some months before, which described Memphis as a "decaying Mississippi river town." "If I may be permitted to add a light touch to a solemn occasion, I would like to paraphrase the great and eloquent Winston Churchill, who in defiant reply to the Axis threat to wring England's neck like a chicken, said, 'Some chicken—some neck.' I would like to reply to our Memphis critics, 'Some river—some town.' Anything else?"

But there was really nothing else.

It was all over a few minutes after noon.

In Canale's office, a little later, as they prepared to go out to lunch and then resume, they hoped, a normal life again—Ray would be on his way to the state penitentiary in Nashville before dawn the next day—Canale turned to Dwyer and Beasley.

If he had had any lingering doubts about the possibility of conspiracy, he said, Ray's unexpected performance in court had gone a long way to dispel them. If it were a conspiracy, would Ray have dared proclaim in open court that he disagreed with those who said it was not? For if there were conspirators, Ray had deliberately endangered them, putting them into the spotlight again after both state and defense said they did not exist. Why had Ray implicated others *when there was no need for it?* He had pleaded guilty, he had taken the responsibility for the murder upon himself, he was accepting the punishment. There was nothing for him to gain by it save to keep alive the talk about conspiracy and so perhaps increase the value of his story. But that was a terrible price to pay if as a result the conspirators, fearing that at some time in the future he might break and reveal their names, decided to make sure that this would never happen by arranging his murder inside the penitentiary, and so silencing him forever. If they could order King killed, they could order Ray killed.

Ray could say what he had said in court with impunity because he feared no retaliation, because there were no others whose wrath and revenge might fall upon his head. He had no one to fear. He could proclaim conspiracy to the housetops for the rest of his days. Chances were, he would.

With that, the three men went out to lunch.

CHAPTER XXXVI

Any student of Ray could have anticipated it.

Within an hour of his departure from Shelby County Jail for the state penitentiary in Nashville, Ray reverted to pattern.

He denied everything.

He had not killed Dr. King. He was not guilty. He had been pressured into pleading guilty by Percy Foreman. He dashed off a quick, sarcastic letter to Judge Battle, dated March 13—three days after he pleaded guilty:

> Dear Sir: I wish to inform the honorable court that that famous Houston Att. percy Fourflusher is no longer representing me in any capacity. My reason for writing this letter is that I intend to file for a post conviction hearing in the very near future and don't want him making any legal moves unless their in Mr. Canale behalf.
>
> Sincerely
> James Earl Ray

Battle could only sigh. The seventy-two hours since Ray had left had been bad enough—the wave of outrage from one end of the country to the other, altogether unexpected in its fury, denouncing him, Attorney General Canale, Foreman, all who were involved in this "prearranged deal," assailing them for what the New York *Times* declared angrily was "a shocking breach of faith with the American people, black and white."

Now Ray, the jailhouse lawyer, riding this wave of indignation, was running true to form. He was trying to will away all that had happened: that he had admitted firing the fatal shot, that he had pleaded guilty, that he had given up the right to a new trial. . . .

This was precisely what he was now going to demand.

Ray's letter required no action from Battle, who left a few days later on a badly needed vacation.

When he returned Monday, March 31, he found another letter on his desk from Ray. It was dated March 26 and had arrived in his absence. He called in Beasley and showed it to him. In it Ray formally asked Battle "to treat this as legal notice of an intent to ask for a reversal of the 99-year sentence that petitioner received in afore-mentioned court," and also requested Battle to appoint an attorney or public defender "to assist me." A letter had also arrived from a Chattanooga attorney, Robert W. Hill, Jr., saying that he was ready to represent Ray if appointed.

Would Beasley, Battle asked, telephone penitentiary officials in Nashville and ask them to determine whom Ray wanted? Two other lawyers were seeking to enter the case—J. B. Stoner, who had been consulting with Ray at intervals, and Richard J. Ryan, a Memphis attorney who had been George Wallace's campaign manager in Shelby County.

Beasley made his calls, to learn that Ray wanted all three to represent him in the various suits he planned. When Beasley called Battle back to inform him of this, there was no answer. At five o'clock, having been unable all afternoon to reach Battle by telephone, Beasley walked down to the judge's chambers on the floor below. He noticed a light inside, under the door. He knocked, and when there was no answer, pushed open the door, to find Battle slumped at his desk, dead, his face resting on the latest Ray correspondence.

Dr. Jerry Francisco, the medical examiner who had almost a year earlier to the day performed the autopsy on Dr. King, now carried out the same duty for Judge Battle. An autopsy was imperative: the sudden death of the judge in the Ray case could only stimulate talk of conspiracy and of mysterious forces at work. Had there not been a number of sudden deaths in the wake of President Kennedy's assassination—deaths of persons who had been associated with the case and its investigation? Dr. Francisco made a most careful examination. There was no question: Judge Battle had died of a heart attack—of coronary insufficiency. He suffered from high blood pressure and, as he told friends, from "a touch of diabetes." There was one other factor. Coronary insufficiency was a form of heart disease "in which emotions can cause a fatal outcome." One could never be sure, of course, but Dr. Francisco concluded that the strain of the long case, over which Battle had labored so conscientiously, intensified by the violent reaction to what had happened in his courtroom, might have hastened his death.

Battle's death spurred Ray to new legal activity. From his cell in Nashville, where he was equipped with a typewriter and lawbooks, and kept abreast of developments by means of his radio, portable TV, and daily newspapers, Ray moved at once for a new trial. His letter to Battle was the legal equivalent of a request for a new trial, he argued; and under Tennessee law, if a judge died while a request for a new trial was pending before him, that request must be granted.

This led to a full-dress hearing nearly two months later—May 26, 1969—before Judge Arthur J. Faquin, Jr., Judge Battle's successor.* Once more Ray was in court—paler, thinner, more peaked, his left hand playing nervously with his jaw and nose while the clerk read, at Faquin's request, the questions Battle had posed to Ray and he had answered when he pleaded guilty: Do you understand that you have all these rights? Yes, sir. Has any pressure been placed upon you . . . ? No. Are you pleading guilty because you killed Dr. Martin Luther King, Jr. . . . ? Yes . . . Yes . . . Yes.

Then, as if to make even more irrevocable what had taken place, Faquin read for the first time from the minutes of the case which Judge Battle had dictated and signed only days before his death: ". . . He does not elect to be tried by a jury . . . of his own free will, without any threats . . . Waives his right to a new trial and for an appeal."

Judge Faquin ruled against Ray's motion. The record was clear and unmistakable, he said.

Now Ray, through his trio of new lawyers—Stoner's National States Rights Party had set up a Patriotic Legal Fund to collect money for Ray's appeals—moved to withdraw his guilty plea. He wrote the American Bar Association in Chicago, to inform its Standing Committee on Professional Grievances that he wanted to file charges against Foreman "for unethical conduct." Then, working industriously on his typewriter, he drew up a long bill of particulars, not only against Foreman but against virtually everyone who had acted for him.

He charged that Art Hanes told Huie everything that he, Ray, told Hanes; that Huie, in turn, passed this on to the FBI, who in turn passed it on to Attorney General Canale, so that everything Ray gave his lawyers in his defense ended up on the desk of his chief prosecutor. He charged that Foreman forced him to plead guilty "when I was not guilty," not because the defense had a bad case but because

---

* Faquin, one of Battle's four criminal court colleagues, had drawn the next lowest number when lots were drawn to see who would preside. Since then he had acted as Battle's backstop, and Battle had kept him au courrant with all developments.

Foreman and Huie expected to make enormous sums from exclusive book and movie rights to his story, and if he went on trial and told his story on the stand, he would be giving it away free, and their rights would be worth nothing. He had finally yielded to Foreman, he said, because he feared that Foreman would deliberately sabotage his case if he insisted on a trial, and railroad him to the chair. So he pleaded guilty, he said, promising himself that he would reopen the case later.

Ray's motion before Faquin had been argued by the youngest of the three lawyers—twenty-nine-year-old Robert Hill, Jr., of Chattanooga. Hill had graduated *cum laude* from Chattanooga University, had been first in his class at the University of Tennessee Law School, and was known for the excellence of his legal briefs. Through the remainder of 1969 Hill met repeatedly with Ray in his cell and learned to his surprise that Ray now had changed his story of what happened in Memphis on Thursday, April 4, 1968.

Ray had always maintained that, when King was killed at 6:01 P.M., he was standing next to his white Mustang parked near 422½ South Main Street, waiting for Raoul, who was washing up in Ray's room, 5B, preparatory to going to dinner with him. Suddenly he heard a shot, a moment later saw Raoul dash down the stairs into the street, drop the evidence in Canipe's doorway, leap into the back seat of his car, cover himself up with a white sheet and order Ray to drive on, only to jump out a few blocks farther when Ray had to stop for a red light, fling over his shoulder, "See you in New Orleans" and disappear—never to be seen or heard from again.

Now Ray said that he was not waiting outside the rooming house when King was shot—he was actually blocks away. At 5:30, a half hour earlier, he said, he had been in Room 5B with Raoul. Raoul told him he was expecting "a contact" to visit him, and "it might be better if I wasn't there." Said Ray: "I told Raoul I'd go downstairs, get a bite, and maybe go to a movie." When he got downstairs, he noticed one of his old tires had a slow leak. So he drove about a mile to a service station to buy a tire. The station, however, had none for sale. An attendant fixed his flat. When he drove back to South Main Street, he saw, about two blocks from the rooming house, a police car parked at an intersection, halting traffic. He wasn't sure what had happened and "I headed south in the direction of New Orleans," planning to call Raoul later and learn what had happened. He had gotten miles into Mississippi, he said, when he heard that King had been shot and the police were looking for a white Mustang, so he drove to Atlanta, where he abandoned his car.

Hill stared at him, perplexed. Why had he told the other story all along? Huie had printed it, and Ray had told it to both Hanes and Foreman. Why would a man tamper with his alibi? Well, said Ray, he wanted to make money for the defense, so he said he was outside the rooming house when all the excitement took place because he thought that would sound more interesting and sell better.

What was significant was that Ray did not give the new version until there had appeared an item in a Memphis newspaper reporting that an employee of a gas station some blocks from the rooming house said that on April 4 he remembered fixing a tire on a white Mustang some time before six o'clock.

Hill did not know what the Haneses and Huie and Foreman had learned about Ray: how they had discovered that he fed back to one what he learned from the other, that he improvised his story as he went along, incorporating what he had read or heard that he thought might make it more credible.

Hill tried to question Ray but could get no more from him.

Meanwhile, his client was involved in other legal actions. Because Tennessee State Prison officials feared that Ray might be killed if allowed to mix with other prisoners—nearly half of the 2000 inmates were black—he had been kept isolated. Ray protested that this was "cruel and unusual punishment," and it led to his second court appearance since his guilty plea—this time in the U. S. District Court in Nashville, on December 29, 1969, before Judge William F. Miller.

Ray, seated behind his lawyers—Robert Hill, Jr., Richard J. Ryan and J. B. Stoner—listened impassively as his problem was discussed. He showed no reaction when Dr. Roger White, the prison psychiatrist, pointed out that Ray's isolation did not work as much hardship on him as one might think. "The type of prisoner who finds his way into isolation usually externalizes his frustrations," Dr. White said. "Such people seem to need less human companionship because they interact less with people and their relationships with others are quite superficial. They take out their frustrations on others: the anger they hold toward society acts as a vent—it keeps them sane. They really don't need people around them."

Now Ray himself had his opportunity, at last, to take the witness stand and to testify, not about the murder, but about his prison accommodations. He seemed almost gaunt—he weighed 158 pounds, compared to 170 when he left Memphis—but appeared to enjoy his day in court. He sat back, one arm draped over the back of the chair, quite at ease, as he sparred with the state's attorney, Thomas H. Fox.

Was he not aware that he was kept apart for his own protection? "Don't you know you're in jail because you killed a man who has a large following?" Fox asked.

Ray retorted, "I'm in jail because my lawyer sold me out."

Fox went on imperturbably: Did he not realize that many of his fellow prisoners might hate him for what he did, and want to kill him?

Ray's sardonic grin appeared for one of the last times in public. "Then they should be locked up, not me."

Would he wish to talk to the prison psychiatrist? This might help him adjust better to his situation.

Ray was curt. "I don't talk to psychiatrists. What you tell them gets into the papers." Anyway, he added, "They put a sex angle on everything. I got enough troubles without that."

Judge Miller turned to him. Well, what was it he wanted? He could not be given the run of the prison: he must be protected. What would he like done? Would he like to take vocational courses, or to study various subjects, so time would not hang so heavy on his hands?

No, said Ray, he did not want to take any courses.

What then? asked the judge. What did he want prison officials to do for him?

Ray rubbed his cheek. If he was impressed that this entire hearing, involving Judge Miller, the court attendants, the attorneys on both sides, prison officials, probation department psychiatrists, the police, the press, the public, had all been arranged in order to learn how James Earl Ray, the admitted murderer of Dr. Martin Luther King, Jr., could be made more comfortable in prison, he did not show it. "I'm not saying what I want," he told the judge. "They never give you what you want if you ask for it. I'll take whatever they decide."

In the end, he was transferred to Brushy Mountain Prison, the state's maximum security institution, in Petros, Tennessee. Here he was placed in a wing with two dozen long-term prisoners who had been screened and judged not likely to be a source of danger to him. Here he had much greater freedom.

Meanwhile, the defense strategy of Stoner and the National States Rights Party became evident. They pressed for a new trial on the ground that King's death had been arranged by the FBI, and that Ray was used; that Hanes, Huie, and Foreman were then enlisted by the FBI to silence Ray, force him to plead guilty, and so prevent the truth from ever being known.*

By April 1970, two years after King's murder, Hill had withdrawn from the case. He was replaced by Bernard Fensterwald, Jr., executive director of the Committee to Investigate Assassinations. One more attorney, long interested in the King-Ray case, now represented him. Fensterwald continued the fight to reverse his client's guilty plea and get him a new trial.

By April 1971, three years after the assassination, Ray had been successively turned down by the Criminal Court in Memphis; the State Court of Criminal Appeals; and the Supreme Court of the State of Tennessee. The State Supreme Court ruled: "The Court finds that the defendant willingly, knowingly and intelligently and with the advice of competent counsel, entered a plea of guilty to murder in the first degree by lying in wait . . . He made a bargain, swapping a guilty plea for a 99-year sentence rather than face a jury and a possible harsher sentence. And now he must live with that bargain."

On May 4, 1971, Ray was suddenly back in the news. At 3:15 A.M., he was seized in the exercise yard of Brushy Mountain Prison. Another long-term prisoner who worked as a plumber had provided him with a hammer, two chisels and a crowbar. Ray had broken out of his cell by prying loose two concrete wall blocks, then crawling through an air duct to a ventilator opening in the yard, prying off the iron bar across it so that he got into the yard. There he removed a manhole cover over a concrete tunnel leading under the prison to a steam plant outside the walls. But the tunnel was lined with steam pipes, and, once in it, he found the steam, which sometimes reached four hundred degrees, too hot to endure: he was forced to back out and was seized by the guards, alerted by the noise he made as he worked his way through the air duct. As he had done when he tried to escape in 1961 and 1966 from Missouri State Penitentiary, he had arranged his bunk so it would appear that he was curled up in sleep. This time he stuffed clothes to make a dummy, topping it off with a wig he made from hair cuttings he gathered from the prison barbershop.

* All three men, Stoner argued, had associations either with the FBI or the Justice Department. Hanes had been an FBI agent; Huie co-operated with the FBI, giving them information; and Foreman was a family friend of Ramsey Clark, who as Attorney General headed the Justice Department and had authority over the FBI.

But the entire thing was in many ways a comedy of ineptness. There were two manhole covers in the yard. A few feet from the concrete tunnel was a second tunnel, without steam pipes, large enough for a man to crawl through. It led to freedom beyond the walls. Ray, with his knack for miscalculation, had removed the wrong cover. He was in the hands of the guards less than twenty minutes after he had broken out of his cell. The warden, observing that there seemed no point in adding more years to a ninety-nine-year sentence, punished him by placing him in solitary for a month, during which he was deprived of his typewriter, radio, and TV.

But he had almost made good his boast to Percy Foreman that he didn't care how long a sentence he received in Judge Battle's court —he would never serve more than two years of it. His attempt to break out had taken place exactly two years and seven weeks from the day of his guilty plea.

By now Ray had exhausted the state courts. He had no recourse but to pursue his appeals through the federal courts, ultimately, perhaps, to the U. S. Supreme Court—if the funds of the National States Rights Party and those of the Committee to Investigate Assassinations held out.

What must be understood about James Earl Ray is that he is a man utterly alone who made up for his isolation from others by living in a private world of fantasies and, sadly, enacted one of them when he assassinated Dr. King. Were not Dr. King's death such a tragedy, Ray's escape from jail (in a bread box!), his picaresque adventures in this country, Canada, Mexico, Portugal, and London during his nearly fifteen months of freedom, his capture as he was about to board a plane to some never-never land of white mercenaries, his subsequent arrangements with Arthur J. Hanes and William Bradford Huie, then with Percy Foreman, then with J. B. Stoner, Richard Ryan, and Robert Hill, Jr., and finally with Bernard Fensterwald, Jr., executive director of the Committee to Investigate Assassinations, would read like a bizarre satire made even more bizarre by Ray himself, sitting in his air-conditioned six-cell jail block, his every act monitored, with fourteen men assigned to guard and tend him, busy creating a fictional tale to baffle and titillate a world so conditioned to its own violence that it was prepared to accept the fantasies he served up to it. And he was helped in this by what appeared to be the public's appetite for the Satanic, its belief in demonology, its morbid need to fear, its readiness to believe in evil forces forever at work in impenetrable secrecy to deceive and hoodwink it. Ray was the star actor in an international cast of characters which included men over-hearing nonexistent conversations, seeing nonexistent gunmen, investigators hunting down nonexistent evidence, and volunteers offering proof of nonexistent events. Through all of this wandered his two brothers, John and Jerry, appearing at intervals to confuse the public with allegations of mysterious and inexplicable intrigues.

There was another factor that had to be taken into account in the story of Ray and his role. Though constantly talking of escape and constantly attempting escape, he knew in his heart that he could not remain for long outside prison. He simply had been unable to manage this, as was evident from a study of his history.* He was too abrasive—quiet, secretive, unaggressive though he was—too antipathetic to society to be comfortable in it: he was too suspicious and distrustful of the world about him, attributing ignoble motives to every act of others, living too much the fiction of his own superiority to be able to function in any society in which he structured his own life. Thus prison was less an ordeal for him than freedom; in freedom he always got into trouble, always defeated himself, as if by some psychological quirk he was involved in a game with authority, to outwit it but at the moment of victory to yield his triumph.

He was comfortable, therefore, only in a society in which his life was structured for him: that is, in prison. He kept to himself, he was rarely involved in fights, he got along with his fellow prisoners, his jailers, needing no one to talk to, to exchange opinions with, to confide in, to lean upon, for he was supported by his own fantasies, which never failed him and allowed him to tolerate even isolation and solitary confinement. For James Earl Ray, prison was where he now had made it, as he had never been able to make it in the outside world. Now he had pride, and identity, and importance, and the respect he had never had.

As he said to his brothers when they found themselves visiting him in Tennessee State Prison instead of Missouri State Penitentiary: "Hell, I'm no worse off than I was before."

Indeed, he was far better off.

Now he was a man in history.

---

* A year before Ray's escape, Carl White, associate warden, wrote: "[His] record of arrests dates over a sixteen year period. He seems to be pretty well established in this type of anti-social behavior . . . Prognosis for making a successful adjustment to society is considered marginal at best. He may be able to survive a short parole without too much difficulty."

Epilogue

Rev. Samuel B. Kyles spoke slowly and thoughtfully. "Yes," he was saying, "when they finally pointed out Ray to me in that courtroom, I thought, No, he cannot be the mastermind behind all this. I still think so. And so do all of Dr. King's associates to whom I've spoken about it."

Now, nearly four years after Dr. King's death, Rev. Kyles, pastor of Memphis' Monumental Baptist Church, who stood a few feet from Dr. King when he was shot, and to whose home Dr. King was to go for dinner that evening of April 4, 1968, was describing how he and his colleagues in the Southern Christian Leadership Conference felt about the murder and its aftermath.

"I feel quite certain that if Ray pulled the trigger, and all the evidence points to him, that it was a hired job," he went on. "Somebody was behind him. I think that he probably didn't even know who it was, because such persons themselves would not have gotten in touch with him. We have never really speculated who they might be. But we have discussed among ourselves the fact that there were forces in this country that did not want Dr. King's Poor People's Campaign to succeed.

"It's one thing to talk about the right to eat a hamburger in a restaurant, or to get a job here or there, but it's an altogether different matter to bring together the poor peoples of America—the Appalachian whites, the Chicanos, the blacks—and move them on Washington. When the white and red people say to themselves, 'Hey, we're as poor as black folks. Why should we continue to take this?' and you start talking about redistribution of the wealth—that's dangerous and frightening to some people. They didn't want Martin to get to Washington. That's why I think his murder had to take place before April 29, the date of his Poor People's March. It didn't have to happen in Memphis, but it was bound to happen before that date."

Rev. Kyles went on to talk, sadly, about other assassinations. "We almost expect today that when you raise up a leader, you will lose him. There's no question that he will be lost: the only question is, when? It makes us wonder. If such acts are just acts by individual, half-balanced men—why is it that the racists and those who sell hate are never the victims? Why do they always choose the good people, the John Kennedys and Robert Kennedys and Dr. Kings . . . ?

"We—Dr. King's friends and colleagues—have not tried to play detective, or to get caught up in the who and why of it. That would not bring Martin back. We thought it more important for us to try to continue his work—to help change the climate of violence in which a man like Ray felt free to do what he did, and could believe that he'd be received as a hero for doing it. But we still think it must be more than James Earl Ray who was responsible for Dr. King's murder."

In a quiet, old-fashioned parlor in a suburb of St. Louis, Jerry Rayns, born James Gerald Ray, James Earl Ray's father, was talking. A thin, gray-haired man of seventy-two with a grizzled face and a slow, surprisingly contagious smile, he spoke in a Midwestern twang, a kind of musical lilt to his words.

"Nothing to tell you about me," he was saying. "I dropped out of school in the fifth grade. Hell, I was born dumb, I lived dumb and I'll die dumb. But Jimmy—he was an awfully smart little kid, a good kid, always minded me. You tell Jimmy do something, and you could walk away from it." He shook his head. "No evilness in that boy—he wouldn't hurt nobody, he'd rather hurt himself. Why, he wouldn't even carry a gun, and if'n he did, there wasn't no bullets in it. He'd carry it just to bluff—"

Sitting across the room from him was his daughter, Carol—Mrs. Albert Pepper, just turned thirty, mother of two small boys. A big, solid woman in a floral house dress, she had been looking through a scrapbook full of newspaper clippings about her brother. She looked up at her father. "Bruiser, you remember how happy Jimmy was to see us when he came out of the Army? He never looked better—so nice and tall in his uniform—"

Bruiser—it was a name given him when he was a carnival boxer in California, taking on all comers—smiled. Carol said, "He was always young-looking for his age, wasn't he, Bruiser? But when I seen him last, he had that distinguished touch of gray at his temples—" Her father nodded. "Yeah, Jimmy's sure a good-looking fella."

On seeing the elder Ray sitting there on the sofa in his shirt sleeves, his legs crossed, his fists dug deep in his pockets, it was easy to visualize him as his neighbors in Ewing remembered him years ago—walking down the middle of a furrowed country road into town, in his curious, shuffling, bowed-shoulders boxer's walk, cigarette dangling from the corner of his mouth, one eye squinting against the smoke, while behind him, in single file, came his three boys, Jimmy, John, whom the family called Jack, and Jerry.

Over the course of a long afternoon, the two, father and daughter, had been talking—now in a reminiscent mood, now outraged, now bitterly resigned—about the troubles that had come upon them: Jimmy, in jail for a killing he never did—"He was framed by the FBI," said Carol, "and then sold out by that Percy Foreman"; Jack, recently sentenced to eighteen years in Leavenworth for a bank robbery he didn't commit: "They framed Jack, too," said Carol. "They had it in for him because he's Jimmy's brother"; and Jerry, now living in Savannah with J. B. Stoner, Jimmy's lawyer, working as his chauffeur and aide, helping take subscriptions for *The Thunderbolt*, whose editorial offices were in Stoner's home—and constantly harassed by the FBI, like the rest of the Ray family. Jerry had been in and out of trouble in the last couple of years. In 1970 Stoner had run for Governor of Georgia on a white supremacist platform in the Democratic primaries, and Jerry had been his campaign manager.* But that July Jerry had been arrested and charged with attempted murder, as a result of wounding a seventeen-year-old white boy who allegedly broke into Stoner's office one night while Jerry, armed with a .38, was guarding it, and tried to make off with a box of National States Rights Party files. Jerry was tried in November 1970 and acquitted. He told the family the boy carried a card showing membership in the competing American Nazi Party, which wanted the NSRP's large mailing list, but everyone suspected he had really been sent on the job by the FBI.

It was pretty much of a mystery, all these things happening to the Ray family, the father was saying. "Now, take Jimmy—you can't make me believe that Jimmy just walked out of Missouri State Penitentiary.

---

* Jerry had been a guest celebrity at a National States Rights Party dinner, at which he was introduced (the story and his photograph appeared in *The Thunderbolt*) as "the Honorable Jerry Ray, brother of James Earl Ray."

They let him out on purpose—to set him up. They wanted to get Jimmy involved in this King thing, because they knowed he'd never talk." He dug his fists deeper into his pockets. "I don't know who killed Martin Luther King, but it wasn't Jimmy. You couldn't hire him to kill anybody. Maybe somebody done it who was afraid they'd make that fella President. A lot of people might vote for him, to start trouble." He brooded for a moment. "Why, Jimmy had no feeling about black people. Hell, we didn't want them moving in around us, but we paid them no mind. I never raised Jimmy to be a racist."

Rayns warmed to his subject. "He wasn't the way you read about him. I don't know why they write all that dirt about us, like we was a *Tobacco Road* family. They paint us so poor—hell, there were a lot poorer people than us around there. We had hogs and chickens, and Jimmy even had his own horse—"

Carol could not help smiling. "Bruiser, you remember about the chickens—how Jimmy got hold of some cigarettes and he didn't want you to know about it and he hid them under the porch and the chickens dug them up and he was so mad—" She laughed.

Rayns nodded. "And the way they write about him—Jimmy wasn't wild or bigmouthed or mean as a boy. He didn't hate nobody. He believed in his rights, he'll fight for them—any boy will do that without his being plumb scared to death or something. Jimmy was always ambitious. He wanted to buy a filling station but he wanted me to work it for him." Rayns chuckled. "I guess he wanted to be the supervisor."

Carol said, "Bruiser, remember what he said when he left for the Army?"

Rayns' blue eyes, the same color as his son's, lit up. "He went down to enlist and he came back and said he picked out what they call chemical warfare. His mother Lucille said, 'Wait a minute—that's flame throwers. That's no place for Jimmy.' You know," said Rayns, "they must of talked him into it, he wouldn't pick that out himself. So Lucille went down and got it straightened out."

"But what he said, Bruiser," his daughter prompted him. "Don't you remember?"

"That's right," said Rayns. "We drove him down to the depot and he turned to us and said, 'Don't you worry about me. I'll be a sergeant in thirty days. I'm going right to the top.' He sure had a lot of confidence." He didn't know what kind of trouble Jimmy got into in the Army—the boy never talked to him about it, except he knew that he had been demoted. But he did well in some things. He won a medal for marksmanship—he never talked about that, either, but they knew about it because the Army sent the medal home later. "He sure was busy. He didn't smoke—I never let him smoke—so he'd sell the cigarettes and stuff, and buy war bonds with it—" He sent the bonds home to his grandmother Maher to keep for him in her rooming house, and she threw them on a top shelf in a closet, and when he came home, they were gone—the roomers had stolen them. "He got disgusted in the Army, he saw there's no justice, and he just got so he didn't trust nobody," Rayns said.

After that, it was one tough break after another for Jimmy. He was in the Missouri prison when his mother died in 1961. They were ready to let him come to Lucille's funeral under guard, but he wrote bitterly, "I won't go in chains to my mother's funeral," and so he was not there at what was the first family reunion in years.

Lucille had been a good mother to him. She worked hard, she liked the farm, she loved to cook and bake . . . Yes, she drank. Rayns did not know why. He threw a quick glance. "There was a lot of drinking on her side of the family," he said. When they were married, he was twenty-seven, she was seventeen. "She was a girl who was always afraid of things. She had asthma, she took a spell once in Florida—we lived in a tent down there—she like to died, she couldn't catch her breath. . . ." Maybe the drinking began when he got a job working nights on the railroad. "She was scared of the dark and scared to be alone at night." Maybe she'd take a drink to settle her nerves when he'd leave for work at night. Maybe that began it. She tried to follow his schedule, he remembered, working nights, sleeping days, but it was hard to do on a farm, taking care of the children and all the rest. . . .

Just before Jimmy was born, they were living in St. Louis, where he'd made a little business for himself—he'd not only been a fighter and a farmer and a railroad man, but a bootlegger, a used-car salesman, a saloonkeeper, he'd tried his hand at everything—this time he was buying wrecked cars, fixing them up and selling them at a good profit. Lucille found she was going to have a baby, and she was scared to death. "Hell, we was both scared" and "she wouldn't go to a doctor, but went to those old midwives, and I had enough sense to know you could die around people like that, and she was so scared, she said she wanted to go to her mother's place to have the baby, so I took her up to her mother's in Alton." Grandmother Maher gave them two rooms in the basement of the two-story clapboard house and there James Earl Ray was born.

Then there was the death of Marjorie, their little girl. "Marjorie was just six then, and she and Jack, he was about four, they were playing out in the kitchen and somehow they got hold of a match. Lucille's in the front room, sewing on her machine. Marjorie, she was just wearing a little voile dress. I guess Lucille didn't hear her screaming at first. There was a big iron door to the kitchen and Marjorie was pounding on it. I was out in the field cutting timber for fence posts with Jimmy, and all of a sudden Lucille comes running out, Marjorie's in her arms, and she was hollerin, 'She's burned, she's burned,' and she fell over a log with her—I grabbed Marjorie up and took her into the house and put that Vicks VapoRub all over her body—" The doctor took the child to Quincy, twenty-three miles away, and there she died. The soft, musical voice went on, "Lucille wasn't drinking then, she wouldn't think of drinking then. . . ."

Things just got worse after that. Their son, Franklin, everybody called him Buzzy, everyone liked him, he was eighteen, and he drowned when his car drove off the Quincy Bridge, he and some girl he had with him—and there was the charities, which came and took the children, Melba and Susy and Max, and put them in the orphanage. They claimed Max was retarded, but the boy was hit over the head in a fight once, and that probably caused it. "Me and Lucille was separated and I didn't even know when they took the children."

Carol spoke up. "They didn't take me, you notice. I wouldn't let them. But they took Melba with the others."

"Yeah," said Rayns. "They tell me she bit and screamed and kicked but the sheriff said he had to take her. Hell, she was just as sane as anybody, but putting her in that home, that did it—they just messed up Melba's brain. She wasn't the same since."

"My mother did what she could," said Carol. "She was working in the kitchen of the Lincoln-Douglas Hotel in St. Louis, but they bothered her all the time, the charities, coming around and asking her questions where she worked, she couldn't keep her job, she had to quit. When the agency woman came over to the house, my mother took her around to show she had food for the children and that the place was clean. But the woman, she was an ignorant woman, she said to the sheriff, 'Take the kids,' and I fought him and I was the biggest and he let me alone."

It was silent. Outside, in the small backyard, Carol's two boys, both under ten, played and shouted as they flew their kites.

Father and daughter did not know what would happen now. It all depended on the FBI, and the FBI never let them have a moment's peace. Maybe Jimmy would get his new trial—if he lived to get it. Take last May, when he almost broke out of Brushy Mountain

Prison. "I just figure they was trying to get him out where they could kill him," said Rayns. "I think Jimmy's probably been set up to be shut up two or three times before. He was just lucky he didn't make it this time."

Carol said, "Those FBI—remember, Bruiser? I went down to the grocery store, and there's two FBI men at the telephone. I can tell them a mile away. Wherever I go, someone seems to have an eye on me. I went into a department store, I was looking down at some records and I had the funniest feeling—all at once I looked up, and there was a man on each side of me. You don't see men in those big department stores, it's mainly women. I don't know if it's the FBI or somebody big putting all this pressure on us—framing Jimmy, framing Jack, asking questions of all Jerry's friends. What are they following us around for?"

Her father said, "This is going on ever since this thing with Jimmy. You know the FBI, they lie about everything. In Memphis they paid witnesses to tell lies. Said his fingerprints were on that gun—that don't mean nothing, that's just somebody talking. They got to have a goat and James Earl Ray was the goat and that's what it was."

There was a rush of feet, and the two boys burst into the room. The younger wore shell-rimmed glasses, and his small face was a startling miniature of the face that had been in the newspapers so many times. Their mother shooed them out. "You know we don't want you in here when we're talking," she said, and they trooped out again.

She sat for a moment, the scrapbook closed on her lap. She spoke sadly. "It's a strange thing. King is killed down in Memphis. Nobody is really thinking about it. We never thought much about him, it wasn't part of our life, you know. Then all of a sudden they're looking for Jimmy, that's who they're looking for—Jimmy!" She shook her head unbelievingly.

Her father suddenly rose, his hands out of his pockets now. They hung loosely at his sides, and as he moved slowly, his head a little down, it was like a boxer coming cautiously out of his corner. "I don't know," he said. "I can't figure it out. It's too deep for me. Them fellas, the FBI, they got a good education, they study all that stuff, and they know the angles. You can't beat the government." He sighed. "I don't know what the FBI got in mind for us. I think they intend to get rid of the whole Ray outfit, if you ask me. Sooner or later, shut us all up. That's what they're going for, if you ask me."

Notes

CHAPTER I

Page 9

King had expressed himself most eloquently and powerfully on the Vietnam war before an audience at Riverside Church in New York on April 4, 1967—one year to the day before his assassination. Dr. Abraham Heschel, a distinguished religious leader, founder of Clergy and Laymen Concerned about Viet Nam, and his co-chairman, the Rev. John Bennett, of Union Theological Seminary, had wanted to enlist the country's outstanding citizens to protest the war. They decided to ask Dr. King, although he had not yet made a major public statement on the subject. Chaplain William Sloan Coffin, Jr., telephoned King at Dr. Heschel's request: "We have a new organization, we'd like you to join us and perhaps come and speak for us." Dr. King asked to have twenty-four hours to think it over: then he agreed to join. His address at the Riverside Church marked the first time an important figure had tied up the war with the situation of the poor in the United States—had made the point that because so much money was spent on the war, the cities of America suffered.

CHAPTER V

Page 44

When Memphis newspapers reported that Burch had become Dr. King's lawyer, he received a series of abusive telephone calls. An hour after the assassination, Thursday, April 4, a woman telephoned him every thirty minutes, insulting him each time: "You Nigger-loving son-of-a-bitch." After the ninth or tenth call—it was then 12:30 A.M., Friday—Burch said to her, "Now, Hon, you can call me just as well in the morning about this thing. The man is dead, and we both want to get some sleep. Let's take this up tomorrow."

His caller thawed slightly. "Mr. Burch, you didn't have to take that case. You didn't need that money."

Burch said, "There wasn't any money."

She said, "Aw, you got fifty thousand dollars for representing that Nigger."

"No, ma'am, I didn't. I didn't get a penny."

She said, "Mr. Burch, you mean they didn't pay you for representing that Nigger?"

"No, ma'am, not a penny."

She hung up.

Half an hour later, on the clock, she rang him again. "Mr. Burch, didn't you tell me you didn't get paid for representing that Nigger?"

Burch said, "No, ma'am, I didn't get a penny."

"Mr. Burch, you're a lying son-of-a-bitch," and she hung up. But he did not hear from her again.

Page 51

Dr. King was stabbed in the L. M. Blumstein, Inc., department store at 230 West 125th Street, in New York, at 3:30 P.M., September 20, 1958. He was seated at a desk in the rear autographing copies of *Stride Toward Freedom: The Montgomery Story*, the first book he had written, and which had been published a few days earlier. The woman, Mrs. Izola Curry, forty-two, who lived in Harlem, said she stabbed Dr. King "because then he'd listen to my problems, because

I've been followed in buses, and people have been making me lose my job." She had been working as a maid; she had never seen Dr. King before. In her dress police found a loaded .25-caliber revolver.

CHAPTER VII

Page 68

Through the years there were scores of threats against Dr. King's life. In 1964 the FBI reported that a group of Klansmen were seeking to hire an ex-convict to kill Dr. King for a fee of two thousand dollars. In July of that year a plan was reported to shoot Dr. King when he came to Monroe, Louisiana, in a civil rights campaign; in February 1965 the FBI reportedly foiled a scheme to kill Dr. King in his SCLC headquarters in Atlanta. That same month when Dr. King spoke at a World Affairs Council luncheon at the Hollywood Palladium, an anonymous telephone caller warned that 1400 pounds of stolen dynamite would be used "to blow up every Nigger Black Muslim temple in town and that Nigger Martin Luther King at the Palladium today when he speaks."

Dr. King spoke anyway. But he asked luncheon officials to seat Mrs. King in another part of the room. If the bullet or bomb came, at least it might not take them together. (The stolen dynamite was later found in an apartment belonging to a man who had said he belonged to the Minutemen of America, a paramilitary group. His whereabouts were unknown.)

On February 12, 1966, Daniel Wagner, nineteen, appearing before the Committee on Un-American Activities, testified that Mrs. Eloise Witte, Grand Empress of the Ohio Ku Klux Klan, told him that the Klan had hired a gunman for $25,000 to kill Dr. King, "but the man couldn't go through with it."

Page 70

At one point this pressure had been so great that in the privacy of a New York hotel room, and among his most intimate friends, he broke down and wept. It was shortly after he returned from Oslo with the Nobel Peace Prize. Hoover's attack on him as "a notorious liar" had come only a few weeks earlier. Now he was certain that at some point Hoover, or someone close to Hoover, would inspire a story in the newspapers that would demean him.

CHAPTER IX

Page 103

Jowers' report that at 6:15 P.M. the white Mustang in front of his restaurant was no longer there was misread: many believed he had said that he saw it *leave* at 6:15 P.M. Since Canipe and his two customers had seen a white Mustang speed away a moment after the bundle of evidence was dropped in Canipe's doorway—perhaps at 6:02 or 6:03 P.M.—this was immediately taken as proof that there had been two white Mustangs. Actually, Ray had driven his car from his spot in front of Jim's Grill shortly before four o'clock, when he drove to the York Arms to buy the binoculars. Then, on his return, he found another car in the place he had vacated, and was forced to park his white Mustang some sixty feet south, the other side of Canipe's.

CHAPTER X

Page 107

The slug was in one piece when Dr. Francisco placed it in the envelope to be sent to the FBI Laboratory in Washington. But when it was returned to Memphis with other evidence to await the trial, it was in two pieces: a small chip, loosened by the impact when it struck Dr. King, had separated from it either in transit or when it was examined in Washington. This led to a rumor that Dr. King had been struck by two bullets.

This rumor, in turn, grew when word seeped out that those who had seen Dr. King's body had observed two wounds—the huge one in the jaw, and an even more massive wound below the collarbone. What had happened was that surgical procedures taken in the emergency room had enlarged the lower end of the wound. Only those familiar with what had been done would know that it was not a second wound.

The rumor was one more piece of misinformation to confuse the story and add to the belief that evidence was being suppressed in order to hide a conspiracy.

CHAPTER XII

Page 134

Although CB operators in Memphis never learned Whitney's identity—police did not disclose it—the man was denounced by many of his fellow CB'ers for his attempt to help the police catch Dr. King's murderer. More than three years after the event, Whitney still wished to keep his anonymity, explaining apologetically, "Many people around here still feel very strongly about the incident and I would rather not have my name publicly connected."

CHAPTER XIII

Page 139

Although the fine lines and grooves by which a ballistics expert matched a slug to the bore of the barrel of the rifle from which it was fired were blurred when it struck Dr. King, the FBI specialist concluded that the slug taken from Dr. King's body "contained land and groove impressions consistent with those present in the barrel of the rifle."

The cartridge case, or shell, was believed by many to have been found in the bathtub. This was not true. It was in the rifle. The Remington 30.06 is a pump-action rifle, which requires the user to eject each shell after he fires the weapon in order to fire a second shot. Since Ray had put only one bullet in the rifle, there was no point in ejecting the shell or casing.

The Remington 30.06 cannot be fully loaded quickly. The chamber holds only one bullet: this can be done swiftly. But additional bullets must be inserted into a removable magazine. To load this, one has to press a button, causing the magazine to drop out, then insert four shells into it, then push the magazine back into place in the weapon.

Page 140

Ironically enough, Ray's prison number, from Missouri State Penitentiary, was on the small radio found in the bundle he dropped in Canipe's doorway. He had bought it the day before he escaped, so he could follow any search for him. Ray tried to file away the number—00416—but it was still visible under a microscope. It meant nothing to Memphis police or the FBI when they found it. But when Galt was identified as Ray, it became one more link in the chain of evidence.

CHAPTER XIV

Page 158

The many sketches of Ray, done by artists, would have to bear their blame for contributing to talk of conspiracy. There had been reports that the sketches appearing in the newspapers, presumably distributed by the FBI, did not resemble the James Earl Ray who was caught in London. This seemed to point to two Rays.

Contrary to general belief, the FBI had never distributed an "authentic" sketch of Ray. None existed. Those appearing in the newspapers had been "artists' conceptions" based upon oral descriptions. Many thought these were sketches from life. None had ever been made from life: none of the artists whose sketches appeared in the newspapers had ever seen Ray.

As was to be true throughout the case, errors, discrepancies, and ordinary human bungling were seized upon as proof of conspiracy. On Wednesday, April 10, the FBI sent to all state police in the country, to be relayed to their stations, a teletyped bulletin reading: WANTED FOR QUESTIONING BY FBI ST. LOUIS—ERIC STARVO GALT DRIVING WHITE 66 FORD MUSTANG. It gave Galt's description and the Mustang's license number, but no explanation why Galt was wanted. This message was relayed over the air by all state police, except the Florida State Police. By some oversight the teletyped FBI bulletin lay unnoticed on a cluttered desk there until Thursday, at 3:10 P.M., when it was immediately put on the air. By that time, however, the Mustang had been found in Atlanta. The Florida police thereupon sent out a second message less than two hours later: CANCEL CALL 3:10 P.M. ERIC STARVO GALT NO LONGER WANTED.

This at once aroused suspicion that Government higher-ups had ordered the cancellation in order to suppress information—most likely, that Galt was hiding out in Florida, waiting to be smuggled aboard a plane to be hijacked to Castro's Cuba, presumably to meet those behind the conspiracy.

CHAPTER XVII

Page 184

The discrepancies between the descriptions of Galt and Ray, the differences in their life-styles, were all explicable. Galt was born in 1931, Ray in 1928. This was a lie told by Ray, posing as Galt, to throw people off the track. He said 1931 because he knew that he looked younger than his age. Ray was said to have a Midwest twang, Galt, a Southern drawl. Southerners hearing him speak thought it was Midwest; Mideasterners, Southern. Galt took dancing lessons in 1964 and 1965 in New Orleans, according to his record as given out by the FBI; Ray was in Missouri State Penitentiary then. This was simply an error. The FBI had been told by dancing instructors in Long Beach, California, where Ray took dancing lessons in early 1968, that he also took dance lessons in New Orleans in 1964–65. It was made more believable because the owners of the Birmingham dancing school where Galt had taken lessons while rooming at Cherpes' also owned a school in New Orleans. It also seemed plausible because Galt had told Cherpes that he worked on Mississippi river barges between New Orleans and St. Louis. Galt was free with his money, buying expensive alligator shoes, and custom-made clothing, his nails manicured; while Ray was a penny pincher. Again, error. Galt's shoes were imitation alligator, worth eleven dollars; his custom-made suit cost sixty-nine dollars. He had his nails manicured once; otherwise they were kept in shape with a nail clipper.

In short, the FBI simply reported the background Ray had built up for himself as Galt. There was obviously no way to check Galt's background until they discovered that he was Ray.

Page 187

Some idea of the exhaustive FBI investigation in New Orleans may be gained from the following. Ray had a telephone in his room, Room 216, at the Provincial Motel, where, as Galt, he stayed December 17 and 18, 1967, during his trip there with Charlie Stein. He made no calls on it. The motel had a pay station phone outside the office, in a small alcove between the office and a swimming pool. One long-distance call to Los Angeles had been made on December 18. It was checked out on the assumption that Ray might have called a confederate. It had been made to the home of Sidney N. Elias, 916 South Ogden Drive, Los Angeles. Questioned in Los Angeles, Elias said he had stayed at the Provincial that night, en route to Miami, and had telephoned his home to talk to his son.

Every person who stayed at the Provincial when Ray was there was interrogated. The telephone directory in Ray's room had pages 47, 373, 375, and 377 bent down at the corner, and two blank sheets of hotel stationery were found stuck into the book at page 47.

Although Room 216 had been occupied by others before and after Ray, on the chance possibility that he had turned down the pages every name listed on them was checked. The stationery was sent to the FBI Crime Laboratory because the faint impression of writing with a ball-point pen covered almost every inch of both sheets. This turned out to be lists of names and telephone numbers, mostly of building and construction companies. Checking further, the trail led to an organization called Parents Without Partners. It met once a month at the New Orleans YMCA. Its membership was thoroughly checked: no Eric Starvo Galt, no John Willard, no Harvey Lowmyer were found.

Perhaps Ray, as Galt, had used New Orleans as a jumping-off place after killing King. The FBI looked for a Galt, Willard, or Lowmyer in the passenger and crew lists of every ship—there were fifty-three—that had sailed from the Port of New Orleans between April 4 and April 9, as well as those of the hundreds of planes, commercial and private, that took off from New Orleans Airport during that period.

This was in addition to an exhaustive interrogation of alleged Mafia leaders and New Orleans underworld personalities.

Page 197

When Ray was captured in London, on his person and in his luggage were found:

A .38 Liberty Chief revolver, five rounds of ammunition, comb, pencil, key, white metal wrist watch on white metal bracelet, tie clip, Polaroid 220 camera, writing pad, printed information on gun silencers, six shirts, three pairs shorts (all darned), five handkerchiefs, three pairs socks, two motel towels, two bars motel soap, five ties, hi-fi radio, two pairs sunglasses, a Collins dictionary, map of London, map of Portugal, bottle opener, screwdriver, nail clipper, deodorant, skin cream, shampoo, hair dressing, toothpaste, shaving foam, safety razor, inhaler, liniment, fifteen Aspros (aspirin tablets), suede brush, shoe polish, hand mirror, book of matches, ten safety pins, spool of brown thread, two paper clips, needle, adhesive tape, three plasters, man's black belt, man's plastic wallet, two pair slacks, vest, brown suit (English & Scotch Woolen Company, Tailors, Toronto, label inside reading "Eric Galt"), a 1967 Almanac, a picture magazine, a book on Rhodesia, a paperback novel, *The Ninth Directive*, number of paperback books including four dealing with hypnosis, fifty-one pounds, nine shillings and six-pence in British money, one Portuguese fifty-centavo piece.

CHAPTER XXIII

Page 263

The affidavit Renfro Hays later obtained from Grace Hays Walden, Charlie Stephens' common-law wife, and signed by her as Grace Hays Stephens, read as follows:

"Statement taken November 5, 1968, from Grace Hays Walden at Western State Hospital, Bolivar, Tennessee:

"My name is Grace Hays Walden and at this time I am a patient in a hospital. I was living at 422½ South Main, Memphis, Tennessee, on 4 April, 1968. I was living in the apartment next to the bathroom at that address. I was ill at that time in bed. During that afternoon, before six o'clock I heard the man in the room next to me go to the bathroom several times, and try to get in, but evidently its door was locked.

"At about six o'clock I heard a shot. I cannot tell where the shot came from. I know it echoed in the arcade beneath my window. At this time Charlie Stephens was in the kitchen fixing a radio. Right after the shot a man left the bathroom and went down the hall and down the steps to Main Street. I saw this man as he passed the door of my room. My best guess of the man's age was in his 50's. This man was not quite as tall as I am. He was small bone built. He had on an Army colored hunting jacket unfastened and dark pants. He had on a plaid sport shirt. His hair was salt and pepper colored. He had something long in his right hand but I cannot swear what it was. Charlie was still in the kitchen then but he got to our door by the time the man had gotten to the head of the stairs. Charles Stephens went out into the hall and looked down the hall. In about two minutes Charlie came back into the room. We heard screaming at the motel but it was quite some time before anyone came up to our rooms.

"Newspaper reporters came up to our room before the police came. Around 10 P.M. the police came and we went down to Police Headquarters. I believe I gave a statement to Inspector Zachary. This statement was more than one page. Charles Stephens had not had much to drink that day. He was drinking dark port wine. Within two or three days after this a London newspaperman gave Charlie some money for his story. He gave him more than one bill. Someone else gave him a single bill.

"I have read this statement of one and two/thirds pages and it is true to the best of my knowledge and belief. I have not been promised any reward or threatened in any way.

"Witness: Dorothy Staunch (Supervisor, Nursing). Grace Hays Stephens."

Renfro added a note. Miss Staunch, he said, told him that Grace Stephens was in full possession of her mental faculties, and "there's nothing at all wrong with her mind."

There was, however, the court record explaining her commitment: July 31, 1968. Probate Judge Peston found that Grace Walden, also known as Grace Stephens, "is mentally ill (not mentally retarded) and because of said illness is likely to injure herself, or others if not hospitalized, and is in need of custody, care or treatment in a mental hospital and should be committed to a hospital . . ." She was judged "mentally ill and incompetent" and committed to Western State Hospital for an indeterminate period.

Page 267

Martin Waldron of the New York *Times,* who had devoted many weeks to the case, was checking out reports that while Ray was said to be staying in Jimmy Garner's Atlanta rooming house, a man fitting Ray's description was staying in a motel near the Birmingham airport—a motel whose records for that period, he discovered, had been confiscated by the FBI. Bernard Gavzer of The Associated Press, who was to spend many weeks preparing an extensive series of articles on the case, was meeting with Institute of Defense Analysis experts in Arlington, Virginia, to examine the problems involved in solving it. In Center, Missouri, Daniel Greene of *The National Observer* had traced Jerry Rayns (only the FBI then knew that Rayns was not dead) to his farmhouse one night, to discover Rayns, hiding behind the door, shouting at him, "I got a rifle—you get off my property or I'll use this!" In Atlanta, Henry P. Leifermann of United Press International was checking out a report that Ray had registered in a motel there, and a few minutes later a pretty, 30-year-old woman picked up his room key and vanished. On all these matters, the FBI refused comment.

CHAPTER XXVI

Page 290

Ray constantly falsified his background through the years. He changed the facts and improvised on his biography as he went from prison to prison, as later he was to change and improvise on his story to his various attorneys in the King case. Prison files show some of his claims: that both parents were dead and he was an only child; that he had an aunt, Lucille Ryan, in Quincy (this was his mother); that he had completed eight grades in St. Mary's School, in Alton; that he had dropped out of the tenth grade in Ewing public school; that after his Army discharge he had graduated from a Chicago night school with the equivalent of a two-year high-school education. None of this was true. But where the truth might be sought out, and the records were immediately available—as, for example, his Army tenure and the dates of his prison terms—he did not lie.

Page 297

If Ray dealt in large sums in prison, as reported by some inmates, one must take this with a certain hesitation. The amounts of money he received from his family were minuscule, and the amounts of money he sent out were equally small.

The record of money orders received by James Earl Ray at Missouri State Penitentiary and the senders:

February 20, 1963, from John, $35; April 16, $65, John; August 23, $25, Jerry; June 19, 1964, $50, Philip L. Baker, 516 Guitar Building, Columbia, Mo.; June 19, $50, John; July 10, $15, Jerry; August 15, $1, West Publishing Company; August 20, $30, Jerry; August 28, $35, Jerry; January 3, 1965, $5, Mrs. M. Fuller; March 11, $1, Jerry; March 25, $10, Mrs. Mary Maher; April 5, $4.50, Jerry; May 18, $8.50, Jerry; May 27, $40, Jerry; June 14, $8.50, Jerry; July 9, $15, Jerry; August 11, $1.50, Jerry; August 31, $30, Jerry; September 1, $13.50, Jerry; December 8, $1.50, Jerry; December 20, $10, M. Fuller; December 24, $10, Mrs. M. Fuller; February 10, 1966, $1, Jerry; March 24, $8.50, Jerry; April 1, $8.50, Jerry; May 7, $3.50, Jerry; May 27, $10, Jerry; August 18, $6.75, Jerry; December 20, $5, Mary Maher; December 20, $5, Jerry; February 3, 1967, $15, John.

Records from March 22, 1960, show him withdrawing and sometimes sending amounts of $3, $2.25, $20. Once he sent $80.25 to Jerry. Total balance in his account in prison ranged from a high of $93.12 on June 3, 1962, to a low of $.65 on December 9, 1966.

CHAPTER XXVIII

Page 309

Although Ray was going about his plan with businesslike efficiency, now and then a glimpse of his own feeling about himself could be seen. He took out time to telephone a woman who had placed a curiously humble ad in *The Single Peoples Advertiser*, a Los Angeles underground publication:

"Tall, skinny, auburn-haired divorcée, 41, seeks prospective husband with patience."

At least twenty other ads appeared that day in the newspaper, each more seductive and enticing than the other: "Fascinating femme, agile, alive, athletic," and "Attractive feminine female seeks dating and companionship with man," and others like these. But Ray chose to phone the skinny, forty-one-year-old divorcée. Nothing came of the call. The woman received about one hundred answers to her ad, but, for whatever reason, she and Ray made no connection.

Page 310

Ray did not allow King's murder to disturb his locksmithing lessons. He continued them all through the period immediately before and after the assassination. He mailed his ninth and final lesson on April 5, from Atlanta—the day after the murder. He had returned to Atlanta, mailed off his lesson, went to the dry cleaner's to pick up his clothes and laundry before leaving for Canada.

Page 318

The fact that when Ray hid out in London, a city totally unfamiliar to him, he went at once to the "Kangaroo Valley" section, where he could easily lose himself among the Australians living there, was cited as proof that a confederate must have helped him. Again, the answer is surprisingly simple. Ray flew from Lisbon to London aboard a Portuguese Air Lines plane, landing at Heathrow. The waiting airport bus he boarded took the passengers to the W. London Air Terminal on Cromwell Road—which happens to be in the heart of "Kangaroo Valley." Ray stayed in hotels convenient to the terminal.

CHAPTER XXIX

Page 323

Dr. King's peripatetic activities at the Lorraine Motel—though he was registered in Room 306, he spent time in 307, 201, and other rooms—led to reports that he had been shifted from room to room before being deliberately placed in 306 so as to be clearly exposed to an assassin's bullet from the South Main Street rooming house. But since virtually any room in the motel was equally exposed, the choice of Room 306 was meaningless.

Page 327

It was impossible to state precisely where the broadcast emanated from, because two listeners would have had to monitor it and, while monitoring it, make a cross-fix on it. But Carroll Satchfield, an audio expert and a well-known CB operator in Memphis, had been at his set when the mysterious broadcast was made.

His memo, sent to Inspector Zachary, read:

"When he first began broadcasting I looked at my meter. It read 8.6, a strong, clear station. But when he said he was at Summer and Highland, and the strength of the meter was still 8.6, I told a friend with me, 'Something is wrong here. The signal is constant and clear, and no noise of any kind.' If he was sending from a mobile unit and moving east on Summer, the signal strength would have to diminish, and there would be noise from the mobile unit. Also, the time he gave from one point to another was impossible: he would have had to be in a jet plane to get from one place to another so swiftly. The voice sounded to me like some real, smart, exceptional high IQ boy that has been listening to the Broderick Crawford TV program, 'Road Patrol,' and is just brilliant enough at that age to concoct something of this nature. It was a young, shallow voice, high-pitched, youthful-sounding, that did not have power behind it, as an older man would; like a youngster from 15 to 18, with his voice on the verge of changing. The studio or room in which he was operating was dead silent— as if he were completely sealed off from everything else. No music, no sound of others in the room, no sound of a police monitor, just as clear as if he were broadcasting all by himself."

Once or twice Satchfield had broken in, to ask questions of the sender. He received a reply: he was going north on Jackson at 100 miles an hour. Satchfield knew at once this was a lie: there was no change in carrier level, no change in modulation: the sender obviously was broadcasting from a fixed location. When the sender said he was being shot at, Satchfield broke in a second time: "State your license number and name of operator" and heard: "Oh, no, with the general situation I don't want to give my name or call."

Then there was silence. Satchfield broadcast to any other CB'ers who might be listening: "Boys, you won't hear any more from that station because he's not changed his location since he started. This is a hoax or a plot. Someone ought to prosecute this guy."

Later, during Zachary's investigation, the boy's transmitter was turned on. Satchfield, alerted at his receiver, checked the signal strength on his meter. It was 8.6—identical to the false broadcast.

Page 328
The report of ashes in the white Mustang came from Mrs. Riley's young son, Johnny, who had peered through the windows of the locked Mustang on his way to school that morning. He told Bernard Gavzer that he saw ashes both in the pulled-out ashtray and on the floor: "It was like someone thumping a cigar and cigarette on the ashtray and missing," he said. He was certain of it. But he was also certain that the Mustang was a 1964 Mustang. Since it was actually a 1966 model, Gavzer asked how he knew this. "I saw a tag on the back that had the year." There was no tag on the back of the car. The boy said the trunk was empty. This, too, was not true. The trunk held much of Ray's property. The fact was that Johnny had not been present when the FBI opened the trunk in the basement garage where they had secretly taken the car. In addition, the FBI report on the Mustang had no mention of ashes—this after a microscopic examination of the vehicle.

CHAPTER XXX

Page 333
Foreman's financial arrangements with Ray were put in written form in two letters which Foreman brought to Ray on Sunday, March 9, 1969, the day before the guilty plea. Ray signed each in the lower left corner to indicate his agreement with it:

Dear James Earl:
You have heretofore assigned to me all of your royalties from magazine articles, book, motion picture, or other revenue to be derived from the writings of William Bradford Huie. These are my own property unconditionally.

However, you have heretofore authorized and requested me to negotiate a plea of guilty if the State of Tennessee through its

District Attorney General and with the approval of the trial judge would waive the death penalty. You agreed to accept a sentence of 99 years.

It is comtemplated that your case will be disposed of tomorrow, March 10, by the above plea and sentence. This will shorten the trial considerably. In consideration of the time it will save me, I am willing to make the following adjustment of my fee arrangement with you:

If the plea is entered and the sentence accepted and no embarrassing circumstances take place in the courtroom, I am willing to assign to any bank, trust company or individual selected by you all my receipts under the above assignment in excess of $165,000. These funds over and above the first $165,000 will be held by such bank, trust company or individual subject to your order.

I have either spent or obligated myself to spend in excess of $14,000, and I think these expenses should be paid in addition to a $150,000 fee. I am sure the expenses will exceed the $15,000, but I am willing to rest on that figure.

Yours truly,
Percy Foreman.

Dear James Earl:

You have asked that I advance to Jerry Ray $500 of the "$5,000" referring to the first $5,000 paid by William Bradford Huie. At that time I had spent in excess of $9,500 on your case. Since then I have spent in excess of $4,000 additional.

But I am willing to advance Jerry $500 and add it to the $165,000 mentioned in my other letter to you today. In other words, I would receive the first $165,500. But I would not make any other advances—just this one $500. And this advance also is contingent upon the plea of guilty and sentence going through on March 10, 1969, without any unseemly conduct on your part in court.

P.S. The rifle and the white Mustang are tied up in the suit filed by Renfro Hays. Court costs and attorney fees will be necessary, perhaps, to get them released. I will credit the $165,500 with whatever they bring over the cost of obtaining them, if any.

Yours truly,
Percy Foreman.

CHAPTER XXXI

Page 345

Solomon Jones was to find himself in many difficulties later. In early 1971 he was sentenced to an eight-year term in Leavenworth Penitentiary after he was found guilty of stealing social security and other government checks from the mails and cashing them. Jones maintained that Memphis police had been "out to get me" because he had told a story that contradicted the "official" version of King's murder.

Not long after the guilty plea a visitor called on John McFerren, who overheard the mysterious telephone call. He found him busy at his gas station—a burly, blue-eyed black man with a wry smile who appeared to be in his mid-fifties. McFerren later sat in a small office in the rear of his grocery and told of his puzzling experiences since revealing the telephone call. One caller drove up to his place in an enormous blue Cadillac, and McFerren filled his tank. The driver was from Chicago, he told McFerren, who studied him and concluded that he was a millionaire—"You could tell it by the way he talked." Instead of driving away, the stranger began questioning him. McFerren, telling the story, chuckled. "He got nothing out of me. He thought I was stupid. I always play dumb—I let them think that, and I end up getting more out of them than they get out of me."

His Chicago caller made his big mistake, he went on, when he suggested they go into McFerren's lunchroom and have coffee. McFerren looked quizzical. "You see, he didn't know I wasn't a coffee drinker. He didn't do good enough research on me. He thought I'd have a cup of coffee with him—why, I'd only have to glance away for a couple of seconds and he could have dropped poison into my cup. I'd never taste it, never know it. He could have had the pellet hidden in the crook of his little finger"—McFerren demonstrated—"and you can't taste anything like that in coffee."

He shook his head. "You should have seen his face when I said, 'No, I don't want any coffee. I never drink it.' I could see the perspiration break out on his forehead."

That was not the only incident. Some days before, he had received a telephone call from a woman with a deep Southern accent. She told him, "I want to order some vegetables, chicken, potatoes—a big order." After a minute or two, her conversation became personal. "You want to be my honey boy?" she asked. "I'll come up tonight to pick up the groceries." He knew immediately then that she was out to spy on him. She obviously must have been calling long distance—"Because if she was from around here, she wouldn't have said, 'I'll come up'—she would have said, 'I'll be over.'" McFerren looked triumphantly at his visitor. "She just made a slip and I caught it." He meditated for a moment. He had to be extremely watchful these days. "Every time I get out on the road in my truck, they try to gun me down or push me off the road."

He shook his head and went back to work.

Like Bartlett and others who insisted that they had private information, Frederic Myers appeared repeatedly in the course of the case. The would-be informants followed the same procedure: as Ray changed lawyers, they approached each in turn with their stories. They also tried to sell their stories to newspapers and magazines.

In October 1968, six months before Ray pleaded guilty, Myers approached the Chicago *Daily News* and offered, for a price, to lead their reporters to the conspirators he had overheard plotting to kill Dr. King. He could identify their car, he said. He asked an enormous sum of money, a guarantee of a job later, and protection for his wife.

The editors of the *Daily News* discussed the proposal. It seemed farfetched, but if the man was telling the truth, it would mark a tremendous break in the case, as well as an exclusive story for the newspaper. Two reporters, Jerry Lipson, who had been covering events in Memphis, and John Linstead, were assigned to meet with Myers and explore the subject.

Myers, accompanied by his wife and his attorney, met them in a nearly deserted motel in Indiana, not far from his home. The attorney was present to draw up any financial agreement that might be worked out.

But Myers now changed his proposal. Instead of leading them to the men he had overheard plotting in the truck stop, he now offered to lead the two reporters to the elusive Raoul. He knew the man, Myers said. He had met him and talked with him.

"What about the other men—if they're the conspirators?" Lipson demanded.

Myers, a huge, powerfully built man, grinned sheepishly. "I made that all up," he said. "I wanted to see if you people were serious about dealing with me, or were just taking me for a nut. Now I'll tell you the real story."

Some months before, he said, he had met a group of oil men from Baton Rouge who offered him a revolver and a fee of $100,000 if he would "take care of Dr. King." He refused. He was not a gunman, he said.

About a week later, at a bar, a man approached him and began a conversation. Myers realized at once that the stranger knew of the offer from Baton Rouge, because he warned him, "You better keep your mouth shut about you-know-what," and walked away. *But this man perfectly fitted the description of Raoul.*

Myers said he was now prepared to go to New Orleans and track down Raoul, for a down payment of $10,000, and a much larger sum later if he was successful. He wanted the other guarantees as well— assurance of a job later, and protection for his wife.

Once more the *Daily News* editors met. Myers' tale bordered on fantasy, but . . . There was always that but. Given the strange events of recent years, the murders of John Kennedy and Robert Kennedy as well as Dr. King, and a nagging general belief that there *had* to be a conspiracy lurking somewhere, there was reluctance to dismiss Myers completely.

Lipson decided to investigate the man. He knew nothing of Myers' earlier history, his belief that he was being pursued on the road, his frantic telephone calls to his wife, Mrs. Myers' reports of her husband's experiences. Myers had told Lipson little about himself but had remarked that he suffered from a respiratory ailment and had been taking treatments at a Veterans Administration hospital. Although hospital rules prohibited divulging any information about patients to strangers, Lipson explained the circumstances—and learned that Myers was a patient in the psychiatric ward. He had been able to come to the meeting with the two reporters, his wife, and his lawyer only because he had been given a home visiting privilege that day.

Further research revealed that Myers had been a patient in a number of state hospitals and also had a record of arrests for passing worthless checks and for mail fraud.

Myers next appeared in the case nearly a year later, this time calling upon Ray's newest counsel—Robert Hill, Jr., in Chattanooga after Hill had joined J. B. Stoner and Richard Ryan as Ray's attorneys.

Hill, too, knew nothing of Myers' earlier activities. Myers told Hill that Ray had been ordered to kill King by foreign Communists, in the hope that King's murder would bring such chaotic conditions in the United States that this country would have little will to continue its war in Vietnam. (This thesis had also been advanced by others.) Ray was considered a hero in North Vietnam for what he had done, Myers continued, and he had reason to believe that the North Vietnamese government would be prepared to trade a number of American prisoners of war for Ray. Myers offered to act—under a pseudonym, Gus Marks—as the agent in such an exchange.

The result was a letter of agreement, dated September 21, 1969, in which Hill appointed "Mr. Gus Marks" as his "sole agent" to carry out the idea. Hill's letter read in part:

"As attorney for James Earl Ray, it is my express desire that his freedom be legally effected as soon as possible. He has made the statement to me that at the culmination of whatever procedures are necessary for his release, he does not wish to reside in the United States . . . It is my understanding that negotiations are presently being contemplated, said negotiations taking the form of possible exchange agreements whereby Mr. James Earl Ray obtains freedom and political asylum for himself. In return thereof the United States of America would by this negotiation secure the safe release of twelve or more prisoners of war held in Viet Nam."

Marks would be entitled "to set up meetings and obtain funds to facilitate or otherwise expedite such an exchange," and Hill reserved for himself the right "to act as an intermediary or arbiter" if "the welfare of the United States and James Earl Ray and any third party nation or nations" needed to be assured.

Within a few months, however, Hill had withdrawn as one of Ray's attorneys, and nothing further was heard of the plan. Nor was anything further heard from Mr. Myers.

Page 346

The two James Earl Rays-two Ramon George Sneyds rumor gained credence because of a mistaken report that Ray was arrested as he came off British European Airways Flight 075 from Lisbon. He was seized, the report said, as he walked through the in-transit area bound for the gate at which he would pick up BEA's Flight 466 for Brussels. Even this was confused: one story had it that he was arrested while walking through the area by an alert Scotland Yard man who recognized him from his photographs; the other, that he was arrested after presenting his passport to the clerk at the immigration desk.

Page 350

The strike was settled on April 16—at the end of sixty-five days—when the 1300 striking members of Local 1733 ratified a "memorandum of understanding," which included the city's recognition of the union "for negotiations on wages, hours, and conditions of employment"; payroll deduction of union dues; a raise of ten cents an hour for the first three months and another five cents an hour thereafter. It was the city's first formal recognition of any labor union.

CHAPTER XXXII

Page 358

The belief in conspiracy was nurtured in many ways. Repeatedly conjecture was stated as fact. One of the most widely syndicated features, Walter Scott's Personality Parade, which seeks to answer authoritatively questions sent in by readers, presented the following question and answer on January 26, 1969:

"Question: Doesn't the U. S. Justice Department plan to arrest shortly the men who financed the assassination of Martin Luther King, Jr.?

"Answer: Two prominent New Orleans businessmen reportedly contributed $25,000 through intermediaries who arranged for James Earl Ray to murder Martin Luther King. These men expected the assassination would cause a war between blacks and whites in this country with the eventual subjugation of the black population. How much the Justice Department knows of the plot and the personalities involved is difficult to tell at this point. On March 3, when James Earl Ray stands trial in Memphis, the plot may begin to unfold. Ray of course was a pawn of limited intelligence unaware of his true financial backers or their diabolical motivation."

Page 361

Interestingly enough, Rhodesia, the white supremacist country in Africa to which Ray wanted to go, was a constant subject of news stories and editorials in *The Thunderbolt*, the publication which Ray read and for which his brother Jerry was later to work. *The Thunderbolt* repeatedly inveighed against "United States efforts to destroy

Rhodesia" by refusing to trade with her. This, wrote the paper, "is but more proof that the government in Washington is run by men who hate the White race. They would bring down a peaceful, civilized nation like Rhodesia because they will not allow Black savages to run the country. They would rather trade with the Communists and build their economy. Thus our government is part and parcel in promoting Russian domination of the world."

CHAPTER XXXIV

JAMES EARL RAY'S SIGNED STATEMENT

Page 379

The fifty-five-paragraph "Stipulation as to Material Facts that State will prove with Lay and Expert Witnesses," which Ray signed on Thursday, March 6, 1969—and stands as his confession to the murder of Dr. King—reads as follows:

1. That on April 21, 1967, James Earl Ray bought a six transister Channel Master radio in Missouri State Penitentiary, No. 00416 scratched on one end, and the same radio was found in a blue zippered bag dropped in front of Canipe's Amusement Co., on April 4, 1968.

2. That as John L. Rayns, defendant was employed at the Indian Trail Restaurant, Winnetka, Illinois, from May 3 to June 24, 1967.

3. That on July 17, 1967, defendant as John L. Rayns registered at the Beaugard Motel, Montreal.

4. That on July 18, 1967, defendant executed lease at Har-K Apartments, 2589 Notre Dame, E., Montreal, using the name Eric Starvo Galt.

5. That on July 19, 1967, defendant purchased suit from Tip-Top Tailors, Montreal, which was recovered from defendant's luggage after arrest in London on June 8, 1968.

6. That on July 21, 1967, defendant fitted for suit at English & Scotch Woolen Co., Montreal; suit later shipped to defendant as Eric S. Galt at 2608 S. Highland, Birmingham.

7. That on August 26, 1967, as Eric Galt rented a room at 2608 S. Highland, Birmingham.

8. That on August 28, 1967, as Eric S. Galt, defendant rented a safe deposit box at Birmingham National Bank.

9. That on August 30, 1967, defendant purchased white Mustang from Paisley and as Eric Starvo Galt transferred registration on said vehicle, obtained Alabama driver's license in name of Eric Starvo Galt.

10. That on October 2, 1967, defendant purchased 1968 Alabama license for the Mustang.

11. That as Eric S. Galt, on October 5, 1967, defendant wrote letters to Superior Bulk Film Co., advising them that defendant would leave for Mexico on October 7, and would have Mexican address.

12. That as Eric S. Galt defendant entered Mexico on a tourists' permit on October 7, 1967, remaining in that country until the middle of November, 1967.

13. That on October 22, 1967, defendant wrote Superior Bulk Film Co., requesting refund check be sent to Eric S. Galt, Hotel Rio, Puerto Vallarta, Mexico.

14. That on November 19, 1967, defendant rented Apartment 6 at 1535 N. Serrano, Los Angeles, as Eric S. Galt.

15. That on November 20, 1967, defendant wrote letter to Superior Bulk Film Company, requesting refund be sent to him at Serrano address.

16. That as Eric S. Galt defendant took dancing lessons at National Dance Studios, Long Beach, California, December 5, 1967, through February 12, 1968.

17. That on December 15, 1967, defendant drove to New Orleans with Charlie Stein and brought Rita Stein's children back to Los Angeles.

18. That on December 17, 1967, defendant registered in Provincial Motel, New Orleans, as Eric S. Galt.

19. That as Galt defendant used Avalon Cleaners and Laundry, Los Angeles, and sheets laundered by this company were recovered from Mustang in Atlanta.

20. That as Galt defendant had shorts and undershirt recovered from bag in front of Canipe's laundered at the Home Service Laundry, Los Angeles.

21. That as Galt defendant enrolled in the International School of Bartending, Los Angeles, from January 19 to March 2, 1968.

22. That defendant took up residence at the St. Francis Hotel, Los Angeles, on January 21, 1968.

23. That on March 5, 1968, defendant had plastic surgery performed on his nose by Dr. Russell C. Hadley, in Hollywood, California.

24. That on March 17, 1968, defendant executed change of mailing address card from St. Francis Hotel, Los Angeles, to General Delivery, Atlanta, Georgia.

25. That en route from Los Angeles, defendant dropped off a package of clothing belonging to Marie Martin's daughter in New Orleans.

26. That as Eric S. Galt defendant spent night in the Flamingo Motel, in Selma, Alabama, on March 22, 1968.

27. That defendant rented room at Jimmy Garner's rooming house in Atlanta, Georgia, on March 24, 1968.

28. That on March 29, 1968, as Harvey Lowmyer, defendant bought .243 calibre rifle and Redfield Scope, from Aeromarine Supply Co., Birmingham, Alabama.

29. That on March 30, 1968, defendant returned above rifle and exchanged it for 30.06 calibre rifle which defendant subsequently used to shoot Dr. Martin Luther King and dropped in front of Canipe's shortly after 6 p.m. April 4, 1968.

30. That on March 31, 1968, defendant paid Jimmy Garner for second week's rent and wrote name Eric S. Galt on envelope and gave it to Garner.

31. That on April 1, 1968, defendant left laundry at Piedmont Laundry in Atlanta.

32. That on April 3, 1968, defendant purchased shaving kit from Rexall Drug Store, Memphis.

33. That defendant registered as Eric S. Galt in New Rebel Motel, Memphis, on April 3, 1968.

34. That on April 4, 1968, as John Willard defendant rented room 5B from Mrs. Bessie Brewer at 422½ S. Main Street, Memphis.

35. That on April 4, 1968, defendant purchased Bushnell binoculars and case from York Arms Co., in South Main Street, Memphis.

36. That defendant parked his white Mustang on Main Street just south of Canipe's.

37. That at approximately 6:01 p.m. April 4, 1968, defendant fired a shot from the second floor bathroom in the rooming house at 422½ S. Main Street and fatally wounded Dr. Martin Luther King, Jr., who was standing on the balcony of the Lorraine Motel.

38. That defendant ran from the second floor bathroom and

dropped rifle, box, nine rounds of ammunition, green and brown bedspread, blue zipper bag containing:

1. Tack hammer and plyers
2. April 4th issue, Memphis *Commercial-Appeal*
3. Bushnell binoculars, case & box
4. Shaving kit from Rexall Drug Store
5. Channel Master pocket-size radio, No. 00416 scratched on end
6. Two unopened cans of Schlitz beer
7. Hair brush and miscellaneous toiletry items
8. Pair of men's shorts and undershirt.

39. That defendant left scene in 1966 white Mustang and on morning of April 5, 1968, left this car parked in Capitol Homes parking lot, Atlanta, Georgia.

40. That defendant picked up laundry from Piedmont Cleaners and left note for Jimmy Garner on April 5, 1968.

41. That on April 8, 1968, defendant as Paul Bridgman rented room at 102 Ossington St., W., Toronto, Canada.

42. That on April 10, 1968, defendant wrote letter as Paul Bridgman requesting copy of birth certificate.

43. That on April 11, 1968, as Paul Bridgman defendant had passport photo made in Toronto.

44. That on April 16, 1968, defendant as Ramon George Sneyd rented room at 962 Dundas St., W., Toronto.

45. That defendant applied for passport and booked passage at Kennedy Travel Bureau on flight to London as Ramon George Sneyd.

46. That defendant obtained birth certificate in name of Sneyd.

47. That defendant as Sneyd flew to London on May 6, 1968.

48. That defendant as Sneyd flew to Lisbon, Portugal, on May 7, 1968.

49. That in Lisbon on May 16, 1968, defendant obtained new passport correcting last name from Sneya to Sneyd.

50. That on May 17, 1968, defendant flew back to London.

51. That in London defendant as Sneyd lived respectively at Heathfield House, New Earls Court, and Pax Hotel until June 8, 1968.

52. That defendant was arrested at Heathrow Airport, London, as he was preparing to go to Brussels on June 8, 1968.

53. That in addition to the two passports and birth certificate of Sneyd, several items of correspondence from Kennedy Travel

Bureau and cash ticket from Andy's Mens Shop, Toronto, Canada, defendant had in his possession a .38 revolver, Japanese make, at time of arrest.

54. That defendant's luggage contained suits from Tip-Top Tailors and Scotch Woolens, as well as Polaroid camera and other items on list.

55. That defendant was fingerprinted by Inspector Brine of Scotland Yard at Heathrow Airport; that various items were obtained from 1966 white Mustang in Atlanta on April 11, including clothing, bedlinen, sweepings and various items from Room 5B in Memphis, items from room of defendant in Jimmy Garner's rooming house, Atlanta, from bag dropped at Canipe's—as well as other physical evidence heretofore mentioned, on basis of expert testimony regarding handwriting, fingerprints, fibers, plus state experts plus one or two lay corpus witnesses, county medical examiner, law enforcement officers.

CHAPTER XXXV

Page 386

Political considerations, too, lay behind Ray's anger in London. He stood up in the London court to deny indignantly that he had said, "Oh, God, I feel so trapped." Part of his outrage stemmed from the fact, as he said then, that "this would be made much of in the so-called liberal press back in the States." He also anticipated a great ground swell of conservative political support to develop in the United States to defend his killing of Dr. King. This explained his insistence to Michael Eugene, the British solicitor, that Eugene "make clear to the people back home" that he, Ray, had not talked with Assistant Attorney General Fred Vinson, Jr. Vinson, as part of the "liberal" Johnson administration, was anathema to Ray, and, as a Wallace man, who expected support from millions of Americans who, he believed, thought like him, he did not want them to think he had betrayed his beliefs by having anything to do with Vinson.

All three Ray brothers were alert to the political consequences of the case. Not only had John and Jerry also insisted that all reference to James's visit to Wallace headquarters be deleted from the stipulation, but they, too, were Wallace supporters. They were also concerned about the political leanings of the newspaper correspondents who were to cover the hearing. Shortly before the hearing Jerry Ray complained to Huie that there were too many "liberal" reporters covering James's trial. He asked if Huie could use his influence to get better seats for three conservative reporters whose politics the Rays approved of, and who "will be friendly to Jimmy."

Page 387

Renfro Hays had found the cabdriver, James McGraw, who claimed that he had been telephoned to come to 422½ South Main Street and pick up Charlie Stephens about 5:30 P.M. April 4, 1968—about half an hour before the murder—and found Stephens so drunk that he refused to transport him in his cab. However, around 3 P.M. Stephens was not drunk when he opened his door and spoke to Mrs. Brewer, while Willard was looking into Room 5B. Anschutz, who spoke to him just before and after the shooting, Captain Ray, Lieutenant Papia, and other police who spoke to him minutes after the shooting—all found him sober and in full control of himself.

CHAPTER XXXVI

Page 393

In February 1969, Renfro Hays sued Ray for $11,000 for his "investigative services" and sought to attach the white Mustang and the rifle. He had heard, he told friends, that the car in which Bonnie and Clyde had been shot had earned more than $100,000 for its owners, who took it on a display tour of the country. Ray's reply denied owing Hays any money, and Ray denied he owned the rifle: as for the car, he had only a small part-ownership in that. Part of the $1995 he used to buy it, he said, came from the sale of his Plymouth; but the majority interest in the car belonged to Raoul, who, he said, gave him most of the money to buy it with.

On January 27, 1970, Hays won a judgment of $6625 in chancery court. Since he could not collect the money from Ray, he continued his suit to attach the white Mustang.

Page 396

For the record: Ray's affidavit relating his own history of his case, typed by him in his cell at Brushy Mountain Prison and filed in Memphis Criminal Court on August 31, 1970, reads in full, with his spelling as he typed it*:

THE FOLLOWING AFFIDAVIT IS TRUE TO THE BEST OF MY KNOWLEDGE. COMMENCING WITH MY ARREST AND IN-CARCERATION IN LONDON ENGLAND ON OR ABOUT JUNE, 6, 1968; TERMINATING WITH THE GUILTY PLEA TO HOMOI-CIDE AND INCARCERATION IN THE TENNESSEE STATE PRISON AT NASHVILLE TENNESSEE.

THE ABOVE PLEA IN THE COURT OF THE HONORABLE W. PRESTON BATTLE, MEMPHIS TENNESSEE, MARCH, 10, 1969. ON OR ABOUT THE 6TH. DAY OF JUNE, 1968, I WAS AR-RESTED AT THE HEATHROW AIRPORT, LONDON ENGLAND, SUBSEQUENTLY I WAS CHARGED WITH HOMOICIDE IN THE UNITED STATES AND ORDERED HELD FOR AN IMMIGRA-TION HEARING. AFTER BEING HELD INCOMMUNICADO FOR APPROXIMATELY 4 DAYS I WAS TAKEN BEFORE AN ENGLISH MAGISTRATE AND ORDERED HELD FOR AN EX-TRADITION HEARING.

SHORTLY AFTER MY INCARCERATION IN THE ENGLISH PRISON I WROTE TO BIRMINGHAM ALABAMA ATTORNEY, AUTHOR J. HANES, VIA THE BIRMINGHAM BAR ASSOCIA-TION ASKING HIM IF HE WOULD MEET ME IN MEMPHIS TENN, WHEN I WAS EXTRIDATED BACK TO THE UNITED STATES. AT THIS TIME I DIDN'T ASK MR. HANES TO TAKE THE CASE JUST MEET ME IN MEMPHIS, AS I WAS CON-CERNED ABOUT FALSELY BEING ACCUSED OF MAKING AN ORAL STATEMENT IF I WAS ALONE WITH PROSECUTION AGENTS IN MEMPHIS.

* Virtually every allegation made by Ray of undue influence, illegal behavior and the like was denied by those named: that Ray had not written Hanes asking him to take his case (Hanes had Ray's letter specifically asking him to represent him); that Vinson "was calling the shots" in London; that Sheriff Morris refused Ray "access to legal counsel or sleep until I submitted to palm prints"; that Huie was giving what Ray wrote him to the FBI; that Foreman told him he could break the contracts with Hanes and Huie, and later, that he knew he was not guilty but would not be able to get him a fair trial; that Huie, Attorney Lucian Burch, and the FBI insisted that Canale insert certain stipulations, etc. Ray was also confused as to the date of his arrest in London, putting it as June 6. He was arrested June 8.

MR. HANES IN TURN WROTE TO THE ENGLISH SOLICITOR WHO WAS REPRESENTING ME IN ENGLAND, MR. MICHEL EUGENE, INQUIRING ABOUT HIS FEE. THEN LATER MR. HANES WROTE TO ME DIRECTLY SAYING HE WOULD TAKE THE CASE.

ALSO, I HAD WRITTEN TO MY BROTHER, JOHN L. RAY, ST LOUIS, MISSOURI–NOT WILLIAM BRATFORD HUIE–ASKING HIM TO GIVE MR. HANES ENOUGH MONEY TO MEET ME IN MEMPHIS.

LATER MR. HANES CAME TO LONDON ENGLAND TO CONFER WITH ME ON LEGAL QUESTIONS. HOWEVER THE ENGLISH GOVERNMENT REFUSED MR. HANES REQUEST TO SEE ME.

WHEN I COMPLAINED TO SUPT. THOMAS BUTLER–WHO WAS THE POLICE OFFICER IN CHARAGE OF INVESTIGATION AND CUSTODY–ABOUT NOT BEING PERMITTED TO CONFER WITH COUNSEL HE SAID UNITED STATES ATTORNEY FRED M. VINSON WAS CALLING THE SHOTS.

THEREFORE AT MY NEXT COURT APPEARANCE I COMPLAINED OF NOT BEING PERMITTED TO CONFER WITH COUNSEL.

THEREAFTER I WAS TOLD BY PRISON AUTHORIES THAT MR. HANES COULD SEE ME.

ON JULY 5TH. 1968, MR. HANES DID VISIT ME IN THE ENGLISH PRISON. HE SUGGESTED I SIGN TWO CONTRACTS– ONE GIVING MR. HANES MY POWER OF ATTORNEY, THE OTHER 40% OF ALL REVENUE I MIGHT RECEIVE–AT THIS TIME NO MENTION WAS MADE OF ANY NOVELIST, AND NO NOVELIST NAME, INCLUDING WILLIAM BRATFORD HUIE, APPEARED ON THE CONTRACT.

THE REASONS MR. HANES GAVE FOR THE CONTRACTS WERE THAT (ONE) HE WAS ALLREADY OUT CONSIDERABLE FUNDS. (TWO) HE WOULD NEED CONSIDERABLE MORE FUNDS FOR HIS SERVICES.

I HAD ALSO WRITTEN THE BOSTON MASS. ATTORNEY, MR. F. LEE BAILEY–AT THE SAME TIME I HAD WRITTEN MR. HANES–ON THE POSSIBILITY OF REPRESENTING ME.

IN A LETTER TO ENGLISH SOLICITOR EUGENE, MR. BAILEY DECLINED ON POSSIBLE CONFLICT OF INTREST GROUNDS.

I SPOKE TO MR. HANES AGAIN BEFORE BEING DEPORTED BUT NO FURTHER MENTION WAS MADE OF CONTRACTS. MR. HANES DID ADVISE ME TO WAIVE FURTHER EXTRADITION APPEALS: WHICH I DID.

AFTER I WAS RETURNED TO MEMPHIS TENN. AND CON-
FINED IN THE SHELBY COUNTY JAIL I WAS DENIED ACCESS
TO LEGAL COUNSEL, OR SLEEP, UNTIL I SUBMITTED TO
PALM PRINTS.

WHEN SUBSEQUENTLY ATTORNEY AUTHOR HANES SR. DID
VISIT ME, SPECIFIALLY THE SECOND VISIT, HE HAD WITH
HIM CONTRACTS FOR VARIOUS ENTERPRISES BEARING HIS
NAME AND THE NOVELIST, WILLIAM BRATFORD HUIE OF
HARTSELL ALABAMA.

MR. HANES URGED ME TO SIGN THE CONTRACTS TO FI-
NANCE THE SUIT. I SUGGESTED RATHER THAT A SEGMENT
OF THE PUBLIC INTEREST IN A FAIR TRIAL MIGHT FI-
NANCE THE TRIAL. THEN AFTER THE TRIAL WAS OVER,
AND IF IT WAS FINICALLY NECESSARY TO FURTHER SUP-
PLEMENT MR. HANES FEE, HE COULD CONTRACT A
NOVELIST.

MR. HANES DISAGREED WITH THIS SUGGESTION AND TOLD
ME TO CONSIDER THE CONTRACTS AS THE ONLY METHOD
TO FIANANCE THE TRIAL.

AFTER CONSIDERABLE THOUGHT, AND BELIEVEING IT
USUALLY NECESSARY TO FOLLOW COUNSEL'S ADVICE IN
THAT TYPE SITUTAION, I SIGNED THE CONTRACTS ON OR
ABOUT AUGUST 1ST. 1968; APPROXIMATELY TWO WEEKS
AFTER MR. HANES RECOMMENDED I DO SO.

MY FIRST DISAGREEMENT WITH MR. HANES WAS (ONE) I
ASKED MR. HANES AND, WROTE THE NOVELIST, WILLIAM
BRATFORD HUIE, REQUESTING $1.250.00. EXPLAINING I
WANTED TO HIRE TENN. LICENCE ATTORNEY IN THE
EVENT I WAS CONVICTED OF SOMETHING, OR HAD A MIS-
TRIAL; AS THEIR WAS SOME QUESTION AS TO WHEATHER
MR. HANES COULD HANDLE AN APPEAL OR, A RETRIAL, UN-
DER THE TENN.+ALABAMA RECIPROCAL AGREEMENT
WHICH MR. HANES DESCRIBED AS A "ONE SHOT DEAL".

I FURTHER STATED IN THE LETTER TO MR. HUIE THAT I
WOULD PROBABLY BE HELD IN CONTINUED ISOLATION AS
LONG AS I WAS INCARCERATED AND WOULD NEED TENN.
COUNSEL TO GET RELIEF.

"FURTHER, I WANTED TO HIRE AN INVESTAGOR TO GO TO
LOUISANA TO CHECK ON SOME PHONE NRS. AND I DID'NT
WANT ANYONE CONNECTED WITH WILLIAM BRATFORD
HUIE DOING THIS SINCE I KNEW THEN THAT MR. HUIE WAS
A CONVEYOR, AN ADMITTED CONVEYOR, OF INFORMA-

TION TO THE F.B.I.—HENCE THE PROSECUTING ATTOR-NEY."

MR. HANES TURNED DOWN THIS REQUEST AND THE ISSUE WAS CLOSED.

(TWO) THE OTHER DISAGREEMENT CONCERNED WHETHER I SHOULD TESTIFY IN MY BEHALF. I FAVORED TAKING THE WITNESS STAND BECAUSE I HAD TESTIMONY TO GIVE WHICH I DID'NT WANT THE PROSECUTION TO KNOW OF UNTIL AS LATE AS POSSIBLE SO THEIR WOULD BE NO TIME TO ALTER RECORDS, SUCH AS PHONE NRS., AND AT THIS STAGE OF THE PROCEEDINGS I HAD REASONS TO BELIEVE MR. HANES WAS GIVING "ALL" INFORMATION I WAS GIVING HIM TO NOVELIST HUIE WHO IN TURN WAS FORWARDINGS IT TO THE PROSECUTION VIA THE F.B.I.

MR. HANES ALSO TURNED DOWN THIS REQUEST STATING, WHY GIVE TESTIMONY AWAY WHEN WE CAN SELL IT. AND THAT ISSUE WAS ALSO CLOSED.

THE ONLY OTHER DISCORD MR. HANES AND I HAD CON-CERNED PUBLICITY.

DESPITE TRIAL JUDGE BATTLE'S ORDER BANNING PRE-TRIAL PUBLICITY THEIR WERE MANY PREJUDICIAL ARTI-CLES PRINTED IN THE LOCAL PRESS AND NATIONAL MEDIA.

(AS EXAMPLE THE STORY BY-LINED BY CHARLES EDMOND-SON IN THE COMMERCIAL APPEAL DATED NOV. 10TH. 1968. JUST TWO DAYS BEFORE TRIAL WAS SCHEDULED TO START, AND MR. HUIE'S FREQUENT NEWS CONFERENCES ON MEMPHIS T.V.) THEREFORE I SUGGESTED TO MR. HANES THAT WE ASK FOR A CONTINUENCE UNTIL THE PUBLICITY STOPED.

MR. HANES ANSER WAS THAT OUR CONTRACTS WITH NOV-ELIST HUIE SPECIFIED A TIME LIMIT FOR THE TRIAL TO BEGIN IF WE WERE TO RECEIVE FUNDS TO PROSECUTE THE DEFENSE.

"ALSO, I WROTE A CERTIFIED LETTER TO TRIAL JUDGE BATTLE COMPLAINING OF THE STORIES MR. HUIE WAS DISSMINATING IN THE MEDIA. I TOLD THE JUDGE IF SUCH PRACTICES WEREN'T STOPED I MIGHT AS WELL FORGET A TRIAL AND JUST COME OVER AND GET SENTENCED."

HOWEVER, DESPITE THESE DIFFERENCES WITH ATTOR-NEY AUTHOR HANES SR. I WAS PREPARED TO GO TO TRIAL WITH HIM ON NOV. 12TH. 1968.

BUT TWO OR THREE DAYS BEFORE THE NOV. TRIAL DATE

MY BROTHER, JERRY RAY, CAME TO VISIT ME. DURING THE COURSE OF OUR CONVERSATION JERRY TOLD ME HE HAD RECENTLY SPOKEN WITH THE NOVELIST, WILLIAM BRATFORD HUIE, AND HUIE HAD TOLD HIM THAT IF I TESTIFIED IN MY OWN BEHALF IT WOULD DESTROY THE BOOK HE WAS WRITING. MY BROTHER ASK ME IF HE SHOULD TRY TO FIND ANOTHER ATTORNEY. I TOLD HIM NO IT WAS TO LATE. WHEN THE VISIT ENDED I WAS STILL ASSUMING I WOULD GO TO TRIAL WITH ATTORNEY AUTHOR HANES SR. ON NOV. 12TH. 1968.

HOWEVER, ON OR ABOUT NOV. 10TH. 1968. MR. PERCY FOREMAN, A TEXAS LICENCED ATTORNEY CAME TO THE SHELBY COUNTY JAIL AND ASKED TO SEE ME.

I AGREED TO SEE MR. FOREMAN ALTHOE I NEITHER CONTACKED HIM DIRECTLY OR, INDIRECTLY, REQUESTING ANY TYPE LEGAL ASSISTANCE.

AFTER THE AMENITIES I SAW THAT MR. FOREMAN HAD THE CONTRACTS I HAD SIGNED WITH MR. HANES & MR. HUIE.

I ASKED HIS OPINION OF THEM. MR. FOREMAN CAME RIGHT TO THE POINT, HE SAID HE HAD READ THE CONTRACTS AND HAD CONCLUDED THAT THE ONLY THING HANES & HUIE WERE INTERESTED IN WAS MONEY. HE SAID THEY WERE PERSONAL FRIENDS AND IF I STUCK WITH THEM I WOULD BE BAR-BE-CUED.

I TOLD MR. FOREMAN I WAS CONCERNED WITH CERTAIN ASPECTS OF THE CONTRACTS, SUCH AS THE INFERENCE OF A TRIAL DATE DEADLINE, BUT THAT SINCE I HAD SIGNED THE DOCUMENT THEIR WASN'T MUCH I COULD DO.

MR. FOREMAN REPLIED THEIR WAS SOMETHING I COULD DO, THAT HE COULD BREAK THE CONTRACTS IF I HIRED HIM: SINCE I HAD BEEN TAKEN ADVANTAGE OF DUE TO A LACK OF EDUCATION IN SUCH MATTERS.

I ASK HIM WHAT HIS POSITION WOULD BE IF I DID ENGAGE HIM IN RELATION TO CONTRACTS WITH BOOK WRITERS AND, RETAINING A TENN. LICENCED ATTORNEY.

HE SAID THEIR WOULD BE NO STORIES WRITTEN UNTIL AFTER THE TRIAL WAS OVER AND THAT IT WAS NECESSARY THAT TENN. LICENCED COUNSEL BE RETAINED TO ADVISE AND ASSIST WITH TENN. LAWS.

I ALSO ASKED MR. FOREMAN HOW HE WOULD FINANCE THE TRIAL, HE SAID LET HIM WORRY ABOUT THAT. THAT

WHEN THE TRIAL WAS OVER HE WOULD MAKE A DEAL WITH SOME BOOK WRITER BUT THAT HE WOULDN'T COMPRISE THE DEFENSE WITH PRE-TRIAL DEALS.

HE SAID THAT HIS FEE WOULD BE $150.000. FOR THE TRIAL, AND APPEALS IF NECESSARY, AND THAT AS A RETAINER HE WOULD TAKE THE 1966 MUSTANG I HAD, WHICH I SIGNED OVER TO HIM. MR. FOREMAN ALSO ASKED ME TO SIGN OVER TO HIM A RIFLE THE PROSECUTION WAS HOLDING AS EVIDENCE. ALTHOE THEIR WAS A QUESTION OF OWNERSHIP I ALSO SIGNED THIS ITEM OVER TO HIM. I THEN WROTE OUT A STATEMENT FOR MR. FOREMAN DIS-MISSING MR. HANES AND STATING I WOULD ENGAGE TENN. COUNSEL.

AFTER MR. FOREMAN BECAME COUNSEL OF RECORD, AND ON ONE OF HIS EARLIER VISITS HE SAID HE WOULD RETAIN NASHVILLE ATTORNEY, JOHN J. HOOKER SR. TO ASSIST WITH THE LAW SUIT.

"LATER, MR. FOREMAN TOLD ME IN THE COURTROOM—ON DEC. 18TH 1968—THAT THE COURT WOULD APPOINT THE PUBLIC DEFENDER TO THE CASE. WHEN I QUESTIONED THE APPOINTMENT MR. FOREMAN SAID HE, JUDGE BAT-TLE, AND MR. HUGH STANTON SR. HAD AGREED BEFORE THE HEARING TO BRING THE PUBLIC DEFENDER'S OFFICE INTO THE CASE. THAT HE (FOREMAN) HAD ALSO DIS-CUSSED THE DEAL PRIVATELY WITH MR. STANTON AND IT (THE APPOINTMENT) WOULD SAVE US MONEY BUT, THAT HE WOULD STILL RETAIN JOHN J. HOOKER SR."

IN DECEMBER 1968 WHEN MR. FOREMAN BECAME ILL, AND TRIAL JUDGE BATTLE APPOINTED—ON JAN. 17TH. 1969—MR. HUGH STANTON SR. FULL COUNSEL, MR. STANTON CAME TO THE JAIL TO SEE ME. I TOLD CAPT. BILLY SMITH I DID NOT WISH TO SEE MR. STANTON. HE WAS PERMITTED IN THE CELL BLOCK ANYWAY.

I INFORMED MR. STANTON I DIDN'T WANT TO DISCUSS ANYTHING WITH HIM AND THAT I WOULD WRITE HIM A LETTER EXPLAINING WHY.

HE LEFT THE BLOCK SAYING HE DIDN'T HAVE TIME FOR THE CASE ANYWAY.

"I THEN WROTE A LETTER TO MR. HUGH STANTON SR. SAYING I DIDN'T WANT JUDGES AND PROSECUTING AT-TORNEYS DESIDING WHO WOULD DEFEND ME."

DURING THIS EARLY PERIOD OF MR. FOREMAN TENURE HE ONCE SUGGESTED I CONFIRM, IN WRITING, SOME

THEORIES BEING PROPOUNDED BY ANOTHER NOVELIST, ONE GEORGE McMILLIAN WHO, IN COLLABORATION WITH A PHRENOLOGIST, WAS WRITING ANOTHER NOVEL CONCERNING THE CASE.

MR. FOREMAN SAID THE PAIR WOULD GIVE US $5.000.00 TO USE FOR DEFENSE PURPOSES. I REJECTED THIS SUGGESTION.

THEN LATER MR. FOREMAN TRANSPORTED A CHECK TO THE JAIL FOR $5.000.00 FOR ME TO ENDORSE. HE SAID HE HAD RECEIVED THE CHECK FROM THE NOVELIST WILLIAM BRATFORD HUIE AND THAT WOULD I LET HIM HAVE THE MONEY TO GIVE TO NASHVILLE ATTORNEY, JOHN J. HOOKER SR. AS A RETAINER FEE. I AGREED TO THIS.

"ALSO DURING THIS PERIOD I SUGGESTED TO MR. FOREMAN THAT RATHER THAN PRINTING MORE PRE-TRIAL STORIES WE INSTIGATE SOME TYPE LEGAL ACTION TO PREVENT THE PUBLISHING OF STORIES, ESPECIALLY THE MORE RANCID TYPE ARTICLES SUCH AS WAS APPEARING IN LIFE MAGAZINE.

MR. FOREMAN REJECTED THIS SUGGESTION SAYING: "WHY STIR UP A BARREL OF RATTLE SNAKES."

STILL LATER, ON OR ABOUT JAN. 29TH. 1969. MR. FOREMAN TRANSPORTED A CONTRACT TO THE JAIL AND ADVISED ME TO SIGN IT. "SEE CONTRACT CT. RECORDS."

MR. FOREMAN SAYING IT WOULD TAKE CONSIDERABLE FUNDS TO FINANCE THE SUIT AND PAY JOHN J. HOOKER SR.'S FEE.

ON OR ABOUT FEBRUARY 3RD. 1969—MR. FOREMAN TRANSPORTED STILL ANOTHER CONTRACT TO THE JAIL AND ADVISED ME TO SIGN IT. HE TOLD ME THE LAW SUIT WAS PROGRESSING WELL, THAT HE COULD PROVE I WAS INNOCENT, AND THE TRIAL WOULD START IN THE NEAR FUTURE.

I ALSO SIGNED THIS DOCUMENT BEING REASSURED BECAUSE THE DOCUMENT STIPULATED THAT MR. FOREMAN WOULD REPRESENT ME AT 'TRIAL OR TRIALS' PENDING IN SHELBY COUNTY TENNESSEE: IN EXCHANGE FOR ME SIGNING THE DOCUMENT. "SEE CONTRACT CT. RECORDS."

THEIR WAS NO MENTION OF "COP-OUTS" IN THE CONTRACT AND IT SEEMS "COP-OUTS" ARE NOT LEGALLY CLASSIFIED AS TRIALS IN TENNESSEE.

BEFORE MR. FOREMAN TERMINATED HIS VISIT THAT DAY OR, MAYBE IT WAS THE NEXT TIME HE VISITED ME, HE

SHOWED ME VARIOUS PICTURES. HE SAID EITHER HE (FOREMAN) HAD RECEIVED THE PICTURES FROM THE F.B.I. OR THAT HE HAD RECEIVED THEM FROM THE NOVELIST, WILLIAM BRATFORD HUIE, WHO IN TURN HAD RECEIVED THEM FROM THE F.B.I.

HE SAID THEY WERE PICTURES OF PEOPLE THE F.B.I. WANTED TO GET OUT OF CIRCULATION.

HE SHOWED ME ONE PICTURE CONTAINING WHITE MALES —SUPPOSELY TAKEN IN DALLAS TEXAS IN NOVEMBER 1963, HE SAID THEY WERE EITHER ANTI COMMUNIST CUBANS OR, ASSOCIATED WITH ANTI COMMUNIST. FOREMAN ASKED ME IF I WOULD IDENTIFY ONE OF THE MEN AS THE MAN WHO SHOT MARTIN LUTHER KING IF THE F.B.I. ARRESTED HIM AND TRANSPORTED HIM TO MEMPHIS.

I TOLD MR. FOREMAN NO, THAT I DIDN'T WANT TO GET INVOLVED IN THAT TYPE THING FOR VARIOUS REASONS.

WHEN READY TO TAKE LEAVE, AND FAILING TO CONVINCE ME TO FOLLOW THE AFOREMENTION ADVICE, MR. FOREMAN ASK ME IF THAT WAS MY LAST WORD ON THE SUBJECT: I REPLIED YES.

THEN AT A LATER DATE WHEN ATTORNEY FOREMAN VISITED ME HE HAD SEVERAL DUPLICATED TYPEWRITTEN SHEETS OF PAPER WITH HIM, ONE CLAUSE IN THE SHEETS CLEARED THE NOVELIST, WILLIAM BRATFORD HUIE, AND LOOK MAGAZINE, OF DAMAGING MY PROSPECTS FOR A FAIR TRIAL BECAUSE OF THEIR PRE-TRIAL PUBLISHING VENTURES, ANOTHER CLAUSE; THAT IF I STOOD TRIAL I WOULD RECEIVE THE ELECTRIC CHAIR.

"I TOLD MR. FOREMAN THAT MR. HUIE AND LOOK MAGAZINE WERE ABLE, LEGALLY & FINICALLY, TO LOOK OUT FOR THEIR OWN INTEREST".

MR. FOREMAN MONOLOGUE WAS VERY STRIDENT THAT DAY IN INSISTING THAT I SIGN THE PAPERS AS I HAD TO ASK HIM SEVERAL TIMES TO LOWER HIS VOICE TO KEEP THE GUARDS, AND OPEN MIKE, FROM OVER HEARING OUR CONVERSATION.

I THOUGHT THEN THAT MAYBE I HAD BEEN "HAD" BELIVEING IT WAS FINICALL, THE SUGGESTION OF A GUILTY PLEA SO SOON AFTER SIGNING THE FEBRUARY, 3RD. CONTRACT.

THE NEXT TIME I SAW MR. FOREMAN HIS MONOLOGUE HADN'T CHANGED SO I SIGNED THE AFOREMENTIONED PAPERS BUT, NOT WITH THE INTENTION OF PLEADING GUILTY; AS I TOLD FOREMAN.

LATER I TRIED TO PERSUADE MR. FOREMAN TO STAND TRIAL, I ASKED HIM WHY IT WAS NECESSARY TO PLEAD GUILTY WHEN I WASN'T GUILTY.

MR. FOREMAN GAVE ME THE FOLLOWING REASONS WHY A GUILTY PLEA WAS NECESSARY.

(ONE) HE SAID THE MEDIA HAD ALLREADY CONVICTED ME AND CITED THE PRE-TRIAL ARTICLES WRITTEN IN LIFE MAGAZINE AND THE READERS DIGEST, WITH THE HELP OF GOVERNMENT INVESTAGATIVES AGENCIES AS EXAMPLES. HE ALSO CITED VARIOUS ARTICLES PRINTED IN THE LO-CAL PRESS, PARTICULAR THE STORY IN THE COMMERCIAL APPEAL DATED NOV. 10TH. 1968, JUST TWO DAYS BEFORE TRIAL DATE.

FURTHER, FOREMAN CITED THE RECORD OF THE AMICUS CUREIA COMMITTEE SAYING NEITHER THE COMMITTEE OR TRIAL JUDGE WOULD ATTEMPT TO HALT PUBLICITY UNLESS IT REFLECTED ON THE PROSECUTION CASE.

(TWO) FOREMAN SUGGESTED, SPECIOUSLY, THAT IT WOULD BE IN MY FINICIAL INTEREST TO PLEAD GUILTY.

(THREE) THAT THE PROSECUTION HAD PROMISED A WIT-NESS CONSIDERABLE REWARD MONEY FOR TESTIFYING AGAINST ME, THAT THIS WITNESS HAD ALLREADY BEEN GIVEN A RAISE IN A WELFARE CHECK HE WAS RECEIVING FROM THE GOVERNMENT, THAT THE PROSECUTION WAS ALSO PAYING HIS FOOD AND WINE BILLS.

FURTHER, THAT TWO MEMPHIS ATTORNEYS HAD SIGNED A CONTRACT WITH THIS ALLEDGED WITNESS FOR 50% OF ALL REVENUE HE RECEIVED FOR HIS TESTIMONY. THEY IN TURN WOULD LOOK OUT FOR HIS INTEREST.

MR. FOREMAN ALSO GAVE ME THE FOLLOWING REASONS WHY THE PROSECUTION WANTED, AND WOULD THERE-FORE LET ME PLEAD GUILTY.

(ONE) THAT THE CHAMBER OF COMMERCE WAS PRESSUR-ING THE TRIAL JUDGE AND THE ATTORNET GENERALS OFFICE TO GET A GUILTY PLEA AS A LONG TRIAL WOULD HAVE AN ADVERSE EFFECT ON BUSINESS, BOYCOTS AND SUCH.

FURTHER, THAT THE CHAMBER WASN'T UNHAPPY ABOUT DR. KING BEING REMOVED FROM THE SCENE—HENCE THE ACCEPTANCE OF A GUILTY PLEA.

(TWO) THAT TRIAL JUDGE BATTLE WAS CONCERNED ABOUT THE EFFECTS A TRIAL WOULD HAVE ON THE

CITY'S (MEMPHIS) IMAGE, AND THAT THE JUDGE HAD EVEN DISPATCHED HIS AMICUS CURIEA COMMITTEE CHAIRMAN, MR. LUCIAN BURCH, TO PERSUADE SOME S.C.L.C. MEMBERS TO ACCEPT A GUILTY PLEA.

"ABOUT THIS TIME PERCY FOREMAN ALSO HAD ME SIGN ANOTHER PAPER SANCTIFYING HIS DEALINGS WITH THE ATTORNEY GENERAL'S OFFICE."

LATER, AFTER CONSIDERING ALL THAT MR. FOREMAN HAD TOLD ME I SAID I STILL WANTED TO STAND TRIAL.

I TOLD FOREMAN I AGREED THAT THE MEDIA HAD HAD AN ADVERSE EFFECT ON THE PROSPECTS OF MY RECEIVING A FAIR TRIAL BUT I DIDN'T THINK THE PUBLIC ANY LONGER BELIEVED EVERY FABRICATION THEY READ OR, SAW ON T.V.–THEREFORE A POSSIBLE FAIR JURY VERDICT.

MR. FOREMAN REPLY WAS THAT IF I PLEAD GUILTY HE COULD GET ME A PARDON, AFTER TWO OR THREE YEARS, THROUGH THE OFFICE OF NASHVILLE ATTORNEY, JOHN J. HOOKER SR. AS A RELATIVE OF MR. HOOKER WOULD THEN BE GOVERNOR.

"AFTER THE SIGNING OF THE FEB. 3RD. 1969. CONTRACT NO FURTHER MENTION WAS MADE BY FOREMAN CONCERNING ENGAGEING ATT. HOOKER ALTHOE ON MARCH 9TH. 1969 FOREMAN TRIED TO GET ME TO SPEAK WITH HOOKER, BARRING THAT, TO HAVE HOOKER PRESENT AT THE PLEA. I DECLINED BOTH SUGGESTIONS."

BUT, IF I INSISTED ON A TRIAL HE (FOREMAN) WOULD HIRE FORMER MEMPHIS JUDGE, MR. BEN HOOKS, AS CO-COUNSEL.

I KNEW FROM NEWSPAPER ACCOUNTS THAT MR. HOOKS HAD RESIGNED A JUDGFSHIP TO ACCEPT A POSITION WITH S.C.L.C.

THEREFORR I TOLD FOREMAN THAT HAVING MR. HOOKS AS CO-COUNSEL WOULD BE A CLEAR CONFLICT OF INTEREST, MORE SO THAN THE GROUNDS ATTORNEY F. LEE BAILEY REFUSED THE CASE ON. FOREMAN REPLY WAS THAT AS CHIEF COUNSEL HE HAD THE RIGHT TO PICK CO-COUNSEL.

BY THIS TIME MR. FOREMAN HAD FINALLY GOT THE MESSAGE OVER TO ME THAT IF I FORCED HIM TO TRIAL HE WOULD DESTROY–DELIBERATELY–THE CASE IN THE COURT ROOM.

"I DIDN'T KNOW HOW HE WOULD FAKE THE TRIAL UNTIL I READ THE ARTICLE HE WROTE FOR LOOK MAGAZINE, PUBLISHED APRIL, 1969"

IT WAS ALSO MY BELIEF THAT I WOULD ONLY RECEIVE ONE TRIAL—THAT APPELLANT CTS. PROABLY WOULDN'T BE LOOKING TO CLOSE FOR TECHNICAL ERROW IN CASE OF CONVICTION—THEREFORE I DID'NT WANT THE ONE TRIAL FAKED.

CONSIDERING I HAD NO OTHER CHOICE, AT THE TIME, I TENTATIVELY AGREED TO ENTER A GUILTY PLEA TO A TECHNICAL CHARGE OF HOMOICIDE.

MR. FOREMAN THEN PRESENTED ME WITH VARIOUS STIPULATIONS TO SIGN WHICH HE CLAIMED HE RECEIVED FROM THE ATTORNEY GENERAL'S OFFICE.

I OBJECTED TO A NUMBER OF THE STIPULATIONS: TWO IN PARTICULAR.

THE FIRST, A STIPULATION WITH NO LEGAL QUALIFICATIONS, MEANT TO BE AN EMBARRASSING REFERENCE TO GOVERNOR GEORGE WALLACE AND INSTIGATED BY A CALIFORNIA HIPPIE SONG WRITER NAMED CHARLES STEIN. MR. FOREMAN HAD THE STIPULATION REMOVED. HE SAID THE NOVELIST, WILLIAM BRATFORD HUIE, HAD GOT THE ATTORNEY GENERAL TO INSERT THE STIPULATION. THE SECOND, THIS STIPULATION CONCERNED MY PEREGRINATIONS BETWEEN MARCH, 30TH. 1968 AND APRIL, 4TH. SAME YEAR.

MR. FOREMAN SAID HE COULD'NT GET THIS STIPULATION REMOVED AS EVERYONE ASSOCIATED WITH THE PROSECUTION, DIRECTLY AND INDIRECTLY, INSISTED IT BE INCLUDED, INCLUDING ATTORNEY LUCIAN BURCH AND THE F.B.I.

LATER DURING ONE OF MR. FOREMAN'S VISITS TO THE JAIL IN EARLY MARCH, 1969, I MADE A LAST ATTEMPT TO HAVE A JURY TRIAL.

I ASKED MR. FOREMAN TO WITHDRAW FROM THE SUIT IF HE DID'NT WANT TO DEFEND ME FOR POLITICAL OR SOCIAL REASONS. "HE HAD MADE THE PUBLIC STATEMENT, AND MENTIONED TO ME SEVERAL TIMES THAT HE WAS CONCERNED THAT THE NEGROS WOULD THINK HIM A JUDAS FOR DEFENDING ME." I TOLD FOREMAN I WOULD SIGN OVER TO HIM THE ORIGINAL $150.000 WE HAD PREVIOUSLY AGREED ON FOR HIM TO DEFEND ME, AND I

WOULD SIGN ANY FUNDS OVER THAT AMOUNT FROM THE CONTRACTS TO ANOTHER ATTORNEY TO TRY THE SUIT BEFORE A JURY.

"I ALSO ASK HIM TO GIVE MY BROTHER, JERRY RAY, $500.00 TO FIND SUCH AN ATTORNEY."

I STATED OTHERWISE I WAS GOING TO EXPLAIN MY FINICIAL SITUATION TO THE COURT AND ASK EITHER TO DEFEND MYSELF OR, ASK OTHER RELIEF.

MR. FOREMAN REFUSED TO WITHDRAW AND REMINED ME OF TRIAL JUDGE BATTLE'S RULING AS OF JANUARY 17TH. 1969, SAYING, IT WOULD EITHER BE HIM AS COUNSEL OR, THE PUBLIC DEFENDER. HOWEVER, MR. FOREMAN SAID IF I WOULD PLEAD GUILTY HE WOULD COMPLY WITH THE AFOREMENTIONED REQUESTS.

HE SAID THAT I COULD GET A TRIAL IN A COUPLE YEARS IF I WANTED ONE AND HE IMPLIED THAT AFTER THE PLEA WAS OVER HE WOULD DISASSOICATE HIMSELF FROM THE SUIT.

THEN ON MARCH 9TH. 1969, ATTORNEY FOREMAN PRESENTED ME WITH TWO CONTRACTS—SEE CT. TR.—WITH THE AFOREMENTIONED STIPULATIONS INCLUDING A CLAUSE STATING IF I REFUSED TO PLEAD GUILTY THE DEAL WAS OFF.

THE NEXT DAY, MARCH 10TH. 1969, I PLEAD GUILTY UNDER THE ABOVE RELATED CIRCUMSTANCES.

I DID OBJECT DURING THE PLEA PROCEEDING WHEN FOREMAN ATTEMPTED TO USE THE OCASSION AS A FORUM TO EXONERATE HIS FRIEND, FORMER ATTORNEY GENERAL MR. RAMSEY CLARK, OF INCOMPETENCEY OR FRAUD AND, TO EXPAND ON WHAT I HAD AGREED TO IN THE STIPULATIONS.

LATER THAT DAY, MARCH. 10, 1969, WHEN I SAW MR. FOREMAN ON T.V. NEWS I KNEW HE WASN'T DISASSOCIATING HIMSELF FROM THE SUIT, RATHER HE WAS TRYING TO PRESENT THE PROSECUTION VERSION OF THE CASE. IN REPLY TO ONE REPORTER'S QUESTION AS TO WHY MY PAST RECORD WOULDN'T INDICATE SUCH A CRIME, MR. FOREMAN WENT INTO A LONG DISSERTATION ON HOW EVERY FIVE YEARS ALL THE CELLS IN THE HUMAN BODY CHANGE, HENCE A DIFFERENT PERSON MENTALLY EVERY FIVE YEARS. "FOREMAN WAS APPLYING THIS SCIENTIFIC QUACKERY TO HIS CLIENT."

THIS PRESS CONFERENCE COUPLED WITH MR. FOREMAN'S COURT ROOM SPEIL AT THE PLEA INDICATED I COULDN'T WAIT ANY TWO YEARS UNTIL I MIGHT POSSIBLE RECEIVE FUNDS FROM CONTRACTS TO HIRE OTHER COUNSEL AS BY THEN FOREMAN & HUIE IN COMPANY WOULD HAVE HAD ME CONVICTED VIA THE MEDIA WHICH THEIR TYPE ALWAYS SEEM TO HAVE READY ACCEST.

AFTER ARRIVING AT THE PRISON IN NASHVILLE TENN. ON MARCH, 11–1969, AND HEARING MORE OF MR. FOREMAN'S CONTINUIOUS MONOLOUGE I THEN "KNEW" I COULDN'T WAIT TWO YEARS BEFORE ATTEMPTING TO GET A TRIAL.

"SHORTLY THEREAFTER THIS VIEW WAS REINFORCED BY THE REMARKS OF TRIAL JUDGE BATTLE AT A NEWS CONFERENCE WHEREIN HE IMPLIED THAT THE REASON HE (THE JUDGE) WANTED THE GUILTY PLEA WAS THAT THE DEFENDANT MIGHT HAVE BEEN AQUITTED BY A JURY."

THEREFORE ON MARCH, 13TH. 1969, I WROTE A LETTER TO TRIAL JUDGE W. PRESTON BATTLE STATING MR. PERCY FOREMAN NO LONGER REPRESENTED ME AND, THAT I WOULD SEEK A TRIAL.

I THEN CONTACKED OTHER COUNSEL AND ASK MY BROTHER, JERRY RAY, TO SEND COUNSEL ENOUGHT FUNDS TO VISIT ME IN ORDER THAT COUNSEL COULD ATTEMPT TO SET ASIDE PLEA.

HOWEVER DESPITE CONFORMING TO PRESCRIBED PRISON PROCEDURE TENNESSEE CORRECTIONS COMMISSIONER, MR. HARRY AVERY, REFUSED TO LET COUNSEL INTO THE PRISON TO PERFECT A PETITION TO SET ASIDE THE PLEA— SEE CT. TR.

AFTER, AND BECAUSE, COUNSEL WAS REFUSED ADMITTANCE ON MARCH, 26TH. 1969, TO THE PRISON, I WROTE A PETITION TO TRIAL JUDGE BATTLE ASKING FOR A TRIAL— THAT SAME DAY. MARCH, 26TH 1969.

"AFTER I WROTE THE MARCH, 13TH. LETTER TO JUDGE BATTLE INDICATING I WOULD ASK FOR A TRIAL CORRECTIONS COMMISSIONER HARRY AVERY STRONGLY ADVISED ME NOT TO SEEK A TRIAL.

HE SAID IF I DIDN'T I WOULD BE TREATED LIKE ANY OTHER PRISONER AND, WOULD BE RELEASED FROM ISOLATION AT THE END OF THE PRESCRIBED SIX WEEKS BUT, IF I PERSISTED IN ASKING FOR A TRIAL HE COULDN'T PROMISE ANYTHING—HE SAID HE WAS SPEAKING FOR THE HIGHEST AUTHORITY."

I WAS ALSO CONCERNED AT THIS PERIOD THAT COMMIS-
SIONER AVERY WAS TRYING TO PUT ME IN A POSITION
TO FALSELY QUOTE ME AS MAKING AN ORAL STATEMENT.

THEREFORE I SENT AN AFFIDAVIT TO UNITED STATE'S
SENATOR JAMES O. EASTLAND, CHAIRMAN SENATE JU-
DICARY COMMITTEE, STATING I WOULD ONLY DISCUSS
THE SUIT IN COURT.

LATER I SENT A SIMULAR AFFIDAVIT TO THE HONORABLE
BUFORD ELLINGTON, GOVERNOR OF TENNESSEE.

SIGNED: JAMES E. RAY 65477.
STATE PRISON
PETROS, TENNESSEE.

FOR ATTORNEYS.
P.C. HEARING.

3.13-69

Dear Sir,

I wish to inform the honorable court that that famous Houston art, peny Saufflesber, is no longer representing me in any capacity. My reason for writing this letter is that I intend to file for a post conviction hearing in the very near future and don't want him making any legal moves unless their in Mr. Cooke behalf.

Sincerely,
James Earl Ray

FILED 4-1-69
J. A. BLACKWELL, CLERK
BY J A Blackwell D. C.

FROM ESCAPE TO CAPTURE--
THE TWISTED TRAIL OF JAMES EARL RAY

27 London, England ▶
May 7, 1968

28 Lisbon, Portugal ▶
May 8-May 17, 1968

29 London ▶
May 17, 1968 to
June 8, 1968
(capture by
Scotland Yard)

▶ 30 Memphis
July 19-20, 1968

① April 23, 1967. Escapes from Jefferson City, Mo.
② St. Louis Arriving (reportedly) April 28, 1967
③ Edwardsville, Ill. presumably same day.
④ Chicago April 30, 1967-June 25, 1967
   worked Winnetka, Ill. Chicago suburb—May 7-
   June 25 (living in Chicago northside all the while)
⑤ Quincy, Ill. Presumably last week of June.
⑥ Chicago Early July, 1967
⑦ East St. Louis, Ill. July 14, 1967 (?).
⑧ Indianapolis July 15, 1967
⑨ Detroit, Windsor, Toronto July 16, 1967
⑩ Montreal July 18, 1967-August 21, 1967
⑪ Windsor Aug. 21, 1967
⑫ Chicago Aug. 21, 22
⑬ Birmingham August 25, 1967-Oct. 7, 1967

⑭ Nuevo Laredo, Mex.
   (across border from Laredo, Texas)
⑮ Acapulco, Mex. (for one week, mid-October)
⑯ Puerto Vallarta, Mex. For one month to mid
   or late November.
⑰ Los Angeles To Dec. 15, 1967
⑱ New Orleans Dec. 17-19
⑲ Los Angeles Dec. 18? or 21? to March 17?
⑳ Selma, Ala. March 22, 1968
㉑ Atlanta March 23
㉒ Birmingham March 29 and 30
㉓ Atlanta March 31
㉔ Memphis April 3 and 4
㉕ Atlanta April 5-6?
㉖ Toronto April 8?-May 6

Ray's trail from his escape on April 23, from Missouri State Penitentiary, Jefferson City, Missouri, to his capture on June 8, 1968, in London, published some time after he was captured. His activities were precisely defined later as follows: #2, James Earl Ray did arrive in St. Louis on April 28, 1967, and traveled to Edwardsville, Illinois on the same day (#3); #4, he worked in Winnetka from May 3 through June 24; #7, he was definitely in East St. Louis, Illinois on July 14, 1967; #12, he was in Chicago August 21–25; #13, he was in Birmingham August 26; #16, he stayed in Puerto Vallarta, Mexico, until mid-November; #19, after his trip to New Orleans, he was in Los Angeles from December 21 to March 17; #25, he arrived in Atlanta on April 5; #26, he was in Toronto from April 8 to May 6; #27, #28, he flew to London May 6, arriving early on May 7, and that night flew on to Lisbon, arriving early on May 8. (*Associated Press*)

Sketch of murder scene. Ray went up the flight of stairs of the rooming house at 422½ South Main Street, crossed over through the passageway (dotted line), and rented Room 5B in the other building, from which he watched for Dr. King's appearance at the Lorraine Motel, behind and to the right of the rooming house. He shot Dr. King from the window of the bathroom (circled), then ran out into the hallway (hash lines) and down the staircase between the two buildings. He dropped the rifle and other evidence in the entrance of Canipe's Amusement Company at 424 South Main Street (Maltese cross). He had originally parked his white Mustang at A; later, after driving down the street to purchase binoculars, he parked it at B, because another car had taken space A. This led to reports that there had been two white Mustangs. (*United Press International*)

ACKNOWLEDGMENTS

The writer who undertakes to write a contemporary history, depicting what occurred at the time it occurred, does so in two separate roles. In one he is as much as possible an eyewitness of the events he describes; in the other he is a reporter who, seeking to learn what happened, how it happened, and why, goes behind the scenes to those who participated in the events. He must, therefore, be in debt to many people.

It is impossible for me to thank adequately all who have co-operated so generously and so patiently with me, many allowing me to interview them innumerable times. Some of their names will be apparent to the reader by the very nature of this book, and to them, and to those unnamed, I express my deep gratitude.

I must also particularly thank William Bradford Huie. My thanks, too, go to my colleagues of the press for their interest in my project and their co-operation, among them Martin Waldron of the New York *Times*, Bernard Gavzer of The Associated Press, Henry P. Leifermann, Jr., then of United Press International, Daniel Greene of *The National Observer*, Jeremiah O'Leary of the Washington *Star*, Jerry Lipson of the Chicago *Daily News*, Jim Killpatrick, Charles Thornton, and Gregory Jaynes of the Memphis *Commercial-Appeal*, James Squires of the Nashville *Tennesseean*, Ernestine Cofield of the St. Louis *Sentinel*, Andrew F. Yakstis of the Alton *Evening Telegraph*, and Ian Colvin of the London *Daily Telegraph*.

INDEX

ABOUT THE AUTHOR

GEROLD FRANK was born in Cleveland and received his B.A. from Ohio State University, his M.A. from Western Reserve University. He was a newspaperman in Cleveland and New York, and a contributor to *The New Yorker*, *The Nation*, *Life*, *Saturday Evening Post*, and other magazines before serving as a war correspondent in the Middle East. Later he was Overseas News Agency correspondent in Europe and at the United Nations. He has collaborated on a number of books about Israel and the Middle East, including Bartley Crum's *Behind the Silken Curtain* and Jorge García-Granados' *The Birth of Israel*. Mr. Frank wrote *I'll Cry Tomorrow* with Lillian Roth and Mike Connolly; *Too Much, Too Soon*, with Diana Barrymore; *Beloved Infidel*, with Sheilah Graham; and *My Story*, with Zsa Zsa Gabor. More recently Mr. Frank wrote *The Deed*, dealing with terrorism and political assassination in Cairo, which won the Mystery Writers of America "Edgar" award for the Best True Crime Book of 1963; and *The Boston Strangler*, dealing with a series of crimes in Boston, which also won the "Edgar" as the Best True Crime Book of 1966. Mr. Frank lives in New York City.